# The Criminal Justice System

## an introduction

# The Criminal

## an introduction

HOUGHTON MIFFLIN COMPANY · BOSTON
*Atlanta*
*Dallas*
*Geneva, Ill.*
*Hopewell, N.J.*
*Palo Alto*
*London*

# Justice System

RONALD J. WALDRON

*Texas Department of Corrections*

JAGDISH C. UPPAL

*The Council of State Governments*

CHESTER L. QUARLES

*University of Mississippi*

R. PAUL McCAULEY

*University of Louisville*

HILARY HARPER

*University of Southern Florida*

ROBERT L. FRAZIER

*Lamar University*

JAMES C. BENSON

*University of Houston/Clear Lake*

JOHN R. ALTEMOSE

*Lamar University*

Printed in the U.S.A.

Library of Congress Catalog Card Number: 75-26098

ISBN: 0-395-18592-0

# Contents

## PART FOUR Courts



## PART FIVE Corrections

## PART SEVEN The Future of the Criminal Justice System



## APPENDIXES

# Illustrations

# Preface

THE 1960s brought forth a new era for the American criminal justice system. Rising crime rates and social unrest strained the system to near breaking point, and because of the inadequacies in the system, it began to grind to a halt. It became quite apparent that the American criminal justice system was in need of major repair and reform. One of the responses to improving it was the establishment of criminal justice programs on college campuses.

Over the past decade the number of college programs in criminal justice has grown from a small handful to a point where criminal justice courses are now offered on almost every college campus. The growth of college criminal justice programs has, unfortunately, exceeded the development of comprehensive introductory textbooks in this field. The few textbooks that exist on the system reflect the strengths or weaknesses of one or two authors. Because this field broadly encompasses law and law enforcement, the prosecutor, the courts, and corrections, it was decided to bring together a group of specialists from the various areas of criminal justice to write a comprehensive textbook on the criminal justice system. A project management approach was utilized and sufficient controls and procedures were implemented to ensure the accuracy, consistency, and continuity of the textbook. By utilizing this approach, we were able to develop what we feel is a sound and complete introduction to the criminal justice system.

*The Criminal Justice System: An Introduction* was written primarily for the introductory course in criminal justice. This book is designed to provide students with basic information on the system. The first part of the text places the criminal justice system in proper perspective. The student is introduced to law and society in general, the criminal justice system, and the criminal justice process. Sections on the police, the prosecution, the courts, corrections, and probation and parole all follow a basic pattern. Within these sections the history, present structure, current functions, and contemporary problems of each major area are thoroughly discussed. The text concludes with a section on the future of the criminal justice system. In this section the student is introduced to some of the trends and directions of the American criminal justice system.

### Textbook Approach

There are many valid approaches to writing an introductory textbook on the criminal justice system. One could write from a legal, criminal process, or sociological point of view. These are but a few of the numerous approaches that one could take. We chose to write from the criminal justice *system* perspective.

We view the criminal justice system as a whole composed of many subsystems—the police, the prosecutors, the courts, and corrections, including probation and parole. Our task, as we saw it, was to describe the subsystems of the criminal justice system. We have tried to describe these subsystems, and therefore, the system, as we know it to be—not as it should be.

We have not dealt at length with the law as we believe this material properly belongs in criminal law, constitutional law, and criminal evidence courses that a student takes later in the criminal justice curriculum. Because law is essential to the criminal justice system, we have presented a brief introduction to the law and the part that it plays in the system. For those who care to further investigate the legal aspects, we have provided an appendix on individual rights under the Constitution.

### Pedagogy

The chapters are presented in the order that we suggest they be covered. Students are first introduced to the nature of law and society. From there they are presented a brief overview of the criminal justice agencies and the criminal justice process. The criminal justice agencies are then discussed in the order in which they would usually be encountered when an individual goes through the criminal justice process. The final section of the text speculates on what the future will bring for the criminal justice system.

THE AUTHORS

# PART ONE

# Overview: The Criminal Justice System

# 1: Law in Society

*DEFINITION OF LAW • NATURE OF LAW • GENERAL FUNCTIONS OF LAW • RULE OF LAW • DIVISIONS OF LAW • SOURCES OF LAW • NATURE, FORMULATION, AND DEVELOPMENT OF CRIMINAL LAW • SCOPE OF CRIMINAL LAW • CLASSIFICATION OF CRIMES*

PURPOSE: *TO DEVELOP AN UNDERSTANDING OF LAW AND ITS FUNCTION IN AND RELATIONSHIP TO SOCIETY.*

THE DEVELOPMENT of a highly organized, industrialized society has made possible many of the important technological advances directly influencing the lifestyle and standard of living of every individual in this nation. The average American household now maintains a standard of living unparallelled in any other nation in the world. However, with such technological, scientific, and industrial advances and their attendant benefits for the individual, there have come many social problems. Increased mobility, while aiding in the development of large industries, has contributed to the deterioration of traditional American institutions, as reflected by an increasing divorce rate and rising crime levels. The stress of modern industrialized society has led to a substantial increase in alcohol abuse and alcoholism in the average American worker. Industrial wastes have so polluted the atmosphere in some cities that factories must curtail production to protect the health of the residents. The list of social problems goes on.

Although it would be difficult to determine which one of these social ills is of the greatest concern to the American populace as a whole, the fact that the press devotes substantial coverage to the social problem of crime and delinquency seems indicative of America's concern about this increasing menace to society. Traditional means of social control—churches, communities schools, families, and so on—seem to be losing their position as the foundation of order maintenance, with the ever-increasing burden of order maintenance falling on a more formal means of social control, the criminal justice system. This ever-increasing burden on the criminal justice system has placed fresh emphasis on the role of criminologists in American society. The life work of these individuals is "concerned with the study of the phenomenon of crime and of the factors or circumstances—individual and environmental—which may have an influence on, or be associated with, criminal behavior and the state of crime in general."[1] Their goal is to acquire knowledge about the causes of crime in order to achieve the reduction, if not ultimate elimination, of this monumental plague on our society.

In general, modern criminologists approach their study of crime from three directions: (1) the "sociology of law," an analysis of the origin, development, and definition of criminal law in our society; (2) "criminal etiology," a scientific analysis of the causes of crime; and (3) "penology," a study of the methods for controlling crime and criminals.[2] Because criminal law is the principal weapon utilized by the present system of criminal justice in America for combating crime, a discussion is necessary of the general nature, development, and functions of law in society, particularly that of the criminal law.

## *DEFINITION OF LAW*

For centuries, legal scholars have struggled with the problem of defining law. The fact that law is a very complex social institution, varying in nature according to different societies and different stages of historical development, places barriers in the way of developing a universally accepted definition. Some scholars have argued against efforts to define law, expounding the belief that total immersion in a legally based profession will itself provide each individual with a sound feeling for law. While this observation may hold true for people already employed in the criminal justice system, an adequate understanding of the essence of law and its relation to society is necessary for the student contemplating a career in one of the criminal justice professions (police officer, probation officer, etc.).

Turning to your fellow classmates and asking the question "What is law?" will probably elicit a variety of responses. Some may visualize law as a police officer apprehending a criminal or writing a traffic citation, while others may picture a judge sentencing a person to prison. Another may visualize the efforts of the family attorney to arbitrate a property dispute with a neighbor, and still another may visualize law as the many law books contained in the local public library. While none of these hypothetical responses gives a complete picture of the law, each contains certain elements and all are part of the law.[3]

Common to each of these responses is the basic effort to order the affairs of society. The police officer, the judge, the lawyer, all attempt to minimize social conflict by applying the rules set forth in the many legal texts. These rules, as an element of law, not only govern the actions and activities of the judge, the lawyer, and the police officer, they also provide the individuals involved in these hypothetical disputes with some means of gauging the legal consequences of their actions when brought before the court. In short, the law is a means of social control. More specifically, law may be defined as "a formal means of social control that involves the use of rules that are interpreted and are enforceable by the courts of a political community."[4]

The history of law in relation to society reveals that humanity's earliest efforts at lawmaking were prompted by the basic desire of self-preservation. Although engulfed by a society that necessitated such combinations as clans and tribes for protection, as well as for social and economic advancement, the nature of the individual led to the development of certain expressed general rights with regard to person and property. Generally, these unwritten rules governing social and economic interaction recognized the right to defend oneself from injury as well as to enjoy property without outside interference. While sufficient for primitive societies, unwritten rules of social control were ineffective in a rapidly developing and advancing society. Consequently, an effort was made to clarify and reword them so that all people would know their definitions, limits, and applications. Some of these rules became the laws that later received further breadth and expression through the growth of courts and legislative bodies. For example, the right of defense from personal injury was gradually qualified by the rule that if an individual attempted to injure the person of another, and was personally injured while doing so, the attacker could not claim any compensation. These laws—laws that create, discover, and define the right and obligations of each person in society—are referred to as *substantive laws.*

## *NATURE OF LAW*

To best understand the nature of law, further analysis of its definition is necessary. Law, as a means of social control, is but one of the many social institutions that help give order to social life. On a daily basis, the norms or standards of other social institutions such as church, community, family, and school influence a person's patterns of social behavior. What differentiates law from these other social-ordering institutions is the formal and general nature of its ordering process. Take for example a violation of the social norm dictating that a husband provide his wife and children with adequate support. The failure of a husband to fulfill this social obligation will normally activate informal social pressures in the form of public opinion, which may originate from local clergy members, elder family members, or neighbors. If these more personal measures of informal social control fail, then a legal solution to the problem may be sought. Law will be more "formal" and "general" in its handling of the violation. Before a court of law, the issues involved will be clearly defined by highly structured, often time-consuming, court procedures. The legal process facilitates an objective decision reflecting a community judgment as opposed to a personal judgment. Law, then, is a special kind of formal ordering process that is characterized by the carefully chosen steps it follows in an effort to create, maintain, or restore social order.

## *GENERAL FUNCTIONS OF LAW*

In all but the most simplistic societies, a system of law performs social functions, similar to the aforementioned, that are essential to the maintenance of the society itself.[5] If a society could exist without potential disputes, then there would be no need for institutional procedures to define the rights and obligations of each person. Since this is not the case, *one of the first functions of law is to re-establish order in society when disputes arise.* The conflict may simply be a quarrel between two neighboring families over the issue of disciplining one another's children without appropriate consent. The dispute may be immediately resolved through the informal pressures of neighborhood families, church, or other social institutions; but if it is not resolved, one of the injured parties may seek a legal remedy to the problem, bringing this social function of law into play. From society's point of view, a legal remedy serves as a means of settling a dispute that may further deteriorate into acts of personal violence and possibly private revenge. Inherent in a legal solution is that it also serves as a means of reaffirming the social norms that may have been violated.

Although law performs an important social control function when the norms of society have been violated, the primary method for controlling certain patterns of behavior still rests with the social institutions of family, community, church, and school: people base their behavior on calculations of probable reward or punishment for conformity or nonconformity to society's rules. Instilled in each member is the knowledge of the consequences of personal actions when they violate acceptable patterns of behavior. Although this kind of social control is important, it is limited in its effectiveness by the complex nature of society and the problems and consequences that can stem from this complexity. As society becomes more diverse, community consensus (the shared belief in basic norms) becomes more difficult to achieve and sustain. The current level of geographic mobility, coupled with urbanization and social evolution, has reduced the effectiveness of community consensus as an element of social order. *Thus, a second major function of law is to reinforce these informal methods of control by further enabling each individual to calculate the consequences of personal actions.* This function makes it possible to predict with more assurance what others will do, adding rationality and efficiency to social interaction. For example, laws perform an important function in governing everyday vehicle traffic in this nation. A driver entering a major highway complex has a legal obligation to yield the right of way to the main flow of traffic. The "yield" sign provides a driver entering the highway with specific instructions as to what to do and, in turn, provides the motorist speeding down the highway with certain expectations about the conduct of the motorist approaching the entrance ramp. If an auto accident results because a motorist fails to yield, then the first function of law is brought into play in an effort to resolve the dispute.

*A third function of law is its role as an instrument of social change.* Law emerges not only to codify existing norms but also to modify behavior, to remold moral and legal conceptions, as well as to convey the new emerging attitudes, standards, and beliefs of a rapidly changing society. This educational function of law, an extremely important function in light of the many social problems plaguing our society, depends on two interrelated processes: the institutionalization and the internalization of patterns of behavior. "In this context, institutionalization of a pattern of behavior means the establishment of a norm with provisions for its enforcement, and internalization of a pattern of behavior means the incorporation of the value or values implicit in a law."[6] Although law can directly affect behavior solely through the institutionalization process, resistance to the institutionalization process greatly diminishes the successful internalization of attitudes and beliefs. Such was the case with the passage of the Volstead Act, which provided for federal enforcement of liquor prohibition as defined by the Eighteenth Amendment of 1919. The law was enacted to fulfill both a social control and an educational task, but it failed to achieve the latter goal. This failure can be attributed to the fact that people did not believe in the law. Consequently, no internalization of the values implicit or explicit in the Volstead Act took place.

This discussion of the function of law

could be expanded on, but the basic point is that when a society reaches a certain level of complexity, mobility, and diversity, it can no longer rely as heavily on the traditional social institutions of family, church, school, and community to perform the functions of social control. Contemporary society in the United States has reached a level of social evolution that makes it increasingly dependent on a highly structured, formalistic system of law and government that act as agencies of social control.

## RULE OF LAW

Other societies rely as heavily as American society on well-ordered legal systems for the maintenance of their civilizations, but a vast difference exists in the way different systems affect the lives of the people under their control. The United States operates under a legal system that recognizes the *rule of law* or "government under law." These phrases

> describe the willingness of a people to accept and order their behavior according to the rules and procedures which are prescribed by political and social institutions—such as legislatures and universities—and enforced, where necessary, either by those bodies or by other institutions—such as governors, police, and courts. The "rule of law" expresses the idea that people recognize the legitimacy of the law as a means of ordering and controlling the behavior of *all* people in a society, the governors and the governed, the rich and the poor, the contented and the discontented.[7]

The totalitarian form of government of he Soviet Union stands in contrast to his system of "government under law." Γhere, *rule of force* or "rule by law" tends to be accepted, with the government stepping above the law to enhance its own position as the ruling authority. Although the use of force is common to both systems of government, some totalitarian regimes, often use force as a weapon to advance the goals of the state at the expense of the welfare of its citizenry. As the major criminal justice subsystems are reviewed—police, courts, and corrections—the role that force plays in allowing institutions of law and government to maintain social order will be further clarified. Generally, it may be said that the use of this social tool has been benevolent in the hands of those in authority in America's criminal justice system. If this should cease to be the case, under the American system of *rule of law* the rules governing the conduct of those in authority will be changed. In essence, this constitutes a fourth general function of the law: *determining who will maintain the authority to "exercise physical coercion as a socially recognized privilege/right, along with the selection of the most effective forms of physical sanction to achieve the social ends that the law serves."*[8] In short, law functions to make rules for the rulers, as well as the ruled, whether they be the president, the Congress, or the judiciary.

## *DIVISIONS OF LAW*

To this point, the analysis of law has concentrated on a number of the functions of the law and its nature as a formal means of social control. There is another aspect of law that must be considered: the various divisions of the law.

### Substantive Law and Procedural Law

*Substantive law* has been defined as the body of law that creates, discovers, and defines the rights and obligations of each person in society. Included in the general body of substantive law is the substantive law of crimes and punishments, or *criminal law.* In criminal law, the statutes that set forth and define the crimes and specify the punishments for each crime are found in the penal codes of the various states and the federal government. When a crime, such as an act of armed robbery, is committed, *procedural law* (also referred to as *adjective law*) is activated. As the "action arm" of the law, procedural law sets forth the rules that govern the enforcement of the substantive criminal law, the law of crimes and punishments. These rules, found in the criminal procedure codes, govern not only the conduct of the police officers investigating a crime but also the orderly operation of the courts. Procedural criminal law is of great importance, not only in controlling the orderly enforcement of substantive criminal law, but also as a significant part of the protection of the rights of individuals within America's system of social order.

### Civil Law and Criminal Law

Another general division of the law is criminal law and civil law. *Civil law* adjusts conflicts and differences between individuals, such as disputes involving inheritances and divorces; *criminal law* deals with crimes and the apprehension and trial of people suspected of violating the criminal laws of the community. In general, both civil and criminal law have a similar function as institutions of social control. However, there are two basic differences between these two bodies of law concerning the nature of the wrong committed and the consequences of the court proceedings. Criminal law deals with crimes that are "public wrongs," and civil law deals with "private wrongs" or injuries, more commonly referred to as *torts.* Secondly, in civil proceedings the redress for a private injury may simply be money payable to the injured party or a court order prohibiting or ordering certain action. In criminal proceedings, however, the result may be a fine, a prison sentence, or both. These penalties and certain others can be levied only by the state, by specific order of its courts.

### Civil Law and Common Law

Since the Middle Ages, a majority of the English-speaking world has followed a system of *common law* that originated in England. Common law concepts were formulated through the written opinions issued from cases tried before the various royal judges as they traveled throughout the districts and circuits of England. These traveling judges ensured that the legal principles developed and applied in one area of England were equally applied in other parts. Over a period of time a common body of law developed, generally referred to as the Common Law of England. This was the body of law carried by the earliest English settlers to the American colonies. "Common law, as the term is correctly used in the United States, means the basic principles developed in England from the time of the Norman Conquest to the date of the American Revolution."[9]

One often hears common law referred to as *case law*. This is because the body of common law originated from decisions handed down by the traveling royal judges. The promulgation of the written opinion of the judges led to the doctrine of *stare decisis*, sometimes referred to as the *doctrine of precedent*. This means that judges and lawyers refer to decisions of past cases to determine the actual state of the law for the case they are handling. Such opinions or rulings of the court often lead to the development of *statutory law*—laws that are made by Congress and state legislatures. For example, when the United States Supreme Court decided that suspect or accused individuals were entitled to be informed of their constitutional rights at the point during a criminal investigation when suspicion focuses on them, the legislatures of the various states enacted criminal procedural laws to meet the new requirements. Case law is frequently used to interpret legislative intent when a particular statutory law is unclear.

Civil law originated in the Roman state as early as 449 B.C. Through the efforts of the Roman Senate, under the guidance and direction of Justinian, all Roman legislation was codified to include excerpts from legal literature and the decisions of the Roman courts. One of the products of this effort, known as the "Code of Justinian" (A.D. 529), supplemented by various later publications, became known in the seventeenth century as *Corpus Jurus Civilis*.[10] This code forms the basis for most of the legal systems of continental Europe with the exception of the Soviet Union and other communist countries. In the English-speaking world, only Scotland, the Province of Quebec, and the state of Louisiana adhere to a civil law system. All judicial reasoning under this system has as its starting point the appropriate codes or statutory provisions. Decisions from similar or related cases are not considered because previous judgments under this civil law system are not viewed as a rule to follow. "When a French court for instance, decides a case, the judge does not purport to be laying down a rule for future cases; he is merely deciding a case between the litigants before the bar. Theoretically, if a person in like difficulties in the future wishes to know what the law is, he must go back to the code and the commentators."[11]

## SOURCES OF LAW

Before analyzing the nature, formulation, and development of criminal law, a few brief comments are necessary on the sources of law that constitute the legal foundation of this text and the legal hierarchy of authority in American jurisprudence. Although somewhat of an oversimplification, some authors have classified the sources of law as "original" and "secondary."[12]

Primary or original sources of law may be placed in three categories: constitutions, statutes, and cases. Generally, constitutions govern the organization of the political state and its relations with its citizenry. The United States Constitution specifies that the federal government be divided into three branches—executive, legislative, and judicial—operating under a system of checks and balances that ensures a government of and by the people. Statutes are continuously enacted by Congress and the legislatures of the fifty states in response to the ever-changing requirements of environmental protection, crime control, social security benefits, civil rights, and the like. Case law, the rules announced in the decisions of the various state and federal courts, serves to answer questions not answered by legislative enactments; it determines the proper application of ambiguous statutes; and, most importantly, it declares those statutes unconstitutional that do not fit the provisions of state and federal constitutions.

In order of legal hierarchy of authority, the constitutions of the several states are supreme in their jurisdictions and subject only to those provisions of the United States Constitution made applicable to the states through the Fourteenth Amendment. Next in the legal hierarchy of authority are the statutes that are subject only to the constitutions, and finally, the decisions made in court cases.

Secondary sources of law include commentaries on the three primary sources of law. Here there is no formal hierarchy of authority as secondary sources of law have no legal authority. Secondary sources include articles such as those found in the *Harvard Law Review*, various legal texts devoted to selected topics, treatises on law, and official comments such as the United States attorney general's opinions on the interpretation of statutes. The value of secondary sources of law lies in the expertise of the authors and the understanding and clarification their writings may contribute to a fuller knowledge of the law.

## *NATURE, FORMULATION, AND DEVELOPMENT OF CRIMINAL LAW*

The *substantive law of crimes* is the body of law that declares what conduct in a society is criminal and prescribes the punishment to be imposed for such conduct. As the oldest branch of law, its origins can be traced to the earliest of ancient civilizations. Edwin Sutherland, a noted criminologist, advances four principal theories regarding the origin of the criminal law as an agency of social control. He proposes that criminal law originated

1. in torts, or wrongs to individuals;
2. in the rational processes of unified behavior;
3. in a crystallization of mores; and
4. in conflict of interests of different groups.[13]

Taken alone, any one of these theories is an inadequate explanation of the development of criminal law. In total, they account for the development of criminal law at various stages in the growth of a politically organized society.

### Controlling Crime in Primitive Societies

Earliest primitive societies maintained control over human behavior through folkways and mores—not law. Each person's life centered around personal rights rather than property rights. As tribes emerged and governments developed, people took a greater interest in both personal and property rights and protected these interests through personal acts of vengeance.

> The concept of criminal law emerged only when the custom of private vengeance was replaced by the principle that the community as a whole is injured when one of its members is harmed. Thus, the right to act against a wrongdoing was taken out of the hands of the immediate victim and his family and was, instead, granted to the state as the representative of the people.[14]

This new system of criminal justice, however, constituted nothing more than a mere substitution of public vengeance for private vengeance. Calhoun points out that true criminal law contains several legal concepts that further distinguish it from elementary tort and primitive law:

1. It will recognize the principle that attacks upon the person or property of individuals, or rights thereto annexed, as well as offenses that affect the state directly, may be violations of the public peace and good order.
2. It will provide, as part of the ordinary machinery of government, means by which such violations may be punished by and for the state, and not merely by the individual who may be directly affected.
3. The protection it offers will be readily available to the entire body politic, and not restricted to particular groups or classes of citizens.[15]

These legal concepts of criminal law emerged and developed principally from three different societies of the Western world: Greek, Roman, and English.

### Criminal Law in Ancient Greece

Richard Quinney states that the turning point in the development of criminal law in the Western world took place in Athens, Greece, around the sixth century B.C. Living under economic and political oppression, the lower classes threatened revolution and were appeased by the ruling aristocrats through legal reforms, which "established popular courts, provided for appeal from the decisions of magistrates, and assured the right of all citizens to intitiate prosecutions."[16] Thus, each citizen was protected from the wrongdoings of the others as well as those perpetrated by the government.

### Criminal Law in Ancient Rome

Unlike Greek law, Roman criminal law did not emphasize the protection of the rights of the individual from the state. This was because Roman society placed great emphasis on private legal matters and civil procedure. Early Roman society, a rural community, operated under a system of customary or unwritten law. It was not until 450 B.C. that the Roman Senate ordered these laws to be collected and put into written form so that the injustices they had brought about could be rectified. Under the control of the *Decembri* (the Ten Men), this codification process produced the Twelve Tables, a system of private criminal law that was well received by the plebeians of Roman society.[17] However, with the rapid growth of Rome from a rural community to a city-state, the Twelve Tables became inadequate as a means of controlling the internal threats that grew with the development of the Roman state.

> Subsequently, during the third century B.C. and the beginning of the second century, a criminal jurisdiction was established for the control of those engaged in such politically threatening activities as violence, treason, arson, poisoning, and the carrying of weapons, and the theft of state property. Tribunals and courts were instituted to deal with such cases.[18]

### Criminal Law in Medieval England

The Norman conquest of England in A.D. 1066 revealed that the administration of law in England, although well coordinated and long established, lacked a unified national character. Three main bodies of law were in existence—the *Wessex law*, the *Mercian law*, and the *Dane law*—all of which were similar, but greatly influenced by local custom and tradition.[19] Because this was largely a system of tribal justice, long blood feuds had often raged among neighboring families and within the same family. The only political consolidation that touched this warring kingdom of the Anglo-Saxons was provided by the Roman Catholic Church and the rise of feudalism. As kinship groups declined in importance and the role of the landlords, kings, and bishops increased, all disputes fell under the jurisdiction of the appropriate ruling authority for its disposition. It eventually became "a breach of the King's peace to resort to the feud before compensation had been demanded from the offender or his family."[20]

This was the tribal feudal system of law encountered by William the Conqueror in 1066. His contribution to the development of criminal law resulted from his unification of England under one head of state. Under his rule and the leadership of William II (1087–1100) and his brother, Henry I, The Lawgiver (1100–1135), national sovereignity was to emerge.[21] The Charter of Liberties, which was endorsed by Henry I in 1100 and set the stage for the eventual signing of the famous *Magna Charta* in 1215, recognized the sovereign's obligations to his subjects.[22] In turn, the state centralized its authority over the affairs of its subjects. There were created thirty judicial districts, eventually to be traveled by the royal judges appointed under Henry II (1154–1189).

> By the end of the reign of Henry II . . . the law of England was in the hands of the Crown. A court of "common law" was established for the justice of all men. A new procedure and a new conception of offenses had been created. Now for the first time some offenses were regarded as clearly in violation of the peace of king and country. A criminal law had emerged in England.[23]

Not too many years later criminal laws began to emerge in response to conflict between interest groups. In 1349, the first full-fledged British vagrancy statute was passed, making it "a crime to give alms to any who were unemployed while being of sound mind and body."[24] Unlike some of the earlier vagrancy statutes enacted to provide financial relief for religious houses swamped by the poor, sick, and feeble, this statute was created to force laborers "to accept employment at a low wage in order to insure the landowner an adequate supply of labor at a price he could afford to pay."[25] Such a law also served to discourage the movement of serfs from the rural communities into the cities, where the rapid growth and development of industry promised a new and better style of life for the underprivileged working classes.

### Criminal Law in Colonial America

Many people have said that the United States has the most moralistic law of any society. This special emphasis on the enforcement of morality by the criminal law can be traced to the first settlers of the Massachusetts Bay Colony, who in 1630 sought freedom of custom and religion here. Although greatly influenced by the English common law, they based their early legal codes on the Old Testament.[26] Morality and its enforcement became the keynote of their lives and established a pattern still visible in American life styles. The desire of Americans to maintain a certain level of morality by enacting and enforcing criminal laws, coupled with the desire of special interest groups to advance their own beliefs and enhance their own positions in society, has produced legislation such as the Volstead Act, which was enacted to control the use of alcohol.

Historically, then, criminal laws have emerged and been formulated within a social context that "involves the promotion of the interests of certain groups in society,"[27] a crystallization of mores that has resulted in our heavy emphasis on morality and law, the development of criminal legislation paralleling the development of national sovereignity. As Quinney says "This is the social nature of criminal law."[28]

## *SCOPE OF CRIMINAL LAW*

The term *criminal law* has often been used to include everything involved in the "administration of criminal justice." For our purposes in this text, "the scope of criminal law" will encompass three different areas:[29]

1. the substantive criminal law, which declares what conduct in our society is criminal and prescribes the punishment to be imposed for such conduct;
2. criminal procedure, which is the formal machinery for the enforcement of the substantive law of crimes; and
3. special problems in the administration of criminal justice, problems peculiar to the three major areas of the criminal justice process: police, courts, and corrections.

**Basic Premises of Criminal Law**

To fully understand the essential nature of criminal law, one must go beyond the concepts of law, crime, and punishment. Underlying the very nature of American criminal law are certain basics that "have been more or less strictly observed by courts and legislatures when formulating the substantive law of crimes."[30] They are: (1) legality, (2) act, (3) mental state, (4) concurrence, (5) harm, and (6) causation.

*The Principle of Legality* Essentially, the principle of legality is synonymous with rule of law. Earlier it was stated that rule of law expresses the willingness of a people to accept and order their behavior according to the rules prescribed by political and social institutions. As long as the people recognize the legitimacy of the law, it will remain a means of ordering and controlling the behavior of all people. To ensure this legitimacy certain legal maxims have evolved to govern the definition of a crime in our society: (1) No Crime without Law: *Nullum Crimen sine Lege;* (2) No Punishment without Law: *Nulla Poena sine Lege;* and (3) No Crime without Punishment: *Nulla Crimen sine Poena.* Together these maxims constitute the "principle of legality": the premise that conduct is not criminal unless forbidden by a law that provides advance warning that such conduct is criminal. (An example of a violation of this principle is an *ex post facto* law, one which creates a new crime and applies it retroactively to an act not criminal at the time committed.) A crime, then, in our society, "is any social harm defined and made punishable by law."[31] It is also a public injury, an offense against the state, created by the state, punishable only by the state, by either fine or imprisonment.

*Guilty Act (Actus Reus)* A second basic premise of criminal law is that no crime can be committed by bad thoughts alone. Simply thinking about breaking into a friend's house to steal an expensive stereo unit does not constitute a crime if one does not take action to achieve the desired results. If, however, one were in fact to break the lock on the front door of a neighbor's house and enter with the intent to steal the stereo unit, a criminal act or *actus reus* has been committed, which can give rise to legal action. Definitions of acts that are considered criminal or constitute wrongful conduct vary from one code to another. According to the following criminal definition from the Texas state penal code, the conduct described would constitute the crime of burglary: The offense of burglary is consituted by entering a house by force, threats or fraud, at night, or in like manner by entering a house at any time, either day or night, and remaining concealed therein, with the intent in either case of committing a felony or the crime of theft. Another state's code might well differ in details.

While this example involves an act of "commission," an "omission," a failure to act when there is a legal duty to act, may also constitute a crime. Such would be the case if a motorist involved in an automobile accident failed to stop and render aid, or a taxpayer avoided filing an income tax return each year. In both examples, the criminal statutes impose the duty to act, and breach of the duty constitutes the wrongful act.

*Mental State (Mens Rea)* Just as there can be no crime without a guilty act, there can be no crime without a guilty or wrongful purpose in mind. This is often referred to as criminal intent or *mens rea.*

> Since the modern concept of crime assumes the rational ability of the particular violator to undertake an act designed to harm either an individual or property, legal punishment can only be enacted against the violator if his action was "intended" and "apparent" to his mind. While intent presupposes that the individual desires to complete whatever act he originates, *mens rea* assumes that the intent was knowledgeable and intelligible to the person as he undertook his particular action.[32]

For some crimes—burglary, for example —the controlling penal statute defines not only the wrongful act but also the "specific intent" necessary to make the act a crime. In this case, the breaking and entering must be done with the "specific intent" to commit a felony or theft. Other statutes defining criminal conduct often use such phrases as "knowingly" or "willfully" to indicate the type of mental state required. Thus, the important point to remember is that both *actus reus* and *mens rea* are elements of a crime and both must be present simultaneously in a crime.

*Concurrence in Time* For those crimes whose definitions require both a wrongful act and a guilty mind, no crime is committed unless the mental state concurs with the act, in the sense that the guilty mind actuates the wrongful act.[33] Take, for example, John Doe, who decides to visit his next door neighbor, Mary Roe. Because they are good friends, John Doe simply opens the front door and enters Mary's home with completely innocent intentions. While inside, John decides to steal Mary's expensive stereo system. Has John committed the crime of burglary? No, because by most definitions of the crime of burglary, John would have had to enter Mary's house by means of force, fraud, or threats with the "intention aforehand" to commit a felony or crime of theft.

*Harm (An Injury or Result)* To be constitutional, a criminal statute must have been enacted to protect the public health, the public morals, or the public safety. If it is determined that there is no real relation between the criminal statute and the protection of the public from some harm or injury, the statute may be declared unconstitutional. Such would be the case if a statute were enacted making a physical state such as being fat or short or tall a criminal offense. As an element of crime and very possibly the most important element, harm or injury resulting from a criminal act determines the statutory penalties affixed to that specific violation.

*Causation* An essential element of every crime is that a causal relationship exists between the offender's conduct and the harm or injury sustained by another. In the usual sense, there is very little difficulty in demonstrating this connection. Take, for example, Mary Roe, who has returned home and found her expensive stereo stolen. Questioning of her neighbors reveals that John Doe was seen leaving her house with the stereo set. Taking her pistol, she goes to John's house with the intent to kill him and does in fact shoot and kill John. Mary not only legally caused John's death but also intended to do so and therefore is guilty of murder.

**Illustration 1.1** PUNISHMENT

How do you feel about punishment, capital and otherwise? Should the criminal offender be punished for committing a crime or should society attempt to rehabilitate the criminal offender? Can society punish and at the same time rehabilitate the offender? If society is going to punish an offender, how severe should the punishment be for a given crime? Does the threat of punishment actually deter individuals from committing crimes? Does punishment deter offenders from committing further crimes? These are not easy questions to answer, yet if our criminal justice system is to work, answers must be found.

The definition of the crime of murder specifies that the defendant's act must cause a death.

These basic premises underlie American criminal law and so have been extremely important in shaping the development of the substantive law of crimes. Although the definition of each crime stipulates a different combination of act and state of mind, each major crime has two elements, a "criminal act" and "criminal intent." Neither alone is sufficient to constitute a major crime; the two must concur to establish criminal responsibility.

The categories of crimes that are punishable without *mens rea* (a guilty mind) involve for the most part violations of regulatory statutes punishable by light monetary fines rather than imprisonment. Many of these violations are such that establishing the defendant's state of mind at the time of the violation is particularly difficult, if not impossible. Regulatory offenses like traffic violations or violations of motor vehicle laws fall into this category. Even if intent could be established, the vast number of people who commit such violations would thwart any efforts at enforcement.

### Purpose and Object of Criminal Law

If the purpose of law is the regulation of an individual's conduct as it relates to society as a whole or in part, then from this general purpose originates the primary objective of criminal law: the prevention of certain specified undesirable conduct with resulting protection for various interests of society. Because these results are achieved by punishing the criminal for infractions of the criminal law whenever they occur, some authors have ventured so far as to say that the purpose of criminal law is to punish.

The purpose of punishment, however, is not so clearly defined. Various theories have been advanced: prevention, restraint, rehabilitation, deterrence, education, and retribution, any one or all of which may secure the aims of criminal law.[34] Which one of these theories or what combination thereof best achieves the goal of a minimum standard of conduct on the part of each individual in society has yet to be determined.

*Prevention* The advocates of this theory feel that if the criminal offender is aware of a punishment for a crime, such as prison, he or she will not wish to endure the punishment and therefore will not commit a crime.

*Restraint* This theory is based on the belief that society may protect itself from persons whom it deems dangerous either by execution or by life imprisonment.

*Rehabilitation* By far the most popular of the recent concepts of penology to be advanced, this theory emphasizes that criminal behavior is the product of causes that can be identified and treated.

*Education* According to this theory, the criminal justice process itself—from arrest to final punishment—teaches the general public what conduct is or is not socially acceptable. This kind of education is particularly important when the crime committed is relatively unknown or misunderstood.

*Retribution* This is by far the oldest societal theory: punishment is imposed by society on criminals in order to obtain revenge for the harm one person has inflicted on another person or on his or her property.

## *CLASSIFICATION OF CRIMES*

Crimes can be classified in several ways: the social harm caused; the grade of the offense, whether *mala in se* (wrong in themselves) or *mala prohibita* (wrong because prohibited); crimes of infamy; crimes of moral turpitude; common law crimes or statutory crimes; and with reference to procedure. Regardless of the classification, however, crimes are always offenses against the state and are always prosecuted by the state (at whatever level, federal, state, or local).

### Crimes of Social Harm

The following definitions of the seven major offenses of the Federal Bureau of Investigation's *Uniform Crime Reports*[35] make it apparent that crimes are classified according to the protections against harm afforded by the criminal law to the various interests of society: protection from physical harm to the person (1 through 4), protection of property from loss, destruction, damage (5 through 7).

1. *Criminal homicide:* (a) Murder and nonnegligent manslaughter: all willful felonious homicides as distinguished from deaths caused by negligence. Excludes attempts to kill, assaults to kill, suicides, accidental deaths, or justifiable homicides. Justifiable homicides are limited to: (1) the killing of a person by a peace officer in the line of duty; (2) the killing by a private citizen of a person while that person is in the course of committing a felony.
   (b) Manslaughter by negligence: any death that police investigation establishes as primarily attributable to the gross negligence of some individual other than the victim.
2. *Forcible rape:* Rape by force, assault to rape, and attempted rape. Excludes statutory offenses, when no force is used and the victim is under the age of consent.
3. *Robbery:* Stealing or taking anything of value from a person by force or violence or by putting a person in fear as in the case of strong-arm robbery, stickups, armed robbery, assault to rob, and attempt to rob.
4. *Aggravated assault:* Assault with intent to kill or for the purpose of inflicting severe bodily injury by shooting, cutting, stabbing, maiming, poisoning, scalding, or by the use of acids, explosives, or other means. Excludes simple assault, assault and battery, fighting, etc.
5. *Burglary—breaking or entering:* Burglary, housebreaking, safecracking, or any unlawful entry to commit a felony or a theft, even though no force was used to gain entrance. Burglary followed by larceny is not counted again as larceny.
6. *Larceny—theft* (except auto theft):
   (a) $50 and over in value; (b) under $50 in value. Theft of bicycles, automobile accessories, shoplifting, pickpocketing, or any stealing of property or article of value that is not taken by force and violence or by fraud. Excludes embezzlement, "con" games, forgery, worthless checks, etc.
7. *Auto theft:* Stealing or driving away and abandoning a motor vehicle. Excludes taking for temporary use when actually returned by the taker or unauthorized use by those having lawful access to the vehicle.

### Felonies and Misdemeanors

This is presently the most important classification of crimes in use in the United States. A *felony* is generally any crime that is punishable by death or imprisonment in a penitentiary, whether it be state or federal. Any other crime is a *misdemeanor,* normally punishable by fine or imprisonment in a local jail. Some penal codes distinguish between felonies and misdemeanors according to the length of sentence imposed—a felony being considered a crime punishable by imprisonment for more than one year or by death.

The importance of this distinction for the criminal offender is threefold in nature. First, as far as the substantive criminal law is concerned, certain crimes such as burglary require as an element of the offense the intent to commit a felony, and hence the intent to commit a misdemeanor will not constitute the crime of burglary. Secondly, this distinction is important to the offender in terms of criminal procedure because a court's jurisdiction over a crime is determined by whether the crime committed is a felony or a misdemeanor. The third effect is in legal consequences, which will generally be different for a convicted felon and for an individual who has sustained a misdemeanor conviction. A felony conviction may constitute grounds for loss of professional license (doctors, lawyers, and so forth), divorce, loss of civil rights, and numerous other penalties.

### Crimes *Mala in Se* and *Mala Prohibita*

This classification of offenses (one of the most ancient) can be traced back to the common law. A crime *mala in se* at common law was considered to be an offense that was inherently wrong or inherently evil. A crime *mala prohibita* is an offense that is wrong only because it is prohibited by legislation. Most regulatory crimes such as traffic violations fall into the second category, whereas felony offenses are usually crimes *mala in se.* One author has suggested that the distinction between these classifications of offenses can be made by determining whether intent is an element of the offense.[36] If no criminal intent is required, as in the case of regulatory crime (traffic offenses), then the clasification is *mala prohibita.* Where intent is specified as part of the definition of the crime, as it is for burglary, the classification is *mala in se.*

### Infamous and Noninfamous Crimes

Under the early common law, certain crimes were considered *infamous* because of the shameful status that resulted after conviction for the offense. Initially, infamous crimes included treason, all felonies, offenses involving obstruction of the administration of justice, and any crime included within the scope of the Roman term *crimen fals,* that is, all crimes involving deceit or falsification. In this country, before the adoption of the Constitution, two kinds of infamy were recognized, one based on the mode of punishment to be inflicted and the other related to the future credibility of the defendant. The accepted modern view is that a crime punishable by imprisonment for more than one year in a state penitentiary is an *infamous crime.*

### Crimes of Moral Turpitude

The distinction between crimes that are crimes of *moral turpitude* and those that are not is similar to the distinction between crimes *mala in se* and crimes *mala prohibita*. Moral turpitude can be defined as an act that goes against the contemporary standards of conduct and decency, a base, depraved act that shocks the conscience of society. Most theft crimes, such as grand larceny and embezzlement, as well as such criminal acts as bigamy and rape, are generally held to involve "moral turpitude." Other crimes such as fornication and adultery are crimes of moral turpitude in some states but not in others. The importance of this distinction to the criminal offender rests in the extraordinary legal consequences that result from conviction for a crime of moral turpitude. These consequences are similar to those following a felony conviction—disbarment, loss of professional license, and so forth.

### Common Law Crimes and Statutory Crimes

This distinction was touched on briefly during the discussion of the various divisions of law. Under the system of the common law, many of the definitions of criminal conduct were developed from specific cases. As the power of the legislative branches developed, many of these common law crimes were redefined by statute and others added. Today the majority of our crimes are defined by statutory law.

### Major Crimes and Petty Offenses

The final classifications to be touched on here involve the distinction between major cimes and petty offenses. Whereas a felony is a major crime, a misdemeanor may be either a major crime or a petty offense according to the punishment allowable. If the criminal violation is deemed a petty offense, then the offender in most jurisdictions is tried by a magistrate through summary procedure. In most states this procedure does not involve the processes peculiar to the trial for a major crime (preliminary hearings, indictments, trial by jury, and so on).

In this chapter, the relationship between law and society has been briefly explored with particular emphasis on the development of the substantive law of crimes, its nature and function. Criminal law has been described as an important instrument of social control by which organized society defines certain human conduct as criminal and attempts to prohibit or restrain such conduct by a system of procedures and penalties. If a "crime" is committed, criminal prosecution will begin, governed by the appropriate code of criminal procedure. This operational side of criminal law, greatly influenced by the doctrine of *stare decisis*, determines the nature and extent of criminal liability for each offender involved. Criminal law, then, is the instrument of criminal policy whereby the rules are set forth for determining whether a crime has in fact been committed; whether the accused person has committed that offense; and, finally, what prescribed penalty is to be imposed if the accused is found guilty after criminal prosecution.

## DISCUSSION QUESTIONS

1. Can a society exist without law?
2. What are the major differences between common law and statutory law? Which do you prefer?
3. If police officers could maintain order without regard to legality, their short-run difficulties would be considerably diminished. Discuss the merits of this argument.
4. It is often said that swift and certain punishment will deter crime. Is this a true statement? If so how swift and certain must the punishment be? What is swift and certain punishment?
5. Should a law be general or specific? What are the dangers inherent in each approach?

## NOTES


1. Leon Radzinowicz, *In Search of Criminology* (Cambridge: Harvard University Press, 1962), p. 168.
2. Donald R. Cressey and Edwin H. Sutherland, *Criminology* 8th ed. (Philadelphia: J. B. Lippincott, 1966), p. 3.
3. Bernard F. Cataldo, *Introduction to Law and the Legal Process* (New York: John Wiley & Sons, 1965).
4. F. James Davis et al., *Society and the Law* (New York: The Free Press of Glencoe, 1962), p. 41.
5. Harold J. Berman and William R. Greiner, *The Nature and Functions of Law* (Brooklyn: Foundation, 1966), pp. 31–34.
6. Jerry D. Rose, *Introduction to Sociology* (Chicago: Rand McNally, 1971), p. 44.
7. *Law and Order Reconsidered: Report of the Task Force on Law and Law Enforcement to the National Commission on the Causes and Prevention of Violence* (Washington, D.C.: Government Printing Office, 1970), pp. 8–9.
8. Joel B. Grossman and Mary H. Grossman, eds., *Law and Change in Modern America* (Pacific Palisades, Calif.: Goodyear Publishing, 1971), p. 13.
9. Hazel B. Kerper, *Introduction to the Criminal Justice System* (St. Paul, Minn.: West Publishing, 1972), p. 27.
10. Frank Day, *Criminal Law and Society* (Springfield, Ill.: Charles C. Thomas, 1964), p. 35.
11. Cataldo, *Introduction to Law*, p. 24.
12. Cataldo, *Introduction to Law*, pp. 15–16.
13. Cressey, *Criminology*, pp. 10–11.
14. Richard Quinney, *Crime and Justice in Society* (Boston: Little, Brown, 1969), p. 5.
15. George M. Calhoun, *The Growth of Criminal Law in Ancient Greece* (Berkeley: University of California Press, 1927), p. 5, quoted in Quinney's *The Social Reality of Crime* (Boston: Little, Brown, 1970), p. 44.
16. Richard Quinney, *Social Reality of Crime* (Boston: Little, Brown, 1970), p. 46.

17. Day, *Criminal Law and Society*, p. 34.
18. Quinney, *Social Reality of Crime*, p. 47.
19. Day, *Criminal Law and Society*, p. 36.
20. Quinney, *Social Reality of Crime*, p. 49.
21. Day, *Criminal Law and Society*, p. 37.
22. Day, *Criminal Law and Society*, p. 38.
23. Quinney, *Social Reality of Crime*, p. 49.
24. William J. Chambliss, *Crime and the Legal Process* (New York: McGraw-Hill, 1969), p. 52.
25. Chambliss, *Crime and the Legal Process*, p. 54.
26. Quinney, *Crime and Justice in Society*, p. 7.
27. Quinney, *Crime and Justice in Society*, p. 9.
28. Quinney, *Crime and Justice in Society*, p. 9.
29. Rollin M. Perkins, *Criminal Law* (Brooklyn: Foundatión, 1957), p. 1.
30. Wayne R. LaFave and Austin W. Scott, Jr., *Handbook on Criminal Law* (St. Paul, Minn.: West Publishing, 1972), p. 1975.
31. Perkins, *Criminal Law*, p. 5.
32. Richard D. Knudten, *Crime in a Complete Society: An Introduction to Criminology* (Homewood, Ill.: Dorsey, 1970), p. 42.
33. LaFave and Scott, *Handbook on Criminal Law*, p. 238.
34. Herbert L. Packer, *The Limits of the Criminal Sanction* (Stanford: Stanford University Press, 1968), pp. 35–62.
35. Federal Bureau of Investigation, U.S. Department of Justice, *Uniform Crime Reports for the United States, 1973* (Washington, D.C.: Government Printing Office, 1974), pp. 2–30.
36. LaFave and Scott, *Handbook on Criminal Law*, p. 29.

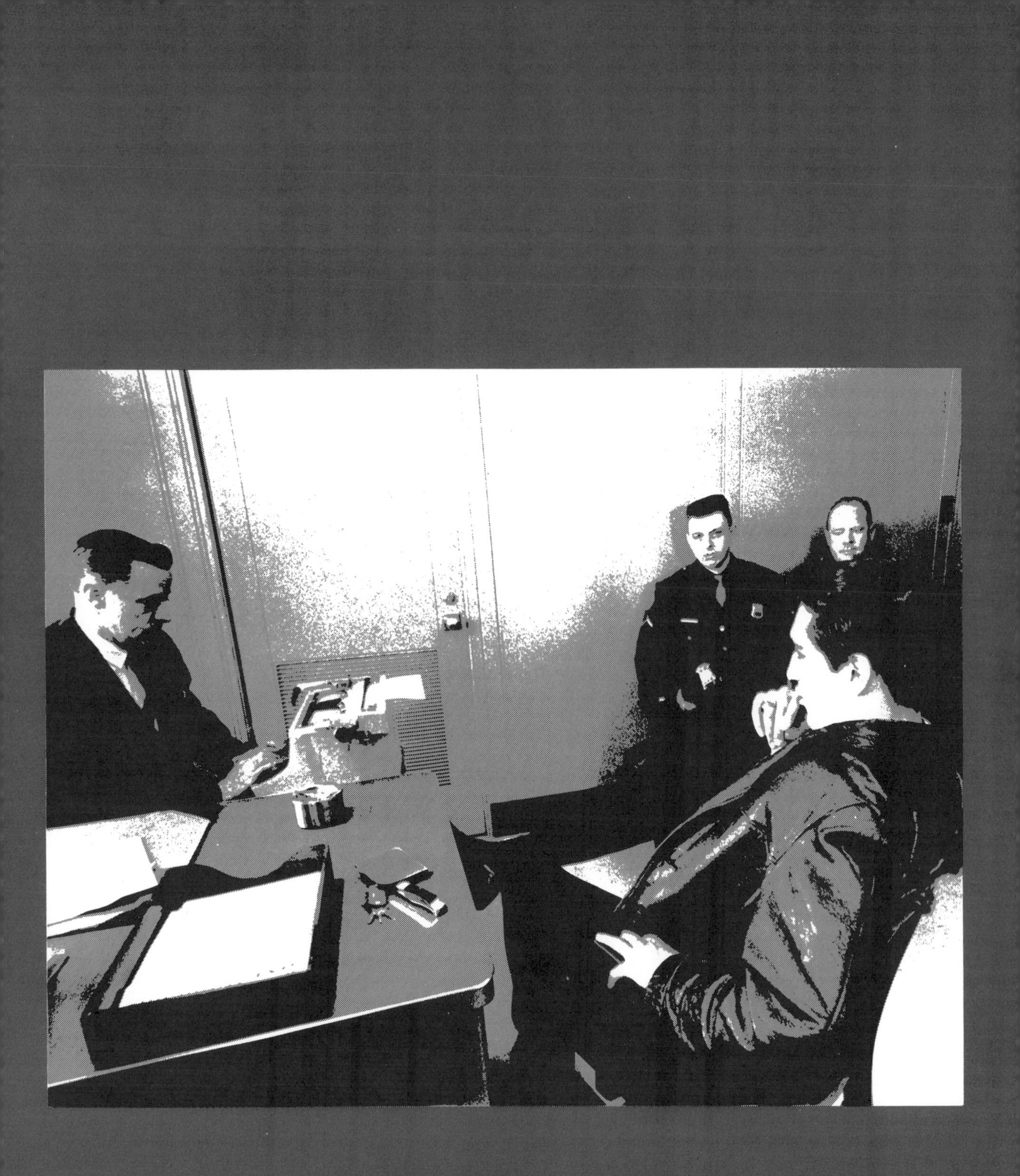

# 2: The Criminal Justice System

*ADVERSARY SYSTEM AND DUE PROCESS OF LAW • CRIMINAL JUSTICE SYSTEM AS A SYSTEM • PRIMARY FUNCTIONAL AREAS*

PURPOSE: *TO PROVIDE A BRIEF OVERVIEW OF THE AGENCIES OF THE CRIMINAL JUSTICE SYSTEM AND THEIR RELATIONSHIPS. TO PUT THE AGENCIES OF THE CRIMINAL JUSTICE SYSTEM IN THEIR PROPER PERSPECTIVE.*

THE SYSTEM of criminal justice in the United States today, like any such system, is the apparatus whereby "society identifies, accuses, tries, convicts, and punishes offenders against the norms of society expressed in law."[1] As a crime control *process*, this system of criminal justice strives to achieve three purposes beyond the immediately punitive one: "It removes dangerous people from the community; it deters others from criminal behavior; and it gives society an opportunity to attempt to transform lawbreakers into law-abiding citizens."[2]

In order to accomplish these purposes, America's system of criminal justice is divided into three major parts: the *law enforcement community*, consisting of the police (both state and federal), county sheriffs, marshals, and so forth; the *judicial community*, consisting of local, state, and federal judges, prosecutors, and defense lawyers; and *the corrections community*, made up of prison officials and parole and probation officers. Each one of these components in turn contributes to the criminal justice process, which is a well-defined continuum through which each offender may pass: from detection and investigation of the criminal act, to arrest and accusation, to trial, conviction, sentencing and possible incarceration, to eventual release.

Although the three major components of the criminal justice *system* are common to each level of government—village, town, city, and county; state; and federal governments—the criminal justice *process* is tailored to meet the individualized needs at each level. Within the governments of some fifty-five states and territories, there are as many varied goals, standards, penal codes, and codes of criminal procedure.

Isolating and analyzing any single state reveals that various components of the criminal justice system are controlled by different branches of the state government. For example, state police organizations are part of the executive branch, whereas the court system falls under the control of the judicial branch. Consequently, when a state police officer arrests a suspect, the suspect may in fact become a defendant in the court system, which is controlled by the judicial branch. If convicted and sentenced to incarceration, the defendant moves from the realm of the judicial branch of government back to the executive, which controls the correctional institution. Closer analysis of this entire process will reveal that it sacrifices much in the way of efficiency and effectiveness in order to protect the rights of each individual as guaranteed by the United States Constitution as well as to ensure and preserve local governmental autonomy.

## *ADVERSARY SYSTEM AND DUE PROCESS OF LAW*

The movement of an offender through the criminal justice process is a struggle from start to finish because the American legal system is an *adversary system* of law. When a criminal law violation is at issue before a court, a battle ensues, the state as plantiff on one side and the accused offender as the defendant on the other. Until evidence is introduced by the state that proves the defendant's guilt "beyond a reasonable doubt," he or she is considered innocent of all accusations.

> Beyond a reasonable doubt means just what it says, a *reasonable* doubt. It does not mean beyond any doubt whatsoever. Thus, it does not require proof amounting to absolute certainty to convict an offender, or to adjudicate a juvenile delinquent. A reasonable doubt is a doubt such as a reasonable man would have after hearing all the evidence in the case and the arguments of counsel, and after applying the law to the case as instructed by the court.[3]

This adversary system of justice is based on the philosophy that "a person may be punished by the government if, and only if, it has been proved by an impartial and deliberate process that he has violated a specific law."[4] The rules that make this philosophy a reality, the rules that guarantee each individual in society a fair trial or hearing in matters concerning life, liberty, or property are to be found in the United States Constitution and the Bill of Rights. (See Appendixes B and C.) These include, but are certainly not limited to, the right of each individual to a public trial conducted in an orderly manner before an impartial tribunal; the right to reasonable notice of charges as well as notice of the time and location of the trial; protection against involuntary self-incrimination; the right to counsel; the right to confront and cross-examine hostile witnesses; and the opportunity to speak in one's own defense. The maintenance of these rights, as contained in the United States Constitution and the constitutions of all the states, is generally summed up in the legal concept known as *due process of law*. Without due process, the adversary system of justice would lack fundamental fairness and fail to represent a community judgment as to an individual's guilt or innocence.

## *CRIMINAL JUSTICE SYSTEM AS A SYSTEM*

To refer to anything as a system implies "some unity of purpose and organized interrelationship among the component parts."[5] In the criminal justice system the parts are the police, the courts, and corrections. Although much current debate focuses on what some authors have referred to as the "nonsystem" of criminal justice in America, it is correct to say that each of these components, as a part of the whole, has a direct effect on the work of the other two. For example, as the police become more professional, additional crimes will in all likelihood be detected; therefore more cases will be brought before the courts; and possibly more business will be generated for the prisons. If the correctional personnel can rehabilitate the offender, then the offender will be out of the system. Any failures will once again encounter the police and the courts, however, and compound the crime problem. Any change in a part of the criminal justice system affects the whole.

This interrelationship becomes more apparent when one examines the *process* of criminal justice administration—the sequence of events from an individual's

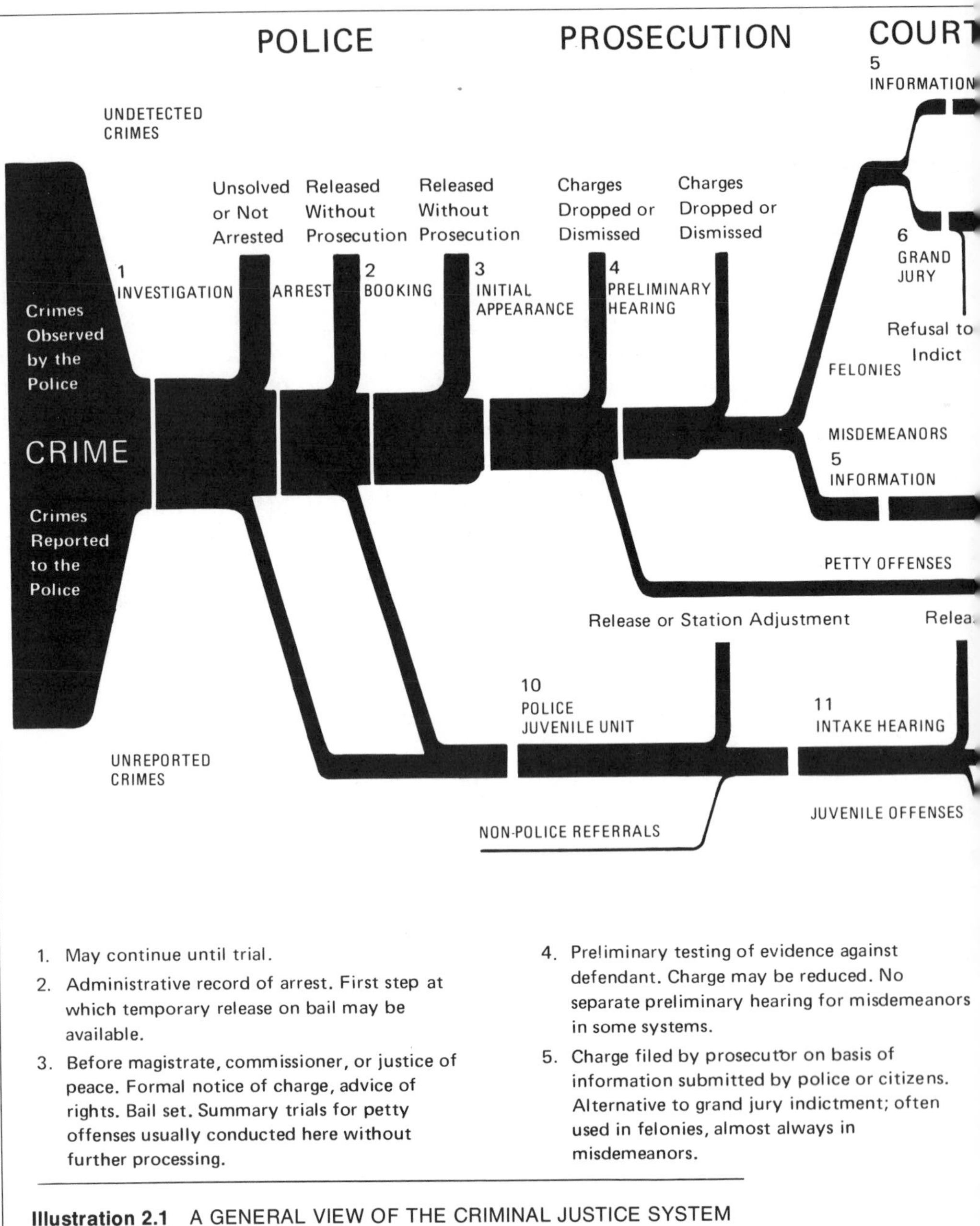


1. May continue until trial.
2. Administrative record of arrest. First step at which temporary release on bail may be available.
3. Before magistrate, commissioner, or justice of peace. Formal notice of charge, advice of rights. Bail set. Summary trials for petty offenses usually conducted here without further processing.
4. Preliminary testing of evidence against defendant. Charge may be reduced. No separate preliminary hearing for misdemeanors in some systems.
5. Charge filed by prosecutor on basis of information submitted by police or citizens. Alternative to grand jury indictment; often used in felonies, almost always in misdemeanors.

**Illustration 2.1** A GENERAL VIEW OF THE CRIMINAL JUSTICE SYSTEM

Source: President's Commission on Law Enforcement and Administration of Justice, *Challenge of Crime in a Free Society* (Washington, D.C.: Government Printing Office, 1967), pp. 8–9.

This chart seeks to present a simple yet comprehensive view of the movement of cases through the criminal justice system. Procedures in individual jurisdictions may vary from the pattern shown here. The differing weights of line indicate the relative volume of cases disposed of at various points in the system, but this is only suggestive, since no nationwide data exists.

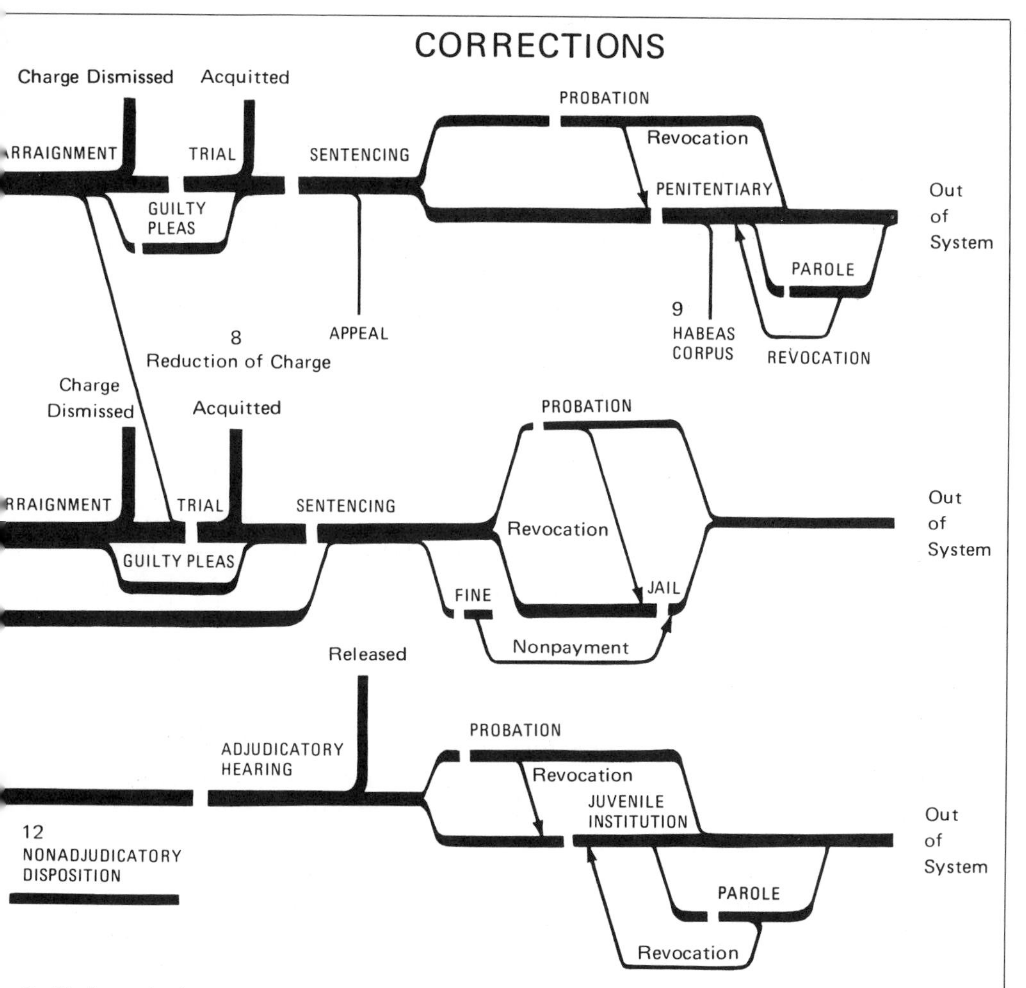


6. Reviews whether government evidence sufficient to justify trial. Some states have no grand jury system; others seldom use it.
7. Appearance for plea; defendant elects trial by judge or jury (if available); counsel for indigent usually appointed here in felonies. Often not at all in other cases.
8. Charge may be reduced at any time prior to trial in return for plea of guilty or for other reasons.
9. Challenge on constitutional grounds to legality of detention. May be sought at any point in process.
10. Police often hold informal hearings, dismiss or adjust many cases without further processing.
11. Probation officer decides desirability of further court action.
12. Welfare agency, social services, counseling, medical care, etc. for cases where adjudicatory handling not needed.

apprehension, to prosecution, conviction, and sentencing. Illustration 2.1 outlines the process of criminal justice administration as it currently operates in most jurisdictions.

Generally, when a crime is committed, the police are notified and an effort is made to determine whether a crime has been committed and who has violated the law. If a suspect is detected and an arrest made, the police bring the suspect before a magistrate as quickly as possible. If a petty offense is involved and if the defendant pleads guilty to the offense charged in the complaint, the magistrate normally disposes of the case at once. However, when a more serious offense is involved or when the defendant does not choose to plead guilty, the magistrate files an information in the court where the defendant is to stand trial and a date for the trial appearance will be set. When a felony offense is involved, the defendant is given a preliminary hearing before a judge in order to review the charge and the evidence that alleges to support it. In those states requiring an indictment in order to bring an accused to trial on a felony charge, a grand jury reviews the evidence and the charge and either affirms the charge by delivering it to the judge in the form of an indictment or dismisses it. Once at trial, the state, operating by the rules that govern the adversary system of justice, attempts to prove the defendant's guilt beyond a reasonable doubt. Should the state succeed and the jury find the defendant guilty, sentencing is done either by the jury or by the presiding judge. If the sentence is a term of years in the penitentiary, a systematic effort is made to rehabilitate the defendant. Should the sentence be a term of years on probation, the defendant is returned to the community conditional upon good behavior.

This brief description of the *process* can be considered "typical" (although it may be something of an oversimplification, depending on the gravity of the criminal offense involved). For the majority of criminal violations that the police encounter, the process for the disposition of the case is far less formal. It should be noted in Illustration 2.1 that the process an offender is subjected to is broken down according to the classification of the crime committed.

## PRIMARY FUNCTIONAL AREAS

There exist within the overall criminal justice process six primary functional areas or subsystems of the criminal justice system. Illustration 2.2 sets forth these six subsystems—police, prosecution, criminal court system, probation services, corrections, and parole—each of which contributes to the overall criminal justice process.

### Police

The two primary functions of the police are law enforcement and general community service. As part of their law enforcement function, police assume both a preventive role and a protective role. Through active patrolling, both on foot and in vehicles, the police attempt to pro-

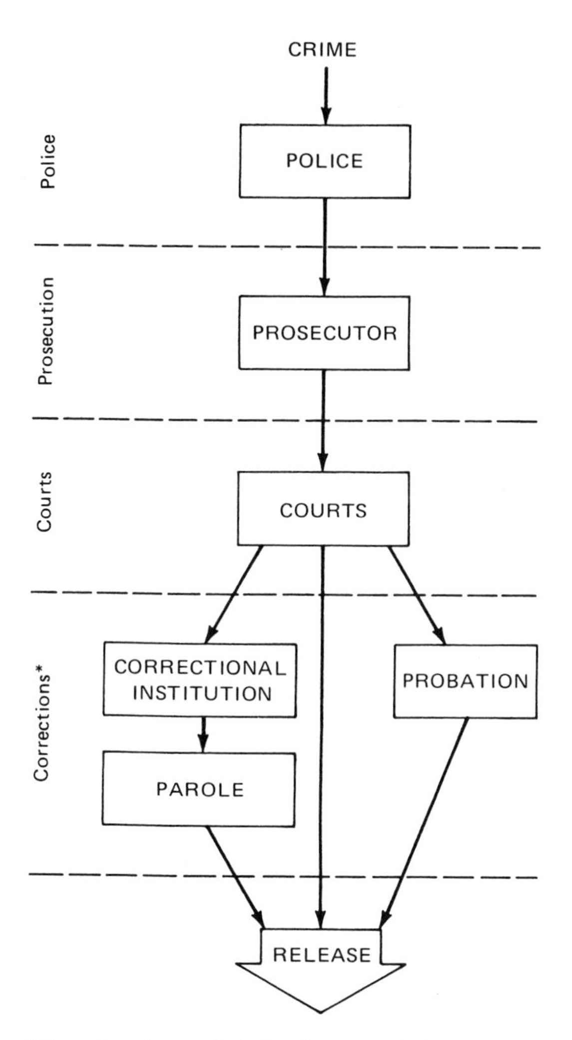


*Though primary functional areas of the criminal justice system, probation and parole are generally considered subsystems of corrections.

**Illustration 2.2** PRIMARY FUNCTIONAL AREAS OF THE CRIMINAL JUSTICE SYSTEM

vide the general public with a blanket of security that will act as a deterrent to potential criminals, while simultaneously providing means of rapid response to reported criminal activity. To further their efforts at providing the community with adequate protection, many police agencies are engaged in community programs that provide the public with firsthand information about the extent of crime in their neighborhoods; educate them about their roles as responsible citizens in crime prevention; and provide them with up-to-date information on basic security measures available to them the better to secure their persons, homes, and properties. In addition, police may provide such services as driver education programs, which help ensure public order by the prevention of accidents.

Although these efforts at crime prevention, detection, general public ordering, and security constitute the primary function of police—law enforcement—this function is not easily separated from the other main function of police—community service. The average patrol officer, who is the heart of every police department, spends a disproportionate amount of time in noncriminal situations. These may range from finding lost children, settling marital disputes, helping a drunken citizen find the way home, to counseling the lonely citizen who has no family to talk to. Many have argued that this social work aspect or community services aspect of police work should be left to the social agencies designated to handle such problems. Unfortunately, such agencies are either nonexistent or do not operate on a twenty-four-hour basis or do not cover as wide a geographical area as do the police. *Task Force Report: The Police* of the President's Commission on Law Enforcement and Administration of Justice (hereafter referred to as the

National Crime Commission) views both the law enforcement function of the police and the community service function as inseparable elements of crime control. Citing as an example the numerous cases of drunks who fall victim to criminal attacks while in a stupor, the National Crime Commission points out that although this is a social problem, the only agency currently available to deal with these people and the crime-related aspect of their drinking problems is the police.

Because a full discussion of whether police officers should or should not be involved in both law enforcement and community service is not appropriate here, suffice it to say that it is the police officer's law enforcement function that initiates the criminal justice process. To fulfill this obligation, police are given formal authority to invoke the criminal process through their power of arrest.

**Prosecution**

The duties of the prosecutors in the criminal justice process entail numerous responsibilities. More commonly referred to as district attorneys, the officials and the offices that they represent are charged with the responsibility for seeing that justice is done. This function brings prosecutors into contact with the criminal justice process from arrest to sentencing. It is the district attorney who decides whether to continue the prosecution of a criminal case where arrest has been made without a warrant. When arrest warrants or other related legal documents such as search warrants are issued, the district attorney participates in the decision-making process about their issuance. When an arrest is made, it is the district attorney who makes the decision to charge, determines the specific criminal offense or offenses with which the individual will be charged, and influences the bail bond process. The district attorney represents the state before the grand jury when seeking an indictment and at the preliminary hearing and arraignment, ready with the evidence gathered in cooperation with the appropriate law enforcement agencies and his or her own investigative staff. Before the trial the district attorney develops still more information and prepares the appropriate legal documents to support the state's position. When appropriate, the district attorney engages in plea negotiations. During the trial phase he or she must prove the defendant's guilt beyond a reasonable doubt with the expertise of a trial lawyer. If the defendant is found guilty, the district attorney is influential in determining the severity of the sentence (within the legally prescribed limits) handed down by the court.

Because of the position district attorneys occupy in the criminal justice system, they and their offices can have a very positive influence on the other participants in the criminal justice process, particularly on police practices and policies. Because many prosecutors' offices maintain a staff of police officers who conduct investigations, secure evidence, and initiate prosecutions, these police officers' practices and conduct, as well as those of their fellow officers, come under the close scrutiny of the district attorney's office. This vigilance aids police by providing them with up-to-date information concerning the rapidly changing laws that govern arrest practices, search and seizure, and so forth. It has been determined in many jurisdictions that "investigations and prosecutions for crimes such as homicide, consumer fraud, governmental corruption, and organized crime, which typically involve difficult problems of proof and require lengthy and careful investigations, are best conducted under the direct supervision of the prosecutor's office."[6] In this position, the prosecutor is both criminal investigator and initiator of the criminal process. This dual role has led many to consider the district attorney the chief law enforcement agent in the criminal justice process.

### Criminal Court System

"The courts are the pivot on which the criminal justice system turns."[7] Although varying in details of organizational structure and jurisdiction, the state court systems of the United States are generally structured in the following manner: *Lower courts,* such as magistrates' courts, justice of the peace courts, and municipal courts, render judgment when petty offenses are involved and set bail and conduct preliminary hearings in felony cases. *Trial courts,* such as county courts and district courts, occupy an intermediate level in the court system. As courts of record, that is, the court in which a written transcript of the trial is kept, trial courts with general jurisdiction handle appeals from the lower courts and try cases outside the jurisdiction of the lower courts, such as felony offenses. *Appellate courts* and *supreme courts,* which occupy the highest level in the state court structures, hear appeals from the trial courts and exercise restricted original jurisdiction.

In their formal organization, the courts are concerned with the punitive sanctions for violations of the criminal law. This concern is reflected in the activities of the court personnel, as well as in the very trial process itself, a process that has as its goal the determination of the guilt or innocence of the accused.

There is, however, an informal court organization that allows the court a certain degree of discretion about whom it should or should not punish and about the nature and extent of the punishment to be imposed. This informal side has made possible some new approaches to the control of crime, for example, by treatment instead of punishment. As the court system now operates, an attempt is being made to be as nonpunitive as possible by the use of such programs as probation and halfway houses coupled with warnings of punishment for the offender who ventures outside the rules of those programs. Further analysis of the formal and informal organization of the criminal court suggests that eventually the conflicting functions of punishment and treatment may lead to a criminal court system that will have as its sole function the determination of the guilt or innocence of the accused, a separate organizational system evolving to prescribe the appropriate treatment for the offender, whether it be punitive or otherwise.

### Probation

When an individual is convicted of a crime, the criminal court involved must determine what sentence to give the defendant. Probation provides for the suspension of a prison sentence by the court in order to allow the offender to remain in the community while the length of sentence continues. To help the courts make this decision there is a tool known as the presentence investigation, which, if thoroughly and professionally done, can furnish the court with a factual basis for granting or refusing probation. If probation is granted, the defendant is released by the judge without imprisonment on the basis of a number of conditions, which may include such things as continued good conduct, adequate support of family, and steady employment.

The responsibility for aiding and supervising the probated offender rests with the court's probation department. Its role or function in the criminal justice system begins with the drafting of the presentence report and continues until those offenders who have been put on probation successfully complete their probationary period. Probation officers aid those offenders who constitute their caseload so they may provide sound advice on matters ranging from finances to family matters, and they provide moral support for the offender, who must confront a society that will punish an offender far beyond the punitive action taken by the courts.

### Corrections

"'Corrections,' America's prisons, jails, juvenile training schools, and probation and parole machinery, is the part of the criminal justice system that the public sees least of and knows the least about."[8] Its isolated nature can be attributed to its normally rural location, its nondramatic activities, and the fact that it is the collection point for many of society's problems and outcasts. So total has this isolation been that only recently have the courts attempted to open correctional institutions to public scrutiny and reform. All this is astounding considering the fact that on any given day "there are well over a million people being 'corrected' in America, two-thirds on probation and parole, and one-third of them in prisons or jails."[9]

The trend reflected in the history of the correctional institutions in the United States has been away from punishment toward treatment and rehabilitation under supervision. Within the crime control process, society expects these correctional institutions or agencies to reform the offender, act as a means of retribution, and simultaneously reduce crime rates. What is readily apparent is that performance of the first task immediately develops a conflict with the two other objectives. It is generally assumed today that the conditions conducive to reformation of the offender by treatment do not in most cases include the intentional infliction of suffering, while the objectives of retribution and deterrence necessitate conditions punitive in nature. Even a probated sentence can be considered punitive by an offender because of its restrictions on freedom of movement and the standards of conduct it imposes. It is this conflict of objectives with which all correctional officials must deal in the daily administration of their agencies.

### Parole

The true test of the success of institutional corrections programs, whether the goal is rehabilitation, retribution, or deterrence, comes when the offenders are released to the community. Some offenders are released directly from prison on completion of their sentences without further supervision. However, ever-growing numbers, now more than 60 percent of adult felons in the nation as a whole, are released on parole before completion of their entire prison sentences.[10] With the exception of sentencing, no decision in the criminal process has more impact on the convicted offender than the parole decision. Ironically enough, the parole board, which must make this all important decision, usually can spend no more than a few minutes with each potential parolee before determining whether to parole or to continue detention.

When an offender is paroled, he or she faces a situation similar to that of a probationer. Under the supervision of a parole officer, the parolee will be required to work at approved jobs, avoid companions who have criminal records, adequately support his or her family, and so forth. If these and other parole conditions are violated, the offender may be returned to the penal institution to serve the remainder of the sentence. The function of the parole officer is to help the parolee return to employment, family life, and the community in general. This period is very critical in the life of the offender, who must once again face the problems from which he or she has been temporarily separated and encounter the additional problems that arise from the new status of ex-offender.

The parole function, then, is at the end of the criminal justice system. The offender has by now been processed by the agencies of the police, the prosecution, the courts, in some cases probation, and the correctional institution. Theoretically, if these agencies have been effective in carrying out their respective responsibilities one would expect that the offender on parole is now ready to assume his or her rightful place in society. It is the responsibility of the paroling authority to ensure that the offender is given every possible chance to assume this law-abiding role.

Briefly then, the adversary system of criminal justice in America today is the apparatus whereby society identifies, accuses, tries, convicts, and punishes offenders for violations of the criminal law. As a sequential crime control process, the system attempts to remove dangerous people from the community, deter others from law violation by punitive sanction, and make the offender into a law-abiding citizen. To achieve these purposes, the system is divided into three major components—the *law enforcement community*, the *judicial community*, and the *corrections community*. At the various levels of government, the law enforcement community is composed of police officers, sheriffs, state troopers, FBI agents, and other functionaries, who are responsible for enforcing the laws. In addition to enforcing the laws, police officers are responsible for a number of community services such as providing ambulance service, resolving domestic problems, and performing other numerous service functions. The judicial community includes the prosecution and the courts. It is the prosecution's responsibility to represent the government in court and to see that the proper persons are appropriately charged. The courts, which consist of judges, magistrates, juries, and so forth, are responsible for the trial process. The courts must ensure that the law is properly applied to the case at hand and that all parties to the proceedings receive justice. The corrections community comprises probation, prisons, and parole. Probation is a process whereby a convicted offender is released after trial to the community under certain conditions. A probation officer supervises the offender to ensure that he or she adheres to the conditions of the sentence, and provides the probationer with assistance should it be necessary. Prisons, or corrections, are the many institutions that house convicted criminal offenders. Correctional workers are responsible for detaining and rehabilitating the offender. Finally, parole is a process whereby the offender is released from prison to the community under certain conditions. A parole officer supervises the offender to ensure that the specified conditions are met, and also assists the parolee should it be necessary. All of these agencies, the police, the prosecution, the courts, probation, corrections, and parole, are major functional areas of the criminal justice system. They are the agencies that we shall be dealing with in the following chapters.

## DISCUSSION QUESTIONS

1. Would you call the police the "catchers" or "gatekeepers" of the criminal justice system? Why?
2. Does the action of one agency of the criminal justice system affect another agency of the criminal justice system? How?
3. Recognizing that the agencies of criminal justice are sealed off from each other by boundaries of legal jurisdiction, political allegiance, and budgetary responsibility, discuss the feasibility of creating a full-time "criminal justice office" to help alleviate these roadblocks to an effective criminal justice system.
4. The American legal system is an adversary system of law. Discuss alternatives to this adversary system for implementation of the legal processes in America.
5. After a close inspection of Illustration 2.1, determine where your local agencies of criminal justice are located in this illustration. Do your local agencies perform the processes indicated in this illustration? How do they differ?
6. Should the police be concerned only with law enforcement? Who should provide the many social services that police officers provide?
7. Probation and parole are similar processes. Should they be performed by one agency, as they are in some locations, or by separate agencies? Why?
8. As you may have noticed judges wear black robes, the bench or desk is elevated, and some of the court procedure is ritualistic. What psychological affect does this have on the trial process? Is this a good or bad affect?

## NOTES

1. Hazel B. Kerper, *Introduction to the Criminal Justice System* (St. Paul, Minn.: West Publishing, 1972), p. 171.

2. President's Commission on Law Enforcement and Administration of Justice, *The Challenge of Crime in a Free Society* (Washington, D.C.: Government Printing Office, 1967), p. 159.
3. Kerper, p. 188.
4. *Challenge of Crime*, p. 154.
5. *Law and Order Reconsidered: Report of the Task Force on Law and Law Enforcement to the National Commission on the Causes and Prevention of Violence* (Washington, D.C.: Government Printing Office, 1970).
6. President's Commission on Law Enforcement and Administration of Justice, *Task Force Report: The Courts* (Washington, D.C.: Government Printing Office, 1967), p. 72.
7. *Task Force Report: The Courts*, p. 1.
8. *Challenge of Crime*, p. 159.
9. *Challenge of Crime*, p. 12.
10. President's Commission on Law Enforcement and Administration of Justice, *Task Force Report: Corrections* (Washington, D.C.: Government Printing Office, 1967), p. 60.

MARCH
18

# 3: The Criminal Justice Process

*PREARREST INVESTIGATION • ARREST • BOOKING • INITIAL APPEARANCE • PRELIMINARY HEARING • GRAND JURY INDICTMENT OR INFORMATION • ARRAIGNMENT IN COURT OF TRIAL • FILING A MOTION • TRIAL • APPEALS • HABEAS CORPUS • JUVENILE PROCEEDINGS*

PURPOSE: *TO OVERVIEW THE CRIMINAL JUSTICE PROCESS AND PLACE THE PROCESS IN ITS PROPER PERSPECTIVE.*

ONE of the primary functions of an organized society is to protect its members from the criminal element. In the United States this function is handled through the crime control process known as the "administration of criminal justice." The entire process involves those agents and agencies of the government that have been assigned crime control functions; those statutes and the case law that define criminal conduct; and, most important of all, the concept of due process, guaranteed to every individual in the society by the federal Constitution.

When a crime is committed, the criminal justice process begins with the police, who have the primary obligation of investigating the criminal act and apprehending the criminal offender. If the police collect sufficient evidence, the prosecutor prepares the formal charges and initiates the court action. The trial proceeding itself assumes the innocence of the defendant until the state can prove guilt beyond a reasonable doubt. This constitutionally prescribed minimum requirement of proof is ensured not only by the court itself but by the defendant's counsel, whether that counsel is privately retained or assigned by the court. Each step of the process of arrest, evidence gathering, and pleadings is carefully scrutinized by the court so that due process is upheld. If a verdict of guilty is returned against the accused, sentencing approximates as closely as possible the rehabilitative needs of the defendant as outlined in the presentence report and allowed by law. Regardless of whether the sentence is probation or incarceration, each defendant has the right to appeal all lower court decisions to the appropriate court of higher appeal. These courts of appellate jurisdiction may review the case in its entirety and, if the situation warrants it, reverse the decision of the lower court.

In order to explain fully the inner workings of this criminal justice process, the cases of two individuals will be traced through its continuum from incident to release. The criminal justice process outlined in this example is typical, but in actuality details would vary from state to state. For the purposes of this chapter, the criminal justice process of a major metropolitan city somewhere in the United States is used. Although the characters are fictitious, as is their armed robbery of a liquor store for $600 in cash, this walk-through is intended to bring the criminal justice process to life. From incident to release, this process is filled with constitutional safeguards, enforced by the procedural law, to protect both the innocent and the guilty so that justice may be served. Although the time lapse between stages varies according to jurisdiction, Illustration 3.1 (pp. 42–43) provides a sequential frame of reference for the hypothetical armed robbery.

## *PREARREST INVESTIGATION*

The process began after the commission of the crime, when the store manager quickly notified the police by phone of the robbery. A local patrol unit, dispatched to the scene of the crime, was able to get a fairly complete description of the two suspects. Subsequent on-the-scene interviews with witnesses to the crime provided these officers with a description of the vehicle used by the robbers and a license plate number. This information was dispatched to other patrol units in the area while the crime-scene investigation was continued.

Although this is a very common beginning for prearrest investigations, not all police investigations start this way. Some are initiated through a citizen's complaint, perhaps a complaint about a noisy party. Others unfold through the routine police patrol function; that is, this robbery might have been detected by a local patrol unit and the robbers apprehended at the scene of the crime. All these examples reflect daily police investigations that may or may not lead to an arrest.

## *ARREST*

In their efforts to flee the scene of the crime rapidly, the two armed robbers committed a number of traffic violations, one of which brought them to the attention of a traffic patrol unit. The officers stopped the fleeing vehicle for the violation and, armed with the information of the recent robbery, began to question the driver and the passenger. Sufficient probable cause was established on the basis of matching license plate number, description of the vehicle, and description of the suspects. *Probable cause* is an apparent state of facts, sufficient in themselves to warrant a person of reasonable caution to believe that an offense has been or is being committed. After establishing probable cause, the officers took both suspects into custody.

The act of taking a person into custody is ordinarily known as an *arrest*. Although the situation described may suggest that an arrest is a very simple procedure, in actuality the rules that govern an arrest are complicated. The standards that all law enforcement officials must comply with in order to legally arrest an individual have their foundation in the Fourth Amendment to the federal Constitution, which reads as follows:

> The right of the people to be secure in their persons, houses, papers, and effects, against unreasonable searches and seizures, shall not be violated, and no warrants shall be issued, but upon probable cause, supported by oath of affirmation and particularly describing the place to be searched and the persons or things to be seized.

Readily obvious is the fact that this amendment safeguards these two suspects from unreasonable seizure not only of their persons, but also of their property. The key word is "unreasonable"; the Constitution does not prohibit lawful arrests, searches, and seizures. Consequently, since these officers had reasonable suspicion that these men had committed armed robbery, they were authorized to conduct a "stop and frisk." A *frisk* is a "pat down" search of the person to see if he or she is carrying a weapon. "An officer is justified in detaining one who he 'reasonably suspects' is committing, has committed, or is about to commit certain specified crimes."[1]

For these officers to progress from

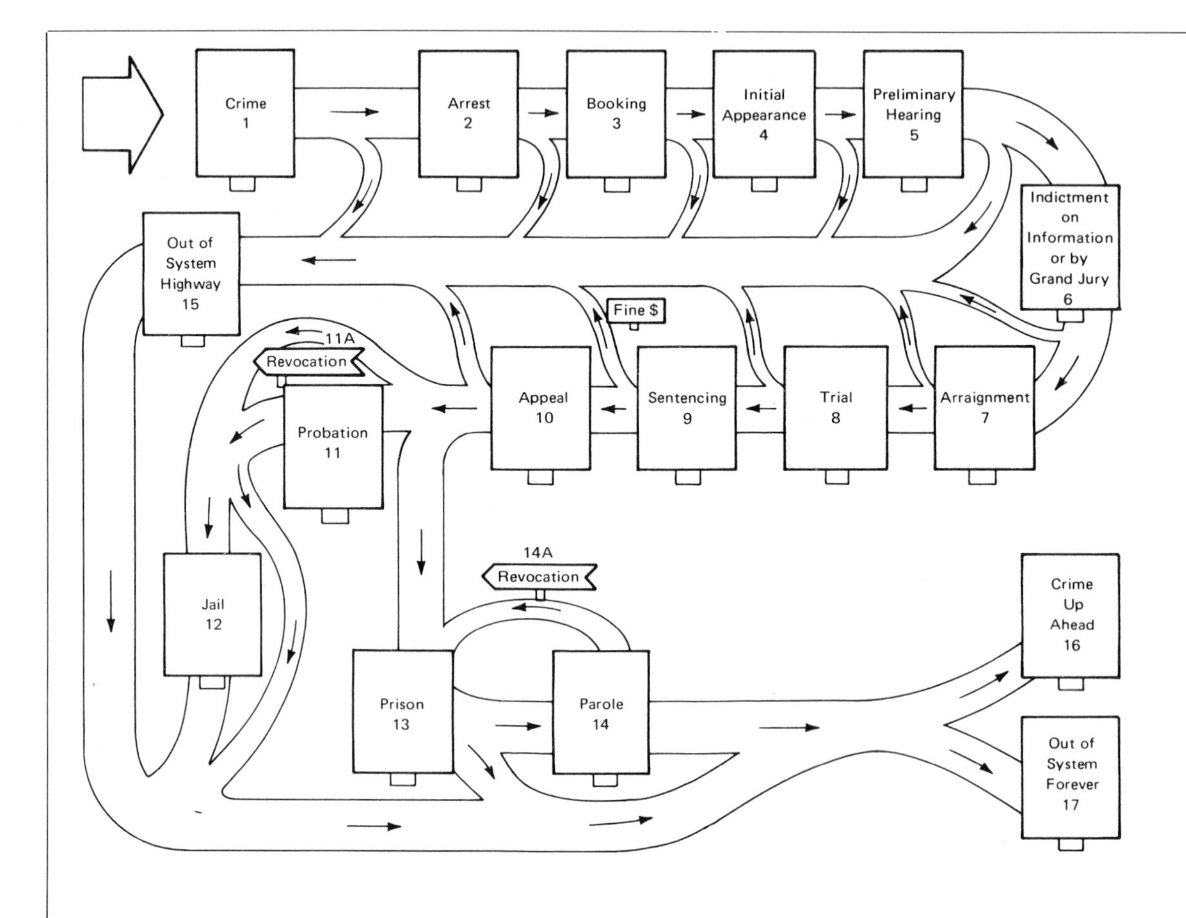

**Illustration 3.1** CRIMINAL JUSTICE HIGHWAY

The Criminal Justice Highway represents a simplified version of the criminal justice process. The road signs represent the major points along the highway. As you will note, one can leave the Criminal Justice Highway at almost any point along the way. For the most part, it is a one-way highway.

1. *Crime* is an act committed or omitted in violation of a law forbidding or commanding it, and to which, upon conviction, there is some form of punishment.
2. *Arrest* is the apprehending or detaining of a person in order that he or she may be forthcoming to answer an alleged or suspected crime.
3. *Booking* is the preparation of official police records of the arrest or an administrative record of arrest.
4. *Initial Appearance* is a formal notice of

charge and advice of rights. Bail and the date for a further hearing are set. For petty offenses, this may be a summary trial without further processsing.

5. *Preliminary Hearing* is the examination before a magistrate of a person charged with a crime to determine whether there is evidence to warrant and require the commitment and/or holding to bail of the person accused.
6. *Indictment* is a written statement charging a person with committing a crime. It is arrived at through a grand jury or information.
   *Grand Jury* is a body of people who listen to charges presented usually by the prosecutor and then determine whether to indict or dismiss the case.
   *Information* means that on the basis of facts that the prosecutor has, charges may be filed directly with the court and the case may go to trial.
7. *Arraignment* is the appearance for plea by the defendant who then elects trial by judge or jury. It is during arraignment that counsel is appointed for those defendants who cannot afford to retain a lawyer. At this point plea bargaining usually begins. The defendant and counsel negotiate with the prosecutor for a lesser charge in exchange for a plea of guilty. Plea bargaining usually brings the defendant a lesser charge, and it removes the case from the trial process.
8. *Trial* refers to adversary proceedings in which the prosecution tries to prove the defendant's guilt, and the defendant's counsel tries to prove innocence either before a judge or jury.
9. *Sentencing* If found guilty, the defendant may be condemned to a punishment by the judge or, in some states, by a sentencing jury. Sentences may include fines, suspended sentence, probation, jail, prison, or whatever punishment is deemed appropriate. The sentence, of course, must be within procedural guidelines.
10. *Appeal* is the defendant's request for a review of the trial to a higher court. Such court may reverse the decision, confirm the decision, or remand for new trial.
11. *Probation* is a sentence of a person for a specified period of time, under supervision of the court, restricted to certain conditions while living in the community. If the conditions are violated, the probationer may have probation revoked (11A) and be sent to jail or prison.
12. *Jail* is a facility usually operated by a local government for short-term misdemeanant offenders. A jail usually holds persons whose sentences are a year or less. Persons awaiting trial are also held in jail when not on bail.
13. *Prison* is usually a state-operated institution that holds offenders who have committed a felony and whose sentence is longer than a year. Offenders may be released to parole or released directly from prison.
14. *Parole* is the offender's release from prison into the community under supervision, under certain conditions, and for a specified length of time. Parole may be revoked (14A) and the parolee returned to prison if the conditions of parole are violated.
15. *Out of System Highway* At almost any point along the way a person can leave the Criminal Justice Highway providing the legal authorities cannot show cause as to why one should continue on the Criminal Justice Highway.
16. *Crime up Ahead* Some people commit new crimes and find themselves back on the Criminal Justice Highway.
17. *Out of System Forever* Some persons and ex-offenders never become involved in the Criminal Justice Highway again.

merely detaining these suspects to a lawful arrest, four distinct elements are involved:

1. the purpose or intention to make an arrest
2. the communication of this intention to the person to be arrested
3. the accomplishment of an actual seizure or constructive (implied or expressed) seizure or restraint by the arresting person of the individual to be arrested
4. the understanding by the arrested person that he or she is being arrested

## *BOOKING*

The stop and frisk conducted by the traffic patrol officers revealed that both suspects were armed, and the search incidental to their arrest also revealed a sizable amount of cash in a paper bag. With both suspects in custody, the patrol officers proceeded to their district station. There an administrative record of the arrest was made, a procedure formally known as *booking.* A cursory identity check by the arresting patrol officers revealed that one of the suspects was only fifteen years of age. Since a fifteen-year-old is a juvenile, this individual was not taken through the same booking process as the adult. The police handed over this youth to the appropriate juvenile intake personnel of the county juvenile court, and his encounter with the criminal justice system will be dealt with later in this chapter.

The booking process for the adult member of this criminal team entailed entry on the official arrest record of the suspect's name, the offense with which he was being charged, and the time and place of the occurrence of the offense. The arresting officer completed a detailed report of the nature and circumstances of the arrest for later verification of "probable cause" because an arrest warrant had not been issued. To positively establish the arrestee's identity, he was both fingerprinted and photographed, and police records were subsequently checked for any warrants outstanding on him. Before the suspect's detention in a cell, he was thoroughly searched, a record was made of any personal belongings taken from him, and, to protect his valuables, he was given a receipt for them. Once again he was informed of his right to remain silent, warned that anything he says may be used against him, and that he has a right to counsel. The entire procedure was noted in the arrest record. After it was completed, the suspect was allowed to notify one individual of his detention in jail—a relative, his attorney, etc.

## *INITIAL APPEARANCE*

When a person is arrested, with or without a warrant, both state and federal statutes require that this individual be taken without "unnecessary" delay before the nearest magistrate or judge.[2] This, of course, does not preclude law enforcement officials from first carrying out such postarrest processes as booking, and the legality of the arrest is not put in jeopardy if delay occurs because a magistrate is not readily available.

The purpose of this *initial appearance* or, formally, *presentment,* is twofold. First, the defendant or arrested person is informed of the charges pending against him or her, as well as of all applicable constitutional rights. These rights normally include notice of defendant's right to remain silent and right to counsel, as well as the right to have a *preliminary hearing* and to know the date and the time of that hearing. The charge itself, whether it is a felony or a misdemeanor, determines whether the offense is within the legal jurisdiction of that particular magistrate or judge. Most misdemeanor offenses are within the legal jurisdiction of the magistrate or judge at the initial appearance, thereby allowing the same person to hear the case, unless the defendant requests a trial by jury. Felony charges are generally beyond the trial jurisdiction of the lower courts in which the initial appearance is made.

Secondly, the magistrate or judge may set bail for the accused. *Bail* is a guarantee, usually in the form of money, that the accused will appear in court. The amount is traditionally based on the nature of the offense. Time permitting, other factors dealing with the defendant (prior criminal record, employment record, family ties, and so on) will be taken into consideration by the judiciary when setting the bail. Often an individual is released on his or her own recognizance if a background check proves favorable. This simply means that no bail is required; the defendant merely signs his or her own bond and agrees to return for the trial.

For the defendant armed robber of our example, bail was set at $5,000. Unable to post the required bail, the defendant was transferred to the county jail to await his preliminary hearing, which was set for the next day.

## *PRELIMINARY HEARING*

Although the federal constitution does not require that an individual have a *preliminary hearing,* the main function of such a hearing is to ensure that unwarranted detention of an accused does not take place and that sufficient probable cause has been established. (Probable cause is a constitutional requirement.) Thus, the burden falls on the prosecution to establish that a crime has been committed and that there exists reasonable ground to believe that the accused armed robber did, in fact, commit the crime with which he is being charged. This does not mean, however, that the state's evidence must prove the case against our defendant beyond a reasonable doubt at this point; a *prima facie* case (one good on the surface or face) will suffice in most jurisdictions. Failure to establish reasonable belief of guilt results in the discharging of the accused, but does not bar a grand jury indictment on the same evidence or additional evidence at a later date.

Besides ensuring that the constitutional requirement of probable cause is established against the armed robber, the preliminary hearing also indirectly provides two other safeguards for him. One, in order to establish probable cause, the state must reveal some, but not all, of the evidence it has against the defendant, thus providing pretrial information (referred to as pretrial discovery) for the accused and his counsel. Secondly, because much of this evidence is likely to come in the form of testimony by witnesses for the prosecution, the defendant's counsel has an ideal opportunity to pin down the testimony of the witnesses so that any deviation during the trial itself can be brought to the attention of the jury and, counsel hopes, weaken the credibility of the state's case.[3] It should also be noted that in some states, the preliminary hearing can be waived by the defendant if done knowingly and intelligently.

If the preliminary hearing reveals that the accusations against a suspect are reasonable (or if the suspect has waived the hearing), the accused is *bound over* to the grand jury. This simply means that our armed robber was held in jail until the charges against him were presented before the grand jury. If this suspect had been able to make bail, he would have been freed until the time designated for him to appear in court.

## *GRAND JURY INDICTMENT OR INFORMATION*

The United States Constitution requires that the handling of offenses carrying penalties in excess of one year go through the indictment process.[4] Subsequently, the Supreme Court established in *Hurtado v. California* [110 U.S. 516 (1884)] that it was the option of each state to use either an *indictment* or an *information* as a charging vehicle in felony proceedings. For our suspect, the charging vehicle was an indictment.

The *grand jury* itself is a body of men and women numbering between six and twenty-three, depending on the state in which the grand jury is summoned. Its function is another step in the screening process: the state must once again put its evidence to the test in an effort to demonstrate that a crime (in our example, armed robbery) has been committed and that probable cause exists to believe that the defendant committed it. If the requisite number of jurors concur in an indictment, a *true bill* will be returned. This means that the prosecution of the defendant will continue on to the arraignment. A *no bill* occurs when an insufficient number of the jurors concur as to the sufficiency of the indictment. Thus, the prosecution's case against the defendant will be dropped.

In no way is a grand jury indictment a trial. Although the defendant may be called by the grand jury during its hearings, the practice is not common. Traditionally these proceedings are secret and protected by law from public disclosure.

If our suspect had committed a misdemeanor instead of a felony, the charging vehicle in our hypothetical state would normally have been an "information." This legal document is filed by the

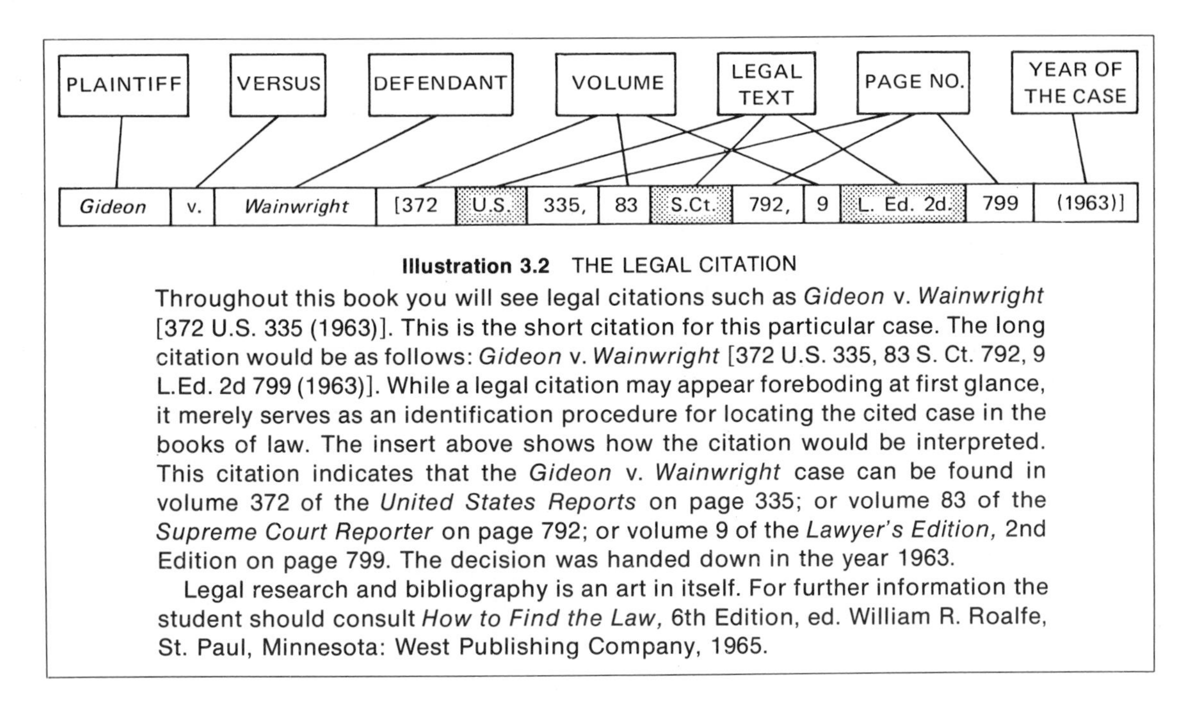


**Illustration 3.2** THE LEGAL CITATION

Throughout this book you will see legal citations such as *Gideon* v. *Wainwright* [372 U.S. 335 (1963)]. This is the short citation for this particular case. The long citation would be as follows: *Gideon* v. *Wainwright* [372 U.S. 335, 83 S. Ct. 792, 9 L.Ed. 2d 799 (1963)]. While a legal citation may appear foreboding at first glance, it merely serves as an identification procedure for locating the cited case in the books of law. The insert above shows how the citation would be interpreted. This citation indicates that the *Gideon* v. *Wainwright* case can be found in volume 372 of the *United States Reports* on page 335; or volume 83 of the *Supreme Court Reporter* on page 792; or volume 9 of the *Lawyer's Edition,* 2nd Edition on page 799. The decision was handed down in the year 1963.

Legal research and bibliography is an art in itself. For further information the student should consult *How to Find the Law,* 6th Edition, ed. William R. Roalfe, St. Paul, Minnesota: West Publishing Company, 1965.

prosecuting attorney after a sworn complaint has been received from and considered by the victim of the criminal act or other knowledgeable persons. In substance, an information is no different from an indictment with the exception that it is filed by the prosecutor in the trial court without approval of a grand jury.

## *ARRAIGNMENT IN COURT OF TRIAL*

The *arraignment* marks the end of the informal screening process for our robbery defendant and the beginning of the formal trial process. Standing before the trial court, the defendant is once again informed of his rights and the nature of the charges filed against him. The major purpose of the arraignment on indictment or information is to confirm the name of the defendant as stated in the charge and to record his "plea" as to those charges. The Supreme Court in *Hamilton* v. *Alabama* [368 U.S. 52 (1961)] declared that because the specific purpose of the arraignment is the entering of the plea by the defendant, it is a "critical stage" in the criminal process and thus necessitates the presence of counsel for all defendants unless knowingly and intelligently waived. Consequently, the defendant, aided by counsel, will stand in open court and enter a plea of *guilty, not guilty,* or *nolo contendere,* as permitted by the laws of our hypothetical state. A plea of *nolo contendere* means that the defendant will not contest the charge.

These three pleas are the most common among those authorized by the statutes of the various states and the federal judicial system. A plea of guilty or *nolo contendere* by any defendant is the equivalent of a verdict of guilty and is so noted on the back of the indictment.[5] Because these two pleas constitute an admission by the defendant to the entire nature of the charge set forth in the indictment, the court must exercise great caution when accepting them. A judge should never accept a plea of guilty or *nolo contendere* without first personally addressing the defendant and

1. determining that he understands the nature of the charge;
2. informing him that by his plea of guilty or *nolo contendere* he waives his right to a trial by jury; and
3. informing him:
   a. of the maximum possible sentence on the charge, including that possible from consecutive sentences;
   b. of the mandatory minimum sentence, if any, on the charge; and
   c. when the offense charged is one for which a different or additional punishment is authorized by reason of the fact that the defendant has previously been convicted of an offense, that this fact may be established after his plea in the present action, if he has been previously convicted, thereby subjecting him to such different or additional punishment.[6]

The tremendously frequent use of plea bargaining in the American system of justice gives added importance to the role of the presiding judge in determining whether each defendant has made his or her plea voluntarily, knowingly, and accurately. This is particularly important when the defendant is pleading guilty after "bargaining" with the prosecution over the nature of the charge and possible penalties stemming from that charge. The risks that surround plea negotiations are many. The judge may not concur with the prosecution's recommendation as agreed upon in the bargaining with the defendant; the prosecution itself may go back on the promises made to the defendant in exchange for a plea of guilty; or the defendant may not fully comprehend the nature of the charge and the attendant penalties. Such misunderstandings, whether they are intentional or not, normally result in a withdrawal of the original plea by the defendant with court's permission.

In our example, the armed robbery defendant, represented by counsel, chose to plead not guilty to the charge as set forth in the indictment. Such a plea puts in motion the entire criminal trial process (procedural law), wherein the state will be called upon to prove beyond a reasonable doubt that the defendant did, in fact, commit the alleged offenses as set forth in the indictment.

## *FILING A MOTION*

Prior to the actual trial stage, the defendant has a number of options that can be explored through the legal procedure known as filing a "motion." This motion is simply a request for a court order. For example, a "motion to suppress evidence" may be filed by the defendant in an effort to prohibit the introduction of certain evidence at trial that the accused believes to have been seized in violation of his or her Fourth Amendment rights. Other motions that may provide legal relief are "motion for a change of venue" (change the place of trial), "motion for a bill of particulars" (provide more specific information than contained in the charging vehicle), "motion to dismiss" (dismiss the indictment, information, or complaint on such ground as the court does not have jurisdiction over the offender or offense), and "motion of continuance" (request for additional time to prepare for trial). Such motions, whether filed by the prosecution or defense, are normally heard during a pretrial hearing without the trial jury being present. To counter such motions, an affidavit showing why such grounds do not exist may be filed.

## *TRIAL*

Lacking sufficient "good cause" for the entry of any pretrial motions, the defendant armed robber had to prepare for the trial process. Initially, he had to decide whether or not to have a trial by bench (that is, the judge alone) or a trial by jury as guaranteed by the Sixth Amendment. Waiving a jury trial is usually a defendant's option, but not in all states. In this model state, the defendant may waive the right to trial by jury for this particular offense. Note that if the defendant had pleaded guilty to the allegations set forth in the indictment, judgment would have been rendered automatically by the presiding judge without a jury because no question of fact exists for a jury to decide.

Having elected to proceed with a jury trial, our armed robbery defendant will encounter the following sequence of events:

1. selection of the jury
2. opening statements by the prosecution and the defense, in that order
3. presentation of government's evidence including witnesses and exhibits in an effort to establish proof beyond reasonable doubt (This entails the direct examination by the prosecution of its witnesses and the cross-examination of these witnesses by the defense.)
4. presentation and arguments of defense motions
5. presentation by the defense of evidence that will create a reasonable doubt as to the evidence presented by the prosecution (This entails the direct examination by the defense of its witnesses and cross-examination by the state.)
6. presentation of rebuttal evidence by the government if the defense raised affirmative defenses that were not negated by the prosecution in the presentation of its case
7. instructions of the court to the jury
8. arguments to the jury by prosecutor and defense counsel
9. charging of the jury by the judge
10. jury deliberations and verdict
11. judgment and posttrial motions
12. sentencing

How soon after arraignment this trial process will begin depends on many factors: the trial court's caseload, granted pretrial motions, whether the defendant is being held in jail, etc. The Supreme Court recently commented on the constitutional safeguard of speedy trial as set forth in the Sixth Amendment:

> This guarantee is an important safeguard to prevent undue and oppressive incarceration prior to trial, to minimize anxiety and concern accompanying public accusation, and to limit the possibilities that long delays will impair the ability of an accused to defend himself. However, in a large measure because of many procedural safeguards provided to an accused, the ordinary procedures for criminal prosecutions are designed to move at a deliberate pace. A requirement of unreasonable speed would have a deleterious effect, both upon the right of the accused and upon the ability of society to protect itself. Therefore, this court has been consistently of the view that the right of a speedy trial is necessarily relative. It is consistent with delays and depends upon circumstances. It secures rights to a defendant. It does not preclude the rights of public justice.[7]

Some states, for example Illinois, have enacted statutory provisions that prescribe that an individual must be brought to trial within 120 days if held in custody and within 160 days if out on bail. Motions for continuance can be granted for a period not to exceed 60 days.[8] Failure to comply with this statutory provision may result in the dismissal of the case for want of prosecution, depending on the circumstances of the delay.

### Prosecution Case

Success for a prosecuting attorney lies in the ability to introduce evidence[9] that will prove the state's case beyond a reasonable doubt. As the burden of proof rests on the plaintiff (the state), the plaintiff is entitled to the first and last word during the evidence-presentation phase of the trial.

A prosecuting attorney begins the state's case by first calling witnesses who can establish the elements of the offense, and then proceeding to witnesses who will introduce real evidence (physical or demonstrative objects). For example, in our robbery case, the manager of the liquor store on duty the night of the robbery could provide the jury with a detailed account of the criminal act as he saw it. The arresting officers could supplement this testimony with pertinent testimony regarding the weapons and money that they seized from the two armed robbers on the night of the crime. To be relevant, evidence must bear some relationship to the contested issues of the case and must have a tendency to prove some fact that is material in the dispute. If the arresting officers had found marihuana in the suspect's vehicle, testifying to that fact would not be relevant to the issue at hand, and the defense counsel would normally object to such testimony as irrelevant and immaterial. There are "rules of evidence" in statutory law and in case law to protect the defendant from evidence that is irrelevant, immaterial, and incompetent.

The prosecution's direct examination of its witnesses is followed by the cross-examination of the same witnesses by the defense. At this stage, counsel for the defense is restricted to the facts brought out by the prosecution in the direct examination phase, so here the defense attempts to discredit the prosecution's efforts to establish proof beyond a reasonable doubt.

### Defense Motion

At the close of the prosecution's case, the trial judge may dismiss the case from the jury (referred to as a "directed verdict") when the state has failed to provide enough proof to sustain a conviction. Or the defense may enter a motion to this effect. The granting of such a motion by the trial judge results in the defendant's *acquittal*, which means dismissal of charges against the defendant. He or she is released from custody, with immunity from further prosecution for that specific crime. This motion may also be entered at the conclusion of the introduction of all evidence.

### Defense Case and Prosecution Rebuttal

Having failed to secure a directed verdict of acquittal, the defense begins its case. Like the prosecution, the defense counsel presents witnesses for direct examination. The state has the option of cross-examination if it sees fit. When the defense has exhausted all its evidence in an attempt to establish the accused's innocence, it will rest its case.

The prosecution may, at the termination of the defense's presentation of evidence, feel that various aspects of its case have been weakened and need to be bolstered. Consequently, the prosecution is allowed to rebut the defendant's evidence with new witnesses or the re-examination of those previously called. Rebuttal is not, however, a privilege only of the prosecution. The defense, in an effort to strengthen its case, may also call additional witnesses or re-examine those previously called.

Occasionally, the defense may feel it necessary to have the accused testify in his or her own behalf. This decision involves the waiver of the defendant's privilege against self-incrimination as guaranteed by the Fifth Amendment to the Constitution. The failure of a defendant to testify cannot be commented on by either the trial court or the prosecution in the presence of the jury.[10]

### Instructions of the Court to the Jury

When the court does not direct or grant a motion for dismissal after the evidentiary stage of the proceedings, the case goes to the jury, and the judge delivers to the jury a written charge, which sets forth the law applicable to the case. These instructions are prepared by the judge and the attorneys in the case after all the evidence has been received. In these instructions, the judge is not allowed to express any opinion as to the weight of the evidence presented or to summarize the testimony or discuss any of the facts or arguments that might arouse the sympathy or excite the passions of the jury.

### Arguments to the Jury

Usually this segment of the trial proceedings is by far the most dramatic and critical stage for the defense and for the prosecution. It is now that each side attempts to persuade the jury to reach a verdict favorable to its position. They attempt to influence the jury by reviewing the evidence presented, interpreting the instructions to the jury, and condemning the credibility of the opposition's witnesses. Generally, the state is allowed the final argument.

**Charging the Jury**

On completion of the argument, the judge instructs the jury as to its responsibility for rendering a true and just verdict in light of the facts of the case, the instruction of the court, and the arguments of counsel. The jury is told the possible verdicts it may render according to the statutory provisions governing the case. Possible verdicts may be guilty, not guilty, not guilty by reason of insanity, and so forth.

**Deliberation and Verdict**

After being charged by the court, the jurors retire to the jury room, where they deliberate on the issues of the case. It is one of the duties of the bailiff of the court to ensure that the deliberations are carried out in complete privacy. Requests for transcripts of the testimony, additional instructions from the court, and other necessary information may be made directly to the presiding judge. Because deliberations very often take more than one day, the bailiff is also in charge of securing food and housing for the jury.

When the jury has reached a decision, it advises the bailiff and returns to the courtroom. The verdict may be returned either orally or in writing by the foreman of the jury. In some cases the verdict in written form is read by the court itself, instead of by the foreman. A jury that fails to reach a unanimous verdict is known as a *hung jury* and results in a mistrial. Before the court declares a mistrial, the jurors are normally questioned in open court about their inability to reach a unanimous decision.

If either the state or the defense feels that the verdict rendered does not represent the considered voluntary judgment of all the jurors, it is possible to poll the jury in open court. Normally the request is made by the defense after a guilty verdict has been entered. A declaration by any juror that he or she was pressured to gain an early release of the jury or to make a verdict unanimous results in a mistrial. A finding of not guilty would have resulted in the immediate release of our armed robbery defendant, but the jury brought in a verdict of guilty.

**Sentencing**

To the defendant who has been found guilty either by bench or by jury, the sentencing phase of the criminal justice process is the most critical. Before issuing the penalty, most judges order a *presentence investigation* of the defendant's background. This report, which is normally compiled by the court's probation officer, covers such things as the family history of the accused; educational and work background; and, particularly important, criminal background. Many states stipulate increased sentences for offenders who have repeated the same or similar offenses. For the first offender, such a report may reveal that the defendant can best be rehabilitated by serving sentence on *probation*. In that case, instead of incarcerating the individual, the court permits him or her to retain freedom under the conditions set forth by law. Before passing sentence, the judge conducts a hearing, at which time the prosecution and the defense are allowed to advance opinions as to the severity of the sentence that should be imposed.

At present, in all but thirteen states, the sentencing function rests with the trial judge.[11] However, when the crime carries an extremely heavy penalty, as in the case of murder and rape, this responsibility is often turned over to the jury. In some states, the defendant is permitted to choose between judge and jury sentencing. Regardless of who has the authority to decide the penalty, any sentence imposed must be within the limits prescribed by law. Many states have adopted the "indeterminate sentence," which allows the trial judge to sentence for the maximum term allowed by law and gives the parole board authority to determine the exact amount of time to be served. For our armed robbery defendant, the sentence was fifteen years in the state correctional institution.

## *APPEALS*

After sentence has been pronounced, the defendant may appeal the conviction to a reviewing court. Although there is no constitutional right to appeal, every state and the federal courts grant a convicted person the right to appeal a lower court's decision.[12] The process of appeal is set forth in the statutes or judicial rules of the jurisdiction involved. In general, appeals are carried from the lower courts to a court of general jurisdiction and from this court of general jurisdiction to an intermediate appellate court or the highest state court.

After a review of the case, the appellate court involved can make any one of a number of decisions. The court may simply *affirm* the lower court's decision, or it may go so far as to *reverse* it. Reversal means that the conviction is nullified and the defendant cannot be retried. A less drastic ruling by the court has the decision *reversed and remanded,* which means that the defendant may be retried if the state elects to do so.

Until recently, state prosecutors had the right to appeal a judgment of acquittal when the trial judge had improperly terminated the proceedings before the prosecution had sufficient opportunity to present its evidence. Today, however, the state may only appeal such pretrial orders as motions to dismiss indictments and motions to suppress evidence. Some jurisdictions do allow the government to appeal judgments for the sole purpose of clarifying questions of law to provide guidance for future criminal cases.

## *HABEAS CORPUS*

To a defendant who has been convicted, has exhausted the appeal processes, and is incarcerated in the appropriate state or federal penitentiary, the hope of a reversal of the original court's verdict seems all but lost. In our society, however, the government must always be accountable to the judiciary for the imprisonment of one of its citizens. A petition for a writ of *habeas corpus*, filed by the prisoner, questions the legality of the detention of the petitioner by alleging violations of the petitioner's rights during the trial process. Such violations may involve denial of counsel at the preliminary hearing or appeal, use of false evidence by the prosecution, use of an involuntary confession, denial of transcript on appeal, and so on.

Normally, these petitions are filed with the court of general trial jurisdiction, which will conduct a hearing to determine if legal authority exists to hold the petitioner. But state prisoners may also file for *habeas corpus* relief in the federal district court having jurisdiction over the penal institution or in the United States Supreme Court. In such a case, the petition normally challenges the original trial court's jurisdiction over the defendant or the legality of the process under which the state is holding the petitioner. While a petitioner may find relief under *habeas corpus,* it is not unusual for the court hearing the petition to give the state the option to retry the petitioner.

## *JUVENILE PROCEEDINGS*

With the adult armed robber convicted, sentenced, and in the state's correctional institution, the juvenile member of this criminal team, left in the hands of the intake personnel of the county juvenile court, remains to be dealt with. In conjunction with the arresting officers, the intake officer prepared a complete report of the circumstances of the arrest and the juvenile's parents were notified of his detention. The report was forwarded to a juvenile probation officer, who made a preliminary decision as to whether the youth was to be held for a court hearing. Often, the conduct of the juvenile is such that the probation officer decides that the child can be handled nonjudicially, whereupon the child is returned to the parents with or without minimum supervision by the probation officer. Because of the nature of the offense involved in our hypothetical incident, the juvenile probation officer conferred with the prosecuting attorney's office and together they elected to file on the youth and proceed with a court hearing. This decision resulted in both the parents and the youth being served with a written copy of the charges being brought against the child, charges that would bring them before the local juvenile court.

### Juvenile Courts

The juvenile court is not a criminal court, nor is it an ordinary civil court. It is in fact a special statutory court that has among its responsibilities the hearing and disposing of cases against juveniles who either offend against the criminal law or who transgress against other rules especially set forth for juveniles. Under the juvenile court's philosophy of individualized justice for each child rest two principles that distinguish the juvenile court system from the adult court.

1. A child in a juvenile court is not regarded as responsible for criminal acts until he or she has attained a much greater age.
2. Under the jurisdiction of the juvenile court a child is never accused of a crime and suffers no conviction or stigma. A child brought before the juvenile court is declared to be a delinquent child needing the care and protection of the court. This is referred to as the court's "delinquency jurisdiction." It also has "dependency jurisdiction," the power to hear cases involving dependent and neglected children.

### *Kent* and *Gault* Decisions

Like the criminal justice system, the *juvenile court system* has come under close scrutiny by the courts of this nation over the past years, particularly the United States Supreme Court. Of the opinions handed down by the Supreme Court, the three decisions having the greatest impact on the juvenile process are *Kent* v. *United States* [383 U.S. 541 (1966)], *In re Gault* [387 U.S. 1 (1967)], and *In re Winship* [397 U.S. 358 (1970)].

*Kent* was the first case in which the Supreme Court touched on the juvenile court process. Previously, the proceedings in the juvenile courts were informal to the point of complete negation of the minimum standards of justice or due process. While fully recognizing the juvenile courts' doctrine of *parens patriae*,[13] the Supreme Court felt this doctrine should be and could be implemented within the constitutional protections and rights afforded every adult. Specifically addressing the question of whether a child would be tried in a juvenile court or in an adult court the Court decided:

1. a child must be given a full hearing on the question of transferring the case to an adult court
2. a child must have the assistance of an attorney at the hearing
3. a child and lawyer must have full access to the social record used by the court to determine whether or not there should be a transfer for certification as an adult
4. juvenile court judges must state in writing the reasons why they chose to waive jurisdiction and transfer a child to an adult court

The following year the Supreme Court in *Gault* re-emphasized and expanded on the constitutional rights of juveniles to be observed and guarded by the juvenile courts. In addition to the right to counsel, the Court emphasized the need for each child and his or her parents to be given proper notice of the scheduled delinquency proceedings and the charges to be heard. The Court felt that juveniles like adults are protected by the constitutional privilege against self-incrimination and have the right to be confronted by those accusing them of criminal law violations or juvenile misconduct.

Questions as to the level of proof necessary before *adjudication*, that is, judgment by a court, were not resolved until the *Winship* case. Here the Supreme Court stated that the standard to be followed was "proof beyond a reasonable doubt," the same minimum requirement that governs adult proceedings. In most states, the determination of whether or not this level of proof has been achieved rests with the juvenile judge, because it has been ruled that juveniles have no constitutional right to trial by jury.[14]

### Adjudicatory Hearing

The purpose of the *adjudicatory hearing* is to determine whether the juvenile did in fact commit the delinquent act with which he or she is charged. Evidence is admitted by each side, state and defense, in an effort to get a ruling in its favor.

One of the many questions left unanswered by *Gault* surrounds the use as evidence of confessions made by juveniles who have not been given a *Miranda* warning.[15] Although there is no requirement to give this warning, its absence may jeopardize the state's evidence if the juvenile is transferred to adult prosecution because of some particularly heinous offense such as murder. In addition, in those states where the jurisdiction of the juvenile court is determined by the age of the juvenile at the time of trial, without the warning evidence may be lost because the juvenile has reached adulthood. In all cases, then, it seems wise to provide even the juvenile offender with a *Miranda* warning in order to preserve important evidence for the state.

### Dispositional Hearing

After the adjudicatory hearing and if the juvenile is found to be delinquent, the juvenile court either makes an immediate decision about the child's future or sets a date for a *dispositional hearing*. How the court chooses to handle the juvenile is greatly determined by the social history report compiled on the child by a juvenile probation officer. Our young delinquent had a negative report, and the juvenile court elected to send him to a state school for boys, a maximum security unit for the control, treatment, and training of chronic, serious juvenile offenders. Other possibilities, not appropriate in his case, are supervised probation, release of the juvenile to the custody and supervision of parents, and other sanctions like the imposition of a fine or a payment of restitution. Unless the juvenile court transfers the case to the adult criminal court, its power to exercise control over the offender lasts until the child becomes an adult as specified in the laws of the state conducting the hearing.

There is no constitutional right to appeal in juvenile cases. However, many states have ventured beyond the minimum standards of due process set forth in *In re Gault* and have extended the right of appeal to juveniles. Should our young delinquent choose to appeal the adjudication of the juvenile court, then a petition can be entered with the Court of Civil Appeals, which in our hypothetical state is an intermediate appellate court below the state supreme court.

The criminal justice highway down which the adult armed robber has passed is one of many paths, numerous detours, countless exits, and alternate routes. Each step in the process is highlighted by constitutional safeguards guaranteed each individual by the due process clause of the Fourteenth Amendment, United States Constitution. Procedural criminal law ensures the protection of the individual liberties of the adult offender and the juvenile by regulating the conduct of those officials engaged in the criminal justice process. The carefully chosen steps that have been described constitute America's crime control process, better known as the administration of criminal justice.

## DISCUSSION QUESTIONS

1. How would you improve the criminal justice process?
2. Can a defendant delay the criminal justice process? Is this to the individual's advantage?
3. Many states have discontinued the use of the grand jury as a way of indicting a suspect. Discuss the pros and cons of this decision relative to the criminal justice process.
4. What impact have the following three Supreme Court decisions had on the juvenile justice process?
   a. *In re Gault* [387 U.S. 1 (1967)]
   b. *Kent* v. *U.S.* [383 U.S. 541 (1966)]
   c. *In re Winship* [397 U.S. 358 (1970)]
5. List the major processes of the criminal justice process from arrest to parole. How would you change this process?

## NOTES

1. John C. Klotter and Jacqueline R. Kanovitz, *Constitutional Law for Police*, 2d ed. (Cincinnati: W. H. Anderson, 1971), p. 100. The Supreme Court in *Terry* v. *Ohio* [392 U.S. 1 (1968)] held that "a police officer may in appropriate circumstances and in an appropriate manner approach a person for purposes of investigating possible criminal behavior even though there is no probable cause to make an arrest" (p. 97).
2. Mallory v. United States, 354 U.S. 449, 454–455 (1957).
3. John Henry Coleman and Otis Stephens, Petitioners v. State of Alabama, 399 U.S. 1 (1970).
4. Fifth Amendment to the U.S. Constitution: "No person shall be held to answer for a capital or otherwise infamous crime, unless on a present or indictment of a Grand Jury."
5. In federal courts and some state courts a defendant may plead *nolo contendere*, which means "no contest." Although it is equal to a plea of guilty, it is not an admission of guilt. Such a plea is most often used when parallel civil action is being filed against the defendant, thereby avoiding the use of a guilty plea as part of the trial for civil offense.
6. American Bar Association Project on Standards for Criminal Justice, *Standards Relating to Pleas of Guilty* (New York: Office of Criminal Justice Project, Approved Draft, 1968), p. 7.

7. United States v. Ewell, 383 U.S. 116 (1966).
8. Illinois Revised Statutes, Chapter 38, Article 103-5 (1965).
9. Evidence includes all legally admissible proof that may be in the form of eyewitness testimony, physical objects of the crime, documents, etc.
10. Griffin v. California, 380 U.S. 609 (1965).
11. American Bar Association Project on Standards for Criminal Justice, *Standards Relating to Sentencing Alternatives and Procedures* (New York: Office of Criminal Justice Project, Approved Draft, 1967), p. 43.
12. The Supreme Court has ruled that where a state has established procedures for appeals, they must be equally available to all defendants. More specifically, the Court states than an indigent defendant must be provided with counsel on appeal plus a free transcript. Griffin v. Illinois, 351 U.S. 12 (1956).
13. *Parens patriae* is the doctrine that the juvenile court acts as a kind and loving parent toward the child.
14. In re Barbara Burrus, 403 U.S. 328 (1971).
15. Miranda v. Arizona, 384 U.S. 436 (1966). In the *Miranda* decision the United States Supreme Court held, "when an individual is taken into custody or otherwise deprived of his freedom . . . he must be warned prior to any questioning that he has the right to remain silent, that anything he says can be used against him in a court of law, that he has the right to the presence of an attorney, and that if he cannot afford an attorney one will be appointed for him prior to any questioning if he so desires." This is known as the *Miranda* warning.

## PART ONE ANNOTATED BIBLIOGRAPHY

Carlson, Ronald L. *Criminal Justice Procedure for Police*. Cincinnati: W. H. Anderson, 1970.

*This excellent text provides the student of criminal justice with a working knowledge of the processing of criminal cases through the varied and sometimes intricate stages of the criminal justice system. Selected court decisions have been reprinted to amplify the reader's understanding of the important points made in the text.*

Day, Frank D. *Criminal Law and Society*. Springfield, Ill.: Charles C. Thomas, 1964.

*This text provides an excellent cornerstone on which some of the more technical aspects of criminal law can be built. Easy to read and understand, this text takes the reader behind the rules of criminal law to their very foundations and origins.*

Kerper, Hazel B. *Introduction to the Criminal Justice System*. St. Paul, Minn.: West Publishing, 1972.

*Intended as a textbook, this is an excellent book for both reference and reading for curiosity. The use of the first person and the lucid style renders complicated information into simple prose. Heavy on law and, therefore, on courts.*

National Advisory Commission on Criminal Justice Standards and Goals. *A National Strategy to Reduce Crime*. Washington, D.C.: Government Printing Office, 1973.

*This volume, one of six reports of the National Advisory Commission on Criminal Justice Standards and Goals, presents a synopsis of the commission's work and its strategy for the reduction of crime in America.*

President's Commission on Law Enforcement and Administration of Justice. *The Challenge of Crime in a Free Society*. Washington, D.C.: Government Printing Office, 1967.

*One of ten reports of the President's Commission on Law Enforcement and Administration of Justice, this report presents a summary of the commission's studies and findings on the American criminal justice system and is probably the best comprehensive report on the criminal justice system in America.*

# PART TWO

# The Police

# 4: History and Development of Police

*POLICE DEVELOPMENT IN ANGLO-EUROPEAN SOCIETIES • ORIGIN OF MODERN POLICING • POLICE DEVELOPMENT IN THE UNITED STATES*

PURPOSE: *TO BRIEFLY TRACE THE HISTORICAL DEVELOPMENT OF THE POLICE AND THE ORIGINS OF THE AMERICAN POLICE FORCE AS WE KNOW IT.*

LAW ENFORCEMENT almost certainly had its beginnings in the lost centuries of prehistory. Undoubtedly early man felt the need to protect his territory and crude possessions. It was not, however, until city states evolved, as exemplified in the Mesopotamian and Egyptian civilizations (3500–700 B.C. and 4500–500 B.C. respectively), that formalized methods of community protection became necessary.

Before then, and as early as 7000 B.C., farming communities like the permanent settlement found at Jarmo, Iraq, had appeared. Although history failed to record much of the culture of such a community, its general protection, as well as the enforcement of its "rules," was probably the responsibility of each individual. Perhaps a community head or clan head was established, but this point is not clear.

Self-policing was probably the first form of law enforcement. The patriarch maintained the order of his family or community by putting the responsibility for maintaining order equally on each member. As centuries passed, however, and the communities increased in both numbers and sophistication, the concept of self-policing proved inadequate and so deteriorated. The complexities of ever-increasing social systems created the need for social protection. About 3700 B.C. cylinder seals were used to identify ownership of documents and vessels. Formal contracts for land sales were drawn up, written in cuneiform, approximately 2750 B.C. Implicit in these developments is the effort to combat crimes of theft and land fraud.

Apparently the folkways and mores were not being complied with; thus they became ineffectual as implements of social control. This fact is substantiated by the attempt in 2150 B.C. of Ur-Nammu, a Sumerian, to establish a code defining societal conduct. Scholars attribute to the Babylonian King Hammurabi (2100 B.C.) the first set of codified laws, commonly known as the Code of Hammurabi.

The development of law is of basic importance to the function of law enforcement. It is the provisions of the law that determine expected conduct and provide for the law's enforcement. Therefore, because Hammurabi's code did provide penalties for noncompliance, it is reasonable to assume that it was to be enforced. To ensure that violators of the code were apprehended and punished, the king in all likelihood designated someone to take what measures were necessary to deal appropriately with such offenders. Whether this someone was an officer of the king's army or a newly appointed official is unclear. Nevertheless, the Code of Hammurabi can be considered a foundation for the development of law enforcement.

Similar developments occurred in ancient China. About 1500 B.C. the Shang Dynasty established and maintained a loosely organized military authority over the settlements in the Yellow River valley. Although this control was accomplished by military and political power, it illustrates compliance with rules established by a central authority. Later the Chou Dynasty (1000–221 B.C.) established a written legal code.

Early Greek civilization (800–600 B.C.) gave birth to the coinage of money and the severe legal code of Draco. Solon, a statesman and reformer, prepared a legal code that opposed tyranny and injustice and laid the constitutional foundations of Athenian democracy. Of great importance in Solon's model was the concept of local autonomy. Note, however, that during that period in history the cities of Athens and Attica combined to form a single political unit. In contemporary law enforcement, such mergers have significant effects.

Roman law was codified by the publication of the Laws of the Twelve Tables (450 B.C.), and enforcement of these laws was carried out by units of the Roman legions. Maintaining order in the city, frequently disrupted by the early Christians, was in later years a major task for the Roman centurions.

Before the Anglo-European developments are addressed, several factors should be reiterated. Thus far it has been observed that compliance to the rules and customs in the early farming communities was a product of self-policing, that is, each person was individually responsible for his or her conduct. Later, as societies became more complex, laws and legal codes were developed. The development of formalized law created a more formal means of enforcement: It delegated enforcement powers to designated officials of the established military, or it simply put the responsibility for social order on a designated individual in the community or on the community as a whole (that is, the entire community might suffer a penalty should a violation occur therein). The point is that responsibility for the enforcement of the law was being delegated to someone or to some group.

At the fall of the Roman Empire (A.D. 395) the enforcement of law by military components was well established, and to this day, the military model prevails in much of continental Europe. This is an important point: The police service in many European countries is in fact part of the military forces. In England and the United States, on the other hand, police services are totally independent of the military organization. They are created by legislative enactments; they are accountable to civilian authority; and their authority, powers, and jurisdiction are defined by the legislature. In spite of this distinction, the organizational structure of many police departments in the United States falls along military lines.

## *POLICE DEVELOPMENT IN ANGLO-EUROPEAN SOCIETIES*

### Early English Development

After the Roman Empire crumbled, the continent was an array of fragmented peoples attempting to maintain some sort of identity. With the leadership of Rome gone, small nations began to form. The desire of most was additional territory, wealth, and power, and this obsession created conflict—war, death, and misery. To avoid the barbarian invasions and the unbearable civil strife, many families migrated in various directions. The continent of Europe became a scene of bloodshed and suffering.

England, however, prospered during this time. Groups formed in small settlements called *tuns*. For protection the principle of "hue and cry" was originated. This concept required every able-bodied man to help in the chase and apprehension of lawbreakers. Failure to take part could force payment of restitution or punishment equal to that of the lawbreaker. This informal method for maintaining peace and order prevailed until the seventh century.

**Frankpledge System (A.D. 800)**

The *frankpledge system,* which was the progenitor of the tithing system, required every freeman above the age of twelve years to belong to a group of ten families (a *tithing*) for the purpose of maintaining the peace and harmony of the community. At the head of each tithing was the chief tithingman, elected from the ten families. The duties and responsibilities of the chief tithingman were to ensure the protection of the tithing as he deemed necessary.

At this point reconsider the patriarchial system employed by the farming community some nine thousand years earlier. The difference lies not in the duties or responsibilities of the clan head or his counterpart the chief tithingman, but rather in the formal system that stipulates, in explicit terms, the protective measures that the tithing must employ. The tithing system can be considered among the earliest attempts to formalize the means by which the community maintains peace and harmony and apprehends and punishes offenders by established customs and laws.

Ten tithings were called a *hundred,* headed by a *reeve.* Several hundreds formed a *shire,* headed by a *shire-reeve* (from which the word "sheriff" was derived). The shire-reeve was given military, judicial, and civil powers, which were frequently exercised inequitably. Although the duties of the shire-reeve were many, the enforcement of the law and the maintenance of the peace are of most significance to us. To provide him with the help necessary to adequately meet the demands of the shire or county, the shire-reeve was vested with *posse comitatus* or "power of the county." This power permitted the shire-reeve to assemble any or all able-bodied men to respond to a "hue and cry" and to seek out and return the offender for trial and punishment.

With all its failures and imperfections, the frankpledge system endured for some time. As society became more complex and the population more mobile, however, the system became inadequate. Growth of the cities added greatly to the deterioration of the tithing system.

**Early Foundations of Anglo-American Police**

With the conquest of England in 1066 by William, Duke of Normandy (William the Conqueror), the pendulum swung away from community responsibility for maintaining peace, as established by the tithing system, toward a concept of "state" responsibility. The Norman Conquest did not remove completely the concepts of the tithing system, but supplemented and supervised the system through military officers who had defined geographical areas of responsibility. The frankpledge system was in effect reaffirmed by the Assize of Clarendon (1166), which required all citizens to pursue by "hue and cry" and by "horn and hounds" any offender fleeing from justice.

During this same period the *comes*

*stabuli* (constable) came into being. His duties were actually to assist the shire-reeve in his duties and to maintain the weapons of the shire.

King Edward I made an authentic attempt to establish a bona fide police organization. The Statute of Winchester (1285) provided a form of police for every community in the empire. The Statute of Winchester tried to cope with rising crime and provide domestic security. It required that city gates be closed between the hours of sunset and sunrise and instituted a night watch. The watchmen, called *bailiffs* (who are today's officers of the court), guarded the city's gates and made tours through the inner city, keeping vigil over all residents and lodgers. The *police des moeurs* was a unit of the night watch responsible for regulating streetwalkers and prostitutes and containing them in the areas of the city where such activities were permitted.

The origin of the word *police* can be traced to either the Greek word *polis*, meaning "city," or to the Roman word *polites*, meaning "citizen." Whatever the case, the Statute of Winchester uses the term *police* in the context of law enforcement, and the genesis of police control and crime prevention through curfews, physical security, and vice control lies with Edward I.

To place these events in proper perspective, note that, America had not been discovered—Columbus had not yet been born—and Asia was in turmoil—Temujin (Genghis Khan) was attempting to unify the Mongol nation. Europe and England, however, were more secure. The University of Paris and University College, Oxford, were established. The European and English atmosphere favored increased urbanization, trade, affluency, and, unfortunately, crime. The need to confront the increasing crime problem became more apparent.

Edward III created an act establishing the *justice of the peace* in 1361. This official was a peace officer appointed by the crown, and his duties were twofold: first, to replace the shire-reeve as the county peace officer; and second, to act in a judicial capacity. In fact, the justice of the peace was both a law enforcement official and a judge (*magistrate*). Although this was at first a means of achieving greater efficiency, it led to the office of the justice of the peace becoming an office of injustice and corruption.

To understand the methods used in selecting persons to occupy the positions of constable, shire-reeve, night watch, and bailiffs is to realize the cause of the system's disintegration. "Citizens who were bound by law to take their turn at police work gradually evaded personal police service by paying others to do the work for them . . . they were usually ill-paid and ignorant men, often too old to be in any sense efficient."[1]

Lack of police efficiency, increasing crime, and public rejection of compulsory police service created a profound dilemma, especially for the city's merchants, who were in dire need of protecting their businesses. Consequently, they began to employ their own private police to protect their establishments and to seek and return stolen goods. This new form of policing was called the *merchant police*.[2]

Cities and towns attempted to combat crime through the formation of distinct territorial divisions (*parishes*) and every member was required to take his turn in the *parochial police.* This system was short lived because of the development of the *paid police.*

England was in a state of lawlessness when her civil war ended in 1655. Oliver Cromwell was in power and had placed the country under military police rule—martial law. Cromwell first divided England and Wales into twelve districts and put each under the direction of a *provost marshall.* The provost marshall acted as the judge in his district and at the same time controlled the civilian population with mounted troops. Military rule was maintained for two years (1655–1657).

In 1663, Charles II created a new system of night watch for the City of London. "The act provided for 1,000 watchmen or 'bellmen' to be on duty from sunset to sunrise. They were ineffective and bore the brunt of English humor, being called 'Charlies' and the 'Shiver and Shake Watch.'"[3]

It was not until 1737 that any significant advancement was made. King George II authorized town councils to levy taxes for the expressed purpose of providing police protection, the first instance of taxation for police protection.[4] Salaries remained deplorable, however, and were reflected in the quality of personnel.

## *ORIGIN OF MODERN POLICING*

Many scholars consider the noted novelist and playwright Henry Fielding (author of *Tom Jones*) the father of modern policing. Fielding was appointed justice of the peace for Westminster in 1748, and he and his half-brother, Sir John Fielding, sat at the Bow Street Magistrates Court.

Henry Fielding took his work seriously and devoted much of his energy to reform. His "Inquiry into the Cause of the Late Increase of Robberies, etc." attracted considerable attention in Parliament, and he was granted funds to implement his suggested remedies. Recruiting an elite group of constables having the qualities of "champions of character," he paid them a salary sufficient to make it possible for them to withstand bribes.[5] The *crème de la crème* became known as the Bow Street Runners. The Runners were equipped with a tip-staff or hollow baton, handcuffs, and pistol, as well as being smartly uniformed.

Nevertheless, crime increased beyond the remedial capabilities of the Bow Street magistrates' efforts. After the Fieldings, other attempts were made to combat crime—without noticeable results.

### Nineteenth Century: A Model for Modern Policing

By 1800 it was evident that the tithing system, hue and cry, constables, justices of the peace, Bow Street Runners, and other provisions were ineffectual. Crime was increasing in unprecedented numbers. This phenomenon can perhaps be attributed to the overwhelming influx of rural people to the cities. Although industrialization, with all its opportunities, also had its consequences—crime—the Industrial Revolution was upon the British nation.

Sir Robert Peel, then England's Home Secretary, recognized that severe punishment for lawbreakers was in itself not the solution to the crime problem, nor was a mere increase in the number of persons vested with the duties of enforcing the law of any real value. Peel presented to Parliament in 1829 "An Act for Improving the Police in and near the Metropolis," now called the Metropolitan Police Act of 1829. On September 29, 1829, the Metropolitan Police became operational with a strength of 3,000 qualified and trained men. Although selection of personnel had over the centuries been based on established criteria, it was under the Police Act of 1829 that the selection criteria, along with mandatory training provisions, became formalized.

To appreciate fully the meticulousness, depth, and far-sightedness of Peel's innovations, the following extract from the first *Instruction Book* (1829), a copy of which was given to each member of the "new" Metropolitan Police in October 1829, should be studied.

> It should be understood, at the outset, that the principal object to be attained is "the Prevention of Crime." To this great end every effort of the Police is to be directed. The security of person and property, the preservation of the public tranquility and all the other objects of a Police Establishment, will thus be better effected, than by the detection and punishment of the offender, after he has succeeded in committing the crime. This should constantly be kept in mind by every member of the Police Force, as the guide for his own conduct. Officers and Police Constables should endeavour to distinguish themselves by such vigilance and activity, as may render it extremely difficult for any one to commit a crime within that portion of the town under their charge.
>
> When in any Division offences are frequently committed, there must be reason to suspect, that the Police is not in that Division properly conducted. The absence of crime will be considered the best proof of the complete efficiency of the Police. . . .
>
> He [the Constable] will be civil and attentive to all persons, of every rank and class; insolence or incivility will not be passed over. . . .
>
> He must be particularly cautious, not to interfere idly or unnecessarily; when required to act, he will do so with decision and boldness. . . .
>
> He must remember, that there is no qualification more indispensable to a Police Officer, than a perfect command of temper, never suffering himself to be moved in the slightest degree, by any language or threats that may be used; if he does his duty in a quiet and determined manner, such conduct will probably induce well-disposed by-standers to assist him, should he require it. . . .
>
> But the first duty of a Constable is always to prevent the commission of a crime.[6]

Command of the Metropolitan Police was initially entrusted to two commissioners: Sir Richard Mayne and Sir Charles Rowan, who were *ex officio* justices of the peace. The Metropolitan Police soon replaced the many independent organizations that existed in the city of London.

The first commissioners impressed upon the force that they were public servants and sent them out unarmed and dressed in a uniform resembling the civilian attire of the period—a suit of blue cloth and a stovepipe hat. This was contrary to Fielding's Bow Street Runners, who were armed with pistols and wore uniforms resembling the military. In 1829 the civilian character and traditions of the modern English police were founded.

Headquarters for the Metropolitan Police was finally established at 4

Whitehall Place, along the Thames. The building was adjacent to the courtyard that had accommodated the kings of Scotland centuries before and was commonly called Scotland Yard by the press. (The Metropolitan Police remained there until 1967, at which time they moved to a modern high-rise, steel and glass structure several blocks away. However, tradition firmly rooted, the name Scotland Yard moved with them to their twentieth-century skyscraper.)

Experience proved that the number of commissioners should be reduced to one. Nominated by the secretary of state, the commissioner was appointed by the crown and given the title Commissioner of Police of the Metropolis. The London Police Act of 1839 established a separate police force for the city of London, headed by its own commissioner.

The Municipal Corporations Act of 1835 required all boroughs in England, regardless of size, to establish a police force, but some of the smaller boroughs did little if anything to comply with this act until the provisions for inspection were introduced by the County and Borough Police Act of 1856. The 1856 act converted to mandatory the permissive powers of the Municipal Corporation Act of 1835 and the County Police Act of 1839 and required each county and borough to establish a police force. To ensure compliance with the provisions of the act, the appointment of H. M. Inspectors of Constabulary was provided for in the act. It also stipulated that a grant be paid by the Exchequer of 25 percent of the approved annual local police expenditure, including pensions. (In 1890 a comprehensive pension plan was introduced.) By the end of the nineteenth century a defined police system had clearly taken shape in England, that is, police forces were established, locally controlled and financed, but with some financial assistance from and some supervision by the central government.[7]

### Twentieth-Century Development in England

A committee was created in 1919 to determine what measures, if any, should be taken by the police with regard to methods of recruiting, rates of pay, and conditions of service. Subsequently the Police Act of 1919 addressed these issues. Further, it established the Police Federation for the purpose of affording members of all police forces of England the opportunity to consider all matters affecting their welfare and enabling them to transmit their views as a body to the secretary of state.[8]

As World War II drew to a close and thousands of qualified men returned to the British labor market, a general review of the police services was essential. The Police Post-War Committee, which sat from 1944 to 1949, considered immediate as well as long-term policy questions. The committee issued four reports, which dealt with the following topics: (a) facilities for training members for higher police ranks, which ultimately led to the creation of the Police College, now located at Bramshill; (b) female police officers, qualifying examinations for promotion, recruitment and training, police prosecutions, and the beat system; (c) police buildings and facilities, and police welfare; and (d) responsibilities in the higher police rank, and a special constabulary.[9]

The Police Act of 1946 was directed toward administrative and operational efficiency. It merged each borough police force with its county force and made possible the amalgamation of two or more forces.[10]

Several other committees were convened to consider the state of the service. However, the Royal Commission on the Police, established in 1960, undertook perhaps the most comprehensive and influential study in the twentieth century, issuing several reports from 1960 to 1967. The various acts that resulted from the several reports dealt with such provisions as the appointment and retirement of chief officers, the duties and powers of the police, the strengthening of the Inspectorate of Constabulary, a central planning and research unit, the consolidation and amalgamation of police forces, district training centers, forensic science laboratories, and regional crime squads.[11]

## *POLICE DEVELOPMENT IN THE UNITED STATES*

History produced many police models that the United States might have emulated. But when our founders established police in the new land, perhaps the common language was the primary factor in the adoption of the English system of government and later the English police model. It should be noted, however, that while our police are similar, they are not an exact copy of our British neighbors'. The American political scene and American police systems are unique, and many factors contribute to the nature of our police forces.

Understanding law enforcement in the United States rests on knowledge of the general political and cultural development of the nation as a whole. The English colonists were apprehensive of central authority. Their migration was, in fact, an attempt to flee the king, who sought to intimidate and suppress political and religious opposition. From such governmental intimidation and suppression of opposition, by means of a formally organized police force, a "police state" evolves. It is obvious then that our founders would go to considerable lengths to limit the power of a central government.

By virtue of geographical factors the Atlantic coastal region took two distinct forms. The Northeast depended chiefly on timber and fishing, and thus small coastal villages and towns matured. On the other hand, the southeastern settlers found fertile soil, and there rural-agrarian communities prevailed. It was logical that the colonies should adopt protective methods known to them from their native England. Therefore, it is not surprising that the New England towns instituted the office of constable and the sparsely populated South relied upon the county sheriff.

Although at least two types of law enforcement existed in Colonial America—the constable (urban) and the sheriff (rural)—as the nation's population, area, and political and cultural base changed so did the number and types of protective arrangements.

PHOTO AND BIOGRAPHY COURTESY OF THE BERKELEY POLICE DEPARTMENT, BERKELEY, CALIF.

**AUGUST VOLLMER**
*1876–1955*

August Vollmer was born March 7,1876 in New Orleans, Louisiana. His father died in 1884 and his mother took August ana his younger brother to California where the family settled in San Francisco in 1888. In 1890, the family moved to North Berkeley where his mother died in 1938.

While living in New Orleans, August Vollmer attended the New Orleans Academy. His move to California brought an end to his formal education, although anyone who met him later would recognize him as a highly educated man.

At the outbreak of the Spanish American War, Vollmer liquidated a fuel and feed store partnership in North Berkeley and enlisted. He participated in the battle for Manila in 1898 and served as one of ninety volunteers on the gunboat Laguna de Bay, keeping the rivers open to travel, convoying troops, and assisting in the capture of river towns.

Returning to Berkeley from the Philippines in 1899, Vollmer received an appointment as a letter carrier, which he held until his friends, believing that he was the only person qualified to deal with the vice conditions then existing in Berkeley, were successful in convincing him to file for the position of Town Marshal. Despite the objections of his family, who thought that service as a policeman would bring disgrace, he was elected to the position on April 10, 1905, thus crossing the threshold of a law enforcement career that was to last a lifetime.

During Vollmer's four-year term of office as Marshal, the city adopted a new charter and a form of government that provided for a police chief to be appointed by the City Council. On August 13, 1909, he was appointed Berkeley's first police chief, a position he filled with distinction until his retirement on July 1, 1932.

Almost immediately after his election in 1905, Vollmer adopted the first of many innovative practices: he mounted his officers on bicycles, followed in 1910 by mounting them on motorcycles. In 1914, with half of his force in the hospital as a result of injuries received in motorcycle accidents, he placed them all in automobiles.

Late in 1905, Vollmer requested an appropriation from the City Council for the installation of a system of flashing lights throughout the city to be used in conjunction with telephones conveniently installed in boxes on telephone poles so that his headquarters might summon officers on patrol for dispatch on police calls. The council was reluctant to grant such a large appropriation but instead, put the issue before the voters in a $25,000 bond issue that carried. In 1906, Vollmer had a communication system in operation that enabled the speedy dispatch of bicycle-mounted officers to the scene of action.

In 1919, during the period of crystal radios

and headsets, Vollmer experimented with a radio receiver installed in a patrol car.

Vollmer immediately recognized the need for complete and accurate police records and set about the development of such a method of record keeping. His system, including a modified British *modus operandi* file, has been widely adopted by other police departments.

In 1907, as president of the California Police Chiefs' Association, he urged the state legislature to create a State Bureau of Criminal Identification. The California State Bureau, created in 1917 after ten years of persistent promotion, has served many other states as a model in the creation of similar clearing houses of information relating to crimes and criminals.

On a national level, a uniform system for the classification and collection of crime data was developed by the International Association of Chiefs of Police some years after Vollmer served as its president in 1921.

Vollmer assisted personally in the reorganization or modernization of the operating methods of scores of police departments, including San Diego, Detroit, Chicago, Kansas City, St. Paul, Minneapolis, Portland, Dallas, Syracuse, and a number of other cities. He served as chief of police of Los Angeles while on a year's leave of absence from Berkeley in 1923. He served as a police consultant to the Wickersham Commission on Law Observance and Enforcement.

Children invariably received sympathetic attention from Vollmer. He organized a junior police before the First World War and later the School Boy Patrol. Under his leadership, Berkeley organized the first Community Coordinating Council for the Prevention of Delinquency in 1919.

He concerned himself with the treatment accorded convicted criminals; he took an active part in promoting the creation of the Youth and Adult Authorities in California. In 1923 he constructed a minimum security prison in Los Angeles, a superior practice that has spread throughout the country.

An awareness of the need for police training prompted Vollmer to establish a police school in the Berkeley Department. Instruction was principally provided by his friends on the faculty of the University of California. A three-year program was designed; each officer was required to complete the program.

At the same time, he interested his University friends in a plan to offer police and other criminology courses at the summer sessions. The plan was inaugurated in 1916 and such courses were given every year (except 1927) until 1932 when the University offered similar courses during the regular school year. Police officials from all parts of the West Coast attended the summer session courses.

Vollmer was appointed Professor of Police Administration at the University of Chicago in 1929, a position he held until 1931 when he accepted a similar appointment at the University of California. He continued in this capacity until he resigned in 1938.

Nearly a dozen West Coast universities and colleges were strongly influenced by Vollmer to institute police and other criminology courses. The program started at the University of California in 1916 developed into a School of Criminology, offering Bachelor's and Master's degrees in Criminology.

Vollmer wrote numerous articles for technical and scientific journals as well as four books: *Police and Modern Society; The Criminal; Crime, Crooks and Cops;* and with A. E. Parker, *Crime and State Police.*

His service as a citizen has been acknowledged by three awards. In 1929 Vollmer received the Harmon Foundation Medal for the most notable contribution to Social Science in the last year. In 1931 he received the Benjamin Ide Wheeler "Distinguished Citizen of Berkeley" award. And in 1934 he received the Academy of Science "Public Welfare Medal" awarded in recognition of the application of scientific principles to police administration.

Unlike England, the United States does not have a centralized system or arrangement for regulating the duties, functions, and organization of its police service. Article X of the Constitution delegates this power to the states. In effect, American law enforcement is composed of many semi-independent systems. Every level of government—municipal or local, county, state, and federal—maintains some form of law enforcement function.

**Municipal and County Law Enforcement**

The first "modern" city police organization in the United States was established in 1844—The New York City Police Department. Before this, many attempts had been made to protect the citizens in every major city. As early as 1636 Boston had a night watch, followed by Philadelphia's in 1700. Philadelphia in 1833 established the first daytime paid police. Five years later Boston followed. Crime problems and subsequent police remedies instituted by our cities were very much like those of England, and they often met with equally disturbing results.

Sir Robert Peel's Metropolitan Police provided the model from which New York City and later the other major cities molded the first American city police departments. Although the basic Peelian principles beaconed the way, several modifications became apparent, primarily because of the differences in national governments. In the United States the establishment and administration of each political subdivision's police department are relatively free from any controls by the next-higher level of government. (Local identity and community autonomy—"home rule"—have not been compromised in the tradition of American government.)

The major cities could provide some form of law enforcement, although the problems of recruiting qualified personnel, training, obtaining police buildings, establishing policy and procedures, and much more had to be solved. But what about the vast majority of America's citizens? Who was to protect them? Certainly New York City, Philadelphia, Boston, and the other cities could not provide police services to the entire population of the United States. There were no state police agencies at this time. Consequently, the rural population looked to their local governments for police service.

County sheriffs typically provided what service they could. However, because both the county sheriff and the town or municipal constable were elected officials, they demonstrated political rather than professional police qualities. Most early state constitutions specifically provided for these offices, making their abolishment or even their dismissal virtually impossible. These constitutional deficiencies still plague the improvement of law enforcement in many states.

The western expansion brought still other peace officers, ranging from citizen groups (vigilantes) to the frontier sheriff. Many exciting tales are told about the frontier sheriff. His duties were comparable to those of the peace officers in eastern counties, but his methods were often somewhat different, as were those of town marshals. Town marshals were often elected by the people of the community, as was the chief of police in the larger cities. Today, with few exceptions, the chief of police is an appointed official.

### State Law Enforcement

Areas outside the cities were likewise becoming more populated, and the need for protective services was apparent. Sheriffs could not provide the necessary law enforcement. Thus, the state governments were pressed for a remedy. The Texas Rangers were established in 1835 in response to this need and became the first form of state law enforcement. Massachusetts in 1865 and Connecticut at the turn of the century organized varieties of state law enforcement. In 1905, Pennsylvania established a force that became the model of later state police organizations. Although the official title of Pennsylvania's police force organization has been changed several times in its history, its functions from the beginning have the essential characteristics of a modern state police unit. The old Pennsylvania State Constabulary today bears the title Pennsylvania State Police.

The need for state law enforcement agencies had been recognized. In 1901 the Arizona Rangers were established, and in 1905 the New Mexico Police were established. A 1917 study by the New Jersey Bureau of State Research recognized that there were a number of statewide police problems.

> The most pressing problems of a statewide nature, which seem to indicate the need for additional protection in New Jersey, are the number of unapprehended criminals, the rural and suburban crime element, the policing of riots, the foreign element, the loss from forest fires, and the enforcement of the road, fish, and game laws.[12]

New Jersey went on to establish a state constabulary in 1921, later to be known as the New Jersey State Police. Other states followed suit and by 1930 twenty-two states had created state police agencies. By 1939 another twenty-four state police agencies were created. Today, all states have some form of state law enforcement under various names and titles.

### Federal Law Enforcement

The United States marshal was the first law enforcement officer in the federal government, created by the Judiciary Act of September 14, 1789. The Revenue Cutter Service was also established in 1789 to prevent smuggling along our seacoasts.

In 1865 legislation was passed to create the Secret Service within the Treasury Department. Counterfeiting of currency had reduced public confidence in the country's money and the Secret Service was to restore it by enforcement of the counterfeiting laws. After the assassination of President McKinley in 1901, the Secret Service was assigned, informally, the task of protecting the president, and in 1903 Congress appropriated funds to the Secret Service for the formal assumption of these duties. John F. Kennedy was the first president to be assassinated while under the protection of this specialized branch of the United States Secret Service.

With the passing of time other federal law enforcement agencies evolved. The forerunner of the Federal Bureau of Investigation was organized in 1908. The FBI was a product of a reorganization in 1924 under the directorship of J. Edgar Hoover, who held that post until his death in 1972. In addition, Drug Enforcement Administration, Internal Revenue Service, United States Marshals, Border Patrol, and many other enforcement bodies in the federal government today provide services to the American public.

Early societies used self-policing as their method of law enforcement. Each individual protected his property and person. As social groups such as clans and tribes developed, the law enforcement function became less the responsibility of the individual and more the responsibility of the group. As societies became even more complex and city-states developed, the government assumed responsibility for law enforcement. In England, where most of the roots of American law enforcement are found, the frankpledge system evolved, and from this the office of sheriff and constable developed. Paid police or watchmen were used in the cities of England during this period. In 1829 Sir Robert Peel introduced an act in Parliament that established the Metropolitan Police of London. This police force served as a model for later American police forces. Colonial Americans adopted the English offices of sheriff and constable. Later in the 1800s city police organizations were created in the large cities. Attempts had been made to create police forces in other cities, but the establishment of the New York City Police in 1844 is considered to be the establishment of the first city police organization. Other cities soon followed. The sheriffs and constables continued to provide law enforcement for the rural areas. The states and the federal government also developed law enforcement agencies. The Texas Rangers were established in 1835, and in 1905 the Pennsylvania State Constabulary was established. The Pennsylvania police force set the model for the development of later state police organizations. The federal government established the United States marshal and Revenue Cutter Service in 1789. In 1865 the Secret Service was established and in 1908 the forerunner of the Federal Bureau of Investigation was organized. In time over fifty federal law enforcement agencies have evolved.

## DISCUSSION QUESTIONS

1. Are police salaries sufficient to make it possible for them (the police) to withstand bribes as Fielding stated in his "Inquiry into the Cause of the Late Increase of Robberies, etc."?
2. How did Fielding, Peel, and others know crime was increasing? How was it measured and by whom?
3. What are the advantages and disadvantages of maintaining federal, state, and local law enforcement agencies in the United Sates?
4. Do you find a single police agency for your state a threat? Why or why not?

5. Do we still need the office of sheriff?
6. How, or to what extent, are police agencies in the United States like those of England? Would the English model work in the United States?

## NOTES

1. Cecil C. H. Moriarty, *Police Procedures and Administration*, 6th ed. (London: Butterworth, 1955), p. 18.
2. Private police or contract security organizations provide a multimillion dollar service to today's modern industrial firms. This topic will be dealt with in more detail in Chapter 5.
3. A. C. Germann, Frank D. Day, and Robert R. J. Gallati, *Introduction to Law Enforcement* (Springfield, Ill.: Charles C. Thomas, 1965), p. 57.
4. Germann, p. 13.
5. Ronald Howe, *The Story of Scotland Yard* (New York: Horizon Press, 1965), p. 18.
6. *Manual of Guidance* (London: Her Majesty's Stationery Office, 1966), para. 1.9.
7. *Manual of Guidance*, 1.13.
8. *Manual of Guidance*, 1.14.
9. *Manual of Guidance*, 1.15.
10. *Manual of Guidance*, 1.16.
11. *Manual of Guidance*, 1.18–1.20.
12. Paul Garrett, *The State Police Problem in America* (Newark, N.J.: New Jersey Bureau of State Research, 1917), p. 181.

# 5: Law Enforcement in the United States

*LAW ENFORCEMENT: A LEGAL CONSTRUCT • FEDERAL LAW ENFORCEMENT • STATE LAW ENFORCEMENT • LOCAL LAW ENFORCEMENT • NONGOVERNMENTAL POLICE • COORDINATION AND COOPERATION OF POLICE*

PURPOSE: *TO PROVIDE A DESCRIPTION OF THE VARIOUS GOVERNMENTAL LEVELS OF LAW ENFORCEMENT IN THE UNITED STATES.*

ALTHOUGH it might be convenient to describe the police department of Kansas City or Seattle because either one would suffice as a typical municipal police department, it would be erroneous to submit either one as typical of the whole of the American police service. This point is made clear when one considers the broad spectrum of federal, state, local, and private police services. To appreciate the difficulties involved in presenting a profile of the "typical" police department, one should be aware of the vast diversity in size, function, jurisdiction, as well as role, mission, and other properties inherent in law enforcement.

Today over 500,000 persons are employed in the police service by approximately 40,000 separate law enforcement agencies.[1] The federal government accounts for 50 of these 40,000 agencies, the various states for another 200, and the remaining 39,750 occur at the local level of government (city, township, county).[2] It is therefore apparent not only that law enforcement has diverse jurisdictions but also that police responsibilities are disproportionately distributed among the three levels of government, the largest portion resting firmly on local government.

Confounding the situation further is the fact that local agencies are created under the provisions afforded by their respective states. Significantly, each of the fifty states provides a distinct and unique model on which its portion of the 39,950 state and local enforcement agencies is fashioned. It is not surprising then that our fragmented police service has been referred to as the American Police Nonsystem.

Perhaps the only generalization to be made is that law enforcement is a function of the executive branch, whatever the level of government. The president, the governors of the fifty states, and the mayors, commission chairpersons, and other executive officers of the many local political subdivisions (local governments) share these responsibilities.

## *LAW ENFORCEMENT: A LEGAL CONSTRUCT*

The Constitution of the United States does not provide expressly for the establishment and maintenance of police services, nor does it prohibit such services. The implicit powers of Article I, Section 8, Clause 18, which provides for the common defense and for the promotion of the general welfare of the people, has been interpreted as enabling the federal government to establish federal law enforcement organizations. Therefore, the Constitution is the *basis* for federal law enforcement. This is not, however, to be confused with the concept of *source*, which is the act or instrument by which a specific law enforcement agency is created. For all practical purposes, the source of all federal law enforcement agencies is the Congress. It is the Congress that enacts appropriate legislation for the agency's creation and maintenance (salaries, training, and general operating budgets).

At the state and local levels of government the majority of law enforcement organizations are also established and maintained by legislative provisions. Several states, however, provide explicitly for such law enforcement officers as sheriffs and constables in their constitutions.

## *FEDERAL LAW ENFORCEMENT*

Distrust of, and the subsequent limitations placed on, the central government by our nation's founders make the absence of a national police force very conspicuous. In the United States there is no single federal agency responsible for the enforcement of all federal laws. In actuality, the enforcement of federal laws is distributed among some fifty or more federal law enforcement agencies.

When a law enforcement agency is created by a congressional act, that piece of legislation defines the jurisdiction and authority of the agency. For example, the Federal Bureau of Investigation has authority to deal with about 185 federal crimes. Geographically, its authority is restricted to the United States and its possessions. In addition, legislation specifically provides that when, say, murder, which as such is not a federal offense and is usually the responsibility of the state or local police authorities, occurs on a military installation, it does fall within the jurisdiction of the FBI.

It is not surprising that the average American is unaware that approximately fifty law enforcement agencies exist at the federal level or that the majority of interested people seeking federal enforcement positions apply to those few agencies with which they are familiar. The Federal Bureau of Investigation, Drug Enforcement Administration, and Secret Service are probably the most visible and the most frequently discussed enforcement units at the federal level. Yet, these three perform less than one percent of the federal law enforcement activities. Other federal enforcement and investigative functions are found in these departments:

I. *Department of Justice*
   (a) Immigration and Naturalization Service: Border Patrol
   (b) United States Marshal
   (c) Drug Enforcement Administration
   (d) Federal Bureau of Investigation

II. *Department of the Treasury*
   (a) United States Customs Service
   (b) Internal Revenue Service
   (c) Secret Service
   (d) Treasury Guard Force
   (e) White House Police Force
   (f) Bureau of Alcohol, Tobacco, and Firearms

III. *Department of Defense* (Employing Nonmilitary Personnel)
   (a) Office of Special Intelligency (OSI) United States Air Force
   (b) Office of Naval Intelligency (ONI) United States Navy
   (c) Criminal Investigation Division (CID) United States Army

IV. *United States Postal Service*
   Postal Inspection Service

V. *Department of Transportation*
   United States Coast Guard

Still other law enforcement units are found in the Departments of State; Interior; Labor; Health, Education, and Welfare; Agriculture; and Commerce. In addition, various independent administrative agencies maintain law enforcement units, among them: Atomic Energy Commission (AEC); Civil Aeronautics Board (CAB); Federal Communications Commission (FCC); Interstate Commerce Commission (ICC); and United States Civil Service Commission. This partial list of federal law enforcement agencies or units makes it quite apparent that there are many career opportunities in federal law enforcement.

## *STATE LAW ENFORCEMENT*

Unlike the federal government, many states maintain an enforcement agency that has the responsibility and jurisdiction to enforce all state criminal laws anywhere within the state (general police powers). State law enforcement agencies are the creations of the state legislature. Even when a state law enforcement agency is expressly provided for in the state constitution, supplemental legislation is required to maintain contemporary training, salaries, budget, etc. Usually such agencies are referred to as state police or state highway patrol, but it should be noted that the official designation of a police organization is often misleading. Even though the official title of the organization does not reflect it, these agencies may or may not have general police powers. Therefore, it is not the title that should be of concern, but rather the functions performed and the organization, authority, and jurisdiction.

State police organizations can be categorized as having either general police powers or restricted police powers. The Pennsylvania and Michigan State Police are in the first category and enforce "all" laws in their respective states. The North Carolina and California Highway Patrols illustrate the latter category and are restricted to the enforcement of the traffic laws, accident investigation, accident prevention, and general highway safety.

Several states maintain more than one state enforcement organization, each having restricted police powers. Florida maintains a state police as well as the Florida Department of Law Enforcement; the former is responsible for traffic and minor criminal offenses, whereas the latter provides specialized investigation and enforcement in the more serious crimes. Similar to this is the North Carolina State Bureau of Investigation, which is the investigating agency in the state and deals with criminal offenses (remember that traffic enforcement is the responsibility of the North Carolina Highway Patrol).

Texas exemplifies another modification. There, the Texas Department of Public Safety has general police powers, which are functionally distributed between two enforcement units: the highway patrol for traffic and criminal enforcement, and the Texas Rangers for specialized investigating assignments. Texas law enforcement is very much like that of Florida. The rather subtle organizational variations, although not necessarily important, are still worth notice.

As a law enforcement officer, my fundamental duty is to serve mankind; to safeguard lives and property; to protect the innocent against deception, the weak against oppression or intimidation, and the peaceful against violence or disorder; and to respect the Constitutional rights of all men to liberty, equality and justice.

I will keep my private life unsullied as an example to all; maintain courageous calm in the face of danger, scorn, or ridicule; develop self-restraint; and be constantly mindful of the welfare of others. Honest in thought and deed in both my personal and official life, I will be exemplary in obeying the laws of the land and the regulations of my department. Whatever I see or hear of a confidential nature or that is confided to me in my official capacity will be kept ever secret unless revelation is necessary in the performance of my duty.

I will never act officiously or permit personal feelings, prejudices, animosities or friendships to influence my decisions. With no compromise for crime and with relentless prosecution of criminals, I will enforce the law courteously and appropriately without fear or favor, malice or ill will, never employing unnecessary force or violence and never accepting gratuities.

I recognize the badge of my office as a symbol of public faith, and I accept it as a public trust to be held so long as I am true to the ethics of the police service. I will constantly strive to achieve these objectives and ideals, dedicating myself before God to my chosen profession . . . law enforcement.

**Illustration 5.1** LAW ENFORCEMENT CODE OF ETHICS

Various other law enforcement functions exist in state government, particularly within the regulatory and administrative bodies. Alcoholic beverage control boards, liquor control boards, public utilities commissions, agriculture commissions, public health services, fire marshals, departments of fish and wildlife, insurance commissions, pollution control boards, and scores of other such governmental bodies maintain law enforcement units. Admittedly, the scope of each of these enforcement functions is greatly limited and highly specialized. However, the combined efforts of all these functions are extremely broad and account for a considerable number of law enforcement personnel in the state governments, all of which are continually seeking qualified personnel.

## *LOCAL LAW ENFORCEMENT*

Law enforcement at the local level has frequently been described and categorized as urban, suburban, or rural. Such terminology more accurately portrays the characteristics of the population being served rather than the formal governmental structure from which it is created, maintained, and regulated. To be more precise, we shall refer to the various local law enforcement agencies as either municipal (city, town, borough, village, township) or county, as determined by their charters or origins and not by demographic properties.

### County Law Enforcement

County law enforcement, which accounts for 3,050 agencies,[3] is of two major types—the county sheriff and county police. Typically, the county sheriff, a constitutional officer (provided for by the state constitution), is the chief law enforcement officer of the county. The sheriff is usually an elected official and may or may not possess those qualities considered essential to perform the complex tasks of his office. Deputy sheriffs are appointed by the sheriff and serve at his pleasure. However, in some sheriff's departments deputies must meet established selection criteria. For example, the Los Angeles county sheriff's deputies are among the best trained and most respected officers in the nation today.

A great disparity exists in the many hundreds of sheriff's departments throughout the United States. In the northeastern states, the county sheriff functions generally as an officer of the court. Traffic enforcement and criminal investigations are left to the state or other local agencies. In the western and southern states it is more common to find sheriff's deputies engaged in both traffic enforcement and criminal investigation duties. The size of a sheriff's staff may range from one to several thousand deputies and civilian personnel. Likewise, the levels of technical sophistication attained by the sheriff's departments vary from those with no training facilities and minimal equipment (some sheriffs must use their private automobiles to perform their duties) to departments that maintain training academies, crime laboratories, helicopters, and a fleet of vehicles. Such extreme diversity prohibits any attempt to describe the typical or average sheriff's department, and each department must be evaluated individually on its own merits and deficiencies.

County police are not synonymous with the county sheriff. Usually they are not provided for by state constitutions, but are created by the county commissioners (county legislative body). County police units are generally headed by a chief of police, who in turn is directly accountable to a county manager, county prosecutor, county director of public safety, or to a county commissioner. The county chief of police is normally an appointed officer and traditionally has been promoted from within the ranks of the department. County police for all practical purposes have general *county* police powers. Unfortunately, the degree of sophistication and expertise in such departments again varies from meager to excellent.

Another county law enforcement officer, found in Pennsylvania and some other states, is the county detective, who is appointed by and serves directly under the district or county attorney. County detectives may be a special unit of a county police department assigned to the district attorney, although it is more common for the district attorney to maintain a unit of special investigators distinct from either the sheriff's office or the county police department. It is possible for a county sheriff, county police, and a county detective in the district attorney's office to exist in a county simultaneously. Difficulties are likely to arise under such conditions, however, and lead to duplication of effort and organizational friction and animosity.

**Municipal Law Enforcement**

Law enforcement at the municipal level (city, town, borough, village, or township) accounts for 36,700 agencies—clearly a majority of the 40,000 total agencies currently providing public protective services to America.[4] This means there are 36,700 separate jurisdictions, each having its own departmental policies, organization, police chiefs, as well as pay scales, pension funds, retirement plans, police headquarters, and many other related factors. Perhaps the full impact cannot be appreciated until one considers the variety of guidelines (municipal and state laws) that are applicable to these thousands of agencies.

Because municipalities are creations of the state, the state obviously retains the power to regulate them. Thus, state legislatures establish certain guidelines in the form of charters and codes for cities and towns to follow. The degree of regulatory action is determined in a large measure by the size (population) of the municipality or political subdivision. States commonly classify political subdivisions in accordance with population and provide specific guidelines in the form of codes and charters accordingly. Among these many provisions are those involving law enforcement.

Pennsylvania, for example, categorizes cities by class. Philadelphia is a first-class city; Harrisburg is a third-class city. Town and townships are also denoted by class. Kentucky classifies cities in a similar way. For each city, town, or township there is a charter or a code of state regulations that must be met. Almost always included in these codes are requirements related to police civil service commissions, retirement, and pension arrangement. But equally important is the fact that some political subdivisions are not required by law to maintain any law enforcement while others must establish and maintain police services.

To illustrate the many forms of law enforcement, consider the state of Kentucky: The Kentucky State Police have general police powers. However, certain class cities may, by law, remove themselves from the jurisdiction of the state police. In effect, these cities have at their discretion the right to keep the state police out of the city.

Another form of law enforcement is seen in Connecticut. Towns may request the state police to assign a *resident trooper* to provide local law enforcement. Under this arrangement the town is billed by the state for the salary and other expenses of the resident trooper as agreed upon. The mechanics of this scheme result in a town-state police officer.

Contract law enforcement is similar to the resident trooper concept, and its most extensive application is found in Los Angeles County, California. A municipality in Los Angeles County, rather than maintaining its own police department, may request the county to provide the required services. The city and the county enter into an agreement whereby the city promises to pay the county for police services. In some cases, the conditions of this agreement may require the county to provide one mobile police officer to patrol between the hours of sunset and sunrise. In others, the conditions may be quite extensive, calling for a comprehensive study of the city and full-time police service, which may require many police officers and even a police building.

### Special and Auxiliary Police

Many police departments throughout the country maintain a body of officers to serve in a reserve capacity. Although some states make a legal distinction in the duties and authority of special and auxiliary police, they are for all practical purposes a supplemental force to serve at the pleasure of the chief of police. The qualifications required to become a special or auxiliary police officer range from none to a comprehensive selection process and extensive training. Many times these officers volunteer, and receive little or no pay. In other cases, when on duty, they may receive a salary equitable to the salary of the regular officers.

## *NONGOVERNMENTAL POLICE*

Law enforcement at the federal, state, and local levels of government represents a variety of police models. Still another segment of protective services exists and increases the milieu of law enforcement: private security or private police agencies.

Early in the developmental stages of British law enforcement the merchant police were introduced. Likewise, in the United States the Pinkerton's and Burn's detectives achieved notable productivity and popularity. Apparently the services rendered by these and similar organizations are regarded as assets to the task of public protection. Such a conclusion can be derived from the fact that an estimated $3.3 billion is expended annually for private security services,[5] and the number of private security personnel is estimated at approximately 290,000.[6]

Private security personnel, according to their descriptive title, should have little impact on public law enforcement. If their functions were represented by their titles, they might not be major contributors to contemporary police problems. But these functions do create difficulties and conflicts.

Normally private police have no police powers. Their function is to observe and report to proper authorities any incident detrimental to the safety and security of their employer's property and personnel. However, this condition is not practiced universally. In many areas, private security personnel are deputized police officers or sheriffs; others have been appointed special and auxiliary police officers. Another common situation is that in which a regular police officer, having full police powers, is employed part time (moonlighting) as a security officer in industry or elsewhere in the private sector of the community. It becomes impossible to determine what authority a security officer possesses by mere visual inspection of the uniform.

Critical to this issue is the quality of

personnel employed in private security, especially when they have the authority to engage in the enforcement functions, regardless of how limited such authority may be. Typically, private security personnel are not adequately trained in the technical aspects of law enforcement. Often they have received no formal instruction about the specific duties they are expected to perform for their employers, let alone general police instruction. Often armed with a weapon and having minimal or no training, they engage in the duties of police officers to the limits prescribed by the laws that permit these organizations to exist and to function.

## *COORDINATION AND COOPERATION OF POLICE*

Local autonomy, which has been so basic an element in American government, is a concept of fundamental importance to the study of the fragmented system of policing. Reducing the number of police agencies in this country is a monumental effort, and any significant reduction will probably not be achieved in the near future. The fragmentation of the police service was recognized by Raymond B. Fosdick as early as 1921[7]; by the Wickersham Commission's "Report on Police" in 1931; by the National Crime Commission in 1967[8]; and as recently as 1973 by the National Advisory Commission on Criminal Justice Standards and Goals.[9] Attempts to compromise the principle of home rule have generally failed, however. Thus, instead of consolidating police services, attention has turned to coordination and cooperation, and to this purpose, several important institutions have developed.

### *Uniform Crime Report (UCR)*

At the national level the *Uniform Crime Report* was developed for the collection, compilation, and distribution of crime statistics. This program was instituted as early as 1930. The Committee on Uniform Crime Records of the International Association of Chiefs of Police (IACP) acts as an advisory body. The *UCR* is a nationwide index of documented law enforcement information on crime and criminals. From this data it is expected that the extent, fluctuation, and distribution of crime can be measured more meaningfully. Further, such information should be valuable in determining and adjusting police activities, policies, and procedures at *all* levels of government. In January 1967, a separate program for the systematic computerization of active crime information, the National Crime Information Center (NCIC), became operational at FBI headquarters. The *UCR* and NCIC are major contributions to synthesizing not only crime statistics but consequent modification of enforcement operations and strategies based on these data sources.

### **Law Enforcement Assistance Administration (LEAA)**

As a result of the rising crime of the 1960s, the President's Commission on Law Enforcement and the Administration of Justice and the Office of Law Enforcement Assistance (OLEA) was established. (The name has since been changed to the Law Enforcement Assistance Administration (LEAA).) In the reports of the National Crime Commission many problems confronting law enforcement were isolated, of which fragmentation was but one. Noting the discrepancies the federal government provided financial grants, through LEAA, to the states to develop programs in an effort to increase the effectiveness and efficiency of law enforcement. The availability of financial support was the impetus for innovative programs at all levels of government. Local government was enabled to implement such programs as regional training centers and area crime laboratories, thus improving quality and at the same time minimizing unnecessary duplication of effort. Small police departments whose separate budgets were unable to support such high-cost facilities can now in many geographical areas collectively finance and share these common services, which are essential for modern policing.

**Recent Developments**

The creation of a single police force to serve the entire United States (or fifty agencies each to serve its respective state) is not probable, and perhaps not desirable. However, local control has been compromised to a degree by state minimum standards acts, which requires all police officers in the state to achieve certain levels of proficiency, regardless of their departmental affiliation. California is an excellent example of a state's establishing minimum police standards in its Police Officers Standards and Training (POST).

As in the past, voluntary interdepartmental cooperation will continue to be a common ingredient by which the police achieve a semblance of unity. Recent police developments commencing at the federal level have flowed to the state and local governments in such a way as to foster greater degrees of cooperation. In the final analysis, they may prove to be the means of perpetuating the fragmented police systems, rather than a stage in the process of reshaping the system into a more comprehensive and unified model.

## DISCUSSION QUESTIONS

1. What is (are) the mission(s) of the police? What kinds of organization, personnel, and philosophy are needed to meet the mission(s)?
2. Discuss the concept of home rule. What implications does it have for the police service?
3. Does the disparity of the quality of law enforcement on the American police scene compromise public trust in the police? Should this disparity be reduced?
4. What is the relationship of public police and private police? How can the image of one be affected by the other?
5. Could your city police be consolidated with the neighboring city police or county sheriff's office?
6. Do we need federal, state, and local police forces? Would a national police force be more efficient?

## NOTES

1. James S. Kakalik and Sorrel Wildhorn, *Private Police in the United States: Findings and Recommendations* (Santa Monica, Calif.: Rand Corporation, 1971), p. 11.
2. President's Commission on Law Enforcement and Administration of Justice, *Task Force Report: The Police* (Washington, D.C.: Government Printing Office, 1967), p. 7.
3. *Task Force Report: The Police*. p. 7.
4. *Task Force Report: The Police*. p. 7.
5. *Kakalik and Wildhorn*, p. 12.
6. *Kakalik and Wildhorn*, p. 11.
7. Raymond B. Fosdick, *American Police System* (New York: Century, 1916).
8. *Task Force Report: The Police*.
9. National Advisory Commission on Criminal Justice Standards and Goals, *A National Strategy to Reduce Crime* (Washington, D.C.: Government Printing Office, 1973), pp. 258–266.

DALLAS POLICE
DEPARTMENT

# 6: Police Administration and Operations

*PRIMARY LINE FUNCTIONS • SECONDARY LINE FUNCTIONS • NONLINE FUNCTIONS • PRINCIPLES OF ORGANIZATION • POLICE OPERATIONS*

PURPOSE: *TO PROVIDE AN INTRODUCTION TO THE ADMINISTRATIVE AND OPERATIONAL ASPECTS OF CONTEMPORARY POLICE, INCLUDING SUCH FUNCTIONS AS PATROL, TRAFFIC, AND CRIMINAL INVESTIGATION.*

All police functions and activities can be categorized as either line or nonline. *Line functions* are those tasks that directly facilitate the accomplishment of organizational goals, whereas *nonline functions* are those tasks that supplement the line in its task performance. Line activities are further broken into subcategories: primary line and secondary line functions, both of which are field services.

## *PRIMARY LINE FUNCTIONS*

The primary line function is police patrol; that is, the patrol activities of a police organization are considered basic and of first priority. The patrol division has the initial responsibility for crime prevention and detection and the apprehension of offenders. It also assists in the preparation of the facts for presentation in a court of law. Theoretically, if the patrol force were 100 percent effective in the execution of its assigned tasks, the need for specialized units (traffic and detective) would be eliminated. The patrol function is accurately called the "backbone" of the police service.

## *SECONDARY LINE FUNCTIONS*

Historically, police departments were established only as police patrols. However, as municipalities increased in population, area, and technology (for example, the invention of the automobile), the burden on these patrols was greatly increased. The departments, unable to provide additional personnel because of budgetary limitations, were unable to increase the number of officers on a patrol beat in proportion to the rising population and rate of crime and were forced to enlarge each officer's beat.

It soon became evident that traffic control and crime investigation were consuming a great deal of the officers' time and removing them from their primary patrol activities. Further, the sophistication of many police problems was above the level of competence normally expected of patrol officers. The need for specialized, trained units became apparent. As a product of the patrol force's inability to respond adequately to its prescribed tasks, spin-off elements evolved, for example, traffic units and criminal investigation. Although others exist in some departments, these two are the major elements often designated as secondary line functions. The important fact is they are spin-offs of the patrol force. What has resulted is a "rob Peter to pay Paul" situation—a major fault of specialization. The patrol force is depleted to provide the supportive services of specially trained officers with expertise in a given area: traffic, vice, juvenile, narcotics, and so forth. Specialization is a luxury most often enjoyed in larger police departments. It can be abused, however, to the extent of reducing the effectiveness of the patrol force. In smaller departments, generalization prevails: the patrol force has total responsibility for all line services, and the patrol officer is traffic controller, detective, or undercover man when the situation arises. An absolute formula for the degree of generalization or specialization has not been developed.[1]

## *NONLINE FUNCTIONS*

Simply put, *nonline functions* are those services that support the line. Whereas the line provides services directly to the citizen, nonline activities help the line to accomplish its primary tasks. Traditionally nonline or support activities consist of two major categories: staff and auxiliary services.

### Staff Services

Those activities that have the responsibility of personnel development and departmental management are *staff services.* Personnel development includes recruitment, selection, promotion, training, and supervision. Budget, planning and research, inspection, and similar activities fall under the heading of managerial activities.

### Auxiliary Services

All nonline activities not regarded as staff services are classified as *auxiliary services.* Typically, they provide support services of both a technical and nontechnical nature to both line and nonline activities. Polygraph examiners, photographers, fingerprint and crime-scene technicians, and the police laboratory are technical auxiliary services that support the line

| *Line Functions* | | *Nonline Functions* | |
|---|---|---|---|
| *Primary* | *Secondary* | *Staff* | *Auxiliary* |
| Patrol | Criminal Investigation | Planning and Research | Police Records System |
| | Vice Investigation | Inspection | Identification Service |
| | Traffic Regulation and Control | Personnel Administration | Property Control |
| | Crime Prevention | Training | Communications |
| | | Budgetary Control | Crime Laboratory |
| | | Purchasing | Jail |
| | | Public Relations | Supply |
| | | | Transportation and Maintenance |

**Illustration 6.1** POLICE FUNCTIONS: LINE AND STAFF

activities. The jail and the communications system are nontechnical auxiliary services that support both the line and nonline (staff) activities. Some activities are extremely difficult to classify as either staff or auxiliary. In many instances they perform a dual service. Police community relations units, although performing secondary line services, may be designated as an auxiliary or even a staff function. Illustration 6.1 presents the various functions graphically.

## *PRINCIPLES OF ORGANIZATION*

To understand the organization and operation of police departments certain general basic principles of organization must be understood. These principles of organization were generated by the experiences of industry, business, and the military services. They have no absolute values, but they do provide a check list against which an organization can be structurally and functionally evaluated. This notion will become more clearly defined as each principle is considered. Illustration 6.2 will be referred to frequently in the discussion of principles of organization.

Police functions are subdivided into units that are described as follows:

*Bureau:* usually the largest unit within a municipal, state, or federal department (Richmond Bureau of Police, in the Department of Public Safety; Federal Bureau of Investigation, in the Department of Justice).

*Division:* part of a bureau having a department-wide function (Detective Division; Traffic Division).

*Section:* basically one of several functional elements of a division (robbery section of the Detective Division; traffic accident investigation section of the Traffic Division).

### Homogeneous Assignment (Division of Labor)

For a police organization to be effective, work assignments must be designed so that similar (homogeneous) tasks, functions, and activities are given to an individual or group for accomplishment. In Illustration 6.2 Internal Investigation, Operations Bureau, Services Bureau, Community Relations, Administration Bureau is each assigned its own kind of task (for example, the Service Bureau does not engage in patrol operations because they are a dissimilar task).

### Unity of Command

Unity of command requires that an individual be directly accountable to only one superior. No one person can effectively serve two superiors at a given time. (It is interesting that Peel's Metropolitan Police violated this principle, because when he established the department, two commissioners, or chiefs of police, were appointed. This dual command arrangement was, however, short-lived.) Note in Illustration 6.2 that only one line connects any organizational block with another block.

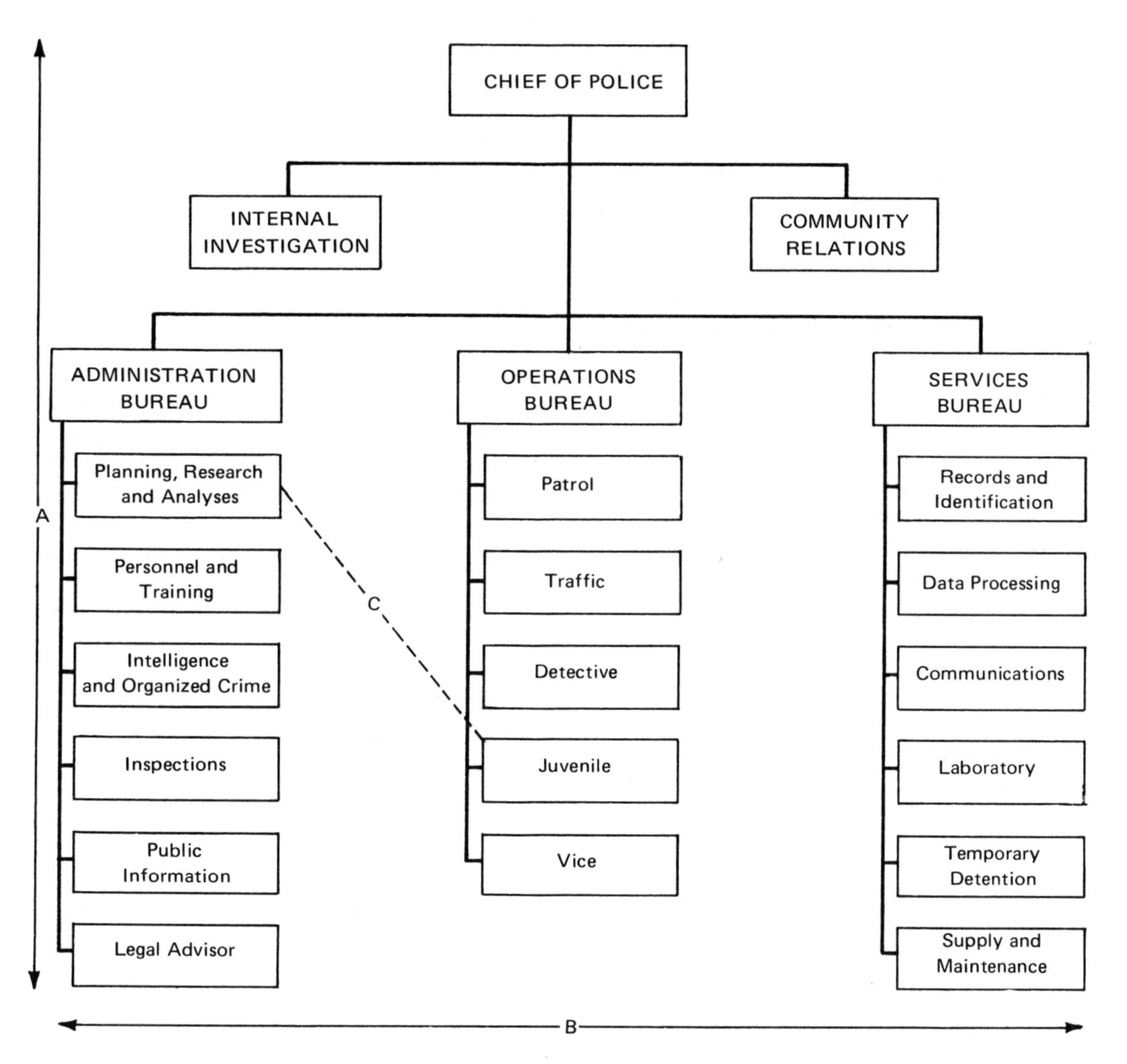


**Illustration 6.2** A WELL-ORGANIZED MUNICIPAL POLICE DEPARTMENT

Source: President's Commission on Law Enforcement and Administration of Justice, *Task Force Report: The Police* (Washington, D.C.: Government Printing Office, 1967), p. 47. Lines A, B, and C added.

### Chain of Command

Primarily this principle provides for the vertical movement of authority up and down established channels in the organizational hierarchy. To illustrate this concept, consider a directive originating in the patrol commander's (captain's) office intended for the patrol force (downward movement). Two levels of authority fall between the captain and the patrol officer—lieutenant and sergeant. Because both levels are held responsible for various aspects of patrol supervision, both must be aware of such directives. If either supervisor is by-passed, that one cannot be held accountable for the lack of knowledge. Further, performance of supervisory duties is greatly hindered, and a potentially serious morale problem is created. Line A in Illustration 6.2 represents the chain of command.

### Delegation of Responsibility and Authority

There must be a clear line of formal authority running from top to bottom of every organization. Ultimate authority and responsibility for a police organization lies at the top of the chain of command—with the chief. However, if a subordinate is to be held responsible for the accomplishment of a given task, he or she must be given the authority to carry out those responsibilities. It is important, also, that the responsibility and the authority be clearly defined. If a patrol officer is given the responsibility for evaluating police response time on a given day or in a specific situation, the officer must be given the authority to procure the communications logs from the communication center. Without this authority, the entire task cannot be accomplished.

### Delineation of Responsibility and Authority

A clear-cut delineation of responsibility and authority is essential to prevent confusion of lines of authority. If responsibility and authority are not clearly defined, conflicts, duplications, and overlaps of functions lead to confusion and inefficiency. Each officer and each organization segment must clearly understand what is to be done and the extent of authority delegated to accomplish the job.

### Span of Control

The number of officers or units reporting directly to a supervisor should not exceed the number that can be feasibly and effectively coordinated and directed. There are innumberable factors that limit the span of control including distance, time, knowledge, personality, and the complexity of the work to be performed. It is not unusual to find fifty or sixty workers who perform identical functions reporting to one supervisor. On the other hand, as we ascend the chain of command and the diversity of functions increases, the number of individuals that a police executive supervises decreases rapidly. In Illustration 6.2 the chief of police has a span of five, as does the commander of operations. However, the commander of the administrative bureau has a span of six.

### Objective

All organizational elements must contribute, directly or indirectly, to the accomplishment of the objective of the enterprise. Each organizational element should be formed for a definite purpose, and this purpose must be to accomplish the major objective. Any police function or organizational element that is not required in the accomplishment of the overall objective should be eliminated.

### Coordination

The organizational structure must facilitate the development of close, friendly, and cooperative relations, especially between line and staff activities. Effective coordination is dependent almost entirely upon adequate communication among all elements of a police organization. Line B in Illustration 6.2 represents the horizontal dimension of the organization. Often, it is necessary to function horizontally and diagonally (Line C) within the organization to achieve the objective. This movement is provided for through departmental orders and regulations.

### Time

The police service is among the few public services that maintain a twenty-four hour schedule. It is necessary for the department to assign officers in sufficient numbers to meet the demands at any given time. The allocation of personnel is a complex problem. On the surface, it would appear logical to divide the total police complement into three equal parts or shifts. However, for any given city, experience indicates that during certain hours of the day activities requiring police services increase and decrease. For example, on a normal weekday in a city the vehicular and pedestrian traffic is heaviest from 7:00 to 9:00 A.M. and 4:00 to 6:00 P.M., when people are going to and coming from work. Therefore, the distribution of the traffic function must be regulated to take these rush periods into account.

It is important to remember that this principle is applicable to *all functions* of the organization; this is an organizational principle and is not confined only to line units. It may be necessary to increase or decrease the number of personnel in the records or jail sections in accordance with pay periods of local industry. In many small towns where there is a single industry, payday means increased social activity, some of which may necessitate police services. The police administrator must take this timetable into account. Police personnel are assigned during the day in the following manner:

*Watch or shift:* a time division of the day to ensure proper allocation of personnel. Shifts are normally eight consecutive hours, five days a week, giving an officer a forty-hour work week. However, longer working hours and work weeks are common. Further, shifts frequently overlap to provide additional personnel during peak periods.

*Platoon:* personnel assigned to a given shift or watch. A platoon may serve an entire city or only a portion of it. Usually, a platoon is determined by the hours worked rather than its assigned area or task.

### Territory

Territorial distribution is necessary to ensure the availability and general suitability of the patrol service throughout a jurisdiction. Geographical or territorial divisions of the department can be described as follows:

*Post:* a fixed or stationary point or location (e.g., a specific street intersection, surveillance site, or an assigned desk or office).

*Route or line beat:* a length of street normally assigned to a traffic and patrol officer (whether foot or mobile). The route has the characteristic of being continuous, in a straight line, or in line of sight.

*Beat:* a geographical area, once again assigned to either foot or mobile patrol and traffic officers. To illustrate a beat, visualize one square city block and arbitrarily designate this a beat. The patrol officer assigned to this beat is responsible for all patrol activities within it, all the streets, side streets, and alleys and any specific calls to which he or she may be required to respond. Assume for a moment that a major street is within this beat and requires a major portion of the patrol officer's time and energies. Under these conditions, the major street could feasibly be assigned to another officer, who would devote full attention to this single length of street (a route), while the beat officer would be better able to patrol the now reduced beat. The beat is the basic unit of police organization, and is among the terms most commonly referred to in the police service.

*Sector:* two or more beats, routes, posts, or any combination thereof.

*District or Precinct:* geographical subdivision of the city for police patrol purposes. (A district for a state police department usually consists of several counties.) Typically a district has a station and perhaps other physical facilities.

*Area:* two or more districts.[2]

### Clientele

The distribution of patrol services with respect to the characteristics of the population served must be recognized and dealt with in contemporary law enforcement. The development of specialized functional units expresses the principle of organization by clientele. For example, the juvenile division is a product of a young community. In contrast, a police department in a retirement community has less need for a juvenile division, but ambulance service may be a necessary police service and have great effect on police organization. The development of police community relations units is, to a great extent, an indication of earlier police failure to comply with this organizational principle.

## *POLICE OPERATIONS*

Another word in the large collection of police service terminology is *operations.* For the most part, operations is synonymous with *line functions.* In accordance with previous definitions, operations is inclusive of both primary and secondary line functions.

Although a comprehensive study of

police operations is not within the construct of an introductory textbook, it is necessary to examine the major points: patrol, traffic, and criminal investigative functions. Illustration 6.3 illustrates the operational structure of a police department. Compare Illustrations 6.2 and 6.3.

### Patrol

Patrol officers are the most important element in the police service. Their reason for being is to *serve*. In their efforts to fulfill this demand, their jobs can become extraordinarily complex. It may be surprising to learn that the patrol officers devote relatively little time to enforcing the law, that is, detecting crime, apprehending criminals, and preparing facts for presentation in court. The primary task of crime prevention is not easily measured because of the absence of qualitative and quantitative indexes. Traditionally, patrol officers spend the majority of their working hours in nonenforcement or peace maintenance activities: directing traffic, routinely covering the assigned beat, engaging in interpersonal communications with the clientele, and so on. General administrative duties and special assignments further remove patrol officers from the law enforcement function.*

Traditionally patrol officers are responsible for all criminal activity on the beat. It is important that they use all resources with optimum efficiency. The most valuable resource is the people with whom the officer has official and casual contact. Ironically, this reservoir of knowledge and assistance often is not developed.

Prudent officers realize their inability to cope with every incident independent of the community in which they work. The alternative is to seek the assistance of those persons who have entrusted their protection to the police. In the final analysis, law enforcement and public protection cannot be defined as the sole responsibility of the police; it is a joint venture of both the police and the public. Theoretically the police could reduce its enforcement function by refining and making its peace maintenance function more productive in terms of crime prevention.

Because patrol officers are expected to be "on the street" and always close at hand, it is reasonable that they should be the first to respond to public need. Being the first at the scene places patrol officers in a rather precarious position: What should they prepare for? What special knowledge should they possess? Their obligation to respond to all incidents does not afford them the luxury of selectivity. They must, therefore, be generalists, and be prepared academically, physically, and emotionally to meet the demands of any given situation. An understanding of human behavior is crucial when confronting the emotionally disturbed, the alcoholic, the juvenile, and the quarreling family. Likewise, a general knowledge of the broad range of police technology must be acquired; patrol officers can mean the difference in a criminal investigation

*Studies such as the *Kansas City Preventive Patrol Experiment* have attempted to evaluate the effectiveness of patrol. As with many studies, there were as many questions raised as answered. The interested student should see: *The Kansas City Preventive Patrol Experiment* (Washington, D.C.: Police Foundation, 1974); and *Police Chief*, Vol. 17, No. 6, June 1975.

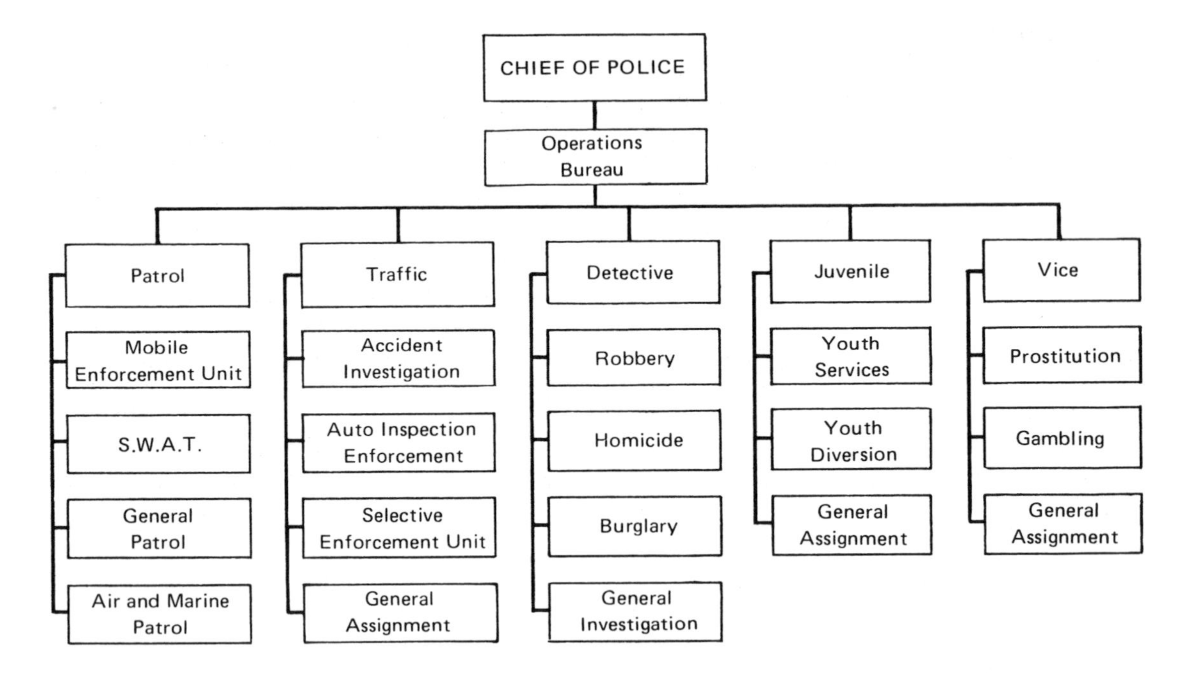


**Illustration 6.3** ORGANIZATIONAL STRUCTURE OF A POLICE OPERATIONS BUREAU

simply by providing investigators with accurate and detailed factors. Patrol officers must observe and record the smallest details in the initial investigation. They must protect the crime scene to ensure investigators as much first-hand information as possible. Undoubtedly, the patrol function is the foundation on which the department is built.

### Traffic

Typically, the traffic function encompasses three tasks: traffic control, accident investigation, and law enforcement. Just who assumes these various tasks is an organizational decision. In smaller departments the patrol division is responsible for all police operations including traffic. In such situations the total traffic function belongs to the patrol officer. Larger cities, on the other hand, establish specialized functional traffic units, usually at the bureau level. Then the traffic control and accident investigation are, for all practical purposes, the responsibility of the traffic bureau, and the enforcement function is shared, at least to the extent of not excluding patrol. Likewise, traffic officers are not totally excluded from the patrol function. Imagine a traffic officer observing a serious crime and not attempting to apprehend the offender because his or her job is directing traffic at a certain intersection. On the other hand, the patrol officer who observes a traffic accident and does not render assistance because patrol is his or her specialty has failed to meet the basic obligation of service.

*Traffic Accident Investigation* Sound traffic safety programs are a necessary and vital product of the collection and tabulation of facts acquired at the scene of traffic accidents through investigative techniques. Often it has been said, however, that police traffic accident investigation is in fact not investigation but simply reporting. At issue, perhaps, is the lack of agreement on the definitions of investigation and reporting—an issue that cannot be addressed here. Nevertheless, anyone taking notice of the investigative techniques employed by the Civil Aeronautics Board (CAB) to determine the cause of aircraft accidents could become skeptical of the phrase "traffic accident investigation" as it is used in most police departments.

*Traffic Control* The importance of the traffic control function is two-fold: first, it assists in expediting the safe movement of vehicular and pedestrian traffic; second, it is the way in which the police make the most direct contact with the greatest number of the public. Many people have never talked to a police officer, and chances are that when they do it will be in a traffic control situation.

*Traffic Law Enforcement* By definition, traffic law enforcement is the total of those actions taken by the police in dealing with violators of traffic laws and ordinances. Its function is to reduce traffic accidents and encourage voluntary compliance with laws and ordinances. Determining the quantity or quality of the traffic law enforcement function is a difficult task.

The *traffic law enforcement index* is merely a quantitative measure: the ratio of the number of citations, arrests, and subsequent convictions for moving violations to the number of vehicle accidents that involved personal injury or death. A traffic enforcement index of twenty is the accepted norm. Although this figure is not absolute, it is a widely used criterion. Some departments may have an index of eighteen, while others maintain an index of thirty. The index must be formulated on the basis of local conditions and experiences.

*Selective enforcement* is a quality measure based upon the principle that enforcement efforts must be applied at specific times and places against those violations that appear to be causing accidents. It further maximizes the proper allocation and distribution of personnel. Good traffic law enforcement can provide to the police department considerable information, which when properly analyzed yields significant results concerning the causes of traffic accidents, trends, and so on. The police department, from this data, can and must take remedial steps to further reduce accidents. This remedial process functions in two ways: education and engineering.

Two segments of the community must receive current *traffic enforcement education:* the private citizen and the police officer. Public and police awareness of the many aspects of traffic law enforcement and traffic safety is crucial in the fight against damage and loss of life on the highways. Instances of traffic education are common in the schools, for example, school safety patrols and driver training programs. Auto safety inspection, driver retraining programs, television and radio presentations, and public addresses by police officials are other means by which the public can become and remain informed and knowledgeable in the many areas of traffic law enforcement.

*Traffic engineering* is a very real part of the total traffic picture. The traffic engineer requires information concerning the flow of traffic, problem areas (dangerous intersections, road surface conditions), and so on. No other unit of government is more qualified to provide this information than are the police. Police officers travel over the majority of the streets, twenty-four hours a day. They are in a prime position to observe and report meaningful traffic information to the traffic engineer for structural change or evaluation. It is logical to assume that improved engineering reduces traffic accidents. Therefore, increased input to traffic engineering from police accident investigation summaries indicating engineering problems should logically play a significant role in the reduction of traffic accidents.

In conclusion, it is not difficult to justify the traffic function. Annually more than 50,000 Americans lose their lives on our nation's highways. Property damage is calculated at hundreds of millions of dollars. Human agony and personal grief are not measurable, but certainly they exist in abundance.

### Criminal Investigation

Criminal investigation is a line function and traditionally a task for patrol. However, the type and frequency of crimes may necessitate a specialized organization component, commonly referred to as the detective division. Remembering that the criminal investigation division is a secondary line element will be helpful as its relationship to the patrol function is shown. Normally the patrol officer is the first police representative to arrive at a crime scene. His or her first obligation is to render assistance to injured parties. Second, the crime scene must be protected so that relevant facts can be observed and recorded. This second requirement can be subdivided into two phases: protection and recording.

Crime-scene protection is simply protection. It ensures that the physical properties of the scene are not disturbed or altered until all the facts have been properly noted. The patrol officer, who is usually the first at the scene of a crime, must be trained to protect the crime scene. Whenever a serious crime occurs it usually attracts a number of spectators. The patrol officer must keep these individuals from removing or possibly destroying evidence. Crimes have been solved by the mere presence of a dropped match or cigarette. Failure to protect the crime scene could easily result in the loss of such valuable clues.

Crime-scene data collection is, as are most aspects of criminal investigation, an art and a science. Because the actual crime scene is a short-term phenomenon, it is imperative that its general characteristics and specific properties are quickly and

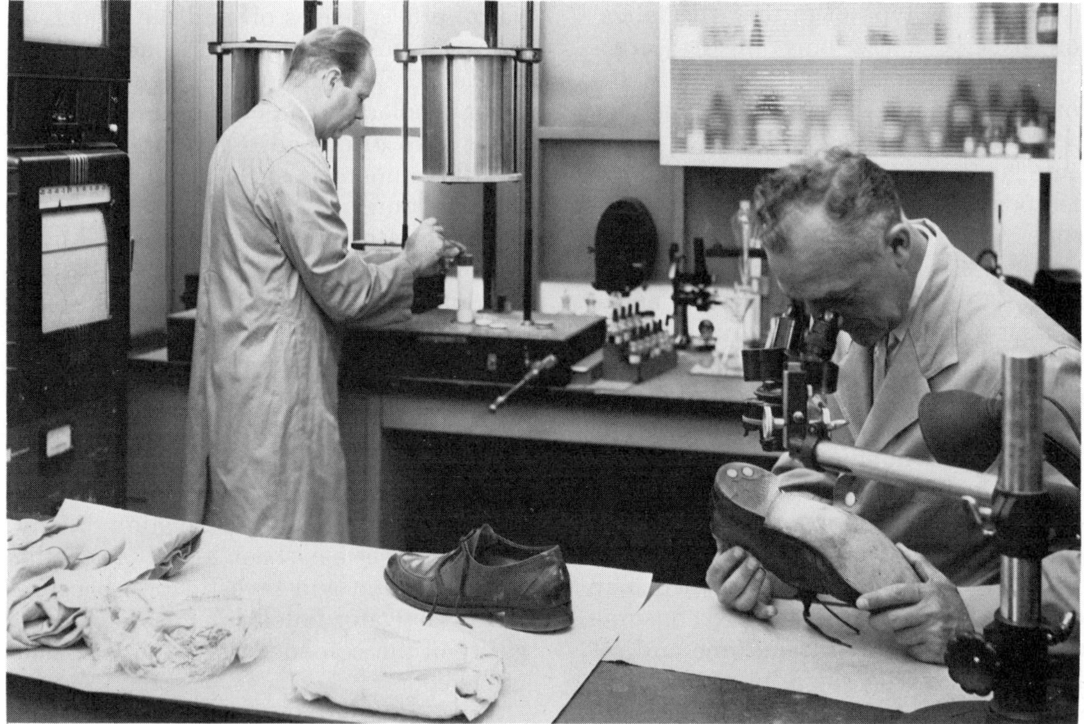

COURTESY OF FBI LABORATORY, WASHINGTON, D.C.

**Illustration 6.4** LABORATORY TECHNICIANS PROCESSING SOIL COLLECTED ON SUSPECT'S SHOES

accurately recorded. Consequently, a detective must be an accurate note taker and have good reporting skills. Only with such information can the crime scene be reconstructed at a future time. Should one investigating officer be removed from the department by retirement, death, or other reasons, the basic facts would be largely lost; they would be available to the newly assigned officer only if the crime scene was carefully recorded.

In the larger police departments, where specialized detective divisions have evolved, the detective divisions have undertaken further specialization. These specialized sections of the detective division take various forms. One approach is to divide the detective division into specialized units according to specific types of crimes. For example, some large detective divisions have a robbery squad, a homicide squad, a burglary squad, an auto theft squad, and so on. Other detective divisions may be organized by general categories. For example, a crimes against person section, a crimes against property section, and a general assignment section may be created in a detective division. This type of further specialization usually exists only in the larger police departments. It is generally believed by these departments that this specialization allows the detective to become familiar with the criminals and the methods associated with a given type of crime. A given criminal's method of operation, for example, may consist of "peeling" a safe with a sledge hammer and a crowbar. A detective who works full time on burglaries is more likely to be familiar with this technique and the individual criminals who use this technique, than is the detective who investigates all types of crimes. Hence, he or she should be able to solve the crime more quickly than the nonspecialist.

The investigative duties outlined here in a few words may in reality consume hours of the patrol officer's time and seriously detract from the primary responsibility, patrol. It is precisely for this reason that the specialist—the detective or investigator—is created.

Departmental organization and policies regarding patrol/detective relationships are almost as many as the number of police agencies. The point at which the patrol officer leaves off and the detective takes up an investigation is not always defined. O. W. Wilson, V. A. Leonard, and other scholars in the field of law enforcement have discussed this issue in detail, and the student is encouraged to review this literature.

Whether the crime is investigated by a patrol officer or a detective, there can be no doubt that there is a need for some degree of investigative specialization.[3] Today more than ever before the criminal investigator relies on scientific investigative techniques—techniques that require special training to master. Also, the investigator must be familiar with the law as it relates to criminal investigation. Many criminal cases have been lost after months of preparation and investigation because the investigator failed to consider the legality of the evidence that he or she had gathered.

The criminal investigation function is a difficult and important one—difficult because it requires special skills and training, and important because crime can never be stopped or deterred if the police cannot detect, apprehend, and successfully prosecute the criminal offender.

## DISCUSSION QUESTIONS

1. Is contemporary police organization effective? Is it efficient? How would you change it? Why?
2. Is the patrol officer the backbone of the police department? Should this be the case?
3. How can a police organization become more responsive to the community as well as to its own needs?
4. If you had your preference, for what assignment would you volunteer in a police department? Why? How does this task relate to the other units of the department and to the community?

5. Discuss the factors that contribute to determining the span of control in a large police organization?
6. Should a large police organization be administered like a big business? Why or why not?
7. The detective is the police officer most often seen in the movies and on television shows. Why do you suppose this is so?
8. How is your local police department organized? Do you consider this organization a proper one?

## NOTES

1. See *Municipal Police Administration*, George Eastman, ed. (Washington, D.C.: International City Management Association, 1969); V. A. Leonard, *Police Organization and Management*, 2d ed. (Brooklyn: Foundation Press, 1964).
2. Any discussion of territory introduces the question of centralization versus decentralization. Answers to this controversy are extremely complex and by no means absolute. It is suggested that the student refer to texts in business, industrial, public, and police organization and management for in-depth coverage of this material.
3. O. W. Wilson and Roy C. McLaren, *Police Administration*, 3rd ed. (New York: McGraw-Hill, 1972).

# 7: Contemporary Issues in Law Enforcement

*ROLE OF THE POLICE • PERSONNEL • INTERAGENCY COOPERATION • PLANNING AND RESEARCH • ADMINISTRATIVE POLICY VS. INDIVIDUAL DISCRETION • WORKING IN THE COMMUNITY • ISSUES IN PERSPECTIVE: AN INTEGRATED SOLUTION*

PURPOSE: *TO PROVIDE A DISCUSSION OF CONTEMPORARY PROBLEMS AND ISSUES IN TODAY'S LAW ENFORCEMENT COMMUNITY.*

THE POLICE service today is confronted with diverse problems. Attempts are being made at every level of government to identify them, to establish priorities, and then to solve them. However, in many instances, the problems are not new but recurring and age-old. This chapter, then, is a search for contemporary solutions to age-old problems.

As early as 1931, the Wickersham Report discussed an impressive assortment of discrepancies relating to the police service. These shortcomings were further expounded by a variety of scholarly works. Again in 1967, many of these same issues were reiterated by the National Crime Commission. However, in addition to merely restating the problems confronting the police service, federal money was made available in abundance in the 1960s, through LEAA, in an effort to study, define, and ultimately remedy many of these complex police issues. In 1973, the National Advisory Commission on Criminal Justice Standards and Goals issued a comprehensive list of standards for police. Again, many of the same issues covered by the Wickersham Commission (1931) and the National Crime Commission (1967) were covered by the National Advisory Commission (1973). The comparison of the recommendation of the National Crime Commission (1967) and the National Advisory Commission (1973) in Illustrations 7.1 and 7.2 clearly illustrates the recurring nature of many of the problems confronting law enforcement. This comprehensive list demonstrates the difficulties of the police role.

## *ROLE OF THE POLICE*

Police administrators, patrol officers, and the community at large are experiencing tremendous difficulties in defining the role of the police service. In recent years the "advancements" in law enforcement have been the results of reaction to specific situations; for example the riot-torn 1960s apparently indicated the need for more equipment, for the establishment of police-community relations units, and for stronger police training and educational requirements. Increased crime indicated the need for "better" law enforcement. The community demanded improvement of the police, but without suggesting direction. It failed to put priorities on their demands, and the police in most instances lacked the knowledge necessary to properly evaluate the problems and establish sound priorities themselves. The lack of priorities resulted in the police service operating without direction. It was required to enforce the law more intensely and at the same time establish and maintain the support of the community. Although such a task is realistic in many areas, it would appear that in some minority communities strong enforcement of the law and strong community support are not compatible.

The police role is determined by community priorities. If major emphasis is placed on crime detection and apprehension of lawbreakers (criminal law enforcement), then police public service activities such as directing traffic may

**Illustration 7.1** RECOMMENDATIONS OF THE NATIONAL CRIME COMMISSION (1967)

Source: President's Commission on Law Enforcement and Administration of Justice, *The Challenge of Crime in a Free Society* (Washington, D.C.: Government Printing Office, 1967), pp. 294–295.

**Community Relations**

Establish community relations units in departments serving substantial minority population.
Establish citizen advisory committees in minority-group neighborhoods.
Recruit more minority-group officers.
Emphasize community relations in training and operations.
Provide adequate procedures for processing citizen grievances against all public officials.

**Personnel**

Divide functions and personnel entry and promotion lines among three kinds of officers.
Assess manpower needs and provide more personnel if required.
Recruit more actively, especially on college campuses and in inner cities.
Increase police salaries, especially maximums, to competitive levels.
Consider police salaries apart from those of other municipal departments.
Set as goal requirement of baccalaureate degree for general enforcement officers.
Require immediately baccalaureate degrees for supervisory positions.
Improve screening of candidates to determine character and fitness.
Modify inflexible physical, age, and residence recruitment requirements.
Stress ability in promotion.
Encourage lateral entry to specialist and supervisory positions.
Require minimum of 400 hours of training.
Improve training methods and broaden coverage of nontechnical background subjects.
Require one-week yearly minimum of intensive inservice training and encourage continued education.
Require twelve to eighteen months' probation and evaluation of recruits.
Establish police standards commissions.

**Organization and Operations**

Develop and enunciate policy guidelines for exercises of law enforcement discretion.
Clarify by statute authority of police to stop persons for questioning.
Include police formally in community planning.
Provide state assistance for management surveys.
Employ legal advisers.
Strengthen central staff control.
Create administrative boards of key ranking personnel in larger departments.
Establish strong internal investigation units in all departments to maintain police integrity.
Experiment with team policing combining patrol and investigative duties.
Adopt policy limiting use of firearms by officers.

**Pooling of Resources and Services**

Provide areawide communications and records coordination.
Pool and coordinate crime laboratories.
Assist smaller departments in major investigations.
Explore pooling or consolidation of law enforcement in all counties or metropolitan areas.

**Illustration 7.2** RECOMMENDATIONS OF THE NATIONAL ADVISORY COMMISSION ON CRIMINAL JUSTICE STANDARDS AND GOALS (1973)

Source: National Commission on Criminal Justice Standards and Goals, *Police* (Washington, D.C.: Government Printing Office, 1973), summary of entire report.

### The Police Role

Formulate policies governing police functions, objectives, and priorities.
Publicize and respect the limits of police authority.
Formalize police use of discretion.
Improve communication and relations with the public.
Enhance police officers' understanding of their role and of the culture of their community.
Publicize police policies and practices.
Promote police relations with the media.

### Role Implementation

Develop workable agency goals and objectives.
Establish written policies to help employees attain agency goals and objectives.
Establish a formal police inspection system.

### Developing Community Resources

Establish geographic team policing.
Involve the public in neighborhood crime prevention efforts.

### Criminal Justice Relations

Coordinate planning and crime-control efforts with other components of the criminal justice system.
Develop cooperative procedures with courts and corrections agencies.
Formalize diversion procedures to ensure equitable treatment.
Utilize alternative to arrest and pretrial detention.
Develop court followup practices for selected cases.
Divert drug addicts and alcoholics to treatment centers.
Allow telephoned petitions for search warrants.
Enact State legislation prohibiting private surveillance and authorizing court-supervised electronic surveillance.

### Planning and Organizing

Establish a police service that meets the needs of the community.
Consolidate police agencies for greater effectiveness and efficiency.
Implement administrative and operational planning methods.
Assign responsibility for agency and jurisdictional planning.
Participate in any community planning that can affect crime.
Assign responsibility for fiscal management of the agency.
Develop fiscal management procedures.
Derive maximum benefit from government funding.
Formalize relationships between public and private police agencies.
Form a National Institute of Law Enforcement and a Criminal Justice Advisory Committee.
Develop standardized measures of agency performance.

### Team Policing

Determine the applicability of team policing.
Plan, train for, and publicize implementation of team policing.

### Unusual Occurrences

Plan for coordinating activities of relevant agencies during mass disorders and natural disasters.
Delegate to the police chief executive responsibility for resources in unusual occurrences.
Develop an interim control system for use during unusual occurrences.
Develop a procedure for mass processing of arrestees.
Legislate an efficient, constitutionally sound crisis procedure.

*(Illustration 7.2 continued)*

Implement training programs for unusual occurrence control procedures.

**Patrol**

Define the role of patrol officers.
Upgrade the status and salary of patrol officers.
Develop a responsive patrol deployment system.

**Operations Specialization**

Authorize only essential assignment specialization.
Specify selection criteria for specialist personnel.
Review agency specializations annually.
Provide state specialists to local agencies.
Formulate policies governing delinquents and youth offenders.
Control traffic violations through preventive patrol and enforcement.
Train patrol officers to conduct preliminary investigations.
Create a mobile unit for special crime problems.
Establish policy and capability for vice operations.
Develop agency narcotics and drugs investigative capability.
Develop a statewide intelligence network that has privacy safeguards.

**Manpower Alternatives**

Employ civilian personnel in supportive positions.
Employ reserve officers.

**Professional Assistance**

Establish working relationships with outside professionals.
Acquire legal assistance when necessary.
Create a state police management consultation service.

**Support Services**

Train technicians to gather physical evidence.
Consolidate criminal laboratories to serve local, regional, and state needs.
Establish a secure and efficient filing system for evidential items.
Guarantee adequate jail services and management.
Establish crime laboratory certification standards.

**Recruitment and Selection**

Actively recruit applicants.
Recruit college-educated personnel.
Ensure nondiscriminatory recruitment practices.
Implement minimum police officer selection standards.
Formalize a nondiscriminatory applicant-screening process.
Encourage the employment of women.
Develop job-related applicant tests.
Develop an applicant scoring system.

**Classification and Pay**

Maintain salaries competitive with private business.
Establish a merit-based position classification system.

**Education**

Upgrade entry-level educational requirements.
Implement police officer educational incentives.
Affiliate training programs with academic institution.
Outline police curriculum requirements.

**Training**

Establish state minimum training standards.
Develop effective training programs.
Provide training prior to work assignment.
Provide interpersonal communications training.
Establish routine inservice training programs.
Develop training quality-control measures.
Develop police training academies and criminal justice training centers.

*(Illustration 7.2 continued)*

**Development, Promotion, and Advancement**

Offer self-development programs for qualified personnel.
Implement formal personnel development programs.
Review personnel periodically for advancements.
Authorize police chief executive control of promotions.
Establish a personnel information system.

**Employee Relations**

Maintain effective employee regulations.
Formalize policies regulating police employee organizations.
Allow a collective negotiation process.
Prohibit work stoppages by policemen.

**Internal Discipline**

Formulate internal discipline procedures.
Implement misconduct complaint procedures.
Create a specialized internal discipline investigative unit.
Ensure swift and fair investigation of misconduct.
Authorize police chief executive adjudication of complaints.
Implement positive programs to prevent misconduct.
Study methods of reducing police corruption.

**Health Care, Physical Fitness, Retirement, and Employee Services**

Require physical and psychological examinations of applicants.
Establish continuing physical fitness standards.
Establish an employee services unit.
Offer a complete health insurance program.
Provide a statewide police retirement system.
Compensate duty-connected injury, death, and disease.

**Personal Equipment**

Specify apparel and equipment standards.
Require standard firearms, ammunition, and auxiliary equipment.
Provide all uniforms and equipment.

**Transportation**

Evaluate transportation equipment annually.
Acquire and maintain necessary transportation equipment.
Conduct a fleet safety program.
Test transportation equipment nationally.

**Communications**

Develop a rapid and accurate telephone system.
Ensure rapid and accurate police communication.
Ensure an efficient radio communications system.
Conduct research on a digital communications system.
Set national communications equipment standards.
Evaluate radio frequency requirements.

**Information Systems**

Standardize reports of criminal activity.
Establish an accurate, rapid-access record system.
Standardize local information systems.
Coordinate federal, state, and local information systems.

become deficient. A basic fallacy in this notion of community-set priorities is the fact that a community is not a homogeneous entity. The suburban and core areas of a city may and normally do have needs peculiar to their location and cultural composition. Even within the confines of a typical suburban or core area, the demands made of the police department may vary greatly within a relatively short distance. The dilemma is one of extreme complexity. For the police to serve any population they must be aware of and understand the root problems of that culture. Inherent in this concept is the need for a more knowledgeable police officer. Education and training, essential to achieve this level of knowledge, is a financial burden that will be placed directly on the shoulders of the taxpayer. Furthermore, since members of the police department are traditionally representative of the middle class, the social disparity between the police and other classes compounds the problem.

Project STAR (System and Training Analysis of Requirement for Criminal Justice Participants), in California, is an attempt to identify the police roles, tasks, and performance objectives, determine knowledge and skill required, formulate educational recommendations, develop training programs, and identify personnel selection criteria for police positions.[1] The project was set up in response to some very basic questions. Before the police can respond to contemporary change, they must determine just what it is they are doing now; the police must find out where they are before they attempt to decide where they want to go.

## *PERSONNEL*

In any organization, the most valuable resource is its members. For years the typical response to increased crime has been to increase the size of the police department. It became apparent, however, that more officers did not necessarily increase the effectiveness of law enforcement. The emphasis on size changed somewhat in the mid 1960s, after the advent of the Office of Law Enforcement Assistance (OLEA; now LEAA) at the federal level. Quality, rather than quantity, policing became the national interest. Efforts were made to develop personnel allocation plans and to use existing police to greater effectiveness.

Great effort was put into elevating the academic level of the police, and the two-year associate degree and later the baccalaureate degree became the goals. Because education was thought by many to be the absolute answer to all police problems, college programs in law enforcement grew rapidly; enrollments increased and ultimately so did the number of graduates. The effects of the increase in degree-holding patrol officers is not yet clear. Although studies comparing the personalities and performance of noncollege and college officers are numerous, the findings of these reports have been less than conclusive.

**Personnel Training**

To state unequivocally that the college-trained officer is a better officer than the noncollege officer is a mistake because a qualitative definition of "better" police performance has long been needed. Attempts to provide such a definition are under way (for example, project STAR). By determining what criteria constitute police performance, the police and the community will be able to determine the qualities needed to perform as a police officer. Likewise, to better prepare the officer, training can be structured around performance needs.

Given the prevailing claim that the police have failed, we must assume that existing performance criteria used to measure the "good" and "not good" officer are in themselves a failure. However, one fact can be stated about the officer considered highly qualified: he is difficult to retain, especially in the smaller municipal agencies.

The apparent need for educated officers, supplemented by federal money for in-service training and later for preservice education, created a reservoir of highly qualified police personnel never before equaled in American police history. However, a new trend was soon established: the recently attained skills and academic degrees opened doors in other agencies, and law enforcement soon experienced a migration from the local, to the state, to the federal law enforcement agencies. This movement was enhanced by higher salaries and more prestige at the state and federal level. Although not all qualified police personnel chose to leave the small municipalities, it was evident that the vast majority of educated officers at the local level were not in the small departments but in the larger urban agencies. It is ironic that the state and federal agencies benefited so greatly when a major objective of LEAA funding had been to improve the effectiveness of the police at the local level, where most of our nation's crime occurs.

**Minimum Standards of Quality**

Minimum police standards legislation is another attempt to remedy several current police problems. With the broad variations among the many police jurisdictions, it is virtually impossible to state just exactly what should be the standards for recruitment, training, and promotion. The concept of minimum standards is rather simple: its purpose is to require every police officer in a given state to attain a specified number of training hours in a certified course of instruction. Initially one problem becomes most apparent: not every state has enacted minimum standard legislation, and those states that have made the effort do not have compatible standards. Furthermore, the legislation, in many instances, fails to give the standards commission (or whatever it may be called in a particular state) the authority and power necessary to ensure quality. Successful completion of the course of instruction is often based on mere class attendance rather than proven proficiency. It is possible for an illiterate to complete some such courses, especially because it is virtually impossible to fail the final test—should one even be required. The philosophy of minimum standards is plausible; however, the actual practice in many states should be subjected to great scrutiny.

**Personnel Selection**

Many of our nation's police agencies are confronted with a critical recruitment problem. Some departments are unable to attract qualified individuals, and these departments need an immediate self-inventory to determine the cause of their unattractiveness. Salaries, fringe benefits, and public opinion of police operations are all factors that make a department desirable or undesirable.

In many departments, police administrators and rookies alike proudly announce: "Out of all those applicants only a handful qualified." The question that must be asked when this comment is heard and the rate of personnel rejected is high is "Are the selection criteria realistic?" This is most pertinent when the department is understaffed and police services are operating below the level of efficiency. Height, weight, and vision requirements are often the cause. If a major portion of the recruits are rejected because of, say, failure to meet minimum height requirements, then an immediate remedy is to reduce the department's height requirement by one or two inches. Although many police officials say a 5′9″ officer can perform better than a 5′7″ officer, they are hard pressed to prove it. In a recent Supreme Court case, *Griggs* vs. *Duke Power Company* [91 S. Ct. 849 (1971)], the Court ruled that promotion tests had to be job related. Recent court actions by the Equal Employment Opportunity Commission have forced many police agencies to remove subjective requirements such as height.

The police selection process may be all but nonexistent, or it may be a very complex, expensive, and time-consuming process. The following is typical of an extensive selection program. The order in which the various phases appear is not necessarily standard, and it does not indicate priority or imply the importance of one phase over another. A complete police selection process may include the following:

1. an application
2. screening of applications
3. written examination
4. physiological and psychological examinations
   a. physical examination
   b. physical agility test
   c. psychological/psychiatric examination
5. background investigation
6. polygraph examination
7. oral interview
8. final selection
9. training academy
10. probationary period of service
11. permanent appointment

Selecting the most qualified personnel for entrance into the police service is of paramount importance to the future of law enforcement. Past experience indicates that personnel resources—the pool of people possessing the basic attributes necessary for a career in law enforcement—increase with the return of military service personnel after a major military build up. This was true immediately after

World Wars I and II, the Korean conflict, and Vietnam.

With large numbers of applicants, any organization becomes more stringent in selection procedures. Even when these numbers are reduced, the objectives of the selection program should remain consistent with the needs of the department. The individuals selected will remain, under current retirement plans, in that organization's employ for twenty to thirty years. Twenty years is a long time for a police department and a community to maintain individuals with qualities less than appropriate to fulfill adequately the organizational needs. The vital issue is: What are the personnel qualities necessary to meet the organization goals? In essence the selection process is complex, and its operation is influenced by many variables. The quality of future police personnel is related to the quality of the selection criteria and process.

### Female Police Officers

The worth of the female in the police service has been greatly underestimated. Female police officers are as much a minority as blacks, Orientals, Mexicans, and other ethnic groups. However, the police are venturing from traditional bounds and meeting contemporary issues with innovative techniques. For example, the Pennsylvania State Police, the Texas Department of Public Safety, the New York City Police, to name but a few, now have women officers. The women of the Pennsylvania State Police perform normal patrol duties and are assigned to both one- and two-officer patrol units. Domestic disturbance teams, police intervention units, police-court liaison offices are using women and minorities to a greater degree. The long-range contributions of these practices will be calculated at a later time, but one thing is certain in terms of personnel development: competition by women for advancement in specialized areas of law enforcement will continue to increase.

### Executive Training

A chief of police in the United States does not enjoy the prestige and social position that is expected for a top executive, and there are many reasons why. One is that the chief of police is traditionally selected from within the ranks of the organization. Thus, the position of chief is actually an extension of the police selection process, and the patrol officer who is selected today may in twenty years or so become the chief administrative officer of the department. Perhaps no single problem looms larger than that of executive selection and development.

In the case of elected county sheriffs, it is readily acknowledged that experience in law enforcement or administration is not a requisite to achieve a majority of the popular vote. As a result, qualified personnel are the exception rather than the general rule. Inept sheriffs appoint deputies with equally poor qualifications, further damaging the image of law enforcement. Where qualified sheriffs are elected they must respond to pressures in order to be re-elected. Because some states prohibit sheriffs from succeeding themselves, a qualified person can serve only one term in office. On the other hand, in some counties highly competent sheriffs have established long tenure and at the same time elevated law enforcement in many respects.

If minimum standards are intended to elevate the quality of personnel at the entrance levels, shouldn't executive minimum standards also be established? Twenty years of patrol experience does not, in itself, cultivate those qualities necessary to be an effective police administrator. A great deal of specific knowledge must be acquired to manage a departmental budget and a large contingent of personnel. If a police department or any organization is in fact the reflection of its leader, a serious examination of law enforcement can provide us with an equally serious message concerning the state of the office of the chief of police. Perhaps this problem can be solved by elevating the standards at each supervisory level.

Although it is generally accepted that to become a police officer one should first undergo training in a police academy, where does a police officer undergo training to become a police executive? The answer to this question is of great importance to the future management of law enforcement. The United States military services have in addition to the various academies, command and staff colleges, the Army War College, and other advanced training centers for senior command officers. The military has recognized the need for an officer to develop special skills in order to perform efficiently and effectively, but we do not have a United States Police Command and Staff College at our disposal.

The Federal Bureau of Investigation provides training for the nation's police personnel at the National Academy, located at Quantico, Virginia, which offers an intensive course in firearms, physical fitness, and classroom studies. This training is not, however, designed for the development of executive talent.

The Southern Police Institute of the School of Police Administration at the University of Louisville is perhaps the command and staff college for the police service. The primary objective of the Southern Police Institute is to develop executive police leadership. The course is open only to active administrative police personnel throughout the world, and since the institute's founding in 1951, Great Britain, Guam, Thailand, and many others have been represented in the administration course. Student officers are required to submit their applications for admission to the University of Louisville. These officers must meet the same admission standards as any student in the university; this factor alone indicates the level of study one can expect. Students' applications that have been accepted by the office of admissions are forwarded to the director of the Southern Police Institute along with the results of the entrance examination and an evaluation of any college work the students may have. A selection board then determines the students who will be accepted. Five areas of study are required of each student officer, and the courses are intense. In addition to formal class lectures, individual and small group research is required, and group seminars and specialized workshops in contemporary problems of police administration are conducted weekly. On completion of the fourteen-week course, the successful student officers have earned fifteen semester hours of college work. Those officers who already hold a four-year degree can enroll in two special courses and receive six semester hours of graduate credit on the successful completion of the program.

States are now beginning to recognize the need for executive development, and several states have initiated special executive development programs and seminars within their general training programs. The larger city and county law enforcement agencies as well as the state police are beginning to implement career and executive development programs.

## *INTERAGENCY COOPERATION*

American society is not static, nor are its lawbreakers. Today, more than ever before, we are a nation of mobility. Automobiles, airplanes, and assorted other forms of land and water transportation virtually remove jurisdictional boundaries. A police officer or government official is naive to believe that law enforcement for any political subdivision can function exclusively within its territorial limits. Not uncommonly lawbreakers come into a city, commit a burglary, for example, and then return to their homes several miles away, perhaps across county or state boundaries. The successful investigation of this violation is greatly inhibited by the existing jurisdictional limitations. The primary means to overcome this blockage has been *voluntary* cooperation between police departments. Such arrangements have been in existence for years; their effectiveness, on the other hand, is difficult to determine. Let us assume that our armed robbers of Chapter 3 return to their home town, where the police department becomes aware of their newly acquired fortunes and excessive spending. The home town police have reason to suspect them, and miles away the "victim police" could provide the necessary facts to successfully bring these violators before the courts. However, the home town police do not know to which of the other 40,000 police agencies they should make inquiry. Hypothetical indeed. Nevertheless, this instance portrays one of the many problems confronting the police service today.

In an attempt to reduce some of the problems created by jurisdictional boundaries, the National Crime Information Center (NCIC) was established as a national clearing house for criminal information. Operated by the Federal Bureau of Investigation, NCIC collects crime data (for example, stolen motor vehicles, wanted persons) and makes them available to state and local authorities. Computerization has made the retrieval of this information reasonably fast; however, a fundamental problem exists: a computer is capable only of providing information that has been fed into it. Crime information is submitted voluntarily to NCIC by state and local police, but a police officer in Utah may have an Ohio vehicle stopped for some reason and, requesting data from NCIC, find no record of this vehicle when in fact it was stolen. The answer is simply that the stolen vehicle information was never submitted to NCIC by the Ohio police.

At the state level similar centers are maintained, usually by the state police, for collection and distribution of state criminal information. With NCIC functioning as the hub, an interstate network of crime data is available—limited by the extent of voluntary participation.

At the local levels and among police departments a variety of staff services have been consolidated under metropolitan or regional agreements. Communications and detention facilities are perhaps the services most commonly amenable to consolidation. Often where several small municipal police departments operate within a county, each municipality maintains its own communications system. Not surprisingly, each system may be on a different frequency, and communications between departments is impossible. Police vehicles of adjoining towns, where jurisdictions are often separated by a street's width, are unable to communicate by radio with one another even in emergency situations. Likewise, if it is necessary to engage in a joint police operation (narcotics raid or roadblock) the problem of interagency communication is a definite handicap. The need for a better system is evident, and, with the availability of federal money, these situations are being remedied. In many instances, however, the lack of proper planning produces a different but not an improved system—a system that will remain incompatible with the demands placed upon an expanding and changing police.

Los Angeles City Police, Chicago City Police, and police in other cities have sophisticated communications systems. In August 1973 the New York City Police Department contracted for a law enforcement data communication system, a federally funded project.[2] These systems are departmental systems and are not usually designed to give support to neighboring police departments. The support that the major cities usually provide neighboring departments is computer terminal linkage with state and federal (NCIC) crime information systems, which is vitally important, and its continuation and expansion are certainly encouraged. The critical lack of communications is apparent at the operational level in situations involving two or more smaller departments and has led to the concept of regional criminal justice planning as a function of the various state planning agencies.

## *PLANNING AND RESEARCH*

The whole area of planning and research, important to communications, must be expanded still further. A majority of the nation's police agencies lack the knowledge to research a given problem scientifically and subsequently plan an effective and responsive program. Although most of the nation's larger police agencies have adequate research capabilities, the small departments, do not have formal planning and research units. There research and planning are secondary functions, if they even exist. Admittedly, research is complicated and its results are more often indications rather than concrete solutions. However, programs based on the product of these scientific indications are more likely to succeed than programs instituted to combat a problem that has in fact not been adequately identified. Because law enforcement is frequently unaware of the nature of its problems, the corrective measures that are instituted are too often hit and miss propositions. Although their intentions have merit the results are less worthy.

Urban planning is a matter of great concern to the police service. Unfortunately, police administrators, community leaders, and government officials have not always realized the need to take the police function into consideration when developing community plans. The construction of a major highway through a municipality can have a great influence upon the police and the community in general. Excluding the obvious change in the traffic function, this highway may be perceived as a line dividing the town into two distinct territories. On a short-term basis the effects may or may not be discernible; over a period of time distinct characteristics may appear. The socioeconomic distribution of the population may fluctuate—with housing deteriorating or improving, with crime increasing or decreasing. Therefore, the development of new subcultures or subcommunities requires recognition by the police. Such factors are not usually considered within the province of the police, because more times than not the police service has failed to provide capable, qualified, and articulate administrators for its organization.

Recognize that the degree of police involvement in urban planning ranges from none at one extreme to major at the other extreme. In the area of crime prevention, however, police are taking an increasing role through their involvement in urban planning and design.[3] If sufficient information can be collected from police crime reports, profiles of crime areas can be developed. These profiles in turn may indicate certain physical characteristics that provide criminal opportunities. A classic example of this point is the improvement of street lighting in areas experiencing a high rate of crime.

## *ADMINISTRATIVE POLICY VS. INDIVIDUAL DISCRETION*

Considerable emphasis has been put on the formulation of administrative police policy to reduce individual discretion at the operational level. Simply stated, the police agencies are being asked, by citizens and police officers alike, to formulate a general course of direction for the agency within which the activities of all personnel and activities must operate. The purpose of establishing policies is to prescribe parameters within which individual police officers and units must function. Policy sets limits but does not remove the elements of discretion, initiative, and flexibility. Policies are guidelines that relate to and complement the total objectives of the department.

At the operational level there appears to be a notable lack of developed procedural guidelines. The issue is whether operational guidelines should be established for the individual officer to follow, or

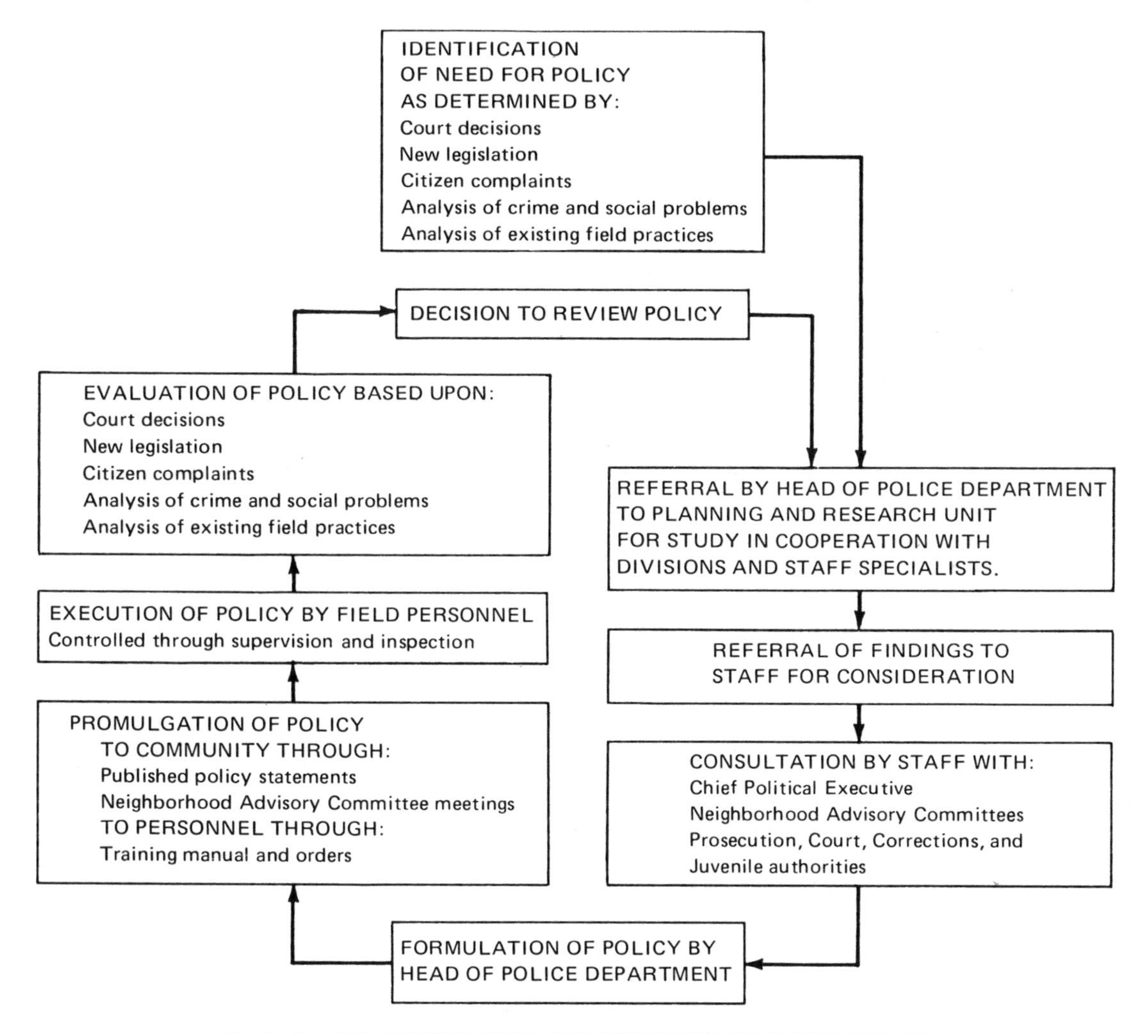


**Illustration 7.3** FORMULATION AND EXECUTION OF POLICE POLICY

Source: President's Commission on Law Enforcement and Administration of Justice, *Task Force Report: The Police* (Washington, D.C.: Government Printing Office, 1967), p. 26.

whether the existing high degree of discretionary tolerance should continue. Many proponents of the former submit that the responsiveness of the police can be ensured only through such policy guidelines. They further argue that individual discretion negates the much desired element of "consistent law enforcement." Established guidelines enhance uniformity of procedures and consistency of enforcement, and at the same time define a legal area in which the officer can function with certainty. This concept is contradicted by the fact that administrative guidelines cannot adequately account for all possible situations. Guidelines, in order to have general applicability, have to be stated in such broad terms as to become meaningless. If the patrol officers' security rests solely with themselves, then their actions should, but may not, have departmental or community support. Every effort should be made to have every officer know what is and what is not acceptable police conduct and procedure.

Nevertheless, the broad latitude of police discretion currently enjoyed by the police could in many instances be reduced through established policy without reducing effectiveness. Judicial decisions and procedural law have definitely influenced police policy. Since the *Miranda* decision, the officer is not given a choice as to whether an arrested felon, for example, has the right to counsel during interrogation. Yet the police continue to function despite the formulation of this policy and the curtailed discretion.

Policy formulation is a complex task involving all the resources of the community and the police department. To illustrate the multivariate nature of policy formulation, examine Illustration 7.3, where everyone seems to have some part in policy formulation. In essence that is accurate, but there are exceptions. One is the right of police to engage in policy formulation through collective bargaining. Because civilian control over law enforcement is so fundamental to the American form of government, law enforcement policy cannot be subject to collective bargaining. Further, local policy cannot be influenced by a state or national police union. Police policy is formulated in response to local requirements and may, therefore, be inconsistent with the policies prescribed by a state or national police union.

Although the complete removal of police discretion is not within the realm of logic, nor has it been insisted upon, guidelines are essential for the proper exercise of police power and authority. Established guidelines offer the police officer protection from unwarranted personal liability suits and protect the citizen from unwarranted police conduct and activities. Properly formulated and executed, police policy is of mutual benefit to police and citizen alike.

## *WORKING IN THE COMMUNITY*

The effective control of crime is not the sole responsibility of the police. On the contrary, law enforcement is a community concern, and the police are merely a formalized supplemental community organization. Bringing this message to the public is undoubtedly a most demanding task for the police service. Surprisingly enough, this principle is frequently not recognized by the police, and consequently, little effort is put into informing and educating the citizenry—and the police themselves—about their roles and positions in the arena of public protection.

### Police-Community Relations

Within the last decade, police-community relations units have been established in many of the nation's police departments. However, this vital function must not be restricted to a single specialized unit: police-community relations is a task for every member of the department. Every officer represents the department by his or her mere presence. Actions and general performance of duty are presumed by the public to represent departmental policy, whether such policy exists or not.

A police officer is a member of the police department; however, he or she is also a member of the community. Unfortunately, both citizens and police officers often lose sight of this fact. The role of the police officer should be a dynamic part in the integration of community-police relations and problem-solving activities. When law enforcement is motivated to seek community support in response to police and crime problems, solutions are more readily attainable, and it is the simple truth that crime control is best achieved through public knowledge, understanding, and awareness of the crime problem.

The community is a complex entity with which the police must interact constantly. Police-community relations must be more than a block on an organizational chart or a written policy statement; they must actively involve the recruitment of qualified minorities and encourage maximum use of their skills and attributes, create positive relationships with the news media to provide an excellent channel for informing the public about police tasks and problems,[4] and otherwise become an integral part of social organization.

A number of myths, as well as many truisms, have evolved over the years concerning the nature of law enforcement. Fear of the police is common, and history has recorded incidents that warrant such emotions. Certain ethnic groups, for example, have experienced police actions beyond the comprehension of any civilized person. Distressing isolated instances still occur, which may or may not have ethnic significance. If it is axiomatic that the community gets the police service it deserves, then change is a future certainty: municipal government is experiencing change, and the police are making the transition with it.

### Community Government

Municipal law enforcement, in many ways, is influenced greatly by the system of local government in which it must operate. The great majority of the 39,750 local police agencies in the United States function under one of three basic governmental models: the mayor-council, the commission, and the city manager. Each has certain properties that either directly or indirectly determine the nature of the police department. More bluntly stated, the degree of police effectiveness and efficiency, whether "good" or "bad," in many cases must not be regarded as solely dependent on the police department; it is determined by the local government. Undoubtedly, the position of the police department in the administrative pattern of present-day municipal organization is of the greatest importance, for without sound administrative structure at the top, no police organization can be administered and controlled efficiently and honestly.[5]

## *ISSUES IN PERSPECTIVE: AN INTEGRATED SOLUTION*

It is difficult to understand the nature and extent of police problems, but understanding is a prerequisite to any formulation of solutions. To best illustrate many, but certainly not all, of the problems currently confronting law enforcement, let us re-examine the hypothetical armed robbery of Chapter 3.

Two armed robbers, one of whom was an adult, the other a juvenile, were stopped by a police traffic unit after committing several traffic violations. The traffic officers, having received the license plate number of the robbery vehicle from the patrol unit investigating the robbery, established probable cause by matching the number of the vehicle that committed the traffic violations and took both suspects into custody or effected an arrest. The traffic officers searched the suspects and found weapons and a large amount of cash. The adult suspect was then booked, fingerprinted, photographed, and jailed, while the juvenile was referred to proper juvenile authorities. The apprehension process as just described is not so simple as it might seem, and Illustration 7.4 shows the various phases in detail.

The above description, although very brief, raises some profound questions that should be discussed because they relate to both the administration of the police and to the individual beat officer. Let us assume the role of the two traffic officers stopping the vehicle that carries the license number of two armed robbery suspects. What are they armed with? Guns, knives, chains, starter-pistols? Perhaps they are not armed at all! How should you approach the suspects' vehicle? What does your partner officer think? What is your partner going to do? These questions and scores of others undoubtedly confront you. Each can be answered in one of three ways—individual discretion, formulated police policy, or a combination of both. Radio communication may provide an answer to the first question, how the suspects are armed, if the patrol officer investigating the robbery reported the information. If not reported, then is the investigating patrol officer available to respond to your radio call? This officer may be involved in the investigation and away from the vehicle radio. The other questions must be answered, but these answers may not be as absolute. In police departments where training is inadequate and policies not clearly established to guide the officers, it is possible that each officer will approach the situation from a different perspective. A very elementary ques-

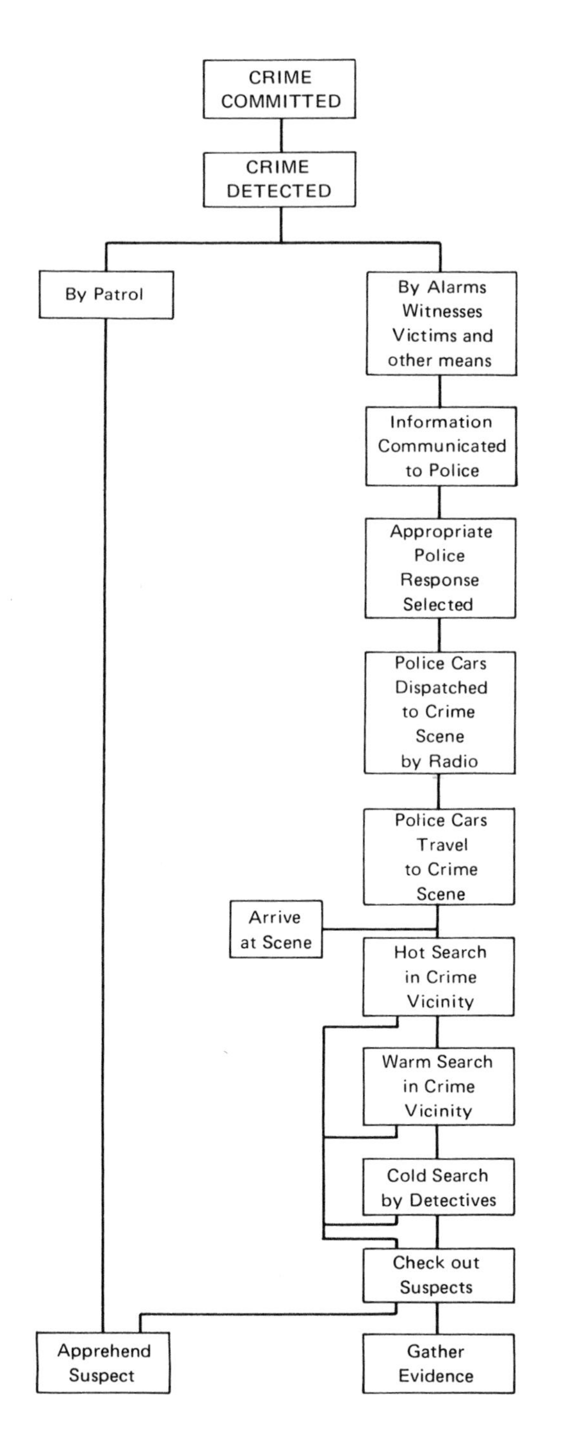


tion these officers will probably ask is should we remove our weapons from the holsters? If such a decision is left to the individual's discretion, the option to remove or not to remove is present. If, however, established department policy and training requires officers to approach a vehicle suspected of being involved in an armed robbery with weapons unholstered, the option to keep the weapon in the holster no longer exists. This requirement may increase the element of personal security for both officers, not because unholstered weapons are necessarily safer, but because each officer is aware of the other's actions and state of readiness.

Without becoming involved in a case study of stop and frisk, arrest, evidence search and seizure, and so on, let us recognize here that every phase of the law enforcement function is based on substantive, procedural, and constitutional law. If the two traffic officers had not had the license number of the robbery suspects, they might not have been able to search the two "traffic violators." Furthermore, the cash and weapons would have been found during an illegal search, because the traffic violations did not give the police probable cause to search for the results of an armed robbery. A search is conducted incidental to an arrest—a suspect is not arrested incidental to an illegal search.

Subsequently, of course, the booking

**Illustration 7.4** APPREHENSION PROCESS

Source: President's Commission on Law Enforcement and Administration of Justice, *Task Force Report: The Police* (Washington, D.C.: Government Printing Office, 1967), p. 26.

procedure, fingerprinting, photograph, arrest information, and lineup procedures are all subject to legal safeguards. Court decisions have firmly established in many legal areas the rules under which the police must operate. The police must know, for example, if and when a suspect is required to have legal counsel present. With regard to the juvenile offender in our robbery case, the officers must be aware of and follow the requirements set forth in another body of law, including *Kent* v. *United States* [383 U.S. 541 (1966)] and *In re Gault* [387 U.S. 1 (1967)] and related cases, which provide guidelines for police dealing with juvenile offenders.

It is absurd to expect every police officer to also become a legal scholar and social scientist. Nevertheless, a police officer must possess a certain level of expertise in both the law and the social sciences in order to perform his or her duties in today's complex community. Attainment of these required levels of expertise is a responsibility of police administration. Every police department must recognize the need for competent police officers and establish a training program to meet that need. The police have a sworn obligation to provide protection and service to the community, and the community has the right to the best possible police service.

## DISCUSSION QUESTIONS

1. How much education does a police officer need? Before you answer, ask: What is a police officer? Keep in mind rank, assignment, and related factors.
2. How does one determine one's role in an organization? How does one change that role? What are the change agents in a contemporary police agency?
3. Have the police failed? How do you measure success or failure in a police department?
4. Of what value can the police be in total urban planning?
5. Why is it difficult for many police agencies to retain college police officers? What steps can be taken to remedy this problem?
6. Why should efforts be made to define the police role?

## NOTES


1. "Criminal Justice Roles, Tasks, and Performance Objectives: Working Document," in *Systems and Training Analysis of Requirement for Criminal Justice Participants (STAR)* (Sacramento: California Department of Justice Commission on Peace Officer Standards of Training, 1973), p. x.
2. "New York City Police Data Communication System," in *Kriston-Bram* (Chanute, Kan.: Kriston Electronics, Inc., 1973), chap. 4.
3. C. Ray Jeffery, *Crime Prevention Through Environmental Design* (Beverly Hills: Sage Publications, 1971).
4. American Bar Association Standards for Criminal Justice, *The Urban Police Function* (New York: Institute of Judicial Administration, 1972), p. 17.
5. V. A. Leonard, *Police Organization and Management*, 2d ed. (Brooklyn: Foundation Press, 1964), pp. 22–31.

## PART TWO ANNOTATED BIBLIOGRAPHY

More, Harry W., Jr., ed. *Critical Issues in Law Enforcement.* Cincinnati: W. H. Anderson, 1972.

*An excellent presentation of current police problems to which students of law enforcement must give careful consideration if law enforcement is to be relevant in contemporary society.*

National Advisory Commission on Criminal Justice Standards and Goals. *Police.* Washington, D.C.: Government Printing Office, 1973.

*Not only presents a list of police problems but also provides goals for which the police should strive. Recommendations are offered in an attempt to make the goals more attainable.*

President's Commission on Law Enforcement and Administration of Justice. *Task Force Report: The Police.* Washington, D.C.: Government Printing Office, 1967.

*One of ten reports of the President's Commission on Law Enforcement and Administration of Justice. This report presents the research and findings of the Commission's Task Force on police topics ranging from administrative problems to police field problems.*

Wilson, O. W., and Roy C. McLaren. *Police Administration.* 3d ed. New York: McGraw-Hill, 1972.

*A textbook on police administration. An in-depth presentation of police organization and administration.*

# PART THREE

# The Prosecutor

# 8: History and Structure of Prosecution

*HISTORICAL PRECEDENTS IN PROSECUTION • DEVELOPMENT OF PROSECUTION IN AMERICA • INFLUENCE OF THE CONTEMPORARY PROSECUTOR*

PURPOSE: *TO TRACE THE HISTORICAL DEVELOPMENT OF PROSECUTION AND DESCRIBE THE PRESENT-DAY STRUCTURE OF PROSECUTORIAL AGENCIES.*

PROSECUTION is the process whereby accusations are brought before a court to determine the guilt or innocence of the accused. The *prosecutor* is an officer of the court whose responsibility it is, under the law, to carry out this legal process. Prosecution is made up of a series of contacts between a government official (who is a lawyer) and criminals and the attorneys representing them, both in and out of legal tribunals or courts of law. From the initial criminal proceedings, through continuances, plea bargainings, *habeas corpus* hearings, at many different levels of the criminal justice system, in the trial process itself, the prosecutor is functioning in behalf of the community he or she serves.

Basically, the prosecutor has the responsibility and the obligation of presenting the government's case in courts of law. If a crime has been committed, it is the prosecutor's task to bring the accused to court. The prosecutor must ensure that sufficient evidence exists to prove the accused is guilty. He must also ensure that the prosecution process is conducted with due process of law. During the trial the prosecutor presents the state's case. The adversary (the defendant's lawyer) is there to protect the defendant's interest and to ensure that the prosecutor does not prosecute unjustly or deprive the client of his or her rights. By analogy, the trial is a battle: the prosecutor is the state's champion, the lawyer is the client's champion, the judge is the referee, and the jury are the deciders of the outcome. It is not, however, a battle without historical precedents.

## HISTORICAL PRECEDENTS IN PROSECUTION

The federal or state prosecutor is known as the attorney general. The origin of the office of attorney general is found hundreds of years ago in the jurisprudential development and the common law of England. The office has evolved from powers derived from the common law, federal and state constitutions, federal and state statutes, and the case law of the various state and federal courts of appeal. In the Middle Ages, the king had attorneys, sergeants, and solicitors to perform some of the functions of the modern attorney general. Before the thirteenth century, the king appointed special attorneys to prosecute criminal cases.[1] The general term *attornatus* was used in English official documents in the Middle Ages to mean anyone who appeared for another as pleader, attorney, or essoiner.[2]

The earliest laws of England defined crimes as being committed against a particular individual, not against the state or other governmental body. The original prosecutor was a victim or an individual representing a victim who stepped forward personally to initiate the prosecution of the alleged offender. The fact that the injured or aggrieved were their own advocates quite often caused the prosecution to be carried out in a zealous quest for vengeance.

Originally all crimes were torts; thus, in early common law, any injury, whether to person or property, was a tort. (A tort today is an injury to an individual that is not an offense against the state.) The historical custom of victim-prosecutors led to so much feuding that eventually the English king took over the obligation of punishing each and every offender, the original declaration or concept being known as the *king's peace*. From this time on, any conduct that resulted in an injury to person or property was considered an offense against the king's peace. Later, the injury was considered an offense against the state.

One way in which "justice" was effected and punishment mandated was the payment of fines. The king could be paid and he could also require that fine monies be paid to a victim or a victim's family. Before law was codified, the punishments meted out by governmental authorities were quite often on a level that would be considered deplorable, barbaric, and inhumane today, but they were quite acceptable by the standards of that period.

Henry V, King of England (1413–1422), required that four specific offenses be classified as felonies, or major offenses, and that all lesser offenses be classified as demeanor offenses. The first four felonies were: treason, counterfeiting, arson, and murder. (In later years the lesser offenses, demeanor offenses, came to be known as misdemeanors.) At the same time, Henry V provided that all crimes be considered crimes against society. The state or government, representing society, was to bear the burden of law enforcement, prosecution of offenders, public trials, and punishment procedures.

There is some disagreement as to who the first attorney general was. However, it was during the reign of Edward IV (1461–1483) that William Husse was appointed attorney general of England, and Husse is recognized by most authorities as the first.[3]

Henry VIII (1509–1547) eliminated the vengeance prosecution system and in its stead provided a system of "sergeants," who were required to act as police prosecutors and to enforce penal statutes. These sergeants were later to become well trained in the law. Even though they received compensation from the king for their services, they were also able to practice in civil courts and criminal courts. Unfortunately, from the outset of this system, prosecutors were able to make much more from pursuits other than prosecution, and so, even from the inception of this publically funded and supported system, divided interests were of primary concern. There was a tendency on the part of many prosecutors to spend very little time on the less financially rewarding prosecution cases as opposed to time spent on the more rewarding cases of private practice.

## *DEVELOPMENT OF PROSECUTION IN AMERICA*

In the United States, development of the prosecutor's office at the state level followed an erratic path. The majority of the colonies created or continued the office of attorney general in their new state constitutions. Territories established the office by law at the time of statehood, though this was not a universal practice.

Hard as it is to imagine a state operating without an attorney general, Virginia waited until 1904 before it legislated the office of attorney general.[4]

The United States attorney general is not a constitutional officer. The office was created by the Judiciary Act of 1789. The attorney general soon became a member of the president's cabinet, but did not head a department until 1870, at which time the Department of Justice was created by an act of Congress.[5]

The agencies of prosecution that eventually developed are like many other elements of the American criminal justice system in that they exist at three distinct levels, the federal, the state, and the local. At the federal level the United States attorney general is the chief law officer. At the state level the state attorney general is the chief law officer. The chief law officer at the local level (city, county, municipal) has such titles as district attorney, prosecutor, and city attorney.

### United States Attorney General

The chief United States prosecutor is given the title United States attorney general and is a member of the president's cabinet, appointed by the president, the appointment confirmed by the Senate. In addition to performing duties related to the chief prosecutional task, he renders legal opinions to the head of the various governmental bureaus and administers the work of all personnel under his command, including the administration of the federal correctional institutions. Agencies coming under his direct supervision and administration include:

Office of the Deputy Attorney General
Office of the Solicitor General
Office of the Nine Assistant Attorney Generals
- The Antitrust Division
- The Civil Division
- The Criminal Division
- The Internal Security Division
- The Land and Natural Resource Division
- The Office of Legal Council
- The Tax Division

The Director of the Federal Bureau of Investigation
The Director of the Federal Bureau of Prisons
The Commissioner of the Immigration and Naturalization Service
The Director of the Community Relations Service
The Executive Assistant to the Attorney General
The Director of Public Information
The Director of Drug Enforcement Administration
The Administrator of Law Enforcement Assistant Administration
The Pardon Attorney
The Board of Parole
The Board of Immigration Appeals
The Office of United States Attorney of the Federal Judicial Districts
The Office of the United States Marshal
The Office of Criminal Justice (See Illustration 8.1.)

The attorney general has a tremendous amount of authority and control over many different branches of the criminal justice system. Although his direction and that of his subordinates in the Justice Department directly affect many different

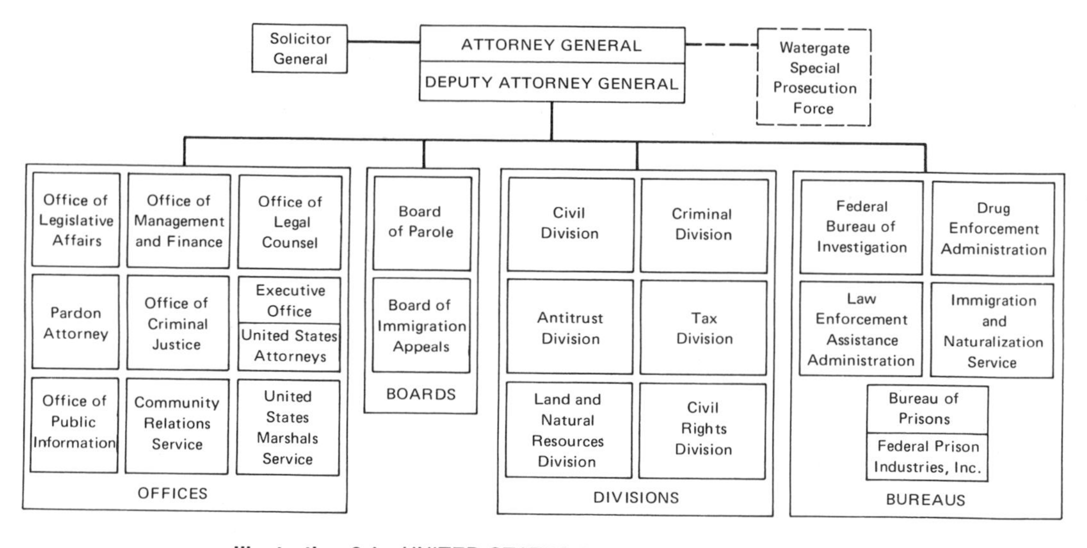

**Illustration 8.1** UNITED STATES DEPARTMENT OF JUSTICE
Source: Office of the Federal Register, *United States Government Manual 1974–75* (Washington, D.C.: Government Printing Office, 1974), p. 299.

units of federal and state government, most federal prosecutions are handled, not in Washington, but locally and directly by the United States attorney or the assistant United States attorney.

Only a small number of the 45,000 personnel who staff the professional and logistical units of the Justice Department are involved directly in the prosecutional process. Many attorneys working under the attorney general are investigators, administrators, inspectors, or law enforcement officers. On some occasions, members of the criminal division and its sections of organized crime and racketeering, administrative regulations, general crimes, fraud, management and labor, and narcotic and dangerous drugs assist the United States attorney general in the prosecution of specific offenses. This gives an attorney who principally serves as an investigator criminal trial and prosecution experience at the various levels of the federal court system.

## State and Local Attorneys General

The attorney general of a specific state is usually elected by the voters of that state. The governors of the states of Alaska, Hawaii, New Hampshire, New Jersey, Pennsylvania, and Wyoming appoint the attorneys general in their states, though in some of these states the legislatures must approve the appointments. The legislature appoints the attorney general in the state of Maine and the state supreme court appoints the attorney general in Tennessee. Illustration 8.2 depicts the method of selection of the state and territorial attorneys general and their terms of office.

The authority of the state attorneys general differs from state to state. In the states

| | Elected | Appointed by | With Consent of | Length of Term (Years) | May Succeed Self |
|---|---|---|---|---|---|
| Alabama | X | | | 4 | No |
| Alaska | | Governor | Legislature | Indefinite | Yes |
| Arizona | X | | | 4 | Yes |
| Arkansas | X | | | 2 | Yes |
| California | X | | | 4 | Yes |
| Colorado | X | | | 4 | Yes |
| Connecticut | X | | | 4 | Yes |
| Delaware | X | | | 4 | Yes |
| Florida | X | | | 4 | Yes |
| Georgia | X | | | 4 | Yes |
| Guam | | Governor | Legislature | Indefinite | Yes |
| Hawaii | | Governor | Senate | 4 | Yes |
| Idaho | X | | | 4 | Yes |
| Illinois | X | | | 4 | Yes |
| Indiana | X | | | 4 | Yes |
| Iowa | X | | | 2 | Yes |
| Kansas | X | | | 2 | Yes |
| Kentucky | X | | | 4 | No |
| Louisiana | X | | | 4 | Yes |
| Maine | | Legislature | | 2 | Yes |
| Maryland | X | | | 4 | Yes |
| Massachusetts | X | | | 4 | Yes |
| Michigan | X | | | 4 | Yes |
| Minnesota | X | | | 4 | Yes |
| Mississippi | X | | | 4 | Yes |
| Missouri | X | | | 4 | Yes |
| Montana | X | | | 4 | Yes |
| Nebraska | X | | | 4 | Yes |
| Nevada | X | | | 4 | Yes |
| New Hampshire | | Governor | Council | 5 | Yes |
| New Jersey | | Governor | Senate | 4 | Yes |
| New Mexico | X | | | 2 | Yes |
| New York | X | | | 4 | Yes |
| North Carolina | X | | | 4 | Yes |
| North Dakota | X | | | 4 | Yes |
| Ohio | X | | | 4 | Yes |
| Oklahoma | X | | | 4 | Yes |
| Oregon | X | | | 4 | Yes |
| Pennsylvania | | Governor | Senate | 4 | Yes |
| Puerto Rico | | Governor | Senate | Indefinite | Yes |
| Rhode Island | X | | | 2 | Yes |
| Samoa | | Governor | | 2 yr. min. | Yes |
| South Carolina | X | | | 4 | Yes |
| South Dakota | X | | | 2 | Yes |
| Tennessee | | Supreme Ct. | | 8 | Yes |
| Texas | X | | | 2 | Yes |
| Utah | X | | | 4 | Yes |
| Vermont | X | | | 2 | Yes |
| Virgin Islands | | Governor | Legislature | Indefinite | Yes |
| Virginia | X | | | 4 | Yes |
| Washington | X | | | 4 | Yes |
| West Virginia | X | | | 4 | Yes |
| Wisconsin | X | | | 4 | Yes |
| Wyoming | | Governor | Senate | 4 | Yes |
| United States | | President | Senate | Indefinite | Yes |

**Illustration 8.2** THE ATTORNEY GENERAL: SELECTION AND TERM

Source: National Association of Attorneys General, Committee on the Attorney General, *The Office of Attorney General*, 1973, p. 63.

of Connecticut, Florida, Idaho, Illinois, Missouri, Tennessee, Virginia, and West Virginia, the attorney general has no authority over local prosecutors and cannot take over the prosecution of any particular case. All other states have provided constitutional or statutory authority for the state attorney general to initiate local prosecutions. Although this authority is often limited to extreme conditions, the discretionary power, the prosecutor's decision to prosecute those cases over which he or she has authority, is usually not limited.

The number of personnel in the state attorney general's office range from less than four in Montana, Nebraska, and South Dakota to about 462 in the state of New York. Overall, the states employ approximately 3,000 lawyers in the offices of their attorneys general.[6]

The prosecuting attorneys of a district, county, or municipal area are chosen either by election or appointment by a court or governing body. In the vast majority of the cases, however, local prosecutors are elected. Although the prosecutor's office may occur at any level of local government, the county level is the most common.

At the state and local levels today, the public prosecutor usually gains office by local election. Such election makes the prosecutor an independent public official with very little central supervision. While the court may place controls over the prosecutor in the courtroom, the prosecutor can act as an independent entity most of the time. The broad discretionary powers of the prosecutor before any court appearance include: (1) decisions about which cases should be presented to the grand jury or those cases in which the prosecutor will file an information, (2) decisions about those cases that will be pressed for trial or those on which the prosecutor will file *nolle prosequi* (which is a refusal to prosecute), and (3) decisions made in bargaining with the accused and defense counsel as to whether some charges will be dropped to a lesser offense or not prosecuted.

> The district or county attorney in most States is a locally elected official. In larger communities the prosecutor has a staff of assistants, but the great majority of the country's more than 2,700 prosecutors serve in small offices with at most one or two assistants and frequently the prosecutor and his assistants are part-time officials. Their official duties are to prosecute all criminal cases and in most jurisdictions to represent the local government in civil cases, but when not engaged in a case they are free to practice law privately. This pattern of outside practice is common to the rural counties and smaller cities although it may be found in our largest cities.[7]

Because the job is a part-time one in most places in the United States, many prosecutors receive extremely low salaries. In addition, crime is not equally distributed, so prosecutors in many places work much harder for the same amount of money than their colleagues in other places. Salaries not being based on case rates, the district or county prosecutor who receives only a small number of cases to prosecute may be very well reimbursed for this total time whereas the prosecutor in an urban or high crime area may be very poorly paid in hourly terms. An overburdened system encourages plea bargaining and case manipulation, especially when the prosecutor is poorly paid. Private pressures may encourage the part-time prosecutor to keep the prosecution time from interfering with private practice. On occasion this situation may result in a preponderance of negotiated pleas or in poor pretrial preparation.

## *INFLUENCE OF THE CONTEMPORARY PROSECUTOR*

The prosecutor is one of the most influential officials in the American system of criminal justice. The powers of the public prosecutor are such that they exceed all others in the criminal justice system with the possible exception of the judge, and they exceed even the judge in the area of discretionary authority because the authority is less subject to formal review. The prosecutor is entrusted with the basic responsibility of deciding whether or not to charge or prosecute a suspect, determines the nature of the charge, has the authority to reduce the charge, and occasionally recommends the dismissal of an action once it has been filed with the court.

The prosecutor, through the power of discretion, usually determines the direction that law enforcement agencies in his or her jurisdiction will take. While many Americans believe that the prosecutor functions primarily in the courtroom, they are wrong. Many prosecutors have the right to make arrests and even carry weapons, just as a police officer does. Many also have investigatory powers in some areas. Occasionally the prosecutor is the only member of the criminal justice community empowered by legislation to investigate organized crime, gambling, governmental corruption, and ecological problems. In those areas where exceptional prosecution power is granted, the prosecutor may be the initial investigator of an alleged crime as well as the court initiator of the criminal process through an arrest or an investigation. The prosecutor may choose to make his or her own investigations in many cases or supplement the police investigation, especially when the prosecutor perceives the local police or sheriff to be inept, poorly trained, or dishonest.

There seems to be very little correlation of practices in different locations. The discretion of the prosecutor and his or her assistants, the qualifications required for the office, and the relationships of police investigators with the prosecutor are not consistent from state to state or city to city.

## DISCUSSION QUESTIONS

1. Why is the attorney general referred to as the chief law enforcement officer?
2. Should a prosecutor be elected or appointed? Why?
3. The United States attorney general has power over many different criminal justice functions. Is this situation conductive to efficiency in the criminal justice system? Why or why not?

4. Do you believe the state attorney general should have the power to take a case away from a local prosecutor? Why or why not?

## NOTES

1. Allen Harding, *Social History of the English Law* (Baltimore: Penguin Books, 1966).
2. Hugh C. Bellott, "The Origin of the Attorney," *Law Review Quarterly*, 25 (1909), 400.
3. National Association of Attorneys General Committee on the Office of Attorney General, *The Office of Attorney General* (1971), p. 12.
4. *The Office of Attorney General*, p. 18.
5. Office of the Federal Register, *United States Government Manual 1973/74* (Washington, D.C.: Government Printing Office, 1973), p. 289.
6. *The Office of Attorney General*, pp. 209–211.
7. President's Commission of Law Enforcement and Administration of Justice, *Task Force Report: The Courts* (Washington, D.C.: Government Printing Office, 1967), p. 73.

# 9: The Prosecutor at Work

*SCREENING AND DIVERSION • DECISION TO PROSECUTE • PRELIMINARY HEARING • INDICTMENT AND INFORMATION • PRETRIAL NEGOTIATIONS • ARRAIGNMENT • TRIAL*

PURPOSE: *TO PROVIDE AN INTRODUCTION TO THE FUNCTIONS OF THE PROSECUTOR AS THEY RELATE TO THE CRIMINAL JUSTICE PROCESS.*

ONCE an arrest or a complaint has been made, the prosecutor examines the charge and decides whether or not to initiate prosecution against the accused individual. (In only certain states or locales can the case be thrown out by a judge before a prosecutor becomes involved.) The prosecutor's first step is to examine the information contained in the warrant and commitment papers that come to the prosecutor's office from the lower court magistrate. After evaluating all the evidence, the prosecutor decides whether or not to initiate prosecution against the person charged with the crime. In this way he or she performs a screening function by reviewing the sufficiency of the evidence before initiating the prosecution. This independent exercise provides some additional protection against the institution of unwarranted prosecutions or prosecutions based on insufficient, inadequate, or contaminated evidence. The questions asked prior to prosecution are as follows:

1. Is there sufficient "probable cause" of guilt to warrant subjecting the defendant to a trial and a unit of government to the expense of paying for that trial?

2. If there is sufficient probable cause or probability of guilt, is there any reason that prosecution should not then be carried out?

3. If an accused is charged with several offenses, which of the crimes should be chosen for the criminal justice process?

4. Will the particular prosecution be in the best interest of the jurisdiction served?

In deciding whether a prosecution will result, the prosecutor usually makes an initial determination based on the facts known to the police officers making the arrest at the time they took the action. A decision that "probable cause" or "reasonable belief of guilt" does not exist is one of the most common reasons for eliminating a case from court action. The prosecutor thus eliminates cases that are vague, inaccurate, or speculatory. Usually these cases have been handled by poorly trained officers or by officers hampered by an overload of investigative cases. On other occasions, a prosecutor may choose to prosecute an offender whose case has been mishandled because of the nature of the offense or of the intensity of social feeling toward the particular offender and the offense.

When a police officer makes an arrest on probable cause with or without a warrant, then the prosecutor has the immediate basis for a good case (unless there was other investigative ambiguity, perhaps coercion or failure to inform the defendant of his or her rights). In some cases, when a police officer merely serves a warrant on the authority of a magistrate, the officer may not have any personal knowledge of probable cause. In such a case, a private citizen making a complaint to a magistrate on oath or affirmation causes the initial decision to arrest, which in turn leads to the prosecutor's involvement in the case.

## SCREENING AND DIVERSION

Screening usually occurs in any case where there is doubt that a conviction can be obtained. Occasionally evidence may be insufficient, a primary witness may lack credibility, or the police may have mismanaged a particular situation. In other cases, the intent of a criminal action may be very difficult to prove: domestic disturbances, checks that are drawn on insufficient funds, or juvenile pranks that may have violated the letter of the law quite often fall in this category. The prosecutor realizes that the most outstanding indiscretion of office is the institution of formal charges against *all* violators of the law, never screening or diverting offenders to other social agencies.

> The prosecutor who institutes . . . charges against all defendants arrested by the police fails to make the necessary choices at this stage of the proceeding. . . . [A] prosecutor's failure to screen at this level introduces some cases which are not important enough to merit full prosecution. By clogging the courts with marginal cases, he is unfortunately ensuring that the more serious crimes, which merit the full attention of the criminal system will not get the scrutiny they deserve.[1]

Whereas *screening* involves the cessation of formal criminal proceedings by the prosecutor and the removal of the individual from the criminal justice system, *diversion* refers to the halting or suspending, before conviction, of the formal criminal proceedings against a person on the condition or assumption that that person will do something in return. Usually, when the prosecutor determines that alternate methods outweigh the value of treatment or punishment within the criminal justice system, the prosecutor will offer the defendant the opportunity to choose between the alternative methods (join the army, seek psychiatric help, accept informal probation, or the like) or continuation of the criminal justice process. Through the screening and diversion processes the prosecutor eliminates from the criminal justice system many of the marginal cases that do not warrant full attention.[2]

## DECISION TO PROSECUTE

Quite often numerous statutes are violated in a single criminal encounter, and prosecutors are responsible for selecting the crime for which the offender is to be prosecuted. The prosecutor usually picks the offense that is the most serious or one that can be easily proven, at the same time retaining the option to prosecute the other offenses. This option provides firm leverage for plea bargaining. Generally, the initial charge is a little more stringent than the ultimate charge.

The decision to prosecute is a very serious one. In making it, the prosecutor announces that the freedom of the offender must be curtailed for his or her own protection or to protect society against that offender. The individual charged may lose job, status, prestige, and large sums of money. On the other hand, the prosecutor may decide not to charge on the grounds that prosecution is not in the community interests.

If the prosecutor is obliged to choose his cases, it follows that he can choose his defendants. There in is the most dangerous power of the prosecutor: that he will pick people that he thinks he should get, rather than pick cases that need to be prosecuted. With the law books filled with a great assortment of crimes, a prosecutor stands a fair chance of finding at least a technical violation of some act on the part of almost everyone.[3]

## *PRELIMINARY HEARING*

Having decided to proceed, the prosecutor's next step in a felony case is generally the preliminary hearing. Here the prosecutor introduces evidence and tries to convince the court that there is probable cause for believing the accused guilty. At this hearing, witnesses may be presented and cross-examined and other aspects of the adversary process are permitted. If the court finds that reasonable cause exists it will carry the case to the next step in the prosecution. The prosecutor may now take the case before a grand jury or file an information, a formal charge leveled against the accused.

## *INDICTMENT AND INFORMATION*

A grand jury is an investigative body composed of members elected from the community. It serves as a buffer between the state and the citizen. The prosecutor, in many cases, brings before the grand jury the evidence gathered on a particular case. The grand jury must then decide if sufficient evidence exists to hand down an indictment—the indictment being a formal charge against an accused person written by the prosecutor and submitted to a court by the grand jury. With the indictment issued, the prosecutor can proceed to the arraignment.

The prosecutor might instead file an information. The information is a formal document filed by the prosecutor before the court indicating that there is sufficient evidence to proceed with the case. In some states and for certain offenses, the prosecutor is bound to the grand jury system. In other states the prosecutor has the option to proceed by a grand jury indictment or by an information. While the Fifth Amendment holds that "no person shall be held to answer for a capital, or otherwise infamous crime, unless on a presentment or indictment of a Grand Jury," the Supreme Court has not yet ruled that the grand jury system is a necessary element of due process.[4]

## *PRETRIAL NEGOTIATIONS*

Pretrial negotiations may involve plea bargaining as well as giving incentives to defendants to testify or to give information to police about those who conspired with them or about other offenders known to them. These negotiations are much more informal at this stage than in later phases of the criminal justice process when the courts as well as defense and prosecutional efforts are much more formalized. Many prosecutors prefer pretrial interaction and negotiation, because there is more opportunity for flexibility of procedure and because the spirit of competitiveness does not exist in the same way as it does during the adversary phases of the trial process.

Pretrial negotiations have been greatly expanded in the last few years in order to help the courts keep pace with their extremely overburdened dockets or caseloads, especially in high-crime-rate urban areas. Because the court system as it now exists simply cannot handle the huge influx of cases, pretrial negotiations are almost mandatory. The sheer number of cases pressure many prosecutors into accepting pleas of guilty to a lesser offense even when they would be inclined to prosecute for the greater offense.

Many members of the legal profession are very concerned because of the large number of inducements available to the police, the prosecutor, and even to the defense attorney that encourage a plea of guilty when the offender has reason to hope for a particular result. Some specialists believe that the criminal justice process in America today would collapse if substantial inducements to elicit guilty pleas are not continued. While this cannot be easily proven, current statistical studies do show that 85 to 90 percent of all prosecutions in many jurisdictions are "negotiated" pleas of guilty.[5] In many jurisdictions, especially those in which the police are not adequately trained, the only prosecutions initiated are against offenders who were caught red-handed. In other places, for an offender to "force" a trial, he or she must have hopes that the penalty will be lessened by the trial process. If the prosecutor agrees to charge for a lesser offense, the offender may be more willing to take a sure thing than to force the gamble of the much more serious conviction that a trial might bring.

Many prosecutors who labor under an unbearable workload are more than willing to negotiate when each negotiated case means little loss of time, and the possibility of case complications or appeals is almost totally eliminated. Through successful negotiation the defense attorney, too, obtains a very tangible result for the client. Defense and prosecutor negotiations are generally approved because the courts, too, are overburdened.

> The negotiated plea serves important functions. As a practical matter, many courts could not sustain the burden of having to try all cases coming before them. The quality of justice in all cases would suffer if overloaded courts were faced with a great increase in the number of trials. Tremendous investments of time, talent, and money, all of which are in short supply and can be better used elsewhere, would be necessary if all cases were tried. It

would be a serious mistake, however, to assume that the guilty plea is no more than a means of disposing the criminal cases at minimal cost. It relieves both the defendant and the prosecution of the inevitable risks and uncertainties of trial. It imports a degree of certainty and flexibility into a rigid, yet frequently erratic system. The guilty plea is used to mitigate the harshness of mandatory sentencing provisions and to fix a punishment that more accurately reflect the specific circumstances of the case than otherwise would be possible under inadequate penal codes. It is frequently called upon to serve important law enforcement needs by agreements through which leniency is exchanged for information, assistance, and testimony about other serious offenders.[6]

The National Advisory Commission on Criminal Justice Standards and Goals recommended the total abolition of plea bargaining by 1978. The commission viewed plea negotiation as inherently undesirable and maintained that such negotiations should and can be eliminated.[7] Admitting that total elimination could not be quickly effected, the commission suggested that in the meantime the court should more carefully evaluate every negotiated plea with the total power of acceptance or rejection. The commission has recommended that the court take into account the following considerations when evaluating a negotiated plea:

1. The impact that a formal trial would have on the offender and those close to him, especially the likelihood and seriousness of financial hardship and family disruption;
2. The role that a plea and negotiated agreement may play in rehabilitating the offender;
3. The value of a trial in fostering the community's sense of security and confidence in law enforcement agencies; and
4. The assistance rendered by the offender:
   a. in the apprehension or conviction of other offenders;
   b. in the prevention of crimes by others;
   c. in the reduction of the impact of the offense on the victim; or
   d. in any other socially beneficial activity.[8]

In addition, weaknesses in the prosecution's case should not be considered in determining whether to permit a defendant to plead guilty to any offense other than that charged. And a statement of policies should be made available to the public.[9]

In reference to the prosecutor, the commission has recommended that no prosecutor should, in connection with plea negotiations, engage in, perform, or condone any of the following:

1. Charging or threatening to charge the defendant with offenses for which the admissible evidence available to the prosecutor is insufficient to support a guilty verdict.
2. Charging or threatening to charge the defendant with a crime not ordinarily charged in the jurisdiction for the conduct allegedly engaged in by him.
3. Threatening the defendant that if he pleads not guilty, his sentence may be more severe than that which ordinarily is imposed in the jurisdiction in similar cases on defendants who plead not guilty.
4. Failing to grant disclosure before the disposition negotiations of all exculpatory evidence material to guilt or punishment.[10]

## *ARRAIGNMENT*

The prosecutor represents the people and the government. The defense attorney represents a particular defendant or defendants against the resources of governmental prosecution. The arraignment is usually, though not always, the first "formal" opportunity for the defense and prosecutor to meet. Simply defined the *arraignment* is the formal opportunity for a defendant to answer the charge or charges of which he or she is accused. The most common options in pleading are: (1) guilty; (2) not guilty; and in some states (3) *nolo contendere,* which means no contest; (4) *non vult,* which means to stand mute; and (5) not guilty by reason of insanity. (In some state statutes, the term *nolo contendere* means that the accused simply does not understand the charge.) The primary purpose of *nolo contendere* is to give the criminal court an indication of the defendant's willingness to accept a conviction and the resultant penalty rather than go to trial. Especially in criminal actions that may later involve civil litigation the plea is helpful, for a guilty plea might possibly be entered into the record of the subsequent civil litigation. *Non vult* is automatically entered as a plea of not guilty on the transcript in some jurisdictions.

If the prosecutor's case proves defective or if necessary witnesses do not appear for trial, the prosecutor may request a *nolle prosequi,* which is known as a "*nol pros.*" Simply stated this means that there will be no prosecution. Generally it is an acknowledgment of the realization that the prosecutor cannot prove the charges. It may indicate records that have been lost or stolen, witnesses who did not appear, or a primary witness who has died.

At the arraignment, the defendant is brought before the court that is to try him or her and is asked to plead to the indictment. If the defendant pleads guilty, the judge ascertains that certain precautions have been taken. The judge may ask the defendant if the charge is understood or ask the prosecutor to present some of the evidence to assure the court that there are sufficient grounds to continue the criminal justice process. If the defendant pleads not guilty or does not plead, the judge will investigate to see whether a basis exists for the plea. If so, the case is bound over or continued for trial. The prosecutor's role in the arraignment is a limited one. The prosecutor is, if you will, a conductor on the train of the criminal justice process as it moves across the criminal justice system to the trial.

## *TRIAL*

Having been bound over for trial the defendant may elect a court, or bench, trial (without a jury) or a jury trial. In the latter the judge determines the legality of the evidence and hence its admissibility, and the jury determines whether there are reasonable grounds for conviction.

After a court has been called in session

for a jury trial and the announcement of the case made, the *voir dire* (jury examination) is generally the first order of business. In minor cases the examination may take only an hour or two, in difficult cases, several days. The first questions are generally asked by the judge. They are usually of broad application, asking whether any of the potential jury members know the defendant personally or have previous information that might tend to prejudice them in the case. In some jurisdictions the prosecution and defense attorneys conduct the entire examination; in others they limit themselves only to areas not covered by the judge. These examinations are always similar, but the specific set of circumstances governs the completeness of any one of them.

When the prosecutor or the defense counsel can show cause during the jury examination, a potential juror can be dismissed. The cause may be preconceived notions of guilty, personal prejudices, or other matters tending to influence a potential juror's final verdict. Both prosecutor and defense are also entitled to peremptory challenges whereby a potential juror can be dismissed without cause, but peremptory challenges are limited.

With the jury selected, the main event of the advisory process begins—the trial. The prosecutor now makes an opening statement indicating a tentative course of action for this trial. The defense makes an opening statement. The prosecutor calls witnesses and presents evidence. The defense proceeds likewise. Various motions may be entered by the defense. Following the prosecutor's rebuttal to the defense's case, the judge instructs the jury on points of law. The defense now presents its final argument, followed by the prosecutor's final argument. The judge charges the jury to render a just and true verdict. The jury deliberates and issues its verdict. While this trial process may call forth images of Perry Mason, the typical criminal trial is far less dramatic than those presented on television series.

In many cases, the prosecutor's role in the criminal justice process ends with the verdict and the sentencing of the defendant. The defendant goes free or moves on to some form of treatment or punishment. In some cases, the defendant appeals the case, and then the prosecutor appears in a higher court, once again to present the state's case.

The prosecutor's complete role is very complex, much more so than can be presented here. By deciding what cases to prosecute, the prosecutor sets the law enforcement policies for the community. As an elected official, the prosecutor is a "political animal" and must engage in the political processes of the community. In short, the prosecution function is a difficult task requiring skills in law, administration, political science; and it requires above all a person of great determination and high moral and ethical principles.

## DISCUSSION QUESTIONS

1. What are the functions of the grand jury? What should they be?
2. Should the prosecutor engage in plea bargaining without the court's approval?

3. Compare and contrast the practices of *screening* and *diversion*.
4. Is the grand jury a "rubber stamp" for the prosecutor? If not, why not? If so, why so?

## NOTES

1. National Advisory Commission on Criminal Justice Standards and Goals, *Working Papers* (Washington, D.C.: Government Printing Office, 1973), p. 215.
2. National Advisory Commission on Criminal Justice Standards and Goals, *Courts* (Washington, D.C.: Government Printing Office, 1973), pp. 24–38.
3. Livingston Hall et al., *Basic Criminal Procedure* (St. Paul: West Publishing, 1969), p. 561.
4. *Courts*, pp. 11–16. Hurtado v. California 110 U.S. 516 (1884).
5. President's Commission on Law Enforcement and Administration of Justice, *The Challenge of Crime in a Free Society* (Washington, D.C.: Government Printing Office, 1967), p. 134.
6. *Working Papers*, p. 218.
7. *Courts*, p. 46.
8. *Courts*, p. 52.
9. *Courts*, p. 52.
10. *Courts*, p. 57.

Cambridge
& Somerville
Legal Services

# 10: Contemporary Problems in Prosecution

*WORKING WITH THE POLICE • MINIMIZING DISCRETION • DECIDING THE CHARGE • SUGGESTING INFORMAL ALTERNATIVES TO PROSECUTION • IMPROVING THE OFFICE OF THE PROSECUTOR • EXAMINING THE ROLE OF THE GRAND JURY • APPOINTING A PUBLIC DEFENDER • CONTROLLING THE POWER OF THE PROSECUTOR*

PURPOSE: *TO PROVIDE INSIGHT INTO THE MAJOR PROBLEM AREAS OF THE PROSECUTOR'S OFFICE.*

Most contemporary problems in the prosecutional function involve decisions at the outset of a case: the use of discretion about going to trial and the question of time as it relates to prompt prosecution. Prosecutors must make, and do make, every effort to maintain their offices at a high level of efficiency and to use wisely the discretion allowed by law.

A society that holds, as we do, the belief in law cannot regard with unconcern the fact that prosecuting agencies can exercise so large an influence on dispositions that involve the penal sanction, without reference to any norms but those that they may create for themselves. Whatever one would hold as to the need for discretion of this order in a proper system or the wisdom of attempting the refutation of its exercise. It is quite clear that its existence cannot be accepted as a substitute for sufficient law. Indeed, one of the major consequences of the state of penal law today is that administration has so largely come to dominate the field without effective guidance from the law. This is to say that to a large degree we have, in this important sense, abandoned law and this within an area where our fundamental teaching calls most strongly for its vigorous supremacy.[1]

## *WORKING WITH THE POLICE*

Although it is the police, by their execution of specific arrest policies, who usually make the initial decision that leads to prosecution, it is the prosecutor who oversees the police in this role and makes the ultimate decision to continue a case in the criminal justice process. While the police must in most instances make the decision to arrest fairly quickly, the prosecutor's decision to charge may come after months of haggling among lawyers. There seem to be no universal norms for these decisions. Quite often, compassion for a first or youthful offender or a belief that a law is much too harsh in its consequences can influence a prosecutor's decision.

Sometimes the police come to the prosecutor and ask that charges against a person arrested by a member of their department be dropped, perhaps for reasons of politics or influence or because the arrested individual is an informant. Occasionally the reason is a technical or judgment error made by the arresting officer that will inevitably embarrass the department. In some areas the prosecutor has such a poor relationship with the local police that he would refuse such a request in almost all circumstances. In other situations the prosecutor generally endorses the will of the police in matters pertaining to informants.

At times the prosecutor is highly suspicious, as is proper, when an offender confesses to a heinous offense or to multiple offenses. Experienced prosecutors know of the mentally ill person who confesses to someone else's crime. Unless great care is manifested in all investigations, the overzealous prosecutor may misdirect the process of justice.

Recent news articles report situations in which young offenders "clear" several hundred burglaries for a police department, making the police investigator and the department look good. However, a meticulous background investigation should ensure that the subject did in fact commit each particular offense. In crimes against property, every effort should be made to recover as much as possible to ensure that the "fruits of the crime" are admitted along with other evidence into courts of law.

Although some prosecutors want more interaction with the police than they now have, others want a clear-cut separation of authority. The police have their own right of discretion, and many prosecutors do not feel that it is within their power to interfere. By the same token, prosecutors resent efforts by the police to pressure them into prosecuting poorly investigated cases. Although most prosecutors stand ready to advise police officials in the prearrest or precharging phase of the investigation, many, if not most, prefer to remain apart from the enforcement function as much as possible.

Many professionals report that in certain areas the police are so ill-equipped by education, training, or experience that the district or county prosecuting attorney is virtually an *ex officio* police chief, just as many mayors of small towns are automatically made *ex officio* justices of the peace for the purpose of city court and municipal government. In these situations, the chief of police or the officers often do not dare make a major felony arrest without specifically asking the prosecutor. Sometimes this policy is advisable, but in the main a balanced criminal justice system requires that all its members be at least adequately qualified in their areas of endeavor. In cases in which the prosecutor is an *ex officio* police chief, the prosecutor will play an important role in both the fact-finding and the prosecutional role, thus jeopardizing a supposedly unbiased status.

## *MINIMIZING DISCRETION*

Despite the attempts of most prosecutors to use their discretion wisely, abuses do occur. Perhaps one way of overcoming such abuses would be the creation of a "control board," made up of fellow prosecutors and other attorneys thoroughly familiar with the criminal justice process. A board of this type could be approached by citizens or groups who feel that the law has not properly protected them. Today most citizens really have no recourse, except at the polls, against a prosecutor.

A "control board" would not be an alien intrusion in the criminal justice system, for the police have had "police review boards" for years. Publicly and privately many attorneys and others have stated that these review boards have prevented the police from "overpolicing" and that they have helped eliminate the police misuse of force and other indiscretions. Physicians, pharmacists, and attorneys have known regulatory boards for years. The bar associations occasionally call to task one of their members who steps out of the bounds of professional propriety, although formal reprimanding occurs rarely. The criminal justice system needs *enforced* codes of ethics if it is to function satisfactorily. Only these thoroughly familiar with the law would be eligible to sit on any board judging prosecutional discretion.

Prosecutors try to use their discretion under the law. Occasionally prosecutors refuse to charge in cases where a person will have to be extradited and the individual refuses to be extradited. Or the prosecutor may simply decide that the trial of a particular case is too expensive for the taxpayers. The victim of this particular kind of case, however, rarely appreciates this decision because it is the government's responsibility to the victim to assume prosecution and trial efforts. On occasion, the distance, even within a state such as Texas or California, causes a prosecutor to have reservations about charging. In felony cases involving bad checks or lesser offenses, the prosecutor may try to work out a reconciliation between the accused and those making the charge, and in many cases when these pressures or "collection" procedures lead to the recovery of the property of the accusers, they do drop all charges against the accused.

Some authorities in the criminal justice system propose the addition of still another office to the prosecutional unit, the criminal justice official in charge of this office to be called an "assessor." The assessor would oversee the discretion of the prosecutor and make separate decisions on whether to prosecute or not, the prosecutor necessarily having to abide by the decision. While there are some very good reasons for this system, some authorities feel that the assessor would usurp some of the power of the court magistrate, and still others feel that an assessor would add an unnecessary burden to the taxpayer because the assessor too could be bribed, coerced, or politically influenced. Some prosecutors believe that if assessors were not experienced prosecutors themselves, aware of the entanglements of the criminal court process, they might frequently force virtually untriable cases on the prosecutor and cause great waste of time and money to the criminal justice system and to the taxpayers who fund it.

## *DECIDING THE CHARGE*

Prosecutors have a certain latitude in the kind of charge they will make. Some charge a less serious offense to avoid the stigma and sanctions of a more serious charge. For example, if the American Legion or the Veterans of Foreign Wars is caught selling liquor in a dry county or running an illegal gambling operation, many prosecutors, because they are dealing with what is usually a socially acceptable organization, would refuse to charge the organization with a felony offense (should the case be one) and would instead drop it to a misdemeanor. Or if an eighteen-year-old youth is caught selling beer to a seventeen-year-old minor, very few prosecutors would charge the youth with a felony offense (in those states in which this behavior is a felony).

The prosecutor may decide not to charge when there are other social or civil procedures that provide alternative measures other than imprisonment. An example of this type of case would be the civil commitment of an insane person under sexual psychopath laws. Ideally the offender should receive treatment at a prison hospital equipped and staffed to handle these kinds of problems, but because many state prisons do not have the necessary treatment facilities for mental disorders, a mental hospital is selected as the appropriate alternative.

A refusal to charge may also result from the belief that to do so would be unduly harmful to the offender and would obstruct his or her chances for a successful life in society. Usually this approach is taken with juvenile offenders or first offenders, and they are accorded a quasi–judicial probation status, with a probationary accounting that is officially "off the court record." In this way the first offender is not officially labeled a criminal. Conviction for a felony could deprive a youth of some rights of citizenship as well as job opportunities in state, federal, and local government. It could also result in more subtle social harm. In making the decision to use any alternative, the prosecutor considers the seriousness of the offense and the success probability of the person to be rehabilitated.

## *SUGGESTING INFORMAL ALTERNATIVES TO PROSECUTION*

In certain types of cases, informal administrative alternatives are more useful and productive of *justice* than other courses the prosecutor could follow. In nonsupport cases, for instance, the restitution of back alimony or child-support payments is socially more desirable than putting the husband in jail and possibly causing the children to be added to the welfare roles. In family and neighborhood assaults, complainants often later refuse to charge or are persuaded by the prosecutor to forgive and forget.

In *statutory rape,* unlawful sexual intercourse with a female minor, or rape cases in which the victim is well known to the defendant, a prosecutor often counsels marriage when pregnancy exists. Naturally, the prosecutor does not counsel marriage when a forceful rape has occurred or when the victim has not allowed intercourse with the defendant in the past. In a situation involving two high school students and their parents, a prosecutor may counsel marriage instead of prosecution. If the girl does not want to marry, the prosecutor may choose to use discretion and not prosecute even though the girl's testimony would probably convict the boy of the offense of statutory rape. The parents of the girl may demand prosecution in spite of the victim's desire to be married. Should the prosecutor choose to initiate the criminal process the boy may be convicted and have to spend time in a state correctional facility. In the meantime if the girl did not have an abortion, she would have an illegitimate child and her family or society (through subsistence payments) would be charged with her care and the care of her child. Although there are arguments of substance indicating the marriage would have little chance of success and should not take place, the prosecutor, whenever possible, prefers the alternatives to criminal prosecution.

## *IMPROVING THE OFFICE OF THE PROSECUTOR*

The National Advisory Commission on Criminal Justice Standards and Goals (1973) gave a very high priority to the prosecution function in terms of the improvement of the criminal justice system. Particular mention was made of improving the quality of the personnel so that the disposition of each criminal case can be more efficiently and effectively handled.[2] The improvement of the prosecution function will require both moderate and drastic changes in the entire structure of society and not just in the criminal justice system itself.

### Status and Pay

It is evident that society and attorneys themselves do not put career-oriented prosecutors on the status level of attorneys who specialize in torts, tax matters, or international law even though our entire system of government depends on public respect for law and the enforcement of law. Because of social attitudes and role concepts, very few of the "best" young attorneys are attracted to the field.

> The personnel policies, size, and organization of many prosecutor's offices do not promote an effective response to the complex demands of the criminal justice system. The majority of the Nation's 2,700 prosecutors serve in small offices with one or two assistants. Frequently, the prosecutor and his assistants are part-time officials who also engage in outside law practices. Although the salary level of prosecutors and their assistants has been rising, it remains much lower than the earnings of lawyers of similar experience in private practice.[3]

Not only must attitudes change. Prosecutors and other professionals involved in the governmental process should be offered reasonable economic rewards. If this is not accomplished many competent personnel may continue to be attracted to other careers despite the need for them in government service. The National Advisory Commission on Criminal Justice Standards and Goals (1973) recommended that the chief prosecutor of a locality be salaried on the same basic level as the chief judge of the highest trial court of the local criminal justice system. It was reasoned by this research council that because both positions required autonomy and the exercise of broad discretion in the workings of the office, it is reasonable that the compensation for these offices have the same base.[4] The National Advisory Commission on Criminal Justice Standards and Goals (1973) also recommended that all full-time prosecutors be paid out of state funds.[5]

Assistant prosecutors could have their status improved through protection of their position through civil service or some other system of protection such as a merit system.

> The position of assistant prosecutor should be a full time occupation, and assistant prosecutors should be prohibited from engaging in outside law practices. The starting salaries for assistant prosecutors should be no less than those paid by private firms in the jurisdiction, and the prosecutor should have the authority to increase periodically the salaries for assistant prosecutors to a level that will encourage the retention of able and experienced prose-

cutors, subject to approval of the legislature, city, or county council as appropriate. For the first five years of service, salaries of assistant prosecutors should be comparable to those of attorney associates in local private law firms.[6]

### Training

Law schools do not adequately prepare their graduates for the position of prosecutor. The belief that any licensed attorney is capable of handling the duties of this office is no longer true. The criminal justice process and the criminal law are unique and require specialized skills and knowledge. The few criminal law courses that a law student may take in law school are, in most cases, inadequate training for the administrative and law enforcement functions of the prosecutors office. The National Advisory Commission on Criminal Justice Standards and Goals (1973) has recommended:

> Education programs should be utilized to assure that prosecutors and their assistants have the highest possible professional competence. All newly appointed or elected prosecutors should attend prosecutor's training courses prior to taking office, and in-house training programs for new assistant prosecutors should be available in all metropolitan prosecution offices. All prosecutors and assistants should attend a formal prosecutors' training course each year, in addition to the regular in-house training.[7]

## *EXAMINING THE ROLE OF THE GRAND JURY*

The grand jury system originated in England in the twelfth century as a buffer between state and citizen. Its duties were to oversee the prosecutor, evaluate the cases that the prosecutor brought before it, and act as an independent investigative body. Over the centuries, however, the grand jury has become a mere rubber stamp of the prosecutor's indictment. In most cities it indicts in 80 percent or more of the cases brought before it. In addition, when a grand jury launches an independent investigation today, it sometimes turns into a witch hunt. As a result, several authorities have recommended the abolition of the grand jury system.[8] The National Advisory Commission of Criminal Justice Standards and Goals (1973) has recommended that the grand jury not be required in criminal prosecution, but that the system remain available for investigation and exceptional cases.[9]

## *APPOINTING A PUBLIC DEFENDER*

At trial the prosecutor's adversary is frequently a *public defender*, a salaried government employee who provides free legal service to individuals too poor to pay, as many involved in criminal litigation are. By law, if the defendant cannot afford counsel then the court will appoint an attorney, if the defendant so desires. A court-appointed lawyer usually has a private practice and generally receives a standard fee. Landmark decisions such as *Gideon* v. *Wainwright* [372 U.S. 335 (1963)] require that all felony offenders have access to court-appointed counsel if they do not have sufficient funds to hire an attorney. A 1972 case *Argersinger* v. *Hamlin* [407 U.S. 25 (1972)] held that *Gideon* also applies to misdemeanors and that no sentence involving loss of liberty can be imposed when there has been a denial of counsel. Traffic cases and those minor offenses not involving deprivation of liberty usually do not call for the state to provide counsel.

The method of providing counsel varies from state to state. Many states have systems whereby counsel is appointed by the judge from a list of members of the local bar association. Some areas provide compensation, and others simply require this service as a civil responsibility such as jury duty. Several states have created a public defender system. In such a system, the attorneys or public defenders are salaried from tax revenues and generally have no other income.

At the present time many of the weaknesses evident in the prosecution system are also evident in the public defender system. Many of these men and women are part-time public servants rather than fully employed professionals. Their dual roles quite often cause stress within their own practice, and the offender receives the short end of the bargain. The financial rewards of public defense are not nearly so great as those of a successful private law practice. A good salary within the office of the public defender, professional employment standards, and a satisfactory workload could eliminate many impediments to the criminal justice system.

## *CONTROLLING THE POWER OF THE PROSECUTOR*

The strengths of the prosecution system in America are also its weaknesses, for while prosecutors may make independent value judgments in the interest of the individual defendant or of society, the almighty dollar or some other influence is always there to cause or help them make the prosecutional decision on the basis of their own self-interest. In a high-crime-rate jurisdiction or in an environmental area involving gambling syndication or other so called "victimless" criminal activity, prosecutors can become very wealthy men in a short time should they choose to accept the available opportunities.

There are both indirect and direct controls over the prosecutor's use or abuse of discretion. Direct controls are those applied to force the reversal of a decision to charge. A *writ of mandamus* (a court order to stop a specified practice) to compel prosecution is one form of direct control. Direct control may at times and in some states be taken by the attorney general of the state, the trial judge, or a privately employed attorney directing the prosecution on behalf of the individual victim. Indirect control of a prosecutor persistently unwilling to enforce the law may, for example, take the form of removal from office.

Politics may cause certain ambiguous

relationships between the prosecutor and his or her constituents. Perhaps some of the personnel involved in the criminal justice system should be elected as independents rather than as party members. However, the individual politician is still obligated to the electorate, so separation from political parties may have little or no effect.

Because so many local prosecutors are so remote from state offices and administrations, it appears that few consistent statewide policies are applied and that the differences among the several states are even greater. Many authorities suggest that a state or regional office, whether of the state attorney general, a prosecutors' council, or an assessor, should have final coordinating authority over policy. Of course, constitutional or legislative enactments would be necessary before the inauguration of any of the alternative solutions.

The powers of investigation and the power over confidential information that comes to the district attorney from the police and other sources are easily abused and represent a constant threat to the rights of the individual. Prosecutors also have the freedom to manipulate charges as they see fit, insofar as judicial and public pressure is concerned. In this way they can maintain control over the decision-making processes of the police. While this power, when used as it was statutorily intended, may enhance the probability of justice, it also too often leaves the door open for graft.

It should not be inferred that prosecuting attorneys should become rubber stamps, constantly endorsing the recommendations of a police unit. The prosecutor's office is not and should not be an automatically cooperative agency, for our system of criminal justice was founded on the principle of a balance as well as separation of powers. To amalgamate any two or more parts will cause the system to function in an unjust manner.

The members of each part of the system have to exercise considerable amounts of discretion and judgment and do so efficiently. Each subsystem is a small but vital unit of the whole, and only with each subsystem working correctly and well can our system of justice function as intended. To accomplish the desired end each section within the criminal justice system must instill respect for the law and must maintain justice within the system. It is to this end that the prosecutor must proceed.

## DISCUSSION QUESTIONS

1. Should we keep or get rid of the grand jury system?
2. Should we limit the prosecutor's discretionary powers? If so, to what extent? If not, why not?
3. Where does the danger of aggressive prosecution lie?
4. In what ways could prosecution be made more effective?
5. What do you consider to be the most important problem in the area of prosecution?

## NOTES

1. Herbert Wechsler, "Challenge of a Model Code," *Harvard Law Review*, 65 (1952), 1102.
2. National Advisory Commission on Criminal Justice Standards and Goals, *Courts* (Washington, D.C.: Government Printing Office, 1973), chapters 1, 2, 3, 12, and 15.3.
3. *Courts*, p. 227.
4. *Courts*, p. 229.
5. *Courts*, p. 230.
6. American Bar Association, *Project on Standards for Criminal Justice: Standards Relating to the Prosecution Function* (Washington, D.C.: American Bar Association, 1970), Standard 3.1(B).
7. *Courts*, p. 239.
8. *Courts*, pp. 74–76.
9. *Courts*, p. 74.

## PART THREE ANNOTATED BIBLIOGRAPHY

American Bar Association. *The Prosecution and the Defense Function: A Report Prepared by the Advisory Committee on the Prosecution and Defense Functions of the Project on Standards of Criminal Justice.* New York: Institute of Judicial Administration, 1971.

*Contemporary research worth reading. The manuscript was the result of research directed to, and the philosophy of, functionalists in the field of prosecution. It also serves as a standard-bearer and a guide manual for the prosecutor in contemporary America.*

Grossman, Brian A. *The Prosecutor.* Toronto: University of Toronto Press, 1967.

*Written by a former prosecutor, the text deals with the sociology of the prosecutor function. The political, social, and monetary pressures are indicated as well as a scholarly analysis of the use and abuse of the negotiated plea.*

Miller, Frank E. *Prosecution.* Boston: Little, Brown, 1969.

*A most persuasive text on the positive and negative effects of plea negotiation and the philosophy of the American prosecution format currently in use.*

National Association of Attorneys General, Committee on the Office of Attorney General. *The Office of Attorney General.* 1971.

*The most comprehensive contemporary report on the present status of state attorneys general, district attorneys, and county or city prosecutors. While much of the text is purely descriptive, it is of the utmost importance in any survey of the prosecution system.*

# PART FOUR

# Courts

# 11: Developmental History of Courts

*CHRONOLOGY OF DEVELOPMENT • COURT LAG*

PURPOSE: *TO TRACE THE DEVELOPMENT FROM THE COURTS OF ANTIQUITY TO THE PRESENT-DAY COURTS OF THE UNITED STATES.*

A useful history of the courts cannot be just a collection of names and dates. It must be a narrative of the changes that have transformed the courts into what they are today. It must be an account of how the courts have developed. And it should point toward the directions of their future development. Some basic definitions are needed, however, before the history can be told. Then the history of the courts can be put in the larger framework of sociology so that the deeper significance of the courts and their development can be appreciated.

Although *court* is a commonly understood word, it is used in several ways: A court may be a person—the judge—or persons—the entire judicial assembly. A court may be a building, or room, in which cases are heard and determined. A court may be a session of a judicial assembly. A court may be a regular organization that does not have to be in session in order to be a court.

The judicial business of a criminal court is essentially to determine whether the accused is guilty and, if so, to pass sentence. Courts are said to enforce the law and are therefore a necessary complement of the law. Indeed, they are sometimes included in the definition of law. An important aspect of courts is that they are a formal, nonviolent means of settling disputes.

A *tribunal* is either a place where judges sit or a court, or it has a meaning broader than court, as in, for example, "the tribunal of public opinion."

A *court system* involves a group or groups of interrelated courts. These groupings are based on the kinds of offenses with which the courts deal (from least serious to the more serious) and by the stage of a case that they handle (for example, the initial appearance before a *justice of peace court*, a trial before a *trial court*, an appeal of a conviction before an *appellate court*). These interrelationships are defined by statutory law. Each state has its own statutes and is regarded as having its own separate court system. There is distinction enough between the states and the federal government to warrant the concept of a dual court system in the United States: the states have one court system, the federal government has another. The *court system of the United States* is a phrase used to distinguish United States courts from the courts of another nation.

A *judge* is the official who presides over a court, and may be called a *justice* in some kinds of courts. A *magistrate* is a judge who handles judicial matters other then jury trials or appeals. A magistrate may be limited by law to certain duties or may be a fully empowered judge who is performing the duties of a magistrate in a given instance.

## *CHRONOLOGY OF DEVELOPMENT*

A chronological history of the courts' development has its beginning in the forgotten past and ends with a picture of the courts as they are today.

## Origin of Courts

For an appreciation of the origins of courts, the court concept must be viewed in relation to society. The sociological perspective is closely allied to the historical perspective, as is evident in any elaboration of the definitions of courts. One reason this nation has not been wracked by unrelenting conflicts at the interpersonal level is that the courts provide a way to contain or control conflicts by their acceptance as formal or official means for the settlement of disputes. Social control is necessary for the maintenance of social order.

Informal means of social control exist in families and groups of families (clans, tribes) and are based on the strong desire of members to stay in good standing with their fellows. These kinds of groups of people are called *primary groups.* You and your friends form a primary group. In very large primary groups or in cultures in which primary groups continue to predominate—even though the primary group ties may be weakened by the existence of specialized secondary groups (hunters, craftsmen, farmers, merchants, and so on)—elders or other rulers may listen to disputes and arbitrarily decide how they are to be resolved. These tribunals may become fairly involved. They are sometimes referred to as courts governed by customs.

With the advent of codes of law, genuine courts of law came into being. All cultures too complex and too large for the informal means of social control exercised by primary groups have doubtless evolved a code of law and a corresponding court system. The culture's standards or norms can then be partially maintained by force, impersonal and formal force. The first courts, therefore, may predate recorded history.

Courts are units of government or, more accurately, units of a political community, such as the United States. The significance of this is that the courts have the support of the overwhelming physical and moral force that rests in the political community. This is the fundamental source of the courts' social power, although the power that judges wield in a community is a product of many other factors as well.

It should be clear that the courts are part of society. They are not merely instruments of law, as they have sometimes been described. It has been said that the degree of civilization possessed by a society can be gauged by the quality of justice meted out by the courts. The wavering development of the quality of courtroom justice can be traced down through history.

## Courts from Antiquity through the Middle Ages

From a rudimentary form of court, ancient Greece developed a tribunal in which there might be hundreds of "judges" or "jurors." In 300 B.C. the Jewish nation had a supreme council called Great Sanhedrin, composed of seventy-one members and having a chief justice, which interpreted Hebrew law and enacted decrees of religious observance. Today, Israel's courts are still closely tied to religion. Rome also began with a rudimentary form of court, but by 300 B.C. had developed the mature form of Roman law (a comprehensive law code) and a correspondingly sophisticated court system.

In the early part of the Middle Ages, ancient codes of law continued to have some effect. The idea of a law above people, even above sovereigns, continued to lurk in the minds of a few Europeans. Nonetheless the kings and nobles, or their designates, held court and made binding decisions as suited their whims. The word *court* comes from this time. Originally, *court* meant a kind of enclosure or partial enclosure, usually without a roof, and it retains this meaning in the lexicon of the architect. In addition to the ancient codes and the practices of the nobility, religion played a role in European criminal justice. The Roman Catholic Church was a growing force in court activity. It provided priests who officiated at many of the criminal trials and provided, too, a legal framework for judicial activity.

By contemporary standards these early medieval courts were lacking in sensitive, systematic law. They were riddled with supersitition, and their processes and sentences produced what would today be called atrocities. Criminal trials were frequently by ordeal, with the Church officiating. Some of the ordeals probably worked as primitive lie detectors; for example, bread held in the mouth of a guilty person would remain dry because one physical reaction of fear is the cessation of salivation. Many of the ordeals, however, would have required miraculous intervention to prove innocence; for example, placing rocks on a man's chest until he confessed or died. If a confession was obtained the punishment might be more of the same torture until death intervened. If people died without confessing, they might be exonerated in memory and a small compensation allotted the family. People were held totally responsible for their actions, and even minor theft might be punishable by death. From time to time, children and animals were likewise held to be totally responsible, and a small child or a pig could be hanged for a minor offense.

These courts were neither in form or in philosophy like the courts of today. They were governed completely by custom whereas today's courts pay token homage to custom. Nevertheless, they were the forerunners of the modern courts. As time passed, the body of legal practitioners not directly connected with the king and the nobles would grow, and with it there would grow a highly complicated body of legal practices.

### Development of Modern Courts

England and continental Europe gradually evolved different court and legal systems, and these two systems had a profound influence on courts virtually the world over.

*England* The courts of the United States are traced to the courts of England, which did not begin to come into their own until the eleventh century. The centuries of Roman rule apparently had little influence on England's courts. The Norse invaders in the succeeding six centuries did not alter the system of custom-governed law and local magistrates. It was the Norman conquerors of the eleventh century who began to gather the various laws and the informal and private tribunals into a central system. Henry II (1154–

1189), often called the Father of Common Law, declared that no man could be denied a freehold (inheritable land) without a royal writ (written order bearing the king's signature). Centralized control of the courts became inevitable. The power of feudal courts, both Anglo-Saxon and Norman, lessened. Records were kept, and consequently the concept of precedent was to be firmly established. By 1178 the King's Court could no longer handle cases brought to it. Five judges were appointed, and circuits were established for some of them.

In England, in June of 1215, King John's nobles forced him to sign Magna Charta. This charter was reactionary in that it was a blow to the development of the courts into a unified court system. Its intent was to return power to the nobles where it had been before the arrival of the Norman kings, and in time Magna Charta came to mark the subordination of the king to law and thereby to the people. By the fourteenth century, however, the English courts had stabilized, and the process of unification of the British courts continued until this century.

In 1215, there occurred another major event: Pope Innocent III at the Fourth Lateran Council forbade the clergy to officiate at trials. As a result, laymen, already important, became still more important in England's judicial process. One body of laymen used their own knowledge of the investigations of the royal coroner to level formal accusations against suspects, and over time this body became the grand jury. A second body of laymen was charged with deciding whether the accusation was true, and this body became the petit jury.

During the fourteenth century, courts that handled only criminal cases came into existence. These courts were run by local landowners. In another development, people who claimed they had not received justice from a court could appeal for help from the king or his chief administrative officer, the chancellor; and between the fourteenth century and the seventeenth century, this process of appeals evolved into an appeals court. This court also established the branch of law known as *equity*, which means to fairly settle conflicts that are not covered by other law. Other courts answered the needs of diverse systems of law, notably, the admiralty courts, which dealt with ships and sailors, and the church courts, which continued to govern matrimonial cases and the estates of the deceased. Vestiges of these and other courts remain in the courts of the United States, including the Supreme Court.

For the most part, the courts made their own law and attempted to maintain consistency by keeping new decisions in close agreement with decisions made in the past in similar cases. These legal processes, identified as common law, case law, the doctrine of *stare decisis*, were to become the distinguishing characteristics of Anglo-American law and courts. Knowledgeable lawyers tried to win cases for their clients through the use of writs. These lawyers were very sensitive to the procedure of the courts; and although they were not alarmed by a public hanging, if the procedure leading to the hanging was not proper as they understood it, they were vociferous in their complaints. The confrontation between the courts with their "proper methods" and the king with his royal whims could not be altogether prevented by the growing profession of lawyers. This conflict led to the development of the concept of *due process of law*.

Lord Chief Justice, Edwin A. Coke, probably did more than any other single person to establish due process. When early in the seventeenth century he informed his monarch, King James I, that the law was above any king, James had Coke supplanted by Sir Francis Bacon. In fact, during the Tudor and Stuart dynasties there were other setbacks to the due process of law. For example, a maverick court called the Star Chamber that ostensibly dealt with traitors was much feared. It sometimes convened in the middle of the night, and held and tried individuals far from their homes and neighborhoods, without their friends' and relatives' knowledge of their whereabouts. In the end, though, the traditions of the courts as well as their autonomy prevailed.

*Europe* In continental Europe the evolution of the courts followed different lines. Pope Innocent's ruling prevented clergy from officiating here too, and in addition the use of laymen declined. The governing bodies of the cities, the city councils, established an inquisitorial procedure in which the accused was questioned about the truth of the accusations prior to the trial. The inquisition may have been largely responsible for the maintenance of police state methods by which confessions were routinely obtained through torture. If the accused denied guilt at the formalistic trial, a witness present at the confession was produced and the case was closed. In the early sixteenth century, the demand for reform brought about change but no relief. The change burdened the courts with a heavy weight of procedure, rendered the trial nonpublic, and left the same inquisitorial methods. Only with the revolutions that wracked Europe in the eighteenth and nineteenth centuries was modern Continental law established. The European courts do not make their own law through precedent-setting decisions, but they do retain the responsibility to question the defendant at length before trial.

*Other Continents* Curiously, Western civilization has been the chief repository for the concepts of individual liberty (or equal rights) and of law transcending the sovereign. In much of Africa and Asia, the courts were ruled by custom, and other means of social control were heavily relied upon, until colonialization brought courts modeled upon those of Britain and continental Europe. The Russian courts in the days of the czar were sophisticated and contributed to his downfall. Today, the communist countries claim a different development from that of Britain and the rest of Europe.

### Development of Courts in the United States

The original thirteen colonies were British, and the court system that worked in England served in America. The populace was particularly familiar with the lower levels of the court system. With independence, however, there came a renunciation of things British and a common recognition of the legislature as the lawmaking body, rather than the courts.

With the adoption of the Articles of Confederation in 1779, the Continental Congress established the Court of Appeals in Cases of Capture. Both Congress and the new court tried cases, a total of 109 cases. On June 20, 1788, the Constitution was ratified, and state courts immediately became subordinate to the United States, although they continued to exercise a high degree of independence.

The sole constitutional basis for the Supreme Court is found in the brief clause popularly called the "judiciary clause," Article III of the Constitution. The clause was too brief, and an act of Congress was required to fill in the details necessary to establish a federal judiciary, the famous Judiciary Act of 1789. It formalized the Supreme Court by (1) defining its authority and limitations (jurisdiction) within the guidelines provided by the Constitution, (2) establishing the number of judges, and (3) establishing a system of "inferior" or "lower" federal courts. Many of the details of the original act have been modified by subsequent acts of Congress, but the Judiciary Act of 1789 has set a pattern that remains unchanged in essence. The Congress could have insisted that all cases be tried in the states' courts before going to the federal courts, as indeed it was urged to do. (Later, in Canada, Australia, and the German Empire, federal court systems were established to hear only cases that had already been tried in provincial courts.) Had Congress limited the federal courts in this way, it would have changed the essential pattern. It is clear that the legislative branch of government can take away what it has given and make other changes, but because the checks and balances of the Constitution, sometimes regarded as a myth, do have a force that is real, it is unlikely that Congress will ever abolish all "lower" federal courts.

In the 1800s the population's conception of the lawmaking body shifted from the Congress to the courts. The British model was firmly entrenched, the lower court system of England was already in effect, and it seemed inevitable that the British system would prevail. Other countries did have some influence, however. Traces of the Dutch remain in New York's legal system and of the Spanish in the southwestern states. Louisiana, because of its French settlers, was pronouncedly affected by the legal system of continental Europe, and its courts are the only ones significantly different from the courts of other states. All the varied peoples who have come to the United States since these early times have not radically altered the model provided by the British heritage.

**Overview of Contemporary Courts**

The functions of the states' courts are very similar from state to state, but the structure of the courts differs widely. Gaps in statutory law result in the courts' occasional reliance on the old common law of England, though rarely in criminal cases. Indeed, the direction seems to be increasingly toward reliance on statutory law. Political science textbooks commonly consider only the federal system in any detail, thereby implying that the states have miniaturized replicas. The state systems may bear some resemblance to the federal, but they are not closely patterned on it. Although the Supreme Court of the United States has long been subject to intense attention, it is in the states' courts, for example, that nearly all criminal cases begin and end. Within the states the number of rural courts, like justice of the peace courts, has decreased and a proportionally huge increase in municipal courts, such as magistrates courts and traffic courts, has occurred.

Because of the diversity and autonomy of the courts there has been no centralized record keeping in the past. With their antiquated methods, many courts have kept little statistical information or have so buried it in a crude filing system that it is inaccessible. Statistics on most of the courts, therefore, are suspect. According to one source there were 548,000 people employed in the judiciary in 1970; 451,000 of them were in local or city judicial systems; not all of them were full time.[1]

The dual court system of the United States appears clear-cut: there are one federal court system and fifty state systems. The court systems of some metropolitan areas, however, are more extensive than the court systems of some states. It is estimated that there are over one hundred systems of major size.[2] The term *metropolitan courts* is used by some authorities to describe patterns of courts in urban areas where there may be several cities and towns and one or more counties.

How many cases are tried in the courts of the United States each year? No one knows the actual number, although it is in the millions. Only a small percentage of the total number are criminal cases.

Judicial statistics are not compiled by all of the states. The federal courts compile their own. These statistics are principally on the flow of cases through the courts from beginning to end (filing to disposition) and on categories of cases handled by judges. Each year the *American Law Journal* publishes an issue containing court statistics. The *U.S. Abstracts* and the *Book of the States*, found in most college libraries, also contain information on the courts in statistical form. Illustration 11.1 gives a breakdown of the number of judges in the various courts in the state system. This illustration provides a feeling for the number and the different kinds of courts and the number of judges associated with them, but it is an illustration, and not to be regarded as literally accurate for any time other than 1974. Florida, for example, has a law that for each addition of 50,000 to the population another judge is to be added to the judiciary.

The National Criminal Justice Statistics Center, a bureau of the United States Department of Justice's Law Enforcement Assistance Administration, is engaged in creating a system to enable the various states to rapidly obtain any information they may need from any criminal history files possessed by any state. This will not only help the courts, it will require a streamlining of their statistical procedures. The system will probably be effective nationally in the early 1980s.[3] The Center for State Courts, created in 1972, has begun compiling information about the different court systems.

| | Appellate Courts | | Major Trial Courts | | | | |
|---|---|---|---|---|---|---|---|
| State or Other Jurisdiction | Court of Last Resort | Inter-mediate Appellate Court | Chancery Court | Circuit Court | District Court | Superior Court | Other Trial Court |
| Alabama | 9 | 8 | ... | 98 | ... | ... | ... |
| Alaska | 5 | ... | ... | ... | ... | 16 | ... |
| Arizona | 5 | 12 | ... | ... | ... | 60 | ... |
| Arkansas | 7 | ... | 25 | 28 | ... | ... | ... |
| California | 7 | 48 | ... | ... | ... | 477 | ... |
| Colorado | 7 | 6 | ... | ... | 81 | ... | ... |
| Connecticut | 6 | ... | ... | ... | ... | 40 | ... |
| Delaware | 3 | ... | 3 | ... | ... | 11 | ... |
| Florida | 7 | 20 | ... | 263 | ... | ... | ... |
| Georgia | 7 | 9 | ... | ... | ... | 52 | ... |
| Hawaii | 5 | ... | ... | 13 | ... | ... | ... |
| Idaho | 5 | ... | ... | ... | 24 | ... | ... |
| Illinois | 7 | 34 | ... | 610 | ... | ... | ... |
| Indiana | 5 | 9 | ... | 87 | ... | 63 | 4 |
| Iowa | 9 | ... | ... | ... | 83(a) | ... | ... |
| Kansas | 7 | ... | ... | ... | 63 | ... | ... |
| Kentucky | 7 | ... | ... | 83 | ... | ... | ... |
| Louisiana | 7 | 26 | ... | ... | 118 | ... | ... |
| Maine | 6 | ... | ... | ... | ... | 14 | ... |
| Maryland | 7 | 10 | ... | 57 | ... | ... | 21 |
| Massachusetts | 7 | 6 | ... | ... | ... | 46 | ... |
| Michigan | 7 | 12 | ... | 126 | ... | ... | 20 |
| Minnesota | 9 | ... | ... | ... | 72 | ... | ... |
| Mississippi | 9 | ... | 25 | 24 | ... | ... | ... |
| Missouri | 7 | 18 | ... | 107 | ... | ... | ... |
| Montana | 5 | ... | ... | ... | 28 | ... | ... |
| Nebraska | 7 | ... | ... | ... | 45 | ... | ... |
| Nevada | 5 | ... | ... | ... | 23 | ... | ... |
| New Hampshire | 5 | ... | ... | ... | ... | 12 | ... |
| New Jersey | 7 | 18 | ... | ... | ... | 120 | 103 |
| New Mexico | 5 | 5 | ... | ... | 29 | ... | ... |
| New York | 7 | 31(b) | ... | ... | ... | ... | 257 |
| North Carolina | 7 | 9 | ... | ... | ... | 49 | ... |
| North Dakota | 5 | ... | ... | ... | 19 | ... | ... |
| Ohio | 7 | 38 | ... | ... | ... | ... | 291 |
| Oklahoma | 9 | 9(c) | ... | ... | 138 | ... | ... |
| Oregon | 7 | 6 | ... | 66 | ... | ... | ... |
| Pennsylvania | 7 | 14 | ... | ... | ... | ... | 285 |
| Rhode Island | 5 | ... | ... | ... | ... | 13 | ... |
| South Carolina | 5 | ... | ... | 16 | ... | ... | ... |
| South Dakota | 5 | ... | ... | 37 | ... | ... | ... |
| Tennessee | 5 | 16(c) | 23 | 50 | ... | ... | 29 |
| Texas | 9 | 47(c) | ... | ... | 219 | ... | ... |
| Utah | 5 | ... | ... | ... | 22 | ... | 21 |
| Vermont | 5 | ... | ... | ... | ... | ... | 6 |
| Virginia | 7 | ... | ... | 99 | ... | ... | ... |
| Washington | 9 | 12 | ... | ... | ... | 98 | ... |
| West Virginia | 5 | ... | ... | 34 | ... | ... | ... |
| Wisconsin | 7 | ... | ... | 52 | ... | ... | 126 |
| Wyoming | 5 | ... | ... | ... | 13 | ... | ... |
| District of Columbia | 9 | ... | ... | ... | ... | 44 | ... |

(a) Unified court system with an additional 24 District Associate Judges, 6 Judicial Magistrates, and 191 part-time Judicial Magistrates.
(b) Does not include temporary designations.
(c) In Oklahoma, there are 3 judges on the Court of Criminal Appeals and 6 on the Court of Appeals. In Tennessee there are 9 judges on the Court of Appeals and 7 members on the Court of Criminal Appeals. In Texas there are 5 judges on the Court of Criminal Appeals and 42 on the Court of Civil Appeals.

**Illustration 11.1** NUMBER OF JUDGES

Source: *The Book of States 1974–75*, vol. 20, ed. Paul Albright (Lexington, Ky.: The Council of State Governments, 1974), p. 121.

## *COURT LAG*

The biggest problem area in today's courts is primarily developmental, although it is manifested in structural problems, administrative problems, and so on. The courts are not static; they are always changing. The courts of the United States form a vast system in which delicate, vital decisions are made continuously that affect us all, directly or indirectly. It is a complicated system. The problem rests in the facts that some of the complication is needless and that the pace of development change has been too slow.

### Recognition

This facet of development is given its character by sociology and by philosophy. Around the turn of the century sociology was becoming accepted as a new discipline using scientific methodology. Rosco Pound, the dean of Harvard Law School, was an enthusiastic advocate of the application of sociology to law. In his extensive writings and speeches, he noted that law was taught and practiced as though it were a pure form of logic based on premises that had been established for all time.[4] In other words, like Latin, law was unchangeable, a dead language. Pound felt that the courts and the laws that had been established in the agrarian past had helped usher in the industrial age, but in their old forms the courts and the laws were a hinderance to the functioning of modern society. He called the courts archaic and described the ways in which they were antiquated.

For a generation Pound had the company of great jurists, including Chief Justice Oliver Wendell Holmes, Justice Benjamin Cardozo, Justice Lewis Brandeis, all of whom shared the belief that legal justice should give way to social justice. The bench no longer reigns over the sociology of law. Although the courts were affected by this intellectual ferment, the judiciary has not embraced Pound's thinking or acted on his suggestions. On August 10, 1970, Chief Justice Warren Burger addressed the American Bar Association:

> [Pound] said that the work of the courts in the twentieth century could not be carried on with the machinery of the nineteenth century. If you will read Pound's speech (to the ABA, 1906), you'll see at once that we did not heed his warning, and today, in the final third of this century, we are still trying to operate the courts with fundamentally the same basic methods, the same procedures, and the same machinery he said were not good enough in 1906.[5]

### Theory

In 1922, William Ogburn developed the idea of cultural lag.[6] He held that the material aspects of culture (such as the products of technological advances) would be followed by economic changes, followed by changes in social institutions (such as government or religion), followed, lastly, by important changes in the values of the culture. Changes in the material culture coexisting with *status quo* social structure and values create an incongruency that is experienced as conflict and problems. These problems will continue as long as changes in the nonmaterial culture lag behind the changes in material culture.

The fundamentals of this theory of social change can be readily applied to the courts' failure to develop properly and rapidly. Technological advances in medicine, agriculture, and so on have made possible the increase in the population of the United States from 76 million in 1900 to approximately 215 million in 1975. There is a huge, corresponding increase in court caseload. Technological advances have resulted in a shift from a culture in 1900 based on the small farmer who owned his own plot of land to the culture of 1975 based on the employee who lives in an urban area and is neither farmer nor industrial worker. The courts have grown in number, but their methods, their very structure, go back to the nineteenth century, when they were rural courts, governed by traditions that are centuries old.

The old method of producing more laws to solve problems, used by the courts and by the legislatures, produces still more cases. Technological advances result in new kinds of offenses to be added to the books and a welter of difficult, new kinds of cases with which the courts must deal, ranging from stolen credit cards to skyjacking. These new laws are cumulative, for old laws are seldom removed from the books. Even an increase in police efficiency is likely to mean that there will be more people arrested who must be processed by the courts. The time lapse between arrest and trial in felony cases doubled between 1960 and 1970.

The courts' lagging behind has had many unsavory effects. Here are some of the most important: The jails burgeon with untried defendants who cannot muster the necessary bail to buy their freedom. The rate of cases dismissed is increased because during the years that may pass before defendants reach trial, witnesses move away or die or their memories become untrustworthy, other evidence is lost, juries regard the cases as past history and no longer important, and so forth. The plea bargaining system is informal, often covert, and puts the responsibility for a case largely in the hands of the prosecutor; it has replaced the unworkable slow trial in the majority of felony cases. Due process is disregarded in misdemeanor cases as the courts try a new case each fifteen minutes in order to handle the increased volume.

The courts, of course, are but one part of the criminal justice system, and the other parts are also responsible for lag as a result of not meeting the demands stemming from various technological changes. The courts' lag is a bottleneck, however, whereas if their decision-making power were not restricted by obsolescent values, they could be a powerful modernizing force in criminal justice.

The courts lag because they adhere to the venerable value of individual autonomy, which has been guarded as the source of their impartiality. But unless they are unified into administrative systems they cannot begin to meet the demands placed on them. Slowly but with gathering momentum they have begun to respond to the increased demands. Law journals emphasize the need for unification, better selection methods and training of judges, to be responsive to the public. State constitutions are being revised with court unification in mind; forty-one

COURTESY OF THE LIBRARY OF CONGRESS

**OLIVER WENDELL HOLMES, JR.**
*1841 – 1935*

Oliver Wendell Holmes, Jr. was born in Boston in 1841, the son of a noted American novelist and poet. After attending T. R. Sullivan's Latin School Holmes entered Harvard and graduated with an A.B. in 1861. In that year he joined the Union Army and subsequently fought in the Civil War. Holmes was wounded quite seriously three times and was eventually mustered out of the service in 1864 as a lieutenant colonel. Holmes then entered Harvard Law School and two years later received his law degree. After a brief sojourn in Europe he entered into the practice of law in Boston in 1867. During this time he also taught at Harvard Law School in various capacities. For three years (1870–1873) he was editor of the *American Law Review*. Holmes made numerous contributions in articles, reviews, and editorials, and in 1881 he wrote *The Common Law*, which brought him considerable recognition as a legal scholar.

In 1882 Holmes was appointed to the Massachusetts Supreme Court. After twenty years of distinguished service on this court, Theodore Roosevelt appointed Holmes to the United States Supreme Court as an associate justice. While on the United States Supreme Court Holmes wrote over 1,000 opinions and while he concurred with 90 percent of the cases before the Court, Holmes became best known for his brilliantly written dissents. In *Abrams* v. *United States* [250 U.S. 616 (1909] Holmes wrote one of his more famous dissents. Jacob Abrams had been sentenced to twenty years in prison for the distribution of pamphlets objecting to American policies. The majority of the Supreme Court affirmed the judgment, but Holmes dissented. In his dissent Holmes wrote,

> But when men have realized that time has upset many fighting faiths, they may come to believe even more than they believe the very foundations of their own conduct that the ultimate good desired is better reached by free trade in ideas—that the best test of truth is the power of the thought to get itself accepted in the competition of the market, and that truth is the only ground upon which their wishes safely can be carried out.

Holmes has been called the "Great Dissenter"; yet his major dissents were to become the law in later years.

Holmes served on the Supreme Court for thirty years before resigning at the age of ninety-one. He died shortly after resigning with, as he once said, "the secret isolated joy of the thinker, who knows that, a hundred years after he is dead and forgotten, men who never heard of him will be moving to the measure of his thought."

states have established court administrators at the state level in recent years; several states have abolished their lower courts; and so on. Money is being poured into the courts for research into their problems and to initiate new programs, primarily as a result of the Omnibus Crime Bill of 1968.

**Limitations and Vulnerability**

Not all changes in the courts have a cumulative or developmental character. The phrase "developmental history" implies an unfolding, a maturation, a certain progress. The progress of the courts can be reversed. Setbacks such as the Court of the Star Chamber and Coke's banishment occurred long ago, but vulnerability to regression always exists.

Vulnerability to error also exists, particularly when change is being made. For example, the "criminal law revolution" of the 1960s was called haphazard and ragged by Warren Burger before he became chief justice. Burger would have had the Supreme Court deliberately establish a model guideline to ensure the consistency of case-by-case decisions and to help in the selection of cases to receive the Court's official attention. Others in turn have said that Burger's method would have been slow and cumbersome and negative. Another example of possible error is described by Judge Jerome Frank, who criticized Holmes, Cardozo, Pound, and others who had accented the need for a change in the laws. Frank claimed that the courts' inability to ascertain the correct facts is the problem to which these jurists should have devoted their energies. Still another example may be the effect of *Miranda* on the investigatory procedure in the United States, an effect that has been compared unfavorably with the investigating magistrate procedures defined in Continental law. In the same vein, perhaps Canada's "federal" court system is better than the federal system established for the United States by the Judiciary Act of 1789. The choices have been made in these instances, and there is no way of being sure that the choices were the best.

If the courts continue to lag, radical change is yet another choice or direction that the courts can take in their future development. In the opinion of some radical groups such as the Weathermen, Black Panthers, and the Symbionese Liberation Army, radical change is necessary. To some, the courts represent a symbol of capitalistic suppression of the lower class, the workers. The idea that justice is denied the poor while the rich go free is held to be true by many radical groups, and some not so radical groups. Radicals would suggest reforms such as "people's courts." These courts would be staffed and run by laypeople. Although these radical changes are unlikely, they do represent a minority point of view that could become a majority point of view if steps are not taken to reform the courts. The failure of social institutions to deal with their lag has in some cases led to radical change, and unless the courts recognize and deal with court lag, court reform may be replaced by radical change. The courts are not the exclusive property of the lawyers and judges, nor are they sacred grounds upon which no person may tread. The law and the courts belong to the people, and if the courts do not choose reform, then the people may choose radical change. Former United States Attorney General Herbert Brownell is quoted as saying, "all of the great administrative improvements in New York in recent years came through the efforts of laymen. Citizens forced judges and lawyers to make changes."[7] These were not radical changes but they could well be in the future. Unfortunately, however, radical change may produce a system that is more unworkable and less just than the present court system.

The courts are in serious difficulties; they have begun to respond with reforms; time will indicate whether the adopted remedies or reforms were good. As institutions, courts cannot change with every change that is introduced into the society; institutions, in a sense, help maintain balance. Court lag, then, will never be completely eliminated; nor is its complete elimination desirable. The expression court lag explains nothing by itself. It is a concept that helps organize and focus attention on the developmental problem of the courts. In the next chapters specific attributes of this problem will become evident.

## DISCUSSION QUESTIONS

1. What are some examples of the different meanings of *court* and *tribunal*? How well are the meanings of these words established by context?
2. What similarities are there between the development of courts and the development of law?
3. Discuss the relationship of the court development in America to American society. What might our society be like if it was reflected in our courts, and they had followed various other lines of development that you can name?
4. Discuss the limitations of the courts.
5. Describe what is meant by court lag. Where are the lag's effects felt most keenly?
6. What direction do you believe the courts will take in their future development—reform or radical change? Which do you believe to be the best direction? Why?

## NOTES

1. U.S. Bureau of Census, *Statistical Abstract of the United States, 1972* (Washington, D.C.: Government Printing Office, 1972).
2. Maxine B. Vertue, *Survey of Metropolitan Courts* (Ann Arbor: University of Michigan Press, 1962).
3. This is an estimate made by Dr. Charles Friel, Chairman of the Statistical Steering Committee of SEARCH (the intergovernmental program designed to bring about the new system), during a private conversation with the author, Fall 1972.

4. Roscoe Pound, "The Need of a Sociological Jurisprudence," in *The Sociology of Law: Interdisciplinary Readings*, ed. Rita James Simon (San Francisco: Chandler Publishing, 1968), pp. 9–18.
Roscoe Pound, *The Spirit of the Common Law* (Boston: Beacon Press, 1963).
Roscoe Pound, *Organization of Courts* (Boston: Little Brown, 1940).
Roscoe Pound, *The Development of Constitutional Guarantees of Liberty* (New Haven: Yale University Press, 1957).
5. Chief Justice Warren Burger, "Remarks on the State of the Federal Judiciary," an address delivered to the American Bar Association, St. Louis, Missouri, August 1970.
6. William F. Ogburn, *Social Change with Respect to Cultural and Origional Nature* (New York: Dell, 1966; originally published 1922).
7. Howard James, *Crisis in the Courts* (New York: McKay, 1971), p. 209.

# 12: Structure of the Courts in the United States

*FEDERAL COURT SYSTEM • MILITARY COURT SYSTEM • STATE COURT SYSTEM • JUVENILE COURT SYSTEM • UNIFICATION OF FEDERAL AND STATE COURT SYSTEMS*

PURPOSE: *TO DESCRIBE THE STRUCTURE OF THE FEDERAL, STATE, AND LOCAL COURT SYSTEMS AND THEIR RELATIONSHIPS TO ONE ANOTHER.*

COURTS are defined, basically, in terms of their structure, the relatively stable framework within which action takes place. The courts in the United States are frequently described as consisting of a "federal" system and a "state" system. This chapter will examine this dualism, as well as the need for unification. The different kinds of federal courts will be treated individually as will be the different levels of the state courts. The military court system and the juvenile courts will be singled out for special attention. Before these courts systems can be considered, however, some specific information is needed.

Court structure is determined largely by the legal limitations imposed on its ability to deal with a case—and a court's authority as described by these limitations is defined as *jurisdiction.* Different sets of limitations or kinds of authority are frequently identified by an adjective preceding the word jurisdiction. Thus, *original jurisdiction* means that a court has the right to try a case, while *appellate jurisdiction* means that a court has the right to hear a defendant's appeal that it set aside a conviction. A court with original jurisdiction may have appellate jurisdiction. An example of this would be the United States Supreme Court. A court with *special jurisdiction* is a court of special original jurisdiction. An example of a special original jurisdiction court is a magistrate's court that has original jurisdiction over civil and criminal matters when the amount in controversy, or fine, does not exceed $200. The jurisdiction is original but special because the cases the court may try are limited by a dollar amount. Special jurisdiction courts are sometimes referred to as *limited jurisdiction* courts. A *general jurisdiction* court is one that has the power to try a wide class of cases. Whereas the special jurisdiction court is limited by a prescribed sum or class of cases it can try, the general jurisdiction court is not. Jurisdiction is frequently used to identify a geographical area in which a court has the authority to hear a case, although technically this is not considered proper usage. Jurisdiction should not be mistaken for the concept of *venue,* the requirement that the trial for an offense be held in the same area in which the offense occurred. The point to remember is that jurisdiction refers to a court's authority to take notice of and decide a case (see Illustration 12.3, p. 190).

The courts are frequently divided into higher, or superior, and lower, or inferior, courts. This division reflects a hierarchy of prestige that has been attached to the courts and ranges from the courts of limited jurisdiction at the bottom (the lower courts) to the courts with appellate jurisdiction at the top (the higher courts). Sometimes the trial courts, the courts that can engage in a jury trial, are included in the higher courts, and sometimes they are included in the lower courts. *Court of last resort* means the highest court to which a case can be appealed. The trial courts used to be the first level of court to keep a record of court activity in a case, and *court of record* is an expression used to separate them from the courts with limited jurisdiction. Any court, however, that on an appeal hears a case on the record of the trial in the court below, without a new trial, has identified the court below as a court of record.

## *FEDERAL COURT SYSTEM*

The federal judiciary was set up on the basis of two sources in the law. These two sources are reflected in the terms *constitutional courts* and *legislative courts.* Constitutional courts are the Supreme Court and "such inferior Courts as the Congress may from time to time ordain and establish" (Article III, Section 1), that is, the courts of appeals, the district courts, and various specialized courts. Legislative courts are based on the "legislative article," Article I of the Constitution, which states, "The congress shall have the power . . . to constitute tribunals inferior to the Supreme Court . . . ." Most legislative courts have subsequently been declared by Congress constitutional courts and thus have been given a slightly different relationship to the Supreme Court.

### United States Supreme Court

The United States Supreme Court—or the "the Court," as it is often called—is composed of nine justices (judges), one of whom is the chief justice, who acts in the capacity of chairperson. The chief justice has no formal authority to make the other justices do anything, although in practice the chief justice determines who will write decisions and do certain other work. These nine people are appointed by the president of the United States, subject to confirmation by the Senate. The president also names the person who will be the chief justice. It is not necessary for the justices to have a background in law, and they may have attracted the attention of the president by their activity in politics. Nonetheless, most of the members have been lawyers, and since 1946 they have generally had the approval of the American Bar Association. If the Senate feels that an individual lacks the stature for the position or that there is something distasteful in his or her background, it may refuse to confirm the president's choice, and another choice must be made. The Constitution establishes tenure for "life or good behavior." The only ways to remove a justice are through impeachment or by securing voluntary retirement. The Constitution does not permit Congress (which controls the budget) to reduce the justices' salaries once they start receiving them.

Besides the justices there are six other regular officers of the Court: the clerk, the chief deputy clerk, the deputy clerk, the marshal, the reporter of decisions, and a librarian. The functions of clerk, reporter, and bailiff (whose functions parallel the marshal) are described elsewhere. Each justice usually selects one or two recent law school graduates to serve for a year as a legal aide or law clerk. The Court has its own library.

The term of the Court is required by statutory law to begin on the first Monday in October of each year. It continues as long as there is business before it, usually until the middle of June. A quorum consists of six members. The caseload has been increasing, and roughly 3,000 cases are being passed upon in each term.

Despite its appearance of stability and power, the Supreme Court has undergone many changes since it was founded. President Washington had trouble filling the positions, and of the first justices some were out-of-work politicians, some left the position for other jobs, and one justice never attended any of the sessions. Chief Justice John Jay declared on his resignation that the Court would always be weak, of little consequence, lacking the stature it should have to be ranked with Congress and the executive branch. Each justice faced the possibility of a yearly ride on horseback through the wilderness to preside over the circuit courts (now called courts of appeals), one reason for the early lack of interest in serving on the Court.

It was not until 1815 that the Court formally established its authority over the states in case law. A number of strong justices were to add to the Court's status, the most crucial role being played by Chief Justice John Marshall. Marshall was successful in his legal fight with President Jefferson in *Marbury* vs. *Madison* [1 Cranch 137 (1803)] and thereby established the authority of the Constitution (as interpreted by the Court) over the laws passed by Congress. The Court is thus said to possess the "power of judicial review" of legislative law. The list of other famous justices includes Brandeis, Cardozo, Holmes, and Warren. (A number of justices have described Chief Justice Hughes as the most effective.) (See Illustration 12.1 for the present make-up of the Court.) The Court has on a number of occasions been under attack by either the executive branch or Congress.

With the expansion of the federal judiciary and the states' judiciaries the Supreme Court's workload has increased. It gets most of its cases from these other courts and has not itself expanded. In 1962, for example, the federal judiciary was enlarged 25 percent by the addition of judges, but the Supreme Court continues unchanged. This has led to a proposal for a National Appeals Court to supplement the Supreme Court, a proposal that gained the support of the American Bar Association in 1974.

The jurisdiction of the Supreme Court is limited as is the jurisdiction of every other court. "I will fight it all the way to the Supreme Court" may be impossible because of the restrictions imposed by the Constitution and the Congress. The Constitution is remarkably concise in its passage on the Court's jurisdiction:

> The Judicial power shall extend to all Cases in Law and Equity, arising under this Constitution, the Laws of the United States, and Treaties, made, or which shall be made, under their Authority;—to all Cases affecting Ambassadors, other public Ministers, and Consuls;—to all Cases of admirality and maritime Jurisdiction;—to Controversies to which the United States shall be a Party;—to Controversies between two or more States;—between Citizens of Different States;—between Citizens of the same State claiming Lands under Grants of different States, and between a State, or the Citizens thereof, and foreign States, Citizens, or Subjects.
>
> In all Cases affecting Ambassadors, other public Ministers and Consuls, and those in which a State shall be Party, the Supreme Court shall have original Jurisdiction. In all the other cases before mentioned the Supreme Court shall have appellate Jurisdiction, both as to Law and Fact, with such Exceptions, and under such Regulations as the Congress shall make.[1]

Congress has conferred appellate jurisdiction upon the Supreme Court, but has no authority to change its original jurisdiction as set up in the Constitution. Actu-

FROM THE BOOK *EQUAL JUSTICE UNDER LAW*, PUBLISHED BY THE FEDERAL BAR ASSOCIATION FOUNDATION

**Illustration 12.1** UNITED STATES SUPREME COURT

Standing (left to right): Lewis F. Powell, Jr.; Thurgood Marshall; Harry A. Blackmun; and William H. Rehnquist
Seated (left to right): Potter Stewart; William O. Douglas (resigned November 12, 1975); Chief Justice Warren E. Burger; William J. Brennan, Jr.; and Byron R. White

ally, cases of original jurisdiction account for fewer than one percent of cases heard in a term. Congress has granted the Supreme Court the power to prescribe rules of procedure to be followed by the federal courts of appeal, district courts, and other specific federal courts. And the Court has established rules to govern various procedures, including criminal cases in district courts, appellate proceedings in criminal cases, and criminal petty offense proceedings before United States magistrates.

**United States Courts of Appeals**

All federal courts other than the Supreme Court are sometimes called the *lower federal courts.* The highest of these are the United States courts of appeals, also referred to as *intermediate appellate courts,* for they are intermediate between the Supreme Court and the district courts. They were created in 1891 to relieve the Supreme Court of hearing all appeals of cases decided by the federal district courts. The courts of appeals can review all final decisions and some interlocutory or temporary decisions of the district courts, except for the few cases that are appealed directly to the Supreme Court. Like the district courts they have responsibility for reviewing and enforcing decisions by certain quasi-judicial tribunals —nineteen of them, in fact; examples are the National Labor Relations Board and the Securities and Exchange Commission. The decisions of the courts of appeals are final unless the Supreme Court chooses to review them or unless they are heard on appeal to the Court.

The United States courts of appeals were known as the United States circuit courts of appeals until 1948. The United States is divided into eleven areas known as judicial circuits, and there is one court of appeals in each circuit. Each court has from three to nine permanent judgeships, depending on the amount of work required of the court. Ten of the circuits are identified by number, and each state and territory is assigned to one of them. The eleventh circuit is the one in which the District of Columbia alone is located. (See Illustration 12.2 for a breakdown of the circuits.)

The member of a court of appeals who has been a judge for the longest period of time and who has not yet reached seventy is the chief judge of the court. One of the Supreme Court justices is assigned as circuit judge for each circuit, but is seldom active in this role. Three to nine judges may sit to hear a case, but usually only three do sit because of their heavy workloads; two is a quorum. The judges are appointed for "life or good behavior." Each circuit has a judicial council to handle administrative business.

**District Courts**

The district courts are the lowest in the hierarchy of the Supreme Court, appellate courts, and district courts. The district courts are the trial courts with general federal jurisdiction. There is a United States district court in each state, and some states have as many as four. Each district court has from one to twenty-four federal district judges. A single judge presides over one trial except in a few kinds of cases, when three judges are called together to form a court. The purpose of the district courts is to relieve the Supreme Court of conducting jury trials (an activity in which it was sometimes engaged in its early history).

The district court in the District of Columbia has jurisdiction over local matters (those usually heard in state courts), as well as its other duties. This jurisdiction is in keeping with the exclusive sovereignty that Congress has over the District of Columbia. In Puerto Rico the district court is called a United States district court, and Puerto Rico's local cases are controlled by the country's system of local courts. The territorial district courts are located in the territories of Guam, the Virgin Islands, and the Canal Zone, and they have federal jurisdiction and, as in the District of Columbia, jurisdiction over local cases. The territorial district court's judges are appointed for terms of eight years except in the Commonwealth of Puerto Rico, where they are appointed for "life or good behavior."

The original jurisdiction possessed by district courts is fourfold: they have jurisdiction in all cases in which a federal criminal law has been broken. They have jurisdiction in cases that give rise to a

| Identifying Number | States |
|---|---|
| First Circuit | Maine, New Hampshire, Massachusetts, Rhode Island, Puerto Rico |
| Second Circuit | New York, Vermont, Connecticut |
| Third Circuit | Pennsylvania, New Jersey, Delaware |
| Fourth Circuit | West Virginia, North Carolina, South Carolina, Maryland |
| Fifth Circuit | Texas, Louisiana, Mississippi, Alabama, Georgia, Florida, (Panama) Canal Zone |
| Sixth Circuit | Ohio, Kentucky, Tennessee, Michigan |
| Seventh Circuit | Wisconsin, Illinois, Indiana |
| Eighth Circuit | North Dakota, South Dakota, Nebraska, Missouri, Arkansas, Iowa, Minnesota |
| Ninth Circuit | Washington, Oregon, California, Nevada, Arizona, Idaho, Montana, Alaska, Hawaii |
| Tenth Circuit | Wyoming, Utah, Colorado, New Mexico, Kansas, Oklahoma, |
| Eleventh Circuit | District of Columbia |

**Illustration 12.2** UNITED STATES JUDICIAL CIRCUITS

federal question and the amount in controversy exceeds $10,000. They have jurisdiction in suits between citizens of different states and the amount in controversy exceeds $10,000. They have jurisdiction in suits between a citizen(s) of one state and other states when the amount in controversy exceeds $10,000. The repeated $10,000 limitation was established as a means of limiting cases to serious ones, and that figure has been waived in special circumstances.

Historically, the district courts made their own law in preference to following the conflicting laws of the many states. They were forced to renounce this authority prior to the 1900s, and now they apply the law of the appropriate states in given cases. The district courts are empowered to review and enforce actions of certain quasi-judicial agencies (five of them) and they handle tort claims against the United States. Most of the cases they deal with are civil, not criminal, cases. The federal crimes with which they are concerned are the offenses against the national revenue, postal, patent, copyright, trademark, bankruptcy, and civil rights' laws. Kidnaping, killing a president, crossing a state line in a stolen vehicle, and so on, are federal crimes.

Each district court has a clerk, a United States attorney, a United States marshal, referees in bankruptcy, probation officers, court reporters, and assistants. The district court judges appoint other judges, called United States magistrates (formerly called United States commissioners), who handle preliminaries, issue warrants for arrest, decide whether an arrested person should be held over for the attention of a grand jury, set bail, and so on. The magistrates are appointed to serve for a term of eight years.

Cases from the district courts are reviewed by the United States courts of appeals. Certain criminal decisions, however, along with certain decisions holding acts of Congress unconstitutional and injunction orders of the special three-judge district courts, may be appealed directly to the Supreme Court.

## *MILITARY COURT SYSTEM*

The military courts have a unique structure and a different procedure from civilian courts. Military justice extends to many kinds of cases besides those involving military personnel on active duty. Jurisdiction even extends to civilians in certain circumstances. These courts, though not limited to criminal cases, do handle many and deserve special attention.

The military courts for the most part exist within the Department of Defense. Congress is, of course, the major policy-making body for both organizations. In 1952 the Congress approved the Uniform Code of Military Justice (UCMJ), the authority for the courts and judicial procedures, which are the same for each branch of the service.

### Grades of Court-Martial

A person in the armed forces who would ordinarily be punished for some kinds of offenses by his or her commanding officer can request and receive a trial by a *summary court-martial.* This is the lowest of three grades of court-martial. Usually the court is convened at the discretion and by the authority of any one of a number of officers. The court does not exist until convened, and the officer or panel of officers appointed to hold court may vary from trial to trial. Large military bases, however, frequently have established a regular summary court-martial. The accused is investigated by the commanding officer, who may then send a report to the convening authority for that area. This officer may choose to investigate the charges still further before convening a court or send the investigatory reports to a convening officer of the next highest court, the *special court-martial.* This officer is higher in rank and may also have the authority to convene a *general court-martial,* the highest court. If he or she does not have the authority but deems a trial to be necessary, the material will be sent to a still higher ranking officer, who will convene the highest grade of court-martial. Of course, most cases go directly to the correct convening authority.

The grades of the court-martial are not defined by the seriousness of the offense as is the case in civilian court systems. They are determined by the seriousness of the penalty. The summary court is limited to cases dealing with enlisted personnel, and the maximum penalty that it may impose is one month's confinement and loss of two thirds of a month's pay. The maximum penalty a special court-martial can impose is six months' confinement and loss of two thirds of six months' pay. Both courts would seem to correspond to civilian courts that are limited to trying misdemeanor cases. The general court is reserved for cases involving the penalties for serious offenses. The offenses are given in the UCMJ, but the president of the United States establishes the penalties. Offenses are described as either military or criminal. Death, imprisonment, and various forms of discharge, rank reduction, and pay reduction are included among the more serious penalties.

The president of the court-martial is similar to the chief judge in a civilian court, although the president lacks the authority over the minimum of five other officers impaneled on the court that a civilian judge has over a jury. The military judges are highly qualified. Officer lawyers present at the trial for either the defense or the prosecution must be approved by the judge-advocate general of whichever branch of the military is involved. They, like the military judges, are highly qualified. The judge-advocate general, similar to a prosecutor, is the highest ranking legal authority within the service. Civilian lawyers may serve as defense attorneys at the defendant's request and expense.

### Safeguards

The military system has been critized because of the investigatory power granted a fellow commissioned officer of the military judge. This power may be abused, not necessarily deliberately, because at one stage the investigating officer is the accused's commanding officer. These investigations tend to have negative psychological affects on the military judges and may lead them to feel that the accused is guilty or he or she would not have been charged. A safeguard that enhances judicial impartiality lies in the rigid rules on the conduct of the military judges; failure to follow these rules can result in the military judge being court-martialed.

Another safeguard rests in the review system. Every court-martial is automatically reviewed, sometimes as many as three times, by trained legal staffs for the sole purpose of examining verdicts of guilty. The reviewing staff or board may include the accused's own civilian defense counsel. The number of verdicts modified by these boards suggests that they are not perfunctory. Nonetheless, they are controlled by military officers and therefore are not always above suspicion. In 1950, Congress created the United States Court of Military Appeals, one of the reforms in military justice subsequently reflected in UCMJ.

### United States Court of Military Appeals

The United States Court of Military appeals operates for administrative purposes as part of the Department of Defense but is judicially independent. It is composed of three civilian judges appointed for fifteen-year terms by the president with the approval of the Senate. The court was designed to be the final appellate tribunal in court-martial convictions, although cases can go to the Supreme Court. The court can review only matters of law (did the trial adhere to due process of law), not of fact (did the facts presented at the trial prove guilt). It receives only cases that have been to a board of review. The judge-advocate general may forward the case, or the accused may attempt to obtain review by a petition to the court. The general counsel for the Department of Transportation may certify a case to the court on behalf of a defendant who is a member of the Coast Guard. Cases automatically appealed to the court are those in which a general or flag officer has been convicted and those in which the sentence is death.

Boards of review are limited by UCMJ. The Court of Military Appeals, however, has the power to interpret the code—thereby creating law, solving some of the problems that arise because of the inability to cover all possible contingencies in statutory law. The court's value for criminal justice may be special, for it is not bound by centuries of tradition as are civilian courts, and it faces problems requiring innovative approaches. Its actions may suggest to civilian courts new approaches for handling criminal cases.

## *STATE COURT SYSTEM*

The structure of the courts in any given state is established by that state's constitution and by its statutory law. As a result, the court systems of the various states contain a bewildering variety of court names and a varying number of levels in the case hierarchy.

### Variety of State Courts

At the county level in Pennsylvania, for example, there are common pleas courts (usually for civil cases involving $5,000 or more), oyer and terminer courts (criminal courts for capital crimes and other felonies), quarter sessions courts (predominantly criminal courts meeting periodically and sometimes consisting of the same judges as oyer and terminer courts), orphans courts (for cases involving orphans), equity courts (for equity cases), probate courts (for cases concerning wills and estates), domestic relations courts (for family legal problems such as divorce), surrogate courts (similar to probate courts), chancery courts (which specialize in equity), and juvenile courts. Other states will have courts that correspond closely or correspond roughly or do not correspond at all. These courts will have the same names or different names, but similarity of name does not guarantee similarity of function. Confusing the matter still more is the fact that people in the criminal justice field commonly use a name as though its meaning was fixed and universal; thus, they speak of a justice of peace court, county court, superior court, as though everyone knows exactly what they mean.

Another element of confusion is conveyed to the nonprofessional by the word *court* because the inexperienced associate one court with one judge. The fact is that a particular kind of court located in a specified area may be represented by several judges. For example, a county courthouse may contain offices (called *chambers*) and courtrooms for both the county court and a state district court, and that county court involves one county judge while the district court involves six district judges. In another county the numbers may be just the reverse.

Criminal courts are not generally distinguished from civil courts, but if they happen to be, distinction is more likely to be made in the lower courts. All courts that handle criminal cases usually fall into one of two categories, determined by the basic kinds of offenses they try: misdemeanors (drunkeness, traffic violations, simple assaults, petty theft, disorderly conduct, prostitution, homosexual acts, possession of certain drugs, and countless other minor infractions of the law) and felonies (murder, arson, kidnapping, robbery, burglary, rape and other serious assaults, and so on.) Courts that are often restricted to dealing with misdemeanor cases are police courts, justice of the peace courts, special sessions courts, and the like. Courts that are concerned with trying felony cases are county courts, superior courts, district courts, circuit courts, and so forth. Too much weight should not be attached to the name of the court, however; for example, the county courts of many states do not try felony cases. In addition, the definition of felony and misdemeanor vary from state to state; for example, as late as 1973 marijuana possession in Texas was a felony with a sentence from two years to life, whereas it was a misdemeanor in Ann Arbor, Michigan, where a person caught smoking marijuana was fined five dollars, payable by mail.

### Levels of State Courts

Some of this confusion is easily resolved by ranking the courts in a three or four-tiered hierarchy based on jurisdiction as is shown in Illustration 12.3.

*Court of Last Resort* Each state has a court that is usually known as the supreme court (note the lack of capitalization that differentiates the states' supreme courts from the federal Supreme Court). In Texas the supreme court hears only civil cases, and a court of criminal appeals is the highest court that hears criminal cases. Each, however, is a *court of last resort*, or *of ultimate review*, for there is no other court to hear the case on further appeal or petition (except a federal court when certain conditions are present). These courts hear appeals from lower state trial courts or courts of intermediate appeals (depending on the structure of the court system in a particular state). These courts, not the Supreme Court, generally have ultimate jurisdiction over controversies involving interpretation of a state's constitution and its statutes. The number of justices who are members of the court of last resort ranges from three to nine, depending on the state.

*Intermediate Appellate Courts* Between the court of last resort and trial courts, *intermediate appellate courts* have been established in twenty states to handle appeals. These courts exist in all the larger states, and they relieve courts of last resort of some of their ever-increasing

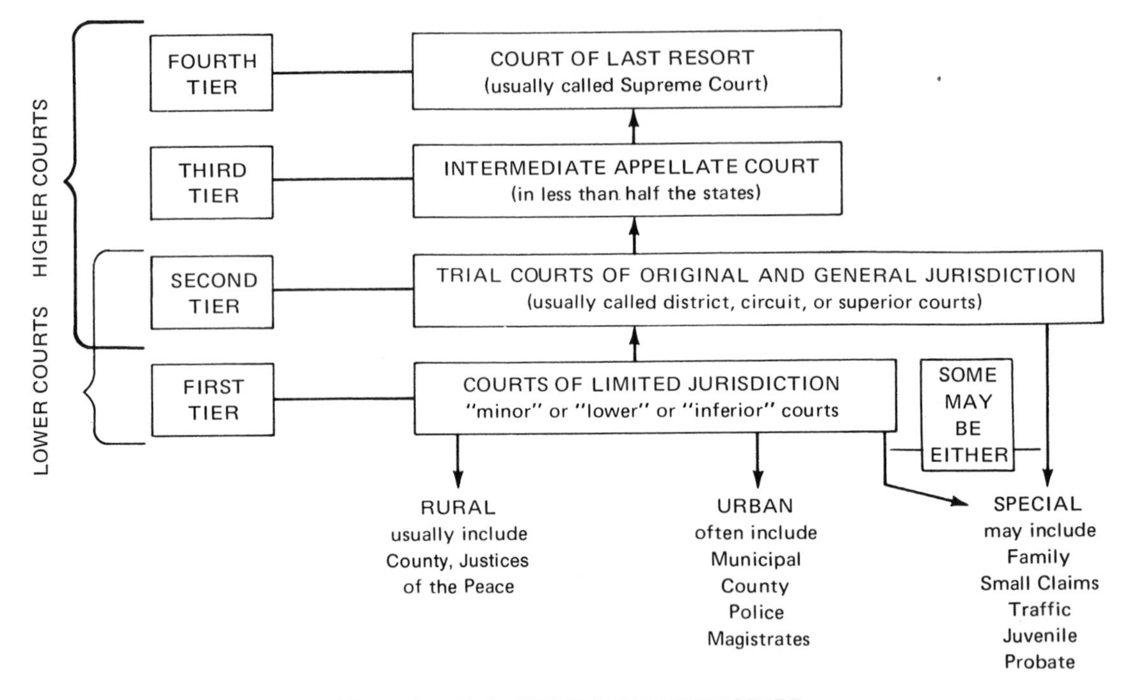


**Illustration 12.3** STATE COURT STRUCTURE

burdens. They are often known as courts of appeal.

Courts of appeals have original jurisdiction in some kinds of cases in some states, but are generally limited to appellate jurisdiction. The defendant generally has the right to appeal regardless of whether the court of appeal wants to hear the appeal. Although most states allow the court of last resort extensive rights to review cases that have been heard or tried by another court, most cases that get as far as the court of appeals end there. States without this level or tier in their court system have a three-tiered court system rather than a four-tiered one.

*Trial Courts of Original and General Jurisdictions* The level of courts in which cases may be tried to the fullest extent of the law are frequently called, simply, *trial courts.* They can and sometimes must use juries. Some states have separate criminal courts at this level and may also have separate courts for civil litigations, equity suits, probate cases, and other matters. The jurisdiction of some of the larger trial courts overlaps with the courts of limited jurisdiction (concurrent jurisdiction). The jurisdiction of any one trial court may be difficult to ascertain without reference to the state constitution and statutory law that lies behind it. Many court systems are remarkably complex at this level and the level below it. In some states a defendant may have to carry what he or she believes to be a single case to more than one court because of the fragmented jurisdiction of the courts. These courts try felony cases and all significant civil cases, and they usually hear appeals from such lower courts as the justice of the peace courts. The number of judges may be restricted by the state's constitution, but in most states the legislature have increased the number as cases or population increases. See Illustration 11.1 for the typical number of judges at this level for the different states.

Trial courts within a state may be assigned districts that include several counties. The early trial courts tended to be county courts, housed in the county courthouse, because of the limited mobility of a small population scattered over a wide geographical area. Today, however, a regional system of trial courts is more practical.

*Courts of Limited Jurisdiction* Historically the courts of special or limited jurisdiction in the United States were courts held by justices of the peace (J.P.). Then, early in the 1800s, different kinds of limited courts began to appear. In many areas, county courts were given jurisdiction concurrent with J.P. courts and cities developed city courts, magistrate courts, and so on. J.P. courts continue to be important, although by 1973 seventeen states had abolished them entirely, and in at least four more states, they have in many of the cities been replaced.

Typically, the J.P. court is the lowest state court. It is usually a *court of non-record*. Indeed, the duties of the office frequently make the name *court* questionable; notary work, the performances of marriages, and other nonjudicial duties done for a fee reveal its quasi-judicial character. Calling a J.P. a magistrate does not alter this character. In some places, the J.P. is called squire, a title that reflects the history of the office and its origin in fourteenth-century England, where then as now it was to aid in the administration of justice in minor matters at the local level.

Although the J.P.'s jurisdiction usually extends throughout the county, the court may be restricted to the town in which the J.P. is elected. The term of office is generally from two to six years. In some cities the J.P. is appointed by the city administration. Pay is low as a rule, but inasmuch as it is frequently collected in the form of a fee paid by the defendant or by the person seeking a service, the office can be a lucrative position in some locales. Backgrounds of J.P.s are extremely varied, and the J.P. often has a "regular" job in addition to holding office. Apparently inherent in the structure that includes and defines the J.P. court are factors that result in an approximate 80 percent conviction rate in criminal cases. The witticism that *J.P.* means "justice for the plaintiff" is as much to the point as it is pointed.

The minor or lower courts that have replaced the justices of the peace with magistrates do much the same kind of work: the issuance of warrants, presentments, setting bail, holding preliminary hearings in felony cases, settling petty misdemeanor cases, and other matters (to be discussed in the next chapter). It is important to note, however, that in one state J.P.s may be so limited that they do not even perform magistrate duties, whereas, in another state, they may be the equivalent of a higher level court. In addition, courts of limited jurisdiction include many specialized courts—traffic courts, juvenile courts (in many places), and so on. These lowest level courts do not make an official transcript of court proceedings; they are not, therefore, courts of records; and, on appeal, a case will be retried—a procedure known as *trial de novo*.

Trial courts have been called the workhorses of the court system. Certainly most of the people who appear before a court charged with an offense against the law appear before a court of limited jurisdiction. In the huge bulk of these cases, the case begins here and ends here. These courts are often *inferior* courts in the common sense of the word. The National Crime Commission in 1967 echoed the Wickersham Commission's recommendation, made forty years earlier, that the lower courts be abolished in an effort to do away with a dual system of justice that treats alleged petty offenders with less regard than alleged felons. Illinois was the first state to do so.

## *JUVENILE COURT SYSTEM*

Juvenile courts are in a special class, neither civil nor criminal, but having characteristics of both. Juvenile courts are statutorially defined. They have less basis in common law than do many other courts. Seemingly their relation to criminal justice is close, for they deal with delinquency, but is delinquency equivalent to criminal behavior?

In medieval England the Church declared that a child not yet seven could not be guilty of a sin, and the king's court concurred. Children over seven who fell into the hands of the law were treated as adults: they were arrested for the same offenses, tried in the same courts, meted the same sentences, assigned to the same prisons. The prisons were the first to be differentiated; one kind for adults, another kind for children. It was not until 1899 that, with the support of the Chicago Bar Association, the women of the Chicago Settlement Houses managed to have the first juvenile court in the United States established in Cook County, Illinois. It was twenty-five years before any other state followed suit, and two of the states continued to hold out for many more years.

The Supreme Court upheld the unique character of juvenile courts in a case in which it set forth the idea of the courts as kind and loving parents—to replace genetic parents, if need be—in the famous doctrine of *parens patriae.* The object of the court's attention in this philosophy is manifestly to rehabilitate, not to punish.

Juvenile courts do not convict children; they declare some children to be delinquents and some merely dependents of the court. Dependency jurisdiction is not of direct interest to criminal justice professionals, but cases in which children are labeled delinquent are of direct concern. What is delinquency in the eyes of the court? Perhaps the working definition used by the Children's Bureau of the Department of Health, Education and Welfare describes the relationship between court and delinquency best:

> Juvenile delinquency cases are those referred to courts for acts defined in the statutes of the State as the violation of a state law or municipal ordinance by children or youth of juvenile court age, or for conduct so seriously antisocial as to interfere with the rights of others or to menace the welfare of the delinquent himself or the community. This broad definition of delinquency includes conduct which violates the law only when committed by children, e.g., truancy, ungovernable behavior, and running away. Also included, but reported separately are traffic violations whenever a juvenile court has jurisdiction in such cases.[2]

As a consequence of the doctrine of *parens patriae,* the structure of the juvenile court approached that of a social welfare agency with social workers, social worker's language rather than legal language, and an informal model in which due process was not regarded as necessary. The court all too often failed to live up to its ideal of being a loving parent, and the child and the parents were at the mercy of a court with totalitarian powers. In a number of famous decisions in the late sixties, the Supreme Court demanded that due process be followed in juvenile courts.[3]

Another criticism of the juvenile court is that it cannot possibly meet all the needs of the juvenile in trouble because of the structural nature of courts as instruments of law. A clear example is the school truant, or the child who is claimed by the parents to be unmanageable; both are treated as criminals to be punished. The child whose freedom is abridged for such a problem may feel that the punishment would be no different for robbery, murder, or rape. Whatever the value of "training school," for example, the child is aware of locked doors, guards, and insistence on certain forms of behavior "or else" additional detention. Others—parents, teachers, peers, and prospective employers—are inclined to see the child who appears in court as a little criminal. All this is true even though the child in a few months or perhaps weeks would have been old enough to play truant or run away from home with impunity. The National Council on Crime and Delinquency has taken the position that juveniles not be brought before the courts and sentenced for "status offenses," that is, offenses that would not be considered criminal for an adult.

It is for these kinds of reasons that youth service bureaus have been urged as a replacement for juvenile courts as the chief agencies to help children who might otherwise be classified as delinquents. The National Crime Commission (1967) stated that juvenile courts had failed and should be used only as a last resort. In many instances they have been of genuine benefit to children, but their original purpose is not being achieved.

"Juvenile court age" varies widely. It may begin with birth, age seven, ten, eleven, or twelve, and it may end anytime from age sixteen through age twenty-one, depending on the court in question. Juvenile court age may differ with the sex of the juvenile. Moreover, the state-defined juvenile court age does not need to bear any relation to other statutory age limitations, such as those for marriage, consent, drinking, driving, or executing a will. The age of criminal responsibility, the age at which one becomes subject to adult court procedures for certain criminal acts, is independent of juvenile court age.

Chicago, New York, Philadelphia, and other large cities have *youth courts* as well as juvenile courts. These courts are adult courts, but they use the techniques of juvenile courts. They exist for youth from sixteen to nineteen or twenty-one who have committed specified kinds of misdemeanors—and, rarely, felonies. Because youth courts lack exclusive jurisdictions, older boys and girls are frequently tried in the regular criminal courts.

The language in various areas of the country contains distinctions between juvenile delinquents, minors, and minor delinquents. Family courts have been advocated as a form of specialized court that would handle juvenile delinquents along with other problems in which children are directly involved, and many cities do have family courts. Appeal from juvenile courts, interestingly enough, goes to a civil court, because the juvenile court technically is a civil court, although it does, in effect, sentence individuals to imprisonment.

## *UNIFICATION OF FEDERAL AND STATE COURT SYSTEMS*

The federal court system is maintained for the prosecution of federal crimes, and the state system, for the prosecution of state crimes. Unfortunately, this dual court system contains overlapping jurisdictions that give rise to conflicts, confusion, inefficiency, and injustice. Furthermore, within a state court system there is frequently an overlap of jurisdictions that can only add to the problems of an already confused dualism. A single court system, with a unified administration, would reduce the inner problems of overlapping jurisdiction.

### Overlap and Conflict

Congress created the federal court system, even though it could have allowed the states to retain all original jurisdiction in their trial courts. On the other hand, when they ceased being colonies, the states could have given up their courts just as they gave up so many of their other rights and privileges to the new federal government. They chose, however, to retain their already established court systems.

The bulk of criminal cases, perhaps 85 percent, are handled by the state courts because most crimes are defined by state law. A single crime, however, may be both a federal and a state crime. Whenever Congress creates a federal law, the state laws dealing with the same offenses remain untouched. Federal laws cannot be prosecuted as such in a state court. A single act, however, may be prosecuted by both federal and state governments independent of one another. For example, if a national bank is robbed and the bank robber is convicted and sentenced by a state court, he may later be convicted by a federal court, and vice versa. Double jeopardy applies within court systems, not across court systems.

Although federal district courts exist in all states, neither their number nor their location means that they have authority over the states' courts or the states. Cases involving state crimes get into federal courts through the back door, so to speak, as when they are heard on a writ of *habeas corpus*. No state court is bound to regard the decisions of a federal district court as a precedent to be followed. The federal district courts and the federal court of appeals in any one circuit, oddly enough, are not bound by the decisions made in other circuits. If a state court disregards federal law in the prosecution of a case, the defendant may obtain the aid of the federal courts, which are empowered to dictate the state court's behavior or reverse its decisions. Federal intervention may also occur if the defendant is a federal officer or a foreign official. Whenever state courts have declared a federal law unconstitutional, the Supreme Court has reacted quickly by reviewing the case and, usually, by striking down the state court's decision.

In the early 1970s the federal court system was being swamped with petitions by defendants for their cases to be heard, largely because of the liberalization of petition requirements in the federal courts. Because states that have strong appeals systems do not have nearly so many cases reaching the federal courts, the federal courts have urged the states to adopt specific appeals measures.

### Court Unification

The independence of each court had led to its maintenance of absolute control over hours, scheduling, and other aspects of administration, and along with autonomy goes the absence of fixed responsibility for court management. The specific results are inept, quixotic, or archaic methods of administration in some courts. The generalized results include systematic and structural disorganization of entire court systems.

It is true that there is a hierarchy in a state court system (or in any court system). Classically, however, the hierarchy is based on jurisdiction and does not extend to administration. No one is in charge; there is no administrative authority independent of the individual judge; there is a lack of centralization. Even the courts within a county may have no coordinated administration.

The consequent disorganization is experienced in many ways. The National Crime Commission refers to the confusion and illegal practices exemplified by one state. Only three of more than two hundred city courts had jurisdiction to imprison offenders; the rest were limited to levying fines. Yet a study of ninety-nine city court judges showed that forty-eight of them believed that they had the power to imprison violators of city ordinances. In another instance a practicing attorney was also a city judge, a two-hat role that is unethical and in this instance illegal. Communication of precedent-setting decisions is not expedited by a fragmented court system. In one state a number of justices of the peace were unaware of changes made in their power to apply contempt rulings, and two-thirds apparently continued to neglect to inform defendants of their right to be silent.[4] A Texas study indicated that a goodly percentage of judges handling juvenile cases were unaware of the revolutionary

Supreme Court decision *In re Gault* [387 U.S. 1 (1967)] two years after the decision.[5]

Lower courts frequently lack the wherewithal to support the probation officers, social workers, and clinical psychologists that enable larger and higher courts to mitigate the charge of arbitrariness in judical decisions. A city court, a county court, and a district court, all may have the jurisdiction to handle a given offense such as petty larceny. The handling of the case and all too often its outcome is likely to be affected by the differences in the various courts' administrations. They may have different rules, policies, traditions. In one court the docket may be so overloaded that the case would never reach the trial state; in another court the case could be tried without great delay, and in the third court the judge might have an excess of time. The support personnel (probation officers, social workers, etc.) will exist in various quantity and quality depending on the court. The arresting police officer or the prosecutor may select the court to deliberately govern the outcome of the case, as of course may the defense. Delayed justice and a resultant overabundance of guilty pleas occur.

The public, of course, pays for this wasteful disorganization, just as it pays for an appeal system that is not only inefficient but frequently overly time-consuming and thus unfair to the innocent defendant. The entire system is also unfair to police, witnesses, and jurors, who also must give up their valuable time and submit to a needlessly unpleasant experience.

The framework necessary for good administration is a court system within each state that is unified administratively. Generally, unification requires more than administrative decisions; it requires change at the policy-making level. Legislatures have to pass laws, constitutions have to be changed. State constitutions frequently last a hundred years, and major changes in the state courts are seldom made between times. It is surprising, therefore, to find that a number of states have made great strides toward unification. Model constitutional provisions have been developed by the National Municipal League and also by the American Bar Association's affiliated American Judicature Society. Most important is *The Model State Judicial Article*, approved by the American Bar Association in 1962 and revised in 1973. Furthermore, the National Advisory Commission on Criminal Justice Standards and Goals developed model standards in 1973.[6]

Typical of the unification that has taken place is the consolidation of courts at the same level and the strengthening of the states' hierarchies. Frequently the venerable county court units are superceded by district trial courts encompassing several counties. Courts that have been sources of town or city income (and it is not uncommon for cities to regard courts as sources of income) are transformed by having the fines and fees paid to the state. Courts that could not afford a probation officer or that did not have access to a competent prosecution office find their problems alleviated by districting. Many other benefits occur.

The earliest unified court system within the states occurred in 1947, when the people of New Jersey, over the local bar association's objections, approved a new state constitution. It established a supreme court, a superior court, county courts, and courts of limited jurisdiction. Justice of the peace courts were abolished, as were a few others. The supreme court was given a free hand to administer and make rules governing the other courts of the state. It is noteworthy that most states—like New Jersey—have given some policy-making power to the courts that would formerly have belonged to the legislative branch.

## DISCUSSION QUESTIONS

1. What examples of court lag can be discerned in the structure of the courts?
2. How are the federal court system and the state court system different?
3. Discuss ideal court structure for federal and state systems. How far are present courts from this ideal?
4. Compare and contrast the military justice system with the federal and state systems. What might be the advantages of the military model? The disadvantages? Should military and civilian models be the same?
5. What is the structure of the courts in your state? How could the state system be improved?

## NOTES

1. United States Constitution, Article III, section 2.
2. Children's Bureau, *Juvenile Court Statistics, 1966*, Statistical Series 90 (Washington, D.C.: Government Printing Office, 1967).
3. These cases are among those identified as part of the "criminal law revolution" of the 1960s and include such major cases as Kent v. U.S. 383 U.S. 541 (1966); In re Gault 387 U.S. 1 (1967); and In the Matter of Winship 90 S.C.T. 268 (1970).
4. President's Commission on Law Enforcement and Administration of Justice, *Task Force Report: The Courts* (Washington, D.C.: Government Printing Office, 1967), p. 82.
5. Sarah Holden, "A Pre-Post Analysis of the Effect of *Gault* on the Juvenile Court of Harris County, Texas: The Juvenile Probation of Harris County," unpublished master's thesis, Sam Houston State University, Huntsville, Texas, 1969.
6. National Advisory Commission on Criminal Justice Standards and Goals, *Courts* (Washington, D.C.: Government Printing Office, 1973), Standard 8.1, pp. 132–136.

# 13: Functions of The Courts

*PRETRIAL • TRIAL • SENTENCING • POSTCONVICTION*

PURPOSE: *TO DESCRIBE THE FUNCTIONS OF THE COURT IN THE CRIMINAL JUSTICE PROCESS FROM THE COURT'S POINT OF VIEW.*

COURT function refers to the judicial work the courts do, and it is the procedure peculiar to the courts that gives them their life, their flavor. The basic process that is described here is fairly similar throughout the states, the variations being responses to statutory law and to location, rural or urban.

The basic process is reductionary, that is, beginning with a large number and ending with a few. It begins with the huge number of people temporarily detained by the police, progresses through the much smaller number of those who have an initial appearance before a magistrate and those tried for misdemeanors, through the much smaller number who, charged with a felony, have a preliminary hearing, through the still smaller number who pass through arraignment and pretrial motions and reach trial, to the still smaller number who are sentenced and who are not granted appeal or other postconviction remedies. Illustration 13.1 presents a flow chart of the various court functions. It also provides the ideal time-lapse maximums formulated by the National Advisory Commission on Criminal Justice Standards and Goals (1973). Each of the functions is discussed in this chapter.

The flow chart illustrates something else that is important: the way the courts are related to the rest of the criminal justice system by their functions. The criminal justice process follows its well-defined path, but the court's role begins to blend with and shift to other segments of the criminal justice system at either end. The role of prosecution is intricately interwoven with the rest of the court procedure. The courts are dependent on the police at one end of the process and on corrections at the other end,

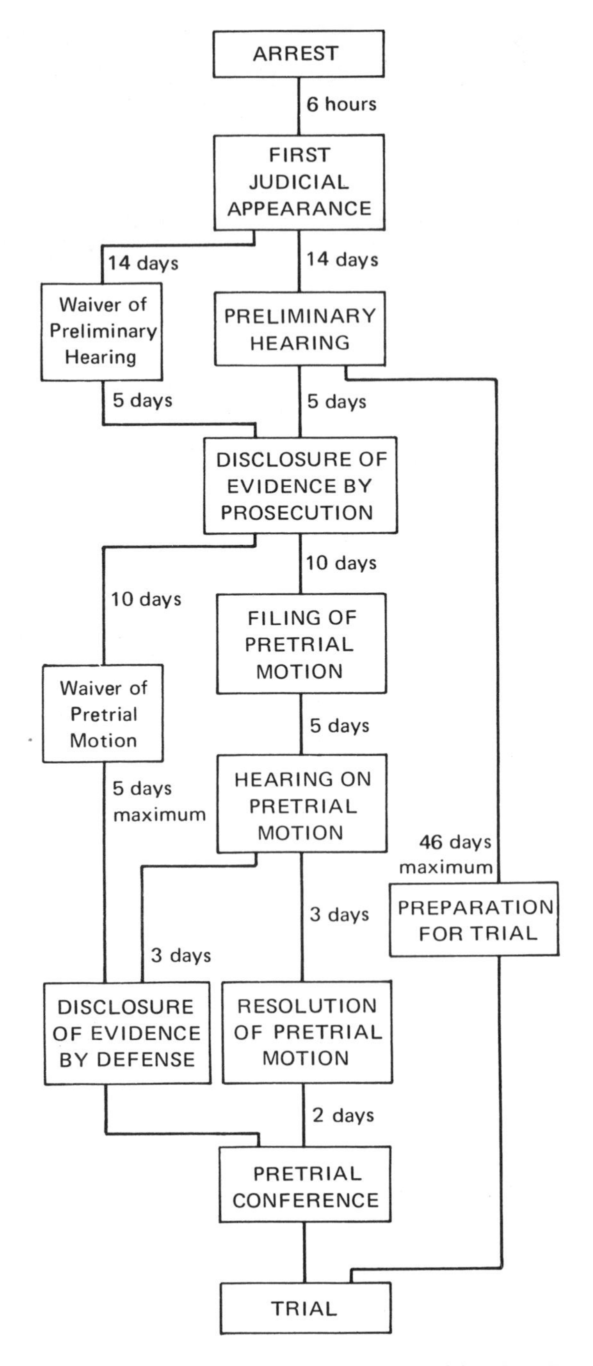

**Illustration 13.1** FELONY CASE TIME SCHEDULE

The flow chart depicts the recommended time limits for processing a felony case.

Source: National Advisory Commission on Criminal Justice Standards and Goals, *Courts* (Washington, D.C.: Government Printing Office, 1973), pp. xx–xxi.

but because they are vested with decision-making authority and responsibility, the courts are pivotal in the criminal justice process.

## PRETRIAL

A number of well-specified court functions either culminate in a trial or the release of the accused. The National Advisory Commission on Criminal Justice Standards and Goals (1973) states that the time lapse from arrest to trial generally should not be more than 60 days in felony cases and not more than 30 days in misdemeanor cases.[1] Florida's highly regarded 1973 speedy-trial law sets a time-lapse maximum of 180 days in felony cases and 90 days in misdemeanors. The order of functions presented here varies slightly from state to state; Illustration 13.2 shows the order in one state by way of example.

Courts indirectly influence police behavior by defining what is permissible in court as evidence against a defendant (although it is to be noted that the police may be guided by statutory codes of evidence also) and by the courts' insistence that due process be observed in developing cases before adjudication. The courts are bound to these considerations by constitutional and statutory law. Particularly in the 1960s, the Supreme Court, using various Bill of Rights amendments in conjunction with the due process clause of the Fourteenth Amendment, arrived at a number of decisions that seem to be directly intended to control the methods of the police.[2] The Court, therefore, was accused of functioning as a police administrator, a role that it could not have wanted or handled. Ranging from prearrest investigations through the initial appearance of the defendant before a magistrate, the criminal justice air echoes with such phrases as "Miranda Warning," and "Exclusionary Rule," referring to these famous decisions. The emphasis in these decisions has been on safe-guarding the rights of the suspect.

### Warrants and Presentment

The decision to issue a warrant is a judicial decision, although in practice this fact is not always manifest. Police searches are common; but as they usually are "reasonable" limited searches of persons or automobiles, or are preceded by arrest, or are consented to by the person who is searched, the use of a search warrant is infrequent. The Constitution conveys the idea that search warrants are generally required, but they are not. A *search warrant* is a written demand by a magistrate that a peace officer search the premises (which are described) of a person (who is named) for the goods (which are listed). The reason for the search must be specified, and it must be based on probable cause, a reasonable belief by the magistrate that criminal evidence can be found. A formal affadavit, the *complaint*, must be signed and sworn to by the person who has the information leading to the request for the warrant. The search warrant may be combined with an *arrest warrant*. To protect the identity of informers the person with the necessary information for the warrant may be called a

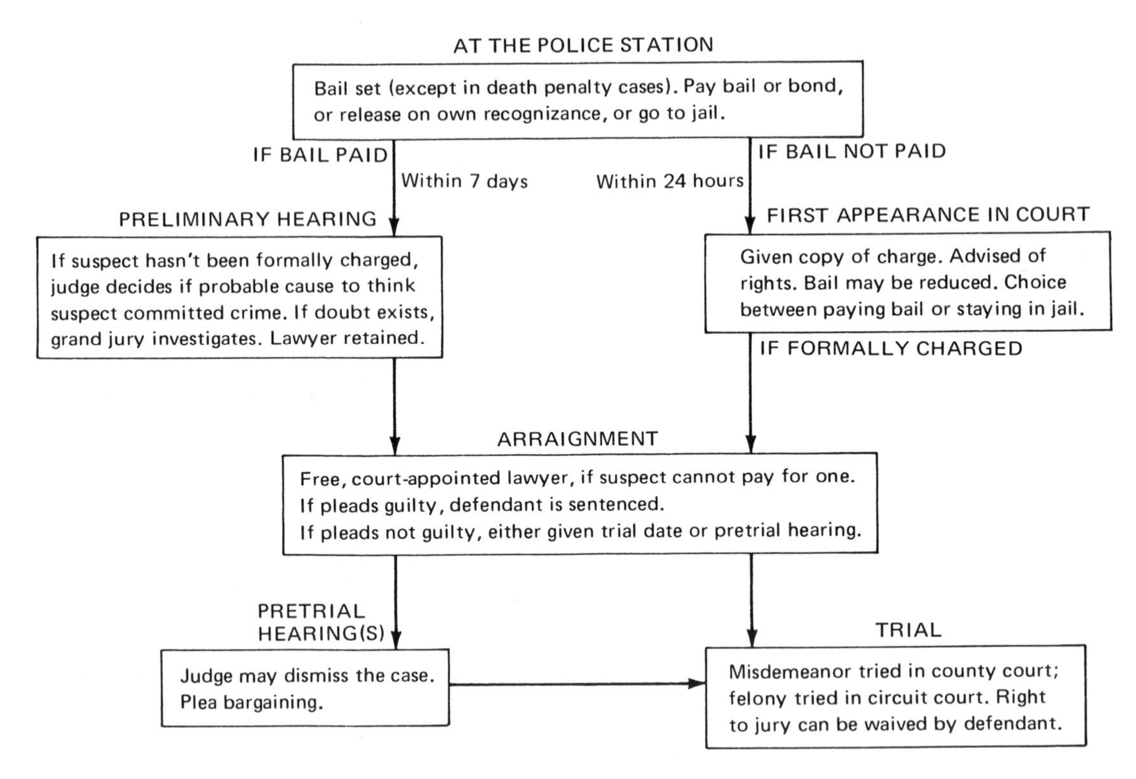


**Illustration 13.2** THE PATH TO TRIAL IN FLORIDA
Source: Adapted from chart prepared by the League of Women Voters of Florida, 1973.

"credible person" and the warrant sworn to by the police officer.

Once a complaint charging the suspect with a violation of criminal law has been signed by an officer or a complaining witness (depending on the nature of the alleged offense), an arrest warrant is usually issued by a magistrate. The purpose of the arrest warrant is to provide official sanction for arresting the alleged offender. The warrant declares that, in the name of the state, any person with official authority to do so is to place a named person in custody and to accompany that individual to court to answer to the charge specified. The arrest date is noted on the back of the form, and it is then returned to the magistrate as a permanent record of the arrest.

One other kind of warrant needs mentioning. A *bench warrant*, also called a *capias*, is an order for someone to be brought into custody although that person is not being arrested for committing a crime. For example, a person previously arrested, perhaps out on bail, or a witness may be brought before a court on a *capias*.

The arresting police officer, the desk sergeant, and the prosecutor all possess considerable discretion to let a detained person go without bringing him before a magistrate. This "judicial" authority is sometimes exercised with an accompanying stern warning.

At the federal level and in most states, the initial appearance before the magistrate is called "presentment." In all states an initial appearance is required if a person is to be detained longer. The time lapse between arrest and initial appearance is variable, but it may be unconscionably long. The reasons for delay include the desire of detectives to interrogate the suspect, an arrest occurring on Sunday or a holiday, and the sheer numbers of people being processed by the police. The maximum delay recommended by the National Crime Commission (1967) is one day.[3]

At the initial appearance the magistrate establishes the defendant's identity and informs him or her of the charge(s) and of his or her constitutional rights. If the defendant is indigent, a defense lawyer is in many states appointed at this time. (In at least one state, a defendant able to post bail is declared not to be indigent.) If the defendant is charged with a felony, he or she is notified of the right to a preliminary hearing. If the arrest was made without a warrant, the complaint and the warrant may be handled at this time. Usually, the prosecutor or an assistant prosecutor is present, if the prosecutor's office is large enough to permit it, and the decision whether to proceed with the prosecution may be made. If the offense is a petty misdemeanor, it is usually disposed (that is, the case is concluded, ended) at the initial appearance. In a more serious misdemeanor case, or a case with a plea of not guilty, or a felony case in which the defendant waives the right to a preliminary hearing, an information may be filed. In some places the case may go to a grand jury instead of a preliminary hearing. One of the magistrate's most important functions is the setting of bail.

### Bail

*Bail* is a term for the assurance sought by the court that the accused not being held in jail will appear for trial. It is a word that is equated with a sum of money. The magistrate's court holds the bail money (or a bond in lieu of money) until the accused appears for trial, at which time the bail money (or bond) is returned. The magistrate generally decides the amount of bail by using a table or schedule listing various amounts for various offenses, sometimes fixed by statute. In some instances, the police may determine proper bail at the police station. Bail may be denied a defendant who is likely not to appear in court if not detained. It is often denied to murder suspects.

A *bail bond* is a document signed by the defendant and by others on his or her behalf providing a guarantee to appear in court for trial. Those who "go his bond" are called the "sureties," and they are supposed to show that they have property as great or greater in value than the bail. If the accused cannot raise the bail or get a friend to go his or her bond, it may be possible to get a bond from a *bail bondsman* or *bondsman,* a person who is in the business of acting as a surety in return for a fee, generally between 10 and 20 percent of the amount of bail. The bondsman frequently is granted by law unusual powers to take into custody a defendant who has "jumped bail," that is, has not appeared in court for trial. The hold bondsmen may have over clients and the power they have to bring in nonpaying clients lead to abuses of this service. Clients have been known to commit crimes to get money for the bondsman! Bondsmen are poorly regulated in many states and may use a piece of property of small value as collateral for large amounts of bail set for several defendants. On the other hand, some courts do not always demand that bondsmen make good a bond when a defendant fails to appear in court.

If a person has bail at $500.00 and is required to pay $50.00 to obtain a bail bond but does not have the $50.00, he or she may be left in jail until the trial. The trial may be months away, and the person may be innocent. Most people who must pay $50.00 to obtain a bond are unable to do so.

Studies have shown that many people unable to make bail would have appeared for trial had they been released. In one project during the 1960s, case workers obtained brief information from jailed defendants and had the court release certain categories on their own recognizance, their word that they would appear in court. (Release on own recognizance is often abbreviated ROR.) The project was successful and is being emulated in many areas of the country. But because of the misgivings of the judiciary, pressures from the public, and perhaps the influence of bail bondsmen, ROR programs have not been universally accepted. Indeed, the success rate of ROR varies over time and in different locales and is highly dependent on the category of criminal offense involved. Nonetheless it has been seriously proposed that the money bail system be eliminated altogether.

Bail set extremely high to keep dangerous offenders locked up and unable to commit crimes while awaiting trial is called *preventive bail.* Well-to-do burglars and criminals with connections to organized crime, however, simply buy their way out. It is frequently difficult to properly define *dangerous offender*, and preventive bail is technically unconstitutional. *Preventive detention* is a term sometimes used instead of preventive bail, but it is the broader term and does not necessarily have anything to do with bail.

The Eighth Amendment of the Constitution states "Excessive bail shall not be required, nor excessive fines imposed, nor cruel and unusual punishment inflicted." Yet thousands of poor people, some of them innocent, are in foul, dangerous jails, with no consideration given to their families' needs or their job requirements, their trials weeks and months away, locked up because they cannot buy their freedom. This condition exists even though it has been shown that many of them would not commit another crime and would appear for trial if they were to sign their own bonds and be released. The direct cost to the taxpayers for maintaining this many people in jail is enormous; the indirect cost to society in terms of human suffering and the criminalization of accused persons are far more enormous. Not only could release on recognizance alleviate this problem; a speed-up of the trial process would do away with many abuses.

The first opportunity to secure release from custody may come at the initial appearance when bail is set. If bail has been set by the police immediately following arrest, as is possible in some states, the magistrate may reduce bail. Or if the bail is excessive the accused may be able to have it reduced through a *habeas corpus* action, although most accused persons are ignorant of this fact, do not know the procedures, and cannot afford a lawyer to pursue this action. Bail is reset at the preliminary hearing and at the arraignment. A person appealing conviction may secure release on an appeal bond.

### Disposition of Misdemeanors

Cases of petty offenses or misdemeanors are usually settled at the initial appearance of the accused before the magistrate. This is the "trial" that most people have experienced. Serious misdemeanors, higher misdemeanor cases, are also settled in the magistrate's court, although they may not be disposed at the initial appearance. The lower court may have the power to hear cases in which the fine does not exceed $200 or some other amount; it may have jurisdiction that overlaps with higher courts; petty offenses particularly may be handled by specialized courts in cities, such as traffic courts.

The incidence of misdemeanor cases is unknown. Studies of certain courts are revealing. In one year's time three judges in Atlanta disposed of more than 70,000 cases. In one year's time, the District of Columbia Court of General Sessions had four judges to process 1,500 felony cases, to hear and determine 7,500 serious misdemeanor cases, 38,000 petty misdemeanors, and about 38,000 traffic violation cases.

Traffic violations are sometimes considered misdemeanors. Nationally, the number is in the millions per year. It is estimated that prosecutors dismiss about 5 percent, as many as 85 percent plead guilty, as many as 25 percent of those tried will be acquitted, and more than 75 percent of those convicted (including those who plead guilty and those who are tried) will be fined, placed on probation, or released.[4]

A person charged with a misdemeanor who can afford a defense attorney tends to be released on bond to prepare for trial at a later date or to engage in plea bargaining. However, the overwhelming majority are without legal representation, and when asked how they plead, reply "guilty." Some of them are aware that they may be returned to jail to await a later trial date if they plead otherwise. Rules of evidence in misdemeanor trials are sometimes ignored; there is seldom a court reporter present; the "due process" safeguards present at felony trials are, at best, strained. The emphasis in many of these lower courts, particularly those in the cities, is on speed. Trials typically last from five to fifteen minutes and, despite complexities, are unlikely to exceed an hour. The defendant is seldom allowed to talk at any length and may not be allowed to offer any defense. Trial records are incomplete or nonexistent.

Jail sentences of several months are common in misdemeanor cases. Probation services and presentence investigations are rare. Fines are the usual result. If a fine cannot be paid, the "$30 or 30 days" rule was once applied, but a court ruling ended this practice. Sentencing is based on the charge and the defendant's appearance and what little of his or her manner the judge may ascertain. Trial and sentencing are affected by the quality of personnel and a multitude of administrative problems, not the least of which is the volume of cases a relatively few judges must process.

### Preliminary Hearing, Information, Return of Grand Jury Indictment

Following the initial appearance, a felony case is typically scheduled for a *preliminary hearing,* also called *examining trial* and *preliminary examination.* The purpose of the preliminary hearing is to protect the accused from an unjustified prosecution. The prosecutor must produce the evidence to enable the magistrate before whom the hearing is held to decide whether there is probable cause for believing that a felony was committed by the accused. Proof of guilt is not necessary. In all but a few cases the defendant is "bound over" by the magistrate for trial before a court of general jurisdiction.

In many jurisdictions not all defendants in felony cases are given a preliminary hearing. Defendants frequently waive it and in jurisdictions in which the grand jury procedure is used, a preliminary hearing may or may not be used. If the preliminary hearing has been waived, an information is usually prepared, often by the prosecutor. An information is like an indictment in that it is a formal charge. Defendants who have lawyers often want preliminary hearings, because these hearings allow defense attorneys to "discover" the state's case against the defendant. (The adversary system in criminal cases is marked by an absence of formal means for the defense to discover the prosecution's case against the defendant.)

The time between presentment and preliminary hearing, information or indictment is ideally from three to seven days. In actuality weeks and even months may elapse.

### Arraignment

The day the information is filed the defendant is generally arraigned, but several days may elapse between an indictment and arraignment. Any formal appearance before a magistrate before a trial is loosely referred to as an *arraignment.* The better usage is the appearance of the defendant in a felony case before a magistrate who takes the defendant's plea. Arraignments are plea sessions. The arraignment takes place in the court in which the case would be tried. This means that if the magistrate processing the case has a lower court jurisdiction, as is nearly always true, the defendant appears before a different magistrate. Counsel must be present, and counsel will be appointed in indigent cases at this time if the appointment has not been made earlier. The plea may be guilty, not guilty, or in some states, *nolo contendere,* a Latin phrase meaning "no contest." There is no plea of innocent. Other pleas such as former jeopardy and not guilty by reason of insanity are permitted in some states. Also, at the arraignment the formal charge is read to the defendant.

For the plea of guilty to be accepted by the court, the judge is required by law to endeavor to determine that the plea is voluntary, that is is made with full awareness of its implications, and that it is accurate. The guilty plea is usually equated with a verdict of guilty, although the judge does follow certain guidelines before accepting a guilty plea. The plea is entered on the back of the information or indictment form, and the defendant is either sentenced or a date is set for the sentencing. A plea of *nolo contendere* is treated the same as a guilty plea by the court. The only benefit that accrues from it is that certain civil penalities that accompany a guilty plea may not be attached. A plea of not guilty places the burden on the state to prove beyond a reasonable doubt that the defendant is guilty. The plea is entered on the back of the information or the indictment form, and a trial date is set. Federal and state law require a "speedy trial," but unless "speedy" is specifically defined this law is flouted.

Nearly all the convictions obtained in felony cases in many jurisdictions result from guilty pleas; in roughly 70 to 80 percent of the felony cases that reach this point the plea is guilty. These fantastic figures reflect the pervasiveness of plea bargaining. Although it has been denied that judges are a part of the plea bargaining process, they are indirectly involved at the very least because communications regarding the bargain must be good if the bargain is to be kept. The National Advisory Commission (1973) would have the courts abandon plea bargaining.

**Pretrial Motions**

The court's functions are referred to as the judicial process. The centerpiece of the judicial process is the trial.

If the plea has been not guilty, much time will be spent in preparation for trial. The National Crime Commission recommends that the maximum amount of time be nine weeks, but the time that frequently elapses is measured in months, sometimes in years. Long delays are frequently sought by defendants who would rather spend a year in jail than five or more years in prison; the more time that elapses between the occurrence of the crime and the trial, the more likely there is to be a dismissal or acquittal because witnesses and evidence have faded or disappeared. Long delays are not always desired: In 1972, the inmates of the Washington, D.C., jail seized a number of hostages, including the Director of Corrections, and released them only after being promised immediate court hearings.

The defense counsel seeks to win the case, or to at least delay the trial, by pretrial motions. Plea bargaining may be going on during delays. The National Crime Commission recommends ten days be allowed for filing motions with the court, up to seven days before a court hearing is held on the plea motions, and up to twenty-one days before the court makes its decisions whether to sustain the heard motions. The actual times in which these steps take place, of course, are frequently much longer.

Even before the plea is entered the defense counsel will generally raise an objection to the sufficiency of the indictment or information. Objections based on the statute of limitations, double jeopardy, and the improper composition or irregular procedures of the grand jury may be made before the plea is to be entered. Each of these is a motion to dismiss.

Following the plea, a request for a change of venue may be made. Change in venue is usually requested if it is felt the emotions of citizens in the locale where the offense occurred might prejudice the case against the defendant. When there are codefendants, a request may be made for separate trials. These two motions are made in only a small percentage of the cases.

Motions requesting information that the state has against the defendant are more common. Called a *motion for a bill of particulars,* it is a chief means of "discovery." Motions to suppress evidence because it has been illegally obtained result in a high dismissal rate, particularly in cases involving narcotics. A motion for continuance may be granted for a number of reasons and results in a postponement of the trial. Motions for continuance may be made by the defense simply to improve the odds for winning the case by delay, but in itself this reason is not grounds for sustaining the motion.

## *TRIAL*

The trials, the sentencing, perhaps some of the pretrial motions, and the system of appeals are what people tend to associate with the word *court.* Final responsibility for the way a person is treated by the criminal justice system classically depends on the judges' decisions at these levels.

The percentage of criminal cases that reach the trial stage is small, but the total number of trials each year is large, and trials require much of the courts' time, civil cases requiring much more than criminal cases. Major factors distinguishing criminal trials from civil trials include the presumption of innocence, the requirement of proof of guilty beyond a reasonable doubt, the right of the defendant not to testify, the exclusion of evidence obtained in an illegal manner, and the frequent use of the defendant's admissions. The case is always the *state* versus the *defendant.* The rate of acquittal in felony cases in large cities is likely to be less than one third regardless of whether the trial was by jury (jury trial) or judge (bench trial).

Felony cases and often serious misdemeanor cases will be tried by jury unless the defendant waives the jury, as is done in a large number of cases. In capital cases, statutory law may require a jury.

### Evidence

Trial procedure is largely governed by rules of evidence, some of which are defined by state law and some by court-made law. *Law of evidence* has its complexities and is offered as a separate course in law schools. The objective of the rules of evidence is to enable the adversary system to reveal the truth in a case. *Evidence* is defined as the legal proofs presented through records, witnesses, objects, or any other vehicle, intended to sway the beliefs of judge or jurors toward the prosecutor's side of the case or toward the defendant's side. *Real evidence* is the term for concrete objects; *testimony* is the term for the statements of sworn witnesses; *direct evidence* is evidence observed at first hand; *circumstantial evidence* refers to a web of facts that form a tendency toward accepting or refuting a point. The court will not accept anything as evidence unless it is relevant, material, and competent, and the adversaries frequently raise objections for the court to sustain regarding material offered as evidence.

The order in which evidence is presented during a trial differs from state to state but always follows a legally established procedure. For example, once the jury is selected, the prosecution makes an opening statement, stating what the case is about. The defense may follow with a statement or make its statement later in the trial. Typically, the prosecution follows its opening statement with a presentation of witnesses for the state, and the defense follows its statement with a presentation of witness for the defense. The defense may argue for various motions following the prosecution's presentation. In rebuttal to the defense the state may counter with another presentation of witnesses, and the defense in turn may counter the state with another presentation of witnesses. The state and the defense then present their final arguments before the jury.

Privileged communications and confidentiality are aspects of evidence that are often confused with one another by the public. *Privileged communications* are communications that the person who is the receiver cannot be legally made to divulge. *Confidentiality* has no legal protection in a court of law. For example, a social worker may be legally and ethically bound by the principle of confidentiality to keep private communications obtained from a client, but these communications are not privileged by law, and a court could command the social worker to tell what he or she heard. Husbands and wives cannot testify against one another (unless the case is a family court matter) because of the privileged communication laws of most states.

### Witnesses

Persons who are ordered or subpoenaed by a court to appear as witnesses for the state or volunteer to do so are "examined" by the prosecutor and then cross-examined by the defense attorney. The witnesses, like the defendant, are guaranteed constitutional rights during the trial. Witnesses called by the defense may be cross-examined by the prosecutor. The examination is a question-and-answer method of eliciting information. The cross-examination is a question-and-answer method for challenging the veracity of the witnesses' accounts. Leading questions ("Have you stopped beating your wife?") and other abrasive techniques are allowed in conducting cross-examinations, and they make the cross-examination a psychological tool for trying (ostensibly) to get at the truth. Witnesses may be impeached, that is, their testimony discredited by cross-examination. They may also be impeached by showing through other witnesses that the testimony was wrong.

Witnesses are generally limited by a rule of evidence to testifying to what they have observed. Lay witnesses (*lay* means anybody not an expert) can express opinions supported by factual material that is recognized as being in the realm of common experience. An opinion that the defendant was sleeping, for example, may be supported by information that he was lying down at night, snoring, after having fought a fire all day. Expert witnesses may give opinions and support them without having observed the defendant at the time of the criminal action. Police officers who are crime lab technicians or ballistics experts or professional investigators may act as expert witnesses. Any person who can be shown to have relevant expertise may act as an expert witness. Psychiatrists who try to define the mental state of defendants, particularly at the time of their criminal behavior, have become fairly common expert witnesses, although controversy about legal insanity rages in the criminal justice field.

Hearsay evidence is information that witnesses have obtained at second-hand. It is not acceptable as evidence because there is no opportunity for determining the veracity of the information through cross-examination. Exceptions to the rule against hearsay evidence includes *res gestae*, "things done," which means that things said that are closely tied to an account of the event are allowed as evidence. For example, an investigation of a homicide in which the victim's wife at the scene of the crime sobs, "My son didn't mean to do it," would result in her words being included in the testimony. Admissions against the interest of a defendant may be accepted also; for example, the above mentioned son may say, "I was there when the murder took place." A confession is also permitted; for example, "Yes, I hit him and his head struck the corner of the table and he died." The judge, however, attempts to ascertain the circumstances surrounding the confession before allowing it to be admitted as evidence. The written confession is desired by the prosecution because, under the rules of evidence, the defendant cannot be required to testify, the Constitution providing protection against demands for self-incrimination.

### Closing the Trial

At the close of the evidence the judge in a jury trial gives written instructions to the jury regarding the law as it applies to the facts in a case. The jury is to decide what the facts may truly be. The arguments by the prosecution and defense counsel to the jury follow. The procedure is prescribed by law and varies from state to state.

The judge then charges the jury to consider the merits of the case and return a just verdict on the written forms supplied. The foreman or forewoman is to sign the verdict the jurors agree on and return it to the judge. The jury is isolated (*sequestered* is the word commonly used) from other people and put in the custody of the bailiff to deliberate (that is, discuss the case) and vote on a verdict of guilty or not guilty. In some states the jury must decide on the type of homicide of which the defendant is guilty, and it may have to decide what a sentence is to be. In some trials the jury vote need not be unanimous for a conviction to be obtained. In other instances, if all the jurors do not finally vote the same way, then the jury may be called a *hung jury*, and the trial will be declared a mistrial. The defendant will have to be tried again with a new jury, unless the prosecutor elects not to prosecute. The court then renders the official judgement as to guilt based on the verdict. Sentence is usually imposed by the judge at a later date, but not long after the verdict or the plea of guilty. If the defendant has been convicted (found guilty), the conviction may be appealed.

## *SENTENCING*

A *sentence* is an official judgment declaring the penalty in an individual case in which there has been a conviction for a criminal offense. The legislature in some states fixes only the maximum penalty, allowing the judge to sentence the defendant for any amount of time less than or equal to the maximum. In some states maximum and minimums are established for each offense. The judge is then restricted to sentencing between the minimum amount and the maximum amount.

Offenders who repeat an offense or one similar to it may receive a more severe sentence if the state has provided *enhancement* or *habitual criminal statutes.* The more severe sentence is called an *enhanced sentence.* The repeater is usually eager to engage in plea bargaining for the sake of getting a reduced sentence. A *fixed* or *definite sentence* is one in which the years it is to be in effect are specified. An *indeterminate sentence* specifies a range of years, for example, one to twenty. A high minimum can prevent early parole, and indeterminate sentences tend to result in confinement for the maximum figure, although this was not anticipated by the proponents of indeterminate sentences. A *concurrent sentence* is one in which a defendant convicted for more than one offense during the same trial is sentenced for each offense but serves the sentences for each offense simultaneously. The alternative is *consecutive*; the defendant serves the sentences one after the other.

### Objectives of Sentencing

The general function of the court is to determine whether the accused has broken the law and, if so, to decide what should be done to or for the convicted person. Sentencing objectives are not clearly settled, either in the general sense or in individual cases. These objectives include revenge, incapacition, general deterrence and individual deterrence, and rehabilitation. Rehabilitation goals may be constructed either to include or to exclude punishment. It is clear, however, that the circumstances surrounding cases in which the offense is the same may differ so markedly that justice requires individualized sentences. By smoking cigarettes in secret behind a haystack, two boys might set the haystack on fire in a game of "I dare you." A man might burn down an apartment building to try to collect insurance money. A woman might burn a house to get rid of her husband. The boys, the man, and the woman may be found guilty of arson, but to sentence all parties who set fire to people's property to life imprisonment for arson would be unconscionable. Although carefully composed and ordered statutes can eliminate much of the present need for sentencing discretion, discretion cannot be eliminated completely if sentencing is to be fair.

### Sentence Hearing Factors

In a sentence hearing following conviction, a judge typically pronounces that an individual shall be incarcerated for a given amount of time (or range of time), or be placed on probation, or be sentenced to imprisonment but have the sentence suspended. The factors that go into the decision include the legal factors, of course; but there are many more, some of which may be determined by presentence investigation reports. Important factors have been shown to include the nature of the offense, the number of offenses for which the person was tried, and the previous criminal record. Other factors include whether the defendant pleaded guilty or was found guilty by verdict, whether he or she was represented by a defense attorney, and whether sentencing alternatives were available and known to the judge. Factors such as the defendant's race, youthfulness, sex, and social status are closely linked to the prejudices of the judge.

These last factors are hotly argued as the source of unfair individualized sentencing, called *sentencing disparity*. There is no question that sentencing disparities occur, for sentencing is a difficult decision-making process that is highly subjective, and judges are human and, therefore, prone to error according to their biases. Carefully done studies would seem to indicate that there is less sentencing disparity in felony cases than many social critics believe.[5] If the sentence itself, as distinguished from the verdict, could be appealed (and in most states it cannot be), it is thought that sentencing would become more certain of being fair. Probably appellate review of sentences will become standard procedure for all the states in years to come. Some states now have automatic review of death and life sentences. Judges' conferences on sentencing and regular visits by judges to correctional facilities have already become common.

### Alternatives to Sentencing

Judges are often in a quandry when they must pass sentence, for in many instances their only choices are to lock up the convicted person or, in essence, to let him or her go. Neither choice may be desirable. In some places, a growing number of sentencing alternatives are available to the judge, for example, work-release programs, halfway houses, and schools for drunk drivers.

Diversion programs have been developed with the court's help. For example, rather than incarcerate a youth for assaulting a relative, he or she may be allowed or directed to begin therapy with a psychiatrist. The National Advisory Commission on Criminal Justice Standards and Goals (1973) states that in appropriate cases offenders should be diverted into noncriminal justice programs before formal trial or conviction. Diversion programs are informal, usually, and there is generally no provision for them in statutory law. This fact gives the court discretion to make unusual demands of offenders. In cases in which on-going programs are established, however, the diversion is apt to take place before the offender becomes a court's responsibility. Police or juvenile probation officers may refer juveniles picked up for minor offenses to youth service bureaus instead of processing them through the courts. Police may take a public drunk directly to a detoxification center instead of booking him. An office of prosecution may have a fraud division that frequently allows restitution in lieu of seeking imprisonment through the courts. There are many other programs; they are local, however, and not available in every jurisdiction.

## *POSTCONVICTION*

### Appeal

Defendants who wish to do so may ask a higher court to overturn their convictions. They can do this through the right to appeal (although it is not a right guaranteed by the Constitution) and through the right to writs of *certiorari* and *habeas corpus*. An *appeal* is a limited review of a case; that is, the appellate court restricts itself to examining the record of the trial and does not hear testimony on matters of fact. If a convicted offender wants to appeal and cannot afford to pay for a transcript of the trial proceedings, or for counsel, they will be provided free by the court. In some states, the prosecution has a limited right to appeal some lower court decisions that favored the defendant. Appeals within the states are time consuming; six months to two years may elapse before they are heard.

An appeal may result in the appellate court's agreeing with the trial court's decision in the case, in a reversal of the decision (that is, finding not guilty a defendant whom the lower court had found guilty), or in a remand of the case back to the trial court for a new trial based on guidelines set by the appellate court. Because of the expense and difficulties associated with a new trial, it may not be held and the once convicted offender is then released. Decisions of appellate courts are frequently expressed in what is called an *opinion*. The best known of these opinions and dissenting opinions come from the Supreme Court justices and are scholarly works of some literary merit.

### Appellate Review

As commonly used, the phrase *appellate review* is a broader term than appeal. An attempt is being made to get the states to adopt a unified review proceeding that would grant every convicted offender the opportunity to obtain one comprehensive judical review of the conviction and sentence by a court other than the court of trial. The review would extend to all matters of legality and proceedings leading to the conviction and the legality and appropriateness of the sentence. It would also extend to errors not apparent in the trial record that might otherwise be used in efforts other than appeal to overturn a conviction or change a sentence. For example, if a juror later testified to something that a judge said "off the record" during a trial and the judge's comments were contrary to due process of law, a conviction could be overturned. The courts are not now geared to handle such a unified review proceeding, but it is believed to be worth the effort it would take to implement it. (It works in England.) It would streamline a creaky, bureaucratic system and probably reduce procedural time and enhance justice. In special circumstances a second review could be granted.

The National Advisory Commission on Criminal Justice Standards and Goals (1973) worked out details for a proposed unified review procedure. It declared that the dispositional time in a reviewing court should range from sixty days after sentence for insubstantial issues to ninety days in complicated cases. Initial action should begin within thirty days following the sentencing.[6]

### Other Postconviction Remedies

The most famous of the other remedies is the *writ of habeas corpus*, "you have the body." It is a court order demanding that a person who is restraining the body produce it in court and explain why the body should continue to be restrained. Almost any judge at the trial court level or the appellate court level can issue this writ. The writ of *habeas corpus* has been described as making the single most important distinction between a free democracy and a tyranical country: in a democracy anyone can petition a court or judge to issue a writ seeking to obtain the release of anyone whose freedom is anyway physically restricted. As a logical consequence, prisoners deluge the courts with their petitions.

Also commonly used is the *writ of certiorari*. This is a court order asking that an issue raised in the writ be made certain or clear by a higher court. It permits such a court to review a case, but the court is not obligated to do so (as it is with an appeal). Most petitions for the writs are simply stampled "*certiorari* denied." Most of the cases heard by the United States Supreme Court are heard on writs of *certiorari*, not on appeal. Another use of this writ, at any level, involves a challenge that a trial court does not have jurisdiction on a particular case. Such a challenge forestalls trial while it is examined by a higher court.

## DISCUSSION QUESTIONS

1. What examples of court lag can be discerned in the functions of the courts?
2. Is sentencing fair? How could it be improved?
3. Discuss the importance of the court's functions prior to trial relative to the importance to the trial.
4. Discuss the ways courts function to protect the innocent. In what ways do they fail to protect the innocent?
5. Describe the abuses of bail. What can be done about it?

## NOTES

1. National Advisory Commission on Criminal Justice Standards and Goals, *Courts* (Washington, D.C.: Government Printing Office, 1973), Standard 4.1, p. 65.
2. These cases are among those identified as part of the "criminal law revolution" of the Sixties and include such major cases as Mapp v. Ohio 367 U.S. 478 (1964); Miranda v. Arizona 384 U.S. 436 (1966); Terry v. Ohio 392 U.S. 1 (1968); Chimel v. California 395 U.S. 752 (1969).
3. President's Commission on Law Enforcement and Administration of Justice, *The Challenge of Crime in a Free Society* (Washington, D.C.: Government Printing Office, 1967), p. 258.
4. President's Commission on Law Enforcement and Administration of Justice, *Task Force Report: The Courts* (Washington, D.C.: Government Printing Office, 1967), p. 31.
5. The best-known study is Edward Green, *Judicial Attitudes in Sentencing: A Study of the Factors Underlying the Sentencing Practices of the Court of Philadelphia* (London: Macmillan, 1961). A number of theses have been completed at Sam Houston State University, Huntsville, Texas, during the late 1960s under the guidance of Dr. Charles Friel in which more elaborate statistical procedures were used in exploring various aspects of sentencing disparity.
6. *Courts*, Standard 6.4, pp. 101–108.

# 14: Court Participants

*ACTIVE PARTICIPANTS • INDIRECT PARTICIPANTS*

PURPOSE: *TO DESCRIBE THE ROLES OF VARIOUS PARTICIPANTS IN THE COURTS AND TO PRESENT THE PROBLEM AREAS OF THE COURT AS RELATED TO THESE PARTICIPANTS.*

"THIS court looks with disfavor . . . ." In a statement that begins thus, there can be no question that a judge is speaking and referring to himself or herself as "the court." The judge is the chief figure of the court and embodies it—even when the judicial role appears to be reduced to that of a referee for two nonjudicial adversaries.

The adversaries are the prosecutor and the defense attorney, and their prestige is second only to that of the judge. The jury may be of key importance, particularly in more serious felony cases. The same is true of witnesses, regardless of whether they are for the state or whether they are for the defense. There is the "administrative" staff—bailiffs, chief clerks, and so on—who can be crucial, and yet their roles are often overlooked by the individuals concerned with the condition of the courts.

The list is by no means exhausted; there are grand juries, probation officers, social workers, researchers, psychiatrists and psychologists, secretaries and bookkeepers, and an endless stream of others—all in the direct employ of the courts or supervised by them. It is sometimes doubtful that the defendant is a participant, although there have been spectacular exceptions.[1]

The courtroom is a public place, despite the frequency of closed-door hearings found particularly in quasi-judicial settings. This means that there is an audience, and by its presence it exercises influence. The audience, therefore, is a participant, however passive it may be. In this audience are news media people, and by their participation they bring the court out of the courtroom and into the living rooms of the public. The public then, by its reaction and potential for reaction, becomes a participant.

If folk wisdom is correct, any organization is only as good as its participants. Who, then, are these court participants, and what are the ground rules by which they abide?

## *ACTIVE PARTICIPANTS*

Some of the participants are active within the courtroom, judges, adversaries, witnesses, and jurors among them.

### Judges

Crucial questions about the operation and success of the courts center on the judges. What qualifications they possess, how they are selected, what their duties and powers are, and how they may be terminated are all questions that must be answered one way or another.

*Qualifications and Training* Most kinds of courts are presided over by judges who are lawyers, although many justices of the peace, city judges, and judges of county courts who handle only misdemeanors are not. The value of a law degree in some of the lower courts has been questioned because lawyers are not trained to be judges. On the other hand, an intimate knowledge of law, particularly the law of evidence and how to find material in the law, is generally recognized as necessary in the higher courts, and a law degree is often advocated as a prerequisite for *all* judgeships. Still, unless a judge has been a prosecutor, he or she is unlikely to have had any experience in handling criminal cases and may or may not have had a single course in criminal law in law school. Some of the non-lawyers who are justices of the peace, who routinely sentence people to six months in jail, are unintelligent, easily dominated by police officers and prosecutors, and preoccupied with their regular businesses—which might be anything from being a mechanic to being a homemaker. In short, they seem singularly unfit to be judges.

In many countries people who wish to become judges enter a standard program of training at a recognized school and later become apprentices before becoming fully empowered judges. In the United States, however, the background of judges reflects a startling lack of standards. There is no training for a judgeship, no necessary course in criminal law, no apprenticeship, and, frequently, no standards whatsoever.

In recent years various forms of judicial conferences have been developed that provide some specialized training, and new judges have been given particular attention. For the most part, however, judges do not observe other judges at work. The conferences usually are not limited to criminal cases, but give most of their attention to civil cases. There is no organized system for assuring their acquisition of updated information. (By way of contrast, physicians specializing in family medicine must pass a test every three years to continue to qualify as specialists.)

*Selection* Judges are selected by a wide variety of procedures that fall into three basic categories: (1) elected, (2) appointed, and (3) mixed. Judges at the state level may be either appointed by the governor or by the legislature. They may be appointed from a selected list of names developed by a professional, "nonpartisan" team. They may be appointed and then have to run for election on their records. They may be elected, rather than appointed, either with political party labels or without them. If they have been appointed, they may be screened by a professional team before they take office.

For the most part, judges are actually selected by the dominant political party in private deals, and the spoils system poses a constant threat to ideal selection. There is danger, too, that the judiciary may be to an extent dominated or controlled by bar associations. A carefully selected nominating team helps to lessen the selection biases arising from these two factors.

A merit system called the Missouri Plan, because it was first adopted by Missouri, is advocated by many jurists, and at least ten states have adopted a similar system. The Missouri Plan requires that judges be nominated by a nonpartisan commission. The judge becomes a judge on appointment by the governor. Then, in a general election the public is asked for a vote of confidence to keep the judge in office. He or she does not run against anyone. At the end of each term another vote is taken, and at least 50 percent of the votes must be for the judge to continue.

*Role* The duties of the judge of a criminal court have already been in large part defined, although they vary enormously with the kind and size of the court. Judges must have good knowledge of law, skill in court procedure, and the necessary toughness to control the court and to make the taxing decisions demanded of them. As a group, judges probably have more power to bring about major changes in the criminal justice system than any other group. High prestige is associated with the higher judicial positions. Good lawyers, however, can generally make more money and may have an easier professional life if they do not become judges. The salaries of judges range from token sums to amounts equivalent to the salaries of well-paid executives. Retirement systems are generally attractive. In addition, retired judges may be recalled to preside over time-consuming cases and thus relieve regular judges of heavy caseloads.

*Termination* Until recently, the only ways to remove judges were impeachment and persuasion to retire. This is one reason for good retirement systems, and many states are now able to use a "forced retirement" method. Impeachment is a formal procedure designed to remove a public servant from office. As a means of eliminating bad or poor judges, it is cumbersome and all but unworkable. A judge cannot be removed by impeachment without being touched by scandal (regardless of the truth or falsity of the charge).

In New York, a Court of the Judiciary has been established to hear complaints of judicial misconduct. For smaller states, a court administrator or other special officer has been suggested as a possible disciplinarian. New Jersey, which has a unified court system, apparently has had success with an informal method in which the state's chief justice initially talks with the errant judge. Perhaps the best system that has evolved is the commission plan adopted by California in 1960, by Texas in 1965, and by many other states since then. The Commission on Judicial Qualifications is a permanent body of judges, lawyers, and others which receives complaints about judicial behavior, makes investigations, and recommends to the supreme court of the state that judges be removed or retired. The commission does *not* make periodic, irregular, unannounced inspections like those used by the military as a form of quality control of personnel practices.

**Adversaries**

The opposing lawyers in a case make for many an exciting television drama. Since their actual duties and responsibilities have already been discussed, they will be treated only briefly in this section.

*Prosecutor* Suffice it to say here that prosecutors often wield informal power that dwarfs the power of the other participants. Prosecutors may be held in check by the judge's ability to place them in contempt, but they nonetheless may be tremendously influential in the court. By controlling guilty pleas, they can swamp a judge's docket with trial cases if they wish to put a judge "in his place." By their plea bargaining they determine verdict and sentencing. They can, by exercising their discretionary power, dismiss cases by refusing to prosecute. If a grand jury is used, it is generally a weighty rubber stamp of approval for the prosecutor to apply at will to obtain indictments. Prosecutors typically have a great deal more trial experience in criminal cases and much greater knowledge of criminal law than do defense attorneys. Prosecutors are not always well paid, and they may have political ambitions, sometimes with the result that persons of inferior quality and ulterior motive apply great power in unjust prosecutions. Bad prosecutors denigrate the very real value of dedicated prosecutors of high personal integrity.

*Defense Attorney* Defense attorneys, or defense lawyers, or counsel, or, sometimes, "the defense," represent the defendant's interests during a criminal case. In a typical medium-sized city, only a few lawyers will handle the defense cases. The new requirements that every defendant who may face incarceration has a right to counsel has resulted in a few lawyers who accept appointments by judges to indigent cases as a form of lawyer welfare. Other cities have arrangements, usually made through the local bar association, by which every lawyer will serve a turn as an appointee to the defense in a criminal case.

Government-sponsored offices of defense lawyers have been created in some places. These "public defender" agencies often have a social work flavor and may even work closely with the prosecutor on the defendant's behalf. They have been accused of not always working on the defendant's behalf. The potential for a growing professionalism of a growing body of defense lawyers appears to be good.

**Jurors**

The grand jury is a body of lay people who determine whether there is enough evidence to justify a formal charge that an accused person has committed an alleged crime. The evidence is provided by the prosecutor. (The grand jury's nature and function has been described in Part Three.) Popular opinion frequently equates an indictment with a conviction by a trial court, but newspaper headlines stating that someone has been indicted do not prove guilt, despite what the public may think.

A *petit jury* is a trial jury, the jury everyone thinks of when the word *jury* is mentioned. It is used in civil as well as criminal cases. In felony cases it is usually composed of twelve people; in serious misdemeanor cases, in which it is sometimes used, the number may be less. Until recently a unanimous verdict was required in every state for a verdict of guilty, but now, in some states, a majority vote is sufficient.

*Selection* Originally jurors were knowledgeable witnesses. Today, they are supposed to be impartial and without opinions on the case at hand. The methods for the selection of the *array*, or the *venire* (people who might become jurors), may be made from a list of voters or by some other method. The veniremen answer general questions posed by the prosecutor in the courtroom, for example, "Have you ever been convicted of a felony?" "Can you understand and read English?" From the group who survives this questioning the judge hears any requests to be relieved from serving and excuses some from jury duty. The names of the resulting panel of jurors are typically written on pieces of paper and drawn by chance, one at a time. Then both prosecutor and defense examine the individual and may seek to have the judge disqualify this person "for cause," for example, because he or she is related to the defendant or has already formed an opinion about the case. Once the jury box is full, the prosecutor and the defense attorney are each allowed to request that a certain number of specified jurors be excused from duty by the judge, without giving any reason. These requests are called peremptory challenges. For each one excused another juror is selected to fill the vacant seat. An alternate juror may be selected to take the place of a regular juror if need be.

*Functions* The jury listens to the trial. Regardless of how long the trial takes, and it may be weeks or months, in many states the jury is not allowed to take notes. The jurors may be isolated from other people all during the trial, or they may be isolated only at the closing of the presentation of evidence. They are paid about $5.00 a day. Little concern is shown by the court for the requirements jurors must meet in their daily work and domestic lives—other than to excuse a wide range of competent people from jury duty. Conscientious citizens are sometimes soured on jury duty by this lack of regard and by the court's poor handling of a case.

The jurors either elect a foreman or the first member of the jury automatically becomes the foreman. This role is somewhat similar to that of a committee chairperson. The deliberations of jurors are supposed to be secret, but the accounts of some jurors' behavior during this period have been shocking in the indifference shown to the trial and to the defendant's lot. The jury may also ignore the law in making its decisions of guilt or innocence. It may render sentences (when it has this responsibility) without regard for the usual considerations. For example, a first offender may be sentenced to twenty years while a "three-time loser" in similar circumstances is sentenced to five years' imprisonment. Studies have indicated, however, the verdicts rendered by juries appear to be about the same overall as would have been expected in cases where the jury trial has been waived.[2]

**Witnesses**

A witness is a person who swears an oath or affirmation to tell the truth, sits in the *witness stand* beside the judge, and provides testimony for either the state or the defense, who will either examine or cross-examine the witness. In the courts of the United States, much reliance is placed on witnesses. The oath is traditional, but it also serves to make perjury (lying by witnesses) appear more serious and therefore less likely to occur. Perjury laws do not, however, make witnesses paragons of truthfulness. The laws cannot prevent the coaching of witnesses by lawyers, exaggerated pleading by witnesses, or the deliberate omission of essential facts. Furthermore, a case may reach the trial stage years after the person witnessed a crime, and the vagaries of human memory and perception over time are well documented by science. The form of taking testimony during a trial is one that the witness may find so alien as to be unable to give information. If the prosecutor or defense attorney is at all skilled, the witness can be made to appear to say something totally different from what he or she knows to be true.

Some witnesses may feel used and abused by the judge and lawyers. They may also be dismayed by the lack of regard for their time. Witnesses may be requested or subpoenaed to appear on a certain date, only to find that they were not needed on that date but can be expected to be called again. In many instances, no facilities or services exist to meet their simple needs for comfort. Some people, however, make money by being frequent expert witnesses, for example, psychiatrists whose speciality in forensic psychiatry has made them sought-after expert witnesses.

The most common witness in criminal trials is the police officer, who usually appears as a state's witness. Police officers may report what they observed at the time of arrest, a report that frequently could have been equally well put into writing and read before the court, thereby avoiding the use of off-duty (unpaid) time. Other police witnesses are frequently expert witnesses: ballistics experts, police photographers, polygraph detectors, and so forth. Special treatment, legal and quasi-legal, has evolved to protect the police informer who becomes a witness and in many instances the police officer acts as a witness in the place of the informer. "Turning state's evidence" means that a defendant has decided to act as a witness for the state and provide testimony against codefendants usually in return for the prosecution's word that charges will be dropped or reduced or that the sentence will be light.

## *INDIRECT PARTICIPANTS*

The people behind the scenes, as it were, in every trial include the people who work for the court—the peripheral personnel—and the public—the people for whom the court is supposed to work.

### Peripheral Personnel

The clerk of court, the bailiff, and the court reporter are adjuncts to all higher courts and many lower ones. They are sometimes described as *court administrators.* Their work is administrative rather than judicial, but they are not to be confused with court administrators, professional executives who handle courts' administrative problems.

*The Clerk of Court* The clerk of court is an elected official at the county level. In a federal court or an appellate court, the clerk of court is appointed by the federal judge. In many places the clerk of court has an additional job as the county clerk and does work unrelated to the courts. In such cases there may be an assistant, a deputy clerk, who is assigned responsibility for the work of the courts. There may be many clerks of court, each with a specific role, such as processing appeals. The clerks usually have no particular qualifications for obtaining the job, and tend to stay in office term after term. Professional associations of clerks are working toward standardization of their procedures.

Clerks of court take care of all the records of the court. They keep on file indictments and informations, pleadings from prosecutors and defense, instructions to the jury, verdicts, and sentences. Such documents are bound into huge books of records. Clerks of court also handle warrants. Docketing and scheduling are processes that tend to fall on the shoulders of the clerk of court. During the trial the clerk swears in witnesses and provides records requested by the judge. Duties are not limited to criminal cases, but encompass a multitude of procedures related to civil cases as well.

An elected clerk not directly responsible to a judge can slow a court's handling of cases to a virtual standstill either by incompetence or dislike of the judge.

*Court Administrators* The nature of court activity is twofold in that it is either judicial or administrative. The court administrator manages the administrative operations of the court. There are budgets to manage, personnel to handle, facilities and equipment to maintain, cases to be scheduled, juries and witnesses to be seen to, and so on. By tending to the administrative needs of the court the court administrator allows the judge more time for the judicial operations of the court.

In the past court administration was the province of the judge. However, with the increase of workload and judicial responsibility it became apparent in many courts that administrative assistance was necessary. The Administrative Office of the United States Courts was created in 1932. In the state and local courts, however, much of the growth in court administration occurred during the sixties. By 1970 approximately 80 percent of the existing court administrators had come into existence during the previous decade. Their presence has enhanced the efficiency of the court and, as a result, the judicial operations of the court.

*Court Reporters* Court reporters are also record keepers, but their specific duty is to record accurately the trial or other court procedures. Court reporters are well paid for they are highly skilled. They must listen to witnesses mumble and at the same time write the correct dialogue in shorthand or with a stenotype machine. Obviously, they must be accurate and fast. In cases that are appealed, they may be required to prepare a narrative record, or transcript, of the trial.

Because some court reporters have other jobs and do not give as much time to court reporting as they should, they may interfere with the proper recording of trials and particularly with appeal procedure. Efforts to replace court reporters with tape recorders have not yet been successful, but some people anticipate the replacement of court reporters through the advances of technology.

*Bailiffs* Bailiffs perform duties similar to those of a security guard in a bank. During trials they protect the court from dangerous or unseemly behavior. In less active courts, they may be paid by the trial. They may be hired by the judge, but in metropolitan areas are usually employees of the sheriff's office. The bailiff has custody of the defendant in the courtroom, summons witnesses to the witness stand, has custody of the jury, and assists the judge in maintaining order.

*Interrelationships* There may be many other people employed by a court, but whatever the number, interrelationships are important. Police tend to feel that courts are too lenient and do not have enough respect for the demands and nature of police work. Prosecutors and judges frequently work harmoniously, although prosecutors may feel that judges do not side with them as frequently as is merited. Lawyers, in general, respect the office of the judge. Sometimes conflicts develop between judges and those elected personnel over whom the judges have little authority. And jurors and witnesses may feel mistreated by the court if interrelationships are ignored.

**The Public**

The public is involved with the courts in more ways than are immediately apparent, sometimes in the courtroom, sometimes in its homes, sometimes in the media.

*The Audience* Attending trials was once a traditional pastime in America. The audience sitting in the courtroom contained many faces that over time came to be familiar to the judge. They may have exerted a certain pressure on the judge to be consistent and impartial; certainly, their presence demanded a sharing of understanding about a case with members of the community whose judgments could not be controlled by the judge. Today, people still attend trials out of curiosity, but the faces in the back of the courtroom are likely to be fewer and transient, usually the faces of family and friends of the defendants. Consequently, the judge has greater control over the courtroom and may, for example, be more likely to angrily jail a spectator for contempt of court for failing to speedily obey a no-smoking order.

*The Media* But even as the audiences grow smaller, television cameras in the courtroom may distort a trial from a judicial proceeding geared to judge or jury, who must decide on a verdict, into a trial geared to the vague but massive influence of the uninstructed public. Although television cameras have generally been banned, and what is seen on television sets are sketches by artists accompanied by narrative by reporters, the conflict between the news media and the courts has not ended. For example, in the 1950s, the infamous trial of Dr. Sam Sheppard for the murder of his wife was heavily covered by a newspaper that assumed that Sheppard was guilty and strongly advocated capital punishment. In 1966 the Supreme Court overturned the verdict in an eight to one decision because "virulent publicity" deprived Dr. Sheppard of a fair trial.[3] Sensationalism sells newspapers, but the problem is often complicated by elected officials—sheriffs, prosecutors, and even judges—who try to get free news coverage to further their own careers. This is what happened in the Sheppard case—both the newspaper and some public officials were at fault. In such cases, it is, of course, difficult to find competent jurors unexposed to the prejudicial news. Changing the location of the trial may help, but there may be coverage nationwide that evokes strong emotional respones.

Spectacular displays of the abuse of free speech by the press and by criminal justice officials have resulted in rules and guidelines being suggested or established by various agencies. Police officers may receive formal instructions from the chief about what can be said to the press. The Department of Justice has issued guidelines. The American Bar Association's Project on Minimum Standards and the American Newspaper Publishers Association have conducted studies leading to the identification of the pertinent elements of the controversy. The National Crime Commission recommended that the various agencies and bar associations issue standards concerning the release of information to the media about criminal cases. The National Advisory Commission (1973) recommended that courts establish public information offices. On the other hand, there are a number of examples of restrictive, even repressive, measures taken by courts in limiting news coverage. And the news media have made some effort to police themselves in order to avoid being unduly censored by the courts. (In England the media have established a toothless yet somehow very effective control over the handling of court cases.)

*Society* Ultimately, however, the public controls the media and the courts as much as it is controlled or shaped by either of them. Lynch mobs and vigilante groups did not have to be stirred by the news media to take control of criminal cases from the courts and exercise their own illegitimate tribunal powers. Changes in the nature of Supreme Court decisions over the decades reflect the changes in the attitudes, beliefs, and values of the public. The Supreme Court that upheld slavery at one point gave way to a Supreme Court that abhorred the idea of slavery and so on. Just as crime itself has in some respects been tolerated and encouraged by the public so have the outdated characteristics of the courts. And other changes in the public have resulted in more demands on the courts. Population increases, new technology, and a more complicated society have brought about new laws and more laws, new crimes and more crimes, new cases and more cases. The courts are changing in response to these changes, and it is likely that they will change very rapidly in the near future.

## DISCUSSION QUESTIONS

1. How could we tell a bad judge from a good judge?
2. How could we eliminate *heavy* reliance on the testimony of witnesses? Or could we?
3. Discuss the qualifications and selection procedures for judges in the United States. How could they be improved? In your state?
4. Discuss the relative weight of the general public and the media in influencing the way courts operate.
5. Who are the participants in a court? What should the role of the public be in a sensational criminal trial?

## NOTES

1. The actions of the "Chicago 7" in the courtroom of Judge Julius Hoffman in Chicago, 1969–70, made national headlines for months. The defendants were on trial for conspiracy to incite a riot at the 1968 Democratic Convention in Chicago. In 1973 they were charged with a total of 38 contempt of court charges, most of which the court threw out.
2. The argument against jury sentencing is strongly supported by a study reported in Atlanta Commission on Crime and Juvenile Delinquency, *Opportunity for Urban Excellence 72* (1962), Appendix D–6. Judicial conferences have treated the subject of jury versus bench trials. The FBI's *Uniform Crime Reports* show roughly equal numbers of felons being convicted in the two forms of trials—in proportion to the different figures for those pleading not guilty in the two.
3. Sheppard v. Maxwell 384 U.S. 333 (1966).

## PART FOUR ANNOTATED BIBLIOGRAPY

James, Howard. *Crisis in the Courts.* Rev. ed. New York: McKay, 1969.

*A skilled journalist gives his first-hand impressions of courts across the nation. Frequently indignant in tone, the book is always highly readable. James makes numerous recommendations for improving courts.*

Meyers, Lewis B. *The American Legal System.* Rev. ed. New York: Harper & Row, 1964.

*An excellent book on the courts and the law. Although this book is scholarly, it reads well. It is the only book in which information on the courts is well synthesized.*

National Advisory Commission on Criminal Justice Standards and Goals. *Courts.* Washington, D.C.: Government Printing Office, 1973.

*The report recommends a major restructuring and streamlining of procedures and practices in processing criminal cases at state and local levels. Recommendations, standards, and goals of the commission are included.*

President's Commission on Law Enforcement and Administration of Justice. *Task Force Report: The Courts.* Washington, D.C.: Government Printing Office, 1967.

*Still the best general report on the problems in the courts and what should be done about them. Comprehensive research and analysis of courts and court problems.*

# PART FIVE

# Corrections

# 15: Background and History of Corrections

*THE EUROPEAN HERITAGE • THE AMERICAN HERITAGE • HISTORY OF COMMUNITY-BASED CORRECTIONS*

PURPOSE: *TO TRACE THE HISTORICAL DEVELOPMENT OF CORRECTIONS, INCLUDING EARLY PRACTICES AND THEORIES.*

THE TERM *corrections* as it is used in criminal justice is only now becoming familiar to the general public. Most people, however, equate *corrections* with the penitentiary system. Corrections does include the agencies and people involved in our systems of prisons, jails, and juvenile facilities, but today it also includes probation and parole. Historically, corrections in the United States developed around the prisons, and in fact, the penitentiary as we know it today was developed primarily in America. For this reason, the history of corrections in the United States centers on the development of the penitentiary. Nonetheless, corrections in the United States did receive its impetus from European ideas.

## *THE EUROPEAN HERITAGE*

In a previous section of the text there was a discussion of the early means of controlling crime. Blood revenge was a method that prevailed for centuries. Later theories tied punishment to an appeasement of the gods and made the apprehension and punishment of offenders of general social concern.[1] The development of the theory of deterrence followed at a later date, as did the theory of reformation, which was strongly influenced by the Roman Catholic Church in the Middle Ages.[2]

Early penal methods, which continued to the 1600s, stressed harsh and cruel punishment and relied to a large degree on the theory of deterrence and on the belief that crime was a sin that required punishment of the offender to protect the public. Using prison for incarceration gained favor as an alternative to whipping, killing, and banishment to the colonies.

On the Continent a major development of the 1600s was the workhouse, which was known to early reformers in America.[3] In 1779, with the passing of the Hard Labour Act in England, it seemed that a major change in penal methods was at hand. This act, which called for the establishment of penitentiaries, came at a time when England could no longer deport its criminal problem to the New World.[4] Although reformers in England developed such ideas as separation of prisoners, it was left to America to put these ideas into practice. It was not until the 1800s that incarceration in a system of prisons became the primary means of dealing with the criminal, but England and the Continent were to follow the lead of the New World in this innovation.

## *THE AMERICAN HERITAGE*

### The Prison System

*Early Development (1600–1830)* In the 1600s the Pennsylvania Quakers, under the guidance of William Penn, passed a criminal code that was less severe than the codes originally brought to this country. Prior to this time, the jails and workhouses had the primary purpose of housing paupers, beggars, and persons awaiting trial. Punishment after the trial came in the form of a fine, public whipping, confinement to the stocks, or hanging. Because long-term imprisonment was not an accepted sentence, jails were not required to hold convicted criminals. The action by the Quakers changed this and introduced imprisonment at "hard labor" as a punishment for most serious crimes. As a result prisons were built in Massachusetts and Pennsylvania, although they led to little rehabilitation and even less deterrence of crime.

The period from 1790 to 1830 is the developmental stage in the penal system. A cellblock in the Walnut Street Jail, opened in Philadelphia in 1790, is considered the first prison in America even though the Quakers had opened prisons for a short time 150 years earlier. Most prisons in the 1790s, however, were in buildings in the cities. Prison labor, evolving from the workhouse idea, was introduced during this period as a means of reducing the cost of housing criminals. By the 1820s the prisons were recognized as complete failures in all ways except as training grounds for more crimes.

As a result of these failures, the Auburn (1819) and Pennsylvania (1829) systems were introduced. These two systems were actually quite similar in that they were both based on the theory that separation and work would bring about rehabilitation. The major difference between the two was the use of congregate labor under the Auburn system and the Pennsylvania requirement that prisoners remain segragated in separate cells. The idea of separation was based on the assumption that the opportunity to reflect in solitude on past sins would bring about rehabilitation. Under the Pennsylvania system, only a selected small group of persons were allowed to see the prisoner, to take care of personal needs. The Auburn system also demanded complete silence at all times, but the use of congregate labor gave it a financial advantage over the Pennsylvania system.[5]

*The Systems of the 1800s* Until about 1870, the Auburn system of silence, penitence, and productive labor was the standard in the United States. Although there were many people who endorsed the Pennsylvania system, it did not allow for congregation of inmates for any purpose. As a result, the more economical Auburn system of bringing prisoners out of their cells to work in prison shops during the day prevailed. Some treatment was initiated before 1870, but it was limited mostly to the use of religion. Harsh punishment was frequently used to enforce the rule of silence. Also, the abuse of prison labor for profit was common.

The model of long, hard daily labor was not without theoretical base because failure to observe the protestant work ethic was thought to be a causative factor in criminality. This theoretical base made the practice of contracting with private firms and the establishment of long work schedules the proper method of reforming criminals. The fact that these practices also helped offset the cost of the system was a side effect that was not stressed as a primary feature of the institution.[6]

*The Golden Age* The so-called "Golden Age of Penology" was introduced with the opening of the Elmira Reformatory in New York in 1876. This effort used mass education and religion, parole, indeterminate sentences, and separation of youthful offenders. However, the anticipated result was never fully achieved and most institutions continued to rely upon security rather than rehabilitation.

The sentencing practice of the period helped seal the doom of reform, for long sentences gave prisoners little incentive to change their ways. The prisons faced one dilemma after another, most ending in a reinforcement of the custodial model. The Auburn and Pennsylvania systems had no requirement for classifying prisoners according to how hardened, skilled, or dangerous they were, because the rules of silence and solitude met the need of keeping prisoners from influencing each other. Subsequently, overcrowding, with the resultant breaking of the rule of silence, allowed prisoners once again to influence each other. Conditions deteriorated and prisons became ideal places for the hardened criminal to influence the younger prisoner not yet committed to a life of crime. The reform efforts disappeared completely during this period. Prisoners apparently were treated individually only when they could corrupt prison officials—and such corruption was a common occurrence.

A significant accomplishment of this period was the development in 1870 of the Declaration of Principles by the American Prison Association (now the American Correctional Association).[7] These principles, which have had only minor revision and are applicable today, indicate the foresight of early correctional thinkers.

*The Industrial Era* The period 1900–1935 was characterized by the expanded use of labor for profit in the form of several "systems" of prison labor. These systems included the contract system, the lease system, the public accounts system, the state use system, and the public works system. Prominent during this period was the establishment of meaningful educational, vocational, and medical programs. Emphasis was also placed on improvement of living conditions and on control of brutality, and productive labor was recognized as therapeutic treatment.

Despite this seeming progress, the order for the day in the 1920s was "preserve order, maintain discipline and prevent escape at all hazards."[8] In carrying out this order, guards were not allowed any conversation with inmates except in the line of duty. One state reported that it had had thirty-six wardens in seventy years,[9] and in some states it was common for the warden to be replaced with each change of governor. Although the typical responsibilities of the warden required a knowledge exceeding that of most business managers, some states had no established education standards. The Wickersham Commission concluded in 1931 that the responsibility for the failure of the prison system had to be laid in part to the failure of the wardens to administer their units effectively.[10]

*Recent Prison Development* Modern concepts in penology have come largely as a result of the reorganization of the federal prison system. This reorganization, which was started by Sanford Bates in the 1930s, is considered the beginning of the modern era in corrections. State

COURTESY OF DR. GEORGE KILLINGER, SAM HOUSTON STATE UNIVERSITY

**SANFORD BATES**
*1884 – 1972*

Before entering the corrections field, Sanford Bates practiced law and was admitted to practice before the Supreme Court of the United States. He was elected as a representative and senator in Massachusetts and served as commissioner of corrections in Massachusetts for ten years before being named the first director of the Federal Bureau of Prisons, a position he held for eight years. Mr. Bates held the position of parole commissioner for New York State for four years and resigned to become the executive director of the Boys Clubs of America. He held this position for four years until he accepted the position of commissioner of the Department of Institutions and Agencies for New Jersey, which he held for ten years.

Mr. Bates wrote extensively about corrections. His book *Prisons and Beyond*, published in 1936, should be read by all students interested in corrections. He also received numerous awards and decorations, which included decorations by foreign countries for work as a consultant, the American Prison Association Award, the National Council on Crime and Delinquency Award for distinguished leadership, and the honorary degrees of L.L.D. and L.H.D. by both Northeastern and Rutgers Universities.

Mr. Bates served as president of the International Prison and Penitentiary Commission, president of the American Prison Association, president of the American Parole Association, and as president or member of the board of many other noted associations. He was professor of criminology at the New York School of Social Work, Columbia University, New York University, Rutgers University, and the City College of New York. His work as a consultant or special assistant ranged from assisting the President's National Crime Commission to assisting in the Development of work release procedures for the Federal Bureau of Prisons.

---

prisons have followed the lead of the federal prison system both in building new facilities and in introducing treatment programs.

Different methods of classifying inmates for treatment have been developed, as have methods for treatment on an individual and group basis. Most significant at present seem to be a growing willingness to try new approaches and the slowly evolving baseline of qualified personnel. It seems possible that future historians will look at the 1970s as the start of another "era" in corrections, largely the result of increased funding of programs at the state and national level, advances being made in several states, and continued leadership by the Federal Bureau of Prisons.

### Women's Reformatories

Although separation of prisoners by sex was initiated between 1790 and 1830, separate institutions for women waited for the reform movement following 1870. Yet in 1930 over half the states still maintained women prisoners in the men's prison under the care of the warden.[11]

The recent history of women's reformatories has been an exception to the rule in corrections. A national survey in the 1930s indicated that substantial progress and foresight were shown in construction, health, and education programs and in efforts to prepare inmates for release. A national survey in the 1960s did not report on the women's reformatories, probably because of the belief of their significant progress relative to the rest of the corrections field and because of the relatively few women in prison. The recent attention given to equal rights for women has pointed up the fact that programs for women prisoners may not be as well developed as has been thought.

### Juvenile Training School

The reformatory, or training school as it is commonly called, was introduced to remove the younger prisoners from the adult prison setting. It was intended to concentrate on building the younger prisoner's character, removal from the influence of the older prisoner, and preparation for successful reintegration into society. The first public training facilities exclusively for juveniles probably were established in Massachusetts (1846), New York (1849), and Maine (1853). By the end of the nineteenth century thirty-six states had established separate juvenile training facilities.[12]

By 1930, however, it was concluded that the reformatory was little different in practice from the prison. The similarities extended to number of inmates, size, and type of construction. The reformatories were guilty of handling education without regard for individual differences, and many of the teachers were actually hired as guards who did extra duty as teachers. The vocational and industrial programs were deficient because they were not related to any need of the inmate following release. As a result of these shortcomings, the Wickersham Commission (1931) concluded that the reformatory movement was for the most part a complete failure.[13]

Contrary to the working philosophy of the reformatory, the National Crime Commission's Task Force on Corrections found that in 1965 corporal punishment was still authorized in ten states. Most training schools did not segregate offenders according to a rehabilitation design but maintained a custodial concept contrary to the theory of rehabilitation. The training schools surveyed, representing 86 percent of the total, had a total capacity of 42,423 and an average daily population of 42,389. Twenty-two percent of the jurisdictions had overcrowding of 10 percent or more, and 17 percent were 10 percent below capacity.[14] The variations in the average cost, length of sentence, programs, staff, and so on all indicated a wide difference in application of theory to practice and a resulting inability to make practical comparisons of the relative value of programs. Consequently, it is not uncommon today for the courts to ask training schools to prove their effectiveness. To date, this effectiveness has not been clearly demonstrated for most classes of juvenile inmates, and the courts have ordered some states to close their juvenile institutions.

### Work Camps

Assigning men to work camps was common before the invention of the penitentiary. Contractors in early colonial times paid the state for the use of criminals. The contractor was expected to be responsible for housing and feeding the inmates and in return was allowed to use them or to hire them out to others. The restrictive laws of the 1930s limited prison labor to state needs and put an end to what had come to be considered a form of slavery.

Nevada used prison camps before 1900 and several other states started before World War I. Between the wars, several additional states initiated camp programs, and following World War II, this use rapidly expanded. Although it has been suggested that this expansion was the result of far-sighted administrators, reduced cost must have also been a factor.

Industry and the labor unions had brought an end to the hard labor that was common prior to 1900. The Hawes-Cooper Act in 1934 and the Ashurst-Summer Act of 1935 excluded prison-made goods from interstate commerce, and to reduce the pressure from industry and labor many states further restricted the sale of prison-made goods. Even today, in the use of camps under the state works system to relieve the burden of idleness to the prisoners and cost to the states, the problem of how to use prison labor ethically is a specter to many prison and jail administrators.

## *HISTORY OF COMMUNITY-BASED CORRECTIONS*

The term *community-based corrections,* as currently used, refers to those correctional programs and institutions that are close to the centers of population and depend on this closeness for their operation. It should be kept in mind that the classification of an institution, agency, or program as community-based does not depend on the level of government that operates the program. The United States Bureau of Prisons and other federal agencies are leaders in the establishment of this type of program, and many states operate, or support by funding, such programs. In addition, certain prisons can be classified as long-term community institutions under certain conditions, and jails can be classified as short-term community institutions. For the purpose of this text, jails and juvenile detention centers are discussed under the heading of community corrections.

### Jails

Centralization of control of our system of jails was recommended in 1930 and again in 1967 as a result of the deplorable conditions in most of them. The 1973 report of the National Commission on Criminal Justice Standards and Goals set state control of jails as a specific goal for corrections. It has been generally agreed, in every study of corrections, that the jail systems are the worst evil of corrections. Only in a few instances where public pressure, adequate funding, and farsightedness have had a combined effect, has there been any significant improvement over the jails of hundreds of years ago.

The use of the jail for detention of accused persons can be traced back thousands of years. Its use as a workhouse was developed in the sixteenth century to deal with minor offenses, and this concept came to the United States during the seventeenth century. The reform movement of the nineteenth century led to general changes in the corrections field for everything but the jail. However, the fact that the jail is in essence the "reception center" for correctional institutions and has considerable impact on the persons processed is beginning to have an impact on correctional thinking. The National Jail Census of 1972 indicated that our 3,921 jails housing inmates over forty-eight hours contained 141,600 inmates, an average of forty inmates per jail. California housed the largest number (25,348) at a time when prison population in the state was decreasing. Six states confined about half the total number, although these states accounted for only about one fourth of the United States population.[15]

A national survey in 1965 found that only 3 percent of our jail employees can be identified as professionals. Many of the local administrators are county sheriffs who stand for re-election every two years, and this tends to hinder any effort at building treatment programs. In 1965 only 8 percent of the local jails required the administrator to have a college degree and only 56 percent were under a merit or civil service system. In 53 percent of the counties there were no minimum education requirements for custodial officers and 1 percent required a college degree. In 50 percent of the counties using the service, a social worker with no college training could be hired.[16] This last statistic speaks eloquently for the importance placed on treatment as opposed to custody. As might be expected, salaries, inservice training, and inmate programs in jails have been at the bottom of the corrections totem pole. It is difficult to imagine significant change in this area, short of a major reduction in the number of persons put in jails and some consolidation for administrative and financial efficiency.

Of particular importance in the findings in the jail census is the fact that on average more than 36 percent of the jail population was in pretrial confinement. Studies done in a number of states in 1974 show that little progress has been made in reducing the number of people in pretrial status. This statistic indicates clearly the role that the courts and the prosecution must play in solving the problem of overcrowded jails. Additional problems indicated in the 1972 census were overcrowding, lack of medical assistance, and lack of areas for recreation and visitation. Meaningful vocational and educational programs were almost nonexistent.[17] Many jails are so old and badly deteriorated that even the most hardened of law enforcement personnel hesitate to use them for human habitation. They are so poorly designed that even basic control and protection of inmates is impossible. Yet, many of these jails house juveniles in different stages of judicial processing as well as housing adults.

Also of importance, when considering jails, is the estimate that in many states up to 80 to 90 percent of them cannot meet the minimum standards for health and safety. There is a cost factor of many millions of dollars at stake in deciding how to solve the problem. Although a possibility of relief is in the hands of the judiciary, which could reduce the number of persons in pretrial confinement, there is still an urgent need to replace many jails. Modern penal reformers are calling for extensive use of community programs as an alternative to the building of new jails. These reformers point out that building new jails simply tends to hide the problems behind bigger and newer walls. Also, because of the cost factor, a number of states, including Vermont, Iowa, and Connecticut, have initiated regional systems with primary emphasis on programs within the community. In any case, it appears that any significant progress in improving our system of corrections will revolve around solutions to our age-old jail problems.

### Juvenile Detention Centers

After the establishment of the first juvenile court in Chicago in 1899, state after state made provisions for separate detention of juveniles. However, by 1915 only three jurisdictions had constructed special facilities for detention of accused juveniles being held prior to trial, and as late as 1945 only a few specially designed facilities were available for this purpose. Major construction and program development has occurred only during the past fifteen years. The 1965 survey of corrections found that 93 percent of the country's juvenile court jurisdictions, covering 44 percent of the population, had no place for pretrial detention of juveniles other than a county jail or police lockup, and most did not detain enough children to justify establishing a detention home.[18]

The National Crime Commission's Task Force on Corrections found that in 1965 it was routine in some jurisdictions to detain all arrested children, whether referred to court or not. The total number of juveniles detailed in 1965 amounted to 409,218. In one county, two thirds of the detained children were later placed on probation in their homes. An estimated 100,000 juveniles were still detained in facilities for adults, and only three jurisdictions could claim that youngsters were never detained in jails. The National Crime Commission did, however, report a number of small model programs for detention of children. These model programs are slowly expanding, primarily where state and federal funds are made available to initiate them and where counties are pooling their resources to operate a central detention facility for juveniles.[19] Although since 1967 a number of states have made significant progress in detention of juveniles outside the county jail system, much remains to be done.

### Halfway Houses and Prerelease Guidance Centers

The halfway house concept has been around for many years and has been known by several other names. Many of the early halfway houses and prerelease guidance centers were operated by private, voluntary organizations, and they usually were located close to the prison rather than in the urban area to which the ex-inmate would return. Their primary function was to provide food and lodging to released inmates. The federal government began to enter the halfway-house field in 1946, and several federal and state programs were initiated over the next twenty years.

In 1966, the Bureau of Prisons was operating five prerelease programs. This number has expanded to include fourteen community treatment centers across the country. These programs were forerunners of the halfway house as it is known today. The distinction between these activities is that the prerelease center is normally administered by, and located in, the institution. It is a program designed to ease the change from institution life to life in the community. The halfway house, on the other hand, is designed to be located in the community and provide not only food and shelter but counseling and other services. Persons residing in the halfway houses are allowed to leave the facility to seek and engage in employment. Florida's program requires payment of room and board and has provision for restitution to the offender's victim.

**Programs for Predelinquents**

There have been numerous attempts over the years to reach youths before they commit offenses serious enough to require placement in an institution. However, the youth-services concept that came into being in the late 1960s probably is the first attempt at a full-scale program with sufficient funding to have a chance of making any impact on the delinquency problem.

The youth-services concept calls for the focusing of all the resources of the community on youths who show signs of becoming delinquent. Another similar program, undertaken by the federal government, is designed to focus on the child of five years of age and under. Although several of these concepts have been demonstrated to be theoretically significant, it is only through long-term evaluation in the environment of the community that we will learn if these theories of change actually work in practice.

**Individual and Group Placement**

Foster homes, essentially a placement service, have been used for a number of years in the welfare service area, but are relatively new as employed on a large scale in corrections. The National Crime Commission's Task Force on Corrections found that 42 percent of 233 probation offices studied used foster-home placement. Several states are now actively engaged in establishing foster-home and group-home programs. In 1966, for example, Minnesota was using seven group homes and the Wisconsin Division of Corrections was operating thirty-three. Many states, even today, however, are far behind in establishing this type of alternative to incarceration.[20]

**Special Programs**

The history of corrections would not be complete unless the agencies using special programs, such as guided group interaction, were mentioned. The best known of the early guided group interaction programs was the Highfields project, established in New Jersey in 1950. Follow-on programs were established at Essexfields, New Jersey, and at Pinehills in Provo, Utah. Basically, these programs involved work in the community during the day and special interaction sessions at the home facility in the evening. The idea behind them was that the individual needed to be resocialized in a community program rather than in an institutional environment, but their results are still debated because, like most other correctional programs, they were not adequately evaluated.

Another relatively recent program is the Synanon program for drug addicts. It has received much attention because of its innovative features, but has suffered from a lack of evaluation. Many other drug programs have developed, but they also lack adequate evaluation.

Currently, there is much debate about the future direction of corrections. Some have pointed out that rather than building new large prisons, we should establish small community facilities and programs. Others have insisted that we must build new prisons because so many of our present ones are outdated and in need of replacement. Some have argued that correctional treatment does not work. And some have argued that prisons are for punishment, not treatment. We have also heard the argument that only dangerous offenders should be sent to prison while nondangerous offenders should receive supervision from community programs. Others argue that the sanction of prison is necessary for the nondangerous offender and that prisons are needed in order to make less punitive sanctions function. The direction that corrections will take is not yet clear. There are valid points to both sides of the argument that are much more complex than those presented here. One thing is clear, however: today's students of criminal justice will determine the future of corrections.

The development of correctional institutions in the United States, that is prisons, jails, and juvenile facilities, can find its impetus in Europe. However, corrections as we know it is primarily an American invention. Early development began with the Quakers who established jails and workhouses. The early 1800s marked the development of the Auburn system (congregate labor) and the Pennsylvania system (separate cell labor). In 1876 the Elmira (New York) reformatory opened with programs for religion, education, parole, indeterminate sentences, and separation of youthful offenders. The period of 1900 through the 1930s was characterized by the widespread use of prison labor. The reorganization of the Federal Prison System in the 1930s led to similar reorganization and reform in the states' prison systems. With the advent of separate courts for juveniles, separate juvenile institutions developed. Also separate institutions for women were established. While jails were the forerunners of our state and federal prison systems, they have in many cases remained static in their developments and improvements. Through the years special programs have developed such as halfway houses, prerelease centers, youth service bureaus, and other unique institutions. In the late 1960s and the early 1970s corrections has embarked on a new road to reform and innovation largely as a result of federal funding from the Law Enforcement Assistance Administration. It remains to be seen where the efforts of this new era in corrections will take us.

## DISCUSSION QUESTIONS

1. What is wrong with our system of jails?
2. What is meant by the phrase *community-based corrections?*
3. Why did a system of prisons develop?
4. Discuss whether prison architecture can make a significant difference in the probability of success of rehabilitation programs.
5. Explain the causes of overcrowding in jails. How can this overcrowding best be eliminated?
6. Discuss the pros and cons of state or local control of jails.
7. What does the future hold for corrections?
8. Where is the state prison located in your state? Is it properly located? If not, where should it be?
9. Can we ever have correctional systems that do not, either implicitly or explicitly, punish the criminal offender?

## NOTES

1. W. Davis Lewis, *From Newgate to Dannemora* (Ithaca: Cornell University Press, 1965), p. 7.
2. Lewis, *From Newgate,* p. 7.
3. Lewis, *From Newgate,* p. 12.
4. Lewis, *From Newgate,* p. 23.
5. David J. Rothman, *The Discovery of the Asylum* (Boston: Little, Brown and Company, 1971), p. 82.
6. Rothman, *Discovery of the Asylum,* p. 103.
7. American Correctional Association, *Manual of Correctional Standards* (Washington, D.C.: American Correctional Association, 1959), p. xix.
8. U.S. National Commission on Law Observance and Enforcement, *Wickersham Commission Reports: No. 9, Report on Penal Institutions, Probation and Parole* (Montclair, New Jersey: Patterson Smith Reprint, 1968), p. 19.
9. Wickersham Commission, p. 41.
10. Wickersham Commission.
11. Wickersham Commission, p. 55.
12. President's Commission on Law Enforcement and Administration of Justice, *Task Force Report: Corrections* (Washington, D.C.: Government Printing Office, 1967), p. 141.
13. Wickersham Commission, p. 51.

14. *Task Force Report: Corrections,* pp. 142–144.
15. U.S. Department of Justice, *Survey of Inmates in Local Jails* (Washington, D.C.: Government Printing Office, 1974), pp. 18–19.
16. *Task Force Report: Corrections,* pp. 162–165.
17. *Survey of Inmates in Local Jails,* p. 17.
18. *Task Force Report: Corrections,* pp. 119–121.
19. *Task Force Report: Corrections,* pp. 23–24.
20. *Task Force Report: Corrections,* p. 40.

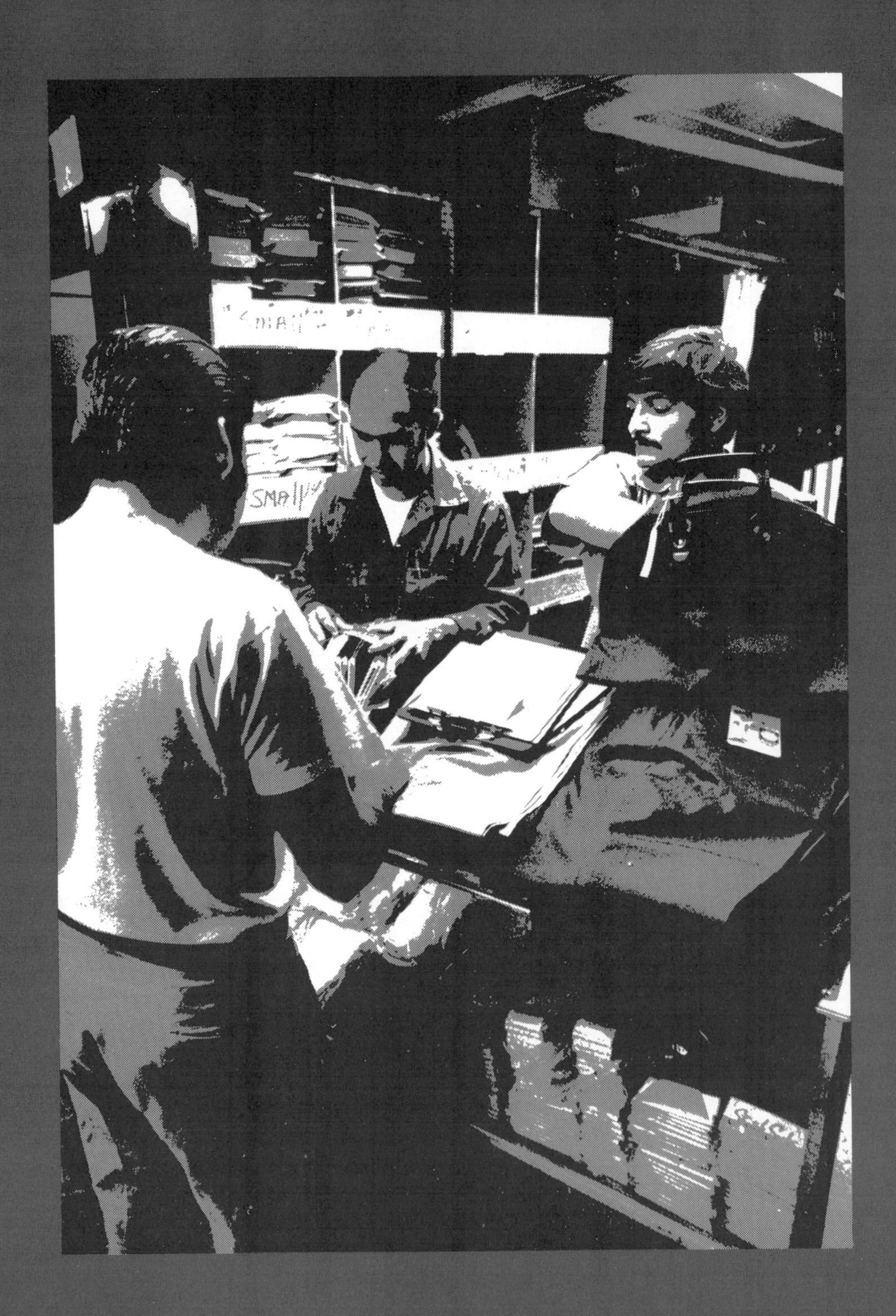

# 16: Correctional Organizations

*CONCEPT OF CORRECTIONS • TYPES OF CORRECTIONAL ORGANIZATIONS • FEDERAL CORRECTIONAL ORGANIZATIONS • MILITARY CORRECTIONAL ORGANIZATIONS • STATE CORRECTIONAL ORGANIZATIONS • LOCAL CORRECTIONAL ORGANIZATIONS*

PURPOSE: *TO DESCRIBE THE VARIOUS LEVELS OF CORRECTIONAL ORGANIZATIONS, INCLUDING FEDERAL, STATE, MILITARY, AND LOCAL CORRECTIONAL AGENCIES.*

THERE ARE several perspectives that can provide a focus for a study of corrections. One of these, history, was used in the previous chapter, which also mentioned several others: (1) functions, (2) organization, (3) theory, (4) facilities, (5) corrections population (inmates, clients, and so forth), (6) treatment programs, and (7) research. The focus of this chapter is organization.

Organization, as related to corrections, can itself be discussed from several perspectives. For example, it is possible to discuss corrections organizations as institutional or noninstitutional. Or corrections organizations can be introduced as community-based and noncommunity-based. Here the perspective is federal, state, and local corrections, but let us first clarify some organization concepts.

## *CONCEPT OF CORRECTIONS*

The word *correction* implies the act or process of correcting. It can include punishment as a tool in the process, but it does not seriously apply to the theories of revenge and retribution. The concept has some meaning within the theory of deterrence, but reaches its full potential only in the theory that the public can best be protected through rehabilitation and careful reintegration of offenders into the community. However, the void between theory, concept, and actual practice remains great.

There is a legal basis for corrections also. The laws of the United States, of each state, and of local governments provide for apprehension, trial, and correction of offenders. And laws are specific in the requirement that correctional organizations and facilities be established. Probation and parole laws and the formal organizations associated with those laws, for example, would not be consistent with a theory of corrections that did not stress rehabilitation. In addition to the organizations established by law, there are voluntary organizations that function directly, or play supporting roles, in the area of corrections. Such organizations include Alcholics Anonymous and crisis counseling centers.

## *TYPES OF CORRECTIONAL ORGANIZATIONS*

Correctional organizations can be generally classified in three types or levels. The first type is that of the planning or policy organization. As the name indicates, this type of organization is primarily concerned with corrections planning and policy (standards and general procedures) on a broad scale. An example is the Board of Corrections in Texas, an organization that does not operate any functional element of the system, but rather is concerned with setting general policy for the Texas Department of Corrections, which in turn operates the state's adult prison system.

The second type of organization is the central or administrative agency. The director and central administrative staff of the United States Bureau of Prisons or of the Texas Department of Corrections fall in this category. These organizations perform the same functions as the policy and planning agency but on a more detailed level. In addition, they are responsible for directing, coordinating, and monitoring the operation of a number of line institutions or agencies. The personnel at this level, like those of the policy and planning agency, normally do not work directly with the inmates or clients.

The third type or level of organization is the line agency or institution. These agencies might also be called operational agencies because they "operate" the system. Included are such prisons as the Glades Correctional Institution in western Palm Beach County, Florida, and the Attica prison in New York, and such community-based agencies as the model system in Des Moines, Iowa. The "operating agency" category of organization works directly with the inmate or client and is responsible for the broadest range of correctional functions, limited only by the assigned goal or mission of the particular agency. For example, the Robert F. Kennedy Youth Center at Morgantown, West Virginia, is concerned with custody and control, as is the maximum security prison, but its facilities and methods of carrying out this function are different from those of the typical prison.

These three levels of organization will appear at each level of government in our discussion of correctional agencies.

## *FEDERAL CORRECTIONAL ORGANIZATIONS*

There are a number of organizations at the federal level that can be classified as policy organizations. Most of them work within the broad framework of the criminal justice system rather than concentrating only on corrections. Although the legislature (establishing laws) and the court (interpreting laws) are agencies that establish corrections policy, our concern here is primarily with the agencies that fall under the executive branch of the government. Within this category are such agencies as the Law Enforcement Assistance Administration (LEAA) of the Justice Department. Portions of this agency are directly concerned with promulgating corrections policy and planning for corrections improvement on a grand scale. This is accomplished by requiring that minimum standards be met as a condition for obtaining federal funds.

### Federal Bureau of Prisons

All the administrative and operational corrections agencies in the federal government are assigned to the Federal Bureau of Prisons. The Federal Bureau of Prisons, like LEAA, is a part of the Department of Justice. The administrative office of the Federal Bureau of Prisons is located in Washington, and its director reports to the Attorney General on a level comparable to the Federal Bureau of Investigation. The bureau exercises general supervision over the operations of all federal correctional institutions and community treatment facilities. It also supervises the commitment and management of federal inmates and the contracting with local institutions (jails) for confinement and support of federal prisoners being held for trial. Its central office is composed of four divisions plus the Federal Prison Industries, Inc., an office of legal counsel, and a regional support office. The regional support office, organized in 1973, is located in Dallas, Texas. The divisions and offices assigned to the bureau are shown in Illustration 16.1.

That section of the bureau called Federal Prison Industries, Inc. is unique. It is responsible for industrial operations in twenty-one institutions across the country, and it provides a variety of goods and services that are sold to federal agencies. The number of operating units in the Federal Prison Industries, Inc. is continually expanding.

The Federal Bureau of Prisons is composed of forty-three penal and correctional institutions, reformatories and institutions for the youthful offender, camps, and medical and treatment centers. McNeil Island, in the state of Washington, was the site of the first federal penitentiary for men. This prison was taken over by the federal government in 1890, although it was constructed approximately twenty years earlier as a territorial prison. It is interesting to note that McNeil Island is still in operation. The bureau is presently responsible for an inmate population of over 22,000—an increase of 2,000 over the last two years.[1] The nine community treatment centers operated by the Bureau are spread across the country in the major population centers.

## *MILITARY CORRECTIONAL ORGANIZATIONS*

The military corrections system is actually made up of three systems, and corrections in the Army, Navy, and Air Force is the overall responsibility of the secretary of each department. The corrections policy element in the Department of the Air Force is under the directorate of security police, which reports in turn to the Inspector General. Corrections policy in the Navy is the responsibility of the corrections division of the Bureau of Naval Personnel. In the Army also, corrections policy is assigned to a corrections division, but the division reports to the office of the Provost Marshal General.

The administrative level organization in the Air Force is the Air Training Command. This organization supervises the 3320th Retraining Group, which is located at Lowry Air Force Base, Colorado. In the Air Force, all persons worldwide who are serving sentences are assigned to the 3320th Retraining Group. Base stockades (operational units) in the Air Force, are used only for short-term purposes, for example, for individuals pending further legal or administrative action. The administrative level organization in the Navy is the United States Naval Disciplinary Command, located at the naval base in Portsmouth, New Hampshire.

The administrative activities in the Army are more extensive than the other branches of the military service because of

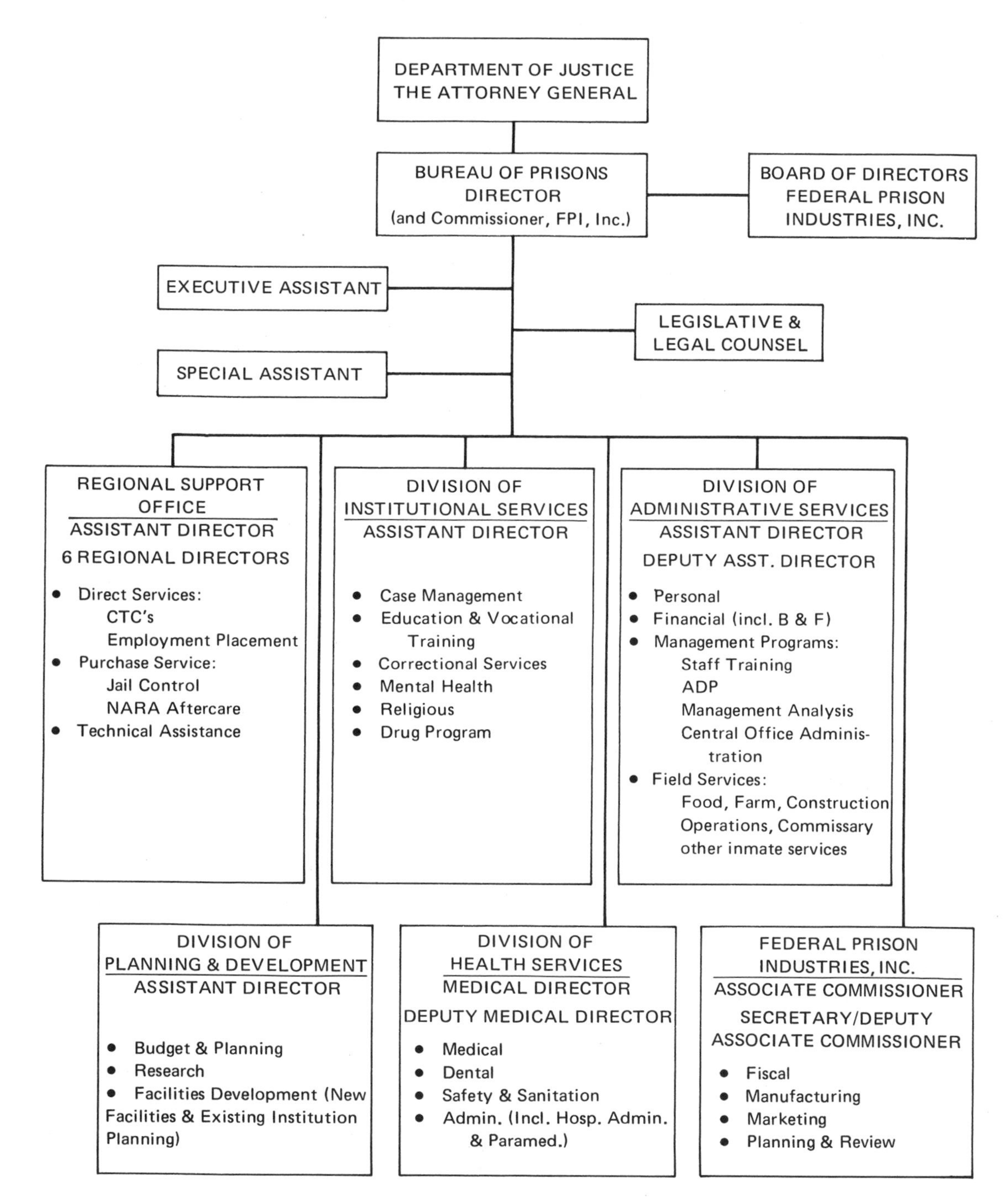


**Illustration 16.1** ORGANIZATION OF THE FEDERAL BUREAU OF PRISONS
Source: Federal Bureau of Prisons, Washington, D.C.

its larger size. The Disciplinary Barracks at Fort Leavenworth, Kansas, has the task of providing correctional treatment, care, and custodial supervision. The Disciplinary Command is under the supervision of an official called the commandant. Directors of administration, classification, training, custody, mental hygiene, and logistic support assist the commandant in supervising a Correctional Holding Detachment and the Disciplinary Barracks.

The Army also operates the United States Army Correctional Training Facility at Fort Riley, Kansas. This facility is used for those who can respond to correctional treatment and for those who have completed a sentence but require additional training before reassignment. Persons who cannot or will not respond to correctional treatment are transferred to the Disciplinary Barracks. The personnel in the Correctional Training Facility supervise and furnish technical guidance to a correctional training battalion, which in turn supervises one or more lower level operational units.

The Army also operates a number of United States Army stockades. There are presently a total of thirty-two permanent stockades. Of these, twenty-four are in the United States and eight overseas (in West Germany, Hawaii, Korea, Okinawa, Alaska, and Panama).[2] The function of the stockade is to provide pretrial and post-trial confinement for persons who have actions pending and to confine prisoners serving short sentences. In this respect, the stockade serves a purpose closely related to that of the city or county jail.

## *STATE CORRECTIONAL ORGANIZATIONS*

There are several policy agencies in the corrections organization at the state level. One of these is the state criminal justice planning agency. This agency, commonly called the Criminal Justice Council or Crime Commission, reports to the governor of the state. These agencies came about as a result of funding by the Law Enforcement Assistance Administration under the Omnibus Crime Control and Safe Streets Act of 1968. This act provided for block grants to be given to the states to fund improvements in law enforcement and the criminal justice system. A state planning agency is organized to work out programs and administer the allocation of these block grants and other funds for all criminal justice components, not just corrections.

Most states also have policy agencies to which the juvenile and adult correctional institutions report, while in a few states the institution directors are responsible to the governor. In Florida, for example, the Division of Corrections (adult) is a branch of the Department of Health and Rehabilitative Service. Sometimes both the juvenile and adult organizations report to one policy agency (commonly called a board), and in other cases there are two separate agencies, each reporting to a separate board. The members of a state

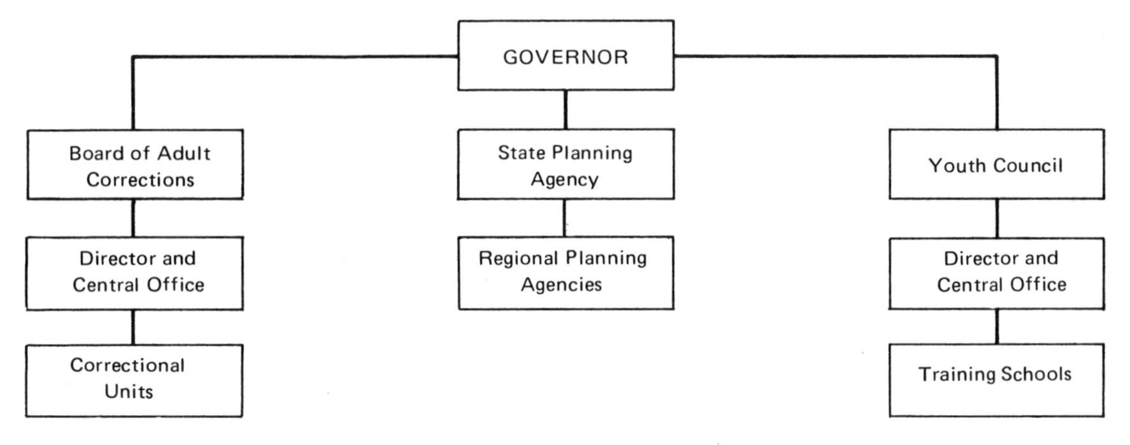


**Illustration 16.2** STATE CORRECTIONS ORGANIZATION

board of corrections are usually appointed by the governor, and the board appoints the institution directors.

Administrative level organizations in the state corrections system are essentially the central offices of the youth and adult penal systems. In some instances, they may include the probation and parole function as well as homes for dependent children and certain welfare and education functions. Generally, the smaller the state, the more functions consolidated under one central organization, but the trend is toward a single state agency controlling all corrective elements. These administrative agencies are organized in a manner similar to the Federal Bureau of Prisons' central office, the principal exception being that juvenile agencies do not normally have extensive agricultural or industrial programs.

Adult prison central offices also vary to some extent, reflecting different perspectives on correction of inmates and differences in state funding support. Texas, for example, has extensive agricultural and industrial programs and inmates in the Texas system are required to work. In California state prisons, such as San Quentin, on the other hand, inmates may choose not to work. The central office organization is different in these two states, reflecting the different approach to corrections. An example of the organization for corrections at the state level is shown in Illustration 16.2. Included in this illustration are all three types of correctional organizations.

Operational or line agencies at the state level are primarily separate penal institutions and training schools that report to the adult or juvenile system's central office, but they include the jail system, as they do in Vermont, and commonly they include community-based agencies. Small states may have only one adult and one juvenile penal institution. Other states have a few large institutions, and a few states have dozens of small, specialized institutions. The layout of a

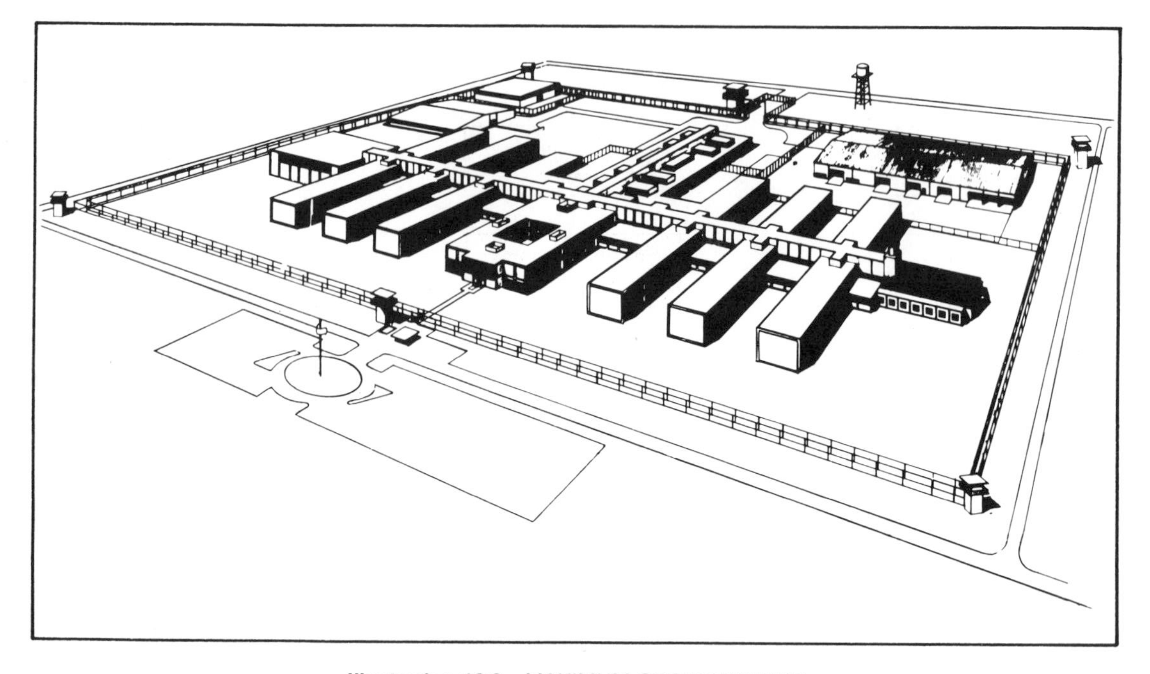

**Illustration 16.3** MAXIMUM SECURITY UNIT
Source: Texas Department of Corrections, Huntsville, Texas

recently constructed maximum security unit that houses approximately 1,500 men is shown in Illustration 16.3. The small institutions (up to 400 inmates) are generally recognized to be preferable to the large units. However, even the smaller institutions tend to be located in rural rather than urban areas, despite the fact that urban areas are preferable because they can support more community-oriented programs.

In the following paragraphs, formal and informal organization of an adult institution is introduced. The formal organization of the training school for juveniles is similar except that more personnel are assigned to education, vocational training, and casework functions instead of farming, external (perimeters and field) security, and industrial programs.

### Formal Prison Organizations

The wardens of prison units are usually the chief executive officers. They are responsible for all the affairs of the unit as defined in policy statements provided by the director and assistant directors of the central office. Among their responsibilities are custody, treatment, training, and discipline of inmates and the administrative duties involved in supervising all employees.

Classification and discipline committees are appointed by the wardens. These committees, which usually consist of five or fewer members, have representatives from a cross-section of the unit staff.

The purpose of the classification committee is to determine the total program for each inmate, which includes job assignment, education, training, and cell-block assignment. Unfortunately, many times these committees do not function in actual practice, and the primary needs considered may be those of the units rather than the individual. In other cases, the committees are active, but the units may lack sufficient programs.

The discipline committees may be semipermanent organizations or they may be organized as the need arises. Their purpose is to consider the more serious breaches of discipline by inmates. Normally, certain punishments, such as solitary confinement, cannot be meted out other than by the discipline committee.

Security sections are usually supervised by correctional officers who have several shift supervisors under their control. Each shift supervisor is responsible for assigning guards to permanent posts in cell blocks and on the perimeter, perhaps in three shifts of eight hours each. The shift supervisor is also responsible for coordinating with the other sections to determine their requirements for shop and field guards. A limited number of guards are held in reserve for special details such as transfer of inmates and supervision of inmates during meals or recreation periods. The security personnel are helped in their function by the classification effort, which predetermines, to a degree, the risk potential of each inmate. The security classification given to each inmate helps guide the security element in making special work assignments.

Vocational training sections are identified as separate elements only in the large systems. Otherwise, vocational training is identified as an element of the industrial or farm enterprises or as an element of the education program. The organization of these elements is critical in determining the relative importance of the different functions. Many times, political considerations influence organization because funds for adult vocational training are more difficult to obtain than funds for an industrial program with emphasis on profit. Actually, vocational training can be adequately achieved for a large number of inmates through industrial programs when the classification committee is active. Problems under this setup exist primarily because profit-making enterprises for a prison (mop-and-broom or license-plate factories, for example) do not always match opportunities for employment in the free world. Although the advantage of active vocational programs is that training can be selected to match more closely opportunity on the outside, much can be said for the emphasis on teaching inmates how to work, no matter what the work.

Education programs are common in prisons, but few are very strong. Of particular interest is the fact that education programs are one of the few prison programs that seem to have an effect on recidivism. In addition to the organization elements discussed above, are such elements as food service, maintenance, supply, counseling, and a chaplain section. The extent of all these elements depends on the size of the unit, the functions stressed, and the funding support given the prison.

### Informal Prison Organizations

Prisons, like all institutions, have informal organizations. Informal organization is just as potent as formal organization and rule making in controlling behavior.

> The prison runs neither by force nor the threat of force alone, but largely by virtue of acceptance on the part of the inmates and their voluntary adherence to rules. These rules are partly the official rules of the prison, partly the mores of the inmate culture developed in the adaption of many generations of convicts to the official code.[3]

Informal inmate organization or subculture has a historical base and is built on the power held by those inmates serving long sentences. It is difficult for treatment personnel to influence individuals once they have been influenced by the inmate subculture and have assumed their roles in that culture. This is a basic element in the belief that rehabilitation is difficult, if not nearly impossible, in the environment of a large prison.

> The inmate social organization . . . is a . . . formidable obstacle to any basic change of character among inmates, for this organization produces, in response to their psychological needs, precisely the conditions that make identification with non-criminal values highly improbable.[4]

The custodial staff also has an informal organization. Guards, like inmates, must protect themselves from the "establishment." Their job is to maintain control among the inmates, and so requires the cooperation of the power factions in the inmate subculture. In reward for cooperation with the guards and as a part of this informal agreement, inmates may be allowed to break certain established rules. Although these relationships help maintain control in the prison, they are also counterproductive when the guards must act as agents of change through treatment.

## *LOCAL CORRECTIONAL ORGANIZATIONS*

There are many organizations at the local level that influence the policy under which correctional units operate. Criminal justice coordinators in the regional planning councils (a multicounty or metroarea planning agency) have some effect on policy through their efforts in planning on a broad basis. One of the functions of the criminal justice coordinators is to provide data to support the state criminal justice plan required yearly by LEAA as a condition for obtaining federal funding under LEAA. The city council is also a policy organization as would be such agencies as the church or social and business clubs that sponsor corrections programs. Many of these agencies play important supporting roles to correctional agencies.

Often, at the local level, it is difficult to distinguish clearly between the policy, administrative, and operational levels of organizations. A county jail, for example, may receive funding, guidance, and planning support from the administrative organization of the sheriff's department of which it is a part. In a small county, the sheriff may be the only full-time person in the organization. In this example, as in the

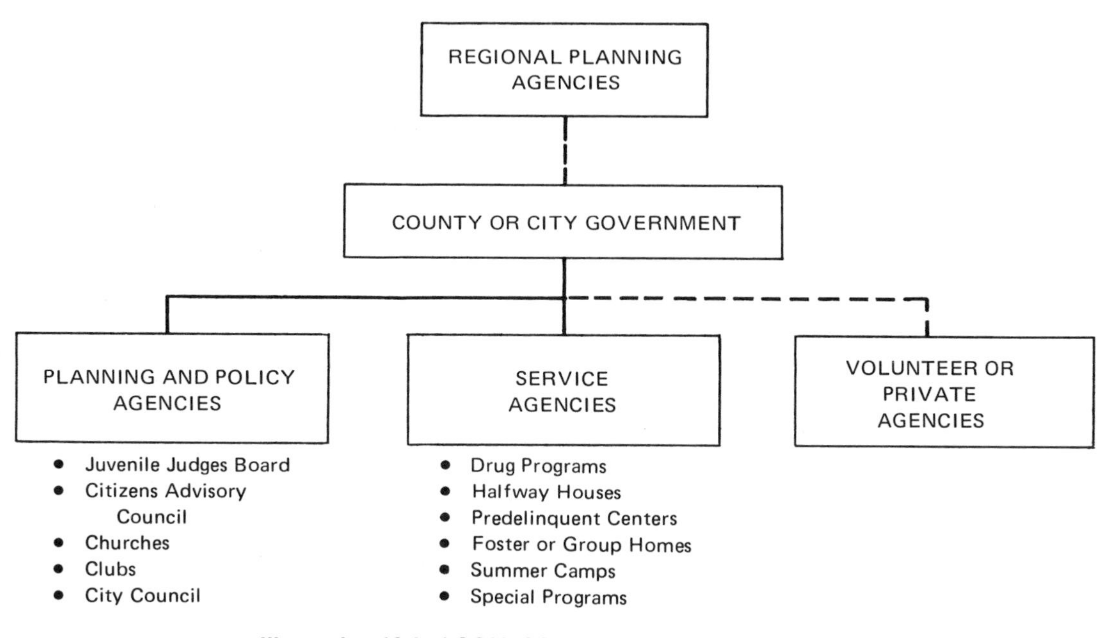


**Illustration 16.4** LOCAL CORRECTIONS ORGANIZATION

case of the chief of police, it would help to think of the individual as wearing several hats. At one time, the sheriff wears the law enforcement hat; at other times, the sheriff is an administrator or operator of a correctional institution and performs the functions normal to that job. The same may be said for the chief of police, who is responsible for the police lockup. (Technically, pretrial detention and lockup are not correctional functions, because the rehabilitation goal is missing.) A typical organization for corrections at the local level is shown in Illustration 16.4

In the paragraphs below, the organizations of several community agencies are presented. With the exception of jails, which are fairly standard, these are only examples of how the corrections functions may be organized in a specific local community. The primary difference between local communities is in the number of staff members (resulting in more or less specialization) and the administrative organization that supports the particular operational unit. These organizations are all classified as community-based, but they may be operated by agencies at levels of government above the city or county.

## Jails

The jail was originally established as a place to detain persons awaiting trial. Over the centuries it has assumed the additional function of housing persons serving short sentences. The jail system that has developed in America has three parts or general classes: (1) the lockup; (2) the jail; and (3) the workhouse, jail farm, or camp.[5] The lockup is used to hold persons for investigation or for preliminary hearing purposes for up to seventy-two hours. It is usually operated by, and located in the same building as, the local law enforcement agency. The workhouse, jail farm, or camp are often used to house minimum custody offenders who are serving short sentences. They may be operated by the city, the county sheriff, or by a separate correctional agency under the city or the county.

Jails are facilities under the control of the police or city or county authorities, and they house both persons awaiting trial and persons serving short sentences. Some jails house both adults and juveniles and, where adequate facilities are not available to provide for separate care, the noncriminal insane. Most jails also serve as lockups for the law enforcement agency operating the facility. A built-in advantage of the jail is that it is normally located in the center of the community so that a full range of community services is within reach. Unfortunately, few jails are administered by professional correctional personnel who utilize the services available, nor are they adequately supported financially so that needed services can be provided by the staff of the jail. In other cases the laws allowing certain programs, such as work release, have not been enacted.

Organizationally and functionally, the jail would typically be much like the prison if the inmate population were the same size and if it held prisoners for the same period of time. Most jails, however, have traditionally been given little financial support, and county jails are usually under the control of a sheriff who stands for election every two to four years. Even under these handicaps, however, there are a number of very progressive jails. The jail in Ingham County, Michigan, for example, operates on an annual budget exceeding $3 million. It has a complete school program, including vocational training, as well as programs for drug offenders, a work release and a school release program. Also available are extensive medical and dental care, arts and crafts, and a closed circuit television network so that inmates under tight security can go to school in their own cells. The staff of this jail includes five professional psychologists in addition to the normal full range of administrative and custodial staff. A jailer in this system is paid more than the deputy sheriffs who work only in law enforcement.

Although the majority of inmates are housed in large city jails, the majority of the jails are in rural areas. The typical small jail is in the care of one man on the staff of the county sheriff's department. Often a police dispatcher is responsible for the jail at night as an extra duty. It is common for a man and wife team to work in the jail, duties being combined to justify a salary large enough to attract two people to take care of the jail functions. In the man and wife team, the man handles the administrative duties and oversees custody of the male prisoners, while the wife acts as both cook and matron, and they may live in the jail. One particular jail in Arkansas that is operated in this manner has a population of ten to twenty inmates.

The jail in the medium-sized county (up

to 300 inmates) is large enough to support shift supervisors under the head jailer. The head jailer is typically responsible for all administrative duties, including such functions as preparing the menu. In jails of this size, the kitchen is commonly operated by inmates, while in small jails meals are often provided by contract with a local cafe. One such medium-sized jail located in southeast Texas is under the control of a jailer who has been given the title of captain, and the staff is composed of approximately sixty employees, who are divided into three eight-hour shifts.

Today, most county jails serve as both lockup facilities and pretrial detention facilities and in addition house convicted offenders for one to two years. There are cases where inmates who are appealing convictions have stayed in local jails for years. Jails have historically provided little treatment and, in fact, are not constructed to allow even adequate control or adequate visitation and recreation. This state of affairs, together with general deterioration with age and problems of overcrowding, has resulted in the need to replace a large number of jails.

The regional jail concept has been proposed as an alternative to building bigger traditional jails. The regional concept calls for the use of holding facilities (lockups) in various locations in a large city or a multicounty area with a central jail to serve the entire region, the central facility to be built around the programs required by the particular area. For example, it might have provisions for diagnostic services, education, vocational training, work and school release, and alcohol and drug detoxification. Or, depending on the area and the size of the inmate population, these activities might he housed in separate facilities, with the detoxification activity, for example, in a local hospital.

The regional concept has been slow in implementation for a number of reasons. One has been a general lack of funding. Jails, like hospitals, are costly to build. Probably the most difficult of the problems to be overcome is that regionalization requires extensive planning and close cooperation between political subdivisions that have not historically been able to cooperate. The advent of regional planning agencies has helped to bring about the cooperation required, but progress continues to be slow. Another problem has been the lack of reform in the courts that causes jails to be crowded with persons awaiting trial. Program activation is difficult when space for programs is at a premium.

**Predelinquent Centers**

The National Crime Commission's Task Force on Corrections reported on several variations of the youth services bureau as a form of predelinquent center.[6] Several of these have sprung up in the past few years on a demonstration basis. Now, many of the larger cities and counties have established their own agencies, assisted in the beginning by federal grants.

One concept is the establishment of an agency primarily concerned with coordinating the services already available in the community. This type of agency is staffed primarily by persons who perform intake and case-summary functions; that is, they are primarily concerned with identifying the problem and referring the individual (or the individual case) to the appropriate agency. Most of the responsibility of this agency is administrative, although professionals in counseling and therapy may be available when these services are not available in other agencies to fulfill specialized needs.

Another type of bureau is one that provides facilities for youth on a live-in basis. In some areas of the country, several counties have pooled their resources to establish juvenile delinquency prevention projects that take potential delinquents from their environment and provide them with a full range of education, training, and counseling services. The factor that distinguishes this project from the typical training school is that participation is voluntary; the youngsters may not have been officially designated as delinquents, and they are allowed to go home on weekends. These individuals are usually controlled by some form of reward structure rather then by guards in locked or barred facilities. Referrals to these projects may come from a variety of sources, among them the family, the schools, the police, and the juvenile court. One such project located in the Southwest has facilities for housing and feeding up to 250 boys. It has full-time teachers, who operate a regular accredited school program, and a diversified vocational program that leads to apprentice status in one of the several labor unions closely associated with the project. The counties that operate this center for boys also operate a similar project for girls.

A third type of bureau is one that has some of the programs of both of the other two approaches. Many projects in this category are under the general control of the juvenile court. They may employ a director, intake workers, caseworkers, a psychologist, and an individual whose responsibility is divided between research and coordination of other community programs. This agency, like the coordinating bureau, maintains close contact with other local social service agencies. In addition, one of its intake workers may be located at the juvenile court and have authority to divert individuals directly to the project prior to juvenile court action. The project maintains close coordination with the police, has daily contact with them, and gives talks during police training programs. Not primarily a referral service, this type of bureau depends more on its own resources but does not provide live-in facilities for clients. The Youth Service Bureau in Waco, Texas, is of this type.

One theory on which these agencies operate is that a juvenile delinquent can be assisted toward a behavior change, if community services are brought to bear at an early stage. Whether the youths are diverted from a life of crime depends to a great extent on the validity of the theory that many of these youths are less likely to continue criminal behavior if kept out of the formal justice system processing and in the community.

### Foster Homes and Group Homes

Foster homes and group homes are alternatives to state schools for dependent or delinquent children. They are more often used for the dependent and the neglected than for youngsters who have committed crimes. Both of these programs are basically instituted to offer a substitute home for a youngster when the former home environment was believed to be unsuitable. Although the use of foster homes is controversial because it takes children away from their natural home setting in the community, there are cases in which this approach is justified.

Group homes are more often used where the alternative is incarceration. They are generally less expensive than an institution and offer the advantages of such community services as the schools. The basic organization of the foster or group home is the family structure, and rehabilitation is expected through the influence that the "parents" can exert on the child. The adults who operate these homes are carefully selected to ensure that they possess the proper traits. The child who goes to a foster or group home is also selected carefully on the basis of expectation that he or she can benefit from this type of treatment or care.

### Community Prerelease Centers and Halfway Houses

The community-based prerelease guidance center or halfway house is normally established to house from ten to twenty-five persons. Since the function of these agencies is to help the inmate through a phased reintegration into the community, a variety of services are required. In addition to providing housing and meals, they provide the important services of counseling and employment assistance.

The typical agency is supervised by a director and, in the large agency, an assistant director. A counselor is available for each ten to twelve persons, and a caseworker or psychologist may be available to oversee the work of the counselors and perform such specialized duties as group therapy. It is also common to employ college interns for counseling and control duties during the night hours. A staff cook is available either half or full time to prepare meals. Also available in the larger agency is an employment counselor, who helps those living in the house with methods and procedures of finding and holding employment and who is also active in the community finding job opportunities and providing funds for tools and equipment that may be needed to obtain jobs in specialized fields. Halfway houses are used most often as a step toward the community after a prison sentence, but they are also used as alternatives to probation or prison.

There are essentially four major systems of corrections in the United States: the federal system, the military system, the state system, and the local system. Within these four major systems there exist planning and policy-making organizations, administrative agencies, and line agencies. Planning and policy-making agencies include the Law Enforcement Assistance Administration (federal), criminal justice commissions (state), and regional criminal justice planning agencies (local). Administrative and line agencies are concerned with the actual operation of correctional systems. The Federal Bureau of Prisons serves this function in the federal system. It supervises the treatment and commitment of federal prisoners, that is individuals who have committed federal crimes. The military prison system consists of the correctional systems of the Army, Navy, and Air Force. Each provides its own system for treatment and commitment of military personnel who have committed acts in violation of the Uniform Code of Military Justice. In the state system of prisons each state has its own unique prison system, ranging from systems with as many as 22,000 inmates in California to as little as 200 inmates in North Dakota. Each state provides for the treatment and commitment of individuals who have violated the state's laws. The local level encompasses the many correctional facilities of the cities, counties, and regional government organizations. At this level we find the police detention cells, the county jails, and the regional correctional centers. These facilities generally serve to hold individuals who have received a short-term sentence or those individuals who are awaiting some form of adjudication.

## DISCUSSION QUESTIONS

1. What role should a research and evaluation unit play in the central administrative organization of a prison system?
2. Explain how special rehabilitation programs can be justified for law violators when they are not available to others?
3. Discuss the education and training needs of a prison warden and prison guards.
4. Describe how to determine the size and program requirements for a new jail.
5. Should an inmate receive benefits, such as a free college education, while in prison?
6. Describe your local correctional organizations. Are they adequate?

## NOTES

1. Bureau of Prisons, *Bureau of Prisons Annual Report 1972* (Washington, D.C.: U.S. Department of Justice, 1973).
2. *Report of the Special Civilian Committee for the Study of the U.S. Army Confinement System* (Washington, D.C.: Department of the Army, 1970).
3. George H. Grosser, "External Setting and Internal Relations of the Prison," in *Prison within Society*, ed. Lawrence Hazelrigg (New York: Doubleday, 1969), p. 18.

4. Grosser, "External Setting," p. 20.
5. American Correctional Association, *Manual of Correctional Standards* (Washington, D.C.: American Correctional Association, 1959), pp. 43–44.
6. President's Commission on Law Enforcement and Administration of Justice, *Task Force Report: Corrections* (Washington, D.C.: Government Printing Office, 1967), pp. 22–23.

BOOK
A
READING
READINESS
M. W. SULLIVAN
SERIES IV
READING
M. W. SULLIVAN

# 17: Functions of Correctional Organizations

*MANAGEMENT AND ADMINISTRATION • CUSTODY AND CONTROL • CORRECTIONAL TREATMENT*

PURPOSE: *TO PROVIDE A DESCRIPTION OF THE FUNCTIONS OF CORRECTIONAL ORGANIZATIONS, INCLUDING ADMINISTRATION, CUSTODY, TREATMENT, PERSONNEL, AND RESEARCH.*

Modern correctional organizations can be categorized as dealing primarily with the function of *treatment* or with the function of *custody and control*. For example, such institutions as the police lockup, housing only persons in short-term, pretrial confinement, are concerned primarily with custody and control. Many community-based predelinquent centers, on the other hand, are concerned primarily with treatment. The prisons, jails, and reformatories generally fall between the two extremes in that they stress both of these functions.

It is almost impossible to explain our modern system of corrections only in terms of these two primary functions. Justifying extensive recreational facilities and legal assistance in a prison, for example, on the basis of their direct relationship to either major function is difficult; probably some programs are justified on moral or other grounds as basic human needs. The presence of these programs (prison employment, education, recreation, adequate food, and so on) may not significantly enhance the treatment or custody and control functions, but their lack may hinder the successful implementation of other programs specifically designed to rehabilitate an inmate. Viewing the functions from this perspective can help explain how the methods used in custody and control can adversely affect treatment. If custody and control methods tend to destroy basic psychological needs of an individual, treatment has little chance of modifying an individual's behavior. In the prison environment, this conflict between control and rehabilitation is not easily overcome.

Historically, corrections organizations have been poorly managed. A complicating factor in accomplishing the treatment and the custody and control functions is the obligation of public officials to operate at a minimum cost consistent with adequate performance. The importance of the cost factor introduces another major function called management and administration. Although proper management and administration are needed by all organizations, their historic neglect in corrections gives them special significance. For this reason the *management and administration function* will be introduced in this chapter along with the functions of *treatment* and *custody and control*.

## *MANAGEMENT AND ADMINISTRATION*

The management and administration function is common to all correctional organizations. It will become evident that the organizations are composed of more than guards and caseworkers. Many technical and professional skills are required. This is shown in Illustration 17.1. And in planning and policy agencies, the management and administration function is everything in that the personnel are not directly involved in treatment and custody functions.

### Planning and Policy

Planning and policy as a part of the management and administration function refer to the establishment of guidelines for

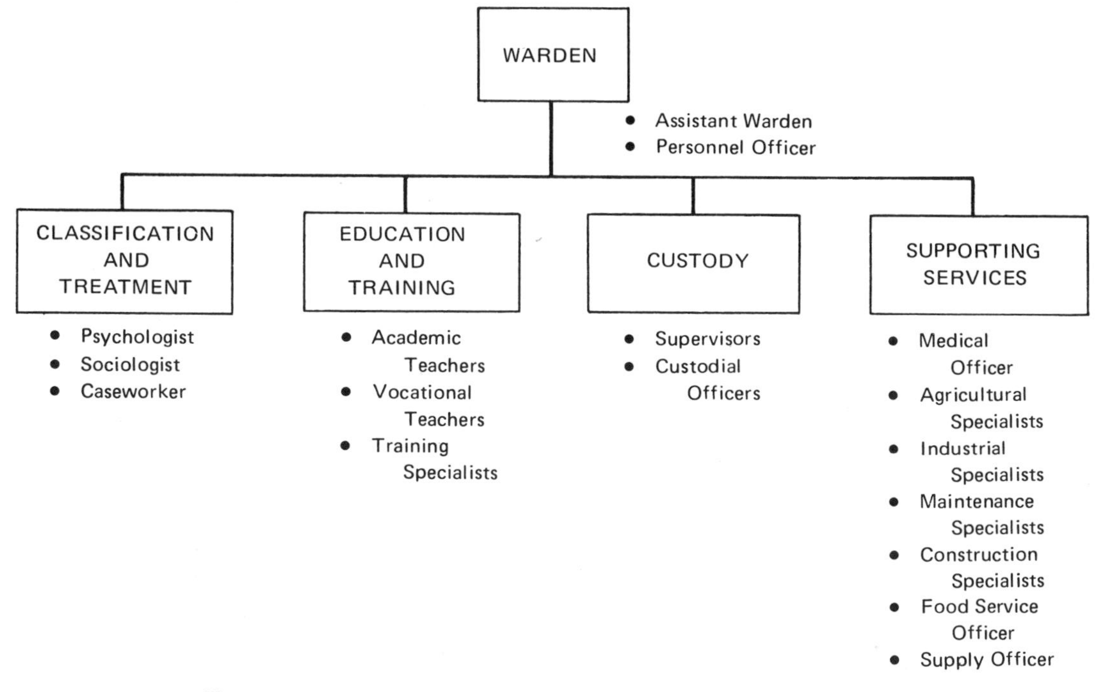


**Illustration 17.1** FUNCTIONAL POSITIONS IN A LARGE PRISON UNIT

the performance of all the programs of an agency or institution, including, for example, the setting of goals and the determination of how success or failure of different programs is measured. Planning and policy are the primary job of the manager, and the job is done at each organization level. The primary difference between levels is in the length of time on which a particular plan is based. For example, the policy agency normally operates on a planning basis of five years or more, whereas the line agency is normally concerned with periods up to one year.

### Fiscal Operations

Fiscal operations include consolidating and monitoring the budget, cost control, accountability for property, and internal auditing. In a small operation, such as a community service project, these responsibilities may be carried out by the project director; whereas, in a large prison, fiscal responsibilities are assigned to the staff.

The fiscal officer ensures that all subordinate agencies submit plans for their monetary needs for the coming year. It is then his or her responsibility, along with the manager, to "sell the product," so to speak, to the funding agency. The funding agency in the case of a state prison system, for example, is the state legislature. Or a community project may require funding from the city government, a state planning agency, or a district office of the Law Enforcement Assistance Administration.

(These funding agencies also have fiscal officers.) Following the receipt of funds, the fiscal officer is responsible for proper distribution of funds and strict accounting of expenditures.

### Personnel Management

The personnel manager works closely with the financial support operation. In the case of small agencies, such as halfway houses, these jobs may be combined and done by the director. The personnel officer may be assigned responsibility for recruitment, records of employees, the retirement plan, job specifications, management development, promotion and selection criteria, and the administration of the staff mail system. The manager is also commonly assigned responsibility for the training of employees and for employee program evaluation.

### Research and Evaluation

The correctional administrator is the important person in any research or evaluation effort. The administrator is responsible for ensuring that the work of the agency or institution is directed, in every phase, toward the achievement of a common goal or mission. To accomplish this task, the administrator must depend on research and evaluation to measure progress toward the objective. Research and evaluation are fundamental elements of effective management.

The scope of research and evaluation in corrections ranges from investigation of the reasons why individuals act as they do and what treatment design best modifies behavior, to methods for improving training and operating procedures. It should be noted, however, that research and evaluation cannot be effective if correctional management is not aware of the utility of the research and evaluation functions.

## *CUSTODY AND CONTROL*

The custody and control functions of institutions and agencies in corrections are primarily those dealing with secure housing, safety of the facility and person, and maintenance of a controlled environment. In some cases, these may be the only functions required of an institution by law. Many of the functions classified as treatment activities in a prison can also help in controlling the inmate; classification is an example. For this reason, it is often difficult, if not impossible, to categorize an activity as one and not the other. The activities identified in this section as belonging to custody or control are traditionally more concerned with custody and control than with treatment. But several could just as well be put in the treatment category, depending on the emphasis, which varies from one organization to another.

### Security

For discussion purposes, *security* is defined as the layout or design of a prison, reformatory, or jail and the programs designed to prevent escape from these institutions. For this purpose, prisons can be described as either *maximum, medium,* or *minimum security*. These terms should not be confused with those used in grading inmates as to security risk, because the modern prison may have facilities suitable for any inmate custody grade.

The maximum security prison is an outgrowth of the Auburn architecture of the last century. Many prisons still in use today were built in the 1800s and thus fall into this category. Their chief characteristic is the high, thick wall surrounding all buildings and activities.

Probably the greatest number of adult prisons today would be classified as medium security. The major differences between this type and the older maximum security prison are the absence of the wall and the fact that some facilities and activities are handled outside the main enclosure. Characteristically, it is smaller than the maximum security unit, and the primary facilities are enclosed by two rows of chain-link fence. (In the past, it was a common practice in military prisons of this type to put folds of concertina wire on top of the fence.) In many ways, the medium security classification is a misnomer, because such a unit may be more escape-proof than the older maximum security unit. Its smaller size and the development of electronic devices to detect escape attempts are effective. Also, most internal doors are electronically controlled from a remote, secure room, and external doors can be unlocked only by electronic means by a guard in a tower removed from the enclosure. Because of the effectiveness of these devices, today most escapes from prisons are likely to be "walk-aways" rather than "breakouts." Walk-aways occur when inmates are allowed to work outside the enclosure.

The minimum security classification unit is found primarily in the juvenile training schools, although the federal government also operates several minimum security units for adults. The Robert F. Kennedy Youth Center in Morgantown, West Virginia, is an example of a minimum security unit. These units do not have fences, and the inmates are free to travel from the dormitory to school, recreation center, or mess hall. Security is provided at night by locking outside doors. The minimum security unit is used primarily for juveniles or for young adults with either short sentences or a short time to go to complete a sentence. An adult felon prerelease center may be of this design.

Classifying jails for security is even more difficult than classifying prisons. The national jail survey of 1970 indicated that 25 percent of the nation's jails were over fifty years old, and many did not provide the minimum essentials for health and safety.[1] Many of these old structures do not have the security devices common in the better prisons, they lack competently trained staff and the basic programs needed to reduce tension and anxiety, and for these and other reasons, security in our jails is a constant problem.

The security functions, as they have been defined for our purposes, are of relatively minor importance in halfway houses and most other community-based projects. There the emphasis is on voluntary control of oneself, and the secure facility in this sense depends on the individual. If rehabilitation of controlled individuals has not progressed to the point where this type of security is sufficient to protect the public and other controlled individuals, then our correctional methods have failed and our modern correctional theories are inadequate.

**Control Procedures**

Another function of custody and control personnel is the development of procedures for the orderly and safe conduct of the institution or agency, those to be followed by inmates or clients and those to be followed by custodial and control personnel. These procedures should be developed on a coordinated basis by all essential elements of the institution so that they represent the best mix of custody and control with the other functions of the institution. In this area of rule making, custody and control commonly conflict with treatment if great care is not taken.

Procedures concerning safety are of paramount importance in controlling the environment and should encompass all areas of the unit. These include work safety, fire prevention, and the proper storage, control, and issue of firearms and other potentially dangerous material. In the modern prison, for example, firearms are maintained only in outside guardhouses (by the pickets) and are issued only when potentially dangerous inmates are escorted to another facility or to work in the field.

Rules and regulations concerning custody and control are established for all phases of inmate processing, work control, and recreation time. Because of the large concentration of inmates found in most prisons and jails, there are rules concerning the personal habits and actions of inmates. Rules generally limit the areas in which an inmate is allowed. Rules also limit loud talking and gathering in groups. Although most of these rules are legitimate requirements for maintaining control, they are also used in some prison and jail situations as a means of repression and punishment in the mistaken belief that control demands complete regimentation in all areas of prison life. The proper use of rules, procedures, and regulations is important not only to insure security and control, but also to complement the treatment programs.

**Reception and Intake**

The initial reception of individuals into the corrections system may be the most critical period in determining their future actions. At this point attitudes toward the corrections system are initiated, and they, to a large degree, control inmates' reactions throughout their stay. *Reception* is used in two senses. In the first, the jails can be considered the "reception centers" of the corrections system, and so the attitudes developed in jail have a great influence on how inmates act in later contacts with the criminal justice system. *Reception* is also used to refer to the processing that individuals receive when they first come in contact with a particular agency or institution, such as a state's adult felony reception center.

*Institutional Reception* The "reception center" concept has been devised to help control the influences operating on individuals during the critical initial phase of their introduction to a penal institution. This concept is common in our prison and reformatory systems but not in our jails. The center may be operated in conjunction with the diagnostic center used for classification; if so, maximum benefit is gained. In addition to the programs that study the background and behavior of the inmate, the reception center may have a program of orientation to remove some of the fear and apprehension found in all individuals. Programs of reading, recreation, and religious training may be available, and special work assignments can be provided to lessen tensions and hostilities.

Typically in the past and in some cases today, the reception center was a shock treatment used to indoctrinate inmates. An inmate, for example a youth of seventeen or even younger, may be forced to undress, after which his body is inspected, his head is shaved, and his personal belongings are taken from him. He then goes through an endless session of days and nights filled with regimentation, forced silence, and loneliness in the middle of a crowd. It is this treatment that forces an inmate to seek relief, and one way is to become an active participant in the inmate subculture. Certainly careful attention is required during the reception process to reduce the possibility of the introduction of weapons, drugs, or physical disease, but it must be remembered that treatment possibilities can be destroyed if consideration is not given to rehabilitation at each stage of administrative processing.

*Reception in Community-Based Corrections* In the setting of the community "helping" agency, the reception process is referred to as "intake." Here an individual's first contact is with the intake worker, who tries to find out what problems an individual has, records basic data concerning age, sex, family situation, and so forth, and determines which particular specialists, either within or outside the organization, are best equipped to work with the client. Essentially, the intake worker handles both the activities associated with intake and many of the activities associated with determining suitable treatment for the individual (classification).

Reception, or intake, assumes great importance in the community helping agency as well as in the institution. Because many of the helping agencies are dependent on the voluntary participation of the client for a successful program, many agencies use their most capable personnel for intake.

### Classification

Classification, in the institutional setting, has a multiple purpose. First, classification supports the overall custody and control function in that an inmate is "classified" according to the amount of custodial control required. Secondly, classification determines a treatment plan for the person based on individual needs. A third use of classification is that of supporting the administrative needs of the institution by placing a person with a particular skill or aptitude in the proper program. Classification in the community helping agency setting, on the other hand, is concerned primarily with designing a treatment plan, which may include a decision to place an individual under a caseworker who will offer intensive supervision or under a caseworker who will provide only minimum supervision.

However, the mere presence of a system of classification indicates little about what it is actually accomplishing. For example, an inmate may be assigned to work in an office or on a farm because that assignment best meets his or her needs or because the institution has a need for labor. Or a juvenile may be put under minimum supervision because all casework loads of the agency were too high to offer close supervision. Classification is a strong tool, and the use to which it is put must be closely monitored.

### Food Service

The food-service function in an institution like a prison or jail can be extremely complicated and costly. Many institutions must procure all the necessary food items from outside sources. A few prison systems, however, operate large farms that provide the bulk of daily needs. And, in some cases, a prison may make excess food available to other governmental institutions, thereby reducing their costs of operation. The prison in Mississippi is an example of a system that has land for extensive agricultural programs.

An effective food-service program combines the essentials of sanitation, menu planning, proper facilities for storage and preparation, and a system of distribution and serving. These specialized activities of necessity require professional food service personnel in all but the smallest institutions. From the inmates' point of view, food service probably ranks with mail and visitation as the most important functions of the prison, reformatory, or jail. The effect on inmate morale of a poorly run food-service program is significant and can be a major factor in the success of control and treatment programs.

### Medical Service

The medical service operates from reception of an individual into corrections to release. In the community agency, the medical condition of a client is one of the first treatment considerations. In the institution, medical services must be available as a part of rehabilitation, but they must also be available for humanitarian and health safety reasons. Usually, a complete medical checkup is one of the first steps in the processing of an inmate into an institution. Minor health problems are corrected immediately, and more costly or time-consuming treatments may be attempted, depending on their seriousness or their potential for forwarding rehabilitation.

Most large prisons maintain a permanent professional staff for medical and dental health purposes. It is difficult to conceive of a more terrifying experience than that of a sick individual locked in a cell knowing that medical assistance is not readily available. Unfortunately, however, such is the case in some prisons and in many jails, both large and small.

### Industry Programs

Although industry programs can be classified under the treatment function, consideration of their cost/savings aspect probably outweighs the treatment aspect in most adult prisons for males. The reverse may be true in juvenile or women's facilities, where the training and work benefits may take precedence over the financial advantage. A properly managed prison industry program can save taxpayers millions of dollars each year while offering job training for many inmates.

Prison industries include such programs as furniture repair and manufacture, license-plate manufacture, cattle and horse operations, farming, building, and road construction. The possible diversification of prison industry is limited only by the effect of law (selling for state use only) and the influence of private industry. Although the possibility for full employment of inmates exists in theory, in practice it has been achieved in very few prison systems and probably in no large jails. Prison industry, however, does offer the multiple advantages of providing the opportunity for proper placement for treatment, reducing discipline problems by the release of tension through productive employment, and reducing costs by a self-supporting operation.

## *CORRECTIONAL TREATMENT*

The treatment program for an individual in prison can actually be thought of as encompassing most correctional functions. For a properly designed and implemented program, all the work, training, education, and custody assignments of an inmate are part of treatment. Even though not designed specifically to aid in treatment, a function may have an effect on the treatment programs; that is, the lack of recreation, medical care, or the like can negate an otherwise successful program.

It is probably in the area of integration of functions that overall institution management fails most often. In a rehabilitative model, a few primary goals have to be the target for all elements of the institution or agency, and treatment may be the one area that can properly integrate all other functions in the development of a realistic and meaningful plan for an individual. The following sections cover some of the current functions normally considered to be primarily treatment oriented. Included are both a discussion of treatment approaches and a discussion of some programs established in the attempt to avoid the pitfalls inherent in the institutional approach to rehabilitation. The fact that many of these functions can also be categorized as control or custody should not be disregarded.

### Prisoner or Client Services

In the institutional setting, the prisoner services category includes those services provided to inmates in the areas of welfare, morale, and daily comfort. Some of these activities, such as providing clothing, may be required by law. Other services, such as visitation privileges, commissaries, pay, vocational rehabilitation, and welfare counseling, may not be required by law, but they may be justified because they provide the maintenance of basic human dignity or are real tools for treatment and rehabilitation.

In many prisons and jails, visitation, commissaries, and certain other activities, including recreation, are considered privileges. As such, the inmate must earn the privilege of their use. In other instances, notably the jails, some of these basic services are completely missing. For example, checkers and cards may the extent of recreation for an inmate serving a year in jail. Most criminologists today feel that all these services are essential for basic health and welfare and that their lack can contribute significantly to the failure of both the treatment and the custody and control functions.

In the setting of the helping agency, client services become a significant activity. Most of these agencies exist for the purpose of providing a specific service or acting as a referral source to the proper service. Some predelinquent control agencies, for example, exist for the sole purpose of seeing that juveniles and their families are channeled to the service organization best suited to satisfy their need. These agencies may not perform any specific treatment activity; rather they refer the client to another agency that specializes in the required service. Among the agencies or programs to which a client or his family might be referred are welfare organizations, employment counseling agencies, remedial reading centers, drug programs, vocational training programs, and individual or group counseling programs.

### Counseling, Therapy, and Individual Evaluation

Professional evaluation of the individual is an essential element in any corrections program. Whether in a community agency or an institution, the experience begins with adequate evaluation so that plans for appropriate treatment and control can be made. In the prison setting, this evaluation is begun by interviewers who are skilled in developing a case history. In the agency setting, this is done by the intake worker. After this processing, a case worker or counselor may be assigned, or the individual may be assigned or referred to a program or agency designed to help him or her toward rehabilitation. These decisions many times are made in conference or with the advice of professional psychologists or others who are trained in behavioral modification programs. Day-to-day counseling may be provided by the case worker, counselor, or correctional officer, who in turn seeks advice from the staff psychologist.

Although many methods and types of counseling and therapy have been attempted in the institutional setting, the success of these programs has been doubtful, to say the least. This doubtful record can be explained in part by the difficulty of measuring success. Many reasons have been advanced for this apparent failure to measure adequately, but we probably have never had both the proper setting and adequate research controls to come to a proper conclusion.

In the community setting, counseling and individual evaluation activities assume a more all-encompassing role than is usual in the institution. Because these programs are not custodial, behavior change through casework and counseling is of primary importance.

### Short-Term Treatment Programs

Several states have employed special short-term treatment programs. California has had extensive experience with such programs, and Florida has recently introduced them. The common practice in these states is to screen all juveniles who have been committed to an institution by the juvenile court for eligibility for immediate release from the reception center on parole or for release after a short treatment program. Those selected may be placed in foster homes or halfway houses, or the may be paroled to a parole officer as part of his or her normal or intensive casework load.

This type of program for juveniles is in striking contrast to the normal process for adults. Adults (normally 17 or 18 and older), when sentenced to a prison term, must usually wait until they have completed a specified portion of the sentence before being eligible for parole. A rigid system of parole eligibility does not recognize that some individuals could be released in a short time and have a high probability of success in staying out of the criminal justice system. This is not to say that we should return to the indeterminate sentence. Rather, some criminologists have indicated that the indeterminate part of the sentence should involve the time before a normal parole date rather than the time after the normal parole date. It has been argued that a system of this kind could offer the best potential for treatment success while maintaining a powerful tool for control in the prison environment.

### Work Furlough

Work furlough or work release is the practice of releasing an inmate from a prison or jail to work in the community. A number of states have initiated such programs in their prison systems, but few jails have tried them (despite the fact that work release was initiated in a very few jails several decades before the United States Bureau of Prisons instituted its program). The normal procedure is for the inmate to be driven to work each day and returned to the prison or jail each night. Part of the inmate's wages may go toward paying room and board, making restitution, and providing family support, or into a savings account. In the jail situation, the program is operated by the jail's chief administrator in a similar manner.

Work release, as a concept, offers the potential for a self-supporting treatment program. It has been strongly advocated by criminologists but meets with considerable resistance from prison and jail authorities, not so much because of their inability to see the benefits, but rightfully because of fear of public opinion in the wake of a failure. Logically, it can be seen that a person on work release is less likely to commit a crime because of the high probability of being caught and the swiftness of the resulting punishment. The problem lies in the fact that the prison or jail administrator has a direct hand in choosing the person for work release and may therefore be held directly accountable for failure. Also, failures in a work-release setting are more visible to the public than are failures within the institution. Nevertheless, the fact that probably 98 percent of all inmates will eventually return to the community is sufficient reason to greatly expand this type of reintegration program.

### Education and Recreation

Education programs, both academic and vocational, and recreation programs are the backbone of the treatment function in most prisons. Many individuals seem only to need this type of "treatment." The lack of these programs in most jails means no treatment program at all. Like many of the other programs in the treatment category, there is very little evidence that they are significantly effective tools in rehabilitation. Most criminologists and administrators feel, however, that they are justified on other grounds and in combination with other treatment programs offer much promise as the foundation for treatment.

The major problem with education programs, where they do exist, is their quality. In many instances, academic classes are conducted on a voluntary basis by off-duty guards. In some cases, they are poorly supported by funding agencies, and teaching materials are limited. There are, however, excellent education programs in several prisons and in many of the juvenile institutions. Those institutions with quality education programs employ qualified teachers and are certified by the state, so that high school diplomas can be issued.

A number of prisons and jails offer college courses for inmates through arrangements with local colleges. Correspondence courses are the most common means of gaining college credit. There are also programs where instructors come to the prison, and in some places, like the Federal Correctional Center in Fort Worth, Texas, groups of inmates go to the college itself.

Vocational training programs, like academic education programs, are used more in juvenile facilities than in adult institutions, partly because of the existence in adult prisons of industry and agriculture programs that relieve some of the need and reduce costs. Because many of the industry programs are not related to employment opportunities outside the prison, much effort is being directed to obtaining funds for realistic vocational programs. Common among these are automotive, radio, and television repair, and programs in such areas as meat cutting, metal work, and other specialized skills.

Recreation by itself is only marginally a treatment program, but it is important as a way of providing a climate for other programs, including the custody and control activities. Recreation programs can range from libraries and books to sports like baseball and rodeo. Several states have regular league play between prison units in baseball and basketball. Organized sports activities are, however, concerned primarily with overall morale building and do not directly involve many inmates. For many jail inmates, there are no facilities for recreation or exercise of any kind.

### Prerelease Counseling

Prerelease counseling includes those activites that take place shortly before an inmate is released from a penal institution and are designed to assist his or her reintegration into the community. A prerelease program is distinguished from a halfway house in that it is normally conducted by the institution and usually within the institution. The other obvious distinction is that it is conducted prior to release from custody, whereas the halfway house usually has ex-inmates, those who have been released on parole or, in some cases, after completion of sentence.

The typical prerelease program is little more than a series of lectures on such topics as general financial management, how to buy major products, the cost of items on the outside, and how to get along with a parole officer. Most prisons operate some type of prerelease program, and they can range from a few talks given by custodial personnel to full-scale programs, several weeks long, with visiting speakers. Inmates may also be allowed limited freedom in the community as a part of the program.

Few jails operate any type of prerelease program, which is unfortunate because jails, like prisons, can hold inmates for a sufficient length of time to justify a need for careful reintegration into the community. An advantage to the prerelease concept, as opposed to the halfway house, is that it can be operated from the institution and so is a reasonable program for jails to operate. Also, an institutional prerelease program can handle much larger numbers than can the halfway house.

## DISCUSSION QUESTIONS

1. Can treatment and control measures exist together?
2. What does cost/effectiveness mean?
3. Is the corrections system in agreement concerning the purpose or goal of corrections?
4. Discuss your concept of the goal of corrections.
5. Is time spent serving a sentence a continuation of punishment or is it the first phase of a rehabilitation program?
6. Discuss whether one of the major penal functions could encompass the other functions.
7. Discuss how security or control measures can influence the rehabilitation process.

## NOTES

1. U.S. Department of Justice, *1970 Jail Census* (Washington, D.C.: Government Printing Office, 1971), p. 1.

# 18: Problems, Controversies, and Modern Concepts in Corrections

*PEOPLE INVOLVED IN CORRECTIONS • INADEQUACIES IN MANAGEMENT AND ORGANIZATION • INSTITUTIONAL AND NONINSTITUTIONAL CORRECTIONS • RESPONSIBILITY*

PURPOSE: *TO PROVIDE AN OVERVIEW OF THE MAJOR PROBLEM AREAS IN CORRECTIONS WITH A DISCUSSION OF THEIR EFFECTS.*

THE MANY problems in corrections are well documented and seem almost insurmountable. After hundreds of years of applying the techniques of punishment and retribution in a system of jails and prisons, failure must be admitted. The negative results are many and the successes are few. The task now is to learn from past mistakes and modern technology and then apply this knowledge to finding better solutions. The overriding problem is that of determining the best method of assuring the protection of society at the price in money and involvement that society is willing to pay.

This chapter is concerned with where corrections stands today in contrast to where it should be. A number of areas are explored: the people who work in corrections, the population being corrected, the tools with which correctional personnel must work, and certain factors influencing the corrections system over which correctional personnel have little control.

## *PEOPLE INVOLVED IN CORRECTIONS*

The people in corrections are both the people being corrected and the people attempting to do the correcting. Each group has it characteristics and its problems. The inmate population has been referred to as "the captive society."[1] In many ways, the rehabilitation potential of the captive is dependent on improvements in the basic corrections system and on improvements affecting the people who are attempting to accomplish the goals of corrections. That is, the inadequate training of corrections workers, among other things, can be counterproductive and actually be a factor in causing more crime rather than diverting a person from a life of crime. For this reason it is important to understand the problems and characteristics of both the captors and the captives.

### Correctional Workers

In October 1973, there were the equivalent of 90,779 full-time employees in correctional institutions at the state level. Of these, 29,628 were in juvenile institutions.[2] There were the equivalent of 28,911 full-time employees working in county jails in March 1970, over 30 percent of them in New York and California. In all jails, the ratio of inmates to employees was 5.56 for the United States. The ratio ranged from 11.44 in Mississippi to 1.31 in Hawaii. The average monthly earnings for these jail employees was $617.00, but for cities under 25,000 the average was $419.00.[3]

The criminal justice system has suffered from a lack of funding support throughout its history, and corrections has had the lowest priority within the system. This low priority has affected the pay and adequate training of correctional workers. Prison and jail employees as a whole are probably one of the lowest paid groups in the economy. Few prisons and jails have education standards for employees, and the pay for correctional workers reflects this lack of standards. Low pay, combined with other factors, makes the attracting and keeping of qualified workers a difficult task. It is common for prison and jail employees to be paid a starting salary of $400–$500 per month, and although the standards for noninstitutional workers in the community (probation, parole, and so on) are often higher (a college degree or more), their pay does not always reflect this higher standard.

Lack of adequate training is also a serious problem. Those persons hired to work directly with the inmates in our institutions are often inadequately prepared either by education or other preservice training to undertake a corrections role. Where in-service training is available, it is primarily concerned with security and administration. Although the Federal Bureau of Prisons sponsors a training program for local jailers, its impact is necessarily low because of the number of jails and the rapid turnover of jail employees. Few states have centrally administered organizations to set correctional standards and offer training. The National Advisory Commission on Criminal Justice Standards and Goals (1973) has recommended the creation of comprehensive training programs for correctional employees to be administered by the states.

Another serious problem for correctional workers is the role dilemma or conflict. Are correctional workers policemen and custodians, or are they primarily concerned with rehabilitation? This role conflict is both a product of inadequate training and lack of agreement on the goals of corrections. When probation and parole officers are asked about their roles, some will concentrate their replies on the supervisory aspect of the job and others will concentrate on the rehabilitation role. The same role conflict is a characteristic of correctional workers in institutions. The custody and control goal may demand a minimum of conversation with inmates, whereas the treatment or rehabilitation goal may call for interaction. When treatment experts explain acting out by inmates in terms of human behavior change, corrections workers understand their own conflict, but they also understand that promotion within the custodial system is based on how they function in the custody and control role, where such acting out may be a threat to the institution. Correctional workers must be able to strike a balance between control measures and treatment measures so that other employees and inmates are not threatened with harm while the rehabilitation goal is served. This dilemma, common to all correctional workers, has not been solved in practice and is not adequately explained in theory.

### Prisoners

It was reported by the National Crime Commission that approximately 426,000 individuals were confined in our correctional institutions on any given day.[4] There was a total average daily population of 1,282,386 in all phases of corrections (includes probation and parole).[5]

More recent studies have indicated that adult prison populations are increasing in some states while they are decreasing in others. The factors of changes in laws, sentencing policy of the courts, added use of alternatives to incarceration, and improved law enforcement can combine in different ways to cause increases or decreases. A decrease in the prison population in California was attributed in part to a comprehensive probation subsidy pro-

COURTESY OF TEXAS DEPARTMENT OF CORRECTIONS, HUNTSVILLE, TEXAS

**Illustration 18.1** CELLBLOCK

A prison guard monitors one-half of a three-tiered cellblock. The other half of the cellblock backs on this portion and is identical. The complete cellblock can house up to 228 inmates with two inmates per cell. All doors are controlled remotely by the guard.

gram. At the other extreme, the Texas system and the federal system have continued to show significant increases in population. Texas does not have a coordinated statewide probation system for adults, and the percentage of people released on parole is one of the lowest in the country.

The jail population is also influenced by a number of other factors. For example, California's probation subsidy program, while decreasing prison population, in some cases had the opposite effect on the jail population. As another example, a 1974 penal code revision in Texas reduced several classes of felonies to misdemeanors; it could decrease prison commitments but will possibly increase jail commitments.

The jail population across the country is made up predominantly of those awaiting trial, or some other form of adjudication.[6] In this respect overcrowding is caused to a large extent by inadequate pretrial release procedures and the overload and inefficiency in the court system. Not uncommonly there is a delay of one year or more between arrest and trial. Our money bail practices obviously discriminate against the poor and in large measure account for the jail population being composed of the poor and uneducated. Drunks are another primary group in the jail population, even though modern correctional concepts call for treatment of drug (including alcohol) users to be handled outside the criminal justice system. Some researchers have described the jail population as being composed of the failures of the public school system. There may be some truth in this statement, but the problem is more complicated and all the blame cannot be laid on the schools.

While much emphasis has been placed on the correction of youth in the community, there is still evidence of increased population in juvenile reformatories. Many are expanding, although at least one state has closed its reformatories. The increase in the population of the juvenile reformatories is a serious concern and reflects a failure in recent efforts to correct youth in the community.

The most significant increase in corrections populations has occurred in probation. Is this a problem? It can be if probation is used as an unsuitable alternative to other community programs rather then as an alternative to prison or reform school. Where probation department funds are based on the number of probationers, there is a natural pressure to maintain a high probation population at the expense of using more appropriate methods or ending a term of probation.

Other problems directly affecting the captive society and indirectly affecting society at large include inadequate programs, unnatural living conditions, and abnormal sexual behavior. These problems are primarily identified with life in an institution as opposed to life in the community on probation or parole. Institutional existence seems to lead naturally to segregation of the sexes, suppression of decision making, and no provision for continuation of normal marital affairs. As punishment, these conditions are effective but as training for reintegration into society they are counterproductive. Modern concepts call for inmates to be exposed to the community to the maximum extent possible.

Lack of adequate rehabilitation programs is also a problem, but it is characteristic of the goal conflict in corrections. Correctional leaders cannot agree on what programs should be mandatory, and research has given them little information on which to base decisions. As a result, inmates leaving institutions are little prepared to assume responsibility in society. They have been separated from society, have not been given basic skills related to work on the outside, and have not even been fully relieved of the "debt" owed society. This situation leaves little hope that they will not recidivate.

## *INADEQUACIES IN MANAGEMENT AND ORGANIZATION*

Although corrections is often referred to as a "system," it is actually composed of a number of systems that seem to be only loosely related. Just as a change in the police or courts can cause changes in corrections, so do changes in correctional elements affect each other. For example, a planned reduction in prison population puts increased pressure on the local institutional system. To talk about a system implies that a number of processes are linked together in pursuit of a common goal. At times, dedication to a common goal in corrections is difficult to find, as is reflected in inadequacies in correctional management and organization.

### Correctional Management

Inadequate management in corrections has been documented from a historical perspective. The recent attention given to corrections both in national surveys and in court cases indicates how little progress has been made. It is a fact that many correctional managers have mishandled their efforts to correct inmates and clients, but they have also mismanaged the resources given to them. It is common to hear cries for more funds and more employees as the solution to problems in institutional and noninstitutional programs alike. However, some correctional leaders are convinced that proper use of existing resources would be more productive. Through better training, correctional officers can be more effectively used, and improved financial management can decrease the cost of operating institutions while providing meaningful work for inmates.

Community agencies often stress a reduction in caseload as a solution to supervision problems, although actually little attention is given to proper classification of clients into supervision categories. The great majority of clients of these community agencies (youth service bureaus, probation and parole, and so on) would do well with little or no supervision.

Institutional management of inmates is undoubtedly worse than noninstitutional management. Even though elaborate classification systems exist, they are typically poorly managed and little utilized. Most prisons and reformatories have diagnostic programs whereby incoming inmates are processed through a testing and case-history procedure, but this information is more often used to classify inmates for security purposes than to plan for long-range rehabilitation.

Another problem associated with management is the lack of adequate planning, research, evaluation, and theory. Large correctional organizations have only recently introduced an integrated planning function. There is a need for planning, both long and short range, to define the goals and objectives and to insure that all elements of the organization are working as a team to reach these goals and objectives. Like the treatment function, planning is often not properly used to bring about an integration of purpose. Research and evaluation are closely associated with planning in that they provide the manager with information about progress toward planned goals. Planning, research, and evaluation are integral parts of effective management.

It has been said that significant, long-term improvement in corrections can only be made within the framework of theory. Theory has the function of providing information about the direction in which to proceed. Theory brings diversified plans together into an understandable network of required actions. To date, however, the results of research raise troublesome questions concerning the adequacy of our theories of behavior change. Just as troublesome are questions about the adequacy of a theory to guide methods of research and evaluation. Attempts to evaluate those programs that are in operation in the community have pointed out the problems associated with using traditional research techniques, and control of the experimental situation is all but impossible in the community setting. Another problem related to research is the use of traditional indicators as measures of success. For example, although recidivism is a common measure of the success of a program, a number of programs can be justified on humanitarian grounds even if they are not demonstrated to have a direct effect on recidivism.

There is little reason to doubt that prisons will always be needed, in that a small percentage of criminals will always require long-term incarceration for the protection of society. However, research indicates that corrections should move away from the institutional concept in the majority of cases. One of the reasons for the slow progress in developing such alternatives as probation, parole, and work release lies in our inability to distinguish between good and bad risks. Most parole boards use a complicated checklist of items that are thought to be predictors of behavior on the outside, but there is little if any research that supports the criteria used to make the selections. This prediction criteria is vital to the success of rehabilitative efforts.

### Correctional Organizations

Organizational problems in corrections could be discussed from several perspectives. For example, most correctional organizations can be classified as "functional" organizations, whereas modern correctional concepts often call for a "team" or "project" approach to treatment. The functional organization is one that is designed around the important functions. A review of the chapter on corrections organizations will indicate that many of the rehabilitation activities do not seem to be important from an organizational perspective. The team or project approach to organization calls for the mixing of skills or functions within one component. Because organizational structure change has not kept pace with modern theory and improved techniques in corrections, problems have developed.

The major problem, is that correctional organizations do not work as a cohesive system. There is a federal correctional system, a state correctional system, and a local correctional system. And within these systems are often found separate systems for probation, parole, adult prison, juvenile reformatories, jails, juvenile detention, *ad infinitum.* Not only is there a lack of coordination between these correctional components, but there is a lack of agreement as to whether they are all a part of corrections and what level of government has responsibility.

In the federal system and the system of several states, probation is administered by the courts. Youth service bureaus are often administered by the juvenile court as an extension of juvenile probation. It will also be remembered that the Federal Bureau of Prisons operates community treatment centers, as do several states. In other states, community treatment is totally the responsibility of the local community. Jails are also commonly the responsibility of local government. Under a "system" of corrections that has little central planning or control, it is not difficult to see why progress has been slow and painful. Significant further progress will depend to a large extent on some consolidation of administration.

## *INSTITUTIONAL AND NONINSTITUTIONAL CORRECTIONS*

Modern correctional concepts call for treatment of convicted offenders in the community, and thus the jails assume an even more important role than in the past.

The jail system of the future, however, will be different in many respects from the present system. Jails and prisons in the past were built to house the correctional population in a custody and control condition; correctional facilities in the future will be built around the needs of that population. These concepts call for confinement only in the most extreme circumstances. A review of some of the problems of the present system will help to focus attention on the needs for the future.

### Prisons

Most prisons were designed to house large numbers of inmates. They are also typically located in rural areas; thus programs of reintegration are most difficult. Large institutions are characterized by regimentation of all areas of daily life, under professional supervision, which is contrary to the ideal of allowing a person to exercise responsibility in an atmosphere like that in which he or she must ultimately live. Prison architecture also detracts from rehabilitation. The Auburn concept of cellblock construction is still in use today, approximately a hundred and fifty years after its invention. In crowded conditions, with inadequate programs of recreation and rehabilitation, without the opportunity for productive employment, and lacking normal sexual relations, prisoners have shown a tendency to riot that is not difficult to understand.

Incarceration is also costly. Prison expenses often exceed $10 per day per person, while probation expense, as a comparison, is commonly less than $1 per day per person. Prison construction cost is another matter. It is estimated that the traditional jail or prison costs over $20,000 per bed to build, not including adequate provision for programs of rehabilitation. When prison populations are reduced, cost per inmate rises drastically, presenting a dilemma; while large populations result in less cost, they are not believed to improve the protection of society by rehabilitation of inmates.

### Jails

Persons coming into the criminal justice system enter through the jail. Most are detained for only short periods of time. Over 50 percent of those detained are drunks, and over 36 percent are pretrial detainees. Jails may house both male and female, adult and juvenile, sane and insane, first offender and habitual criminal. All these classes of offenders are typically housed in cells that were constructed years ago. Plumbling has rusted to the point where it cannot be used. Lighting is inadequate, recreation and education are almost nonexistent, and services like visitation are usually inadequate to maintain any sort of normal family existence.

Inmates housed in prisons and jails are a drag on society. The taxpayer commonly supports the inmate's family while also supporting the inmate. The jail system also is a drag on society in that all evidence points to the jail as a breeding ground for more crime. What is the alternative to the present system? Many believe that it is to be found in a community corrections concept that places emphasis on a combination of coordinated institutional and noninstitutional programs. However, the problems associated with this concept have not yet been solved.

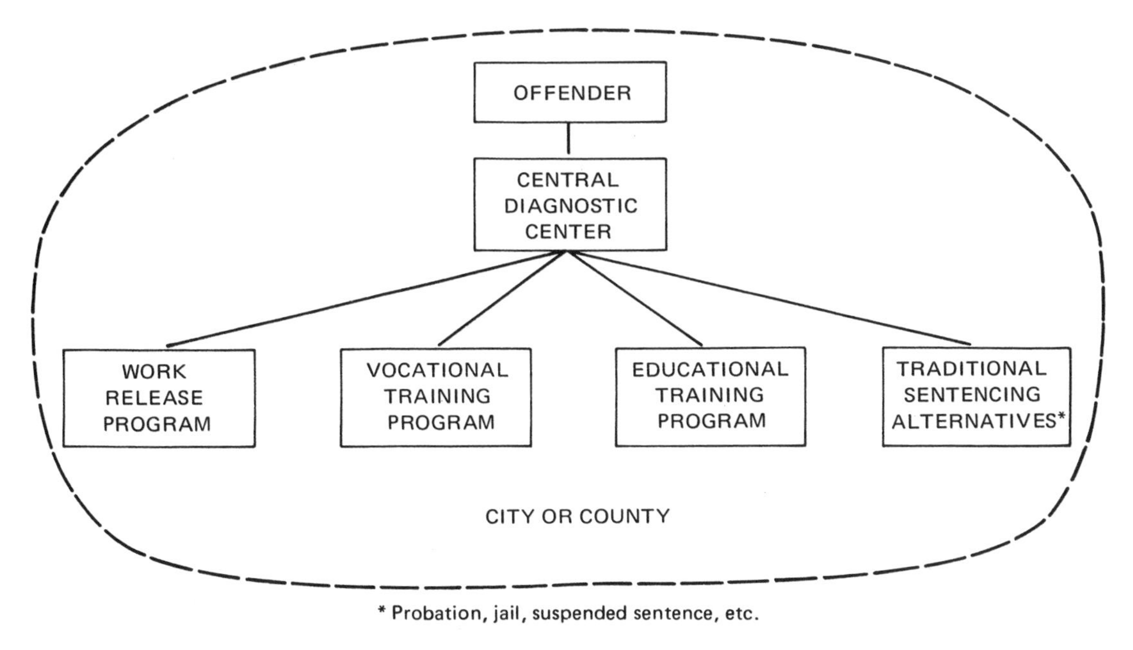


**Illustration 18.2** COMMUNITY-BASED CORRECTIONS

### Community Corrections

Millions of dollars are being spent each year on the construction of new prisons, jails, and reformatories. The problem of our aging institutions has been known for years but several organizations and individuals have indicated that more new construction can create or perpetuate facility problems. A number of cities and counties have built new jails only to find that the population expanded to fill both the old and the new facility. Walls are being built around the expanding population as a substitute for taking action to reduce the population. Some also believe that funds expended on building institutions as opposed to creating community programs are wasted funds. The National Council on Crime and Delinquency has recommended that construction be stopped until adequate community programs have been established in the attempt to reduce institution population. It is possible that there are more new facilities in existence than would be needed if other reform measures were taken.

The failure of the old system has led to a concept of corrections that keeps the client within or close to the community to which he or she will return. For reasons previously stated, the regional corrections concept has developed. Illustration 18.2 is a pictorial description of a regional corrections program based in a large city. Under this concept, a diagnostic center is the primary receiving institution and the jail is considered one of many alternatives.

An alternative design, still under the regional corrections concept, might be a grouping of rural counties. Each county would operate a short-term holding facility. Persons being held longer than forty-eight to seventy-two hours would be transferred to a single regional correctional facility. This facility would have extensive internal diagnostic and program capability and serve as the focal point for all corrections activities in the region, housing as well both law enforcement and court functions in the area.

Not only do current community corrections concepts attack the problems of institutional corrections, but they also tend to force the issue of organization problems. Regional correctional facilities or regional corrections programs require that city, county, and state governments cooperate in the planning of facilities and programs. Also required is cooperation in funding for both construction and operation. Regional councils of government were established to assist in obtaining this cooperation, but progress has been slow. One reason for this has been the failure of state governments to establish standards for facilities and programs.

## *RESPONSIBILITY*

Groups seemingly outside the corrections community have a direct influence on and some responsibility for the problems in corrections, and some solutions rest with these groups: (1) the public, (2) the law enforcement agencies, (3) the courts, and (4) the legislature of each state.

### The Public

Public apathy toward corrections is evident. The very fact that foul jails are allowed to continue to house human beings is a prime example. The difficulty of organizing and funding community corrections programs requiring cooperation between elements of government is another example. Many people pay lip service to correctional programs, but the difficulties uncovered in establishing such activities as halfway houses show that apparent support tends to fade when action is required. A halfway house or other correctional facility is a great idea as long as it is in some other neighborhood. If the public cannot be led to believe that rehabilitation measures require new methods, then our current efforts will be meaningless.

### Law Enforcement Agencies

Law enforcement agencies have traditionally been vocal in calling for longer jail and prison sentences and quick to point out probation and parole failure. Programs of education over the past few years have done much to alleviate this situation, but it still exists.

Law enforcement offficers believe correctional goals are in conflict with law enforcement goals. On the other hand, some correctional personnel believe that law enforcement goals are antagonistic to correctional goals. In the final analysis, however, the overall goals of both these subsystems of the criminal justice system are the same. Each element has a distinct part to play, and each must understand one another's roles.

### The Courts

The majority of the inmates and clients in corrections are products of the activity, or inactivity, of the courts. When the courts effectively and efficiently perform their function, they are not in conflict with corrections. Next to our system of jails, however, the court system in many states suffers the most from failure to keep up with the times. Court backlogs result in inability to prosecute effectively, which results in the overcrowding of the jails. Many prominent persons have expressed the belief that it is the swiftness and surety of justice that can bring deterrence. Until the court system is streamlined, there is little hope that jail problems will be solved.

### The Legislatures

Although corrections, primarily an executive function, is responsible for planning and administering correctional programs, it is the legislatures that must provide the legal basis and the money. The legal basis is primarily the establishment of modern standards, and these standards are needed for facilities and programs at both the state and the local level. Correctional agencies and associations must adequately plan the standards, and the legislatures must recognize their responsibility in this area.

Standards for jail are a typical example. Local communities, with state and federal aid, are spending millions of dollars on jail facilities. However, these facilities in many cases are not adequate to support current correctional needs because the standards to which they are constructed, or refurnished, are inadequate. Most jail standards (if available at all) cover only the existence of utilities and the size of cells. Failure of the legislatures to pass adequate measures or to assign responsibility for standard setting and inspection perpetuates correctional problems, because jails and prisons, once built, will be used for years to come.

If the criminal justice system is to work, it must actually become a network of coordinated subsystems, not just a group of loosely related agencies. In addition it must have the understanding of the public and the support of the legislature.

## DISCUSSION QUESTIONS

1. Under what conditions should incarceration be used?
2. Are community correctional programs usually well coordinated?
3. Is program coordination necessary or desirable?
4. Should certain classes of offenders be given long prison sentences with little chance of parole?
5. Discuss the advantages and disadvantages of community-based corrections programs.
6. What does the future hold in store for corrections?

## NOTES

1. Gresham M. Sykes, *The Society of Captives* (Princeton, New Jersey: Princeton University Press, 1958).
2. Bureau of Census, *Expenditure and Employment Data for the Criminal Justice System 1970–71* (Washington, D.C.: Government Printing Office, 1973). p. 197.
3. Bureau of Census, *Expenditure and Employment Data for the Criminal Justice System 1972–1973* (Washington, D.C.: Government Printing Office, 1975), p. 291.
4. President's Commission on Law Enforcement and Administration of Justice, *Task Force Report: Corrections* (Washington, D.C.: Government Printing Office, 1967), p. 1.
5. *Task Force Report: Corrections*, p. 1.
6. Law Enforcement Assistance Administration, *Survey of Inmates in Local Jails* (Washington, D.C.: Government Printing Office, 1974), p. 17.

## PART FIVE ANNOTATED BIBLIOGRAPHY

American Correctional Association. *Manual of Correctional Standards*. Washington, D.C.: American Correctional Association, 1959.

*Presents a model for organization and reponsibility in carrying out the functions of a prison or jail system.*

Morris, Norval. *The Future of Imprisonment*. Chicago: University of Chicago Press, 1974.

*An excellent sketch of current problem areas in corrections. The author outlines what he considers to be the direction of and trends in corrections.*

National Advisory Commission on Criminal Justice Standards and Goals. *Corrections*. Washington, D.C.: Government Printing Office, 1973.

*Presents the recommendations, and standards and goals established by the commission for corrections. If adopted by the states, these standards and goals should have considerable impact on corrections in the United States.*

National Commission on Law Observance and Enforcement. *Wickersham Commission Reports, No. 9, Report on Penal Institutions, Probation, and Parole, 1931*. Montclair, New Jersey: Patterson Smith, 1968.

*The Wickersham Reports total fourteen volumes and are named for the chairman of the commission. Report No. 9 provides an in-depth review of the conditions of the prisons during the 1920s as well as an analysis of the problems uncovered. These reports are presented in a simple style and are easily read by the beginning student in criminal justice.*

President's Commission on Law Enforcement and Administration of Justice. *Task Force Report: Corrections.* Washington, D.C.: Government Printing Office, 1967.

*A detailed account of the status of corrections in the 1960s with recommendations for improvements that are valid today.*

Rothman, David J. *Discovery of the Asylum.* Boston: Little, Brown, 1971.

*One of the better reference books concerning the early history of prisons. The author presents material on theory and practice in the early years of prison development.*

# PART SIX

# Probation and Parole

# 19: History and Process of Probation

*DEFINITION OF PROBATION • PHILOSOPHY AND OBJECTIVE • HISTORICAL PERSPECTIVES • THE PROBATION PROCESS • PROBATION ADMINISTRATION AND ORGANIZATION • APPLICATION AND ELIGIBILITY • JUVENILE PROBATION • MISDEMEANANT PROBATION • PRESENTENCE REPORT • REVOCATION OF PROBATION*

PURPOSE: *TO PROVIDE A DISCUSSION OF THE HISTORICAL PRECEDENTS FOR PROBATION AND A DESCRIPTION OF THE PROBATION PROCESS.*

PROBATION and parole are a very significant part of the correctional process. While they are similar in their objectives of rehabilitation, the distinctions are important. Probation has evolved as an alternative to imprisonment, whereas parole evolved as an alternative to continued imprisonment. Probation is usually administered at the local level and as a component of the judicial system. Parole, on the other hand, is usually administered at the state level and by an administrative agency that is part of the executive branch. Within statutory limitations, probation rather than a prison term is generally given to those who have committed less serious offenses and when there are indications that no further offenses are likely to be committed.

## *DEFINITION OF PROBATION*

The meaning of the term *probation* can be divided into three components: the sentence, the organization, and the process. As a sentence, probation generally means a judicial disposition in which a defendant is allowed to remain "free" in the community subject to certain conditions imposed by the court. As an organization, it is the agency that conducts the operation of probation. As a process, probation involves a presentence investigation report of each person before the court and his or her supervision, casework for each individual, program management, and guidance for each person placed on probation by the court.[1]

The special Task Force on Corrections appointed by the President's Commission on Law Enforcement and Administration of Justice defines probation as "A legal status granted by a court whereby a convicted person is permitted to remain in the community subject to conditions specified by the court.[2]

The National Council on Crime and Delinquency (NCCD) Standards, in Article 1 section 2 (a), defines probation as follows: "Probation is a procedure under which a defendant, found guilty of a crime upon verdict or plea, is released by the court and subject to the conditions imposed by the court and subject to the supervision of the probation service."[3]

The American Bar Association Project on Standards for Criminal Justice define probation as "Probation means a sentence not involving confinement which imposes conditions and retains authority in the sentencing court to modify the conditions of the sentence or to resentence the offender if he violates the conditions. Such a sentence should not involve or require suspension of the imposition or the execution of any other sentence."[4]

These definitions demonstrate how professional emphasis and orientation can differ. In essence, however, probation is the release of a convicted person by a court, under specified conditions.

The word *probation* comes from the Latin *probare,* which means "to test" or "to prove." Probation is really one of the modern methods for the treatment of offenders and as such, it is rooted in its broader social and cultural trends of the modern age.[5]

## *PHILOSOPHY AND OBJECTIVE*

The dominant purpose of the entire correctional process is the promotion of the general welfare of society. Probation, as an integral part of the correctional process, furthers the welfare objectives by providing for the security and protection of the community. Although traditionally imprisonment was used indiscriminately to reach these objectives, research has shown that it is not only in most instances ineffective and harmful to society, including the offender, but also more expensive financially.[6]

Probation proceeds on the basic notion that taking people out of the community, where they live and work, is not the best way to help them learn to live in it. The general premise underlying the new direction of integration or reintegration into society is that crime and delinquency are symptoms of failure and disorganization in the society as well as failure of the individual offender.[7]

This approach marks a shift from the traditional narrow explanation of crime as the act of an individual. Now the treatment of those lawbreakers who are placed on probation involves a number of different public and private agencies, which, besides providing support, service, and supervision, help the probationers to strengthen their social skills. Confinement, a form of punishment and a method of segregation, deprives convicted persons of their freedom and breaks their lines with family, friends, and employers. Probation, on the other hand, provides an opportunity to maintain the social contacts in a firmer but more helpful environment.

Probation is not intended to be an "easy sentence" or "leniency." It is a positive and firm method of permitting certain offenders to keep functioning in society under specified conditions. Such conditions are primarily designed to prevent further violation of the law. Using probation as a preventative and a corrective tool, society obtains maximum benefit without unnecessarily jeopardizing the family and social obligations of an individual operating as a productive member of society. It is believed that people well-integrated with the community are less likely to commit other crimes, particularly when they have the help and guidance of probation officers and others. Probation, then, offers a positive approach to the attainment of socially and legally acceptable behavior.

## *HISTORICAL PERSPECTIVES*

Probation had its early origin in such practices as right to clergy (*privilegium clericale*), dating back to the thirteenth century; securing sanctuary; judicial reprieve; and recognizance (a bond stipulating an action for a given period). The English common law practice of suspending sentences with certain restrictions is also a forerunner of probation. However, these early informal practices, sometimes called quasi-probationary measures, though similar in some respects, are not in the strict sense probation.[8]

Massachusetts is honored as having given the probation system to the world. During the first half of the nineteenth century, Massachusetts judges sought in a variety of ways to make the administration of justice more humane, and a favorable judicial climate was thus established for the development of rudimentary probation practices.[9] In 1841, John Augustus, a shoemaker, for the first time in the United States used probation when he secured the release of a drunkard from a Boston police court. The court allowed the release with the condition that the defendant be brought back in three weeks for sentencing and when the defendant reappeared, he showed signs of reform. Encouraged by his first experience, Augustus continued his probation work for almost eighteen years until his death in 1859. During these years he worked with men, women, and juveniles charged with a wide variety of offenses.[10]

Augustus established many of the present-day features of probation. When he undertook the responsibility for offenders, he agreed to "note their general conduct" and to see that "they were sent to school or supplied with some honest employment." In addition, he very often provided or arranged for accommodation. The register that he kept of all cases handled shows that he supervised over two thousand persons. Augustus's systematic work was to be the foundation of the modern probation.

In 1878 Massachusetts passed its first law regulating probation and authorized the mayor of Boston to appoint a paid probation officer. It is significant to note that this pioneer statute specifically contrasts probation with punishment by directing that "such persons as may reasonably be expected to be reformed without punishment" should be selected for probation. The criteria for selection was much broader than that of some recent laws. In 1880 appointment of probation officers was extended to all cities and towns in Massachusetts; and in 1890, it was extended to the whole state.[11] By 1900 Vermont, Illinois, Minnesota, Rhode Island, and New Jersey had also introduced laws on probation.

In 1899 the first juvenile court was established in Chicago. This was the beginning of the juvenile court movement, which in turn accelerated the spread of juvenile probation. By 1910, thirty-seven states and the District of Columbia had established juvenile courts and probation for juveniles. By 1925 probation for juveniles was available in every state, whereas adult probation was not available in every state until 1956.[12]

In many states the types of agencies that handle probation are as varied as their philosophies. Some states do not authorize paid probation officers, and in only fifteen states may probation be granted regardless of the type of crime committed. In some places probation is administered only by the courts in cities and counties, and in others it is administered by the state. Some of the statutory restrictions are indicative of a conflict between the punitive and treatment reactions to crime.[13]

The importance of probation, nation-

**JOHN AUGUSTUS**
*1785 – 1859*

Probation, both as a concept and in its development, is the United States' distinctive contribution to progressive methods of handling law offenders. The name of John Augustus stands out for his unique contribution of first using probation for the rehabilitation of men, women, and boys and girls.

John Augustus was born in Benbrighton, Massachusetts in 1785. He operated a shoe manufactory in Boston. It was in his shop at 5 Franklin Avenue near the police court that Augustus received frequent calls from those who sought his help. It was Augustus's practice to bail an offender after his or her conviction, if there was hope for reformation. The person would be required to appear before the court at a specified time. Augustus would accompany the offender to the court and if the judge was satisfied with Augustus's account of the individual's behavior, the offender would be fined one cent and costs, which was usually paid by Augustus.

Writing about his first probationer, a common drunkard, Augustus states, "The case was clearly made out, but before sentence had been passed, I conversed with him a few moments—although his looks precluded a belief in the minds of others that he would ever become a *man* again. He told me that if he could be saved from the House of Corrections, he never again would taste intoxicating liquors; there was such an earnestness in that tone, and a look expressive of firm resolve, that I determined to aid him, I bailed him, by permission of the court."*

In spite of the problems of opposition, misunderstanding, and even physical abuse from the public, he continued this work from 1841 until his death in 1859. During these years he maintained careful records and took great pride in exhibiting the list. Up to 1858 he had bailed 1,946 persons, 1,152 males and 794 women and girls.†

Augustus's work with offenders is characterized by his careful selection of fit subjects for probation. His approach to his critics varied. To some he said that for each person bailed to him, a commitment to a house of corrections was prevented. To those who understood social progress and justice in terms of dollars saved, he pointed out that the public was saved the greater expense of caring for the person in prison. To some others, he replied that his form of treatment was more effective; that it saved offenders for their families and for society and did not disgrace them forever as incarceration would.

---

*John Augustus, *First Probation Officer* (reprint of Report of John Augustus, Boston, 1852) National Probation Association, 1939, p. 4.

†*Probation & Parole Progress*, Yearbook, National Probation Association, New York, 1941, p. 6.

| | 1965 | | 1975 | |
|---|---|---|---|---|
| *Location of Offender* | *Number* | *Percent* | *Number* | *Percent* |
| Probation | 684,088 | 53 | 1,071,000 | 58 |
| Parole or institution | 598,298 | 47 | 770,000 | 42 |
| Total | 1,282,386 | 100 | 1,841,000 | 100 |

**Illustration 19.1** NUMBER OF OFFENDERS ON PROBATION AND ON PAROLE, OR IN INSTITUTIONS (1965 AND 1975)

Sources: 1965 data from National Survey of Corrections and special tabulations provided by the Federal Bureau of Prisons and the Administrative Office of the U.S.Courts; 1975 projections by R. Christensen, of the Commission's Task Force on Science and Technology.

wide, can easily be ascertained when it is considered that over 50 percent of all the offenders sentenced to correctional treatment in 1965 were placed on probation. The figures given in Illustration 19.1 also show the expansion of probation in the recent years. The data from the National Survey of Corrections depict the number of persons on probation on an average day in 1965, and an estimated number of probationers in 1975.[14]

## *THE PROBATION PROCESS*

Over the years probation has developed into a process that does not vary greatly from state to state. Generally the probation process operates in the following way: After the defendant is found guilty by the court, either following a verdict or a plea of guilty, the court has a number of sentencing choices—suspend the sentence, impose a fine, give a term of imprisonment, place on probation, and so on. There are, however, restrictions in most states as to who may or may not be placed on probation. For example, in some states individuals who commit certain serious crimes and those who have previously been convicted of crimes are not eligible. Such restrictions vary from state to state, but where the defendant is eligible for probation, the court has discretionary power to probate the sentence.

When an individual is determined by the judge to be suitable for probation, a probation order is issued. This order carries a set of obligatory conditions requiring the probationer to act in a certain way and/or restraining him or her from doing certain things. A requirement might be that he or she attend school or college, and a restriction might prohibit his or her association with known criminals or visiting a certain area for a period of time. The person's probation officer is responsible for seeing that the probationer adheres to the conditions. The officer also provides assistance, counseling, and guidance. If the probationer violates the conditions of probation or any law, the court may remove him or her from probation and force him to complete the sentence in a correctional institution.

This, in general, is a typical probation process. There are, however, some differences and variations from state to state resulting from the differences in laws.

## *PROBATION ADMINISTRATION AND ORGANIZATION*

Because each state and the federal government has its own basic probation law, there is very little that is standard procedure in every jurisdiction. There are, however, definite patterns in each aspect of probation. In the main, as Illustration 19.2 shows, adult probation services are state functions, while juvenile probation services are local functions.

In thirty-two states, juvenile courts administer probation services. Elsewhere, juvenile services are operated by state correctional agencies in five states, by the state welfare department in seven, and by other state or local agencies in the remainder. In thirty states, adult probation is combined with parole services. In the others, such services are administered by a separate state board or agency or are under local jurisdiction. This diversity is largely the result of historical accident. Because juvenile probation services were developed in the juvenile courts, which were operated by cities or counties, they were administered locally. Services for adults, in the majority of states, were grafted onto existing statewide parole supervision services.[15]

| | | *Number of Jurisdictions* | |
|---|---|---|---|
| | *Type of Agency* | *Juvenile* | *Adult* |
| State: | Corrections | 5 | 12 |
| | Other agencies | 11 | 25 |
| Local: | Courts | 32 | 13 |
| | Other agencies | 3 | 1 |
| Total | | 51 | 51 |

**Illustration 19.2** ADMINISTRATION OF JUVENILE AND ADULT PROBATION BY TYPE OF AGENCY (FIFTY STATES AND PUERTO RICO, 1965)

Source: President's Commission on Law Enforcement and Administration of Justice, *Task Force Report: Corrections* (Washington, D.C.: Government Printing Office, 1967), Table 4, p. 35.

## *APPLICATION AND ELIGIBILITY*

Probation is available to juveniles and adults, males and females, felons and misdemeanants. Over 4.5 million arrests in 1971 were for offenses that would be misdemeanors in most jurisdictions.[16] Yet eleven states have no probation service whatever for adult misdemeanants, six have practically none, and most states furnish service of some kind, but on an irregular basis.[17]

The use of probation is greatly influenced by the requirements imposed by statute or sentencing courts. Its use in juvenile cases is rarely restricted by statute, but the court may have a degree of practical restraint, generally influenced by the prevailing custom or the pressure of community feeling about certain offenses. Theoretically, the courts are free to probate any juvenile. The statutory limitations, on the other hand, make grant of probation for adults less flexible.

Only fifteen states have no statutory restrictions on who may be granted probation in felony cases. In the remaining thirty-five states, probation is limited by such factors as type of offense, prior convictions, or whether the defendant was armed at the time of offense(s). The type of offense is the most commonly used device for restricting probation, as shown in Illustration 19.3; otherwise there is little consistency between the states.

| *Offenses Excluded* | *Number of States* |
|---|---|
| Murder | 19 |
| Capital offenses | 9 |
| Rape | 12 |
| Arson | 7 |
| Robbery | 6 |
| Burglary | 5 |
| Kidnaping | 4 |
| Treason | 3 |
| Embezzlement | 2 |

**Illustration 19.3** LEGAL RESTRICTIONS ON USE OF PROBATION BY TYPE OF OFFENSE

Source: "Corrections in the United States," *Crime and Delinquency*, vol. 13-1, January 1967, Table 2, p. 162.

The National Crime Commission advocated the general reduction of the various outright prohibitions and restrictions on probation and, in their stead, the provision of statutory standards to guide the courts in using their discretion in decision making. This approach is considered logical in that probation legislation cannot take into account all the possible extenuating circumstances of particular offenders. Inflexible restrictions based on narrow criteria may defeat the goals of differential treatment by limiting the options from which a judge may choose. The National Advisory Commission on Criminal Justice Standards and Goals (1973) also recommended that barriers confronting probation be reduced.

## *JUVENILE PROBATION*

Juvenile probation, which permits a child or young person to remain in the community under the supervision and guidance of a probation officer, is a legal status created by a court of juvenile jurisdiction.[18] It usually involves: (a) a judicial finding that the behavior of the child or the youth has been such as to bring him within the purview of the court; (b) the impositions of conditions upon his or her continued freedom; and (c) the provision of means for helping him or her to meet these conditions and for determining the degree to which the conditions can be met by those placed on probation. Probation thus implies much more than indiscriminately giving the youth "another chance." Its central thrust is to give him or her some positive assistance in adjusting in the "free" community.

Within the broad goals of welfare and protection, juvenile probation has the following specific assignments: (a) preventing a repetition of the youth's delinquent behavior; (b) preventing long-term deviate or criminal careers; and (c) assisting the youth through measures feasible to the probation service, to achieve his or her potential as a productive citizen.

While the thrust of probation service is primarily toward the young persons found delinquent by the court, it often extends to a responsibility to help the family and undertake other, broader delinquency prevention programs.

In the main, the modern probation department performs similar functions for adult and juvenile probationers. Juvenile probation, however, is more consequential in the sense that those juveniles who fail on probation tend to become repeaters in the criminal justice system and generally for a longer time than adults. Probation services for juveniles are also more encompassing.

The modern juvenile probation department performs three central functions, and sometimes there are several auxiliary functions involved. Its central services are: (a) juvenile court, probation department, and detention intake and screening; (b) social study and screening; and (c) supervision and treatment.

### Intake and Screening

The scope of jurisdiction of the juvenile court and the probation department is defined and limited by law. The intake limitations imposed by law are not always fully understood. The intervention of the courts, on the other hand, is not effective in all types of cases. The cases referred by those agencies that do not fully appreciate the limitations have to be examined by the probation staff to determine whether the problem can be resolved by referring the case to some other community resource.

Frequently the probation department must also decide or participate in deciding whether the child or the youth should be admitted to, continue in, or be released from detention pending disposition of the case by the court. Removing a child from home and family and holding him or her in a detention facility, even for a temporary period, constitute a major intervention in the person's life as well as the family's. For some young people, this may be necessary and perhaps helpful; for others it may be deeply damaging and may contribute to alienation from the conforming society and its institutions. The problem is complicated by the fact that in many jurisdictions in the early 1970s, juvenile detention is provided in facilities that criminalize, degrade, and brutalize rather than rehabilitate.

### Social Study and Diagnosis

The juvenile court has great power to make authoritative decisions about many vital aspects of the lives of the children and young people and their families within its jurisdiction. Delinquent children may be returned to their homes and families without further intervention, they may be placed on probation, or they may be removed from the families' control for any period ranging from a few weeks to several years.

Such decisions have a great influence on the individuals involved both at the time the decisions are made and in later life. It is recognized that decisions of this nature imply the difficult task of predicting human behavior. For this reason and because of their impact on human lives, such decisions must be made only on the basis of very careful and competent diagnostic study. The focal concern is the nature of young people's response to the necessary demand of society. Will they or will they not offend again? Important questions like this require skilled analysis of the child's perceptions of, and feelings about the violations, personal problems, and life situations. The study must consider the value systems that influence behavior, the degree of motivation, and the problem-solving techniques that often produce deviant behavior. Physical, intellectual, and emotional capacities are also important to the analysis, as are the influences of family members, friends, and the neighborhood.

All this information must be brought together in a meaningful picture of a complex whole composed of the personality, the problem, and the environment. The total situation must then be considered in relation to the alternative dispositions available to the court. From these considerations a constructive treatment plan must be developed.

### Supervision and Treatment

The three interrelated elements of effective supervision are surveillance, service, and counseling. Surveillance, in essence, is keeping in touch with the child or the youth with a view to carrying out the probation plan. It provides individualized treatment and the support and assurance that society, represented by the court and the court officer, is aware of and interested in the probationer's new confrontation with reality. It is also concerned that he or she not engage in future criminal and self-defeating behavior.

Service involves ascertaining what other community services are available and needed by the probationer and the family, for example, employment information or vocational training. The probation officer can coordinate with other agencies so that the probationer and the family can use these services effectively.

Counseling, the third aspect of the probation officer's task, makes it possible to perform the other two more effectively because of the systematic contact with the probationer. Everyone concerned, including the child or the youth, must be helped to understand and face the existence of the personal or environmental problems productive of the delinquency. The probation officer may be asked to listen, respond, and sometimes counsel in situations not strictly related to the probation work, but such attention can win the trust and confidence necessary for a meaningful relationship.

### Auxiliary Programs

In addition to these three central functions, probation departments, both for adults and juveniles, frequently perform auxiliary tasks. Large departments often operate mental health clinics and administer other treatment services like foster homes, forestry camps, group homes, and other residential or nonresidential facilities. Some also engage in community planning and community organization efforts on behalf of children, youth, and adults.

### Application and Eligibility

Juvenile probation service is authorized by statute in each of the fifty states and Puerto Rico. In a recent year some 192,000

| State | Age Under Which Court Has Jurisdiction | | |
|---|---|---|---|
| | 16 | 17 | 18 |
| Alabama | M | | F |
| Alaska | | | M/F |
| Arizona | | | M/F |
| Arkansas | | | M/F |
| California | | | M/F |
| Colorado | | | M/F |
| Connecticut | M/F | | |
| Delaware | | | M/F |
| District of Columbia | | | M/F |
| Florida | | M/F | |
| Georgia | | M/F | |
| Hawaii | | | M/F |
| Idaho | | | M/F |
| Illinois | | M/F | |
| Indiana | | | M/F |
| Iowa | | | M/F |
| Kansas | | | M/F |
| Kentucky | | | M/F |
| Louisiana | | M/F | |
| Maine | | M/F | |
| Maryland | | | M/F |
| Massachusetts | | M/F | |
| Michigan | | M/F | |
| Minnesota | | | M/F |
| Mississippi | | | M/F |
| Missouri | | M/F | |

| State | Age Under Which Court Has Jurisdiction | | |
|---|---|---|---|
| | 16 | 17 | 18 |
| Montana | | | M/F |
| Nebraska | | | M/F |
| Nevada | | | M/F |
| New Hampshire | | M/F | |
| New Jersey | | | M/F |
| New Mexico | | | M/F |
| New York | M/F | | |
| North Carolina | M/F | | |
| North Dakota | M/F | | |
| Ohio | | | M/F |
| Oklahoma | | | M/F |
| Oregon | | | M/F |
| Pennsylvania | | | M/F |
| Rhode Island | | | M/F |
| South Carolina | M/F | | |
| South Dakota | | | M/F |
| Tennessee | | | M/F |
| Texas | | M | F |
| Utah | | | M/F |
| Vermont | M/F | | |
| Virginia | | | M/F |
| Washington | | | M/F |
| West Virginia | | | M/F |
| Wisconsin | | | M/F |
| Wyoming | | | M/F |

Key: M = Male
F = Female

**Illustration 19.4** UPPER AGE LIMITS OF JUVENILE COURT JURISDICTION
Source: Department of Health, Education and Welfare, *Juvenile Court Statistics,* 1973, pp. 14–18.

social studies were conducted and put into writing on behalf of the young people and children referred to the courts, of whom 189,000 were placed on probation. There were approximately 223,800 children and youth under supervision.

The upper age limit for eligibility for the services of juvenile probation is determined by the statue establishing the jurisdictional limits of the juvenile court. The Standard Juvenile Court Act, which was sponsored by the National Council on Crime and Delinquency, the National Council of Juvenile Court Judges, and the United States Children's Bureau, provides that the court shall have jurisdiction over a youth alleged to have committed an offense "prior to having become eighteen years of age." But this is not a universal practice, as Illustration 19.4 shows.

## MISDEMEANANT PROBATION

Originally probation concerned itself primarily with the handling of the misdemeanant offender. As the practice and the use of probation grew, a change took place. The emphasis of probation moved, for some unclear reason, from the misdemeanant offender to the felony offender, and today, probation for misdemeanant, the minor or petty offender, is relatively little used. For example, only an estimated 300,440 persons were placed on misdemeanant probation in 1965 out of a total of over 2.5 million arrested misdemeanants. Reliable data on disposition of misdemeanors are not always available, but for all those convicted in all cities for which data are available, probation, with a range of 2.5 percent to nearly 20 percent, is the least frequently used disposition.[19] These figures are low in spite of the fact that probation costs about one tenth, in direct costs, of the expense of keeping a person in jail. The indirect costs of family support, loss of taxes, and productivity loss are considerably higher. Over and above the monetary costs are the human costs. Logically, it could be assumed that misdemeanant offenders are the best risks for probation. Usually the nature of their crimes is such that they do not present a serious threat to society. Furthermore, the misdemeanant offenders are often just getting initiated into criminal careers, and perhaps the use of probation could help them live more law-abiding lives. The *Task Force Report: Corrections,* in its recommended standards, states: "The statute should authorize the court to use probation at its discretion, following adjudication or conviction, for the best interests of the offender and society."[20]

## PRESENTENCE REPORT

The presentence investigation report is a basic working document in judicial and correctional administration. It performs the following functions:

(1) aids the court in determining the appropriate sentence;
(2) presentence report when available can be helpful to institutions in their classification and treatment programs;
(3) it helps in the release planning of offenders by way of prerelease programs, day-parole, work furloughs, and full parole;
(4) aids the probation officer in his rehabilitative efforts during the probation supervision; and
(5) serves as a source of pertinent information for systematic research.[21]

The primary objective of presentence reports is to obtain as much information as is relevant and available about offenders and their social background, family, friends, school, and employment history. They also assess the strengths, weaknesses, and potentials with a view to working out probation plans.

The content of the presentence report is obtained by interviewing offenders, some family members, and sometimes neighbors. Information also comes from the previous employers, schools, social agencies, and from social control agencies like the police and courts.

The presentence report generally follows a set format, beginning with identification details and circumstances and details of the offense(s), both the official version and the probationer's version. It also contains a brief social history depicting significant events relating to behavior and attitudes, and information about previous disciplinary and/or criminal involvements. This section briefly reports significant family members, information on education, employment record, and general behavior patterns in terms of work habits and leisure-time pursuits. Another important factor generally included is an assessment of community attitudes toward the offender and the offense, and the kind of community reaction to be expected if the offender were to be placed on probation. An unfavorable community attitude can cause difficulties in social functioning. Support from the more significant social institutions like family, police, school, and employers is frequently vital for rehabilitation. Other things being equal, letters offering help from friends, neighbors, and so on are often an evidence of the community support available.

In closing, the presentence report usually contains a rough diagnosis of the problem, whether it is based in the family or in the gang (peer group), whatever the probation officer believes are the important factors that contributed to the offense. An assessment of the strengths available within the family, within the individual, within the community, or elsewhere is of assistance in developing a treatment program. Finally, because most courts expect a specific recommendation regarding disposition by the court, the presentence report includes such a recommendation to the judge.[22]

There is a growing appreciation in the United States of what psychiatric and psychological consultation can do to help the courts and the probation staff in coping with problems that arise in the course of investigation. Professional psychiatric and psychological advice has its role at the time of sentence and also during the period of supervision.[23] Psychiatric and psychological evaluations and psychometric testing are being included increasingly in presentence reports, particularly in the more difficult cases.

The basic function of the presentence investigation is to help the courts resolve the issue of whether to use probation in a given case. Over the years, however, many new and important uses have been found for the information gathered in the report. Now it is used for the entire range of correctional programs—from the appropriate disposition by the court, to the correctional institutions developing treatment programs, to the consideration of parole application.

## *REVOCATION OF PROBATION*

Every probation statute requires that probationers must adhere to certain conditions. Any violations may result in revocation of probation by the court. There are technical conditions imposed by the court (for example, requiring the probationer to report at a given time, to avoid drinking, and so on). And there are legal conditions (for example, no new criminal violations). If a probationer does break a law, then he or she can be ordered to complete the sentence in an institution. The offender whose sentence is suspended, or who is placed on probation, is given a guarantee by law that unless certain defined conditions are violated, he or she will not be placed under more severe restrictions. A few states explicitly allow revocation without advance notice or a hearing. In half the states and in the federal system, statutes stipulate that the probationer whose case is being considered for revocation be given a hearing in the court.

Some courts, interpreting statutory guarantees of a revocation hearing, have held that the defendant has a right to be represented by counsel. The Supreme Court decision in *Mempa* v. *Rhay* [389 U.S. 128 (1967)] has confirmed the probationer's right to counsel at a hearing for probation revocation. In most cases, however, probation revocation is based on a prerevocation report prepared by the probation officer. Revocation is considered an administrative decision; therefore, if undertaken in accordance with established rules and regulations, it is not subject to judicial review. Concern for the protection of individual rights and the general social awareness are some of the factors influencing the trends in formalizing the revocation procedures.

## DISCUSSION QUESTIONS

1. Who was John Augustus?
2. How would you define probation?
3. Discuss probation as an alternative to imprisonment. What are some of the problems and implications involved?
4. Discuss the psychological and sociological consequences of probation as compared with imprisonment.
5. What are the purposes of a presentence report?
6. Do you believe that probation is a "better" alternative than imprisonment? Justify your opinion.
7. Should a probationer be entitled to a probation revocation hearing with full due process in effect? If you believe the probationer should have full due process, who should bear the cost?

## NOTES

1. American Correctional Association, *Manual of Correctional Standards* (Washington, D.C.: American Correctional Association, 1969), p. 98.
2. President's Commission on Law Enforcement and Administration of Justice, *The Task Force Report: Corrections* (Washington, D.C.: Government Printing Office, 1967), p. 206.

3. *Standard Probation and Parole Act,* 1955 rev. (New York: National Council on Crime and Delinquency, 1964).
4. American Bar Association Project on Standards for Criminal Justice, *Standards Relating to Probation* (New York: ABA, 1970), p. 9.
5. Robert M. Carter and Leslie T. Wilkins, *Probation and Parole: Selected Readings* (New York: John Wiley, 1970), p. 3.
6. Edwin H. Sutherland and Donald R. Cressey, *Criminology* (New York: J. B. Lippincott, 1970), p. 517.
7. *Task Force Report: Corrections,* p. 7.
8. Sutherland and Cressey, *Criminology,* p. 463.
9. Carter and Wilkins, *Probation and Parole: Selected Readings,* p. 11.
10. David Dressler, *Practice and Theory of Probation and Parole* (New York: Columbia University Press, 1969), p. 26–27.
11. Carter and Wilkins, *Probation and Parole: Selected Readings,* pp. 12–13.
12. *Task Force Report: Corrections,* p. 27.
13. Sutherland and Cressey, *Criminology,* p. 464.
14. *Task Force Report: Corrections,* p. 27.
15. *Task Force Report: Corrections,* p. 35.
16. Federal Bureau of Investigation, Department of Justice, *Uniform Crime Reports for the U.S. 1971* (Washington, D.C.: Government Printing Office, 1972), p. 115.
17. President's Commission on Law Enforcement and Administration of Justice, *The Challenge of Crime in a Free Society* (Washington, D.C.: Government Printing Office, 1967), p. ix.
18. *Task Force Report: Corrections,* pp. 130–141.
19. *Task Force Report: Corrections,* p. 156.
20. *Task Force Report: Corrections,* p. 206.
21. Division of Probation, Administrative Office of the United States Courts, *Presentence Investigation Report* (Washington, D.C.: Government Printing Office, 1965), p. 1.
22. Vernon Fox, *Introduction to Corrections* (Englewood Cliffs, N.J.: Prentice-Hall, 1972), p. 107.
23. United States Bureau of Prisons, *Trends in the Administration of Justice and Correctional Programs in the United States* (Washington, D.C.: Bureau of Prisons, Department of Justice, 1965).

# 20: Problems and Recent Developments in Probation

*PROBLEMS • RECENT DEVELOPMENTS*

PURPOSE: *TO PROVIDE A BRIEF DISCUSSION OF THE MAJOR ISSUES AND PROBLEMS IN PROBATION.*

A principle of the American Bar Association Project on Standards for Criminal Justice states: "The legislature should authorize the sentencing court in every case to impose a sentence of probation. Exceptions to this principle are not favored, and if made, should be limited to the most serious offenses."[1] This recommendation can be realistically assessed and the advantages of probation determined from the practice and experience of probation in the United States and other countries and by scientific research.

The growing emphasis on community treatment is supported by several kinds of considerations.[2] The main advantage is that the correctional strategy that presently seems to hold the greatest promise, based on social science theory and limited research, is the reintegration of the offender into the community. A key element in this strategy is dealing with the problems in their local context, and this means avoiding as much as possible the isolating and labeling effects of commitment to an institution.

These justifications seem to be borne out by the record of probation services themselves. Although probation services have been characteristically poorly staffed and often poorly administered, the success of those placed on probation, as measured by not having probation revoked, has been high. One summary analysis of the outcomes observed in eleven probation studies indicates a success rate between 60 and 90 percent. A survey of probation effectiveness in such states as Massachusetts and New York and a variety of foreign countries provides similar results, with a success rate of about 75 percent.

The Cambridge Study, published in England in 1958, found that 79 percent of the adults and 73 percent of the juveniles in the research sample successfully completed their periods of probation. A study in Pennsylvania found that 82 percent of a group of 490 probationers were not recommitted within a period of six to twelve years after completion of their probation.[3] More recent figures for the United States federal probation system show success rates in terms of nonviolation while on probation of about 88 percent for nineteen United States district courts. Two recent studies of receptions into California penal institutions support the view that probation might be used more liberally in preference to institutional treatment.[4]

The second advantage is that while on probation the probationer can live a relatively normal life in the community with an opportunity to become, in many instances once again, a responsible and useful person. Probation makes possible the experience of personal and family life, satisfying and gainful employment, and support of his or her family. There is also a possibility of preserving the unity of the family.

The third advantage is that probation inspires self-worth and self-respect, without which it is very difficult to make a good social adjustment. Probation permits changes in attitudes and outlook through the counsel and guidance of a probation officer.

In addition to the social advantages inherent in the community supervision, probation is economically sound. Excellent probation services, with all the other ensuing advantages, can be provided at much less cost than imprisonment. The

National Crime Commission indicated that the average state spends about $3,400 a year (excluding capital costs) to keep a youth in a state training school, while it costs only about one tenth of that amount to keep an individual on probation (see Illustration 20.1).

Objections can be raised about the validity of such comparisons because expenditures for probation services are now much too meager. However, with the 1 to 10 cost ratio prevailing, probation expenditures can clearly be increased sevenfold and still remain less than the cost of institutional programs. This is especially true when construction costs, which now add up to and beyond $20,000 per bed in a correctional institution, are included. The difference becomes even greater if the cost of welfare assistance for the families of the incarcerated and the loss in taxable income are considered.[5] In a recent Texas study, comparing probation cost and imprisonment cost per man per year in a model probation system, which included the cost of facilities and equipment, $274 was spent for probation as against $2,179 for incarceration.[6]

The experience of the European countries has been well summed up by Dr. Roger Hood in the Council of Europe Report entitled *The Effectiveness of Punishment and Other Measures of Treatment* (1967): some offenders can be dealt with in a way that avoids institutional contamination for the offender, offers equal protection to the public, saves the time of those engaged in treatment so that they can concentrate on more difficult cases, and saves public money.[7]

| *Type of Service Institution* | *Juvenile* | *Adult* |
|---|---|---|
| Detention | 11.50 | |
| State institutions | 9.35 | 5.24 |
| Local (including jails) | 10.66 | 2.86 |
| Probation | .92 | .36 |

**Illustration 20.1** AVERAGE DAILY DOLLAR COST PER CASE

Source: President's Commission on Law Enforcement and Administration of Justice, *Task Force Report: Corrections* (Washington, D.C., Government Printing Office, 1967), p. 194.

It seems important to keep all the advantages of probation and the pragmatic considerations in mind especially when the more recent figures for the number of persons on probation are reviewed. The National Crime Commission (1967) estimated a 5 to 6 percent yearly increase in the use of both adult and juvenile probation. This rate of growth exceeds the rate of growth of the United States population as a whole.[8]

## *PROBLEMS*

It must be recognized that it is appropriate to indicate that probation has its critics. Some criticisms and the negative attitudes toward probation are the product of genuine failings and therefore understandable. Even though there are no scientific criteria for what is or is not a failure on probation, probation failures can generally be attributed to any one, or a combination, of several factors. It can result, for example, from improper selection, the limitations of the predictability of human behavior, and other problems like the lack of suitably trained staff and adequate facilities.

The criticisms resulting from such factors can be constructive and can produce favorable and sometimes innovative changes, but when criticism represents the negative and the punitive attitudes of society, the problems become much more complex. These negative attitudes are exemplified by outright public apathy to the practices and policies of hiring former offenders. Certain segments of society have even formalized these unfavorable attitudes toward offender rehabilitation by incorporating legal restrictions against offenders. Such restrictions are particularly noticeable in the area of bonding or licensing.

**Special Issues**

Imprisonment as one of the basic sanctions of criminal justice cannot be abandoned until scientific research positively demonstrates that its alternatives have a greater social value. Even then, incarceration may be the only effective solution for some types of offenders. The views of certain experts, including some who think that imprisonment has failed, often conflict with those of law enforcement and prison personnel and cause wasteful conflicts and controversies. It is possible that the prevailing pessimism regarding imprisonment "may be due to the demise of exaggerated hopes and frustration of ideals."[9]

The Advisory Commission on Intergovernment Relations (ACIR) recognizes the importance of institutional confinement as a means of controlling and deterring certain types of offenders, particularly the estimated 15 to 20 percent who are so-called "hardened criminals"[10] and cannot be handled successfully on probation, parole, or similar types of community-oriented programs.

A recent report of the ACIR aptly summarizes some major problems facing corrections, including probation and parole. The commission concluded that corrections is the step-child of the criminal justice system and that it is essential that greater public attention and funds be directed to this field.

That correctional reform falls low on the agenda of public priorities is obvious from these figures: In fiscal year 1972–73 the police received $7.6 billion in expenditures while corrections received only $2.7 billion. The police employed 623,603 while corrections employed 203,101.[11]

The use of Law Enforcement Assistance Administration (LEAA) money for corrections reflects an equally low priority. In 1969, for instance, in its second-year budget of $268 million, only $3.6 million of LEAA block action grant funds were programmed by the states for corrections. Furthermore, the states later reprogrammed much of the money so that the total amount that went to corrections was closer to $2.0 million, or less than 1 percent. In 1970, out of the total LEAA budget of $480 million only $5 million was spent on probation and parole programs. The National Crime Commission (1967), in one of its seven basic recommendations, stated that "correctional agencies will require substantially more money if they are to better control crime."[12]

The new priorities that LEAA, for example, has established for the commitment of funds and effort to corrections are also generally reflected in the state plans. The emphasis throughout is on community-based programs as alternatives, whenever possible, to the use of institutional facilities.

Another one of the major and frequently encountered hurdles is the generally unfavorable, at times hostile, attitude of the public, which is well represented in the press and in some of the law enforcement agencies. Clarence Schrag put this attitude in these words: "Although the threat of retaliation may have lessened during the ensuing years, there is little doubt that the motive of revenge still plays some part in the public endorsement of repressive measures."[13] The offender merits punishment for wrongdoing, and the traditional and well-known form of punishment is a sentence to an institution. Probation is not really punishment; therefore, how can law and order be maintained if law-breakers or "criminals" are not properly punished? Such "concerns" are apparent in the way people are continually shocked by sentences that they regard as too lenient. This can be particularly observed in the not-too-uncommon occurrence of the "upper class" citizens stealing substantial public or private funds, or committing other crimes, and their sentences being probated. In addition, the media and the police often cite examples of a few probationers who sensationally violate their probation and do not mention the majority who are leading useful lives.

### Lack of Skilled Personnel

The need for trained probation personnel is likely to increase: (1) as the probation services expand; (2) if the official crime rate is not reduced (or perhaps continues to rise); and (3) when probation comes to be viewed as a preferable and more economical alternative to incarceration.[14] "The real crisis in social welfare is manpower not merely quantity but quality; not merely filling jobs but rendering a valuable professional service; not merely being employed in any agency but working in soundly managed agencies in which professional skills are utilized to their fullest extent."[15]

The problem of skilled personnel is not only complex and multifaceted but also closely linked to some of the basic problem areas already mentioned. But there are other problems in probation.

Generally accepted standards to achieve specified goals have not been developed. Starting with the Social Defense Section of the United Nations, the President's Task Force on Corrections and professional organizations like the American Bar Association and the American Correctional Association have recommended standards for probation. Essentially, standard-setting in probation agencies means that there are guidelines to follow so that their services are on more acceptable levels. Unlike the army, where standards are more likely to be enforced, probation agencies are not obligated to meet many standards. Standard review procedure for ensuring that minimum standards are being met by probation officers or administrators is virtually nonexistent.

Probation agencies often have decorative standards only. There are many historical and value-oriented reasons why standards are not or cannot be accepted or implemented. And there are other reasons within the probation departments. Lack of qualified supervisory personnel and training officers is a problem, as is the lack of educational and training facilities. The result of the Pilot Study of Correctional Training and Manpower in 1967 indicated that 17,800 or 67 percent more probation and parole personnel were required than the number actually employed in 1966.[16]

In spite of all these limitations, the number of probationers has been increasing. There is a greater demand by the courts for more and fuller presentence reports. Activities like probation officers' involvement in community programs, in schools, and so forth are imposing heavier demands on mostly overburdened, understaffed, and unsystematically organized probation departments. Under such circumstances, quality is often reluctantly sacrificed, with the result that more serious cases are given greater and sometimes undue attention and seemingly minor matters neglected. Perhaps a probationer who is progressing well gets involved in problems because the probation officer cannot afford the time to help.

Probation in corrections, like many of the other social welfare systems, deals disproportionately with large numbers of minority groups (for example, blacks, Mexican Americans, and Puerto Ricans) who are culturally different from the majority.[17] Sometimes there are conflicts between the goals of probation agencies, which often represent the value system of the majority, and the goals of their minority-group clientele. If sufficient care is not exercised, complex problems can arise because the programs and the personnel instituting and running them do not take into account the minority cultural factors.

Some people also view the cultural differences within the majority group as causing problems. For example, the probation officer usually represents a social milieu and value system different from the clients', who are generally from the "lower" socioeconomic group. Greater understanding among the groups, as well as greater representation of the social and cultural characteristics of the minorities and the minority groups within the majority groups, may not be the answer, but it would be a step in the right direction.

**Case Load**

The effectiveness of probation depends to a large degree on what is done with probationers after they have been put under supervision. There are two significant areas of concern regarding the type and intensity of supervision and the extent of case load. They are significant because the number of cases to be supervised will influence the kind of supervision provided to the probationer, assuming that the probation officer is skilled and competent.

There are divergent views about the ideal size of case loads. There is no magic number. Numerous variables influence the number of cases a probation officer can effectively handle, for example, the policy and the size of the probation agency, the quality and the quantity of expectations for probation officers, and the type of probationers. Ideal case load is also influenced by other services available in the community and whether it is an urban or rural environment.

There are, however, ways of reducing case loads. One, as is obvious, is to obtain more probation staff, provided it is justified and the resources are available. The second is by systematically providing differential supervision, according to the real need, particularly for cases in which it is obvious that extensive supervision will not be particularly beneficial. The third method is through discharge from probation by court order when a probationer has derived the maximum benefit from supervision.

## *RECENT DEVELOPMENTS*

New priorities put added emphasis on the need for alternatives to incarceration for most offenders, and advocates of this new emphasis contend that it is self-evident because two thirds of the offender population are already being handled through probation and parole.[18] The increasing amount of money being devoted to corrections is likewise indicative. Rehabilitation by community-based treatment programs, then, rather than incarceration and isolation, is generally considered a more effective means of controlling crime.

### Probation Subsidy Programs

The state of California took a significant step forward in 1965 by enacting a law to subsidize probation supervision on a performance principle. It recognized quality probation as the most suitable alternative to the massive program of state incarceration. The act was generally viewed as a profitable alternative because of the many human and economic benefits derived from maintaining offenders as functioning individuals in society. The act gave incentive to local probation departments to improve service by providing a substantial financial reward to those who voluntarily participated in the program and reducing their rate of commitment to prison.

The California experience reflects that probation subsidy programs have not only encouraged "more even administration of justice," but have provided strength to the view that probation is as effective, if not more so, than most institutional forms of correctional care. Probation is the least costly correctional service available.[19]

National Advisory Commission on Criminal Justice Standards and Goals (1973) recommends that the purpose of an effective probation subsidy program should be not only to reduce commitment to institutions but to upgrade local probation services. This means the state should set standards that the local agency must meet to be eligible for reimbursement. The state should also provide technical assistant to local agencies, audit their programs, and withhold funds when there is noncompliance.[20]

### Volunteers as Probation Supervisors

Another significant development, especially since 1961, has been the introduction of the use of volunteers to supervise and be friends with probationers. This innovation was followed by conflicts, strains, and differences of opinion, mostly stemming from negative attitudes and skepticism about lay people working with "criminals." In spite of the difficulties involved, the use of local volunteers in court probation programs has spread from three or four courts in 1961 to around 400 courts in 1969. According to one report on volunteer programs, ten thousand court volunteers work in many different capacities. Volunteers exist in all types of communities, in all sections of the United States.[21]

Volunteers, who are generally local citizens working unpaid and usually on a part-time basis, are used to supplement and amplify probation services, and they function under the guidance of a trained probation officer. They are selected on the basis of their interest, willingness, and background rather than their performance in special volunteer training, which is rarely given. Volunteers have contributed new and uninhibited ideas and services and have brought the community closer to the offender.

### Research and Evaluation

Another noticeable trend, one receiving increasing emphasis, is measuring the effectiveness of treatment programs. There are two reasons for this trend, one related to value received for taxpayers dollars and the other to the technology and tools now available for evaluation. This new systematic and more scientific approach has resulted in additional funds being made available for research and for the evaluation of programs.

The setting up of the National Institute of Law Enforcement and Criminal Justice Information Center to disseminate research and demonstrate results proven to be effective in improving the different components of the criminal justice system is an example of the efforts at the national level. At the local levels, besides the closer working cooperation between the universities and criminal justice agencies, autonomous research organizations are being created to exchange and disseminate information and make use of all the existing research resources. In short, more and more studies are being conducted to evaluate the outcome of probation and its effectiveness as a corrective tool.

### Impact of Public Awareness

Another recent development, referred to earlier, which has numerous practical implications, is the public expression of concern about the individual and civil rights. The public is interested in knowing how officials make decisions affecting the lives of many people and their constitutional rights as the government and public institutions seek to extend their aid and apply sanctions. The result is a strong impact not only on the policy and procedures of public agencies but also on the organizational structure. Most of the direct and indirect influences have come from one of the more significant social development agencies—the courts. The decisions of the courts relating to law enforcement, welfare, and corrections reflect greater social awareness about the fundamental principle of fairness in decision making.

Judicial activity concerning the juvenile and adult rights of those under the care of the criminal justice agencies, for instance, has some obvious message for the probation departments. One of the important decisions is *In re Gault* [387 U.S. 1 (1967)], in which the Supreme Court ruled that juveniles had the right to receive notice of charges, the right to counsel, the right to confrontation and cross-examination, and the protection of the privileges against self-incrimination. Probation, like some of the other criminal justice elements, has policy and criteria governing the "grant, the supervisory period, revocation, and termination." However, these are areas needing clearer and more precise definition.[22]

### Establishment of Standards

The introduction of standards, previously discussed in more detail, is another of the major trends. More and more probation departments are joining hands with other criminal justice agencies to set up, implement, and evaluate standards relating to programs and personnel. In this regard, professional organizations like the American Bar Association (ABA), the American Correctional Association (ACA), the National Council on Crime and Delinquency (NCCD), and the various state correctional associations have contributed a great deal. The role of the National Advisory Commission on Criminal Justice Standards and Goals (1973), consisting of about 200 national experts representing different areas of the criminal justice system, which met in January 1973, cannot be overemphasized. The proposed standards not only relate to the quality of service to be provided and the education and training of personnel but also set out ethical guidelines for the probation employees.

### Cooperation and Coordination of Components

Last but not least, the old rhetoric of coordination of efforts among the parts of the criminal justice system is gradually being translated into practice. Rather than each subsystem working on its own and following its individual direction (sometimes nonexistent and often inconsistent with the greater goals), most of the subsystems are now making a greater and a more deliberate effort to consider the offender and his or her environment as pivotal. Many of the new policies, programs, and services being provided or planned by probation and other criminal justice components reflect the new directions being taken. The reorganization of the services and facilities in the court systems (for example, psychiatric clinics, referral services) demonstrates the slow but sure movement toward a more planned system. The establishment of the criminal justice councils in every state, under the Omnibus Crime Control Act of 1968, is yet another definite step toward a more coordinated and planned approach to the whole system. The impact of these and other measures will not be properly felt until the new techniques have been in operation for some time.

Programs are being implemented that combine and coordinate police, prosecutor, defense attorney, diagnostic service, probation, and other court personnel to provide all the relevant information at the decision-making point as a case is dealt with by each unit of the subsystem. For example, the court administration systems are instituting programs to combine and accumulate all the relevant information about the defendants before they are brought to trial. The advantage is that not only does the judge have a more rational basis for disposition but also the defendant does not need to wait or be detained in jail, usually unproductively, while the court orders piecemeal reports and information to decide a case.

To sum up, from the foregoing considerations, both negative and positive, regarding the value and the future of probation, one can conclude that it is one of the more efficient, humane, and economical methods of handling offenders in the community. It is believed that while concerted efforts always resolve some of the problems, some problems remain and some are created because organizations are living organisms particularly those that function with and for human beings.

## DISCUSSION QUESTIONS

1. What do you see as the major contemporary problem of probation?
2. Should probation departments recruit lay persons as probationers?
3. Discuss some of the merits and limitations of a state probation agency. Compare it with the locally controlled probation departments.
4. How can the individual rights of probationers be balanced with the notion of a higher social goal pertaining to the protection of society?

## NOTES

1. The American Bar Association Project on Standards for Probation, *Standards Relating to Probation* (New York: ABA, 1970), p. 9.
2. President's Commission on Law Enforcement and Administration of Justice, *The Task Force Report: Corrections* (Washington, D.C.: Government Printing Office, 1967), p. 28.
3. R. W. England, "A Study of Post-Probation Recidivism among 500 Federal Offenders," *Federal Probation,* 19 (1955), 10.
4. R. F. Sparks, "The Effectiveness of Probation," in *The Criminal in Confinement,* Vol. 3, ed. Leon Razinowicz and Marvin E. Wolfgang (New York: Basic Books, 1971), pp. 211–212.
5. *Task Force Report: Corrections,* p. 28.
6. Robert L. Frazier, "Incarceration and Adult Felon Probation in Texas: A Cost Comparison," thesis, May 1972, Sam Houston State University, Huntsville, Texas, p. 47.
7. Roger Hood, *The Effectiveness of Punishment and Other Measures of Treatment* (Strasbourg, France: Council of Europe, 1967).
8. *Task Force Report: Corrections,* p. 215.
9. Norval Morris and Gordon Hawkins, *The Honest Politician's Guide to Crime Control* (Chicago: University of Chicago Press, 1970), p. 116.

10. Advisory Commission on Inter-Governmental Relations (ACIR), *State-Local Relations in Criminal Justice System* (Washington, D.C.: Government Printing Office, 1971), p. 54.
11. Bureau of Census, *Expenditures and Employment Data for the Criminal Justice System: 1972–73* (Washington, D.C.: Government Printing Office, 1975), p. 17.
12. President's Commission on Law Enforcement and Administration of Justice, *The Challenge of Crime in Free Society* (Washington, D.C.: Government Printing Office, 1967), Summary X.
13. Clarence Schrag, *Crime and Justice: American Style, Crime and Delinquency Issues* (Washington, D.C.: Government Printing Office, 1971), p. 10.
14. Herman Piven and Abraham Alcabes, *Probation/Parole: Vol. 1, The Crisis of Qualified Manpower for Criminal Justice: An Analytic Assessment with Guidelines for New Policy* (Washington, D.C.: Department of Health, Education, and Welfare, 1969), p. 37.
15. Joseph Weber, "Manpower: The Real Crisis in Social Welfare," *Personnel Information,* 11–1 (January 1968), 1.
16. Piven and Alcabes, *Probation/Parole.*
17. *State-Local Relations in the Criminal Justice System,* p. 1.
18. *State-Local Relations in the Criminal Justice System,* p. 238.
19. Robert L. Smith, *A Quiet Revolution: Probation Subsidy* (Washington, D.C.: Government Printing Office, 1971), p. 5.
20. National Advisory Commission on Criminal Justice Standards and Goals, *National Conference on Criminal Justice* (Washington, D.C.: Department of Justice, 1973), p. C–176.
21. *Volunteer Programs in Courts: Collected Papers on Productive Programs* (Washington, D.C.: Government Printing Office, 1969), p. 204.
22. Fred Cohen, *Legal Challenge to Corrections* (Washington, D.C.: Government Printing Office, 1969).

DEPARTMENT OF JUSTICE
QUI PRO DOMINA JUSTITIA SEQUITUR

# 21: History and Process of Parole

*DEFINITION OF PAROLE • PHILOSOPHY AND OBJECTIVE • HISTORICAL PERSPECTIVES • THE PAROLE PROCESS*

PURPOSE: *TO DESCRIBE THE HISTORICAL BACKGROUND OF PAROLE AND TO OUTLINE THE PROCESS OF PAROLE.*

THE WORD *parole* is derived from the French expression *parole d'honneur,* which means "formal promise," or "a word of honor given or pledged." In the French military, it was a promise given by a prisoner of war that he would not try to escape or if freed would return to custody under some stated condition, or would not take up arms against his captors for a stated period.[1] The French corrections system, however, uses the term *libération conditionnelle* rather than parole, which literally means "conditional release."

## DEFINITION OF PAROLE

Robert M. Carter and Leslie T. Wilkins define parole as a procedure by which prisoners are selected for release and a service by which they are provided with the necessary controls, assistance, and guidance as they serve the remainder of their sentences in the free community.[2] Harry E. Barnes and Nagley K. Teeters consider parole a form of conditional release that is granted after a prisoner has served a portion of his or her sentence in a correctional institution.[3]

The National Workshop for Correctional and Parole Administrators, held in New Orleans in early 1972 under the auspicies of the American Correctional Association (ACA), defined parole as:

a decision —by an authority constituted according to statute to determine the portion of the sentence which the inmate can complete outside of the institution, and

a status —the serving of the remainder of the sentence in the community, according to the rules and regulations set up by the Parole Board.[4]

To reiterate briefly the difference between probation and parole: probation involves serving of a probation term in the community without going to a correctional institution, whereas the release on parole follows a specific period in confinement depending upon the rules of parole eligibility.

There are different procedures for releasing a person from a correctional institution. Not only are these methods different procedurely and governed by different rules, but they also affect those to be released differently in terms of the obligations of each person to report and fulfill the conditions. Therefore, their distinctions should be clearly understood. The methods are:

1. executive clemency or pardon
2. mandatory release
3. release at the expiration of sentence
4. temporary release programs, and
5. parole

*Executive clemency* or *pardon* is granting a person a release with or without conditions and/or supervision under an executive order. This method is used sparingly and only in special circumstances. The power to grant a pardon is usually vested in the chief executive (governor) of a state.

*Mandatory release, statutory release,* or *conditional release* provides for the release of all prisoners or some prisoners prior to the expiration of their sentences. There are no selection criteria in this type of release. The basic notion behind mandatory release is that persons released under this system can have the benefit of supervision until the original date of discharge.

*Release at the expiration of sentence* or *discharge* is without any of the selection or supervision that characterizes the other methods of release. Discharge occurs after a person has served the lawful sentence.

*Temporary release programs* (like the prerelease centers), study release (particularly for juveniles), work release, and release based on immediate family needs, are more fully discussed in the section on corrections. The objective of these and other release programs is to enhance the rehabilitation opportunities of the offender, often gradually and under some supervision.

In brief, parole is the release of an incarcerated offender to the community, under supervision of a parole officer and with certain restrictions and requirements, after he or she has completed a portion of the sentence in a correctional institution. Generally, a person becomes eligible for parole consideration after serving one third of the sentence, although some laws permit parole at any time during the sentence.

Parole is concerned primarily with helping the committed offender make the difficult transition from the prison community to an acceptable adjustment in society. The dual purpose of parole is protection of society and rehabilitation of the offender. Society is protected more effectively when an offender is diverted from his or her criminal patterns, and successful diversion is more likely to occur within the community rather than in the artificial environment of prison.

## *PHILOSOPHY AND OBJECTIVE*

Parole, like the rest of corrections and the whole criminal justice system itself, lacks a generally agreed-upon philosophy and objective. Like many other parts in our society, parole is viewed differently according to the perspective of the particular observer and the level of observation. In other words, an average American's reaction to parole varies depending on whether he or she is supposed to respond at the intellectual level or is involved in personal interaction. Even among correctional personnel there are markedly divergent approaches to parole, what it is expected to accomplish, and how. The holders of traditional views about the methods of handling offenders sometimes question the concept of parole.

There is, however, less disagreement with the view that parole represents a changing point of view toward crime and punishment generally and toward offenders and their rehabilitation particularly. Some marked changes can be observed in society's beliefs regarding the causes and the control of criminal behavior, and such changes are reflected in the new developments in the field of corrections and in the system of justice.

The new approaches to dealing with offenders have diverged widely from the principle of an eye for an eye and the age of revenge. Current thinking has also moved away from the eighteenth- and the early nineteenth-century idea of "let the punishment fit the crime." The late nineteenth and early twentieth centuries saw the offender more often as sick and disadvantaged rather than "wicked." Therefore, treatment and training, rather than punishment, became the method of handling offenders. Parole is an outgrowth of the belief that a person can be "redeemed" by a more helping and humane attitude.

From society's point of view, it must protect itself. "But it is obvious that the most profitable way of obtaining this protection is by turning the 'criminal' into a useful citizen. Parole is a means to that end."[5]

No one who is serving a sentence has an absolute right to parole. So far the courts have maintained the rule of noninterference, thus leaving the matter of granting parole solely to the discretion of the paroling authority. In *Tarlton* vs. *Clark* [491 F. 2d 384 (5th Cir. 1971)] the court ruled that it is not the function of the courts to review the discretion of the parole board in the denial of application for parole. Who has and who has not the right to be considered for parole is one of today's actively debated issues. The National Crime Commission in its Standards for Parole states that the law should empower the parole authority to consider all prisoners for parole regardless of the nature of the offense committed.[6]

In keeping with the aims of the protection of society and the fact that over 90 percent of the offenders do eventually return to the community, there are several reasons why parole offers better measures for the objectives of protection.

1. Parole, as a service, aids the released offender during the very difficult time of adjusting to the environment of the community after a period in the prison milieu.
2. By providing supervision and control, reversion to criminal activity is made more difficult and there are more chances of its being prevented.
3. Parole provides an opportunity to return a parolee to prison as soon as he shows indications of unacceptable and illegal behavior.
4. The parole restrictions provide legal authority to compel an ex-offender to live up to certain acceptable standards of conduct.
5. Parole is much less expensive than the cost of keeping a person in a correctional institution. (See Illustration 21.1.)

The success of any parole system, however well designed and well intended, will depend upon how it is administered.

## *HISTORICAL PERSPECTIVES*

Parole as an individualized form of treatment is not new. The scriptures from India, written over four thousand years ago, and Plato's writings, over two thousand

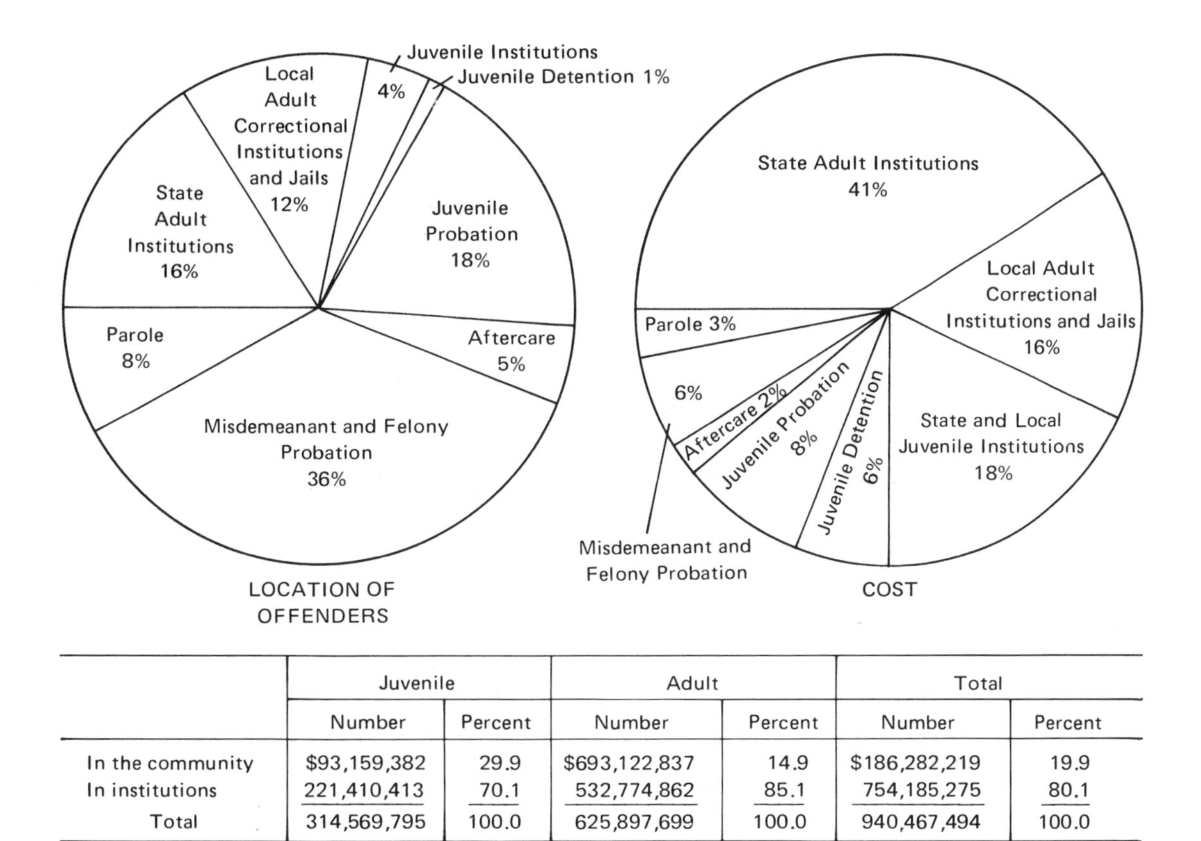


| | Juvenile | | Adult | | Total | |
|---|---|---|---|---|---|---|
| | Number | Percent | Number | Percent | Number | Percent |
| In the community | $93,159,382 | 29.9 | $693,122,837 | 14.9 | $186,282,219 | 19.9 |
| In institutions | 221,410,413 | 70.1 | 532,774,862 | 85.1 | 754,185,275 | 80.1 |
| Total | 314,569,795 | 100.0 | 625,897,699 | 100.0 | 940,467,494 | 100.0 |

**Illustration 21.1** ANNUAL EXPENDITURES FOR CORRECTIONAL SERVICES/COST OF PAROLE

Source: President's Commission on Law Enforcement and Administration of Justice, *Task Force Report: Corrections* (Washington, D.C.: Government Printing Office, 1967), Table 2, p. 193.

years old, referred to individual study, classification, and reform of the deviant individual.

In its more recent history, parole began to develop with the transportation of British criminals to the American colonies and to Australia in the sixteenth century. Initially, convicted persons who were fit enough to work in the colonies were given a reprieve or pardon, if they did not return to England during the term of their sentence. A number of them, however, did return to England without permission and before their sentence had expired. The result was that more conditions were added to such a pardon, which became known as a ticket of leave. "This ticket of leave was merely a declaration signed by the governor or his secretary, dispensing a convict from attendance at government work and enabling him, on condition of supporting himself, to seek employment within a specified district."[7]

By the early nineteenth century ticket-of-leave laws reflected the idea of selection as compared to the earlier indiscriminate use, and prisoners were required to serve a certain portion of their sentences before being granted a ticket of leave. The English Penal Servitude Act of 1853 related to conditional release and gave legal status to the system of ticket of leave.

The developments of parole in the United States contains the same three basic concepts: (1) the principle of shortening the term of imprisonment as a reward for good conduct; (2) the indeterminate sentence; and (3) supervision.

The first concept was recognized by the "good-time" law of New York in 1817. Today there are good-time laws of some kind in every state and the federal jurisdiction. The indeterminate sentence was first introduced in the later half of the nineteenth century with the establishment of the houses of refuge for children.

The concept of parole related to supervision first began with the use of volunteers. The master of an indentured child from a house of refuge was also the child's guardian and supervisor. As early as 1851 the Quakers' Society for Alleviating the Miseries of Public Prison appointed two agents to work with discharged prisoners from the Philadelphia county prison and the penitentiary.

It appears that supervision by a paid public employee was first provided in Massachusetts in 1845, when an agent was appointed by the state to help released prisoners obtain employment, clothing, and other publically funded aid. This was far from what is provided by supervision today, but at least a parolee could obtain some material support during the very difficult and critical parole period.

Although parole had its earlier beginnings in Europe, it is now more fully developed and used in the United States. Today there are fifty-three parole agencies, one in each of the 50 states, the federal system, the District of Columbia, and the California Woman's Board of Terms and Paroles. In twenty-five of the fifty-three jurisdictions, the paroling agency is known as parole board or board of parole (or paroles); in nine jurisdictions, it is known as board of paroles and pardons; in eight jurisdictions, board of probation and parole; and in the remaining eleven jurisdictions by different names.[8]

The first attempt to apply parole in the United States came in conjunction with the opening of the Elmira Reformatory in 1876. Thus, the first parole statute in the United States was enacted only two years before the first probation law was passed in 1878. By 1900, twenty states had provisions for parole, and by 1944, all states had parole laws.

The provisions for parole vary considerably from state to state, and no one statement applies generally to the administration of parole. There is considerable variation in the extent to which parole is used in the different states and the efficiency with which the parole functions are carried out.

Illustration 21.2 represents the use of releases on parole in relation to all releases in 1973 by regions. During the year

| Region | Prison Population | Unconditional Release | Conditional Release |
|---|---|---|---|
| Northeast | 29,823 | 1,615 | 15,356 |
| North Central | 36,072 | 2,426 | 18,429 |
| South | 84,462 | 15,947 | 26,678 |
| West | 31,177 | 1,488 | 10,825 |
| Total | 181,534 | 21,476 | 71,288 |

**Illustration 21.2** PRISON POPULATION AND NUMBER OF RELEASES IN 1973 (BY REGIONS)

Source: U.S. Department of Justice, *Prisoners in State and Federal Institutions* (Washington, D.C.: Government Printing Office, 1975), pp. 12–26.

1971–72 about 34,000 persons were employed fulltime in the United States in probation, parole, and pardon. And during the same period the state governments alone had spent a total of $144 million on probation, parole, and pardon.[9]

## *THE PAROLE PROCESS*

Parole is an executive function and is generally granted by an administrative board or an agency. (Probation, on the other hand, is a function of the courts.) Parole entails supervision and is granted on the basis of such factors as an offender's prior history, sentence served, readiness and suitability for such release, need for supervision and assistance in the community before the expiration of sentence, and the reaction of the community to an offender's release under supervision.

Of those released from state and federal prisons approximately two thirds are released by parole or some other type of conditional release. There were 175,280 persons released on parole in the United States in 1966. As Illustration 21.3 indicates, only two states, New Hampshire and Washington, have provided parole or conditional release for all persons leaving the prisons. In twenty-three states more than 70 percent of releases are by parole or conditional release, and in ten states it is less than 40 percent. These statistics clearly demonstrate the wide use of discretion in paroling of offenders.[10]

Parole is an integral part of the correctional process. As such and as a rehabilitation method it offers continuity of the treatment started in the institution, under supervised guidance, in the normal society. The importance of supervision is further highlighted when it is considered that the period immediately following release from prison is most crucial for acceptable social adjustment and integration in the community. An equally important function of parole is to provide assistance and guidance in finding solutions to many of the problems an "ex-con" faces on his or her return to society.

| STATE | TOTAL RELEASES | PERCENTAGE OF TOTAL RELEASES |
|---|---|---|
| N.H. | 117 | 100.0 |
| Wash. | 1,391 | 100.0 |
| Kan. | 1,199 | 98.2 |
| Utah | 337 | 93.5 |
| Ohio | 4,642 | 93.4 |
| Cal. | 7,766 | 90.7 |
| Wis. | 1,866 | 89.0 |
| Hawaii | 168 | 88.7 |
| N.Y. | 7,602 | 87.3 |
| Mich. | 4,108 | 85.2 |
| Penn. | 2,633 | 84.7 |
| Nev. | 234 | 84.2 |
| N.J. | 2,918 | 83.1 |
| Conn. | 1,114 | 80.7 |
| Ind. | 2,186 | 78.8 |
| Me. | 587 | 78.5 |
| Vt. | 237 | 78.5 |
| N.D. | 152 | 78.3 |
| Colo. | 1,612 | 76.5 |
| W.Va. | 678 | 76.0 |
| Ill. | 3,396 | 73.9 |
| Minn. | 974 | 72.5 |
| Ark. | 1,123 | 71.0 |
| Mass. | 1,327 | 66.6 |
| U.S. | 87,640 | 65.8 |
| D.C. | 693 | 65.7 |
| Idaho | 241 | 63.5 |
| La. | 1,741 | 63.1 |
| Ia. | 1,085 | 61.4 |
| Mont. | 435 | 59.8 |
| Ga. | 2,728 | 51.3 |
| N.M. | 457 | 51.2 |
| Ariz. | 633 | 50.1 |
| Ala. | 2,198 | 47.5 |
| Va. | 1,827 | 47.3 |
| Miss. | 863 | 45.0 |
| N.C. | 2,722 | 44.5 |
| R.I. | 127 | 44.1 |
| Fla. | 2,899 | 42.5 |
| Ken. | 1,340 | 42.3 |
| S.D. | 411 | 41.8 |
| Del. | 204 | 39.7 |
| Ore. | 1,030 | 38.7 |
| Tenn. | 1,558 | 37.2 |
| Tex. | 5,824 | 35.7 |
| Md. | 4,190 | 35.5 |
| Mo. | 1,955 | 35.5 |
| S.C. | 1,323 | 32.8 |
| Neb. | 780 | 27.7 |
| Okla. | 1,822 | 17.3 |
| Wyo. | 187 | 12.3 |

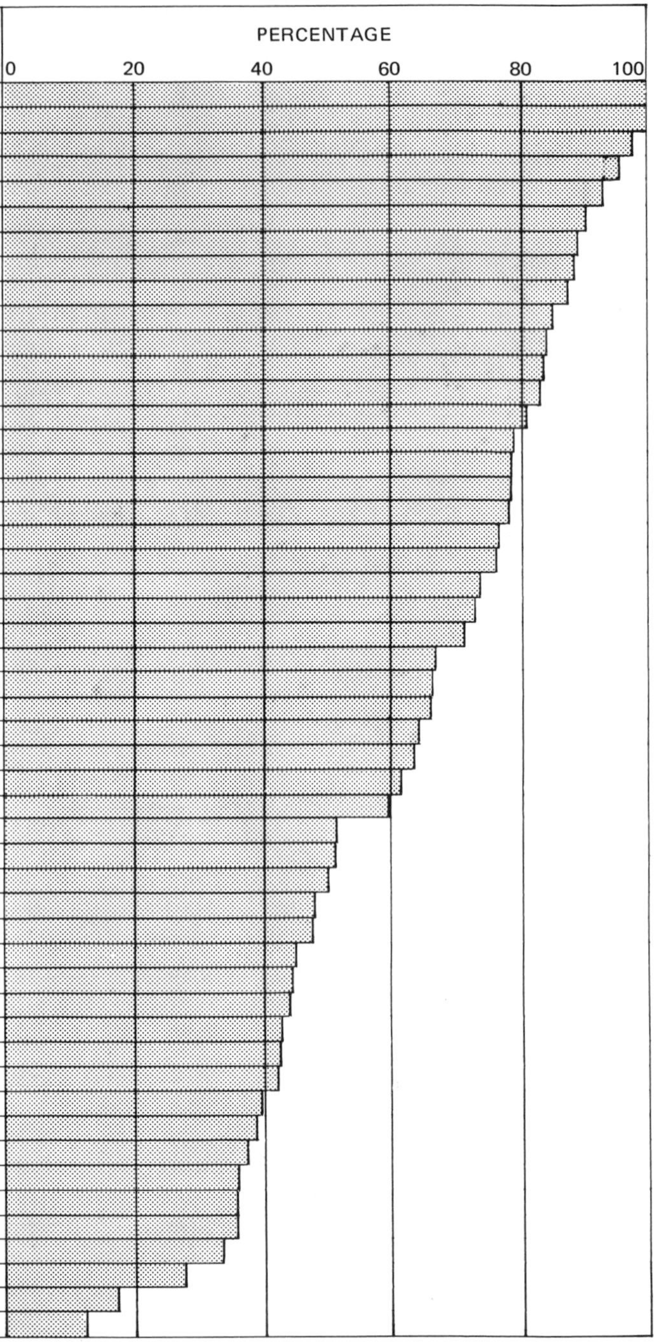

**Illustration 21.3** INMATES RELEASED ON PAROLE FROM STATE PRISONS (1966) (INCLUDES CONDITIONAL RELEASES UNDER MANDATORY SUPERVISION)

Source: Bureau of Prisons, "Prisons in State and Federal Institutions for Adult Felons, 1966," *National Prisoner Statistics* 43 (Washington, D.C.: 1968), pp. 28–29.

To fulfill these functions there are several essential elements in the parole process. All presuppose that there is a duly constituted agency with authority, usually called the parole board, to administer parole. A parole board, established under a statutory authority, usually consists of three to nine or more members. Its functional responsibilities include grant or denial of parole and revocation. A parole board is assisted by staff generally divided into three broad categories: personnel for carrying out the administrative duties, personnel for supervising parolees, and staff stationed in institutions to interview prospective parolees.

The following are considered essential elements in the parole process:

1. part of the sentence served in an institution in order to gain what is referred to as parole eligibility
2. selection for parole
3. supervision, control, and guidance of parolees according to the conditions of parole up until discharge from parole
4. parole revocation when parole conditions are violated

### Parole Eligibility

The legal authority within which parole decisions are made varies widely from one jurisdiction to another. Basically, the parole decision for adult offenders may depend on statutes enacted by legislature, on the sentence imposed by the court, on the determination of correctional authorities, or on independent parole board action. Some statutes require that a certain minimum amount of time be served before parole can be considered. Some statutes prohibit parole for certain types of offenses. Because such restrictions allow no consideration of the individual or the special circumstances, correctional authorities have consistently found that they interfere with effective decision making; at times they cause unnecessary confinement; and at times they result in substantial inequities.

With respect to parole for juveniles, a number of legal issues are involved in commitment and subsequent release. Those which most directly affect parole practice are the restrictions as to when a juvenile can be released. Of these the most important are the stipulated period of time a youth is required to stay in a training school and the necessary approval from the committing judge before release can be authorized. As in the case of adults, rules of parole eligibility for juveniles vary from jurisdiction to jurisdiction.

### Parole Selection

The parole selection criteria, which also vary from one jurisdiction to another, can be divided into: (1) statutory requirements, (2) type of sentence, (3) institutional recommendations, and (4) parole board policy.

*Statutory Requirements* The statutory requirements set the limits for the paroling agency regarding the type of offender who can or often cannot be considered for parole and the length of time an offender must serve before becoming eligible. In some places the laws prohibit parole of offenders who have committed serious crimes. The rules in most cases specify the minimum time, the maximum, or both before a person can become eligible for parole consideration, but usually eligibility comes after completion of one third of the sentence.

In general, the longer the time a person has served, the greater the possibility that he or she will be considered favorably for parole. Some people believe that serving a longer period in an institution corresponds to society's idea of punishment, and others interpret it as an inmate benefiting from the institutional programs. Reality is perhaps somewhere in between the two. Some inmates merely pay lip service to the rehabilitative programs and appear to cooperate because they know that by doing this their chances for an early parole will increase.

*Type of Sentence* The type of sentence influences parole selection. The sentencing judge may impose a special condition requiring the offender to follow a certain course or prohibiting him or her from doing certain things. The judge may also order a specific treatment plan, though it does not happen often. Such considerations, particularly when they are viewed as practical and beneficial to the offender, are taken seriously by parole boards.

Some judges impose longer sentences because they feel that the community expects some offenders to be confined for a longer period, especially those who have committed crimes particularly unacceptable at the time. Naturally, these sentences result in longer confinement before consideration for parole. Perhaps a parole board has full control over a convicted person only when a court imposes a truely indeterminate sentence, neither a minimum nor a maximum being set.

A few applicants cannot seriously be considered because their behavior, attitude, almost every aspect about the case is negative or there are other indications that they will not succeed on parole but will further violate the law. Occasionally, inmates write to say that they are not interested in parole, and such cases are not processed by the parole agency staff.

The cases in which detainers have been lodged, either for violation of a previous parole or for another offense, are handled by parole boards in various ways. (A detainer is a legal order for holding a person who is wanted or for whom a summons has been issued.) Some boards postpone consideration of such applicants till the detainer is lifted, some consider detainers but decide the case on its own merits, and others disregard detainers.

*Institutional Recommendations* Some of the parole laws provide that recommendations from the institution must be considered by the paroling agency. Most paroling authorities not only like to have reports and recommendations but view them as a necessary part of the case preparation, because the institutional personnel usually know inmates, their attitudes and motivations, and their capabilities for functioning with others. They also have a better appraisal of the programs in which the inmates may have participated. The kind of consideration given to reports from the institutional personnel depends upon the board's view of the writer's attitude, whether in favor of or against parole, and the objectivity of the information.

*Parole Board Policy* Parole board selection criteria revolve around two basic concepts: (1) the community is ready and willing to receive a parolee; and (2) the offender is ready and willing to lead a law-abiding life. These are considerations over and above the legal requirements and the institutional assessment. The suitability of an individual for parole and the community's readiness to accept him or her hinge on a number of factors, sociological, psychological, and educational. Sometimes, a specific factor like the availability of employment or the details of a political or deportation case is taken into consideration. In the political category, most often a specific situation may make it politically imprudent to release an inmate even though suitable for release at that time. When nationals of other countries are committed to correctional institutions, they may be granted parole for deportation to their countries after fulfilling certain requirements.

Many parole agencies have a standard form for preparing parole reports and recommendations. Generally these reports provide information regarding the offender's social history and background. The depth and the breadth of information about a potential parolee's personal, family, marital, education, and employment history differs from case to case. The greater the severity of the offense committed the greater the amount of information expected, and often required, for making a sound judgment.

In addition to a thorough social history of a person, which has been prepared by the parole agency staff in institutions and outside, most parole boards have information concerning the criminal record. The previous criminal history not only includes the present sentence and details about the type and circumstances of the offense; it also includes the previous offense patterns. Information may refer to the use of a weapon, whether an injury was involved, and so on. Parole reports often contain information obtained from the institutional files, including their recommendations, if any, indicating the process and conduct of the inmate. There may be other special reports, perhaps a medical report, and letters of recommendations from interested citizens (and sometimes expressing opposition to parole). Of more recent origin are such selection aids as parole hearings and the statistical prediction tables. Parole hearings are used in most jurisdictions. Usually a team of two parole board members visits institutions to interview inmates. The new prediction aids are mostly "unproven" from the scientific point of view, but more and more experiments are being undertaken to improve the techniques used to predict the outcome of parole.

The proportion of those released on parole as against those discharged has been rising steadily during the past few years. Occasionally when a parolee is involved in a bizarre or a well-publicized offense that generates unfavorable community reaction, parole boards are inclined to enforce stricter selection procedures, for a while anyway. For the most part, however, the use of parole has been increasing because of its lower cost and the overall trend toward community-based corrections.

Statutes in most jurisdictions allow parole agencies to adopt their own rules and regulations for selection provided there is no conflict with the statutes. Only a few agencies have written criteria for

**Illustration 21.4** GENERAL FACTORS CONSIDERED BY THE U.S. BOARD OF PAROLE IN PAROLE SELECTION

Source: *Rules of the United States Board of Parole* (Washington, D.C.: Government Printing Office, 1971), pp. 14–16.

According to its rule book, the following factors are considered by the U.S. Board of Parole in making parole decisions.

A. Sentence Data
   (1) Type of sentence
   (2) Length of sentence
   (3) Recommendations of judge, United States attorney, and other responsible officials
B. Facts and Circumstances of the Offense
   (1) Mitigating and aggravating factors
   (2) Activities following arrest and prior to confinement, including adjustment on bond or probation, if any
C. Prior Criminal Record
   (1) Nature and pattern of offenses
   (2) Adjustment to previous probation, parole, and confinement
   (3) Detainers
D. Changes in Motivation and Behavior
   (1) Changes in attitude toward self and others
   (2) Reasons underlying changes
   (3) Personal goals and description of personal strengths or resources available to maintain motivation for law-abiding behavior
E. Personal and Social History
   (1) Family and marital
   (2) Intelligence and education
   (3) Employment and military experience
   (4) Leisure time
   (5) Religion
   (6) Physical and emotional health
F. Institutional Experience
   (1) Program goals and accomplishments in areas:
      (a) academic
      (b) vocational education, training or work assignments
      (c) recreation and leisure time use
      (d) religion
      (e) therapy
   (2) General adjustment:
      (a) interpersonal relationships with staff and inmates
      (b) behavior, including misconduct
   (3) Physical and emotional health, and treatment
G. Community resources, including release plans
   (1) Residence; live alone, with family, or others
   (2) Employment, training, or academic education
   (3) Special needs and resources to meet them
H. Use of scientific data and tools
   (1) Psychological and psychiatric evaluations
   (2) pertinent data from the uniform parole reporting system
   (3) Other statistical data
   (4) Standardized tests
I. Comments by hearing member or examiner
   Evaluative comments supporting a recommendation, including his impressions gained from the hearing.

parole selection, supervision, and technical revocation, and those written criteria are generally considered very broad and vague. Some paroling authorities consider the lack of precise and written criteria helpful because it allows flexibility and individual treatment. In decisions against parole and parole revocation cases, however, persons whose paroles are denied or revoked want to know exactly why, so that they can improve themselves in the deficient areas, and some consider this information their right.

Recently, however, the United States Supreme Court has ordered the chairman of the United States Board of Parole to meet with lawyers to discuss and spell out parole selection criteria.[11] The courts have now begun to take more active interest in corrections, including parole, and to rule in areas once considered strictly administrative. For example, in a recent case, *Morrissey* v. *Brewer* [408 U.S. 471 (1972)] the Supreme Court unanimously ruled that a parolee is entitled to a full due process hearing prior to parole revocation.

The present approach to parole revocation significantly changes the earlier stand that parole was a privilege that could be taken away almost arbitrarily. The new approach is not only evidence of the growing concern for the rights of persons under correctional control; it also recognizes that the correctional system must impress on those working in the system that due process operates fairly and equally for the protection of *all* society.

### Supervision, Control, and Guidance

The principles, concepts, and methods of probation supervision apply equally to the supervision of parolees. One way of looking at what the supervision, control, and guidance functions entail is to relate them to the definition and objective of parole. The task of parole supervision is to provide more favorable opportunities and conducive environment for parolees so that they can readjust life patterns to societal demands, within the limits set by the community, through the parole board.

Although it is recognized that parolees have had the benefit of correctional treatment programs, parolees in general are more difficult to supervise than probationers. This is so partly because parolees usually have a history of long criminal careers and serious offenses, whereas probationers have not had the inmate indoctrination of the correctional institution. Adjustment in the community after prison indoctrination is often made difficult by the community itself and takes special effort and time. Parole supervision, like probation supervision, entails working with the parolee and his or her family, if there is one. It involves establishing a professional working relationship with the police department and the sheriff in the area, an awareness of the social services in the community, and a good knowledge of all the potential employers in the area who will hire parolees.

The case load of parole officers varies greatly. Sometimes probationers and parolees are supervised by one officer. One state reported a probation-parole case load of 314 for each parole officer.[12] Views about the ideal size of a case load differ, the most frequently recommended case load being between thirty-five and fifty, but most parole systems have more than that under the supervision of one parole

**Illustration 21.5** COMPARISON OF CONDITIONS OF PAROLE FOR THE FIFTY STATES, THE UNITED STATES BOARD OF PAROLE, AND THE DISTRICT OF COLUMBIA (1972)

Source: American Correctional Association, *Parole: Origins, Development, Current Practices and Statutes* American Correctional Association Resource Document no. 1, 1972, Appendix C, pp. 196–198.

| *Conditions of Parole* | Alabama | Alaska | Arizona | Arkansas | California | Calif. Women | Colorado | Connecticut | Delaware | Dist. of Col. | D.C. (Federal) | Florida | Georgia | Hawaii | Idaho | Illinois | Indiana | Iowa | Kansas |
|---|---|---|---|---|---|---|---|---|---|---|---|---|---|---|---|---|---|---|---|
| 1. Liquor usage | | 4 | 4 | 4 | | | 2 | 4 | 4 | 4 | 4 | 4 | 4 | 4 | | 4 | 2 | 4 | |
| 2. Association or correspondence with undesirables | 2 | 2 | 2 | 2 | | 1 | 1 | 1 | 2 | 2 | 1 | 2 | 2 | 1 | 2 | 1 | 2 | 2 | 2 |
| 3. Change of employment or residence | 1 | 1 | 1 | 1 | 6 | 6 | 1 | 1 | 1 | 1 | 6 | 1 | 1 | 1 | | 1 | 1 | 1 | 1 |
| 4. Filing report blanks | 3 | 3 | | 3 | | 3 | 3 | 3 | | | 3 | 3 | 3 | 3 | 3 | 3 | | 3 | 3 |
| 5. Out-of-state travel | 1 | | 1 | 1 | 1 | 1 | 1 | 1 | 1 | | | | 1 | 1 | | | 1 | 1 | 1 |
| 6. Contracting new marriage | 1 | 1 | 1 | 1 | | | 1 | 1 | 1 | 1 | | 1 | | 1 | | 1 | 1 | 1 | 1 |
| 7. First arrival report | 3 | 3 | 3 | 3 | 3 | 3 | 3 | 3 | | 3 | 3 | 3 | 3 | | | 3 | 3 | 3 | 3 |
| 8. Operation and ownership of a motor vehicle | | 1 | 1 | 1 | | | 1 | 1 | 1 | 1 | | 1 | | | | 1 | 1 | 1 | 1 |
| 9. Narcotic usage | 2 | | | 2 | 2 | 2 | 2 | 2 | 1 | 2 | 2 | 2 | 2 | 2 | | 2 | 2 | 2 | |
| 10. Support dependents | 3 | 3 | | | | | | 3 | 3 | 3 | 3 | 3 | 3 | 3 | | 3 | 3 | 3 | 3 |
| 11. Possession, use, or sale of weapons | | 1 | 2 | 2 | 2 | 2 | 2 | 2 | 1 | 2 | 1 | 1 | 2 | 2 | | 2 | 2 | 2 | 2 |
| 12. Travel out of county and community | | 1 | | 1 | | | 1 | | | 1 | 1 | 1 | | | | 1 | 1 | 1 | 1 |
| 13. Agree to wave extradition | 3 | 3 | | | 3 | | 3 | | 3 | | | 3 | 3 | | | | | 3 | 3 |
| 14. Indebtedness | | 1 | 1 | 1 | | | 1 | | 1 | | | | | 1 | | | | 1 | 1 |
| 15. Curfew | | | | | | | | | | | | | | 11 pm | | 1-11 pm | | 5 | |
| 16. Civil rights | | | | | | | | | | | | | | | | | | | |
| 17. Street time credit if PV | | | | | | | | | | | | | | | | | | | |
| 18. Gambling | | | | | | | | | | | | 2 | | | | | | | |
| 19. Airplane license | | | | | | | | | | | | | | | | | | | |
| 20. Report if arrested | | | | 3 | | | | 3 | 3 | | 3 | 3 | | | | | | | 3 |
| 21. Keep lawful occupation | 3 | 3 | 3 | | | | 3 | 3 | 3 | 3 | 3 | 3 | 3 | 3 | | 3 | | | 3 |
| 22. Obey the law | 3 | 3 | 3 | 3 | 3 | 3 | 3 | 3 | 3 | 3 | 3 | 3 | 3 | 3 | 3 | 3 | 3 | 3 | |
| 23. Allow home and work visits | 3 | | | | | | 3 | 3 | | | | 3 | 3 | | | 3 | | | |
| 24. Search home, car, and person | | | | | | | 3 | | | | | | | | | | | | |
| 25. Not inform | | | | | | | | | | 3 | 3 | | | 3 | | | | | |
| 26. Undergo treatment | | | | | | 3 | | | | | 3 | | | | | 3 | | | |
| 27. Radio, TV, books, etc. | | | | | | | | | | | | | | | | | | | |
| 28. No common law marriage | | | 2 | | | | | | | | | | | | | | | | |
| 29. Register with the police | | | 3 | | | | | | | | | | | | | | | | |

Key: 1. Must have permission 2. Prohibited 3. Compulsory 4. Allowed but not to excess 5. Reasonable hour 6. Notify

| Kentucky | Louisiana | Maine | Maryland | Massachusetts | Michigan | Minnesota | Mississippi | Missouri | Montana | Nebraska | Nevada | N. Hampshire | New Jersey | New Mexico | New York | North Carolina | North Dakota | Ohio | Oklahoma | Oregon | Pennsylvania | Rh. Island | S. Carolina | S. Dakota | Tennessee | Texas | Utah | Vermont | Virginia | Washington | W. Virginia | Wisconsin | Wyoming |
|---|---|---|---|---|---|---|---|---|---|---|---|---|---|---|---|---|---|---|---|---|---|---|---|---|---|---|---|---|---|---|---|---|---|
| 2 | | 4 | | 2 | | 4 | 2 | | 4 | 4 | 2 | 2 | 4 | 2 | 4 | 2 | | 4 | 2 | | | 2 | 2 | 2 | 4 | 2 | | 4 | | 4 | 4 | 4 | 4 |
| 2 | 2 | | | 2 | 1 | | 1 | 2 | | | 1 | 2 | 2 | 1 | 2 | 2 | | 2 | 2 | | | 2 | 2 | 2 | 2 | 2 | 2 | | 2 | 2 | | | 2 |
| 1 | 1 | 1 | 1 | 1 | 1 | 1 | 1 | 1 | 1 | 1 | 1 | 1 | 1 | 1 | 1 | 1 | 1 | 1 | | | 1 | 1 | 1 | 1 | 1 | 1 | 1 | | 1 | 1 | 1 | 1 | 1 |
| 3 | 3 | | | 3 | 3 | 3 | | | 3 | 3 | 3 | 3 | | 3 | | | 3 | 3 | 3 | 3 | 3 | | 3 | 3 | 3 | 3 | 3 | 3 | 3 | | 3 | 3 | 3 |
| 1 | | 1 | 1 | 1 | 1 | 1 | 1 | 1 | | 1 | 1 | 1 | 1 | 1 | 1 | 1 | 1 | 1 | | 1 | 1 | 1 | 1 | 1 | 1 | 1 | 1 | 1 | | | 1 | 1 | 1 |
| 1 | | 1 | | 1 | | 1 | | | 6 | 1 | 1 | 1 | 1 | 1 | 1 | 1 | 1 | 1 | 1 | | | 1 | | 1 | 1 | 1 | 1 | | | 1 | 1 | 1 | 1 |
| 3 | 3 | | 3 | | 3 | 3 | 3 | | 3 | | 3 | 3 | 3 | | 3 | | | 3 | 3 | 3 | 3 | 3 | 3 | | 3 | 3 | | | | | 3 | | 3 |
| | | 1 | | 1 | 1 | 1 | 1 | 1 | 1 | 1 | 1 | 1 | 1 | 1 | 1 | 1 | 1 | 1 | | | | 1 | | 1 | 1 | 1 | 1 | | 1 | 1 | 1 | 1 | 1 |
| 2 | | | 2 | 2 | | 2 | 2 | 2 | 2 | | 2 | 2 | 2 | 2 | 2 | 2 | | 2 | 2 | | 2 | 2 | 2 | 2 | 2 | 2 | 2 | | | | 2 | | 2 |
| 3 | 3 | 3 | | 3 | | | 3 | | 3 | 3 | | 3 | 3 | 3 | 3 | 3 | | 3 | 3 | | 3 | | 3 | | 3 | 3 | 3 | 3 | 3 | | 3 | | 3 |
| 2 | 2 | 1 | 1 | 1 | 2 | 2 | 1 | | 2 | 2 | 2 | 1 | 1 | 2 | 2 | 1 | 1 | 2 | 2 | 2 | 2 | 1 | 1 | 2 | 1 | 1 | 1 | 2 | | 2 | 2 | 1 | 1 |
| 1 | 1 | 1 | | | | 1 | 1 | 1 | 1 | 1 | 1 | | | 1 | 1 | 1 | | 1 | 1 | | 1 | 1 | | 1 | 1 | 1 | | | 1 | 1 | 1 | | 1 |
| | 3 | 3 | | | | 3 | 3 | | | | | 3 | | | 3 | 3 | | | 3 | | | 3 | 3 | | 3 | 3 | | | 3 | | | | |
| | | | | | | 1 | | | 1 | | 1 | 1 | 1 | | | 1 | 1 | | | | | | | 1 | | | 1 | | | 1 | | 1 | 1 |
| | | | | | | | | | | | | 5 | | | | | | | | | | | | 5 | | | 5 | | 5 | | | | |
| | | | | | | | | | | | 1 | | | | 2 | | | | | | | | | | | | | | | | | | |
| | | | | | | | | | | | | | | | | | | | | | | 2 | | | | | | | | | | | |
| | | | | | | | | | | | | | | | | | | | | | | | | 2 | | | | | | | | | |
| | | 1 | | | | | | | | | | | | | | | | 1 | | | | | | | | | | | | | | | |
| | | | 3 | | 3 | 3 | | 3 | | | | | 3 | 3 | 3 | | | | | | 3 | | | | 3 | | | | | | 3 | | |
| 3 | 3 | 3 | 3 | 3 | 3 | | 3 | | 3 | | | 3 | 3 | 3 | 3 | 3 | | 3 | 3 | | 3 | | 3 | | 3 | 3 | 3 | | 3 | | 3 | | 3 |
| 3 | 3 | 3 | 3 | 3 | 3 | 3 | 3 | 3 | 3 | 3 | 3 | 3 | 3 | 3 | 3 | 3 | 3 | 3 | | 3 | 3 | 3 | 3 | 3 | 3 | 3 | 3 | 3 | 3 | | | 3 | |
| 3 | | | | | | | | | | | | 3 | | 3 | 3 | 3 | | | 3 | | | 3 | 3 | | 3 | | 3 | | 3 | | | | 3 |
| | | | | | | | | | | | 3 | | | | 3 | | | | | | | | | | | | | | | | | | |
| | | | | | | | | | | | | | | | | | | | | | | | | | | | | | | | | | |
| | 3 | | | 3 | | | | | | | | | | | | | | | | | | | | | | | | | 3 | | | | |
| | | | | | | | | | | | | | | | | | | | | | | | | | | | | | | | | | |
| | | | | 2 | | | | | | | | | | | 2 | | | 2 | | | | | | | | | | | | | | | |
| | | | | | | | | | | | | | | | | | | | | | | | | | | | | | | | | | |

Key: 1. Must have permission
2. Prohibited
3. Compulsory
4. Allowed but not to excess
5. Reasonable hour
6. Notify

officer. The type and the intensity of supervision also varies on a number of factors: the type of parolees, the social environment, supervision caseload, the ratio of parole officers to parolees, and other workload.

Once parole is granted, satisfactory completion of the parole period is related to the variations in the regulation and supervision of parole. Nationally, the average parole period for offenders is twenty-nine months. The state averages for parole period range from fewer than twelve months to over eighty-four months.[13]

If the parole board feels that a particular parolee has had the maximum assistance available under parole supervision and can function in the community in a socially and legally acceptable manner without supervision, he or she may be discharged gradually from parole obligation. A discharge from parole means a lifting of parole restrictions in accordance with ability to integrate into the community. Having demonstrated that he or she does not present any risks, the discharge can be complete.

### Conditions of Parole and its Revocation

When parole is granted to an applicant, it contains conditions with which he or she must agree and abide. Any violation of the conditions either by disregarding them (which is referred to as a technical violation of parole) or by breaking any laws or statutes can result in the revocation of parole. In case of violation of a condition of parole, the supervisor may recommend to the parole board that the parolee be returned to prison either because a parole restriction has been violated or because he or she is likely to commit a crime.

Conditions of parole have a three-fold purpose; they represent the expectations of the community; they test a parolee's serious intention to lead a law-abiding life; they offer the parolee an opportunity for self-improvement.

If a parolee is arrested and charged with a new offense, there is little if any problem about declaring him or her a parole violator, as is also the case if the parolee absconds. In both these situations the decision to revoke parole does not present any dilemma, but not all cases are so clear cut. This is one of the sources of criticism of the administration of parole policies: there are no definite criteria. Judicial intervention, previously mentioned, is likely to bring about changes, however.

The decisions of parole supervisors have an important affect on parolees and their families. When supervisors recommend revocation, everything that has been accomplished in terms of treatment, finding employment, and in general making adjustment in the community more feasible is usually negated. Should supervisors be more understanding and more flexible in their control duties? Or should they emphasize performance in accordance with the conditions agreed to with the parolee? These are some of the important considerations that parole supervisors have to deliberate in almost each revocation case.

Illustration 21.5 compares conditions of parole used in different jurisdictions, and the diversity of emphasis is obvious. Yet all inmates granted parole have to sign such an agreement and abide by the conditions listed on their parole certificates. Not only are there divergent views about the number and type of conditions; there is little agreement about what constitutes a realistic approach to enforceability. Some experts believe that it is better to give greater flexibility to the parole supervisor assisting parolees and others believe that the conditions should be more specific so that persons charged with their violation know where they faulted, rather than being told in generalities that their attitudes are uncooperative or that they present risks and it will therefore be safer to send them back to prison.

The courts, on the other hand, have become more concerned, reflecting the interest of the public, with the rights of prisoners, probationers, and parolees. Indications are that the number of parole rules and regulations is increasing, to deal with many special situations, and there is also a tendency for such regulations to be more specific.

**Contract Parole**

Contract parole is also known as Mutual Agreement Programming (MAP). Under the concept of contract parole or MAP the inmate, the parole board, and the correctional institution sign a contract at the beginning of the inmate's sentence. If the inmate fulfills his or her obligations under the contract, he or she will be paroled on an agreed-upon date. If the inmate does not fulfill his or her obligations the contract becomes void and a new contract may be negotiated. The basic elements of contract parole are:

- A written, legally enforceable contract between the inmate, the institution, and the parole authority;
- A target date, which becomes the parole date if all contract provisions are met by the inmate;
- Face-to-face negotiations between the inmate (often helped by an advocate), the institution, and the parole authority;
- The involvement of an outside party who independently determines whether the contract has been fulfilled;
- Contract provisions spelling out measurable goals for inmates in the areas of education, training, counseling and institutional behavior, and a guarantee from the correctional system that programs and services to fulfill these goals will be available as needed.[14]

In 1975 nine states and the District of Columbia were using parole contracts. In some states the target date for parole under the contract system is negotiable. In other states it is set by law. Other variations also exist from state to state. Basically, however, under the contract parole system the inmate enters into the contract voluntarily. The inmate may withdraw from the contract at any time. Those inmates who withdraw from or fail to fulfill the contract revert to the regular parole process. For those inmates who remain in MAP they have the advantage of a definite parole date, specific program objectives, and, in some cases, the possibility of an early release.

## DISCUSSION QUESTIONS

1. How would you define parole?
2. Where did the parole concept develop?
3. Discuss the pros and cons of parole for every prisoner, regardless of the type of offense or offenses committed.
4. Some people believe that parole is just an incentive for good behavior during the imprisonment period, and others believe that it does help parolees not to revert to crime. Discuss the implications, particularly from the point of view of an administrator.
5. What are the criteria that a parole board generally uses for parole consideration? Are they valid?
6. Is a parolee entitled to full due process during a parole revocation process? What is your opinion?
7. Discuss the importance of supervision and counseling skills required of a parole supervisor. What are some of the problem areas?
8. Discuss and outline the rights of prisoners, as they relate to the parole process. Is parole a right or privilege?

## NOTES

1. *Oxford English Dictionary* (London: Clarendon Press, 1933), VII, 489.
2. Robert M. Carter and Leslie T. Wilkins, *Probation and Parole* (New York: Wiley, 1970), p. 180.
3. Harry E. Barnes and Nagley K. Teeters, *New Horizons in Criminology* (Englewood Cliffs, N.J.: Prentice-Hall, 1959), p. 566.
4. William Parker, *Parole: Origins, Development, Current Practices and Statutes*, American Correctional Association Resource Document No. 1, 1972, p. 5.
5. G. I. Giardini, *The Parole Process* (Springfield, Ill.: Charles C. Thomas, 1959), p. 19.
6. President's Commission on Law Enforcement and Administration of Justice, *Task Force Report: Corrections* (Washington, D.C.: Government Printing Office, 1967), p. 208.
7. Parker, *Parole*, p. 13.
8. Parker, *Parole*, p. 38.
9. Bureau of Census, *Expenditure and Employment Data for the Criminal Justice System 1971–72* (Washington, D.C.: Government Printing Office, 1974), pp. 13, 255–309.
10. "Corrections in the United States," *Crime and Delinquency*, 13–1 (January 1967), 213.

11. Parker, *Parole*.
12. Vernon Fox, *Introduction to Corrections* (Englewood Cliffs, N.J.: Prentice-Hall, 1972), p. 274.
13. Richard Quinney, *The Social Reality of Crime* (Boston: Little, Brown, 1970), p. 194.
14. "Parole Contracts: A New Way Out," *Corrections Magazine*, 2–1 (September/October 1975), 4.

# 22: Problems and Recent Developments in Parole

*PROBLEMS • RECENT DEVELOPMENTS*

PURPOSE: *TO DISCUSS THE PROBLEM AREAS IN PAROLE AS WELL AS CURRENT DEVELOPMENT AND TRENDS.*

ANY PROBLEM in the area of parole takes on a different magnitude depending on who is observing it and the reason for so doing. There can be an objective and a realistic review of some of the problems, however, designed not to blame but to understand the system better, as is necessary before any improvements can be effectively incorporated.

## PROBLEMS

Many of the fundamental problems that beset parole are not peculiar to parole alone; they are the problems of our almost goalless, unsystematic, and fragmented system of criminal justice. Therefore, working for solutions, however well designed and well intended, at only one point in the system means fighting half the battle or fighting it half-heartedly.

One of the shortcomings of parole is best stated in the words of the chairman of the United States Board of Parole: "It is important that our goals be better defined and our definitions of terms clarified."[1] The National Crime Commission (1967) listed the following objectives of a parole system:

1. Release of each person from confinement at the most favorable time, with appropriate consideration to requirements of justice, expectations of subsequent behavior, and the cost.
2. The largest possible number of successful parole completions.
3. The smallest possible number of new crimes committed by released offenders.
4. The smallest possible number of violent acts committed by released offenders.
5. An increase of general community confidence in parole administration.

The methods by which those objectives can be achieved must include the following:

1. A process for selecting persons who should be given parole and for determining the time of release.
2. A system of pre-release planning both inside the institution with the offender and outside the institution with others in the community at large.
3. A system for supervision and assistance in the community.
4. A set of policies, procedures, and guidelines for situations in which the question of re-imprisonment must be decided.[2]

These methods, recommended by the National Crime Commission (1967), bring out some of the other problems facing parole. It must be realized that not all parole agencies have all the same problems—the extent and intensity of the problems vary from one agency to another.

### Fragmented System

Tradition is partly responsible for the fragmentation in the criminal justice system, and the result most often has been the pursuit of organizational philosophies, programs, and procedures single mindedly, with little regard for what happens to the offender for whom the programs are essentially set up. A change in this attitude of the handling agencies is long overdue, particularly because the actions of one component of the criminal justice system have a direct bearing on the others.

In terms of parole, this lack of any systematic approach makes it the exception rather than the rule to find a correctional institution and a parole agency effectively coordinating and planning together a treatment program for offenders, this despite the fact that the correctional literature emphasizes the importance of initiating release plans as soon as a person is admitted to an institution. Cooperation, when it does exist, is more theoretical than actual. Not infrequently organizational rivalries and accusations operate at the expense of the persons who are supposed to be helped and, of course, at the cost of the taxpayer's dollar.

Difficulties between the courts and the paroling authorities arise from lack of dialogue and lack of communication about the aims and procedures of parole. Some courts, like some law enforcement agencies, feel that parole functions are contrary to the aims of law enforcement and the judiciary. Community reactions, particularly in the smaller community where practically everyone knows everyone else, can be unfavorable and make problems for a parolee's adjustment. The community must be prepared and its readiness thoroughly investigated.

Unless social services organizations, particularly the police, and potential employers are carefully made aware of some of the problems that ex-offenders face on their release, parolees can have a hard time finding employment. Until parolees have legitimate sources of income they are likely to find comfort and support from people who understand them better, and more often than not, these "buddies" have criminal records. Any association with "undesirables" is in many cases a technical violation of parole and can cause the parolee to be returned to the prison.

### Lack of Skilled Personnel

All functions and responsibilities of parole require that the number of personnel be sufficient, professionally skilled, and properly trained. Parole officers are expected to supervise, guide, and control parolees, the major functions of their job. They are expected to maintain professional contacts with the other criminal justice and welfare agencies. They are expected to be knowledgeable of the employment market, have time for parolees' families, write reports, and perform all the other administrative chores. Given such demands they cannot be expected to be productive and effective when they must look after large case loads. At present, 97 percent of all officers handling adults have case loads above the recommended average.[3]

The shortage of officers in parole is even more acute today than in 1967, when the National Crime Commission (1967) reported an immediate need for almost three times the number of parole officers then employed. Considering the population increase in the coming years, the total requirements will be even greater.[4]

The parole officer's authority to exercise sanctions sometimes creates conflicts not only with the parolee but also within the parole supervisor. Some people believe that the policing functions of control on the one hand and the helping rehabilitative services on the other present an inherent conflict. Whether or not such conflict exists often depends on the orientation and professional training of an individual parole officer and a particular situation. But a skilled parole officer should have no problem reconciling these apparently conflicting duties.

**Parole Board Members**

In forty-three of the fifty-three jurisdictions, state governors are the appointing authority of parole board members. In almost three fourths of the jurisdictions, there are no qualification requirements for the board members or qualifications are stated in broad terms.[5] Absence of any demonstrable knowledge of human behavior among the board members restricts the effectiveness of parole decisions. In addition, their effectiveness is further limited when it is realized that in one half of the jurisdictions, all or part of the parole board serves only on a part-time basis, which means they must usually give time to another job.

**Individual Rights**

Another problem relates to the constitutional issues of the due process of law and rights of individuals concerning matters of parole. Traditionally, parolees have been given few rights concerning matters of parole. Parole has been and still is considered a privilege, not a right. extended to the parolee by a sovereign. As such the sovereign or state could grant or revoke parole at its discretion, and without due process of law. Recent court decisions, however, have indicated that parolees are entitled to at least some rights in the parole process.

In *Morrissey* v. *Brewer* [408 U.S. 471 (1972)] the Supreme Court held that a parolee is entitled to two separate and distinct hearings before revocation of parole. At the first hearing, the one to determine whether to remove the parolee from the street, the parolee is entitled to present relevant information and question adverse witnesses. At the second hearing, the revocation hearing, the parolee is entitled to: (1) written notice of the claimed violation of parole, (2) disclosure of evidence, (3) opportunity to be heard in person and present witnesses and evidence, (4) the right to confront and cross-examine witnesses, (5) an impartial board, and (6) a written statement of the facts and findings of the board. The Court declined to consider the issue concerning the right to counsel in this particular case, but did so in *Gagon* v. *Scarpelli* [411 U.S. 778 (1973)].

In *Gagon* v. *Scarpelli* the Supreme Court held that in some cases the government must provide counsel to parolees at the revocation hearing. The decision as to the need of counsel in each case is left essentially in the hands of the parole board. The Court did not make a "blanket" decision, therefore, the need for counsel must be determined on a case-by-case basis.

In the past few years the rights of the parolee have been expanded. There are, however, many issues concerning the rights of individuals in matters related to parole that are still unresolved. The trend now appears to be toward the expansion of rights. It remains to be seen how far the courts will go.

### Research

Lastly, there is the problem of lack of research into the different aspects of parole. It is recognized that more intensified criminological research has helped formulate the predictive factors for success or failure on parole, but parole prediction is somewhat special in that it has to concern itself with violation of parole agreements. There is need for reliable information regarding the parole officer's method and techniques of handling parolees. A need exists for an inventory of the factors related to the stresses and strains experienced by parolees; for a realistic investigation of the factors that help or hinder their community integration; and for a procedure to establish classes of offenders who are more amenable to treatment and rehabilitation.

## *RECENT DEVELOPMENTS*

### Public Awareness

An overall trend among the public and among criminal justice agencies is toward greater awareness and understanding of parole as a rehabilitative technique. Greater numbers of people are recognizing the advantages and the risks involved in releasing offenders on parole. With two thirds of the total corrections case load under probation or parole supervision today, the central question is no longer whether to handle offenders in the community but how to do so safely and successfully.[6]

### Establishment of Standards

Another overall trend is toward the clarification of standards. Greater numbers of parole agencies have set up standards of some kind for parole selection, supervision, and reporting and standards about the qualifications and training of parole officers. There is a greater recognition for the need for appropriate qualifications and skills among board members. Many parole administrators are cognizant of the deficiencies and would like, if they had the resources and the public's support, to bring about the much needed improvements and changes in the present system.

As standards are incorporated into parole administration and as greater resources are available for research, more evaluative facilities will also be made available. Today, however, most parole systems not only lack evaluative devices for either the quality or the quantity of work; they are not even certain what needs to be evaluated. The only criterion presently used in most places is the number of successes and failures on parole, but even success and failure are defined and interpreted in many ways.

### Court Intervention

A definite development can be seen in the courts, which during the later 1960s discarded the "hands off" doctrine. Now they are intervening to protect the constitutional rights of individuals against the "caprice and whim" of the administrative agencies like the parole boards. For instance, the United States Board of Parole has been required to set more precise criteria for parole selection and intervention in specific cases.

**Community Involvement**

One of the more significant developments in probation and parole has been the involvement of the community at different levels of the rehabilitative process. Community participation is noticeable in the expansion of the use of nonprofessionals, more commonly known as volunteers. A number of new projects involve volunteer opportunities for individual citizens as well as projects for civic organizations. For example, young lawyers in Los Angeles, Sacramento, and Santa Clara counties will work with the California Youth Authority (CYA) as volunteers to help CYA parolees in a new, nationally sponsored program. The project in California is part of the National Volunteer Parole Aide Program sponsored by the American Bar Association Young Lawyers Section, its Commission on Correctional Facilities and Service, and the Federal Bar Association. This program involves over one third of the states. The basic purpose of the program is to provide caseload relief and treatment flexibility.[7]

More recent innovations involve the indigenous nonprofessional in corrections. "Most professional corrections workers agree that a large segment of their clientele are, by virture of their norms, values, and life styles, alienated from the mainstream—middle class professionals. . . . The indigenous worker, conversely, has often experienced situations and problems similar to those that beset certain clients."[8]

With the increasing acceptance and popularity of treatment within the community there is more widespread use of the programs associated with work release or, as they are sometimes known, day parole and work furlough. One of the objectives of such programs is to develop a greater sense of responsibility among the parolees by giving them responsibility gradually. The other objectives of work release or work furlough are to involve parolees in employment, education, and vocational programs. In some jurisdictions work release programs are solely administered either by the institutional or by the parole agency staff, and in others they are jointly administered. The trend, however, is toward increasingly coordinated efforts in program planning.

**Ex-offenders as Advisors**

Another recent development, which is viewed with great caution and sometimes with skepticism, concerns the idea that ex-offenders might be hired to act in advisory capacities, helping plan new programs and making existing ones more effective. Ex-offenders might also be members of reviewing committees and assist legislative committees, the rationale being the use of an existing source of experience at little cost.

Finally, parole agencies with the other correctional components are becoming more competitive and aggressive for their fair share of the resources and support required to carry out the changes that have been neglected or postponed for too long.

Parole, not unlike other agencies of the criminal justice system, is beset by a number of problems. The fragmented criminal justice system, unskilled parole personnel, unqualified parole board members, issues of parolees' rights, and lack of research hamper the effective and efficient operation of parole. However, recent developments in parole standards, community awareness and involvement, court intervention, and the use of ex-offenders offers some hope for the future of parole.

## DISCUSSION QUESTIONS

1. Are there any differences between mandatory release, conditional release, and parole? If so, what are they?
2. Do you believe the courts have the right to tell correctional administrators how to administrate parole?
3. Discuss some of the techniques for tackling public apathy relating to parole and the parolee.
4. Do you believe that ex-offenders have a role to play in the criminal justice system? What are the roles, if any?

## NOTES

1. George J. Reed and William E. Amos, "Improved Parole Decision-Making," *Federal Probation* (March 1972), p. 16.
2. President's Commission on Law Enforcement and Administration of Justice, *Task Force Report: Corrections* (Washington, D.C.: Government Printing Office, 1967), p. 185.
3. President's Commission on Law Enforcement and Administration of Justice, *The Challenge of Crime in a Free Society* (Washington, D.C.: Government Printing Office, 1967), p. 12.
4. *The Challenge of Crime in a Free Society*, p. 167.
5. William Parker, *Parole: Origins, Development, Current Practices and Statutes*, American Correctional Association Resource Document No. 1, 1972.
6. *The Challenge of Crime in a Free Society*, p. 165.
7. National Council on Crime and Delinquency, *NCCD News*, vol. 53-3 (May–June, 1972).
8. Donald W. Belass, William S. Pilcher, and Ellen J. Ryan, "Use of Indigenous Non-professionals in Probation and Parole," *Federal Probation* (March, 1972), p. 10.

## PART SIX ANNOTATED BIBLIOGRAPHY

Carter, Robert M., and Leslie T. Wilkins. *Probation and Parole: Selected Readings.* New York: John Wiley, 1970.

*This can be considered an all-purpose text on probation and parole, both for university study particularly by those who are beyond the introductory stages and for practitioners. The articles deal with the philosophy, scope, process, and problems of probation and parole.*

Dawson, Robert. *Sentencing: The Report of the American Bar Foundation's Survey of the Administration of Criminal Justice in the United States.* Boston: Little, Brown, 1969.

*This book is a good reference for the range of sentencing possibilities, including the granting and revocation of probation and parole. Although the title of this book is somewhat deceptive, it takes a systems approach to consider the specific processes in the total criminal justice system.*

Dressler, David. *Practice and Theory of Probation and Parole.* 2d ed. New York: Columbia University Press, 1969.

*An excellent second book on probation and parole. It contains the current theoretical approaches to correctional functions, particularly those relating to probation and parole. The concern for the individual's treatment and the role of the community in rehabilitation is explained. There is a good deal of case-work detail to support both the theoretical orientation and as a heuristic device in so far as the potential probation and parole officers are concerned.*

National Advisory Commission on Criminal Justice Standards and Goals. *Corrections.* Washington, D.C.: Government Printing Office, 1973.

*This report presents the commission's work on corrections and, therefore, probation and parole. Standards and goals for probation and parole are covered.*

President's Commission on Law Enforcement and Administration of Justice. *Task Force Report: Corrections.* Washington, D.C.: Government Printing Office, 1967.

*The research and findings of the commission on probation and parole are presented in this report.*

# PART SEVEN

# The Future of the Criminal Justice System

# 23: Systems Approach to Criminal Justice

*NEED FOR A SYSTEMS APPROACH • BASIC ELEMENTS OF THE SYSTEMS APPROACH • LONG-RANGE CONTRIBUTIONS OF THE SYSTEMS APPROACH • SHORT-RANGE BENEFITS OF THE SYSTEMS APPROACH • LIMITATIONS OF THE SYSTEMS APPROACH*

PURPOSE: *TO EXPLORE THE CONCEPT AND APPLICATION OF SYSTEMS ANALYSIS, IN LAY TERMS, AS IT RELATES TO THE CRIMINAL JUSTICE SYSTEM.*

THE CRIMINAL justice system is just beginning to make use of a powerful tool for data analysis and decision making—the *systems approach,* sometimes called *systems analysis* or *operations research.* This tool has proved so effective in other governmental operations, especially national defense, that there can be little doubt that the criminal justice system of the future will be affected profoundly by its concepts.

## *NEED FOR A SYSTEMS APPROACH*

The possible benefits of the systems approach are numerous. Perhaps the most needed contribution will be in the area of reducing conflict between the component parts of the criminal justice system—the police, the courts, and corrections.

The most visible conflict in the criminal justice system is between the police and the courts. The present relationship between them has been characterized as a vacuum.[1] The police often see the court as an agency working against them. Within the past decade, courts have ruled that more and more police practices are unconstitutional. Trial judges grant motions to suppress evidence, evidence that the police have often painstakingly collected over periods of weeks or months. Judges have publicly censured individual police officers for actions that both the officers and their superiors have long considered proper police procedure. These encounters and others like them are one-sided; the police feel that they have no opportunity to defend themselves, to present their side of the story. Many police officers have become embittered at this state of affairs, an attitude that serves to further erode what little cooperation exists.

Although these conflicts between the police and the courts have received more publicity in recent years, much the same phenomenon exists in the relationship between the courts and corrections. Judges have ruled that individual prisons, and even entire state correctional systems, violate the constitutional prohibition against cruel and unusual punishment. These judges have ordered prison officials either to improve along the lines ordered by the court or to shut down. Naturally, correctional officials are not happy.

Probation and parole officials have been getting their share of judicial guidance. Although the courts have so far been concerned primarily with the procedures by which probation and parole are revoked, recent cases suggest that the courts are about to exercise some supervision over the whole correctional area.[2]

As in the relationship between the police and the courts and between the courts and corrections, the relationship between the police and corrections seems to be one of conflict. The police have accused prison officials of releasing dangerous felons to prey upon the community and to make the police task more difficult. Prison officials, in turn, have accused the police of harassing parolees, a practice, they say, that might well counteract the rehabilitative effect of parole. Police and probation and parole officers need information and assistance from one another.

All this conflict might seem to indicate that the police, the courts, and corrections work at cross-purposes, that they have goals that are basically different and often antagonistic. It might seem that the three parts of the criminal justice system have little in common beyond the fact that they all deal with criminals. However, the criminal justice system of the future, if it is to be at all effective, must not reflect such fragmentation. The criminal justice system, now as well as in the future, is indeed a *system,* in the sense that all the parts are interrelated and dependent on one another. The courts cannot arrive at just decisions, or for that matter any decisions at all, if the police do not make arrests. If the police arrest the wrong people, if the courts convict the innocent, corrections cannot perform its functions, for how can it correct people who are by definition not in need of correction? On the other hand, if the courts do not convict the guilty, there is no one to correct. And if corrections does not effectively accomplish its function, the police and the courts will deal over and over again with the same individuals.

Because the criminal justice system is interdependent, a change in one part of the system must necessarily affect the operations of the other parts. If the police make more arrests, the courts and corrections have to work faster, expand, or be overwhelmed with cases. If the courts extend their scrutiny to areas that they had previously ignored, police and corrections must alter their operating procedures. A great increase in correctional effectiveness would leave the police and courts with less to do; a decrease in effectiveness would complicate their jobs. Even small changes in one part of the system, such as a change in police patrol procedures, changes the criminal justice system as a whole. Because the system is so interdependent, it simply cannot function effectively with its component parts working at cross-purposes and pursuing independent and conflicting goals. Before examining how the systems approach can help deal with this confusion of goals, it is necessary to examine the important elements of the systems approach itself.

## *BASIC ELEMENTS OF THE SYSTEMS APPROACH*

The systems approach comes with good credentials. Its use in such diverse fields as national defense, medicine, and business management has enabled researchers in these areas to make quantum jumps in their knowledge.[3] In the popular mind, the systems approach is a complicated and confusing field using giant computers, incomprehensible flow charts, and indecipherable jargon. Its basic principles, however, are not difficult to grasp.

### Examining the Whole System and Its Parts

The systems approach is based on the principle that the whole is often more than the sum of its parts and that it is impossible to get an accurate picture of phenomena without examining the relations between the separate parts and the whole. In terms of criminal justice, this means that the overall operation of the criminal justice system must be studied as a unified whole and that the overall objectives of the system, rather than the objectives of the police, or the courts, or of corrections, must be examined. The systems approach holds that since all parts of a true system are interdependent, it is not only inefficient but often counterproductive to study or advocate changes in any one part of the system without examining the effect the changes will have on the whole system.

Perhaps the clearest example of the need for examining systems as a whole is in the fields of medicine and biology. Common sense agrees with systems analysis that an individual organism, such as the human body, should be studied as a whole. It would be a poor physician indeed who cured a diseased stomach with treatment that stopped the heart. It is easy to forget, however, that until the modern era the human body was viewed as a fragmented collection of separate bones, muscles, and glands, much as many people now tend to view the criminal justice system as a collection of police agencies, courts, and prisons. However, no real progress was made in either understanding the body or in treating its illnesses until researchers began to study the body as an integrated system containing functionally related subsystems, the respiratory system, the digestive system, and so on.[4]

If it was difficult to conceive of an individual organism as a system, it is even harder to think of the air defense system of the United States or the Bell Telephone Company as an organism to be studied as a whole. However, viewing the system as a whole is the first requirement of a systems approach to criminal justice.

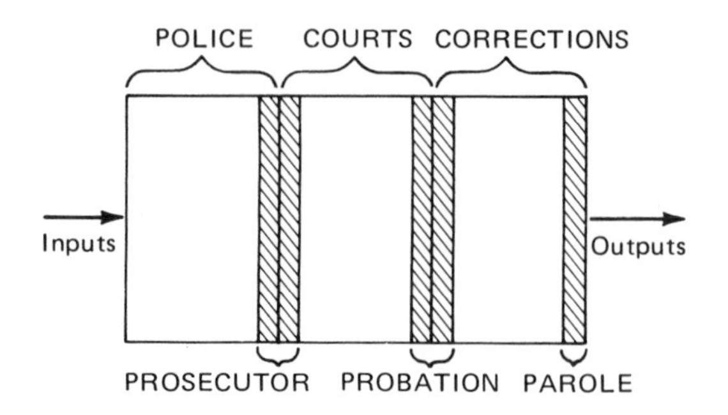


**Illustration 23.1** CRIMINAL JUSTICE SYSTEM

A "black box" illustration is often used to illustrate a system. The criminal justice system is represented above as though it were a box with inputs and outputs. A simple analysis of a system through the black-box approach often provides insight into the systems problems. As an example consider an offender as an input when arrested and then later consider this same offender as an output when released from prison. If you were to examine the offender at the input and output side and find that his or her attitudes were essentially the same you could assume that the criminal justice system had no affect on this individual. This is, of course, an oversimplification but it does illustrate some of the methods of systems analysis.

## Understanding Goals and Objectives

The second requirement of the systems approach is a clear understanding of goals and objectives, both of the entire system and of its component parts. The usual approach to examining the criminal justice system is to analyze separately the goals of police, courts, and corrections. Writers on police tend to emphasize goals that affect only the police, such as crime-solving, patrol efficiency, and professionalization of police personnel. Other police writers emphasize goals stated in such general terms as to be almost meaningless, such as protecting the public or serving the community. The goals of the court system, too, are usually stated in broad, general terms: justice, protecting the individual, protecting society. The goals of corrections, as usually stated, are not quite so broad, but are specific to corrections: rehabilitation, general deterrence, incapacitation. The goals of the criminal justice system as a whole are rarely considered.

A systems approach to analyzing goals attacks the problem from exactly the opposite direction. The first question to be decided is "What is the purpose of the system as a whole?" Once this question is answered, the goals of the police, courts, and corrections can be analyzed in terms of how they accomplish the overall goals of the system. The importance of this distinction cannot be overemphasized. Assume it is decided that the primary purpose of the whole criminal justice system is to reduce crime. Let us further assume that a given objective of one part of the criminal justice system does not further that overall objective. To take a most unlikely example, let us assume that future research demonstrates that providing police with higher education does nothing to reduce crime or accomplish any of the other objectives of the system as a whole. It merely provides the community with educated police. In that unlikely event, the criminal justice system of the future, if operating on the basis of a systems analysis, will deny that educating police is a legitimate goal of the criminal justice system.

This insistence on an overall objective does not mean that the police cannot have specific goals not shared by the other parts of the system. They can and must. However, the acid test of what the police, courts, and corrections do must be the accomplishment of the goals of the overall system. When analyzing individual goals, police administrators, judges, and correctional officials must ask themselves, "If we accomplish this goal, will crime be reduced? Will the other objectives of the system be accomplished?"

**Stating Goals in Measurable Terms**

Since the systems approach is based on a clear understanding of goals and objectives, there must be methods of determining whether or not a given objective is being accomplished, whether or not there is progress toward whatever goal is being sought. The third requirement for a systems approach, therefore, is that goals be stated in terms that allow measurement. In essence, a systems approach requires that goals and objectives be translated, as much as possible, from words like "serving the public" to numbers.

This is an extremely difficult requirement. It is made necessary, however, by the nature of digital computers as well as by the nature of the scientific method. Although up to this point, the description of systems analysis has proceeded with no mention of computers, the interested student will find that almost all the literature in the field of systems is heavily computer-oriented. The reason is that a systems approach to a complex subject like the criminal justice system requires and generates such an enormous amount of information that data-processing systems requiring computers are needed to avoid drowning in the data. Computers, in their speed and in the amount of information they can process, are impressive instruments, but they have their limitations. Basically, they can only add, subtract, multiply, divide, and make simple yes-no decisions. Most information fed into them must be in the form of commands and numbers. Perhaps a police administrator knows what "serving the public" means, perhaps a judge knows what "justice" is, but computers definitely do not. They must be told what to do in the only language they understand, and this language requires that criminal justice officials translate the complex concepts they work with into simple, specific statements that are compatible with some system of measurement.

At the present level of knowledge in criminal justice, the complete statement of objectives in quantitative terms is not possible. Not enough data are available. However, it is vitally important to state goals and methods for achieving them in as objective and measurable terms as we can. The future of systems analysis in criminal justice—indeed, of any scientific approach to studying the criminal justice system—depends on it. Science, like systems analysis, can work only with what can be measured.

To illustrate the difficulty and the importance of stating goals in terms that make it possible to measure accomplishment, it is useful to examine the concept of reducing crime as a principal objective of the criminal justice system. The reduction of crime is certainly one of the basic functions of the system, and it seems that it should be one of the easiest to measure. For many years the Federal Bureau of Investigation has published annually *Crime in the United States: Uniform Crime Reports.* When the news media report that homicide is up 2 percent in a certain city or that crime in the nation is up 8 percent, it is referring to data published in the *Uniform Crime Reports.*

Before it is possible to determine whether the criminal justice system or any of its parts is reducing crime, it is necessary to know how much crime exists, hence the vital importance of accurate information of the amount of crime, the types of crime, who is committing it, and so on. Without such information it is impossible to determine to what extent, or even whether, the criminal justice system is meeting its goals of reducing crime. The *Uniform Crime Reports* are the best available statistics, but they are not accurate enough to serve as the measure of crime that the system needs.

The difficulty with these reports is twofold. First, the FBI is dependent on data supplied by local police agencies. Any change in a department's method of recording or reporting crime can lead to gross errors in statistics. More important, however, is the fact that police agencies can report only crime they know about. The National Crime Commission has documented what has been long suspected by criminologists: the majority—and a very large majority—of crimes never comes to the attention of the police.[5] In fact, the serious crime that does come to police attention can be compared to the tip of an iceberg with the vast bulk submerged. This fact may mean that the increase in crime in recent years reported by the *Uniform Crime Reports* reflects a real increase in the amount of crime, or it may reflect greater reporting of a lesser amount of crime. This defect of the *Reports* makes it very difficult to judge police performance. A city reporting a large increase in crime might discover that their police had declined in effectiveness and were no longer doing their job in such a manner as to reduce crime. On the other hand, the very same statistics could mean that the police were much more effective, had gained the confidence of the public, and therefore had received more reports of criminal activity despite the fact that crime was decreasing.

In recent years several attempts have been made to develop a set of criminal statistics more accurate than the *Uniform Crime Reports.*[6] Perhaps the most far-reaching attempt is an effort by the Law Enforcement Assistance Administration (LEAA) to measure crime by the use of census techniques. The LEAA survey is based on a National Crime Panel consisting of 60,000 homes and 10,000 businesses randomly selected to represent all the nation's households and businesses. Individuals in the panel are interviewed monthly to determine the nature and extent of criminal activity to which they have been subjected. It is hoped that the device of surveying victims will avoid some of the drawbacks associated with the reliance on police statistics to measure crime. Assuming the LEAA survey is effective, as pilot studies seem to show, it may provide the criminal justice system of the future with a powerful tool to indicate the extent to which the system is accomplishing one of its most important objectives, the reduction of crime.

This method of measuring crime is only one of the indicators of performance that will be used by the criminal justice system of the future. After all, a long-term decrease in the amount of crime in a city does not tell us whether the decrease can be credited to better police performance, more efficient courts, a more effective correctional system, or factors outside the scope of the criminal justice process. Each segment of the system has to have its own methods of measuring effective performance in achieving its goals. The importance of the overall measure of the amount of crime is that it will be used as a yardstick to evaluate the individual performance measures used by the police, the courts, and corrections. For example, it is relatively easy for the police to measure the number of arrests. Is such a measure a valid performance indicator for police? To put the question another way, do arrest rates for offenses have anything to do with reducing crime? There is some evidence that increased arrests may lead to more, not less, crime, but with the present inability to measure crime, it is impossible to tell. The criminal justice system of the future, equipped with a more accurate measure of crime, should be better able to determine by experimentation if arrest rates correlate with crime reduction. If they do correlate positively, they are a valid measure of police effectiveness; if they do not, other measures will have to be developed.

### Developing Alternative Systems and Mathematical Models

Once the goals of the system are stated in mathematical terms and a large body of information on the operations of the system has been collected, it is possible to undertake experimentation otherwise impossible. An operating system, such as the criminal justice system, is difficult and expensive to change. To experiment with the actual system would sometimes entail unacceptable risks, as for example, an experiment in eliminating all prisons or in disarming the police. Once the groundwork necessary for the systems approach has been laid, however, it is possible to do these experiments without much expense and completely without risk. A mathematical model of how the system actually operates is developed, a model that serves as a baseline for experiments. Alternative methods of operating the system, for example, doing without prisons or doubling the number of police officers, are examined and transformed into mathematical models. The models are run through a computer to determine how well each alternative system operates to achieve the objectives of the system. If enough data are available, if enough is known about how the criminal justice system actually operates, it is possible to determine in advance the results of major changes in operations and to compare the results of one suggested change with those of another.

## *LONG-RANGE CONTRIBUTIONS OF THE SYSTEMS APPROACH*

The contributions of the systems approach to the criminal justice system of the future are several. Most of them result from the very nature of the approach.

### Measuring Effectiveness of Agencies and Programs

The systems approach requires that the criminal justice system of the future develop a variety of performance indicators, that is, measures of effectiveness, and the resulting ability to measure effectiveness will be perhaps the most important contribution to the systems approach. It will improve the decision-making process throughout the system. Are one-man patrol cars better than two-man cars? Who should be put on probation, who should be imprisoned? Which correctional treatment is the most effective for a given prisoner? Criminal justice officials must make thousands of such decisions every day. Without reliable performance measures and an objective method of determining what works and what does not, these decisions must be made on the basis of hunch and intuition. With the measures of performance available to the criminal justice system of the future, a better decision-making process will be available. All the different methods of accomplishing a goal can be tried theoretically and the outcomes measured to determine which works the best. Decisions about the most effective procedures can be made on the basis of facts, not guesses.

### Resolving Conflicts within the System

The ability to measure performance accurately and in terms of the goals of the whole system will not be the only contribution of systems analysis. This chapter began with a discussion of conflicts between the various elements of the system. At present, there is no satisfactory basis for resolving these conflicts. The police pursue police goals, the judiciary is concerned with quite different goals, and the correctional system pursues its correctional aims. When these objectives conflict, it is not possible now to determine which should take precedence in order to accomplish overall goals. Without any rational means of choosing between conflicting objectives, the decision generally depends on which part of the system has the power to enforce its position. In the case of more or less equal power, an impasse results, benefiting no one. For example, in the case of judicial rulings limiting police practices, the courts have almost unlimited power to decide which actions violate the Constitution. However, since most police practices have low visibility (judges generally do not ride in squad cars), the police often have the power to ignore decisions that inconvenience them. Without police compliance, judicial decisions cannot be expected to protect individual rights. And because the police are concerned almost exclusively with their own objectives, voluntary compliance is not likely.

In the system of the future, with its accurate measures and adequate means for judging performance in terms of larger goals such as reducing crime, a way of rationally adjudging many conflicts will exist. For example, if the police and corrections differ on the best method of handling certain first-time offenders, research will be able to determine whether the "get tough" approach reduces crime more effectively than the liberal use of probation. This does not mean that conflict will be absent. The system has more than one major objective, and these large-scale objectives, such as reducing crime or protecting the rights of individuals, may conflict. Systems analysis has no technique for deciding cases in which basic goals are antagonistic to one another. It can, however, reduce conflict in those situations in which the problem is simply determining the best way to achieve an agreed-upon goal.

### Setting Priorities: Cost-Benefit Analysis

A third contribution of systems analysis to the criminal justice system of the future is its ability to set priorities and allocate money effectively. Which is more important, to increase the number of police or to upgrade parole? What is the better crime-fighting technique, speeding criminal trials or providing halfway houses for convicted offenders? Will an individual police force fight crime better if it has more patrol cars, or should it concentrate on training its detectives? If the federal government has a given number of dollars to spend on reducing crime, should it invest in an experimental narcotics treatment program? On scholarships to enable police to attend college? On upgrading prison systems? Which does the best job of reducing crime for the money?

At the present time, there is no rational method of answering such questions. We cannot measure how much a given program reduces crime, so we cannot compare one program with another in terms of crime reduction. This system of the future, however, using measures of performance in conjunction with relevant research, will have a basis for making decisions about what program should have the higher priority. Using a technique known as cost-benefit analysis, it should be able to make a good estimate of how much crime is reduced per dollar when the dollar is spent, for example, on a certain probation project, and compare it with crime reduction per dollar spent on patrol cars. Within a given police department, the chief will be better able to judge which of the many possible ways of spending the budget has the most crime-reducing potential. Money can be allocated rationally rather than by hunch and political influence.

## *SHORT-RANGE BENEFITS OF THE SYSTEMS APPROACH*

Despite its many benefits, a systems approach to the whole criminal justice system, the approach discussed so far, is not just around the corner. There is simply not enough information about how the present system operates. The accurate measure of crime that the system so desperately needs will take years to develop. Until it is perfected, performance indicators that can determine what is working well and what is not will be extremely difficult to develop. Without information about what the system is actually doing, a full-scale systems approach is not possibe. The Institute of Defense Analysis, an organization with extensive expertise in the systems approach, attempted with little success a preliminary analysis of the entire criminal justice system for the National Crime Commission.[7] Although the Institute seemed surprised at how little is really known about criminal justice, those working in field are not. Luckily, however, some of the benefits of the systems approach are available, not in the far future when the information necessary to analyze the whole system is available, but right now.

### Concentrating on Goals

Even a small-scale and tentative attempt to approach the criminal justice system in terms of the systems approach forces criminal justice officials to concentrate on goals. Criminal justice officials, whether police officers, judges, or correctional officers, are busy people. They are fully occupied coping with day-to-day problems and have little time or energy for reflecting on the big picture, on what it is they are trying to do. This reflection is, however, necessary. If we forget what we are trying to do, if we do not think about our goals hard enough to express them in useful terms, we will not be able to improve significantly our operations or cope with the changes the future will bring. The very first step in a systems approach forces the people working within the system to tell the system analysts exactly what it is the system is trying to accomplish. Experts in systems analysis are not experts in criminal justice, and they must rely on the people in the system to explain goals and objectives. If this requirement does nothing other than require criminal justice officials to examine their goals, it will have made a significant contribution to the system of the future.

### Using a Systems Approach to Criminal Justice Subsystems

Although a systems approach to the whole criminal justice process is now impossible because of the lack of the necessary factual information, an analysis of smaller and less complicated subsystems is possible in the immediate future. The principles and techniques can be applied, for example, to scheduling cases for a single criminal court, or to procedures required to get a patrol car to the location where help has been requested. One advantage of analyzing smaller subsystems is that the question of goals is less difficult. Maximum effectiveness requires that police patrol cars get to the scene of a request for assistance quickly, and the measure of performance for this task is relatively simple: the quicker the better. The National Crime Commission did a systems study on response time in a hypothetical city. To decrease the average time, a police department has a number of ways to spend its money: it can increase the number of patrol cars, install a computerized command and control system, purchase an automatic car-locator system, hire more telephone complaint clerks, and so on.[8] By using a systems analysis of the entire response procedure from the moment the police are notified of a need for help to the point at which the squad car arrives on the scene, it is possible to determine where the money can be spent most effectively. In the hypothetical case used by the National Crime Commission, it was determined that money spent to pay the salary of an additional complaint clerk was over four times as effective as money invested in additional patrol cars. In a real city, the best way to spend money to reduce response time might be to install a system that automatically keeps track of the positions of all squad cars. The point is that without a cost-benefit analysis made possible by the systems approach, there is no good way to determine how to spend most effectively the available funds, even if the department knows what it wants to accomplish.

The benefits of systems analysis of small systems is not limited to police work. The commission experimented with a computer simulation of processing felony cases in criminal courts. If real data were available for a given court system, it would be possible to determine which of the many possible approaches to reducing delay in the judicial process gives the most improvement per dollar.[9] Similar small-scale applications of the systems approach are possible in correctional institutions. For an example, let us consider a systems approach to correctional institutions.

In our correctional subsystem example, consideration will be given to correctional *inputs*, *outputs*, and *feedback*. Inputs are those things that move into a system, outputs are those things that move out of a system, and feedback is information reported back to the system about the outputs.

*Inputs* There are a number of inputs into a correctional system that can affect the system. The many inputs into a correctional system include money, employees, materials, and inmates. Inmates are one of the more important inputs. For example, if court systems continue to divert the less dangerous offenders to community programs they can expect inmates in institutions to be more dangerous. Consequently, greater security and control of inmates in institutions may be necessary. Every input into the system must be taken into consideration in the day-to-day operation of the correctional system.

*Outputs* As with inputs, the inmate is one of the more important outputs of the correctional system. Theoretically, the correctional institution must rehabilitate the inmate while he or she is in the correctional system. The criminal offender is supposed to be rehabilitated when he or she leaves the correctional system, though often this is not the case. It becomes the correctional system's responsibility to effect a change in the inmate from input to output. Therefore, it becomes necessary to measure the inmate as an input and as an output, to ascertain if some change in the direction of more socially acceptable behavior has occurred. If not, we may consider our correctional institution a failure in some respects.

*Feedback* Once the inmate has left the institution, the real test of its effectiveness begins. If the ex-inmate reverts to criminal behavior then in some respects our correctional institution has failed. If not, then perhaps our correctional institution has succeeded. The correctional system must know (have feedback information) who failed or succeeded, and why. If authorities at the correctional institution do not have this information they cannot possibly know what programs effect success or failure of ex-inmates.

This brief exercise in "systems thinking" illustrates some of the utility of the systems approach as applied to a criminal justice subsystem. For a further elaboration of this particular example the student should see, "Systems Approach to Correctional Institutions" in *Federal Probation*, March 1974.

## *LIMITATIONS OF THE SYSTEMS APPROACH*

The lack of concrete information on the criminal justice process has already been mentioned as a limitation of the systems approach. This limitation is quite obvious, but it is one likely to be overcome as more research into criminal justice is done. There are two other limitations, much more serious precisely because they are much less obvious and therefore much more likely to be overlooked.

### Omitting Important Goals of the System

Determining the goals of the criminal justice system or of its subsystems—the police, courts, or corrections—is not an easy task. Some goals, such as reducing crime, are obvious, but others are not and some are a matter of dispute. For example, justice is surely a goal of the system, but is hard to define, difficult to measure, and easy to omit. A further difficulty is that, although the systems model itself is rigidly scientific and objective, goals are determined by value judgments and subject to error. The assumption that the criminal justice system should reduce crime is a value judgment. The assumption that the system should preserve the rights of the people it handles is also a value judgment, but our system of criminal justice would be far different if the preservation of individual rights was not included in its goals. Systems analysis is particularly susceptible to this mistake of ignoring important goals because it is so much easier to analyze systems that have only one major objective. This problem is not completely soluble, for systems analysis, by its very nature, must ignore some aspects of the system it is studying. Systems analysis, like the scientific method itself, must simplify complex reality in order to deal with it.

Perhaps the best rule of thumb for dealing with this limitation is to be very suspicious of any attempt to measure a complex criminal justice function with a single measuring instrument or to proclaim that this particular goal, whatever it may be, is *the* objective of the criminal justice system or *the* objective of the police, the courts, or corrections. The criminal justice system is an extremely complex set of relationships between people and institutions; concentrating on any one objective or trying to measure complex performance with a single measuring instrument can only distort the results.

### Assuming That Only the System Can Be Changed

The other limitation of a systems approach is perhaps even more serious. It is easy to fall into the trap of assuming that only the system can be changed, while all other factors outside the particular system being studied must remain constant.[10] This mistake is particularly easy to make because preoccupation with what is necessary in order to introduce a systems approach makes it all too easy to ignore factors outside the system. For example, a medical systems analysis would analyze a bullet entering a soldier's body as a disruptive outside influence, one that must be handled with whatever success is possible within the system. This is a logical approach, and whatever success is possible with coping with a bullet might well be enhanced by a systematic approach to medicine. However, there might be far better solutions involving changes outside the system that no one would consider while preoccupied with the system itself. In this case, a change in military tactics might prevent bullets from entering so many soldiers' bodies, and a yet broader viewpoint might suggest the desirability of ending the war. This is not to argue that the systematic medical viewpoint is not of value in such a case; given certain assumptions as to the desirability of a particular military tactic and the necessity of a particular war, the medical approach may be the only one possible. The danger is that these broader assumptions may no longer be questioned.

The present criminal justice system is already preoccupied with itself; officials already tend to confine their thinking to improvement of the system and to ignore factors outside of it. The criminal justice system of the future, influenced as it will be by the systems approach, may well go further in this direction, assuming that factors outside the system are given and therefore cannot be changed. To be sure, given the present criminal law, given an economic structure in which a sizable minority of the population lives in poverty while surrounded by luxury, given a value structure emphasizing competitiveness and material possessions, the question of how the criminal justice system can be made to work better to reduce crime may sound logical. However, the criminal justice system is a subsystem of a much larger and more important system: society. Concentrating on the reduction of crime through the improvement of the criminal justice system and ignoring other social institutions and processes may well be making exactly the same mistake as concentrating on the police, or the courts, or corrections and ignoring the rest of the criminal justice system. Emphasis on the criminal justice system may be valuable for certain purposes; in the long run, it may be counterproductive.

## DISCUSSION QUESTIONS

1. What is a system? Does systems analysis offer any hope for the criminal justice system? Why?
2. Is the criminal justice system a system or a nonsystem?
3. Discuss the possible contributions of the systems approach to improving police efficiency.
4. Draw up a set of goals for the local police department. How would you measure the attainment of these goals?

## NOTES


1. Herman Goldstein, "Trial Judges and the Police," *Crime and Delinquency*, 24 (January 1968), 14.
2. President's Commission on Law Enforcement and Administration of Justice, *Task Force Report: Corrections* (Washington, D.C.: Government Printing Office, 1967), p. 83.
3. Richard J. Hopeman, *Systems Analysis and Operations Management* (Columbus: Charles E. Merrill, 1969), 65–76.
4. Hopeman, *Systems Analysis*, p. 74.

5. President's Commission on Law Enforcement and Administration of Justice. *Task Force Report: Assessment of Crime* (Washington, D.C.: Government Printing Office, 1967), pp. 17–19.
6. Thorsten Sellin and Marvin Wolfgang, *The Measurement of Delinquency* (New York: Wiley, 1974).
7. President's Commission on Law Enforcement and Administration of Justice, *Task Force Report: Science and Technology* (Washington, D.C.: Government Printing Office, 1967), pp. 54–67.
8. *Task Force Report: Science and Technology*, pp. 10–12.
9. *Task Force Report: Science and Technology*, pp. 39–44.
10. Robert Boguslaw, *The New Utopians: A Study of Systems Design and Social Change* (Englewood Cliffs, N.J.: Prentice-Hall, 1965).

CHECKED
BY
RADAR

# 24: The Impact of Science and Technology

*TECHNOLOGY IN THE LABORATORY • TECHNOLOGY IN THE FIELD • ELECTRONIC DATA PROCESSING • OTHER TECHNOLOGICAL ADVANCES • EFFECT OF THE BEHAVIORAL SCIENCES ON CRIMINAL JUSTICE • SCIENCE AND THE SHAPE OF THINGS TO COME*

PURPOSE: *TO PROVIDE AN ANALYSIS OF THE POSSIBLE CONTRIBUTIONS OF SCIENCE AND TECHNOLOGY TO THE CRIMINAL JUSTICE SYSTEM OF THE FUTURE.*

THERE can be little doubt that the criminal justice system of the future will be affected tremendously by the application of scientific and technological advances to the problem of crime. Already there are indications that some of the scientific brainpower and resources that went into the space program and the war in Vietnam will be diverted to the criminal justice system. But because the physical and biological sciences were the first to be applied to criminal justice, the discussion will begin with them.

## *TECHNOLOGY IN THE LABORATORY*

The oldest, and still the most common, application of science to crime is in the area of the crime laboratory and its use to solve individual crimes. The capabilities of the police laboratory of today are tremendous.[1] By analyzing a single hair, the criminalist working in the laboratory can determine if it is animal or human, from what part of the body it was taken, whether or not it fell out naturally or was forcibly removed, and other information useful in investigations. Fibers from clothing can be analyzed to determine from what material they came. A blood spot can be analyzed to determine its type and age, the height from which the drop fell and its direction of travel, and sometimes even the part of the body from which the blood came. The use of fingerprints to identify individuals is well known. Impressive as the crime lab of today may be, it has its limitations, which are gradually being overcome by advances in physics, chemistry, biology, and computer technology.

### Fingerprinting

Movies, television, and detective novels have immortalized the use of fingerprints in criminal investigations. In a typical plot, the alert investigator finds a single fingerprint at the scene of the crime. By comparing the print with the FBI files or the files of the local police department, the hero identifies the culprit and justice is triumphant.

In real life, unfortunately, it does not work that way. True enough, if the police have a suspect in mind, a single print or even a partial print is sufficient for identification purposes, but the absence of a particular suspect makes the police task quite different. The FBI maintains more than 190 million identification and fingerprint files, but the system presently used for classification is based on the prints of all ten fingers. Searching through the millions of files for a match-up with a crime-scene fingerprint is a mind-boggling task. Individual police departments maintain single-fingerprint files, but since the search of the files must be done manually, the files are of necessity restricted to a few thousand prints. Therefore, the typical fingerprints left at the scene of the crime are of value to police only as added evidence if they later identify the criminal by some other means or as a way to eliminate the innocent from suspicion.

If it were possible to search the FBI files for a match to crime-scene fingerprints, the police would have an extremely effective tool for crime-solving. The computer, with its almost limitless ability to store and retrieve data, makes it theoretically possible to develop a classification system that can search fingerprint files automatically and compare the files with single prints. Although the technical problems are considerable, the present technology for reading fingerprint cards is sufficiently advanced to make a completely automated system possible in the near future.[2]

### Voiceprinting

Fingerprint-retrieval systems will not be the only contribution of technology to criminal identification. Another system now in use is the technique called voiceprinting,[3] based on the principle that each person's voice, as well as fingerprints, is unique. When the soundwaves produced by human speech are fed into the voiceprinting machine, they are transformed into voice spectrograms or prints. The print of even a single word is sufficient to identify the speaker with a high degree of accuracy, despite attempts to disguise the voice by whispering, talking through a handkerchief, and so on. The value of such a technique is considerable in crimes involving the telephone, such as bomb threats and obscene phone calls. A California district court of appeals has held that voiceprint evidence is admissable in criminal cases. If voiceprinting becomes routinely acceptable to courts, the criminal justice system of the future will have an identification technique useful when no fingerprints are available.

### Lie Detecting

A security firm has developed a device they call the *psychological stress evaluator,* which they feel will be an alternative to the traditional lie detector or polygraph. Polygraphs in common use today measure bodily reactions that usually accompany the telling of a lie, reactions such as increased perspiration and more rapid breathing. The developers of the psychological stress evaluator believe that lying causes a change in voice patterns, particularly by decreasing tones that are inaudible to the human ear, and their device measures these inaudible frequencies. Unfortunately, any form of stress seems to affect the voice, so it is difficult to determine whether a suspicious voice pattern is the result of lying or other forms of stress. This defect becomes an advantage for security work, however. The United States Army has advocated the use of the stress evaluator as an antiassassination aid. It suggests that Secret Service agents ask suspects a few harmless questions, because by using the stress evaluator, agents might be able to tell if a suspect's replies reveal merely the stress associated with personal troubles or the stress associated with a commitment to violence.

The voice lie detector, of course, has a great advantage over the conventional lie detector; it does not have to be hooked up to the individual whose veracity is in question. This makes it theoretically possible to determine if a voice over the telephone is telling the truth about a bomb threat, for example, or to check the truthfulness of a witness without the witness becoming aware of the check. (It might even be possible to evaluate the campaign promises of politicians by checking the inaudible frequency modulation of their radio and television speeches.) Before any of these possibilites come to pass, much research on the technique is needed.

### Germtyping

Another method of identification that may prove valuable is the technique of germtyping.[4] Still in the early experimental stage, the procedure is similar to the typing of blood, saliva, and other bodily fluids. Because a criminal does not always leave fingerprints, blood, or saliva at the crime scene, but always leave microorganisms that constantly cover the body, a workable method of gathering and typing these microorganisms might well play a part in the crime lab of the future.

### Analyzing Physical Traces and Neutron Activation

Neutron activation analysis offers further help with the problem of identification. Using present techniques, it is not possible for the criminalist to state that a certain hair or group of hairs is from a particular person. Nor is it possible to determine whether or not a given spot of blood is from a particular individual, even if the blood can be typed, which is impossible in the majority of cases of dried blood. A ballistics expert can determine that a bullet was fired by a given gun only when the bullet is fairly intact. Neutron activation analysis may well be able to make all these determinations, and more.[5]

Neutron activation analysis is based on the fact that many chemical elements not radioactive in the natural state can be made radioactive by bombarding them with neutrons. These elements then give off distinctive radiation, which can be analyzed to determine the type and amount of the elements present in an object, even when the particular element is present in such a small quantity that it cannot be detected by any other method.

Once the physical evidence found at the scene of the crime is analyzed by neutron activation, the results can be compared with an analysis of the hair, clothing, weapon, or blood of the suspect. At present, there are technical problems involved in the analysis of such organic substances as hair and blood, but there is little doubt that neutron activation analysis will provide the criminal justice system of the future with a powerful crime-solving tool.

## *TECHNOLOGY IN THE FIELD*

Technological advances will not be limited to the crime laboratory. Right now, many police departments are experimenting with the use of space-age and military technology to improve the operations of field units. The future of the criminal justice system will be profoundly affected by the results of these experiments.

### Helicopters

One of the more familiar applications of technology is the use of helicopters in pa-

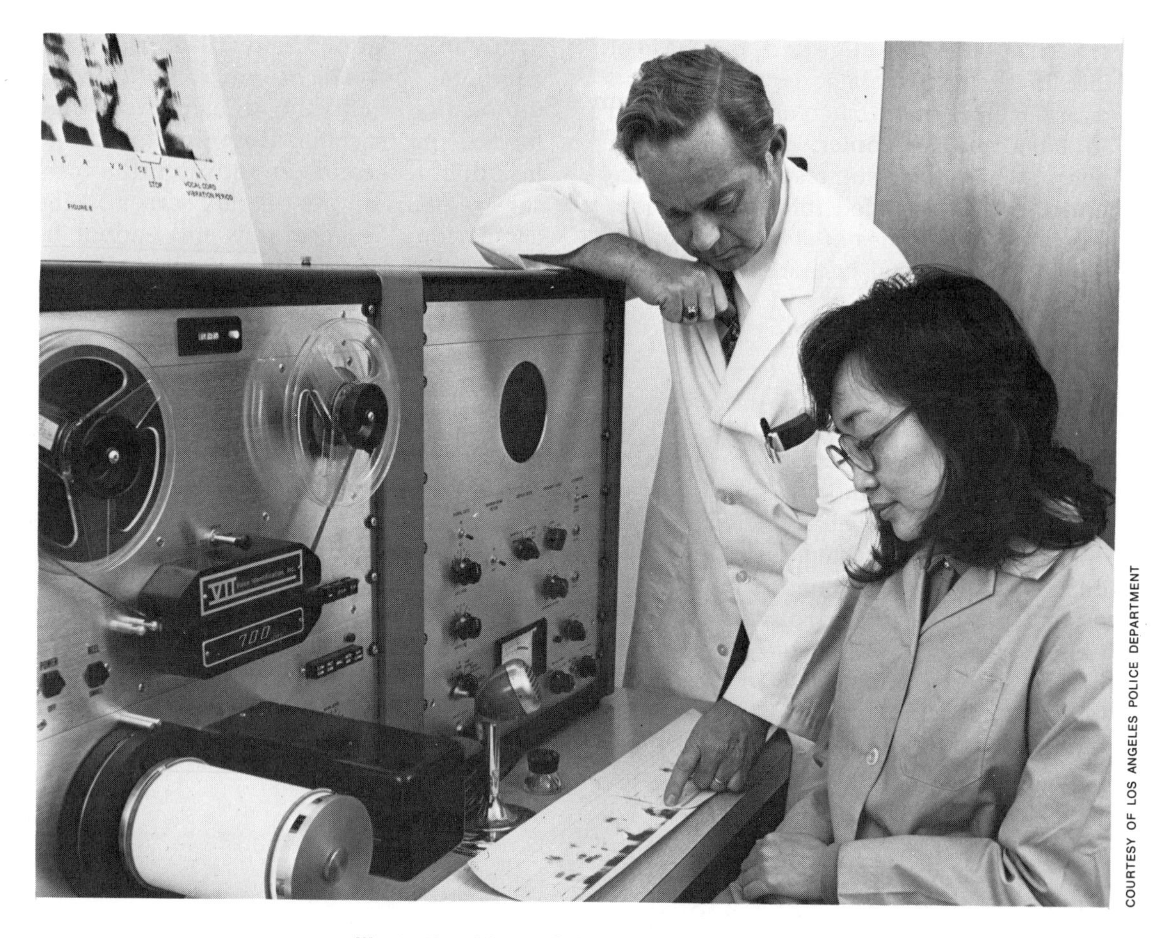

COURTESY OF LOS ANGELES POLICE DEPARTMENT

**Illustration 24.1** VOICE SPECTROGRAPH

A voice spectrograph supplies voiceprints that identify characteristics of an individual's voice patterns.

trol. The Federal Railroad Administration is already experimenting with the use of helicopter patrols to prevent vandalism and cargo theft from the nation's rail network.[6] Four cities in California have formed a regional helicopter patrol system designed to prevent the crimes of burglary, theft from automobiles, robbery, and auto theft.[7] Helicopters are also being used in narcotics enforcement, crowd control, traffic surveillance, evacuation during natural disasters, and pursuit of fleeing felons. They seem to be particularly helpful when patrol cars have limited value, for example, on long stretches of almost-deserted beaches or against vandalism in crowded innercity areas. The major drawback to the expanded use of helicopters is the huge cost: purchase of the "bird," its associated equipment, and maintenance costs can easily approach $100,000 per helicopter. Despite the expense, the enthusiastic response of police indicates an expanded role for helipcopters and other modes of aerial transportation in the criminal justice system of the future.

### Computers

The computer too will be used to increase the effectiveness of patrol. The installation of computer terminals in squad cars is feasible and already being tried by some departments. The system used in Palm Beach County, Florida, consists of a computer terminal, which looks like a typewriter keyboard, connected to a radio transmitter inside the car.[8] This squad car terminal can communicate directly with the computer at headquarters and through it to the computers at the Florida Crime Information Center and the National Crime Information Center. The use of the computer instead of voice radio communications cuts the transmission time for a dispatch signal from one minute to less than a second. In addition, the message remains on the display screen in the car as long as necessary and cannot be intercepted by criminal elements. Since the terminal in the squad car can communicate directly with computers without the use of human intermediaries, the time required to search the records for stolen car license numbers, for example, is cut from three minutes to less than six seconds. Besides these advantages, the system used in Oakland, California, includes an electronic map of the city mounted inside the squad car and connected electronically with a larger map at headquarters. By touching a finger to the spot on the map where the car is located, the patrol officer can keep the map in the dispatcher's office up to date with its exact location.[9]

## *ELECTRONIC DATA PROCESSING*

The use of computers in solving criminal justice problems goes far beyond the installation of terminals in squad cars. One of the most pressing needs of the people in the criminal justice system is information. The police need to know whether or not the man they have stopped for a routine traffic violation is wanted in another state on a felony charge. Judges need to know the criminal record of a suspect in order to make decisions involving bail and sentencing. Court administrators need to know at exactly what point the flow of offenders through the judicial system is bogging down. Correctional officials need to know not only everything possible about the individuals they are trying to correct, but also about successful and not so successful correctional programs used in other jurisdictions. Most of this information is recorded somewhere in the criminal justice system, but the problem of getting it to the decision makers quickly remains. The solution to this problem is within the capabilities of present technology, and efforts in this direction are already being made.

A good small-scale example of the use of computers in data retrieval and analysis is the PATRIC system in use in Los Angeles. The Los Angeles police, like any major police department, have a tremendous amount of data available in their standardized police reports. Unfortunately, quantity itself has made the task of manually going through reports to determine the patterns of crime and the methods of operation of individual criminals all but impossible, and the information less than helpful. In a small department, a police officer can keep much of this information in his or her head, using it to determine who is likely to have committed a particular crime and where a criminal is likely to strike next. In a city the size of Los Angeles, of course, no officer can possibly remember all the important facts. The computer can. The PATRIC computer contains data from standardized reports from all over the city. Officers can query the computer not only on specific facts, such as the description of a suspect or the license number of a stolen car, but also on patterns of criminal activity recognizable by the computer.

On a much larger scale, the FBI's National Crime Information Center (NCIC) has been in operation since early 1967. Tied in with computers in each of the states and in some of the larger local law enforcement agencies, NCIC's computer is a national repository of information on stolen cars, weapons, securities, and other property, as well as wanted persons. Through local or state computers, police can check on stolen property or fugitives wanted anywhere in the United States. Until 1971, however, NCIC did not contain *rap sheets*, that is, criminal histories on offenders. Rap sheets were kept at the local and state levels and typically were not computerized; the process of finding and relaying an individual's criminal history was frequently difficult and time-consuming.

To simplify the process of storing and transmitting criminal histories and other criminal justice data, the Law Enforcement Assistance Administration (LEAA) funded Project SEARCH, an attempt to develop and test a computerized information system suitable for adoption by each of the states. The original proposal sought to avoid a centralized, national data bank by keeping records at the state level while making exchanges of computerized information between the states.

Over the objections of LEAA, the Attorney General in 1971 gave the FBI responsibility for further development of Project SEARCH. This means that while the various states will feed information into the system, the collected data on offenders will be stored in the FBI's National Crime Information Center computer. The FBI hopes the system will soon be completely operational, with computers in all the states tied into NCIC.

Exactly what data will be contained in this centralized data bank is not clear.[10] The information on individuals will be collected by the various federal, state, and local agencies that are tied into NCIC, and these agencies are limited in the type data they can put into NCIC only by an NCIC Advisory Board policy paper, which excludes only juvenile offenses and certain minor offenses. In addition, it is not clear who will have access to the information contained in the NCIC files. The states do not have to limit access to criminal justice agencies; they can make the computerized files available to anyone they like. At least one state is considering making information in the files available to anybody who can pay for it.[11]

A nationwide data bank has few technological limitations. It has been estimated that a 2,000 page dossier on every man, woman, and child in the nation could be coded and stored in a ten-by-twelve-foot room, each one available in five minutes.[12] In addition, there is no technological reason why such information must be limited to criminal histories. Other governmental agencies have computerized information on military records, school files, credit information, income tax forms, bank records, and so on; it is not a difficult task to interface computers and have all this information and more available by the mere process of entering a social security number in one of the computers. Any limitation on computerized information will have to come through laws and regulations.

The National Advisory Commission on Criminal Justice Standards and Goals (1973) has developed a plan for a National Criminal Justice Information System. This system would provide complete criminal career histories (CCH) on offenders. The system's offender based transactional system (OBTS) would also have the capability of tracking an offender through all phases of the criminal justice process—from arrest to release. At this point in time, it is not possible to predict what information will be available or when it will be entered in the National Criminal Justice Information System, but it is safe to say that the information available will be considerable. (This system is presented in Illustration 24.2.)

## *OTHER TECHNOLOGICAL ADVANCES*

Speculation on other technological inventions available to the police of the future runs the risk of making this text sound like science fiction. Some of the more esoteric electronic devices developed for the Vietnamese war are in the process of being adapted for police purposes. Although some are secret, a glance at a catalogue of any of the many firms catering to police shows such electronic marvels as viewers that enable the police to see in the dark and surveillance systems that have the capacity to put large areas of a city under constant police scrutiny. It will not be surprising to see every patrol officer equipped with a two-way radio especially designed for police work. A number of firms are attempting to develop useful nonlethal weapons to bridge the gap between the officer's night stick and handgun. Among the nonlethal weapons proposed are wire guns that release coiled barbed wire, drugs that rapidly immobilize the victim, and such lively ideas as "instant banana peel," a substance that makes it almost impossible to run or even

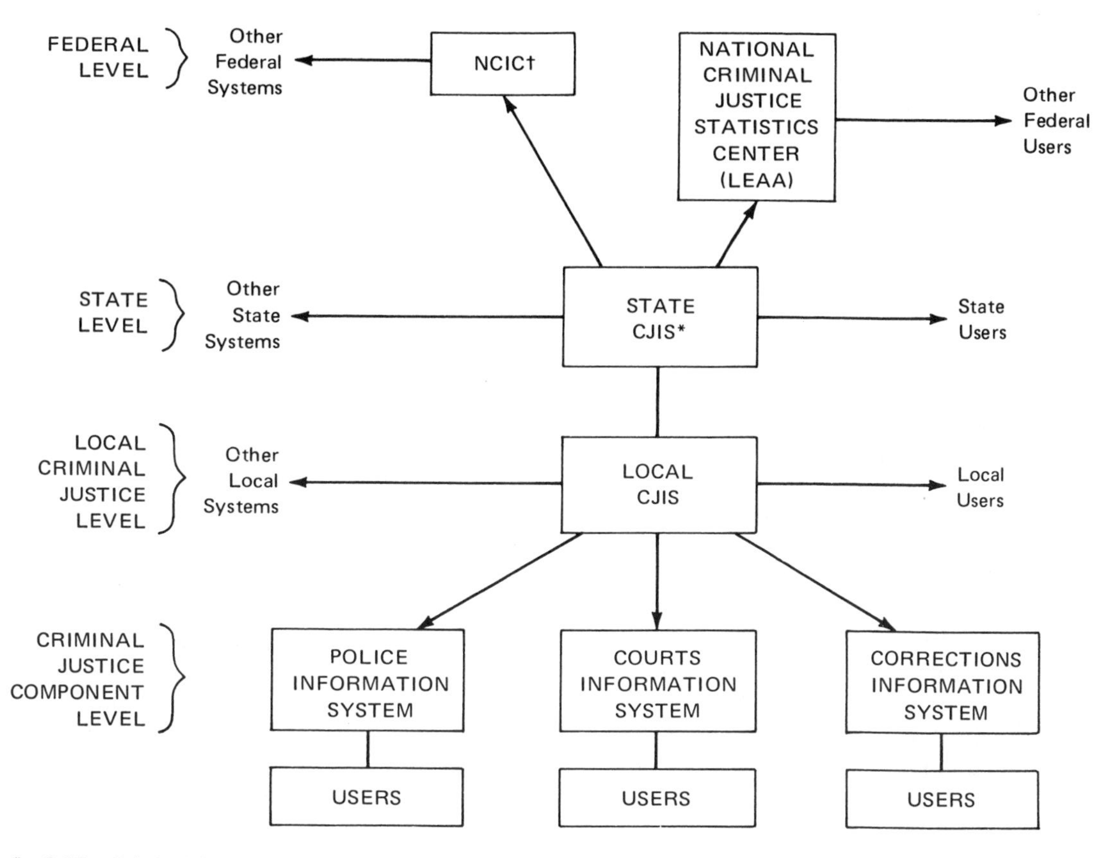


**Illustration 24.2** NATIONAL CRIMINAL JUSTICE INFORMATION SYSTEM
Source: National Advisory Commission on Criminal Justice Standards and Goals, *Criminal Justice System* (Washington, D.C.: Government Printing Office, 1973), p. 42.

walk away from the scene of the crime, and "instant rope" for blocking off small areas.[13]

Although by far the greatest amount of federal money for technological improvements has gone to the police, we may expect other parts of the criminal justice system to profit from technology. For example, courts would benefit from automatic transcription devices for courtroom testimony, and automatic perimeter surveillance systems for prisons are now being installed. These devices sound tame compared to the technological wonderland the police seem to be entering, but they should be useful.

## *EFFECT OF THE BEHAVIORAL SCIENCES ON CRIMINAL JUSTICE*

The impact of the physical sciences and the associated technology on the criminal justice system of the future, though considerable, may well be less than the impact of the social and behavioral sciences. Although criminology or criminal justice is rapidly becoming a scientific discipline in its own right, knowledge and procedures discovered by other behavioral sciences will also be applied to the problems of criminal justice. Although there is much overlap in the subject area of the behavioral sciences, the possible contributions of these disciplines can be more or less arbitrarily divided into seven areas.

### Business Administration

To a great extent, the process of running a police department, a prison, or a parole office is similar to the process of running a business. Personnel must be selected, trained, and paid; supplies and equipment must be ordered; accurate financial records must be kept; and the various activities of many individuals must be managed so that the overall purposes of the organization are accomplished. Insofar as the problems of business and criminal justice agencies are similar, the wealth of information discovered by scholars in the field of business administration is available to be applied to criminal justice.

This application of the principles of business administration to the problems of criminal justice is already under way. Police chiefs, prison wardens, and court administrators throughout the country are attempting to apply solutions that have worked in industry to the management and administrative situations they encounter. As the educational level of administrators in criminal justice is increased, and as more and more criminal justice practitioners are exposed to formal and informal courses in business management, the influence of this discipline will increase.

### Public Administration

Although the administration of a criminal justice agency and a business are similar in many respects, there are differences caused by the fact that criminal justice agencies are governmental organizations. One of the most important differences is in goals: the major goal of a business organization is to increase profit, whereas the goals of a governmental organization are more complicated and more difficult to measure. If X Corporation doubles its profits under a new set of managers, the new people may justifiably pat themselves on the back. The warden of a prison, a judge, or a police chief has no such easily defined and easily measured objective as profit. In the absence of a well-defined objective, it may be next to impossible to determine whether a criminal justice administrator is doing a good job or not. Another practical difference is that the duties and the area of discretion of a criminal justice administrator are much more clearly defined by law than those of a business executive. The management of a company can purchase supplies under any system that appeals to them and may hire and fire personnel with little regard for legal restrictions. The criminal justice administrator, on the other hand, must contend with rigidly specified laws and regulations on such matters as purchases, and civil service regulations usually limit discretion in personnel actions.

Since there are real and important differences between business administration and the administration of a government agency, a separate discipline called *public administration* has increased in importance. Public administration, as the name implies, concerns itself with the problems inherent in the administration of governmental organizations. Because public administration is a much younger field of study than business administration, its contributions to the criminal justice system probably have not been as great. However, because public administration addresses itself to exactly those problems faced by criminal justice administrators, and because criminal justice administrators are showing a real interest in the work of public administration scholars, its contributions in the future are assured.

### Industrial Psychology

Industrial psychology is the application of principles of psychology to such problems as the selection, placing, and training of employees, worker efficiency, organizational management, and consumer behavior. Although the purchasing behavior of consumers is of little concern to the criminal justice system, the other areas certainly are. The problem of selecting from a group of applicants those who will best fulfill job requirements is in principle the same problem whether the hiring agency is a police selection board or the personnel department of a large industry. There is no reason to think that the psychological principles underlying worker efficiency and job satisfaction in factories do not apply to prisons. Unfortunately, there has been markedly little collaboration between industrial psychology and the criminal justice system. Whether such collaboration will benefit criminal justice is a question for the future to answer.

### Experimental Psychology

Experimental psychology is the scientific study of such processes as motivation, perception, and learning. Since individuals involved in the criminal justice system learn, perceive, and are presumably motivated in one way or the other, it is reasonable to assume that the work of experimental psychologists may well be applicable to the problems of criminal justice. There is some evidence that this is the case. For example, psychologists interested in basic research on perception are now studying the problem of eyewitness testimony in criminal cases. It has long been realized that eyewitness testimony is less than reliable, but police and others have had no information on exactly what variables influence its reliability and how these variables operate. Present research indicates that many of the same variables that influence perception in the laboratory—the significance of the event, the length of observation, the method used in questioning, and so on—also influence testimony in criminal cases.[14] When this information is put into a form that can be used by police and court officials, it may well change drastically the criminal trial of the future.

Undoubtedly the aspects of experimental psychology that will have the most effect are the advances in the field of learning theory. A large number of psychologists are working on the problem of applying the principles of behavior discovered in the learning laboratory to the analysis and control of complex human behavior, and some are now focusing their attention on crime problems.

One application of simple learning principles to the improvement of criminal justice operations is the use of programmed learning. *Programmed learning* is based on the concept that certain types of material are better learned in small steps, using immediate reinforcement or reward for correct responses. The program of questions and answers can be contained in a teaching machine that mechanically presents questions and notes correct answers, or it can be contained in a computer program. For example, police cadets at an academy in California are learning case law through a specially programmed computer.[15] After familiarizing themselves with the relevant materials, cadets are questioned on a given case by a computer. The computer evaluates the answers typed in by the cadets and tells where they are right and where they went wrong. A number of correctional institutions are also using programmed instruction for inmates with some success.

A scientific study of the principles of learning promises a more important aid to the criminal justice process than the mere improvement of instructional techniques. Experimenters in learning have determined that by making changes in the environment of an individual, considerable control of behavior is possible. The use of learning principles to control behavior is generally called *behavior modification.* Programs to treat offenders by using behavior modification have shown promise of lowering the frequency of destructive behavior among prison inmates, controlling the antisocial behavior of emotionally disturbed convicts, and decreasing criminal and delinquent behavior of persons on probation. An immense amount of research is presently in progress on behavior modification. For example, the Robert F. Kennedy Youth Center, a federal reformatory in Morgantown, West Virginia, was attempting to base its entire operation on the principles of behavior modification. The potential for the control of criminal behavior by use of behavior modification may well be immense, but limited due to the specter of "A Clockwork Orange" and the refusal of LEAA to fund behavior modification programs.

### Counseling

Counseling is an attempt to improve a person's behavior by expert advice and guidance. Psychologists, psychiatrists, social workers, and other behavioral science professionals have long engaged in the process of trying to change behavior by listening and talking to clients or patients. The use of counseling in criminal justice has a long history, particularly in the field of corrections. Unfortunately, the small number of trained counselors compared to the large number of inmates, probationers, and parolees means that traditional counseling methods are not adequate for the task. One attempt at overcoming this problem is group counseling, in which the counselor's expertise is available to more than one person at a time.

Perhaps the most promising approach, however, is based on the growing realization that effective counseling can be undertaken by individuals without long professional training in the field. A number of programs have been initiated that involve the use of laymen to aid correctional officials in probation and parole projects. For example, a recent pilot project in Salt Lake City has shown that volunteer helpers can get better results than professional probation officers with some types of probationers. Other studies indicate that under the supervision of trained professionals, housewives, businessmen, and other interested members of the community can play an important role in the counseling of offenders.

In addition, there are indications that the police too have a role in counseling. Police officers have, in fact, long served as informal counselors, since the police are often the first public agency notified when people are in trouble. Today, however, police receive little or no training for this role, and many officers dislike and resent the necessity of intervening in emotionally charged conflict situations like disputes between husband and wife. This resentment is justified: family disturbance calls are a major cause of injuries and fatalities among police. The New York City Police Department has experimented with training officers in counseling and the other behavioral sciences to equip them with the tools necessary to handle family crises. In the original study, eighteen officers received an intensive on-campus training course in the application of behavior sciences to intervention in marital disputes. This initial training was supplemented by a continuing program of consultation with behavioral science experts. These officers returned to their regular patrol function, with the additional duty of handling all family disturbance calls in their precinct. It was determined that the operation of the Family Crisis Intervention Unit, as the group was called, was effective in reducing homocides and assaults in the families with which they dealt, as well as preventing injuries to the officers themselves.[16] The New York police feel that the program was of such value that they now include the principles of family crisis intervention in the training program for all officers.

## Sociology

Sociology has undoubtedly been the behavioral science most often applied to the crime problem. In the United States, in fact, criminology and juvenile delinquency courses have traditionally been located in university departments of sociology, and much of the information we now have on crime, criminals, and the operation of criminal justice system has come from the work of sociologists.

Future contributions of sociology to the crime problem can be expected in at least two areas. The first is the accurate description of exactly what goes on in the criminal justice process. Trained sociological observers will be able to give us a more accurate picture of what is really happening in prisons, in police departments, and in the courts. A second contribution will be more precise knowledge about the factors that lead to criminal behavior. Although from past studies sociologists have some familiarity with the effect of poverty, education, housing, family structure, and similar variables on crime, there is a need to know much more so that the criminal justice system of the future can prevent as well as treat criminal behavior.

### Probability and Statistics

Statistical techniques have long been used in criminal justice to describe data, as in the FBI's *Uniform Crime Reports* describing crime rates and trends. Statistical procedures, however, can help decision making in uncertain situations. There are numerous times when decisions in criminal justice must be based on an estimation of probable future behavior. In deciding on probation or parole, in determining the type of treatment program best suited to a given offender, in the use of police patrol to deter specific crimes, criminal justice officials must make decisions based on probabilities, not certainties. Usually these decisions are the personal judgments of officials, for example, a parole board granting or withholding a parole on the basis of an interview with the inmate, or a judge assigning an offender to a certain correctional program on the basis of a "rule of thumb" evolved out of his or other judges' experience. With the proper use of statistical decision-making techniques, the information process used to arrive at decisions can be formalized, tested, and improved. These statistical techniques can be used to help officials make decisions or in effect, could make the decisions for the officials, as in the use of a parole prediction table to decide whether or not a person should be paroled. Once experimentation has produced reliable statistical decision-making strategies, the data deemed relevant could be fed into a computer to produce decisions without human intervention, eliminating the need for parole boards, judges, and even juries. The extent to which statistical decision making will replace or supplement human decision making in the criminal justice system of the future is not clear; it seems likely that human reluctance to entrust life and death decisions to anything but another human may mean that this tool will not be used to its full capacity.

## SCIENCE AND THE SHAPE OF THINGS TO COME

Unquestionably the application of science to the problems of criminal justice will make the criminal justice system of the future different from the system of today. This chapter has barely touched on the possibilities inherent in the application of the methods of science to the crime problem. Tomorrow the system may "correct" criminals, not by throwing them in prison, but by subjecting them to a brain operation that makes further criminal behavior impossible. Police patrol may decline in importance as a result of technological improvements that allow the police to maintain surveillance of all citizens all the time. These things may not come about, of course, but it would be foolish to bet against them.[17] The history of science has shown that once the advance of knowledge makes a new technology possible, the new technology is almost invariably developed. No one has yet said no to a major advance in science, regardless of the possible cost. The hydrogen bomb stands as testimony to the fact that the products of science are ethically neutral: they can be used for good or evil.

It is not difficult to imagine a future in which the criminal justice system, with the help of science, will have succeeded in controlling crime.

It is easy to imagine every citizen carrying his or her own police alarm system or a weapon that will immobilize but not harm a potential attacker. It is easy to imagine our police equipped with weapons that can stun or kill an offender; mobile computer terminals that fit into the police officer's pocket; uniforms that are lightweight yet completely bulletproof; electronic "sniffers" that can place a suspect at the scene of a crime or identify contraband drugs; electronic devices that make the telling of a lie virtually impossible; electronic equipment that can monitor the conversation and movement of persons without their knowledge; and police vehicles that traverse all terrains and carry a sophisticated array of weapons and scientific crime-detection equipment. It is easy to imagine our courts with computers that scientifically select the jurors; recording instruments that transcribe the trial; lie detectors that monitor for perjury during the trial; juries composed not of people but of computers; sentence lengths that are determined by a computer; or computers that can sustain or overrule an objection through an instant analysis of the law. It is easy to imagine a corrections system where drugs are the major rehabilitative program; where adversion therapy alters criminal behavior; where architects using modern materials build jails and prisons that look like college campuses yet are more secure than present prisons. It is easy to imagine a probation and parole system that can select an offender for probation or parole by a computer's statistical prediction of success, or in an instant electronically locate all of its charges at any time of the day or night. All of these things are within our grasp if this is what we desire.

George Orwell's *1984* is a picture of a society in which crime is all but impossible because freedom is all but unknown. Perhaps the best defense against such a future is a commitment to the second word in the much used phrase "criminal *justice* system."

## DISCUSSION QUESTIONS

1. What are some possible future developments in criminalistics?
2. Can science deprive us of our freedoms?
3. Can we have a "1984" in the criminal justice system?

4. How will advances in science and technology affect the police of the future? The courts? Corrections?
5. Discuss the limitations of computer technology and electronic data processing in reducing crime.
6. What recent scientific developments can you think of that may apply to criminal justice?
7. Some states have passed legislation limiting the use of radar, polygraphs, and electronic bugging devices. What does this portend for the future?
8. If science is ethically neutral, how can society protect itself from the misuse of science?

## NOTES


1. Richard O. Arther, *The Scientific Investigator* (Springfield, Ill.: Charles C. Thomas, 1965), pp. 14–58.
2. President's Commission on Law Enforcement and Administration of Justice, *Task Force Report: Science and Technology* (Washington, D.C.: Government Printing Office, 1967).
3. William W. Turner, *Invisible Witness* (Indianapolis: Bobbs-Merrill, 1968), pp. 1–29.
4. M. Gersham, "Preliminary Report: A System for Typing," *Applied Microbiology*, vol. 23, no. 4 (April 1972), 831–833.
5. Jurgen Thorwald, *Crime and Science: The New Frontier in Criminology* (New York: Harcourt, Brace and World, 1967), pp. 417–463.
6. *Crime Control Digest*, 6 (June 23, 1972), 7.
7. *Crime Control Digest*, 6 (June 9, 1972), 10.
8. *Crime Control Digest*, 6 (July 14, 1972), 6–7.
9. *Newsweek*, June 5, 1972.
10. Lawyers' Committee for Civil Rights under the Law, *Law and Disorder III* (Washington, D.C.: Lawyers' Committee for Civil Rights under the Law, 1973).
11. *Law and Disorder III*, p. 45.
12. Turner, *Invisible Witness*, p. 268.
13. *Law and Disorder III*, p. 53.
14. *Behavior Today*, 3 (June 5, 1972), 2.
15. *Criminal Justice Newsletter*, 3 (March 27, 1972), 51.
16. United States Department of Justice, Law Enforcement Assistance Administration, National Institute of Law Enforcement and Criminal Justice, *Training*

*Police as Specialists in Family Crisis Intervention* (Washington, D.C.: Government Printing Office, 1970), pp. 23–33.

17. John R. Altemose, "The Criminal Justice System of the Future," unpublished Ph.D. dissertation, Sam Houston State University, 1973.

# 25: Reform

*NATIONAL CRIME COMMISSION RECOMMENDATIONS FOR REFORM • RESEARCH • PERSONNEL • FUNDING • REFORM AND THE FUTURE*

PURPOSE: *TO PROVIDE A VIEW OF THE EFFECTS THAT NEEDED REFORM WOULD HAVE ON THE CRIMINAL JUSTICE SYSTEM OF THE FUTURE.*

In the last analysis, the shape of the criminal justice system of the future depends on decisions being made today, decisions about what goals to pursue and what changes are most important. Few people involved in the system deny that changes are necessary, but there appears to be basic disagreement on the scope of change required. On the one hand stand those who maintain that reform of the present system is the hope of the future; on the other hand are those who insist that more of the same is not enough and that the system must be drastically restructured if we are to achieve the objective of crime control within a free society. Let us examine the position of those advocating reform within the present system.

## *NATIONAL CRIME COMMISSION RECOMMENDATIONS FOR REFORM*

Reform is the position advocated by the majority, in the sense that most criminal justice practitioners agree with most of the reforms suggested. Perhaps the most comprehensive study of the position of reform was made by the President's Commission on Law Enforcement and the Administration of Justice (the National Crime Commission), which has been mentioned many times throughout this text. The commission presented more than two hundred specific recommendations for reform in its main report and nine task force reports, totaling more than two million words. In the years since, its recommendations have received intensive study and discussion by those interested in criminal justice. A few of the recommendations have even been put into effect. While it is doubtful that many students of criminal justice agree with all the commission's recommendations, it is safe to say that most experts agree with most of the recommendations; the commission report has come to represent conventional wisdom in the field of criminal justice.

Conventional wisdom holds that the criminal justice system should be revised as it stands, with many changes in procedure and a few in priority, but without any radical changes. Its answer to the crime problem is basically more of the same but better: more police, but more professional police; more courts, but more efficient courts; more corrections that actually correct. The means of achieving this goal is improvement in three broad areas: research, personnel, and funding.

### *RESEARCH*

The commission report is insistent on the need for more research in all aspects of the criminal justice system. Commission members seemed surprised at how little is really known about crime and about the criminal justice system. They call again and again for more data, more knowledge, more information. Their concern is well placed. It is a truism that good people, with good information, tend to make good decisions, but the truism serves to remind us that the best qualified police, judges, and correctional officials who can be obtained cannot perform their functions effectively without information, and that can come only through research.

Police officials must know what makes a good police officer. They must know what qualities of mind, body, and character separate the good officer from the bad. They must learn how to select officers with the necessary qualifications and how to train them most effectively. They must know what it is the police should spend their time and effort doing and how to accomplish these tasks more effectively.

Court officials need the information necessary to apply a rapidly growing body of law to a rapidly growing case load. They need a better method of storing and retrieving case law, as well as methods to speed up trials and, more importantly, reduce the delay between arrest and trial. They need information on one of the court's most basic functions: separating the guilty from the innocent. How good a job is done now, how many innocent are convicted, and how many guilty are acquitted? By what process is the decision of guilt or innocence made? How can the process be improved? The courts also need research data on another main function, sentencing. Are sentencing decisions really biased by such factors as race or social class? Is a flat sentence such as five years less effective in rehabilitation than an indeterminate sentence of one year to life? Who should receive what sentence?

Correctional officials need to know how effective a job correctional agencies are now doing. What programs or approaches increases the probability that an inmate will succeed on release? How is it possible to determine when a prisoner is ready to return to the free world?

These are not academic questions. Criminal justice officials need information of this type in order to make rational and just decisions. All these questions are matters of fact and could be answered by research, but the research has not been done, and the answers are not available.

Indeed, the extent of our ignorance about basic and vital questions on the administration of criminal justice is difficult to believe. It is assumed, but it is not known, that more police mean less crime. It is assumed, but it is not known, that solving crime reduces the amount of future crime. It is not known whether probation and parole are effective either in reducing crime or in helping individuals. It is not known whether imprisoning offenders reduces or increases the amount of crime in society.

Imagine the outcry among stockholders if the Ford Motor Company were operating without any idea of what products were being manufactured and without a method of determining whether the company was showing a profit. Imagine taxpayer reaction if the Department of Defense operated with World War I equipment and without any idea what planes, ships, and troops can or should do, or if NASA decided to send men to the moon without bothering to determine where the moon was located before the rocket was fired. Yet there is little outcry when every year the United States spends billions of dollars, arrests millions of people, and puts hundreds of thousands in prison or jail without the research needed to know what it is we are doing.

For years the Department of Defense allocated about 15 percent of its total budget for research. Research allocations in private industry, particularly in the progressive and competitive industries, have been of similar magnitude. And for years the criminal justice system has allocated, at most, a small fraction of 1 percent of its budget for research. The effects of these years of neglect will be difficult to overcome, but they must be overcome if the criminal justice system of the future is to do anything more than an inadequate job.

To leave the impression that the simple expedient of providing more research money will solve the problem of discovering and disseminating the information that the criminal justice system needs would be misleading. It would also ignore the truly impressive ability of the system to resist change. As the National Crime Commission mentions, "Many of the criminal justice system's difficulties stem from its reluctance to change old ways or, to put the same proposition in reverse, its reluctance to try new ones."[1] This resistance to change, of course, is not limited to criminal justice institutions. Organizational resistance to change is in itself a field of behavioral science study, and one that might prove invaluable to the criminal justice system, but as the National Crime Commission concludes, the single greatest need in the criminal justice system is the need to know.

## *PERSONNEL*

If the greatest need is the need to know, the second greatest need of a reformed criminal justice system is personnel: more personnel, but especially better personnel. Although the effectiveness of the system is influenced by the level of technology and equipment available, the most important aspect of the system is the people who work in it. The criminal justice system, both now and in the foreseeable future, is not highly automated; 80 to 90 percent of the total budget of the system is spent on salaries. If the system is to be significantly improved, the people working in it must be significantly improved. There are two distinct but complementary approaches to improving criminal justice personnel. One method is to recruit and hire better people, and the second is to improve the capabilities of the people already there.

### Recruiting vs. Working Conditions

Perhaps the first and most basic step in attracting qualified people to the criminal justice system lies in the improvement of working conditions. The whole system, from the precinct station to the parole office, is characterized by neglect, as reflected in the physical surroundings.[2] Police stations are typically old and run down. Lighting is poor, office equipment inadequate, secretarial help small or nonexistent. Courts, particularly the lower courts, are generally overcrowded and frequently squalid. The average municipal or county jail in this country is not a fit place to house stray dogs, let alone human beings.

The difficulty of working in dirty, overcrowded, and ill-designed surroundings is not improved by the salary level. Although many jurisdictions have significantly improved police salaries in recent years, police in many areas would be financially better off if they were to quit and take a job in the local factory. Many do. Prosecutors in many places, including some of the larger cities, are paid so little they must maintain a private law practice while attempting to fulfill the demands of their office. It is little wonder that the prosecutor's office is frequently looked upon as a place for young lawyers to get experience to qualify them for a good job. The pay of prison guards is typically so inadequate that attracting high-quality personnel is all but impossible.

Money, of course, is not everything. Many exceptionally capable people are working in the system despite the lack of financial rewards. Others, however, work in criminal justice because they cannot get a better job. Some look upon their position as a license to steal. It should not be too surprising that in the matter of criminal justice personnel, as in other areas, society gets what it is willing to pay for. To date, we have not been willing to pay for truly professional people.

Pay and physical surroundings are not the only aspects of working in criminal justice that tend to repel qualified people. Hours are long and frequently irregular. The police officer working the evening shift may rarely get to see his wife, who is working during the day to help make ends meet. The work is often difficult and sometimes dangerous. Police officers, judges, and correctional workers are exposed, day after day, to the least attractive aspects of human behavior. They interact with people who are drunk, enraged, sick, and violent.

Despite or perhaps because of their difficulty and importance, jobs in criminal justice are not afforded a high status among the general public. Many police officials are concerned with the low esteem in which police are held by many segments of the community. They should be concerned. Nearly every police department in the nation that has tried has experienced grave difficulty in recruiting qualified minority group members. This fact should surprise no one, considering the reputation of the police in many minority areas. But the police are not the only part of the system with problems of status. By and large, the most capable graduates of the best law schools avoid the criminal law, and the leaders of bar associations have other legal specialities. In corrections few men are proud of their positions as prison guards. If the criminal justice system of the future is to attract better-qualified personnel, all these aspects of the job must be improved. It will take time and money, and it will be difficult, but the future of justice in the United States depends upon it.

While in the process of improving working conditions, the most promising method of getting qualified personnel into the system lies in recruiting personnel from backgrounds traditionally ignored. Specifically, a reformed system will attempt to mount a campaign to recruit and use women, college graduates, and minority group members.

**Recruiting Women**

With the exception of attorneys, criminal justice personnel are overwhelmingly white males with little or no college background. The attorneys have more education, but they are no less white and no less male. This tradition is so strong that women, college graduates, and minority group members usually never think of joining a police department or a correctional agency. While it is true that many people from these groups would not consider working in existing conditions, it is equally true that the criminal justice system has made little effort to recruit from these groups or to change the operation of criminal justice agencies to provide desirable opportunities for women, college graduates, and minorities.

The typical police department today cannot find enough qualified applicants, but discourages women from attempting police work. Female police officers are usually allowed to type and file, work with juveniles, and serve as matrons, but are kept out of the patrol and detective divisions. Consequently, the department hires personnel under a quota system, with only a certain small percentage of the sworn personnel allowed to be women; nationwide, only 1 percent of police are women. Meanwhile, a number of undermanned departments (with no pun intended) turn away fully qualified female applicants.

The excuse generally given for the failure to effectively use female personnel is that women are not physically or emotionally qualified for patrol and detective work. This view, though widely and frequently expressed, is not backed up by evidence. In fact, research indicates that women are qualified to handle most police jobs. Women are now performing regular patrol work in Washington, D.C. The chief of police in Miami, which has more than twenty female officers performing regular patrol work with men, has stated that women have proved effective in all types of police work and that "in certain situations, they are more effective than men."[3] Women officers appear to have a real role in situations that had been considered too dangerous for them, such as subduing drunks or intervening in family disturbance calls. Many men who under the influence of alcohol would not hesitate to attack a male officer calm down in the presence of a woman. Whether this calming effect is the result of male chivalry or the shock value of seeing a woman police officer answering a disturbance call is a question for future research to decide.

Police work is not the only aspect of criminal justice in which the talents of women are underutilized. The proportion of women serving as prosecutors and judges is considerably lower than the proportion of female lawyers. Women in corrections are usually limited to working with other women and juveniles. The trend in the larger society is toward women taking their places in fields traditionally dominated by men, and there is no reason to think that the criminal justice system of the future will be an exception.

### Recruiting College Graduates

The difficulty experienced by the criminal justice system in interesting college graduates in police and prison work reflects more than the undesirable pay and working conditions. Traditionally, there has been only one place to start in a police department or in a prison system:

at the bottom of the ladder. Nearly every police department in the country starts a new officer at the lowest rank, regardless of education or previous experience. In many departments, it is three, four, or even five years before he or she is even eligible for promotion. If Ford Motor Corporation started college graduates as assembly-line personnel, or the United States Army awarded the rank of private to West Point graduates, the consequent recruiting difficulty would surprise no one. It is not surprising that college graduates avoid jobs in the criminal justice system.

Putting qualified personnel directly into a supervisory position after a period of training is known among police as *lateral entry*. Lateral entry has been discussed for years, recommended by the National Crime Commission, and tried on a very limited basis. The men who now occupy supervisory positions in police departments have come up through the ranks, and most think that their successors should, too. Whether or not the police departments and prisons of the future make more extensive use of lateral entry depends on the willingness of present criminal justice officials to change.

**Recruiting Minorities**

The third group now underrepresented in the criminal justice system are members of minorities other than women. The lack of minority-group personnel may well be the most dangerous failing of the system's personnel selection. The police can get along without women in patrol cars; the police and corrections have been doing without college graduates for years; however, it is becoming more unlikely that a police force or a prison staff made up of whites far in excess of the proportion of whites in the population served can do an effective job in serving all of the people. To truly serve the community, the police must understand and be able to communicate with all sections of that community. A police force serving without the trust and respect of the people is quickly seen as an army of occupation, not as a source of help. To expect a lily-white police force to effectively serve the minority community in times of increasing racial division is to expect the impossible.

The police departments of the United States are not generally lily-white, though some are nearly so. State police forces are about 98 percent white. Few departments in the nation reflect the racial proportions of the people they serve, and no single major department even comes close. The situation in corrections is, if anything, worse. At Attica State Penitentiary at the time of the 1972 tragedy, the inmates were 85 percent black and Puerto Rican, the correctional staff over 99 percent white.

The problem of interesting minority group members in jobs in criminal justice is not an easy one to solve. Although some departments have attempted vigorous recruiting programs in their minority neighborhoods, by and large these programs have not been successful. The only bright spot is that the problem has been recognized.

Recruiting personnel who are better qualified is only one part of the task of providing the system with effective workers. An equally important consideration for the criminal justice system of the future is upgrading the skills of the people already working. The two major tools for upgrading personnel are standards and education.

### Standards for Recruiting

Standards can be either suggested or mandatory. A standard is suggested when a prestigious organization such as the American Correctional Association recommends that probation and parole officers have masters degrees. Suggested standards gives local authorities a goal toward which to work. A standard is mandatory when the organization announcing the standard has the authority to force compliance, as when a state law requires justices of the peace to be lawyers or when a state accreditation agency requires local police to have a specified number of hours of instruction before they can serve.

The criminal justice system does not lack sets of standards toward which to work. Scores of different organizations have published hundreds of sets of standards in criminal justice matters. The American Bar Association and the National Council on Crime and Delinquency have been particularly active in setting standards. Unfortunately, most of the standards relate to only one aspect of the criminal justice process and make little or no attempt to view the problems of the system as a whole. A giant step toward creating a set of standards for the whole criminal justice system has been taken by the National Advisory Commission on Criminal Justice Standards and Goals (1973).[4] The commission used the systems approach, examining goals and objectives in detail before suggesting methods of accomplishing the goals. The result is a report of such scope and quality that, although many criminal justice professionals disagree violently with some of the suggested standards, the report of National Advisory Commission on Criminal Justice Standards and Goals (1973) may well bring about needed change in the criminal justice system.

### Education and Training

The second method of improving the skills of those already in the system is education and training. The police probably lead the subsystems in the attempt to train their personnel. The time when a police officer was hired one day and put on the street the next is fast drawing to a close; almost all the larger departments have at least some academy training for officers, as well as regular training sessions after academy graduation, and the FBI has long held training sessions for local police. Police are also coming to realize the value of academic education for officers. In 1965, there were only twenty states with colleges offering any type of police science courses. Today, junior colleges, four-year colleges, and universities throughout the nation offer education in police science and criminology and grant degrees ranging from the associate to the doctoral level.

Training for court functions has not had the same attention. The effective prosecutor must be knowledgeable in many fields in addition to the law, but training programs for prosecutors are almost nonexistent. Judges too must know more

**Illustration 25.1** MAJOR RECOMMENDATIONS OF THE NATIONAL ADVISORY COMMISSION ON CRIMINAL JUSTICE STANDARDS AND GOALS

Source: National Advisory Commission on Criminal Justice Standards and Goals, *A National Strategy to Reduce Crime* (Washington, D.C.: Government Printing Office, 1973).

## Goals and Priorities

*Goals for Crime Reduction*

The Commission proposes as a goal for the American people a 50% reduction in high-fear crimes by 1983. It further proposes that crime reduction efforts be concentrated on five crimes. The goals for the reduction of these crimes should be:

- Homicide: Reduced by at least 25% by 1983
- Forcible rape: Reduced by at least 25% by 1983
- Aggravated assault: Reduced by at least 25% by 1983
- Robbery: Reduced by at least 50% by 1983
- Burglary: Reduced by at least 50% by 1983

*Priorities for Action*

The Commission proposes four areas for priority action in reducing the five target crimes:

- Juvenile Delinquency: The highest attention must be given to preventing juvenile delinquency and to minimizing the involvement of young offenders in the juvenile and criminal justice system, and to reintegrating juvenile offenders into the community.
- Delivery of Social Services: Public and private service agencies should direct their actions to improve the delivery of all social services to citizens, particularly to groups that contribute higher than average proportions of their numbers to crime statistics.
- Prompt Determination of Guilt or Innocence: Delays in the adjudication and disposition of criminal cases must be greatly reduced.
- Citizen Action: Increased citizen participation in activities to control crime in their community must be generated, with active encouragement and support by criminal justice agencies.

## Key Commission Proposals

*Criminal Justice System*

The Commission proposes broad reforms and improvements in the criminal justice system at the State and local levels. Key recommendations include:

- Development by States of integrated multiyear criminal justice planning.
- Establishment of criminal justice coordinating councils by all major cities and counties.
- Establishment by each State of a Security and Privacy Council to develop procedures and recommendations for legislation to assure security and privacy of information contained in criminal justice information systems.
- Creation by each State of an organizational structure for coordinating the development of criminal justice information systems.

The Commission proposes that all Americans make a personal contribution to the reduction of crime, and that all Americans support the crime prevention efforts of their State and local governments. Key recommendations include:

- Increased citizen contribution to crime prevention by making homes and businesses more secure, by participating in police-community programs, and by working with youth.
- Expanded public and private employment opportunities and elimination of unnecessary restrictions on hiring ex-offenders.
- Establishment of and citizen support for youth services bureaus to improve the delivery of social services to young people.

*Illustration 25.1 (continued)*

- Provision of individualized treatment for drug offenders and abusers.
- Provision of statewide capability for overseeing and investigating financing of political campaigns.
- Establishment of a statewide investigation and prosecution capability to deal with corruption in government.

*Police*

The Commission proposes that the delivery of police services be greatly improved at the municipal level. Key recommendations include:

- Consolidation of all police departments with fewer than 10 sworn officers.
- Enhancement of the role of the patrolman.
- Increased crime prevention efforts by police working in and with the community.
- Affirmative police action to divert public drunks and mental patients from the criminal justice system.
- Increased employment and utilization of women, minorities, and civilians in police work.
- Enactment of legislation authorizing police to obtain search warrants by telephone.

*Courts*

The Commission proposes major restructuring and streamlining of procedures and practices in processing criminal cases at the State and local levels, in order to speed the determination of guilt or innocence. Key recommendations include:

- Trying all cases within 60 days of arrest.
- Requiring judges to hold full days in court.
- Unification within the State of all courts.
- Allowing only one review on appeal.
- Elimination of plea bargaining.
- Screening of all criminal cases coming to the attention of the prosecutor to determine if further processing is appropriate.
- Diverting out of the system all cases in which further processing by the prosecutor is not appropriate, based on such factors as the age of the individual, his psychological needs, the nature of the crime, and the availability of treatment programs.
- Elimination of grand juries and arraignments.

*Corrections*

The Commission proposes fundamental changes in the system of corrections that exists in States, counties, and cities in America—changes based on the belief that correctional systems usually are little more than "schools of crime." Key recommendations include:

- Restricting construction of major State institutions for adult offenders.
- Phasing out of all major juvenile offender institutions.
- Elimination of disparate sentencing practices.
- Establishment of community-based correctional programs and facilities.
- Unification of all correctional functions within the State.
- Increased and expanded salary, education, and training levels for corrections personnel.

*Criminal Code Reform and Revision*

The Commission proposes that all States reexamine their criminal codes with the view to improving and updating them. Key recommendations include:

- Establishment of permanent criminal code revision commissions at the State level.
- Decriminalization of vagrancy and drunkenness.

*Handguns in American Society*

The Commission proposes nationwide action at the State level to eliminate the dangers posed by widespread possession of handguns. The key recommendation is:

- Elimination of importation, manufacture, sale, and private possession of handguns by January 1, 1983.

than the law, particularly in those jurisdictions in which the judge does the sentencing. Unfortunately, the typical judge has received no training whatsoever for the job, beyond the experience picked up in a law practice that all too frequently did not include criminal law. There are signs, however, that the legal profession is recognizing the desirability for training programs for prosecutors and judges, and workshops, courses, and meetings are being held throughout the nation for this purpose. Three universities now have programs especially designed to educate court administrators, specialists trained to take some of the administrative burdens off the judges, freeing them to concentrate on their judicial duties.

The situation in corrections is similar, and there is a small but increasing effort in higher education programs. Bachelors and masters degrees in corrections are no longer unknown. Although junior colleges tend to emphasize police education, a growing number are including courses in corrections. The experience of colleges located near prisons seems to be that a surprisingly high percentage of prison personnel are eager to continue their academic education.

The effect of higher education on the skills of criminal justice personnel is not yet known. Experience in the fields of law, medicine, and business seems to indicate that the best way to truly professionalize an occupation is to emphasize higher education. There was a time when few lawyers had attended a law school and few doctors had seen the inside of a college. The day may well come when the criminal justice professional without a college degree will be the exception, not the rule.

## *FUNDING*

In addition to research and personnel improvement, most advocates of criminal justice reform emphasize the need for more money. Without the necessary funding, it will be extremely difficult to effect the necessary improvements in research, equipment, or personnel.

Because law enforcement and court functions are basically activities of local government, the bulk of the money for these two operations has come from local taxes. State tax sources provide the greatest source of correctional funds. The role of federal money in funding the criminal justice system has historically been limited to federal law enforcement, federal courts, and federal prisons.

However, during the 1960s it was becoming increasingly obvious that state and particularly local governments could not be expected to raise the funds necessary to improve significantly the criminal justice system. Large cities through the country were facing the problem of an increasing demand for services coupled with a decreasing tax base. In 1968 Congress passed the Safe Streets Act, which, among other provisions, set up the Law Enforcement Assistance Administration (LEAA) under the Department of Justice. The basic function of LEAA is to channel federal money to state and local governments for the purpose of fighting crime. In the period from 1968 through 1973, over two billion dollars of federal funds were distributed. To put this figure in perspective, it should be noted that the entire budget of the criminal justice system, the cost of operating all the police departments, courts, and correctional agencies, federal, state, and local, was estimated to be about five billion dollars a year in the period immediately before the passage of the Safe Streets Act.

It is probably too early to evaluate the effect of this massive influx of funds. For one thing, LEAA did not originally demand any scientific evaluation of the effectiveness of the programs funded, so it is not possible now to determine if many of the early programs had any effect whatsoever on crime. Other criticisms of the program have been advanced, some of them with merit. The original emphasis of the program was on grants to law enforcement agencies almost to the exclusion of courts and corrections. In the earlier years, many of the police departments spent their money on hardware, not programs. Some departments invested heavily in automatic weapons and even tanks. In addition, since LEAA money is channeled through the state governments, critics have charged that not enough of the funds went to the larger cities, which have the greatest problem. Birmingham, with the biggest crime problem in Alabama, got less than a hundred thousand dollars of the eight million dollars invested in the state in the early years of the program. The Houston Police Department, which faces more major crime than any other city in Texas, did not apply for or accept its first dollar from LEAA funds until 1974.

On the other hand, the operation of LEAA has improved in recent years. More money is going to courts and corrections and less to hardware of dubious usefulness. LEAA now insists on some form of program evaluation if funds are to be granted. And it is undeniable that, through the funding programs of LEAA, much critically needed money has been put into the system. Whether or not federal funding will be the answer to the system's financial need, it is apparent that it will be of great importance to the criminal justice system of the future.

## *REFORM AND THE FUTURE*

It is, of course, impossible to guarantee that the reforms discussed in this chapter will be put into effect. If they are, it is possible to make a guess concerning what the criminal justice system of the year 2000 will be like. The police patrol officer of our reformed system will be a college graduate, with intensive training in the behavioral sciences as well as in criminology and police science. His or her pay and working conditions will equal or exceed the level of pay and working conditions for college graduates in private industry. If the officer is patrolling one of our major cities, he or she will probably be black, since most the largest cities will probably have a preponderantly black population by the year 2000. The officer will have available all the technology needed to perform the job effectively—

computer-dispatched squad cars and helicopters, mobile crime laboratories, and, through a portable computer terminal, immediate access to the information in national, state, and local files.

The officer's superiors will have advanced degrees in the behavioral sciences and law. The chief will be an expert in management, equal in skills and training to the top management of major industries, and assisted by experts in finance, accounting, law, and psychology. The police research department will know what types of crime are being committed throughout the city and where and will have experimented with the best methods of controlling crime. Decisions will be made on the basis of fact, not hunch.

When the police of the future arrest suspects, they will be turned over to a highly sophisticated system for judging guilt or innocence and for sentencing. Defendants will be provided with an attorney in any situation in which they may be sentenced to imprisonment, no matter how short. The trial will take place in a matter of weeks after arrest, depending on how much time the defense attorney needs to prepare the best possible defense. Because of the improvement of the police, guilt will be established much more on the basis of hard physical evidence and much less on the basis of eyewitness testimony and confession.

If defendants are convicted, their fate will be determined by a judge with intensive training in sentencing. The judge will have available not only the facts about the crime for which the person is charged, but also a presentence report containing the facts from the defendant's life history that are relevant in determining the best possible treatment program. The judge will be aided in this decision by a large body of research on effective treatment for various kinds of offenders. In addition, there will be a variety of sentencing options: a halfway house, a residential treatment center run by charitable or religious organizations, a center for treating drug addicts, an alcoholism treatment center, as well as the prison or the probation department.

The prisons of the future will be much smaller, because all but the most dangerous convicts will be treated in programs outside prison walls. Instead of being located in rural areas, prisons will be close to the major cities from which the offenders come. Prison officials, trained and educated to be experts in human behavior, will have the personnel and physical resources to work individually with each offender. After determining the causes of the individual's criminal behavior, they will design a treatment program for each offender to eradicate whatever it was that caused the individual to turn to crime. Inmates will be released to the free community, under parole supervision, at the moment they have received maximum benefit from the correctional experience.

However, emphasis of the future will center on those correctional programs that treat offenders outside of prisons. Research will have determined which are most effective for which offenders and how to improve effectiveness. These programs will be staffed by probation and parole officers with advanced degrees and training in the behavioral sciences, as well as by social workers, psychologists, and psychiatrists.

The people who advocate reform of the criminal justice system are working toward the goal of making this vision of the future a reality. For example, most of the states are developing standards and goals modeled after those established by the National Advisory Commission on Criminal Justice Standards and Goals (1973). As each state develops its own standards and goals, they will be implemented on a gradual basis. State crime commissions will fund those programs that adhere to the state's standards and goals. State legislatures will, in all likelihood, use these as the basis for criminal justice legislation, and criminal justice agencies of the state will use the standards and goals as guidelines for planning and operation. In short, the standards and goals initially established by the National Advisory Commission on Criminal Justice Standards and Goals (1973) will eventually become a reality.

This will not be the end of the reform process because in 1975 the Law Enforcement Assistance Administration established the National Advisory Committee on Criminal Justice Standards and Goals. This committee will develop standards and goals for the private security industry; criminal justice research and development; and programs to combat juvenile delinquency, disorders and terrorism, and organized crime.[5] The reform process goes on, despite those critics who say we do not need reform, and those who say we need basic change more than reform.

## DISCUSSION QUESTIONS

1. Can reform work, or is radical change needed in the criminal justice system?
2. What effects will women and minority recruitment have on the agencies of the criminal justice system?
3. Discuss various methods of improving criminal justice personnel.
4. Discuss the areas of criminal justice in which the need for research information is particularly acute. What type of research is needed?
5. How can raising the educational level of criminal justice personnel adversely affect the criminal justice system?
6. If research indicates that raising the educational level of prisoners while they are in prison does nothing to reduce recidivism, should prisoner education programs be terminated? Assuming that the research information is valid and reliable, would you consider such a movement reform?

## NOTES

1. President's Commission on Law Enforcement and Administration of Justice, *Challenge of Crime in a Free Society* (Washington, D.C.: Government Printing Office, 1967), p. 14.

2. Ramsey Clark, *Crime in America* (New York: Simon and Schuster, 1970), pp. 115–238.
3. *Houston Chronicle*, June 7, 1972, sec. 2, p. 2.
4. National Advisory Commission on Criminal Justice Standards and Goals, *Report of National Advisory Commission on Criminal Justice Standards and Goals* (Washington, D.C.: Government Printing Office, 1973).
5. "LEAA Launches Second Standards and Goals Effort," *LEAA Newsletter*, vol. 4, no. 10 (May 1975), 24.

# 26: Basic Change

*SOCIETAL REFORM • CRIMINAL JUSTICE SYSTEM AS A CAUSE OF CRIME • INJUSTICE IN THE CRIMINAL JUSTICE SYSTEM • INSTITUTING CHANGES*

PURPOSE: *TO EXPLORE AND DISCUSS SOME OF THE MORE PROVOCATIVE SUGGESTIONS FOR IMPROVING THE CRIMINAL JUSTICE SYSTEM OF THE FUTURE.*

A reformed criminal justice system as described in the preceding chapter does not satisfy everyone. There are those who maintain that the basic problems of criminal justice are not isolated abuses subject to piecemeal correction but are misconceptions of what the criminal justice system really is and what it should be doing.

## SOCIETAL REFORM

Most frequently expressed is their idea that reform of the criminal justice system is of secondary importance; society itself must be reformed if we are to have a real chance of reducing crime. The National Crime Commission, which concerned itself primarily with reform of the system as it now stands, has gone on record as stating that "America must translate its well-founded alarm about crime into social action that will prevent crime. To speak of controlling crime only in terms of the work of the police, the courts and the correctional apparatus, is to refuse to face the fact that widespread crime implies a widespread failure of society as a whole."[1] In other words we need more than reform of the criminal justice system; we need social justice.

Social justice in this context means adequate food, housing, education, and job opportunities for all citizens. It means the end of racial and class prejudice. These goals are seen not only as desirable in themselves, but also as answering the crime problem. Perhaps the foremost spokesman for this position is Ramsey Clark,[2] and his approach deserves further investigation.

While Clark admits that no one has the complete answer to the question of why people turn to crime, he states that scholars are familiar with the conditions associated with criminal behavior. Crime flourishes where unemployment is high and where the inhabitants do not have the skills and training needed to make an honest living. Crime flourishes where education is poorest, where schools are least equipped to teach youngsters, and where most drop out before graduation. Crime flourishes in those areas in which there is inadequate health care, in which the average life expectancy is ten years lower than in the city as a whole.

As Clark points out, people live in areas such as these. Every city has them. The police are very familiar with them; they spend much of their time there. Although it is recognized that to state that poverty causes crime is to oversimplify, Clark and others maintain that slums breed crime, because so much human misery concentrated in such a small geographic area cannot help but be explosive and can result in crime.

That human misery leads to all kinds of undesirable behavior should surprise no one. What surprises Clark and the other advocates of social justice is a nation that thinks it cheaper to hire another thousand police officers rather than to provide its citizens with the education that will enable them to survive without crime, a nation that builds huge prisons while ignoring the housing conditions that breed disrespect for society, a nation that can provide tanks for its police but not decent jobs for its people.

Most people would agree that criminal behavior is caused, that it does not just happen. Most would also agree that the criminal justice system is helpless to do anything fundamental about any of the causes of crime. Arresting a school dropout does not provide him with the education necessary to succeed in a complex society. Bringing an alcoholic before the bar of justice rarely cures the alcoholism. Police, courts, and prisons have proved themselves remarkably ineffective in curing drug addiction. Professional police have created no more jobs for the unemployed than nonprofessional police. The most skilled correctional officials in the nation have not been able to rehabilitate criminals as fast as the slums of the nation turn them out.

For these reasons, Clark is probably correct in insisting that total reliance on the criminal justice system for the control of crime will not work. People obey laws for one of two reasons: they respect their society and its laws, or they are forced to obey. The criminal justice system stands ready to apply the force, but the use of force without justice only creates the need for more force. Already some of our citizens, because of the conditions under which they must live, have lost faith in America's desire to do justice. It is difficult to teach them to respect the law once they come to believe that the law does not respect them. To rely on the criminal justice system to maintain order while ignoring social justice will be to demonstrate to the disaffected that they are correct, that America cares nothing for its poor and its minorities. This will not be an inviting future for the criminal justice system, for no police force, however strong, has been able to maintain order with force alone.

On the other hand, there is a basic flaw in any approach to crime that limits its concerns to adequate education, housing, job opportunities, and so on. If the slums were eliminated tomorrow, and if all Americans were well-educated, responsible members of the middle and upper classes, there would still be crime. Crime is not limited to the poor; the rich commit crimes, and many of them.

## *CRIMINAL JUSTICE SYSTEM AS A CAUSE OF CRIME*

There are others who reject the reformation of the criminal justice system along present lines, not because they think the system is ignoring the causes of crime, but because they belong to a growing group who believe that the operation of the criminal justice system itself causes crime. That the criminal justice system can cause crime is not a new idea; it has long been recognized that the occasional brutal and unlawful procedures of police and correctional officials may increase the amount of crime by provoking disrespect for the law. It has recently been suggested, however, that a well-operated and professional criminal justice system can increase crime by its very operation. There is even some evidence to suggest that the more efficient the system is, the more crime it can create.

### "Labeling" Theory

The theoretical orientation for this position is the sociological theory usually called *"labeling" theory*. The basic tenet of "labeling" theory has been stated by Howard Becker: "social groups create deviance by making the rules whose infractions constitute deviance, and by applying those rules to particular people and labeling them as outsiders."[3] From this point of view, deviance is not a quality of the act the person commits, but rather a consequence of the application by others of rules and sanctions to an "offender." The deviant is one to whom that label has been successfully applied; deviant behavior is behavior that people so label.

Applied to criminal behavior, this means that crime and criminals are created by society in two ways. First, legislators create crime when they pass a law against a certain form of behavior. Without the law, there is no crime, though of course there will still be "objectionable" behavior. Second, the criminal justice system creates criminals when it arrests and especially when it convicts individuals for criminal or delinquent behavior. Until the point of arrest and particularly conviction, individuals are not considered criminals by friends, family, and society as a whole. After conviction they are labeled. If they are sent to prison, they acquire another label, "con," later modified to "ex-con." At this point, these people are full-fledged criminals, having been so defined by the criminal justice system, the institution in our society entrusted with the task of defining criminals.

The effect of this process on future crime is simple, though it has not yet been sufficiently documented by research to be considered a fact. Society expects "criminals" to commit crime, just as society expects people who have been labeled mentally ill to behave in a disordered manner. After someone has been labeled a criminal or a delinquent, family, friends, peer group, school officials, and the cop on the beat are more likely to expect criminal behavior from that person than from one of his or her friends who has not acquired the label. Human beings, more often than not, behave in the manner in which they are expected to behave. This phenomenon is known as a *self-fulfilling prophecy;* if the important people in a girl's environment expect her to turn out bad, she will rarely disappoint them. If a boy considers himself a criminal, his fate is almost assured.

If these assumptions are true, it follows that the process of arresting, convicting, and sentencing individuals leads to future crime. Take the case of two youngsters committing their first felony, say burglary. One of the two is caught by the police, taken to court, adjudged delinquent, and placed on probation. The other is never caught. Since the first boy has now been labeled a "juvenile delinquent," he is expected, by those around him, and perhaps by himself, to commit further delinquent acts. Therefore, he will be far more likely to commit further offenses than the other boy, who was never caught.

### "Labeling" Theory vs. Reform

It should be noted that reform of the system as proposed in the last chapter would only make matters worse. A professional police force solves more crimes. An efficient judicial system convicts more of the guilty. There is evidence to indicate that professional police tend to handle more juveniles by formal methods, that is, they tend to bring more children before the juvenile court rather than reporting them to their parents or lecturing them. The net result, therefore, of a reformed and more efficient criminal justice system in the future may well be that more people will be labeled criminal or delinquent. If the principles of "labeling" theory are true, and other factors remain equal, a reformed criminal justice system will experience more crime, not less.

Critics of the labeling approach point out that, even if convicting people of robbery makes it more likely that they will commit more criminal acts in the future, *something* must be done about people who steal, kill, and rape. While this is quite true, it is important to note that many people labeled criminal by the criminal justice system have physically injured no one and stolen no property. The system spends much time and effort arresting and convicting people who have injured no one except possibly themselves.

### Victimless Crime

The "crimes without victims"—alcoholism, drug addiction, prostitution, sexual "perversions" with consenting partners, and so on—have received much attention from criminologists in recent years. They have received much attention from the police and courts also; anywhere from one fourth to one third of *all* the nontraffic arrests in America are for drunkenness. The policy of using the criminal justice system to suppress behavior that directly injures no other party gives rise to a number of questions that are beyond the scope of this text. One important point, however, is relevant to the future of the criminal justice system, and that is the overreach of the criminal law.

The variety of behavior presently labeled illegal by the law is staggering. A study in a major city indicated that a normal, law-abiding citizen, in the course of ordinary daily activity, will violate enough laws in one day to merit fines of nearly $3,000 and imprisonment for five years.[4] Many of these laws and ordinances are never enforced, of course; it is not likely that Vermont has arrested many citizens for violation of the statute against whistling underwater. Unfortunately, however, many of these laws are enforced upon occasion. One study of self-reported behavior found that over 90 percent of Americans had committed an offense for which they could have been imprisoned.[5]

The problem with having on the books laws that could imprison most of the population is two-fold. First, these laws might be enforced. Marijuana laws, for instance, have been on the books of the federal government and the states since the 1930s. Until the last decade, however, they were rarely enforced, except against occasional blacks, Mexican-Americans, and jazz musicians. Until the last decade, the use of marijuana was not very common. The causal relationship here is not very clear; it may be that increased use led to increased enforcement, or it may be that increased enforcement led to increased use. One fact, however, is clear: a large number of otherwise satisfactory young men and women have been arrested, convicted, and imprisoned for no other offense than the use of marijuana. If nothing else, this enforcement of marijuana laws gives the researcher an opportunity to subject labeling theory to an empirical test: if the theory is true, many of these young "criminals," on release, should become criminals in fact.

### Laws That Cause Crime

It is not necessary to support labeling theory to believe that the enforcement of certain laws directly increases the amount of crime. Prohibition, of course, is the historical example. It is generally agreed that the attempt to enforce the Volstead Act led to corruption of the criminal justice system, disrespect for the law, and more crime. Laws against other victimless crimes, such as gambling, prostitution, and sales on Sunday, have been blamed for present-day police corruption. The shining example of laws that themselves breed crime are those making it a criminal offense to possess narcotics. Harsh penalties for dealing in addictive drugs have one invariable effect: they drive up the price of drugs. The more effective government action against narcotics is the higher the cost of drugs. The higher the cost of drugs, the more muggings, holdups, and burglaries that must be committed by addicts to get the money necessary to support their habit. It has been estimated that over half the street crime in New York City is committed by narcotics addicts, and it cannot be doubted that the need to purchase drugs is a factor in a tremendous number of the crimes committed throughout the nation. In the absence of law enforcement activity to drive up the price, narcotics are cheap. The criminal law has created a reason to rob and kill by making what is essentially a sickness into a crime.

The outlook for the future is not good. Legislatures have shown themselves much more anxious to legislate new crimes than to repeal old ones. Working with a set of laws that make many varieties of typical human conduct illegal, a reformed criminal justice system might well be dangerous. To put the matter bluntly, it is possible to live under a set of ridiculous laws, which make some of the behavior of most of the citizens illegal, only if these laws are not enforced. One hallmark of a reformed and efficient criminal justice system, however, is that it enforces the law. It could hardly be otherwise.

It is by no means unlikely that many of our laws were passed by legislators who thought they would never be enforced. The laws regulating sexual behavior are a case in point; the laws of almost any state make almost all forms of sexual activity illegal. If studies by Kinsey and others are to be believed, most of the legislators who passed these laws would be in prison if the laws were enforced. This was no problem fifty years ago; the police could not have enforced many if they had wanted to, because wiretaps, "bugs," and electronic surveillance devices did not exist. The police of tomorrow, armed to the teeth with technology, may well be equipped to seriously enforce the laws against victimless crimes. To the extent to which they are professionals, they *will* enforce the law; after all, it is their job.

It is not surprising that prostitutes, gamblers, and marijuana smokers hate and fear the police. To them the police represent danger, not safety. Most of our citizens seem to be unconcerned, secure in the knowledge that they themselves are not criminals. But according to the law, most of them *are* criminals, although the police have not got around to them yet.

The criminal justice system of the future either will or will not have a more reasonable set of laws with which to work. If it does not, society will have to decide if it really wants a more efficient criminal justice system, if it really wants better enforcement of the reprehensible laws under which we live. Society's answer to this question more likely than not depends on who is arrested.

## *INJUSTICE IN THE CRIMINAL JUSTICE SYSTEM*

It is now known who gets arrested. By and large, he is disproportionately male, black, young, and, of course, poor. Perhaps the majority of criminals are male, black, young, and poor, or perhaps his arrest is a result of the operation of a factor called *discretion*.

### Discretion

Discretion means that any police officer gets to pick and choose the persons to be arrested. Since our law makes so much illegal, it could not be otherwise; no urban police officer could possibly proceed against everyone seen breaking the law. Discretion also means that the prosecutor gets to pick and choose against whom to proceed, who will be allowed to plead guilty to a lesser charge, and who will be released without trial. Discretion means the judge gets to pick and choose who will get thirty years for an offense and who will get probation for the same offense. Discretion means that the parole board gets to pick who will serve thirty years on a thirty-year sentence and who will serve ten years of the same thirty-year sentence. Discretion means that probation and parole officers get to pick who will live in the community and who will live behind bars.

The primary result of all this discretion is that we have, contrary to the official rhetoric, a rule of men, not a rule of law. Such government occurs when legislatures abdicate their responsibility by passing as many laws against so many different types of behavior that the police must make the decision about what type of crime to proceed against, and by making the maximum penalty for law violation so high that courts and corrections must determine which individuals to subject to the full force of the penalty and which to treat more leniently. The principal reason most legal philosophers prefer rule of law is that rule of men tends to be unjust. It tends toward injustice because human beings exercising unnecessarily broad discretion tend to make decisions on the basis not of the individual's criminal act, but on extralegal considerations such as manner, life style, socioeconomic status, or perhaps the color of skin.

### Discrimination

The question of discrimination in the criminal justice system is a sensitive one. However, there can be little doubt that the operation of the system tends to be biased toward white, middle-class standards. Upper- and middle-class offenders such as polluters, price fixers, violators of health and safety laws, and owners of criminally substandard housing are treated in a manner far different from lower-class offenders who commit lower-class crimes such as purse snatching, prostitution, or petty theft. Nor is there any doubt that there is a systematic class bias throughout the entire criminal justice system in regard to offenders committing the same crime. The doctor's children may be just as likely as the black militants to smoke marijuana, but the reaction of the system to the offenders is quite different.

## *INSTITUTING CHANGE*

This chapter has so far concentrated on problems and has all but ignored solutions. However, there is no lack of solutions proposed by those advocating more or less radical change in the operation of criminal justice. Taken together, these solutions present a far different vision of the future of the criminal justice system than that presented in the last chapter.

### Social Justice

Although there are many points of disagreement, the advocates of basic change unite on the need for social justice. Social justice is seen as necessary, not only as the only effective proposal to attack some of the causes of crime, but as a mandatory step to insure justice within the criminal justice system. Put simply, if the larger society is unjust in its treatment of minorities, it is expecting too much to hope that the criminal justice system can operate in a fair manner. If racial prejudice is prevalent throughout society as a whole, it is unlikely that criminal justice officials will be free of prejudice.

### Change in Criminal Law

The second basic change in the criminal justice system advocated by this view of the future is the change in the criminal law under which the system operates. Many of the present abuses of the system can be traced to the fact that the criminal law overreaches itself and tries to prevent some conduct that it cannot prevent. It makes criminals of people whose problems injure no one but themselves, and it intrudes into some areas that, to put it bluntly, are none of the government's business.

Of course, to remove public drunkenness, possession of narcotics, and sexual deviation from the scope of the criminal law will not cure alcoholics, reduce drug addiction, or eliminate perversion. Alternate treatment methods for these types of behavior must be provided, clinics, hospitals, residential treatment centers, and so on. Adequate facilities are not presently available, and if the police do not haul drunks off the streets, for example, there is no other agency that will. But society has for too long relied upon the police to solve all its social problems. Some of these problems are simply beyond the capabilities of the criminal justice system. As long as the criminal justice system spends its time, money, and effort in the futile attempt to cure addiction, prostitution, alcoholism, and gambling by arrest and imprisonment, the facilities and programs needed to really deal with these problems will not be developed.

### Reduction of Discretion

The third suggestion for basic change is the reduction of official discretion. Once legislators clearly define what actions are criminal and limit the scope of the criminal code to those laws that the public truly wants enforced, it will be possible to insist that the police try to enforce all the laws all the time. While total enforcement of the law is more a goal than a real possibility, the limitation of police discretion and the even-handed enforcement of the laws that remain on the books is probably the very best method of attaining law reform. The reason that there is little public outcry against some of the repressive laws now in effect is that the people who have the ability to make themselves heard, the powerful and the influential, are rarely arrested for violation of these laws. Present practices are so remote from total enforcement of the law that the call for it may sound strange, but the principle seems reasonable: if a law is fair it should be enforced every time it is violated; if this enforcement does more harm than good, the law should be repealed or restated. Any other use of the law is inherently discriminatory; any law that is enforced some of the time against some of the people becomes far too easily an instrument of oppression.

The reduction of discretion in the criminal justice system envisioned here will not be limited to police discretion. The courts and correctional systems of the United States have tremendous discretion, based on the treatment ideal almost universally accepted: individualized treatment, or "treating the criminal, not the crime." Individualized treatment and the judicial and correctional discretion needed to effect it have attained the status of articles of faith; it is difficult for criminologists to think in any other terms. Yet there is little evidence that the model works, that it reduces crime or, for that matter, helps the offender. There is ample evidence, on the other hand, that the discretion involved in sentencing and in decisions about when an offender is ready for release leads to discriminatory and unjust treatment of individuals.

That individuals who have committed exactly the same crime and have similar criminal records can and do receive different sentences is well documented. It is not unheard of to find one sentenced to life imprisonment while another gets probation. The varying motives of the judges in sentencing are open to speculation. Did one man receive lenient treatment because he looked respectable? Did the other man become the recipient of the full force of the law's wrath because he was poorly dressed? Or was it because the probation officer who made up the presentence report was offended by the way the defendant treated his family? Perhaps the judge quarreled with her husband the morning before sentencing. Maybe the judge decided that it was time to "make an example" of somebody. The motives behind the decisions of parole boards and prison authorities are equally obscure. But when society gives these authorities the mandate to treat the whole person, to treat the criminal, not the crime, it is almost inevitable that, because these people are predominantly white and middle-class, they will judge the offender by white and middle-class standards. Is he respectful to authority? Is she punctual? Does he conform?

Regardless of the motive behind the particular decision, the decision is typically based on nonlegal considerations. What business is it of the criminal justice system, when deciding a man's punishment for the crime of armed robbery, if he beats his wife or if he thinks highly of religion? How is it possible to preserve a government of laws, not men, if a woman's fate is decided on the basis of how officials evaluate her total life history, or whatever portion of her life history they may think relevant?

The answer, of course, is that it is not possible. The alternative is to let the punishment fit the crime, not the criminal. To accomplish this, criminal laws will have to be rewritten. For example, the criminal laws of most states include, under the crime of kidnapping, both the abduction of a baby for ransom and the temporary detainment of a wife by her estranged husband in the attempt to talk her out of divorce. It is doubtful that justice is served by envoking the same punishment in each case. However, the various legislatures have not bothered to distinguish between the two crimes, preferring to rely on judicial discretion. This discretion can be avoided by precise law. In addition, if the legislators think that such factors as age, sex, or, for that matter, social position should result in a different sentence, let them write these factors into the law.

### Decentralization of Power

A final series of proposals advanced by those advocating basic change in criminal justice involve decentralization of criminal justice institutions and community control of these agencies. Most frequently expressed is the desire for decentralization and community control of the police. Instead of one police force for a city, there would be one for the black community, one for the white community, and perhaps a separate department for another minority area.

The very fact that this division has been proposed tells us much. It tells us that many in our society doubt that the present police force will do justice. It tells us that many in minority communities despair of their ability to be heard in the operation of their police department. If the big, predominantly white police department will not listen to them, will not consider their desires, perhaps a smaller force, located in the black community and staffed by black officers, will.

So far, the cry for minority control of

courts and corrections, for a black court in the black community, a Chicano prison in the Chicano community, has not been loud. It very likely will be. The police are the most visible part of the criminal justice system and usually the first attacked. To evaluate the movement toward decentralization, it must be remembered that the criminal justice system does not operate in a vacuum; it is affected by all the social trends affecting the larger society. The desire for minority control of the institutions that vitally affect the minority community is not limited to the institutions of the criminal justice system; the movement for minority control of ghetto schools, for example, is growing in strength.

This desire for decentralization is based on two long-term social trends. The first is the growing desire of the powerless to have some voice in the decisions that affect their lives. The rich hire lobbyists to influence the criminal justice process, the influential help elect politicians. The poor and powerless remain silent. It is little wonder that they dream of having their own police department. It should not be surprising that they dream of having their own courts and correctional systems as well, because they have as little control over these as they have over their police.

The second trend leading to demands for community control of criminal justice institutions is the growing racial polarization in America. The basic conclusion of the 1968 report of the National Advisory Commission on Civil Disorders is that "our nation is moving towards two societies, one black, one white—separate and unequal."[6] If this trend continues, the effect on the criminal justice system of the future will be profound. Whether it leads to minority control of criminal justice institutions, a secret police system to fight social change, or some other result is impossible to predict. It is easy to predict, however, that without a firm commitment to justice for all, the criminal justice system of the future could become even more efficient and even less just.

## DISCUSSION QUESTIONS

1. Can the criminal justice system be changed, or do bureaucrats have too much invested in the system as it is?
2. Does the criminal justice system actually create crime by processing "so-called criminals?"
3. What implications does "labeling" theory have for criminal justice reform?
4. What steps can be taken to prevent injustice?
5. Can you have a free society without abuses of freedom?

## NOTES

1. President's Commission on Law Enforcement and Administration of Justice, *Challenge of Crime in a Free Society* (Washington, D.C.: Government Printing Office, 1967), p. 15.

2. Ramsey Clark, *Crime in America* (New York: Simon and Schuster, 1970), pp. 15–114.
3. Howard S. Becker, *Outsiders: Studies in the Sociology of Deviance* (New York: Free Press, 1963), p. 9.
4. L. M. Hussey, "Twenty-four Hours of a Lawbreaker," *Harper's Magazine*, 160 (March 1930), 436–439.
5. John R. Altemose, "A Learning Theory Approach to Crime," unpublished M.A. thesis, Sam Houston State University, 1972.
6. United States National Advisory Commission on Civil Disorders, *Report of the National Advisory Commission on Civil Disorders* (New York: New York Times Co., 1968), p. 1.

## PART SEVEN ANNOTATED BIBLIOGRAPHY

American Friends Service Committee. *Struggle for Justice.* New York: Hill and Wang, 1971.

*A chilling indictment of the basic philosophy behind our system of criminal justice. This book charges that the problem with the criminal justice system is not that it is ineffective in reducing crime, but rather that it does not, cannot, and will not do justice.*

Boguslaw, Robert. *The New Utopians: A Study of Systems Design and Social Change.* Englewood Cliffs, N.J.: Prentice-Hall, 1965.

*A readable, nontechnical study of both the promise and the peril of the systems approach.*

Clark, Ramsey. *Crime in America.* New York: Simon and Schuster, 1970.

*Contains both practical suggestions for reform and an eloquent plea for social justice.*

President's Commission on Law Enforcement and Administration of Justice. *The Challenge of Crime in a Free Society.* Washington, D.C.: Government Printing Office, 1967.

*The most comprehensive study ever made of the operations of the criminal justice system and the need for reform.*

President's Commission on Law Enforcement and Administration of Justice, *Task Force Report: Science and Technology*, Washington, D.C.: Government Printing Office, 1967.

*A comprehensive report on both the present status of science and technology in criminal justice and of the needs of the future.*

# Appendixes

# Appendix A:

## Career Opportunities in the Criminal Justice System

The American criminal justice system provides a wide variety of employment opportunities for men and women of varied interests. There are police officers, parole officers, federal law enforcement officers, probation officers, detectives, prison guards, judges, lawyers, forensic scientists, correctional counselors, and public defenders, to name but a few of the many people who make up the criminal justice system. The criminal justice system encompasses many important professional fields open to people with appropriate education, training, and experience.

Generally speaking, the employment outlook for the near future appears favorable. Retirement and normal attrition of personnel will continue to provide a number of openings, and natural growth and mounting concern over the condition of the system have created an increasing demand for qualified personnel. In order to provide further information on career opportunities in the criminal justice system, a partial listing of major areas of criminal justice employment appears on the following pages.

### *CAREER OPPORTUNITIES IN FEDERAL LAW ENFORCEMENT*

#### Nature of the Work

*Federal Bureau of Investigation* Federal Bureau of Investigation (FBI) Special Agents investigate many types of violations of federal laws: bank robberies, kidnapings, frauds against the government, thefts of government property, espionage, sabotage, and so forth. The FBI, which is part of the U.S. Department of Justice, has jurisdiction over more than 185 federal investigative matters. Special agents may be assigned to any type of case, but those having specialized training in accounting are likely to be assigned chiefly to cases involving complex financial records; for example, frauds involving Federal Reserve Bank records. For further information write

Federal Bureau of Investigation
Room 4306, Department of Justice Building
Washington, D.C. 20535

*Drug Enforcement Administration* Special Agents with the Department of Justice's Drug Enforcement Administration conduct investigations relating to violations of federal narcotics and drug laws. The work may involve surveillance, raids, interviewing witnesses and suspects, searching for evidence, seizure of contraband goods, arrests, and inspecting records and documents. For further information write

Drug Enforcement Administration
U.S. Department of Justice

1405 Eye Street N.W.
Washington, D.C. 20537

*Immigration and Naturalization Service* The Immigration and Naturalization Service, Department of Justice, has officers (Border Patrol Agents) throughout the United States and in Europe, Bermuda, Nassau, Puerto Rico, Canada, Mexico, and the Philippines. Among other duties, they conduct investigations, detect violations of immigration and nationality laws, and determine whether aliens may enter or remain in the United States. They present the government's case at hearings and make recommendations to the courts in such matters as petitions for citizenship. For further information write

U.S. Department of Justice
Immigration and Naturalization Service
119 D Street N.E.
Washington, D.C. 20536

*Alcohol, Tobacco, and Firearms Special Investigators* Alcohol, Tobacco, and Firearms Special Investigators (U.S. Treasury Department) work for the detection, investigation, and prevention of violations of liquor, tobacco, and firearms laws. The duties of a "revenoor" include undercover assignments, investigations of organizations acquiring guns, and much contact with all segments of the American public.

*Secret Service Special Agents* Secret Service Special Agents (U.S. Treasury Department) have both protective and investigative responsibilities. They guard the president and vice president and their families, the president-elect and vice president-elect, and former presidents upon request for limited periods of time. They also work to prevent the counterfeiting of U.S. currency and investigate forged government checks and bonds.

*Internal Security Inspectors* Internal Security Inspectors (U.S. Treasury Department) make up the investigative unit of the Internal Revenue Service. They check out prospective employees of IRS and investigate allegations of serious misconduct or illegal activities on the part of IRS employees, with the aim that only people of unquestionable honesty be employed.

*Special Agents Intelligence Division of IRS* Special Agents, Intelligence Division of the Internal Revenue Service (U.S. Treasury Department), perform work unique in the field of criminal investigations. They dig out the facts in tax fraud cases (particularly for income tax, excise tax, and coin-operated gaming devices) and other criminal violations; assist the United States Attorney General in preparing the government's case; and frequently serve as the key witnesses for the prosecution.

*U.S. Customs Service Special Agents* U.S. Customs Service Special Agents (U.S. Treasury Department) have the responsibility of making sure that proper duty is paid on goods coming into the country and that narcotics, drugs, and defense materials neither enter nor leave the country illegally.

For information on *all* of the above

listed agencies of the U.S. Treasury Department write

Recruitment Coordinator for Law Enforcement
Department of the Treasury
Internal Revenue Service
Washington, D.C. 20224

*Postal Inspectors, Investigators, and Security Force Technicians* Postal Inspectors form the criminal investigations arm of the Postal Service. Their cases involve fraud, burglary, theft, obscenity and bombs, among other activities. Investigators assist Postal Inspectors in criminal investigations. Security Force Technicians are a uniformed force providing security at postal installations. For further information write

Chief Postal Inspector
Post Office Department
Washington, D.C. 20260

**Places of Employment**

Federal law enforcement agents may be employed anywhere in the United States, depending on the agency they are working for and the type of work they perform. Some federal agencies, such as the Drug Enforcement Administration, have agents assigned in foreign countries. As a condition of federal employment one must be willing to serve wherever the agency needs his or her services.

**Training, Other Qualifications, and Advancement**

Jobs with the federal government are organized by grades on a general schedule, with each grade (GS–1, GS–2, etc.) having certain general requirements. Salaries correspond to the grades; the higher the grade, the higher the salary. Appointment grades in federal agencies are based on one's qualifications and the hiring levels of that particular agency. Generally, the more education, training, and experience one possesses, the higher entrance level one can command.

Requirements vary among the agencies. Some federal law enforcement positions have unique requirements. For example, Special Agents (Intelligence, IRS) must have at least twelve hours of college accounting, or equivalent experience, and there are strict physical requirements. Because of these variations, it is recommended that you contact the particular federal law enforcement agency in which you are interested in order to learn their specific requirements.

Federal agencies generally maintain their own training programs. For example, each newly appointed Special Agent of the FBI is given approximately fourteen weeks of training at the FBI Academy. The type of training of each agency is naturally a reflection of the specific function of that agency. Narcotics officers can expect to receive training about narcotics, and postal officers can expect to receive training about postal regulations.

Almost all federal law enforcement agents begin their careers at the bottom of the ladder. However, most agencies fill vacancies, whenever possible, by promoting their own employees. Promotion programs in every agency are designed to make sure that promotions go to the employees who are among the best qualified to fill higher positions. How fast employees are promoted depends on openings in the higher grades and on their own ability and effort.

### Employment Outlook

Although it is impossible to forecast the personnel requirements for federal law enforcement personnel, employment can be expected to increase with the growing concern over crime in our nation. Also, normal attrition will continue to provide openings over the years.

### Earnings and Working Conditions

Salaries in the federal service are based on the civil service grade one holds. For example, if you entered the Secret Service as a Special Agent with a grade of GS–7 you would receive the entrance rate currently being paid federal employees at the GS–7 level. In order to keep federal salaries competitive, the entire salary scale is adjusted from time to time by Congress, based on comparison with salaries in the private sector.

### Sources of Additional Information

The above listing is but a few of the many federal law enforcement agencies. For further general information about law enforcement positions with the United States government, the requirements, the examinations, and the methods of application, the applicant should write the nearest United States Civil Service Commission's *Federal Job Information Center*. If you write to the *Federal Job Information Center*, give a brief description of your education, work experience, and the kind of job you seek. Telephone numbers of *Job Information Centers* may be found under United States Government listings in the telephone directory in cities where *Federal Job Information Centers* are located. Local State Employment Service Centers can also provide you with information on the location of your nearest *Federal Job Information Center*. For further information about federal law enforcement careers you can also write

United States Civil Service Commission
1900 E. Street N.W.
Washington, D.C. 20415

Ask for the following Civil Service Commission pamphlets:

1. "Working for the USA" BRE–37
2. "Law Enforcement and Related Jobs with Federal Agencies" BRE–38

There are many federal intelligence and law-enforcement-related jobs that are not filled through the Civil Service Commission. If you are interested in working for any agency listed below, write directly to the address shown.

Central Intelligence Agency (Intelligence)
Director of Personnel
Washington, D.C. 20505

Federal Bureau of Investigation (Special Agents)
Room 4306, Department of Justice Building
Washington, D.C. 20535

National Security Agency (Investigators, Intelligence)
College Relations Branch
Fort Meade, Md. 20755

Department of State (Special Agents, Security Officers)
Executive Office, Office of Security
Room 25513
Washington, D.C. 20520

Atomic Energy Commission (Investigators)
Divison of Personnel
Washington, D.C. 20545

U.S. Postal Service (Inspectors, Investigators, Security)
Chief Postal Inspector
Post Office Department
Washington, D.C. 20260

Defense Intelligence Agency (Intelligence)
Civilian Personnel Office
The Pentagon
Washington, D.C.

U.S. Army Security Agency (Intelligence)
Civilian Personnel Office
Arlington, Va. 22212

Naval Intelligence Command (Intelligence)
Washington, D.C. 20350

U.S. Air Force Security Service (Intelligence)
Kelly Air Force Base
San Antonio, Texas 78240

1127th U.S.A.F. Field Activities Group (Intelligence)
Attn: AFNIA–2
Fort Belvoir, Va. 22060

For law enforcement positions with branches of the United States Armed Services (e.g., Military Police, Air Police) you should contact your nearest Army, Air Force, Navy, or Marine recruiter.

## *CAREER OPPORTUNITIES IN STATE LAW ENFORCEMENT*

### Nature of the Work

*State Police/State Highway Patrol* State police officers perform general police duties throughout the state. Generally speaking, agencies designated as state police agencies have full law enforcement powers throughout the state, whereas highway patrol agencies have only traffic enforcement powers, although, some of the highway patrol agencies do have statewide law enforcement duties and powers.

State police duties involve all facets of police work. State police officers are involved in traffic enforcement, traffic control and accident investigation, criminal investigation, and other general police duties. In the rural areas the state police may provide all police services, while in the urban areas they perform only traffic functions, special investigative assignments, and, when requested, assistance to the local police forces.

*Other State Law Enforcement Agencies* Just as the federal government has numerous specialized law enforcement agencies so also do the various states. There are Liquor Control Boards, Motor Vehicle Agents and Inspectors, Narcotics Agents,

Welfare Investigators, Marine Police, Fish and Game Officers, to name but a few.

The extent and nature of state law enforcement agencies vary from state to state and therefore no complete or accurate listing can be provided. One is best advised to check with the state civil service commission or the local state employment agency.

### Places of Employment

Officers of the various state law enforcement agencies can expect to find work anywhere within the state. The needs of the service come first, and state law enforcement agents must usually be willing to work anywhere in the state.

### Training, Other Qualifications, and Advancement

*State Police/State Highway Patrol* All state police agencies have vigorous and thorough training programs. State police officers must pass competitive examinations and meet strict physical and personal qualifications. Completion of high school is required by most. State police agencies are for the most part under civil service regulations, and promotions and advancement adhere to merit concepts.

*Other State Law Enforcement Agencies* Training and qualifications vary with the needs and functions of the other state law enforcement agencies. You are best advised to check with the particular agency you are interested in, in order to learn of its requirements and training program. Promotions and advancement are usually under the state civil service regulations.

### Employment Outlook

The employment outlook for state law enforcement agencies through the 1970s is excellent. The growth of the interstate highway system will require additional state police/state highway patrol personnel. The continued public emphasis on crime control will create the need for personnel in all areas of state law enforcement. Normal attrition will also continue to supply a limited number of openings.

### Earnings and Working Conditions

State law enforcement salaries vary from state to state, but they are generally competitive within their state. State police/state highway patrol agencies usually furnish officers' uniforms, firearms, and other necessary equipment, or provide special allowances for their purchase. In some state law enforcement agencies cars are provided. State law enforcement agencies are usually provided with liberal benefits, such as pension plans, paid vacations, sick leave, and medical, surgical, and life insurance.

In most states, the scheduled workweek for state police/state highway patrol officers is forty hours. Although the workweek is longer in some states, weekly hours in excess of forty are rapidly being reduced. In a few states, officers are paid overtime. Since state police/state highway patrol officers must provide protection around the clock, some officers are on duty over weekends, on holidays, and at night.

As is any law enforcement work, the work of state law enforcement officers is sometimes hazardous. They always run the risk of an automobile accident while pursuing speeding motorists or fleeing criminals. Police officers also face the risk of bodily harm while apprehending criminals or controlling disorders.

### Sources of Additional Information

For information about state law enforcement agencies you should write the state law enforcement agency you are interested in. Information may also be obtained from the state employment agency or the state civil service commission. For further information write

International Association of Chiefs of Police
Eleven Firstfield Road
Gaithersburg, Md. 20760

## *CAREER OPPORTUNITIES IN MUNICIPAL LAW ENFORCEMENT*

### Nature of the Work

The police officer who works in a small community handles many police duties. In the course of a day's work, he or she may direct traffic at the scene of a fire, investigate a housebreaking, and give first aid to an accident victim. In a large police department, officers are usually assigned to a specific type of duty. Most are detailed either to patrol or traffic duty; smaller numbers are assigned to such specialized work as accident prevention or operating communication systems. Some officers are detectives assigned to criminal investigation; others are experts in chemical microscopic analysis, firearms identification, and handwriting and fingerprint identification. In very large cities, a few officers may be trained to work with such special units as mounted and motorcycle police, harbor patrols, helicopter patrols, canine corps, mobile rescue teams, and youth aid services.

An increasing number of city police departments include women. These officers work with juvenile delinquents, try to locate lost children and runaways, or search, question, book, and fingerprint women prisoners. They may also be assigned to detective squads, where they work mainly on crimes involving women.

### Places of Employment

Municipal police departments range from as large as New York's 30,000 to departments as small as one or two. Almost every city or community of any size has a police force. Local police forces can be found at all levels of local government. Female police officers can expect to find work only in the larger cities.

### Training, Other Qualifications, and Advancement

Local civil service regulations govern the appointment of police officers in practically all large cities and in many small ones. Candidates must be United States citizens, usually at least twenty-one years of age, and able to meet other minimum requirements. Eligibility for appointment is also determined by performance on competitive examinations, physical and personal qualifications, and education and experience. In large police departments, where most jobs are to be found, applicants usually must have at least a high school education. A few cities require some college credits, and some hire law enforcement students as police interns. Some police departments accept men and women who have less than a high school education as recruits, particularly if they have had work experience in a field related to law enforcement.

Police departments increasingly emphasize post-high school training in sociology, psychology, and minority group relations. As a result, more than 500 colleges and universities now offer major programs in law enforcement. College training may be required for female police officers because of their specialized assignments. Training or experience in social work, teaching, or nursing is desirable.

Before their first assignments, police officers usually go through a period of training. In many small communities, the instruction is given informally as recruits work for about a week with experienced officers. More extensive training, such as that provided in large city police departments, may extend over several weeks or a few months. This training includes classroom instruction in constitutional law and civil rights, as well as in state laws and local ordinances, and in the procedures to be followed in accident investigation, patrol, traffic control, and other police work.

Police officers generally become eligible for promotion after specified periods of service. In a large department, promotion may enable an officer to specialize in one kind of law enforcement activity, perhaps laboratory work, traffic control, communications, or work with juveniles. Promotions to the rank of sergeant are made according to each candidate's position on a promotion list, as determined by performance on written examinations and work as a police officer. Advancement opportunities generally are most numerous in large police departments, where separate bureaus work under the direction of administrative officers and their assistants.

### Employment Outlook

Police employment is expected to rise moderately during the 1970s as population and economic growth create a need for more officers to protect life and property, regulate traffic, and provide other police services. Future police jobs are likely to be affected by changes now occurring in police methods and equipment. Specialists are becoming more essential to the effective operation of city police departments. In an increasing number of departments, for example, electronic data processing is used to compile administrative, criminal, and identification records and to operate emergency communications systems. Many departments also need officers with specialized training to apply engineering techniques to traffic control and social work techniques to crime prevention. Generally, growth, public concern over law enforcement, and normal job attrition will provide numerous openings for the coming years.

### Earnings and Working Conditions

In the past police salaries have been low, but in most cities salaries and benefits are now becoming competitive with private industry. Most police officers receive regular pay increases during the first few years of employment until a specified maximum is reached. Sergeants, lieutenants, and captains are paid progressively higher basic salaries than patrol officers in the same police departments. Police departments usually provide officers with special allowances for uniforms and furnish revolvers, night sticks, handcuffs, and other required equipment. Police officers generally are covered by liberal pension plans, enabling many to retire at half pay by the time they reach age fifty-five. Paid vacations, sick leave, and medical, surgical, and life insurance plans are among the benefits frequently provided.

The scheduled workweek for police officers is usually forty hours, and in localities where the workweek is longer, weekly hours are gradually being reduced. Police protection must be provided around the clock; therefore, in all but the very smallest communities, some officers are on duty over weekends, on holidays, and at night. Police officers are subject to call at any time their service may be needed and in emergencies may work overtime. In some departments, overtime is paid at straight time or at time and a half; in others, officers may be given an equal amount of time off on another day of the week.

Police officers may be assigned to work outdoors for long periods in all kinds of weather. The injury rate is higher than in many occupations and reflects the risks police officers take in pursuing speeding motorists, capturing lawbreakers, and dealing with public disorders.

### Sources of Additional Information

Information about local entrance requirements may be obtained from local civil service commissions or police departments. Additional information on the occupation of police officers may be obtained from

International Association of Chiefs of Police
Eleven Firstfield Road
Gaithersburg, Md. 20760

Fraternal Order of Police
Pick-Carter Hotel
1012 Prospect Avenue
Cleveland, Ohio 44115

Further information on the salaries and hours of work of police officers in various cities is published by the International City Managers' Association in the *Municipal Yearbook*, which can be found in your local library.

## *CAREER OPPORTUNITIES IN CORRECTIONS*

### Nature of the Work

Correctional operations are administered by federal, state, county, and municipal governments. The career opportunities within this diverse system are many. Correctional institutions employ people with an array of occupational specialities. There are psychologists, counselors, sociologists, administrators, custodial guards, parole officers, probation officers, teachers, technicians, and many other skills employed in the correctional system.

Security is an essential element of prisons, and a considerable number of personnel employed in the correctional system are employed as custodial guards. Custodial guards maintain a watch over the inmate population to insure there are no escapes. They enforce the rules and regulations governing the operation of a correctional institution and the confinement, safety, health, and protection of inmates. They may at times require arduous physical exertion in subduing recalcitrant inmates who may be armed or assaultive. Custodial guards also supervise the work assignment of inmates and may counsel inmates on personal and family goals and problems. Custodial guards may be used at any location where a guard is needed to maintain a vigil over the inmate population.

Although security is essential in the prison situation, rehabilitation is considered the ultimate goal of the correctional institution. Various occupational specialities work together to develop programs of rehabilitation for the prison population. Teachers conduct educational programs to improve the educational level of the inmates. Counselors advise inmates on personal problems and available programs within the correctional institution. Sociologists and psychologists delve into the social and psychological problems of the inmates and attempt to develop programs of rehabilitation designed to suit special needs. Correctional administrators develop programs, budgets, personnel plans, and so forth for the running of the correctional institution. Vocational instructors provide job training through work programs. All are attempting to rehabilitate the criminal and make possible a return to society and a normal life.

Probation and parole officers assist persons on probation and parole in readjusting to society. Probation officers investigate the social history and background of persons under the jurisdiction of the court and make reports of this information to the court. The judge uses this information in judicial decisions. Parole officers perform this same service for parole boards. They also counsel and supervise persons on probation or parole, help them secure necessary education or employment, and try to resolve the family problems of probationers and parolees through counseling or by directing them to other services in the community.

This is only a partial list of the many talents used today in the larger correctional institutions. As with most large institutions, clerks, secretaries, accountants, managers, lawyers, computer operators, research teams, and all the many talents that go to operate a large modern business organization are present in many correctional institutions.

**Places of Employment**

There are correctional institutions throughout the United States at the federal, state, county, and municipal level. Correctional facilities are usually located in rural areas; however, there is a trend toward more community-based correctional facilities. The institutional workers in the correctional system are generally employed at the prisons, jails, or where ever the inmates are serving their terms. Probation and parole officers generally work out of a local office in the community. Employment in corrections is nationwide, and positions can be found in all the fifty states.

**Training, Other Qualifications, and Advancement**

There is much variation in the personnel policies of the many correctional systems. However, civil service merit systems cover a majority of correctional systems, with the minority most often being smaller, local organizations.

Entrance requirements for jobs in correctional institutions also vary considerably from one jurisdiction to the next. Custodial personnel are usually required to have at least a high school education and to be in good physical condition. The professional staff of correctional institutions —counselors, sociologists, teachers, and the like—are usually required to have a bachelor's degree at minimum. A number of correctional agencies provide some form of initial training and in some cases continued in-service training for their personnel.

Although promotions within correctional systems tend to stress seniority, and promotions programs for the most part are rather inflexible, there should be excellent chances for advancement for the well-qualified and dedicated correctional worker in the coming years. Personnel requirements in the correctional systems far exceed the present recommended standards. The recent availability of federal funding for correctional systems has provided the impetus needed for many correctional agencies to try to meet recommended standards in personnel.

**Employment Outlook**

Employment opportunities for correctional workers for the next decade should be excellent. The increasing concern over crime and criminal offenders has led to an era of growth and expansion for most correctional agencies. To meet recommended standards, many correctional agencies need to hire additional correctional personnel. As new programs—half-way houses, community-based corrections, work-release, and so forth—are initiated, new personnel will be needed. In addition, normal attrition through retirement and job shifts will continue to provide a steady flow of openings in corrections.

**Earnings and Working Conditions**

Unfortunately, salaries for correctional employees have traditionally been low. Nevertheless, the current emphasis on change and improvement in the correctional field should bring about an improvement in the salaries. Now, the federal agencies pay higher salaries than the state agencies, and the state agencies usually pay higher salaries than the local agencies.

Prison settings are usually in rural areas. Certain prison services like security require twenty-four hour coverage and therefore shift work. Other support services usually work a normal forty hour week. Correctional agencies are government agencies, and as such they usually supply the liberal job benefits given most government employees.

### Sources of Additional Information

Information about local requirements for correctional employees can be obtained from the local correctional agency. Information on state correctional agencies can be acquired from the state civil service commission, the state correctional agency, or the local state employment service office. Information on federal correctional institutions can be obtained from the Federal Civil Service Commission, or write

United States Department of Justice
Bureau of Prisons
Washington, D.C. 20544

General information on corrections can be obtained by writing

The American Correctional Association
4321 Hartwick Road
College Park, Md. 20740

National Council on Crime and Delinquency
Continental Plaza
411 Hackensack Avenue
Hackensack, N.J. 07601

## *CAREER OPPORTUNITIES IN THE LEGAL PROFESSION*

### Nature of the Work

Training in law and the legal profession provides many avenues for entrance into various criminal justice positions. Judges are usually lawyers, as are prosecutors and attorneys general. The FBI employs a large number of trained lawyers as Special Agents. Large police departments and some correctional agencies employ lawyers as legal consultants on their staffs. Criminal justice agencies need expert advice on the law, and the trained lawyer usually provides this service.

Lawyers also provide services to the criminal defendant. Lawyers in private practice represent their clients in criminal matters before the courts. Some, though only a few, specialize in criminal law. Public defenders, who are also lawyers, represent criminal defendants.

A good many lawyers find their way into political life, where they deal with the criminal justice system in many ways. Legislators, a good many of whom are lawyers, create legislation on substantive and procedural law. Numerous other lawyers serving as elected officials in various capacities deal with aspects of the criminal justice system both directly and indirectly.

### Places of Employment

Opportunities for lawyers in the criminal justice system exist mainly in the larger cities. Police departments, district attorney's offices, public defender's offices, and other criminal justice agencies of the larger cities have the need for legal assistance. They also have the size necessary to support the employment of large legal staffs.

The federal government employs a large number of lawyers in the Justice and Treasury departments. Assignments in these agencies could be anywhere in the United States. State and local governments throughout the United States employ lawyers in various positions, for example, as legal assistants to the attorney general or the district attorney.

### Training, Other Qualifications, and Advancement

Before a person can practice law in the court of any state, he or she must be admitted to the bar of the state. In all states, applicants for bar admission must pass a written examination; however, a few states waive this requirement for graduates of their own in-state law schools. Other usual requirements are United States citizenship and good moral character. If a lawyer has been admitted to the bar in one state, he or she can usually be admitted to practice in another state without taking an examination by meeting the state's standards of good moral character and having specified amounts of legal experience.

To qualify for the bar examinations in the majority of states, an applicant must have completed a minimum of three years of college work and must in addition be a graduate of a law school approved by the American Bar Association or the proper state authorities. The most usual preparation for becoming a lawyer is four years of college study followed by three years in law school. Some states will accept study in a law office instead of, or in combination with, study in a law school, although this method of training is now rare. Only one state will accept study of the law by correspondence. A number of states require registration and approval by the State Board of Examiners before students enter law school or during the early years of legal study. In a few states, candidates must complete a period of clerkship in a law office before they are admitted to the bar.

### Employment Outlook

Positions for lawyers in criminal justice agencies are usually specialized in nature, and therefore opportunities for advancement are somewhat limited. However, these positions generally pay above-average salaries from the outset. Positions with federal and state agencies are career positions with growth potential dependent on the size of the agency.

Prospects for the lawyer establishing a private practice will probably continue to be best in small towns and expanding suburban areas. In such communities, competition is likely to be less than in big cities and rent and other business costs somewhat lower. Also, young lawyers may find it easier to become known to potential clients. For well-qualified lawyers, opportunities to advance will be available in both government and private practice.

### Earnings and Working Conditions

Lawyers entering the federal service will usually begin around the GS–10 salary level. In the federal service yearly increments in salary are provided, and with promotion comes advancement in pay grade. State governments operate on a similar scheme.

Beginning lawyers engaged in legal aid work usually receive the lowest starting salaries. New lawyers starting their own practices may earn little more than expenses during the first few years and may work part time in another occupation.

Lawyers often work long hours and are under considerable pressure when a case is being tried. In addition, they must keep abreast of the latest laws and court decisions. However, since lawyers in private practice are able to determine their own hours and workload, many stay in practice until well past the usual retirement age. Lawyers in government service may find themselves working a regular eight-hour day.

**Sources of Additional Information**

The specific requirements for admission to the bar in a particular state may be obtained from the clerk of the supreme court or the secretary of the Board of Bar Examiners at the state capital. Information on law schools and on law as a career is available from

Information Service
The American Bar Association
1155 East 60th Street
Chicago, Ill. 60637

Association of American Law Schools
Suite 370, 1 Dupont Circle N.W.
Washington, D.C. 20036

It should be kept in mind that not all the career opportunities in the criminal justice system or in related professions have been covered. Related professions, like private and public security, similar to those in criminal justice agencies do exist. The growth of criminal justice programs on college campuses has created a need for criminal justice teaching personnel. The courts presently need court administrators, the police need forensic chemists, and most criminal justice agencies need researchers. The American criminal justice system is in a state of change and expansion. New opportunities and new challenges are constantly arising. For the individual who desires a challenging career field that serves other human beings and society as a whole, the criminal justice system offers a wide variety of sometimes difficult but always rewarding work.

## BIBLIOGRAPHY

NOTE: The material in this appendix was in part based on the following government publications:

"Law Enforcement and Related Jobs with Federal Agencies." Civil Service Commission pamphlet BRE–38, June 1972.

Bureau of Labor Statistics. *Occupational Outlook Handbook 1972–1973*. Washington, D.C.: Government Printing Office, 1972.

President's Commission on Law Enforcement and Administration of Justice. *Task Force Report: Corrections*. Washington, D.C.: Government Printing Office, 1967.

"Working for the USA." Civil Service Commission pamphlet BRE–37, January 1972.

# Appendix B:

## The United States Constitution

WE THE PEOPLE of the United States, in Order to form a more perfect Union, establish Justice, insure domestic Tranquility, provide for the common defence, promote the general Welfare, and secure the Blessings of Liberty to ourselves and our Posterity, do ordain and establish this CONSTITUTION for the United States of America.

### ARTICLE I

SECTION 1. All legislative Powers herein granted shall be vested in a Congress of the United States, which shall consist of a Senate and House of Representatives.

SECTION 2. [1] The House of Representatives shall be composed of Members chosen every second Year by the People of the several States, and the Electors in each State shall have the Qualifications requisite for Electors of the most numerous Branch of the State Legislature.

[2] No Person shall be a Representative who shall not have attained to the Age of twenty-five Years, and been seven Years a Citizen of the United States, and who shall not, when elected, be an Inhabitant of that State in which he shall be chosen.

[3] *[Representatives and direct Taxes shall be apportioned among the several States which may be included within this Union, according to their respective Numbers, which shall be determined by adding to the whole Number of free Persons, including those bound to Service for a Term of Years, and excluding Indians not taxed, three fifths of all other Persons.] The actual Enumeration shall be made within three Years after the first Meeting of the Congress of the United States, and within every subsequent Term of ten Years, in such Manner as they shall by Law direct. The Number of Representatives shall not exceed one for every thirty Thousand, but each State shall have at Least one Representative; and until such enumeration shall be made, the State of New Hampshire shall be entitled to chuse three, Massachusetts eight, Rhode-Island and Providence Plantations one, Connecticut five, New-York six, New Jersey four, Pennsylvania eight, Delaware one, Maryland six, Virginia ten, North Carolina five, South Carolina five, and Georgia three.

[4] When vacancies happen in the Representation from any State, the Executive Authority thereof shall issue Writs of Election to fill such vacancies.

[5] The House of Representatives shall chuse their Speaker and other Officers; and shall have the sole Power of Impeachment.

[1] SECTION 3. **The Senate of the United States shall be composed of two Senators from each State, [chosen by the Legislature] thereof, for six Years; and each Senator shall have one Vote.

[2] Immediately after they shall be assembled in Consequence of the first Election, they shall be divided as equally as may be into three Classes. The Seats of the Senators of the first Class shall be vacated at the Expiration of the Second Year, of the second Class at the Expiration of the fourth Year, and of the third Class at the Expiration of the sixth Year, so that one-third may be chosen every second Year; [and if Vacancies happen by Resignation, or otherwise, during the Recess of the Legislature of any State, the Executive thereof may make temporary Appointments until the next Meeting of the Legislature, which shall then fill such Vacancies].***

---

*The part included in heavy brackets was repealed by section 2 of amendment XIV.
**The part included in heavy brackets was repealed by section 1 of amendment XVII.
***The part included in heavy brackets was changed by clause 2 of amendment XVII.
NOTE.—The superior number preceding the paragraphs designates the number of the clause.

[3] No Person shall be a Senator who shall not have attained to the Age of thirty Years, and been nine Years a Citizen of the United States, and who shall not, when elected, be an inhabitant of that State for which he shall be chosen.

[4] The Vice President of the United States shall be President of the Senate, but shall have no Vote, unless they be equally divided.

[5] The Senate shall chuse their other Officers, and also a President pro tempore, in the absence of the Vice President, or when he shall exercise the Office of President of the United States.

[6] The Senate shall have the sole Power to try all Impeachments. When sitting for that Purpose, they shall be on Oath or Affirmation. When the President of the United States is tried, the Chief Justice shall preside: And no Person shall be convicted without the Concurrence of two-thirds of the Members present.

[7] Judgment in Cases of Impeachment shall not extend further than to removal from Office, and disqualification to hold and enjoy any Office of honor, Trust, or Profit under the United States: but the Party convicted shall nevertheless be liable and subject to Indictment, Trial, Judgment, and Punishment, according to Law.

SECTION 4. [1] The Times, Places and Manner of holding Elections for Senators and Representatives, shall be prescribed in each State by the Legislature thereof; but the Congress may at any time by Law make or alter such Regulations, except as to the Places of chusing Senators.

[2] The Congress shall assembly at least once in every Year, and such Meeting shall [be on the first Monday in December,] unless they shall by Law appoint a different Day.*

SECTION 5. [1] Each House shall be the Judge of the Elections, Returns, and Qualifications of its own Members, and a Majority of each shall constitute a Quorum to do Business; but a smaller Number may adjourn from day to day, and may be authorized to compel the Attendance of absent Members, in such Manner, and under such Penalties as each House may provide.

[2] Each House may determine the Rules of its Proceedings, punish its Members for disorderly Behavior, and, with the Concurrence of two thirds, expel a Member.

[3] Each House shall keep a Journal of its Proceedings, and from time to time publish the same, excepting such Parts as may in their Judgment require Secrecy; and the Yeas and Nays of the Members of either House on any question shall, at the Desire of one fifth of those Present, be entered on the Journal.

[4] Neither House, during the Session of Congress, shall, without the Consent of the other, adjourn for more than three days, nor to any other Place than that in which the two Houses shall be sitting.

SECTION 6. [1] The Senators and Representatives shall receive a Compensation for their Services, to be ascertained by Law, and paid out of the Treasury of the United States. They shall in all Cases, except Treason, Felony and Breach of the Peace, be privileged from Arrest during their Attendance at the Session of their respective Houses, and in going to and returning from the same; and for any Speech or Debate in either House, they shall not be questioned in any other Place.

[2] No Senator or Representative shall, during the Time for which he was elected, be appointed to any civil Office under the Authority of the United States, which shall have been created, or the Emoluments whereof shall have been encreased during such time; and no Person holding any Office under the United States, shall be a Member of either House during his Continuance in Office.

*The part included in heavy brackets was changed by section 2 of amendment XX.

SECTION 7. [1] All Bills for raising Revenue shall originate in the House of Representatives; but the Senate may propose or concur with Amendments as on other Bills.

[2] Every Bill which shall have passed the House of Representatives and the Senate, shall, before it become a Law, be presented to the President of the United States; if he approve he shall sign it, but if not he shall return it, with his Objections to that House in which it shall have originated, who shall enter the Objections at large on their Journal, and proceed to reconsider it. If after such Reconsideration two thirds of that House shall agree to pass the Bill, it shall be sent, together with the Objections, to the other House, by which it shall likewise be reconsidered, and if approved by two thirds of that House, it shall become a Law. But in all such Cases the Votes of both Houses shall be determined by Yeas and Nays, and the Names of the Persons voting for and against the Bill shall be entered on the Journal of each House respectively. If any Bill shall not be returned by the President within ten Days (Sundays excepted) after it shall have been presented to him, the Same shall be a Law, in like Manner as if he had signed it, unless the Congress by their Adjournment prevent its Return, in which Case it shall not be a Law.

[3] Every Order, Resolution, or Vote to which the Concurrence of the Senate and House of Representatives may be necessary (except on a question of Adjournment) shall be presented to the President of the United States; and before the Same shall take Effect, shall be approved by him, or being disapproved by him, shall be repassed by two thirds of the Senate and House of Representatives, according to the Rules and Limitations prescribed in the Case of a Bill.

SECTION 8. The Congress shall have Power To lay and collect Taxes, Duties, Imposts and Excises, to pay the Debts and provide for the common Defence and general Welfare of the United States; but all Duties, Imposts and Excises shall be uniform throughout the United States;

[2] To borrow money on the credit of the United States;

[3] To regulate Commerce with foreign Nations, and among the several States, and with the Indian Tribes;

[4] To establish an uniform Rule of Naturalization, and uniform Laws on the subject of Bankruptcies throughout the United States;

[5] To coin Money, regulate the Value thereof, and of foreign Coin, and fix the Standard of Weights and Measures;

[6] To provide for the Punishment of counterfeiting the Securities and current Coin of the United States;

[7] To Establish Post Offices and post Roads;

[8] To promote the Progress of Science and useful Arts, by securing for limited Times to Authors and Inventors the exclusive Right to their respective Writings and Discoveries;

[9] To constitute Tribunals inferior to the supreme Court;

[10] To define and punish Piracies and Felonies committed on the high Seas, and Offenses against the Law of Nations;

[11] To declare War, grant Letters of Marque and Reprisal, and make Rules concerning Captures on Land and Water;

[12] To raise and support Armies, but no Appropriation of Money to that Use shall be for a longer Term than two Years;

[13] To provide and maintain a Navy;

[14] To make Rules for the Government and Regulation of the land and naval Forces;

[15] To provide for calling forth the Militia to execute the Laws of the Union, suppress insurrections and repel Invasions;

[16] To provide for organizing, arming, and disciplining the Militia, and for governing such Part of them as may be employed in the Service of the United States, reserving to the States

respectively, the Appointment of the Officers, and the Authority of training the Militia according to the discipline prescribed by Congress;

[17] To exercise exclusive Legislation in all Cases whatsoever, over such District (not exceeding ten Miles square) as may, by Cession of particular States, and the acceptance of Congress, become the Seat of the Government of the United States, and to exercise like Authority over all Places purchased by the Consent of the Legislature of the State in which the Same shall be, for the Erection of Forts, Magazines, Arsenals, dock-Yards, and other needful Buildings;—And

[18] To make all Laws which shall be necessary and proper for carrying into Execution the foregoing Powers, and all other Powers vested by this Constitution in the Government of the United States, or in any Department or Officer thereof.

SECTION 9. [1] The Migration or Importation of Such Persons as any of the States now existing shall think proper to admit, shall not be prohibited by the Congress prior to the Year one thousand eight hundred and eight, but a tax or duty may be imposed on such Importation, not exceeding ten dollars for each Person.

[2] The privilege of the Writ of Habeas Corpus shall not be suspended, unless when in Cases of Rebellion or Invasion the public Safety may require it.

[3] No Bill of Attainder or ex post facto Law shall be passed.

[4] *No capitation, or other direct, Tax shall be laid, unless in Proportion to the Census or Enumeration herein before directed to be taken.

[5] No Tax or Duty shall be laid on Articles exported from any State.

[6] No preference shall be given by any Regulation of Commerce or Revenue to the Ports of one State over those of another: nor shall Vessels bound to, or from, one State be obliged to enter, clear, or pay Duties in another.

[7] No money shall be drawn from the Treasury, but in Consequence of Appropriations made by Law; and a regular Statement and Account of the Receipts and Expenditures of all public Money shall be published from time to time.

[8] No title of Nobility shall be granted by the United States: And no Person holding any Office of Profit or Trust under them, shall, without the Consent of the Congress, accept of any present, Emolument, Office, or Title, of any kind whatever, from any King, Prince, or foreign State.

SECTION 10. [1] No State shall enter into any Treaty, Alliance, or Confederation; grant Letters of Marque and Reprisal; coin Money; emit Bills of Credit; make any Thing but gold and silver Coin a Tender in Payment of Debts; pass any Bill of Attainder, ex post facto Law, or Law impairing the Obligation of Contracts, or grant any Title of Nobility.

[2] No State shall, without the Consent of the Congress, lay any Imposts or Duties on Imports or Exports, except what may be absolutely necessary for executing its inspection Laws; and the net Produce of all Duties and Imposts, laid by any State on Imports or Exports, shall be for the Use of the Treasury of the United States; and all such Laws shall be subject to the Revision and Control of the Congress.

[3] No State shall, without the Consent of Congress, lay any duty of Tonnage, keep Troops, or Ships of War in time of Peace, enter into any Agreement or Compact with another State, or with a foreign Power, or engage in War, unless actually invaded, or in such imminent Danger as will not admit of delay.

## ARTICLE II

SECTION 1. [1] The executive Power shall be vested in a President of the United States of America. He shall hold his Office during the Term of four Years, and, together with the Vice-President, chosen for the same Term, be elected, as follows:

*See also amendment XVI.

[2] Each State shall appoint, in such Manner as the Legislature thereof may direct, a Number of Electors, equal to the whole Number of Senators and Representatives to which the State may be entitled in the Congress: but no Senator or Representative, or Person holding an Office of Trust or Profit under the United States, shall be appointed an Elector.

*[The Electors shall meet in their respective States, and vote by Ballot for two persons of whom one at least shall not be an Inhabitant of the same State with themselves. And they shall make a list of all the Persons voted for, and of the Number of Votes for each; which List they shall sign and certify, and transmit sealed to the Seat of the Government of the United States, directed to the President of the Senate. The President of the Senate shall, in the Presence of the Senate and House of Representatives, open all the Certificates, and the Votes shall then be counted. The Person having the greatest Number of votes shall be the President, if such Number by a Majority of the whole Number of Electors appointed; and if there be more than one who have such Majority, and have an equal Number of Votes, then the House of Representatives shall immediately chuse by Ballot one of them for President; and if no Person have a Majority, then from the five highest on the List the said House shall in like Manner chuse the President. But in chusing the President, the Votes shall be taken by States, the Representation from each State having one Vote; A quorum for this Purpose shall consist of a Member or Members from two-thirds of the States, and a Majority of all the States shall be necessary to a Choice. In every Case, after the Choice of the President the Person having the greatest Number of Votes of the Electors shall be the Vice President. But if there should remain two or more who have equal Votes, the Senate shall chuse from them by Ballot the Vice-President.]

[3] The Congress may determine the Time of chusing the Electors and the Day on which they shall give their Votes; which Day shall be the same throughout the United States.

[4] No person except a natural born Citizen, or a Citizen of the United States, at the time of the Adoption of this Constitution, shall be eligible to the Office of President; neither shall any Person be eligible to that Office who shall not have attained to the Age of thirty-five Years, and been fourteen Years a Resident within the United States.

[5] In case of the removal of the President from Office, or of his Death, Resignation or Inability to discharge the Powers and Duties of the said Office, the same shall devolve on the Vice President, and the Congress may by Law provide for the Case of Removal, Death, Resignation or Inability, both of the President, and Vice President, declaring what Officer shall then act as President, and such Officer shall act accordingly, until the Disability be removed, or a President shall be elected.

[6] The President shall, at stated Times, receive for his Services, a Compensation, which shall neither be encreased nor diminished during the Period for which he shall have been elected, and he shall not receive within that Period any other Emolument from the United States, or any of them.

[7] Before he enter on the Execution of his Office, he shall take the following Oath or Affirmation:—"I do solemnly swear (or affirm) that I will faithfully execute the Office of President of the United States, and will to the best of my Ability, preserve, protect and defend the Constitution of the United States."

SECTION 2. [1] The President shall be Commander in Chief of the Army and Navy of the United States, and of the Militia of the several States, when called into the actual Service of the United States; he may require the Opinion, in writing, of the principal Officer in each of the executive Departments, upon any subject relating to the Duties of their respective Offices, and he shall have Power to grant Reprieves and Pardons for Offences against the United States, except in Cases of Impeachment.

[2] He shall have Power, by and with the Advice and Consent of the Senate, to make

*This paragraph has been superseded by amendment XII.

Treaties, provided two-thirds of the Senators present concur; and he shall nominate, and by and with the Advice and Consent of the Senate, shall appoint Ambassadors, other public Ministers and Consuls, Judge of the supreme Court, and all other Officers of the United States, whose Appointments are not herein otherwise provided for, and which shall be established by Law; but the Congress may by Law vest the Appointment of such inferior Officers, as they think proper, in the President alone, in the Courts of Law, or in the Heads of Departments.

[3] The President shall have Power to fill up all Vacancies that may happen during the Recess of the Senate, by granting Commissions which shall expire at the End of their next Session.

SECTION 3. He shall from time to time give to the Congress Information of the State of the Union, and recommend to their Consideration such Measures as he shall judge necessary and expedient; he may, on extraordinary Occasions, convene both Houses, or either of them, and in Case of Disagreement between them, with Respect to the Time of Adjournment, he may adjourn them to such Time as he shall think proper; he shall receive Ambassadors and other public Ministers; he shall take Care that the Laws be faithfully executed, and shall Commission all the Officers of the United States.

SECTION 4. The President, Vice President and all civil Officers of the United States, shall be removed from Office on Impeachment for, and Conviction of, Treason, Bribery, or other high Crimes and Misdemeanors.

## ARTICLE III

SECTION 1. The judicial Power of the United States, shall be vested in one supreme Court, and in such inferior Courts as the Congress may from time to time ordain and establish. The Judges, both of the supreme and inferior Courts, shall hold their Offices during good Behavior, and shall, at stated Times, receive for their Services a Compensation which shall not be diminished during their Continuance in Office.

SECTION 2. [1] The judicial Power shall extend to all Cases, in Law and Equity, arising under this Constitution, the Laws of the United States, and Treaties made, or which shall be made, under their Authority;—to all Cases affecting Ambassadors, other public Ministers and Consuls;—to all Cases of admiralty and maritime Jurisdiction;—to Controversies to which the United States shall be a Party;—to Controversies between two or more States;—between a State and Citizens of another State;*—between Citizens of different States;—between Citizens of the same State claiming Lands under Grants of different States, and between a State, or the Citizens thereof, and foreign States, Citizens or Subjects.

[2] In all Cases affecting Ambassadors, other public Ministers and Consuls, and those in which a State shall be Party, the supreme Court shall have original Jurisdiction. In all the other Cases before mentioned, the supreme Court shall have appellate Jurisdiction, both as to Law and Fact, with such Exceptions, and under such Regulations as the Congress shall make.

[3] The trial of all Crimes except in Cases of Impeachment shall be by Jury; and such Trial shall be held in the State where the said Crimes shall have been committed; but when not committed within any State, the Trial shall be at such Place or Places as the Congress may by Law have directed.

SECTION 3. [1] Treason against the United States shall consist only in levying War against

*This clause has been affected by amendment XI.

them, or, in adhering to their Enemies, giving them Aid and Comfort. No Person shall be convicted of Treason unless on the Testimony of two Witnesses to the same overt Act, or on Confession in open Court.

[2] The Congress shall have power to declare the Punishment of Treason, but no Attainder of Treason shall work Corruption of Blood, or Forfeiture except during the Life of the Person attainted.

## ARTICLE IV

SECTION 1. Full Faith and Credit shall be given in each State to the public Acts, Records, and judicial Proceedings of every other State. And the Congress may by general Laws prescribe the Manner in which such Acts, Records and Proceedings shall be proved, and the Effect thereof.

SECTION 2. [1] The Citizens of each State shall be entitled to all Privileges and Immunities of Citizens in the several States.

[2] A Person charged in any State with Treason, Felony, or other Crime, who shall flee from Justice, and be found in another State, shall on demand of the executive Authority of the State from which he fled, be delivered up, to be removed to the State having Jurisdiction of the Crime.

[3] *[No person held to Service or Labour in one State, under the Laws thereof, escaping into another, shall, in Consequence of any Law or Regulation therein, be discharged from such Service or Labour, but shall be delivered up on Claim of the Party to whom such Service or Labour may be due.]

SECTION 3. [1] New States may be admitted by the Congress into this Union; but no new State shall be formed or erected within the Jurisdiction of any other State; nor any State be formed by the Junction of two or more States, or parts of States, without the Consent of the Legislatures of the States concerned as well as of the Congress.

[2] The Congress shall have Power to dispose of and make all needful Rules and Regulations respecting the Territory or other Property belonging to the United States; and nothing in this Constitution shall be so construed as to Prejudice any Claims of the United States, or of any particular State.

SECTION 4. The United States shall guarantee to every State in this Union a Republican Form of Government, and shall protect each of them against Invasion; and on Application of the Legislature, or of the Executive (when the Legislature cannot be convened) against domestic Violence.

## ARTICLE V

The Congress, whenever two-thirds of both Houses shall deem it necessary, shall propose Amendments to this Constitution, or, on the Application of the Legislatures of two-thirds of the several States, shall call a Convention for proposing Amendments, which, in either Case, shall be valid to all Intents and Purposes, as part of this Constitution when ratified by the Legislatures of three-fourths of the several States, or by Conventions in three-fourths thereof, as the one or the other Mode of Ratification may be proposed by the Congress; Provided that no Amendment which may be made prior to the Year One thousand eight hundred and eight shall in any Manner affect the first and fourth Clauses in the Ninth Section of the first Article; and that no State, without its Consent, shall be deprived of its equal Suffrage in the Senate.

ARTICLE VI

[1] All Debts contracted and Engagements entered into, before the Adoption of this Constitution shall be as valid against the United States under this Constitution, as under the Confederation.

[2] This Constitution, and the Laws of the United States which shall be made in Pursuance thereof; and all Treaties made, or which shall be made, under the Authority of the United States, shall be the supreme Law of the Land; and the Judges in every State shall be bound thereby, any Thing in the Constitution or Laws of any State to the Contrary notwithstanding.

[3] The Senators and Representatives before mentioned, and the Members of the several State Legislatures, and all executive and judicial Officers, both of the United States and of the several States, shall be bound by Oath or Affirmation, to support this Constitution; but no religious Test shall ever be required as a Qualification to any Office or public Trust under the United States.

ARTICLE VII

The Ratification of the Conventions of nine States, shall be sufficient for the Establishment of this Constitution between the States so ratifying the Same.

DONE in Convention by the Unanimous Consent of the States present the Seventeenth Day of September in the Year of our Lord one thousand seven hundred and Eighty seven and of the Independence of the United States of America the Twelfth. IN WITNESS whereof We have hereto subscribed our Names,

Go WASHINGTON—
*Presid^t. and deputy from Virginia.*

[Signed also by the deputies of twelve States.]

*New Hampshire*
JOHN LANGDON
NICHOLAS GILMAN

*Massachusetts*
NATHANIEL GORHAM
RUFUS KING

*Connecticut*
WM. SAML. JOHNSON
ROGER SHERMAN

*New York*
ALEXANDER HAMILTON

*New Jersey*
WIL: LIVINGSTON
DAVID BREARLEY
WM. PATERSON
JONA: DAYTON

*Pennsylvania*
B FRANKLIN
ROBT MORRIS
THOS. FITZSIMONS
JAMES WILSON
THOMAS MIFFLIN
GEO. CLYMER
JARED INGERSOLL
GOUV MORRIS

*Delaware*
GEO: READ
JOHN DICKINSON
JACO: BROOM
GUNNING BEDFORD, JUN
RICHARD BASSETT

*Maryland*
JAMES McHENRY
DANL CARROLL
DAN OF ST THOS. JENIFER

*Virginia*
JOHN BLAIR—
JAMES MADISON JR.

*North Carolina*
WM. BLOUNT
HU WILLIAMSON
RICH'D DOBBS SPAIGHT

*South Carolina*
J. RUTLEDGE
CHARLES PINCKNEY
CHARLES COTESWORTH PINCKNEY
PIERCE BUTLER

*Georgia*
WILLIAM FEW, Attest:
ABR BALDWIN
WILLIAM JACKSON, *Secretary*

## RATIFICATION OF THE CONSTITUTION

The Constitution was adopted by a convention of the States on September 17, 1787, and was subsequently ratified by the several States on the following dates: Delaware, December 7, 1787; Pennsylvania, December 12, 1787; New Jersey, December 18, 1787; Georgia, January 2, 1788; Connecticut, January 9, 1788; Massachusetts, February 6, 1788; Maryland, April 28, 1788; South Carolina, May 23, 1788; New Hampshire, June 21, 1788; Virginia, June 25, 1788; New York, July 26, 1788; North Carolina, November 21, 1789; Rhode Island, May 29, 1790. It was declared in operation September 13, 1788; by a resolution of the Continental Congress.

ARTICLES IN ADDITION TO, AND AMENDMENT OF, THE CONSTITUTION OF THE UNITED STATES OF AMERICA, PROPOSED BY CONGRESS, AND RATIFIED BY THE LEGISLATURES OF THE SEVERAL STATES, PURSUANT TO THE FIFTH ARTICLE OF THE ORIGINAL CONSTITUTION

### AMENDMENT I

Congress shall make no law respecting an establishment of religion, or prohibiting the free exercise thereof; or abridging the freedom of speech, or of the press; or the right of the people peaceably to assemble and to petition the Government for a redress of grievances.

### AMENDMENT II

A well regulated Militia, being necessary to the security of a free State, the right of the people to keep and bear Arms, shall not be infringed.

### AMENDMENT III

No Soldier shall, in time of peace be quartered in any house, without the consent of the Owner, not in time of war, but in a manner to be prescribed by law.

### AMENDMENT IV

The right of the people to be secure in their persons, houses, papers, and effects, against unreasonable searches and seizures, shall not be violated, and no Warrants shall issue, but upon probable cause, supported by Oath or affirmation and particularly describing the place to be searched, and the persons or things to be seized.

### AMENDMENT V

No person shall be held to answer for a capital, or otherwise infamous crime, unless on a presentment or indictment of a Grand Jury, except in cases arising in the land or naval forces, or in the Militia, when in actual service in time of War or public danger; nor shall any person be subject for the same offence to be twice put in jeopardy of life or limb; nor shall be compelled in any criminal case to be a witness against himself, nor be deprived of life, liberty, or property, without due process of law; nor shall private property be taken for public use, without just compensation.

AMENDMENT VI

In all criminal prosecutions, the accused shall enjoy the right to a speedy and public trial, by an impartial jury of the State and district wherein the crime shall have been committed, which district shall have been previously ascertained by law, and to be informed of the nature and cause of the accusation: to be confronted with the witnesses against him; to have compulsory process for obtaining witnesses in his favor, and to have the Assistance of Counsel for his defence.

AMENDMENT VII

In suits at common law, where the value in controversy shall exceed twenty dollars, the right of trial by jury shall be preserved, and no fact tried by jury, shall be otherwise reexamined in any Court of the United States, than according to the rules of the common law.

AMENDMENT VIII

Excessive bail shall not be required, nor excessive fines imposed, nor cruel and unusual punishments inflicted.

AMENDMENT IX

The enumeration in the Constitution, of certain rights, shall not be construed to deny or disparage others retained by the people.

AMENDMENT X

The powers not delegated to the United States by the Constitution, nor prohibited by it to the States, are reserved to the States respectively, or to the people.

(Ratification of first ten amendments completed December 15, 1791.)

AMENDMENT XI

The Judicial power of the United States shall not be construed to extend to any suit in law or equity, commenced or prosecuted against one of the United States by Citizens of another State, or by Citizens or Subjects of any Foreign State.

(Declared ratified January 8, 1798.)

AMENDMENT XII

The electors shall meet in their respective states and vote by ballot for President and Vice-President, one of whom, at least, shall not be an inhabitant of the same state with themselves; they shall name in their ballots the person voted for as President, and in distinct ballots the person voted for as Vice-President, and they shall make distinct lists of all persons voted for as President, and of all persons voted for as Vice-President, and of the number of votes for each, which lists they shall sign and certify, and transmit sealed to the seat of the government of the United States, directed to the President of the Senate;—The President of the Senate shall, in presence of the Senate and House of Representatives, open all the certificates and the votes shall then be counted;—The person having the greatest number of votes for President, shall be the President, if such number be a majority of the whole number of Electors appointed; and if no person have such majority, then from the persons having the highest numbers not exceeding three on the list of those voted for as President, the House of Representatives shall choose immediately, by ballot, the President. But in choosing the President, the votes shall be taken by states, the representation from each state having one vote; a quorum for this purpose shall consist of a member or members from two-thirds of the states, and a majority of all the states shall be necessary to a choice. *[And if the House of Representatives shall not choose a President whenever the right of choice shall devolve upon them, before the fourth day of March next following, then the Vice-President shall act as President, as in the case of the death or other constitutional disability of the President.]—The person having the greatest number of votes as Vice-President, shall be the Vice-President, if such number be a majority of the whole number of Electors appointed, and if no person have a majority, then from the two highest numbers on the list, the Senate shall choose the Vice-President; a quorum for the purpose shall consist of two-thirds of the whole number of Senators, and a majority of the whole number shall be necessary to a choice. But no person constitutionally ineligible to the office of President shall be eligible to that of Vice-President of the United States.

(Declared ratified September 25, 1804.)

## AMENDMENT XIII

SECTION 1. Neither slavery nor involuntary servitude, except as a punishment for crime whereof the party shall have been duly convicted, shall exist within the United States, or any place subject to their jurisdiction.

SECTION 2. Congress shall have power to enforce this article by appropriate legislation.

(Declared ratified December 18, 1865.)

## AMENDMENT XIV

SECTION 1. All persons born or naturalized in the United States, and subject to the jurisdiction thereof, are citizens of the United States and of the State wherein they reside. No State shall make or enforce any law which shall abridge the privileges or immunities of citizens of the United States; nor shall any State deprive any person of life, liberty, or property, without due process of law; nor deny to any person within its jurisdiction the equal protection of the laws.

SECTION 2. Representatives shall be apportioned among the several States according to their respective numbers, counting the whole number of persons in each State, excluding Indians not taxed. But when the right to vote at any election for the choice of electors for President and Vice-President of the United States, Representatives in Congress, the Executive and Judicial officers of a State, or the members of the Legislature thereof, is denied to any

*The part included in heavy brackets has been superseded by section 3 of amendment XX.

of the male inhabitants of such State, being twenty-one years of age, and citizens of the United States, or in any way abridged, except for participation in rebellion, or other crime, the basis of representation therein shall be reduced in the proportion which the number of such male citizens shall bear to the whole number of male citizens twenty-one years of age in such State.

SECTION 3. No person shall be a Senator or Representative in Congress, or elector of President and Vice-President, or hold any office, civil or military, under the United States, or under any State, who, having previously taken an oath, as a member of Congress, or as an officer of the United States, or as a member of any State legislature, or as an executive or judicial officer of any State, to support the Constitution of the United States, shall have engaged in insurrection or rebellion against the same, or given aid or comfort to the enemies thereof. But Congress may by a vote of two-thirds of each House, remove such disability.

SECTION 4. The validity of the public debt of the United States, authorized by law, including debts incurred for payment of pensions and bounties for services in suppressing insurrection or rebellion, shall not be questioned. But neither the United States nor any State shall assume or pay any debt or obligation incurred in aid of insurrection or rebellion against the United States, or any claim for the loss or emancipation of any slave; but all such debts, obligations and claims shall be held illegal and void.

SECTION 5. The Congress shall have power to enforce, by appropriate legislation, the provisions of this article.

(Declared ratified July 28, 1868.)

## AMENDMENT XV

SECTION 1. The right of citizens of the United States to vote shall not be denied or abridged by the United States or by any State on account of race, color, or previous condition of servitude—

SECTION 2. The Congress shall have power to enforce this article by appropriate legislation.

(Declared ratified March 30, 1870.)

## AMENDMENT XVI

The Congress shall have power to lay and collect taxes on incomes, from whatever source derived, without apportionment among the several States, and without regard to any census or enumeration.

(Declared ratified February 25, 1913.)

## AMENDMENT XVII

The Senate of the United States shall be composed of two Senators from each State, elected by the people thereof, for six years; and each Senator shall have one vote. The electors in each State shall have the qualifications requisite for electors of the most numerous branch of the State legislatures.

When vacancies happen in the representation of any State in the Senate, the executive authority of such State shall issue writs of election to fill such vacancies: *Provided*, That the legislature of any State may empower the executive thereof to make temporary appointments until the people fill the vacancies by election as the legislature may direct.

This amendment shall not be so construed as to affect the election or term of any Senator chosen before it becomes valid as part of the Constitution.

(Declared ratified May 31, 1913.)

## AMENDMENT XVIII

[SECTION 1. After one year from the ratification of this article the manufacture, sale, or transportation of intoxicating liquors within, the importation thereof into, or the exportation thereof from the United States and all territory subject to the jurisdiction thereof for beverage purposes is hereby prohibited.

[SECTION 2. The Congress and the several States shall have concurrent power to enforce this article by appropriate legislation.

[SECTION 3. This article shall be inoperative unless it shall have been ratified as an amendment to the Constitution by the legislatures of the several States, as provided in the Constitution, within seven years from the date of the submission hereof to the States by the Congress.]*

(Declared ratified January 29, 1919.)

## AMENDMENT XIX

The right of citizens of the United States to vote shall not be denied or abridged by the United States or by any State on account of sex.

Congress shall have power to enforce this article by appropriate legislation.

(Declared ratified August 26, 1920.)

## AMENDMENT XX

SECTION 1. The terms of the President and Vice-President shall end at noon on the 20th day of January, and the terms of Senators and Representatives at noon on the 3d day of January, of the years in which such terms would have ended if this article had not been ratified; and the terms of their successors shall then begin.

SECTION 2. The Congress shall assemble at least once in every year, and such meeting shall begin at noon on the 3d day of January, unless they shall by law appoint a different day.

SECTION 3. If, at the time for the beginning of the term of the President, the President elect shall have died, the Vice-President elect shall become President. If a President shall not have been chosen before the time fixed for the beginning of his term, or if the President elect shall have failed to qualify, then the Vice-President elect shall act as President until a President shall have qualified; and the Congress may by law provide for the case wherein neither a President elect nor a Vice-President elect shall have qualified, declaring who shall then act as President, or the manner in which one who is to act shall be selected, and such person shall act accordingly until a President or Vice-President shall have qualified.

SECTION 4. The Congress may by law provide for the case of the death of any of the persons from whom the House of Representatives may choose a President whenever the right of choice shall have devolved upon them and for the case of the death of any of the persons from whom the Senate may choose a Vice-President whenever the right of choice shall have devolved upon them.

*Amendment XVIII was repealed by section 1 of amendment XXI.

SECTION 5. Sections 1 and 2 shall take effect on the 15th day of October following the ratification of this article.

SECTION 6. This article shall be inoperative unless it shall have been ratified as an amendment to the Constitution by the legislatures of three-fourths of the several States within seven years from the date of its submission.

(Declared ratified February 6, 1933.)

## AMENDMENT XXI

SECTION 1. The eighteenth article of amendment to the Constitution of the United States is hereby repealed.

SECTION 2. The transportation or importation into any State, Territory, or possession of the United States for delivery or use therein of intoxicating liquors, in violation of the laws thereof, is hereby prohibited.

SECTION 3. This article shall be inoperative unless it shall have been ratified as an amendment to the Constitution by conventions in the several States, as provided in the Constitution, within seven years from the date of the submission hereof to the States by the Congress.

(Declared ratified December 5, 1933.)

## AMENDMENT XXII

SECTION 1. No person shall be elected to the office of the President more than twice, and no person who has held the office of President, or acted as President, for more than two years of a term to which some other person was elected President shall be elected to the office of the President more than once. But this article shall not apply to any person holding the office of President when this Article was proposed by the Congress, and shall not prevent any person who may be holding the office of President, or acting as President, during the term within which this Article becomes operative from holding the office of President or acting as President during the remainder of such term.

SECTION 2. This article shall be inoperative unless it shall have been ratified as an amendment to the Constitution by the legislatures of three-fourths of the several States within seven years from the date of its submission to the States by the Congress.

(Declared ratified March 1, 1951.)

## AMENDMENT XXIII

SECTION 1. The District constituting the seat of Government of the United States shall appoint in such manner as the Congress may direct:

A number of electors of President and Vice President equal to the whole number of Senators and Representatives in Congress to which the District would be entitled if it were a State, but in no event more than the least populous State; they shall be in addition to those appointed by the States, but they shall be considered, for the purposes of the election of President and Vice President, to be electors appointed by a State; and they shall meet in the District and perform such duties as provided by the twelfth article of amendment.

SECTION 2. The Congress shall have power to enforce this article by appropriate legislation.

(Declared ratified April 3, 1961.)

## AMENDMENT XXIV

SECTION 1. The right of citizens of the United States to vote in any primary or other election for President or Vice President, for electors for President or Vice President, or for Senator or Representative in Congress, shall not be denied or abridged by the United States or any State by reason of failure to pay any poll tax or other tax.

SECTION 2. The Congress shall have power to enforce this article by appropriate legislation.

(Declared ratified February 4, 1962.)

## AMENDMENT XXV

SECTION 1. In case of the removal of the President from office or of his death or resignation, the Vice President shall become President.

SECTION 2. Whenever there is a vacancy in the office of the Vice President, the President shall nominate a Vice President who shall take office upon confirmation by a majority vote of both Houses of Congress.

SECTION 3. Whenever the President transmits to the President pro tempore of the Senate and the Speaker of the House of Representatives his written declaration that he is unable to discharge the powers and duties of his office, and until he transmits to them a written declaration to the contrary, such powers and duties shall be discharged by the Vice President as Acting President.

SECTION 4. Whenever the Vice President and a majority of either the principal officers of the executive departments or of such other body as Congress may by law provide, transmit to the President pro tempore of the Senate and the Speaker of the House of Representatives their written declaration that the President is unable to discharge the powers and duties of his office, the Vice President shall immediately assume the powers and the duties of the office as Acting President.

Thereafter, when the President transmits to the President pro tempore of the Senate and the Speaker of the House of Representatives his written declaration that no inability exists, he shall resume the powers and duties of his office unless the Vice President and a majority of either the principal officers of the executive department or of such other body as Congress may by law provide, transmit within four days to the President pro tempore of the Senate and the Speaker of the House of Representatives their written declaration that the President is unable to discharge the powers and duties of his office. Thereupon Congress shall decide the issue, assembling within forty-eight hours for that purpose if not in session. If the Congress, within twenty-one days after receipt of the latter written declaration, or, if Congress is not in session, within twenty-one days after Congress is required to assemble, determines by two-thirds vote of both Houses that the President is unable to discharge the powers and duties of his office, the Vice President shall continue to discharge the same as Acting President; otherwise, the President shall resume the powers and duties of his office.

(Declared ratified February 10, 1967.)

## AMENDMENT XXVI

Section 1. The right of citizens of the United States, who are eighteen years of age or older, to vote shall not be denied or abridged by the United States or by any State on account of age.

Section 2. The Congress shall have power to enforce this article by appropriate legislation.

(Declared ratified July 1, 1971.)

## PROPOSED AMENDMENT

Section 1. Equality of rights under the law shall not be denied or abridged by the United States or by any State on account of sex.

Section 2. The Congress shall have the power to enforce, by appropriate legislation, the provisions of this Article.

(Passed Congress March 24, 1972.)

# Appendix C:
## Individual Rights under the Constitution

ARTICLE I, SECTION 9, CLAUSE 2

*The Privilege of the Writ of Habeas Corpus shall not be suspended, unless when in Cases of Rebellion or Invasion the public Safety may require it.*

Habeas Corpus:

This guarantee enables a person whose freedom has been restrained in some way to petition a Federal court for a writ of habeas corpus, to test whether such restraint was imposed in violation of the Constitution or laws of the United States. This right under the Constitution applies to all cases in which a person is confined by Government authority. It can be suspended only when the President, pursuant to congressional authorization, declares that a national emergency requires it and probably only when the courts are physically unable to function because of war, invasion, or rebellion. Habeas corpus is an important safeguard to prevent unlawful imprisonment.

ARTICLE I, SECTION 9, CLAUSE 3

*No Bill of Attainder * * * shall be passed [by the Federal Government].*

ARTICLE I, SECTION 10, CLAUSE 1

*No State shall * * * pass any Bill of Attainder.* * * *

Bill of Attainder:

A bill of attainder historically is a special act of a legislature which declares that a person or group of persons has committed a crime and which imposes punishment without a trial by court. Under our system of separation of powers, only courts may try a person for a crime or impose punishment for violation of the law.

Section 9 restrains Congress from passing bills of attainder, and section 10 restrains the States.

ARTICLE I, SECTION 9, CLAUSE 3

*No * * * ex post facto law shall be passed [by the Federal Government].*

ARTICLE I, SECTION 10, CLAUSE 1

*No State shall * * * pass any * * * ex post facto law.* * * *

Ex Post Facto Laws:

These two clauses prohibit the States and the Federal Government from enacting any criminal or penal law which makes unlawful any act which was not a crime when it was committed. They also prevent the imposition of a greater penalty for a crime than that in effect when the crime was committed. However, laws which retroactively determine how a person is to be tried for a crime may be changed so long as no important rights are lost. Laws are not ex post facto if they make the punishment less severe than it was when the crime was committed.

## ARTICLE III

The Judicial System:

Article III of the Constitution outlines the structure and power of our Federal court system and establishes a Federal judiciary which helps maintain the rights of American citizens. Article III, section 2, also contains a guarantee that the trial of all Federal crimes, except cases of impeachment, shall be by jury. The Supreme Court has interpreted this guarantee as containing exceptions for "trials of petty offenses," cases rightfully tried before court-martial or other military tribunal and some cases where the defendant has voluntarily relinquished his right to jury.

This section also requires that a Federal criminal trial be held in a Federal court sitting in the State where the crime was committed. Thus, a person is given protection against being tried without his consent in some part of the United States far distant from the place where his alleged violation of Federal laws occurred.

## ARTICLE III, SECTION 3

*Treason against the United States, shall consist only in levying war against them, or, in adhering to their Enemies, giving them Aid and Comfort. No person shall be convicted of Treason unless on the Testimony of two Witnesses to the same overt Act, or on Confession in open Court.*

*The Congress shall have power to declare the Punishment of Treason, but no Attainder of Treason shall work Corruption of Blood, or Forfeiture except during the Life of the Person attainted.*

Treason:

Treason is the only crime defined by the Constitution. The precise description of this offense reflects an awareness by our forefathers of the danger unpopular views might be branded as traitorous. Recent experience in other countries with prosecutions for conduct loosely labeled "treason" confirms the wisdom of the authors of the Constitution in expressly stating what constitutes this crime and how it shall be proved.

## ARTICLE VI, CLAUSE 3

* * *[N]*o religious test shall ever be required as a qualification to any office or public trust under the United States.*

Religious Tests:
Together with the First Amendment, this guarantee expresses the principle that church and government are to remain separate, and that a person's religious beliefs are no indication of his patriotism, his ability, or his right to serve his country. Thus a citizen need not fear that his religious affiliation or convictions may legally bar him from holding office in our country.

## The Bill Of Rights

### AMENDMENT I

*Congress shall make no law respecting an establishment of religion, or prohibiting the free exercise thereof; or abridging the freedom of speech, or of the press; or the right of the people peaceably to assemble, and to petition the Government for a redress of grievances.*

Religion:
Two express guarantees are given to the individual citizen with respect to his religious freedom. First, neither Congress—nor a State legislature because of the Fourteenth Amendment—may "make any law respecting an establishment of religion." This means no law may be passed which establishes an official church which all Americans must accept and support or to whose tenets all must subscribe or which favors one church over another. Secondly, no law is constitutional if it "prohibits the free exercise" of religion. A citizen is guaranteed the freedom to worship in the way he chooses.

The Supreme Court has described the establishment clause as providing a "wall of separation between church and state." Governmental activity which leads to "excessive entanglement" with the church or its related institutions and practices has been ruled unconstitutional. Thus, the Court has held that a state may not require prayer in the public schools nor may it supplement or reimburse parochial schools for teachers' salaries and textbooks. To permit or authorize such activities would constitute governmental support of the religious organization affected. On the other hand, the Court has held that it is permissible for public schools to release students, at their own request, from an hour of classwork in order that they may attend their own churches for religious instruction; or for a State to provide free bus transportation to children attending church or parochial schools if transportation was also furnished to children in the public schools. Furthermore, the Court has upheld the tax-exempt status of church property used exclusively for worship purposes, and has sanctioned federal aid programs for new construction at church-related universities. It has also held that the establishment clause does not prevent a State from designating Sunday as a day of rest.

One's freedom to worship as he pleases has been interpreted by the Supreme Court so that the right to worship must not conflict with otherwise valid government enactments. For example, one may not have two wives and escape conviction for bigamy by attributing his conduct to his religious beliefs. Nor could a person commit an indecent act or engage in immoral conduct and then validly justify his actions on grounds of religious freedom. The Supreme Court has also declared that it is an unconstitutional invasion of religious freedom to exclude children from public schools who, because of their religious beliefs, refuse to salute the American flag. The Court has further ruled that requiring attendance of children of the Amish religious sect in public schools beyond the eighth grade was an impairment of the free exercise clause since it prevented education in the traditional Amish framework.

Speech:

As a general rule, a citizen may freely speak out on any subject he chooses. In addition, he may join organizations, wear buttons, buy books, and carry signs which represent his views. And he may take his case to court when he feels he has been wronged.

The Supreme Court has ruled, however, that the protections afforded by the First Amendment do not extend to all forms of expression. Highly inflammatory remarks spoken to a crowd which advocate violence and clearly threaten the peace and safety of the community, or present a "clear and present danger" to the continued existence of the government, have likewise been unprotected. Obscenity, too, has been judged unprotected by the First Amendment, although the Court has held that the mere possession of obscene materials in the home may not be punished.

Courts have also recognized that "symbolic speech," which involves more tangible forms of expression, falls within the protection of the First Amendment. Wearing buttons, or clothing with political slogans, or displaying a sign or a flag, are examples of symbolic speech. The wearing of black armbands by secondary school students in protest against the Vietnam war has been ruled protected by the First Amendment, so long as such activity was not disruptive or injurious to the rights of other students. Display of a black flag in protest to organized government has also been protected. On the other hand, burning draft cards in protest against the Vietnam war has not been protected, since it could be shown to disrupt or undermine the operation of the Selective Service System. Courts have also been reluctant to overturn hair and dress codes of public schools where the schools could show that such codes were designed to prevent disruption or distraction of classes.

Finally, censorship by requirement of official approval or a license in advance for speaking has been condemned frequently by the courts. While a citizen is free to make speeches on the public streets, he may be prevented from doing so when he uses a loud and raucous amplifier in a hospital zone or when the location chosen for his address is such that it is likely to interfere with the movement of traffic.

Press:

Freedom of the press is a further guarantee of the right to express oneself, in this case by writing or publishing one's views of a particular subject. The Founding Fathers recognized the importance of a free interplay of ideas in a democratic society and sought to guarantee the right of all citizens to speak or publish their views, even if they were contrary to those of the government or the society as a whole. Accordingly, the First Amendment generally forbids censorship or other restraint upon speech or the printed word. Thus, a school board's dismissal of a teacher who had protested school board activities in a letter to the editor of the local newspaper was held to infringe upon his First Amendment rights.

As with speech, however, freedom to write or publish is not an absolute right of expression. The sale of obscene materials is not protected nor are printed materials which are libelous to other individuals. The Supreme Court has ruled, however, that public figures cannot sue for defamation unless the alleged libelous remarks were printed with knowledge of their falsity or a reckless disregard for the truth.

The Court has also ruled that the publication of a secret study into the origins of the United States involvement in the Vietnam war could not be prevented due to the First Amendment guarantee. The Court indicated, however, that freedom of the press may not extend to other similar matters which could be shown to have a more direct and substantial bearing on national security.

Finally, it is to be noted that broadcasting, to include radio, television, and motion pictures, receives the protections of the free press guarantee, and is subject to its limitations.

Assembly and Petition:

American citizens, whether they are meeting for political activity, religious services, or for other purposes, have the right to assemble peaceably. Public authorities cannot impose unreasonable restrictions on such assemblies; but they can impose limitations reasonably designed to prevent fire, hazard to health, or a traffic obstruction. The Supreme Court has emphasized that freedom of assembly is just as fundamental as freedom of speech and press. Thus, while no law may legitimately prohibit demonstrations, there may be laws or other governmental actions which legitimately restrict demonstrations to certain areas or prohibit the obstruction and occupation of public buildings.

Picketing has also been protected under the free speech guarantee, however, it may be reasonably regulated to prevent pickets from obstructing movement onto and from the property involved. Picketing on private property has been upheld but only where the property is open to the public and the picketing relates to the business being conducted on the property. Thus, the distribution of antiwar handbills on the premises of a privately-owned shopping center has been held to be unprotected.

The right of petition is designed to enable the citizen to communicate with his Government without obstruction. When a citizen exercises his first Amendment freedom to write or speak to his Senator or Congressman, he partakes of "the healthy essence of the democratic process."

## AMENDMENT II

*A well regulated Militia, being necessary to the security of a free State, the right of the people to keep and bear Arms shall not be infringed.*

The Right to Bear Arms:

The Second Amendment provides for the freedom of the citizen to protect himself against both disorder in the community and attack from foreign enemies. This right to bear arms has become much less important in recent decades as well-trained military and police forces have been developed to protect the citizen. No longer does he need to place reliance on having his own weapons available. Furthermore the Supreme Court has held that the State and Federal Governments may pass laws prohibiting the carrying of concealed weapons, requiring the registration of firearms, and limiting the sale of firearms for other than military uses.

## AMENDMENT III

*No Soldier shall, in time of peace be quartered in any house, without the consent of the Owner, nor in time of war, but in a manner to be prescribed by law.*

Quartering of Soldiers:

Prior to the Revolution, American colonists had frequently been required to provide lodging and food for British soldiers against their will. The Third Amendment prohibited the continuation of this practice.

## AMENDMENT IV

*The right of the people to be secure in their persons, houses, papers, and effects, against unreasonable searches and seizures, shall not be violated, and no warrant shall issue, but upon probable cause, supported by Oath or affirmation, and particularly describing the place to be searched, and the persons or things to be seized.*

Search and Seizure:

In some countries, even today, police officers may invade a citizen's home, seize his property, or arrest him whenever they see fit. In the United States, on the other hand, the Fourth Amendment protects the individual and his property from unreasonable search and seizure by officers of the law. In most instances, a police officer is not allowed to search the home of a private citizen, seize any of his property, or arrest him without first obtaining a court order called a warrant. Before the warrant will be issued to the policeman, he must convince a magistrate that he has "probable cause"—good reason—to believe either that the individual involved has committed a crime, or that he has in his possession evidence related to a crime. Even with a warrant, police cannot typically break into a private home without first demanding entrance, unless such action is permissible under a "no-knock" statute authorizing such entry where there is a reasonable expectation that evidence is being destroyed.

The courts have ruled that in some instances it is permissible to arrest a man or conduct a search without a warrant. For example, if a felony is committed in the presence of a police officer, he has the right to arrest the criminal immediately, without waiting to get an arrest warrant; and, if the policeman makes the arrest, he may then search the suspect and a limited area surrounding him to prevent the suspect from destroying evidence or seizing a weapon. Furthermore, evidence in plain view, whether or not in this area, may be seized.

The courts have also permitted the police to search certain vehicles without a warrant on the grounds that if not when the arrest is made, the vehicle may be many miles away when the policeman returns with his warrant.

The courts have frequently wrestled with the problem of determining what is required to constitute probable cause for a search or an arrest. Generally speaking, the criterion has been one of common sense: Would a reasonable person consider, on the available evidence, that there was a good basis for believing that the person to be arrested had committed a crime, or that the place to be searched contained the evidence of a crime? The Supreme Court, in considering whether a policeman who "stopped and frisked" a citizen without reason to believe that the individual concerned had committed a particular cime had met this test, ruled that the Fourth Amendment did not prohibit such a search if it was reasonable on the basis of the police officer's experience and the demeanor of the individual who was frisked.

Frequently courts have been confronted with the question of what constitutes a search. It has been held that no search has been conducted when a police officer overhears a conversation through a closed door, or when, through an open window, he sees a crime being committed. Intentional and prolonged eavesdropping, however, has been held unreasonable where it "subverts normal expectations of privacy."

Wiretapping—listening in on a telephone conversation by mechanical or electronic means—and electronic "bugging" have been held "search and seizures" under the terms of the Fourth Amendment and therefore they are subject to the same limitations of probable cause and reasonableness, and require a warrant for their use. Congress has enacted legislation which limits the use of wiretapping and bugging to the investigation of specific crimes and restricts those officials permitted to authorize them. The Supreme Court has held, moreover, that electronic surveillance of "domestic subversives" by the federal government is unconstitutional unless a warrant is obtained, even when authorized by the Attorney General in the interests of national security.

Evidence secured by means of an unlawful search and seizure cannot be used in either a State or Federal prosecution. Thus, the adage that "one is innocent until proven guilty" in practice means "until proven guilty by evidence obtained in accordance with constitutional guarantees."

## AMENDMENT V

*No person shall be held to answer for a capital, or otherwise infamous crime, unless on a presentment or indictment of a Grand Jury, except in cases arising in the land or naval forces, or in the Militia, when in actual service in time of War or public danger; nor shall any person be subject for the same offense to be twice put in jeopardy of life or limb; nor shall be compelled in any criminal case to be a witness against himself, nor be deprived of life, liberty, or property, without due process of law; nor shall private property be taken for public use, without just compensation.*

Grand Jury:

The Fifth Amendment requires that before a person is tried in Federal court for an "infamous" crime, he must first be indicted by a grand jury. The grand jury's duty is to make sure that there is probable cause to believe that the accused person is guilty. This prevents a person from being subjected to a trial when there is not enough proof that he has committed a crime.

An infamous crime is a felony (a crime for which a sentence of more than 1 year's imprisonment can be given) or a lesser offense which can be punished by confinement in a penitentiary or at hard labor. An indictment is not required for a trial by court-martial or by other military tribunal. Also, the constitutional requirements of grand jury indictment does not apply to trials in State courts. However, where States do use grand juries in their criminal proceedings, the Supreme Court has ruled that such juries must be free of racial bias.

Double Jeopardy:

The Fifth Amendment also guarantees the individual that he will not be placed in double jeopardy; that is, that he will not be tried before a Federal or State court more than once for the same crime. The Supreme Court has also stated that, under the due process safeguard of the Fourteenth Amendment, State courts may not harass defendants by successive prosecutions for the same act of misconduct.

Double jeopardy occurs when the second trial is for the same offense as the first. A second trial can occur, however, when the first trial results in a "mistrial," for instance, when the jury cannot agree on a verdict, or when a second trial is ordered by an appellate court.

Double jeopardy does not arise when a single act violates both Federal and State laws and the defendant is exposed to prosecution in both Federal and State courts. Nor does a criminal prosecution in either a State or Federal court exempt the defendant from being sued for damages by anyone who is harmed by his criminal act. Furthermore, a defendant may be prosecuted more than once for the same conduct if it involved the commission of more than one crime. For instance, if a person kills three victims at the same time and place, he can be tried separately for each slaying.

Self-incrimination:

The right that every person has not to be compelled in any criminal case to be a witness against himself applies to Federal proceedings and to State proceedings through the Fourteenth Amendment, and signifies that no one is obliged to provide answers to questions tending to convict him of a crime. Such questions may be asked at the very earliest stages of the investigation of a crime and, thus, the Supreme Court has ruled that when an individual is interrogated in the "custody" of the police the guarantees of the Fifth Amendment apply. "Custodial interrogation" can extend to questioning outside the police station and has even been held to include police questioning of a defendant in his own bed in his own boarding house.

To insure that the right against self-incrimination is protected, the Court has ruled that citizens must be warned prior to custodial interrogation of their right to remain silent, that what they say may be used against them in court, and that they have a right to counsel which will be furnished them. Failure to give these warnings results in any statements obtained by the questioning being inadmissible in later criminal proceedings.

Although an accused may waive his rights under the Fifth Amendment, he must know what he is doing and must not be forced to confess. Any confession obtained by use of force or threat will be excluded from the evidence presented at the trial. Furthermore, if a defendant or a witness fails to invoke the Fifth Amendment in response to a question on the witness stand, such a failure may operate as a waiver of the right and he will not be permitted to object later to a court's admitting his statement into evidence on the basis that it was self-incriminating.

Courts have ruled that the guarantee against self-incrimination applies only to "testimonial" actions. Thus, it has been held that handwriting samples, blood tests and appearance, to include repeating words in a police lineup, do not violate the Fifth Amendment.

Courts have ruled in addition that the Fifth Amendment prohibits both federal and state prosecutors and judges from commenting on the refusal of a defendant to take the witness stand in his own defense. The refusal of witnesses to testify to matters which could subject them to criminal prosecutions at a later date has also been upheld. The courts have recognized, however, a limited right of the government to question employees about the performance of official duties and have upheld the dismissals of such employees for their refusal to answer questions so related.

Government regulations which required registration of items such as highly dangerous weapons or narcotics which were a crime to possess have also been invalidated on the grounds that they require information which may be used in a criminal prosecution against the person who registers.

Due Process:

The words "due process of law" express the fundamental ideas of American justice. A due process clause is found in both the Fifth and Fourteenth amendments as a restraint upon the Federal and State Governments, respectively.

The clause affords protection against arbitrary and unfair procedures in judicial or administrative proceedings which could affect the personal and property rights of a citizen. Notice of a hearing or trial which is timely and adequately informs the accused of the charges against him is a basic concept included in "due process." The opportunity to present evidence in one's own behalf before an impartial judge or jury, to be presumed innocent until proven guilty by legally-obtained evidence and to have the verdict supported by the evidence presented are other rights repeatedly recognized within the protection of the due process clause.

The due process clauses of the Fifth and Fourteenth Amendments also provide other basic protections whereby the State and Federal Governments are prevented from adopting arbitrary and unreasonable legislation or other measures which would violate individual rights. Thus, constitutional limitations are imposed on governmental interference with important individual liberties—such as the freedom to enter into contracts, to engage in a lawful occupation, to marry, and to move without unnecessary restraints. Governmental restrictions placed on one's liberties must be reasonable and consistent with due process in order to be valid.

Just Compensation:

The Fifth Amendment requires that, whenever the Government takes an individual's property, the property acquired must be taken for public use, and the full value thereof paid to the owner. Thus, property cannot be taken by the Federal Government from one person simply to give it to another. However, the Supreme Court has held that it is permissible to take private property for such purposes as urban renewal, even though ultimately the property taken will be returned to private ownership, since the taking is really for the benefit of the community as a whole. The property does not have to be physically taken from the owner. If governmental action leads to a lower value of private property, that may also constitute a "taking" and therefore require payment of compensation. Thus, the Supreme Court has held that the disturbance of the egg-laying habits of chickens on a man's poultry farm caused by the noise of low-level flights by military aircraft from a nearby airbase, lessens the value of that farm and that, accordingly, the landowner is entitled to receive compensation equal to his loss.

AMENDMENT VI

*In all criminal prosecutions, the accused shall enjoy the right to a speedy and public trial, by an impartial jury of the State and district wherein the crime shall have been committed, which district shall have been previously ascertained by law, and to be informed of the nature and cause of the accusation; to be confronted with the witnesses against him; to have compulsory process for obtaining witnesses in his favor, and to have the Assistance of Counsel for his defense.*

Criminal Trials:

This Amendment sets forth specific rights guaranteed to persons facing criminal prosecution. Its guarantees apply to both the Federal courts and the State courts by virtue of the Fourteenth Amendment.

The right to speedy and public trial requires that the accused be brought to trial without unnecessary delay, and that the trial be open to the public. Intentional or negligent delay by the prosecution which prejudices the defendant's right to defend himself has been held as grounds for dismissal of the charges. The Supreme Court has ruled that delay in prosecution was not justified by the defendant's confinement on an earlier conviction because he should have temporarily been released for purposes of trial on the later charge.

Trial by an impartial jury supplements the earlier guarantee contained in Article III of the Constitution. The requirement that the jury have 12 members and that these must reach a unanimous verdict were derived from the common law and are not specifically accorded by the Constitution. The Supreme Court has ruled, however, that state juries need not necessarily be composed of 12 members and actually has approved a state statutory scheme providing for only six. Moreover, the Court has ruled that jury verdicts in state courts need not necessarily be unanimous. The right to jury trial does not apply to trials for petty offenses, which the Supreme Court has suggested as those punishable by six months' confinement or less. In all trials where a jury is used it must be impartially selected, and no one can be excluded from jury service merely because of his race, class, or sex.

The Sixth Amendment requirement that a person "be informed of the nature and cause of the accusation" means that an accused person must be given notice in what respects it is claimed he has broken the law, in order that he may have an opportunity to prepare his defense. This also means that the crime must be established by statute before hand so that all persons are aware of what is illegal before they act. The statute must not be so vague or unclear that it does not inform people of the exact nature of the crime. Generally, the accused is entitled to have all witnesses against him present their evidence orally in court; and subject to certain exceptions, hearsay evidence cannot be used in Federal criminal trials. Moreover, the accused is entitled to the aid of the court in having compulsory process issued—usually a subpena—which will order into court as witnesses these persons whose testimony he desires at the trial.

Finally, the Sixth Amendment provides a right to be represented by counsel. For many years, this was interpreted to mean only that the defendant had a right to be represented by a lawyer if he could afford one. The Supreme Court held in 1963, however, that the Amendment imposed an affirmative obligation on the part of the Federal and State governments to provide at public expense legal counsel for those who could not afford it, in order that their cases could be adequately represented to the court. The Supreme Court has held that this right extends even to cases involving "petty offenses" if there is a chance that a jail sentence might result. The indigent were held to have such a right at any "critical stage of the adjudicatory process." Thus, courts have accorded this right at initial periods of questioning, at police lineups, and at all stages of the trial process. In addition indigents were given the right to a free copy of their trial transcript for purposes of appeal of their conviction. Congress enacted the Criminal Justice Acts of 1964 and 1970 to implement this right to counsel by establishing a federal defender system to represent those defendants who could not afford legal counsel. Most state legislatures have enacted similar measures.

## AMENDMENT VII

*In suits at common law, where the value in controversy shall exceed twenty dollars, the right of trial by jury shall be preserved, and no fact tried by a jury, shall be otherwise re-examined in any Court of the United States, then according to the rules of the common law.*

Civil Trials:

The Seventh Amendment applies only to Federal civil trials and not to civil suits in State courts. Except as provided by local federal court rules, if a case is brought in a Federal court and a money judgment is sought which exceeds $20, the party bringing the suit and the defendant are entitled to have the controversy decided by the unanimous verdict of a 12-man jury.

## AMENDMENT VIII

*Excessive bail shall not be required, nor excessive fines imposed, nor cruel and unusual punishments inflicted.*

Bail:

Bail has traditionally meant payment by the accused of an amount of money specified by the court to insure the presence of the accused at trial. An accused who was released from custody and subsequently failed to appear for trial forfeited his bail to the court.

The Eighth Amendment does not specifically provide that all citizens have a "right" to bail, but only that bail will not be excessive. A right to bail has, however, been recognized in common law and in statute since 1791. In 1966 Congress enacted the Bail Reform Act to provide for pretrial release of persons accused of noncapital crimes. Congress thus sought to end pretrial imprisonment of indigent defendants who could not afford to post money bail and who were, in effect, confined only because of their poverty. The Act also discouraged the traditional use of money bail by requiring the judge to seek other means as likely to insure that the defendant would appear when his trial was held.

The lack of a specific constitutional guarantee has, nonetheless, indirectly contributed to legislative enactments which have modified the availability of bail. In 1970, Congress provided for a system of pretrial detention in the District of Columbia for those defendants considered to be dangerous and likely to commit additional crimes if released prior to trial. The law was highly controversial and is considered by many to be a violation of the right to bail which they implied in the Eighth Amendment.

Whether bail, where it is available, is excessive or not will depend upon the facts of each particular case. In a few instances, as when a capital offense such as murder is charged, bail may be denied altogether.

Cruel and Unusual Punishment:

Whether fines or periods of confinement are "cruel and unusual" must be determined on the facts of each particular case. Clearly excessive practices, such as torture, would be invalid. The Supreme Court has furthermore held the death penalty itself to be cruel and unusual.

In addition to excessive forms of punishment, the clause has also been applied to imposition of punishment for a condition which the "criminal" had no power to change. Thus, a law making the status of narcotics addiction illegal was struck down by the Supreme Court as cruel and unusual since it punished a condition beyond the control of the accused. Some courts have held that laws punishing public drunkeness were "cruel and unusual" when applied to homeless alcoholics since it was impossible for them to avoid public places.

## AMENDMENT IX

*The enumeration in the Constitution, of certain rights, shall not be construed to deny or disparage others retained by the people.*

Privacy and Other Rights:

The Ninth Amendment emphasizes the view of the Founding Fathers that powers of government are limited by the rights of the people, and that it was not intended, by expressly guaranteeing in the Constitution certain rights of the people, to recognize that government had unlimited power to invade other rights of the people.

The Supreme Court has on at least one occasion suggested that this guarantee is a justification for recognizing certain rights not specifically mentioned in the Constitution, or for broadly interpreting those which are.

The case which involved the Ninth Amendment was *Griswold* v. *Connecticut* 381 U.S. 479, decided in 1965. At issue was whether the right to privacy was a constitutional right and, if so, whether the right was one reserved to the people under the Ninth Amendment or was only derived from other rights specifically mentioned in the Constitution.

Courts have long recognized particular rights to privacy which are part of the First and Fourth Amendments. Thus, freedom of expression guarantees freedom of association and the related right to be silent and free from official inquiry into such associations. It also includes the right not to be intimidated by government for the expression of one's views. The Fourth Amendment's guarantee against unreasonable search and seizure confers a right to privacy because its safeguards prohibit unauthorized entry onto one's property and tampering with a citizen's possessions or property, to include his very person.

The court in *Griswold* ruled that the Third and Fifth Amendments, in addition to the First and Fourth created "zones of privacy" safe from governmental intrusion and, without resting its decision upon any one of these or on the Ninth Amendment itself, simply held that the right of privacy was guaranteed by the Constitution.

## AMENDMENT X

*The Powers Not Delegated to the United States by the Constitution, Nor Prohibited by It to the States, Are Reserved to the States Respectively, Or to the People.*

Reserved Powers:

The Tenth Amendment embodies the principle of federalism which reserves for the States the residue of powers not granted to the Federal Government or withheld from the States.

## LATER AMENDMENTS DEALING WITH INDIVIDUAL RIGHTS

### AMENDMENT XIII

*Section 1. Neither slavery nor involuntary servitude, except as a punishment for crime whereof the party shall have been duly convicted, shall exist within the United States, or any place subject to their jurisdiction.*

*Section 2. Congress shall have power to enforce this article by appropriate legislation.*

Involuntary Servitude:

This Amendment prohibits slavery in the United States. It has been held that certain State laws were in violation of this Amendment because they had the effect of jailing a debtor who did not perform his financial obligations. The Supreme Court has ruled that selective service laws, which authorize the draft for military duty, are not prohibited by this Amendment.

The courts have also justified certain civil rights legislation which condemned purely private acts of discrimination but which did not constitute "state action," on the basis of the authority granted in Section 2 of this Amendment and Section 5 of the Fourteenth Amendment, which is similar. An example is the civil rights legislation of 1866 and 1964 designed to end discrimination in the sale or rental of real or personal property. Such discriminatory practices were seen as "badges of servitude" which the Thirteenth Amendment was intended to abolish.

### AMENDMENT XIV

*Section 1. All persons born or naturalized in the United States, and subject to the jurisdiction thereof, are citizens of the United States and of the State wherein they reside. No State shall make or enforce any law which shall abridge the privileges or immunities of citizens of the United States; nor shall any State deprive any person of life, liberty or property, without due process of law; nor deny to any person within its jurisdiction the equal protection of the laws.*

*Section 5. The Congress shall have power to enforce, by appropriate legislation, the provisions of this article.*

Due Process:

The Fourteenth Amendment limits the States from infringing upon the rights of individuals. The Bill of Rights—the first 10 Amendments—does not specifically refer to actions by States, but applies only to action by the Federal Government. Through judicial interpretation of the term "due process of law" in the Fourteenth Amendment, many of the Bill of Rights guarantees have been made applicable to action by State governments and their subdivisions, such as counties, municipalities, and cities. Under this principle certain rights and freedoms are deemed so basic to the people in a free and democratic society that State governments may not violate them, even though they are not specifically barred from doing so by the Constitution.

The Fifth Amendment, as already seen, also contains a "due process" clause which applies to actions of the federal government.

Equal Protection:

In addition to the "due process" clause, the Fourteenth Amendment also prohibits denial of the "equal protection of the laws." This requirement prevents the State from making unreasonable, arbitrary distinctions between different persons as to their rights and privileges. Since "all people are created equal" no law could deny red-haired men the right to drive an automobile, although it can deny minors the right to drive. The State, therefore, remains free to make reasonable classifications. There are some classifications, however, which have been held to be patently unreasonable such as classifications based on race, religion, and national origin, for example. Thus, racial segregation in public schools and other public places, laws which prohibit sale or use of property to certain races or minority groups, and laws prohibiting interracial marriage have been struck down.

The Supreme Court has furthermore held that purely private acts of discrimination can be in violation of the equal protection clause if such acts are customarily enforced throughout the state, whether or not there is a specific law or other explicit manifestation of action by the State.

In another vein, the equal protection clause has been held to mean that a citizen may not arbitrarily be deprived of his right to vote and that every citizen's vote must be given equal weight as far as possible. Thus, the Supreme Court has held that state legislatures and local governments must be apportioned strictly in terms of their populations in such a way as to accord one man one vote.

It is also to be noted that Section 5 of this Amendment provides the authority for much of the civil rights legislation passed by Congress in the 1960s.

## AMENDMENT XV

*The right of citizens of the United States to vote shall not be denied or abridged by the United States or by any State on account of race, color, or previous condition of servitude.*

## AMENDMENT XIX

*The right of citizens of the United States to vote shall not be denied or abridged by the United States or by any State on account of sex.*

## AMENDMENT XXVI

*Section 1. The right of citizens of the United States, who are eighteen years of age or older, to vote shall not be denied or abridged by the United States or any State on account of age.*

The Right to Vote:

The intent and purpose of these three amendments are clear. The right to vote, which is the keystone of our democratic society, may not be denied any citizen over the age of 18 because of his race, color, previous condition of servitude, or sex. The Twenty-sixth Amendment which lowered the voting age for all elections from twenty-one to eighteen years of age became law on July 1, 1971. These amendments, together with the Fifth and Fourteenth, prohibit any arbitrary attempt to disenfranchise any American citizen.

## AMENDMENT XXIV

*The right of citizens of the United States to vote in any primary or other election for President or Vice President, for electors for President or Vice President, or for Senator or Representative in Congress, shall not be denied or abridged by the United States or any State by reason of failure to pay any poll tax or other tax.*

*The Congress shall have power to enforce this article by appropriate legislation.*

Poll Taxes:

The Twenty-fourth Amendment prohibits denial of the right to vote for federal officials because a person has not paid a tax. This Amendment was designed to abolish the requirement of a poll tax which, at the time of its ratification, five states imposed as a condition to voting.

The Supreme Court subsequently held that poll taxes were unconstitutional under the equal protection clause of the Fourteenth Amendment on the basis that the right to vote should not be conditioned on one's ability to pay a tax. Accordingly, poll taxes in any election have been prohibited.

## AMENDMENT XXVII (PROPOSED)

*Section 1. Equality of rights under the law shall not be denied or abridged by the United States or by any State on account of sex.*

*Section 2. The Congress shall have the power to enforce, by appropriate legislation, the provisions of this Article.*

Equal Rights:

This amendment was proposed by two-thirds vote of Congress and submitted to the states for ratification on March 24, 1972. As of the date of this printing, it has been ratified by twenty state legislatures, and rejected by none.

The object of the Amendment is to abolish unfair or unreasonable discriminations which the law makes against women, and which the courts have refused to otherwise invalidate under the "equal protection" clause of the Fourteenth Amendment.

## Conclusion

In addition to the specific constitutional rights outlined herein, certain safeguards for the individual are inherent in the structure of American government. The separation of powers between legislative, executive, and judicial branches of government is the basis for a system of "checks and balances," which prevents excessive concentration of power—with the inevitable threat to individual liberties that accompanies such concentration. With respect to the legislative power itself, the existence of two Houses of Congress—each chosen by a different process—is itself a protection against ill-advised laws that might threaten constitutional rights. Similarly, our Federal system, which divides authority between the National Government and the governments of the various States, has provided a suitable soil for the nourishment of constitutional rights.

No matter how well a constitution may be written, the rights it guarantees have little meaning unless there is popular support for those rights and for that constitution. Fortunately, in the United States such support has existed. Indeed, in this country the most fundamental protection of personal liberty rests in the well-established American traditions of constitutional government, obedience to the rule of law, and respect for the individual.

---

Reprinted from *The Layman's Guide to Individual Rights Under the United States Constitution*. Washington, D.C.: Government Printing Office, 1972.

# Appendix D:

## Glossary*

**acquitted** The finding of the court that the accused is not guilty of the crime or crimes charged.

**adjudication** A judgment by the court.

**admiralty courts** Courts originated in England centuries ago to handle maritime cases, those involving sailors, ships, and activities on the high seas.

**adversary system** A legal system that entails a contest between two opposing parties under a judge who acts as an impartial umpire. (In the United States the accused is considered innocent until the pleadings and evidence introduced in court prove guilt beyond a reasonable doubt.)

**appeal** The act of transferring a case from a lower court to one of higher jurisdiction for a new hearing. The request for such a hearing of a case already tried. A case that has been so transferred.

**appellate jurisdiction** The authority to rehear cases and alter lower court decisions.

**appellate review** A comprehensive rehearing of a case in a court other than the one in which it was previously tried.

**arraignment** A calling into court of the defendant to inform him or her of the charge and to ask for the plea.

**arrest** The act of depriving a person of his or her freedom in a significant way.

**arrest warrant** A document issued by a court ordering law officers to arrest a specified individual.

**bail** A guarantee, usually in the form of money, required by a judge or determined by statutes, that must be provided by an arrested person in exchange for freedom from jail prior to trial or an appellate hearing, to be forfeited if the defendant does not appear for trial or hearing.

**bail bondsman** One who provides bail for a defendant, usually a businessman who charges a fee for the service.

**bailiff** A court guard having various duties, such as taking charge of jurors and maintaining order in a courtroom (not to be confused with the British bailiff, whose duties are more like those of a deputy sheriff or constable).

**bench warrant** A document issued by a judge (the bench) and not requested by the police demanding that a specified individual be brought before the court. Also called a *capias*.

**beyond a reasonable doubt** To establish facts sufficient to fully convince an ordinary person that a defendant has committed the crime charged. (The standard of proof required under America's adversary system of law.)

**booking** The process of entering in the official arrest record the suspect's name, the offense charged, and the time and place of the occurrence of the event, usually done at a police station by the arresting officer.

**calendaring** The setting of a date for trial and various other administrative procedures associated with a court's scheduling of a case.

**case law** Law created by judicial decisions in specific prior cases; as opposed to *statutory law*. (See ***stare decisis***.)

**case load** The number of parolees or probationers under the supervision of a parole or probation officer.

**causation** That element of a crime which requires a casual relationship to exist between the offender's conduct and the harm or injury sustained.

---

*Space does not permit a full treatment of all the words specific to the criminal justice system. The student is advised to consult *Black's Law Dictionary*, West Publishing Co., for further reference.

**cellblock** A group of individual or multiple-inmate cells within a locked enclosure.

**chancery courts** A court of equity. (See **equity**.)

**change of venue** A change in the place of trial usually from one county or district to another.

**chief justice** The presiding or principal Justice of a court, possessing nominal authority over the other judges.

**circuit courts** Originally, courts that were held by judges who followed a circular path hearing cases periodically in various communities; however, it now refers to courts with several counties or districts within their jurisdiction.

**circumstantial evidence** Evidence of indirect facts as opposed to evidence of direct facts.

**city courts** Usually lower courts of special original jurisdiction; its rural counterparts are the justices of the peace courts.

**civil courts** Courts that handle civil cases, as opposed to criminal cases. (See **civil law, tort**.)

**civil law** Adjusts conflicts and differences between persons in the area of private and civil law as distinguished from criminal law.

**clerk of the court** A court official who handles much of the routine paper work associated with the administration of a court.

**common law** A body of law originating in England, based on centuries of case decisions. (See **case law** and ***stare decisis***.)

**common pleas courts** Where used in the United States, courts with this title are usually courts of general and original jurisdiction.

**complaint** An official form completed by a plaintiff or a law officer in registering a formal charge against another.

**concurrent jurisdiction** Jurisdiction over a case held in common by two or more courts.

**concurrent sentencing** More than one sentence handed out on the same occasion to be served during a common time period. (See **consecutive sentencing**.)

**consecutive sentencing** More than one sentence handed out on the same occasion to be served one sentence after the other. (See **concurrent sentencing**.)

**constitutional officer** Any law enforcement officer specifically and expressly provided for in either the Constitution of the United States or each state constitution. The offices of sheriff, constable, and coroner are constitutional officers in several states.

**county court** A court whose jurisdiction is limited to the boundaries of a county. May be either a court of special original jurisdiction or a court of general jurisdiction.

**court** A tribunal of one or more judges assembled to conduct the affairs of law and justice.

**court of last resort** The last court that may hear a case. The United States Supreme Court is a court of last resort for many kinds of cases.

**court of non-record** A court that does not make a written record of the trial.

**court of record** A court that records trial activity.

**crime** Any act or omission prohibited by law for which there is a specified fine or punishment.

***crimen fals*** Indicates the class of offenses that involve the perpetration of a falsehood, e.g. forgery, perjury, counterfeiting, etc.

**criminal courts** Courts that handle criminal cases; they may be courts that also handle civil cases, and are called criminal courts only in reference to the criminal cases that they do handle.

**criminal justice process** The series of actions through which each criminal offender may pass: from detection and investigation of the criminal act, to arrest, booking, indictment, arraignment, trial, conviction, sentencing, possible incarceration, and eventual release.

**criminal justice system** The agencies society entrusts to operate the criminal justice system and the apparatus that identifies, accuses, tries, convicts, and punishes offenders against the norms of society expressed in law. Major subsystems include the police, the prosecution, the courts, probation, corrections, and parole.

**criminal law** The division of law that deals with crimes and their punishment as distinguished from civil law.

**criminalistics** The use of scientific techniques derived from physics, chemistry, and biology to solve crimes. Also known as forensic science.

**cross-examination** The examination of a witness by the party opposed to the one who produced him or her.

**defendant** In criminal law, the party charged with a crime; as distinguished from the plaintiff.

**detainer** A hold order filed against a person incarcerated by another jurisdiction, which seeks, upon his or her release from current confinement, to take this individual into custody to answer to another criminal charge.

**detention** To hold in custody. Usually indicates the period of time between arrest and the preliminary hearing. The jails or holding facilities of the police are often referred to as detention facilities.

**district courts** Trial courts at the state or federal level with general and original jurisdiction. The boundaries of their venue do not conform to standard political unit boundaries, but generally include several counties.

**diversion** Refers to halting or suspending, before conviction, formal criminal proceedings against a person on the condition or assumption that he or she will do something in return.

**diversion programs** Programs designed to prevent defendants from being convicted and incarcerated or from reaching the trial state by providing them with specialized treatment resources.

**docket** A court record of the cases scheduled to appear before the court.

**doctrine of parens patriae** The principle that the juvenile court was to be a kind and loving parent to juveniles.

**domestic relations courts** Courts dealing with family problems. (See **family courts**.)

**double jeopardy** The principle that a person will not be properly tried in a court of law more than once for the same crime by the same sovereign.

**dual court system** The courts of the United States can be conceptualized as belonging to one of two court systems: state or federal.

**due process** Those procedures and safeguards necessary to ensure an individual that he or she will have a fair trial or hearing.

**equity** The concept that the relationships between man, woman, and society be just and fair and in accordance with contemporary morality.

**essoiner** A person who appears in court to present an excuse for the absence of the defendant.

**evidence** All the materials or means admissible in a court of law to produce in the minds of the court or jury a belief concerning the matter at issue.

**examination** The initial question and answer session between the defense or the prosecution and a witness during a trial.

**executive branch** That segment of government responsible for the administration, direction, control, and performance of government. Examples: president of the United States, state governors, city mayors. The police and correctional subsystems are under the executive branch. (See **legislative branch** and **judicial branch**.)

**executive clemency or pardon** The removal

of punishment and legal disabilities of a person by an executive (usually the governor) order.

**family courts** Courts of original jurisdiction that typically handle the entire range of family problems ranging from juvenile delinquency to divorce cases. (See **domestic relations courts**.)

**felony** A crime that is punishable by death, life, or a term of imprisonment for more than a year. (See **misdemeanor**.)

**fixed sentence** A sentence for a specified amount of time that is to be served by a convicted person; also called determined sentence.

**forensic** Those things related to law and courts. As an adjective it indicates those professions that specialize in the legal aspects of their profession.

**frisk** A brief search of the person that is usually limited to a "pat down" of the persons outer clothing.

**general court martial** The highest level of court in the military in which the most serious offenses are tried.

**general jurisdiction** The authority that permits the court to engage in the full range of trial activities in a wide variety of cases; as opposed to special or limited jurisdiction.

**"good time" laws** Laws that allow a reduction of a portion of a prisoner's sentence for "good behavior" while in prison.

**grand jury** A body of men and women called together by legal authority to conduct inquiry into matters brought to the attention of the jury.

***habeas corpus*** A written court order to any person, including a law enforcement official who has a person in custody, directing the person or official to bring the individual before the court so that it can determine if there is adequate cause for continued detention.

**hearsay evidence** Evidence that is not firsthand but is based on an account given by another.

**higher courts** Appellate courts and sometimes trial courts of record; as distinguished from lower courts.

**hung jury** A jury that cannot agree on a verdict.

**indeterminate sentence** A sentence in which a range of time (such as one to twenty years) is allotted a convicted person to serve; the actual time served to be at the discretion of the corrections officials, within legal proscriptions.

**index crimes** See **uniform crime report**.

**indictment, bill of** An accusation in writing presented by a grand jury, charging the person named therein with a criminal offense; sometimes called a "True Bill." A "No Bill" indicates the accused was not indicted.

**information** A document issued by a prosecutor constituting a formal charge against the defendant.

**injunction order** A written notice by a court to a party, prohibiting that party from committing some act.

**interlocutory decision** A temporary judgment pending the resolution of the facts at issue.

**intermediate appellate courts** The third level of state courts; appellate courts between trial courts and courts of last resort.

**judge** The official who bears primary responsibility for the activity of a court, whether this be performing the duties of a magistrate, deciding a case, sentencing, regulating the adversaries, or instructing the jurors.

**judicial branch** That segment of government charged with the interpretation of law and the administration of justice. Examples: United States Supreme Court; state supreme, superior, and appellate courts; county courts; and magistrates' courts. The court subsystem falls under this branch of government. (See **legislative branch** and **executive branch.**)

**jurisdiction** (Court) The extent of a court's right and authority to interpret and apply the law.

**jurisdiction** (Police) The established geographical boundaries in which the police of a political subdivision have authority.

**jury panel** The list of jurors summoned to serve at a particular court. From the jury panel, the petit jury is selected.

**justice** Refers to a judge particularly a Supreme Court judge. An ideal concerning the maintenance of right and the correction of wrong in the relations of human beings.

**justice of the peace courts** A court, usually rural, possessing special original jurisdiction in most instances and certain quasi-judicial powers.

**juvenile courts** Courts with special original jurisdiction over juvenile cases.

**law enforcement officer** Any public agency employee empowered and sworn to enforce, full- or part-time, the criminal and/or regulatory laws of their respective jurisdiction. Also known as peace officer, police officer, and sheriff.

**legislative branch** That segment of the government responsible for the consideration, drafting, and enactment of the law. Examples: United States Congress, state legislatures, county commissioners, city councils.

**limited jurisdiction** Authority by which the court is limited in the activity it can engage in when trying a case—for example, it may not be able to call a jury; also called special jurisdiction.

**lower courts** Courts of special original jurisdiction and sometimes trial courts; as opposed to higher courts.

**magistrate** A judge who handles cases in pretrial stages; usually handles misdemeanor cases. An officer of the lower courts.

**magistrate courts** Courts of special jurisdiction; usually urban.

***mala in se*** An offense against common law that was considered to be inherently evil or inherently wrong. (See ***mala prohibita***.)

***mala prohibita*** An offense that is wrong only because it is prohibited by legislation. (See ***mala in se***.)

**mandatory release** The release of an inmate prior to the full expiration of his or her sentence, usually under supervision.

**misdemeanor** A crime less serious than a felony; punishable by fine or imprisonment usually for less than a year. (See **felony**.)

**motion for a bill of particulars** An action before a court asking that the details of the state's case against the defendant be made known to the defense.

**motion for continuance** An action before a court asking that the trial or hearing be postponed.

**motion to dismiss** The action before a court asking that the court dismiss the case against the defendant—for specified reasons.

**municipal courts** Courts of special jurisdiction whose jurisdiction follows the political boundaries of municipality or city.

**original jurisdiction** First authority over a case or cause; as opposed to appellate jurisdiction.

**parole** The administrative act of releasing an offender from incarceration while retaining the legal custody of the offender. This release prior to completion of sentence is conditional upon maintaining standards of conduct prescribed by the parole board.

**parole revocation** The decision of a paroling authority to return the parolee to serve his or her sentence in an institution because he or she did not live up to the conditions of parole.

**peremptory challenge** An arbitrary challenge, requiring no cause to be shown, that is used to dismiss a potential juror during jury selection.

**petit jury** A group of lay people selected from the jury panel to hear a trial and decide on a verdict (usually a verdict of guilty or not guilty) and, in some states, to determine sentences or recommend mercy.

**plaintiff** The person or party who initiates a legal action against someone or some party. (See **defendant**.)

**plea bargaining** The process of negotiation between the prosecutor and the defendant for a reduction of the penalty. The charge is usually reduced (for example, from murder to manslaughter) or the judge agrees to limit sentence time or grant probation in return for the defendant's plea of guilty or cooperating with the state in providing evidence for other cases; circumvents trial time. (Also called "plea negotiation.")

**plea of guilty** A full confession of guilt to the accusation in open court.

**plea of *nolo contendere*** A plea of no contest. While it is equal to a plea of guilty in terms of effect, it is not an admission of guilt. Such a plea provides certain protections in other matters involving the defendant that may be brought before the courts.

**plea of not guilty** A statement by the defendant denying guilt of the offense with which he or she is being charged.

**postconviction remedies** The various means a convicted person has of seeking redress for his or her incarceration or conviction.

**precedent** The principle that the way a case was decided previously should serve as a guide for the handling of a similar case currently under consideration. (See **case law** and ***stare decisis***.)

**preliminary hearing** A preindictment hearing in which the prosecution attempts to show the court that there is probable cause for continuation of the criminal justice process.

**presentence report** A report containing social and historical background information about an offender, usually requested by a court, and usually prepared by a probation officer.

**privileged communications** Communications between two or more people that is privileged in law, in which case the court cannot require either to reveal the communications.

**probable cause** An apparent state of facts sufficient in themselves to warrant a person of reasonable caution to believe that an offense has been or is being committed.

**probation** The release of a convicted person by a court under specific conditions for a specified length of time. It is an alternative to imprisonment. If the conditions of probation are not adhered to, the probation can be revoked and the offender sent to prison.

**procedural law** That which sets forth the rules governing the method of enforcement of the laws of crime and punishment.

**quarter session courts** Originally, courts that met four times a year, usually to try serious cases. Where this old title is still used, it is in connection with a higher or trial court.

**reasonable doubt** Sufficient facts and circumstances to form a belief in the mind of a reasonable person that an offense has not been committed by the accused. Less than the certainty required to convict.

**recidivism** The number of offenders who return to an institution or are again processed by the criminal justice system. It is used as a measure of the effectiveness of programs or institutions involved in corrections.

**rule of law** Describes the willingness of a people to accept and order their behavior according to the rules and procedures that are prescribed by political and social institutions.

**screening** The removal of selected persons from the criminal justice process.

**search warrant** A written order by a judge, ordering law officers to search a designated place or person for specified materials.

**selective enforcement** The enforcement of selected laws by law officers; usually those laws applying to crimes determined by the police administrator to be the most serious or most frequent.

**sentence** The decision of the court (judge or jury), within the framework of statutory law, concerning the judgment imposed upon an individual once he or she has been tried and convicted.

**sentence hearing** A hearing held shortly after conviction in which the judge reviews the circumstances surrounding a case and then renders the sentence.

**sentencing alternatives** The range of possibilities the judge (or jury) has in sentencing an individual, e.g. probation, suspended sentence, prison, etc.

**social justice** The fair distribution of important goods and services such as housing, education, and health care.

**special court martial** The military court that is second in the three grades of court martial in terms of the severity of the penalty that it can impose.

**status offense** An offense committed by a juvenile that would not be an offense if committed by an adult, e.g. truancy, running away from home.

**statute of limitation** A period of time after which a crime that has been committed cannot be prosecuted.

**statutory rape** Sexual intercourse between a man and a women who is not his wife and not yet of legal age; the offense may be either with or without the woman's consent. Legal age varies from state to state.

***stare decisis*** The doctrine of precedent. Under this doctrine, judges are bound by previous court decisions. (See **precedent** and **case law**.)

**substantive law** That body of law which creates, discovers, and defines the rights and obligations of each person in society. Substantive law prescribes behavior and procedural law prescribes how unlawful behavior is handled.

**summary court martial** The military court that is the lowest of the three grades of court martial in terms of the severity of the penalty that it can impose.

**supreme court** The federal court of last resort specified by the United States Constitution; also the court of last resort in most kinds of cases at the state level.

**territorial district courts** The federal trial courts corresponding to the United States district courts but located in the territories.

**testimony** The evidence offered in court as declarations or affirmations of the truth or the facts.

**tort** In civil law, an infraction; parallel to an infraction in criminal law.

**trial** The formal court process in which all the evidence connected with a case is presented and a decision is made as to the guilt of the accused.

**trial *de novo*** A retrial that must take place when a case was tried in a court that did not record the trial. The retrial takes place on the initial appeal.

**tribunal** A court; a place where judges sit; a judicial weighing of information leading to a decision.

**uniform crime report** A statistical compilation of crime in the United States. The report is published annually by the Federal Bureau of Investigation. The main body of the report is limited to several selected crimes, known as index crimes.

**United States commissioners** See **United States magistrates**.

**United States court of military appeals** The highest court in the military system; an appellate court.

**United States courts of appeals** Federal intermediate appellate courts that handle appeals from federal district courts. There are eleven of them, one to each judicial circuit.

**United States magistrates** Formerly, United States commissioners. Judges who fulfill the pretrial judicial obligations of the federal district courts.

**venireman** One member of a jury panel.

**venue** The place of trial; the particular city or county in which the court with jurisdiction will hear and determine the case.

**verdict** The judgment reached by a jury or a judge at the conclusion of a trial.

**warrant** A writ issued by a court ordering specific acts to be carried out by law officers.

**youth services bureau** A diversion program for juvenile courts that eliminates noncriminal cases and petty first offenses from the courts' consideration by providing a resource to help a young person become less troubled or less troubling.

**CHAPTER-OPENER CREDITS**

Chapters 1, 2, 3, 9, 13, and 25, courtesy of the National Council on Crime and Delinquency.
Chapters 4 and 11, The Bettman Archive, Inc.
Chapter 5, Monkmeyer Press Photo Service.
Chapter 6, Cary Wolinsky/Stock, Boston.
Chapters 7 and 24, courtesy of the Los Angeles Police Department.
Chapter 8, R. Norman Matheny, *The Christian Science Monitor*.
Chapters 10, 12, 14, and 23, Philip Jon Bailey.
Chapter 15, Derrick Te Paske.
Chapters 16, 17, 20, 21, 22, and 26, courtesy of Leo M. Dehnel, United States Department of Justice.
Chapter 18, David Powers/Jeroboam, Inc.
Chapter 19, courtesy of Arthur Leipzig, Ford Foundation.

# Index

CDEFGHIJ–VB–79876